THE LAST FLORENTINE REPUBLIC

THE
LAST FLORENTINE
REPUBLIC

CECIL ROTH

NEW YORK / RUSSELL & RUSSELL

TO
YOU

FIRST PUBLISHED IN 1925
REISSUED, 1968, BY RUSSELL & RUSSELL
A DIVISION OF ATHENEUM HOUSE, INC.
BY ARRANGEMENT WITH CECIL ROTH
L. C. CATALOG CARD NO: 68-25048
PRINTED IN THE UNITED STATES OF AMERICA

PREFACE

THE Last Florentine Republic has long awaited its historian. While countless works have been written upon Savonarola and his age, the amazing revival of thirty years later has remained virtually neglected, save for the verbose accounts of contemporary chroniclers and the brilliant inaccuracies of Perrens. A partial exception can be made only with regard to the period of the Siege, which, besides inspiring numerous political tracts of the Risorgimento inadequately disguised as novels, has formed the object of a certain amount of industrious research. Even this, however, has not been utilized hitherto in any continuous account. Yet it is a period second to none even in Florentine history for human interest, and strangely suggestive in many details of the French Revolution. It is Florence's heroic age ; and she seems to summon on to the scene all the greatest of her children that her downfall might be the more epic. The revival was inspired by the teachings and character of Savonarola as if by a resurrection of his personality. Niccolò Machiavelli lived long enough to see the change. Michelangelo Buonarroti acted as Governor-General of the Fortifications. Francesco Guicciardini directed the intrigues of the exiles. The period is more typically represented in Francesco Ferrucci, the solitary military hero of Florence, who fell together with the opposing general in the only real battle in her history. Thus was ended the struggle in which the City of the Arts had resisted the combined forces of Pope and Emperor, backed up by the resources of Italy, Germany, Spain, and Flanders, and by the growing wealth of the New World. Even so, victory might yet have been possible had it not been for the treason of Malatesta Baglione, commander-in-chief of the defending forces, an episode presented in a new light in the following pages. No apology is needed for this, the first study devoted to this heroic period and the first detailed presentation of it to the English public. Recourse has been had consistently, so far as is possible, to original records and authorities, in illustration not so much of the arid details of military history as of the superb morale of the people at bay.

My thanks are especially due to the Directors of the R. Archivio di Stato di Firenze and the R. Biblioteca Nazionale di Firenze for the generous facilities accorded to me in my researches ;

to Mr. Edward Armstrong and Professor Cesare Foligno for their consistent encouragement and help; to Miss Ady for a number of valuable suggestions and corrections; and to my brother David for the peculiarly irksome labour of reading the proofs.

CONTENTS

BIBLIOGRAPHY

of some of the more important works used.

A. PRINTED AUTHORITIES

Benedetto Varchi. *Storia Fiorentina* (ed. Arbib, Firenze, 1843).
Bernardo Segni. *Storie Fiorentine, Vita di Niccolò Capponi* (ed. Masi, Livorno, 1830).
Paolo Giovio. *Istorie del suo tempo* (Venezia, 1557).
Jacopo Nardi. *Le Historie della Citta di Firenze* (Lyons, 1582) [1st Edition].
Scipione Ammirato. *Istorie Fiorentine* (ed. Scarabelli, Torino, 1853).
R. Caggese. *(Storia di) Firenze dalla Decadenza di Roma al Risorgimento d'Italia* (Firenze, 1912–20). 3 vols.
Giambattista Busini. *Lettere sopra l'Assedio di Firenze*, ed. Milanesi (Firenze, 1861).
Francesco Guicciardini. *Opere Inedite* (Firenze, 1860 ff.) ; *Storia d'Italia* (ed. Gherardi, Firenze, 1919).
Albèri. *Relazioni degli Ambasciatori Veneti* (Firenze, 1839).
P. Falletti-Fossati. *L'Assedio di Firenze* (Palermo, 1883). (2 Vols.)
A. Rossi. *Francesco Guicciardini e il Governo Fiorentino* (Bologna, 1899). (2 Vols.)
Donato Giannotti. *Opere Politiche e Letterarie* (Firenze, 1850).
A. Anzilotti. *La crisi costituzionale della Repubblica Fiorentina* (Firenze, 1912).
M. Lupo Gentile. *Studii sulla storiografia fiorentina alla corte di Cosimo I* (Annali di R.S.N.S. di Pisa, Vol. XIX, 1906).
Ricordi Storici di Filippo Rinuccini (Firenze, 1840).
M. Rastrelli. *Vita d'Alessandro de' Medici* (Firenze, 1781).
Nerli (Filippo de'). *Commentarij* (Augsburg, 1728) [1st ed.].
Vasari. *Opere*, ed. Milanesi.
Villari. *Life of Niccolò Macchiavelli* (English translation, London).
Istorie di Giovanni Cambi, Cittadino Fiorentino, ed. P. Ildefonso di S. Luigi, in *Delizie degli Eruditi Toscani* (Firenze, 1786), Vols. XIX–XXII.
L. A. Ferrai. *Lorenzino di Medici e la società cortigiana del Cinquecento* (Milan, 1891).
Le Vite degli Uomini Illustri di Casa Strozzi (Firenze, 1892).
Francesco Ferruccio e la Guerra di Firenze (Firenze, 1889).
L'Assedio di Firenze di Mambrino Roseo da Fabriano, poema in ottava rima, ed. Ant. Dom. Pierrugues (Firenze, 1894).
Albèri. *L'Assedio di Firenze*, illustrato con inediti documenti (Firenze, 1840).
Ulysse, Robert. *Philibert de Chalon, Prince d'Orange, Viceroi de Naples* (2 vol.). (Paris, 1902.)
Pastor. *History of the Papacy* (English Translation).
Négociations Diplomatiques de la Toscane, ed. Desjardins.

Londi : *Appunti di un fautore dei Medici durante l'Assedio di Firenze del* 1529–30 (Firenze, 1911).
Reumont. *La jeunesse de Cathérine de Médicis . . . traduit annoté et augmenté par Arman Buschet* (Paris, 1886).
Gaye. *Carteggio Inedito d'Artisti dei secoli XIV, XV, XVI.*
Lanz (Karl). *Actenstuck und Briefe zum geschichten Kaiser Karl V* (Wien, 1853).
De Leva. *Storia Documentata di Carlo V.*
Hauvette. *Luigi Alamanni, sa vie et son œuvre* (Paris, 1903).
Calendar of State Papers, Spanish.
Calendar of State Papers, Venetian.
Letters and Papers : Henry VIII.
State Papers : Henry VIII.
Sanuto, *Diarii.*
Molini. *Documenti di Storia Italiana.*
Ruscelli. *Lettere di Principi.*
Alvisi. *La Battaglia di Gavinana* (Bologna, 1881).
Pitti. *Apologia de' Cappucci.*

PERIODICALS

Archivio Storico Italiano (abbreviated as A.S.I.).
Studi Storici (Pisa).
Nuovo Archivio Veneto.

B. DOCUMENTARY AUTHORITIES

R. Archivio di Stato di Firenze.

Deliberazioni dei Signori e Collegi.
Otto di Guardia e Balia.
Dieci di Balia, Legazioni e Commissarie, Istruzioni e Lettere Missive.
Dieci di Balia, Legazioni e Commissarie, Istruzioni e Lettere Responsive.
Dieci di Balia : Carteggio Originale.
Registro di Lettere Esterne agli Ambasciadori dal 1529 al 1554 (Signori : Carteggio, Missive, Registri, I° Canc. v. 58).
Signori : Carteggio, Missive, Minutari, I° Canc. v. 21.
Archivio Mediceo avanti il Principato.
Consulte e Pratiche.
Carte Strozziane.
Ricordanze.

BIBLIOTHECA NAZIONALE DI FIRENZE

Carte Strozziane.
Magliabecchiane.

BRITISH MUSEUM

Bergenroth Transcripts of Spanish State Papers. (Many of these have been used by Gayangos in *Calendar of State Papers, Spanish* ; but it has been thought advisable to make use as far as possible of the original and unabbreviated forms.)
Pandolfini Papers.

THE LAST FLORENTINE REPUBLIC

THE
LAST FLORENTINE REPUBLIC

CHAPTER I

THE RE-ESTABLISHMENT OF THE MEDICI

(1) THE RULE OF THE MEDICI

THE tragic pyre of 23 May 1498 in which Savonarola met his fate did not mark the end of his influence in Florence. The Republican regime which the reformer had inspired survived his death by fourteen years, still based upon the three fundamentals which had been laid down under him— the exclusion of the Medici; the maintenance of the new constitution; and alliance with France. It was this last which ultimately proved its undoing. Perilous at the best, it had never secured for Florence, even at the period of the French triumphs, any advantages commensurate with its dangers. The hatred of the Papacy had been earned by the harbouring at Pisa of the French " Conciliabolo." The Cardinal Giovanni de' Medici, elder surviving son of Lorenzo the Magnificent and prominent not at the Papal court alone but also in European diplomancy, never ceased to press wholeheartedly the cause of his family. Thus when in 1511 the Holy League was formed by Pope Julius II to drive the French from the Peninsula, Florence found herself faced with the hostility of almost all the powers of Italy, and indeed of Europe, for her fidelity to her traditional alliance; while the French, doubting her sincerity, failed to provide any succour. In the spring of 1512 the latter won the Battle of Ravenna but lost the campaign by the death in it of their most brilliant general, Gaston de Foix; and by the end of June their forces were driven beyond the Alps. The Holy League determined to punish the contumacy of Florence. A Congress at Mantua decided, under the influence of Medicean promises and payments, to restore the family. Piero Soderini, the titular head of the State, was hoodwinked by the diplomacy of the confederates while a Spanish army under Raimondo da Cardona was sent into Florentine territory. The city refused the proffered conditions of entry

1

into the League, restoration of the Medici, and deposition of Soderini. She even neglected Cardona's private offer to retire on condition that his famished forces were provided with food. But she had over-estimated her strength. Machiavelli's newly organized militia proved itself incapable of defending Prato ; and the place was sacked with a horror which is said to have haunted the last hours of Leo X. A *coup de main* followed within the walls. Soderini weakly fled ; and at last the conditions were agreed to, with the addition of the promise of a heavy indemnity. On 1 September 1512, amid cries of " Palle, Palle," [1] the first representatives of the exiles entered the city. Thus after a lapse of eighteen years the Medici were restored.

With the former rulers, the former methods of sovereignty were re-established. At first the Revolution had been accomplished with only a single constitutional change of importance, in the election of a Gonfalonier for one year to replace Soderini, who had held office for life. Before long, however, more drastic measures succeeded. The very first of these showed a most complete disregard for the legislation of recent years. Mediæval Florence, seldom in fact other than an oligarchy, had justified its nominal democracy in one single constitutional expedient—the Parlamento. Whenever it was considered by the government that a state of emergency had arisen, the populace was summoned by the tolling of the great bell to the Piazza. Here proposals for the betterment of the city were laid before them, to be carried or rejected by acclamation without debate. Thus in theory the people remained the ultimate arbiter in time of stress. The practice, however, was very different. It was easy for a ruling faction to pack the Parlamento with partisans by blocking the entries into the Piazza with troops, and thus to carry whatever measures it desired, however unjust. What was essentially the symbol of liberty was thus made the instrument of tyranny ; and it had become part of the regular machinery of a Florentine revolution. A packed Parlamento would approve, instead of specific proposals, the appointment of a Balia,[2] with authority to carry out any reforms it considered necessary ; and by its means any change desired could be carried out smoothly and with legal sanction.[3] The extreme democratic theory and the notorious tyrannic uses of the Parlamento had alike rendered it objectionable to the bourgeois regime under Savonarola, when it had been formally abolished by law. This act was now disregarded. A Parlamento was held on 16 September under the control of the Spanish troops. A Balia was appointed which immediately did away with the essential parts of the Savonarolan reforms ; and by the November of the following year the constitution had returned to the form in which it existed prior to 1494. For the space of fifteen years the city was ruled by a restoration of the system of Lorenzo the Magnificent.

In outward appearance this was the old Republican constitution, which had been modified only in details since the close of the thirteenth century.   At its head stood the Signoria of eight Priors of Liberty, presided over by the Gonfalonier (i.e. Standard Bearer) of Justice, the titular chief of the State.   Two Colleges, those of the Twelve Buonuomini and of the Sixteen Gonfalonieri of the Companies—a relic of the ancient civic militia—completed the supreme executive authority, supplemented in various departments by a number of committees.   Legislative authority resided in the two ancient Councils of the People and of the Commune ; though since Cosimo's day a smaller Council of One Hundred, nominated by the ex-Gonfalonieri and so more amenable to control, had been set up by their side.

The operation of this free constitution had however been nullified ever since the fourteenth century by a provision which had been in intention essentially democratic.   In mediaeval Italy as in ancient Greece, the principle of election, so natural to us had been considered defective.[4]   Always liable to be warped by influence or by superficial recommendations, as well as by less legitimate forces, it was thought to militate against that essential of ancient democratic theory—the regular rotation of office. For this reason, at the time of the tumults consequent upon the attacks of Castruccio Castracane, the system of *Squittino* or Scrutiny was instituted for the greater security of the city.   In place of the old system of indirect bi-monthly election, it was arranged for the choice to be made at once of a sufficient number for twenty-one times, and for the names thus obtained to be put into a bag and drawn thence by lot as occasion required.[5]   Later, at the time of the expulsion of the Duke of Calabria (1328), the system was revised and made permanent, being extended from the Signoria to the other major Magistracies.   The arrangement, though popular, was always liable to abuse.   The names in the bags could be tampered with, or the extractions could be made fraudulently.   At the time of the exile of Cosimo de' Medici, however (1443), this corruption received legal sanction.   The Albizzi, his enemies, obtained the appointment of ten partisans as *Accoppiatori*, to fill the election bags at will and to control extractions.[6]   The Medici took over the system and made it permanent.   Thus, while all the forms of a popularly chosen magistracy remained, it became to all intents a system of open nomination.   At the counter-revolution of 1512, therefore, the Medicophile Signoria was empowered to appoint twenty permanent Accoppiatori, of whom half, alternating every six months, formed a board for the designation of the Signoria and the Collegi.

This formed the key by which the nominal government of the city was controlled.

The principal work of administration however was now carried out by the Council of Seventy (*Settanta*), an institution of Lorenzo the Magnificent, and the central pivot about which the Medicean constitution worked. Re-established in 1513 by the government from among their own partisans, the continuance of its favourable complexion was assured by the right of keeping up its numbers by co-optation. It elected in rota from among its own members the twelve *Procuratori* who discussed and prepared legislative decrees, as well as the *Otto di Pratica* who attended to diplomatic and military questions. Every provision of the Signoria had to pass one of these two committees or else the general body of the Settanta : by it every act of government, financial, legislative, or diplomatic, had to be approved by a two-thirds majority before passing to the ordinary bodies whose essential offices were thus usurped. By its side stood the Council of One Hundred, essentially legislative, nominated by the Accoppiatori, twenty-five for each quarter of the city. Before this were brought all provisions for imborsation, for the formal election of magistrates, for taxation and finance, and for the special commissions for government ; yet in all these matters the sanction of the twelve Procuratori and of the Settanta was also required. The Councils of the People and of the Commune continued to drag on their existence but with curtailed functions, such as dealing with petitions, concessions of charity, and reforms of the government of dependent towns. The essential work of administration was thus carried out by the Settanta at the dictation of the Medici. Liaison was provided between the nominal government and the real rulers by the right given to one of the supreme family to attend its meetings.

Thus far, the system restored in 1512–13 was that of Lorenzo. One innovation however of the highest importance was made. Originally the Balia appointed by the Parlamento in time of emergency had ceased to function immediately the reforms deemed necessary had been carried into operation. Under the Medici however the system had obtained an extended importance. The Balia which recalled Cosimo was appointed for five years, and was almost continually renewed or reappointed as occasion demanded. Still, it remained in essence a temporary, and there-fore a subordinate, committee. But the Balia of 1512 completed the change in character. Its forty-five members (later increased to sixty-five) were all nominees of the Medici. It was given power " so much as lay in the whole people." Above all, even the pretext of temporariness was thrown off, and the Balia be-came avowedly permanent " for all occasions that can occur and for every requirement or benefit or safeguard of the State." Its power was absolute and unchecked. It met every five days, with plenary power over all matters of government and of public security. It could absolve and condemn unrestrained ; it could suspend the action of the laws ; it approved the commissions of the Accoppiatori ; its members took part in their selection of candidates for office ; it possessed the immense influence entailed by the sole right of conceding the boon of citizenship. On this, too, a member of the ruling family was given a seat. By its means, the Medici, of whose partisans it remained exclusively composed, retained permanent control over every operation of government. From their palace in the Via Larga,[7] they had only to issue their instructions for them to be carried through all the requisite channels ; and they could come to any decision in home affairs or in foreign in the fullest confidence that it would be confirmed and executed by every responsible organ of government.[8]

The instructions for the rule of Florence which Leo X gave his young nephew Lorenzo show the methods by which the influence of the family was exercised. He was advised to fill all the principal magistracies with friends, and to take care to have continual reports on their behaviour. When in case of emergency he was forced to make use of others, he should take care to choose nonentities. He should make sure of a majority upon the executive councils, especially the Otto di Pratica and the Otto di Balia, which controlled foreign and internal affairs respectively, upon the private intercourse of whose members he should be kept informed by some confidant among them. But above all the officials of the *Monte di Pietà*—the public loan bank— should be entirely devoted to him, for " that was the heart of the city." Lesser offices were to be distributed freely as a sop to those who could not serve in those of greater importance. The citizens should be secured by espionage and by disarmament ; yet care should be taken to conciliate them by broad-mindedness and impartiality. Especially was this to be shown towards the populace and the inhabitants of the contado—the broad basis which established and almost justified Medicean rule.[9] The days of Lorenzo the Magnificent seemed to be revived in the splendid pageants and " trionfi " produced under the ægis of the heads of the family—not a negligible consideration for conciliating the Florentine temperament ; yet the general benignity could be varied on occasion by outbursts of harsh repression.

The Medicean rule was thus established at its restoration more securely even than before the expulsion ; and this dependence was accentuated when Lorenzo obtained appointment as Captain of the Republic with the command of a company of men-at-arms.

Responsible and even favourable observers condemned the instability of this growing family, or rather personal, hegemony, as distinct from the " optimarchy " which had characterized their previous rule ; and many of the Florentine statesmen of the time aimed at the re-establishment of the old alliance between the Medici and the other leading families of the city with whom they had formerly shared both the odium and the honours of government. To compensate this growing detachment, however, the Medici were strong in a family alliance which now embraced several of the leading Florentine houses. Two of Leo X's sisters were married to members of the Salviati and the Ridolfi families respectively ; his niece Clarice was wife of Filippo Strozzi. Through this means some semblance of the old rule of the aristocracy was preserved.

Yet there was probably no circumstance which at the commencement strengthened the rule of the Medici in Florence after their return so much as the elevation of the head of the family to the highest dignity in Christendom. Little more than six months after the restoration, Cardinal Giovanni de' Medici was elevated to the Papacy as Leo X. Never before had Florence produced a Pope ; and her joy at the honour was unmeasured. Nor was the appeal only to the patriotic susceptibilities of the citizens. Now, as ever, they were open to approach through the pocket as well as through the intellect. All Florentines, and especially the Pope's multitudinous relatives, pretended or real, could count upon reception and entertainment at the papal court. Many received from their countryman patronage, ecclesiastical or lay. Above all, the banking class found openings which amply recompensed their loss of influence at home ; and this most important section of the Florentine population became the strongest of their supporters. Nor was it easy to question the hegemony of a family now identified with one of the foremost Italian powers and strong in the support of European alliances.[10]

Another type of mind which was neither dazzled by the glamour nor attracted by the profits of the papal dignity welcomed it with scarcely less fervour. To those few to whom their country seemed of greater importance than their city, this close connection of two of the most powerful Italian states provided at last the long-sought opportunity to drive out the foreign invader. Niccolò Machiavelli, who had served the Republican regime and suffered for it, now rallied to the Medici, sought employment under them, and commenced the series of patriotic political writings which made his name famous.

Under these circumstances and by these methods, the Medicean rule continued uneventfully in Florence during the pontificate of Leo. The family influence was exercised by its two foremost

lay members, Giuliano and his nephew Lorenzino, later Dukes of
Nemours and Urbino respectively, whose names have been for
ever linked together by Michelangelo's immortal sculptures in
S. Lorenzo. The one was the youngest son of Lorenzo the
Magnificent and brother of Leo ; the other, his nephew, son
of that Piero expelled from Florence in 1494. But the dynastic
ambitions of Leo were ruined by the death of Giuliano in 1516 and
of Lorenzo three years later. He now entrusted the administration of the city to his cousin Giulio, natural son of Giuliano,
the brother of Lorenzo the Magnificent who had fallen in the
Pazzi conspiracy. But a forged legitimacy had been made out
for him on his elevation to the dignity of Cardinal ; and a
handsome appearance rare in the Medici combined with his high
dignity and prospects to provide such palliation as the Florentines
required for the blot upon his birth. Under these auspices
Florence was ruled with moderation and success from 1512 to
1523.[11]

(2) THE ITALIAN SITUATION

It was in the domain of foreign policy that Florence had felt
the change most acutely. This was a matter in which barely
the forms of independence were left to her. In all the vacillations and tergiversations of papal policy she had been dragged
about with the Pope, and was included in every treaty as if
subject to him. She had come to be considered almost an
appanage of the Papacy ; and it had even been openly formu-
lated that " the state of Florence is joined to the Pope in such a
way that it can be rightly said that it is one thing with the
papal state." [12] This intimate connection kept Florence bound
down to a policy which was not hers.

The restoration of the Medici by Spanish arms had forcibly
detached the city from her traditional French alliance, and had
bound her for the nine years of the pontificate of Leo X to a
policy on the whole Spanish and Imperial : to alliance, that is,
with Charles V, who combined from 1518 the dignity of Holy
Roman Emperor with the actual control of Spain, the two
Sicilies, and the Netherlands with Franche-Comté. The Cardinal
Giulio de' Medici, who had strongly influenced the policy of his
kinsman, continued his exertions in favour of the Emperor under
the brief pontificate of Adrian VI (January 1522–September
1523) ; and he owed his own succession to the Papacy as Clement
VII (November 1523) principally to his reputation as an ardent
Imperialist and to the consequent support of Charles. Yet
though Florence found herself once more a satellite of the Holy
See, her dependence upon the Emperor became nevertheless
modified. As Pope, Clement was subject to considerations to

which he had been impervious as Cardinal. The advance of the Turk and the rise of Lutheranism rendered peace in Western Europe an imperative necessity if headway was to be made against the two forces which were undermining its very foundations. Yet the victory of Charles was to be dreaded, as the Papacy, however much his ally, could not take the risk of lying helpless before his overwhelming strength. At the same time, in case of the victory of the French, the Papal States would be left defenceless and would form the first object for attack. It was necessary therefore in either case to recede from dependence upon the Empire ; and from his very election Clement attempted to follow a policy of compromise which can be traced through all the vacillations and hesitations which were constitutional both to his timidity and to his craft. In the Conclave itself, there were indications that he had modified his attitude in the hope of winning over the French party among the Cardinals. Almost his earliest action as Pope was an endeavour to demonstrate himself no mere puppet of the Emperor by entering into separate negotiations with Venice. By the league of August 1523, his predecessor had entered into a defensive alliance with the Emperor, and had made himself responsible for a monthly contribution of 15,000 ducats to his forces. To the amazement of the Imperialists, Clement refused on his accession to extend the terms of this alliance and to make it offensive as well as defensive. While agreeing to continue the promised payments, he stipulated that they should be kept secret so as not to alienate the French. Finally, in April, he declined to renew the league on the ground that the father of all Christians should observe the strictest neutrality in order to obtain a readier obedience when he summoned them against the Turk. Thus Clement succeeded in detaching himself from the Imperial bondage.

The repulse of Bourbon from Marseilles and the subsequent victories of the French in Lombardy made Clement begin to fear the possibility of the triumph of their cause and to tremble for his own safety. An armistice was proposed to both parties, and was unequivocally refused ; and the Pope then safeguarded his own interests by a peace and an alliance with Francis (December 1524 and January 1525). But at the Battle of Pavia (24 February), the French forces were overwhelmingly defeated and Francis himself was captured. For very safety's sake, Clement was driven to a headlong change of front. On 1 April, he concluded an alliance defensive and offensive with Lannoy, the Imperial Viceroy, and humbly returned to his previous obedience. But this was obviously brought about under constraint. The Imperialists, while enjoying to the full the monetary advantages gained under the treaty, did not fulfil the main condition on their own side of evacuating the territories they had occupied within the papal states. Disappointed in the French and beguiled by the Imperialists, Clement turned for once to an Italian policy. The conspiracy of Girolamo Morone, chancellor of the Duke of Milan, to drive the Spaniards from the Peninsula by means of the defection of their greatest general, met with his fullest sympathy. But its betrayal (14 October 1525) left affairs in a worse condition than ever before. The Spanish seized possession of the Duchy, only the citadel of its capital holding out ; and the Papacy was threatened, as in the days of the Hohenstaufen, from either side. Clement had recourse to desultory negotiations carried on with his usual timidity and irresolution with Louisa of Savoy (Regent of France for her son), with Venice, and with England, in the hopes that he might obtain some advantage by delay. For once his procrastination was of avail. In the following January Francis agreed to the ruinous conditions of the Peace of Madrid, whereby Charles was to recover the whole of the rich Burgundian inheritance and France to be reduced almost to vassalage. But the reciprocal obligation was easier of fulfilment ; and Francis became, as he cried, a King again, as he stepped over the frontier into freedom, leaving his two eldest sons behind him as hostages. It was soon realized that at Madrid he had deliberately perjured away the honour which was all there was left to him (according to his own declaration [13]) after Pavia. The treaty, sworn to under constraint and under a secret protest, was repudiated by the advice of the Estates and with the approval (though apparently not with the formal dispensation) of the Pope. Vigour was immediately thrown into the opposition to Charles ; and on 22 May a so-called Holy League was concluded at Cognac between the Pope, Venice, France, and Francesco Sforza, dispossessed Duke of Milan ; with the sympathy, but not adhesion, of England. All Italian states were to receive back the possessions they had held before the war. France was to renounce its claim to Milan, receiving in compensation an annual tribute with the County of Asti and the suzerainty of Genoa. The Emperor was to be confined to Naples ; and in the event of his refusal even this should be taken from him and conferred on some Italian prince, who should pay a tribute to France. By a secret clause Florence was to enjoy the protection of the league, but did not give nominal adherence for fear of reprisals upon her merchants and commerce in the Emperor's dominions. Thus after a lapse of fourteen years she again found herself in virtual alliance with France, not as before as a free state, but dragged forcibly in the wake of the tortuous policy of a Pontiff whose family had been restored to the city largely on the ground of its anti-French sympathies !

The war which followed showed that Charles was still more than equal to his adversaries, whether in arms or in diplomacy. The support of the French was lukewarm. The citadel of Milan, all that remained of the dominions of Francesco Sforza, fell to the Imperial forces under Bourbon. The Duke of Urbino, in command of the forces of the league, showed a conspicuous lack of resolution and activity, and wasted his time in the capture of Cremona instead of proceeding to the relief of the capital. The Colonna, roused up by Ugo da Moncada, raided Rome and sacked the Borgo, the Vatican, and St. Peter's itself (19–21 September 1526)—a melancholy foretaste of the disaster of the following year. Clement, driven to take refuge in the Castle of S. Angelo, was forced to conclude a truce of four months with the Emperor. But he followed the example of keeping faith which he had licensed in Francis. The hostages which he had given were left to their fate ; the amnesty promised to the Colonna was disregarded, and a force was sent to chastise them ; while Giovanni de' Medici with the best of the papal troops continued to fight for the league in the name of the King of France.

Meanwhile, however, Charles continued to gain successes. Ferrara was now, as ever, easy to attract to the side hostile to the Pope. The famous mercenary leader, George Frundsberg, crossed the Alps with 12,000 German lanzkneckts, mainly Lutherans, and bearing, it was said, silken halters to hang the Cardinals and a golden halter for the Pope. The Duke of Urbino was forced to abandon his tardy blockade of Milan in order to prevent a junction between the two sections of the Imperialist forces. But in a skirmish at Borgoforte near Mantua Giovanni de' Medici was fatally wounded. The inaction of Urbino, whether owing to constitutional weakness or to distrust of his troops or to personal and political motives, became all the more pronounced. Frundsberg and Bourbon were allowed to effect a junction at Fiorenzuola near Piacenza (February 1526-7) and moved towards the papal states, which were threatened also by Lannoy and the Colonna from the South. Clement was again driven to alarm. He attempted in vain to stir up Francis to action, and endeavoured to come to terms with Charles. The arrival of Renzo da Ceri, who had defended Marseilles in 1524, and the consequent stand made by the papal forces in the South at Frosinone, served to strengthen his resolution ; but only for the moment. The Imperial army lying inactive at S. Giovanni between Bologna and Ferrara became increasingly clamorous for pay, and by its actions was giving ample justification for the title of " barbari " which Italy still conserved for its invaders. In March, the troops, Spanish as well as German, broke out in open mutiny ; and their leaders were unable to agree to pay them

even one-half of their arrears.   The sops which could be procured from Ferrara failed to satisfy claims which amounted to
150,000 ducats for the Germans alone.   Religious fanaticism and
greed combined with the wretched weather, the lack of supplies
and the legitimate demands of war, to make Bourbon lead his
forces southwards.   Here, amid the far-famed wealth of Florence
and the splendid luxury of Rome, they counted confidently on
having all their desires satisfied to the full.

Clement meanwhile in an agony of fear entered into negotiations with Lannoy, the Imperial Viceroy in Italy.   Upon the
fifteenth of March he succeeded in concluding a trace for eight
months, to which France and Venice might become parties.
Both sides were to give up their conquests in Naples and in the
papal states ; and above all the dreaded northern army was to
retire into Lombardy.   In return for this and for the release of
the hostages, Clement was to make a contribution of 60,000 ducats
towards the satisfaction of Bourbon's army and to withdraw from
the league.   In the midst of their revolt, the news of the armistice
was communicated to the troops in Lombardy, now (owing to
the death of Frundsberg through a stroke of apoplexy while
endeavouring to calm his troops) under the sole command of
Bourbon.   The articles of the truce were sent by Lannoy for
his confirmation with an open hint that they need not be obeyed.
The captains of the rebellious army were asked for their opinion ;
but, confident that thus alone they could obtain their arrears of
pay, they determined to advance.   Bourbon, after a private
protest, consented to lead them ; and on 30 March 1527 he conducted his forces towards Imola.[14]

(3) FLORENCE UNDER CLEMENT VII

The accession of Clement VII to the throne of St. Peter had
been greeted in Florence with great joy ; yet not so great, we
are informed, as that which celebrated the election of Leo X.[15]
The advantages of the connection with the Papacy were indeed
by now recognized as somewhat qualified ; for Florence had not
been long in finding the truth of the Genoese taunt that to give
birth to a Pope was a burdensome privilege.   The roseate
expectations aroused by Leo's elevation had been in part
disappointed by an extravagance on his part which led
more than one Florentine house to the verge of bankruptcy.
His general opposition to France had been intensely disliked in
the city where the old friendship still beat strong, and was thought
at one time to have endangered the Medicean rule.   But the
French marriages of Giuliano and Lorenzino were very popular,
and served to conciliate public opinion.   The city had indeed
been forced to bear a great part of the cost of Leo's expensive

foreign policy.   In particular, the unprincipled war to deprive the Duke of Urbino of his duchy in order to confer it upon Lorenzo had laid upon her a very heavy burden.[16]   But at the same time Leo's remarkable good fortune had not left Florence unaffected. Out of the spoils of Urbino she received the somewhat inadequate recompense of the fortress of St. Leo, together with the territory of Montefeltro.   Through the Pope's mediation she recovered from Lucca the cities of Pietrasanta and Mutrone, filched from her during the Pisan war.   There was something, therefore, to compensate for the drain upon her purse and sympathies.   Nevertheless, Clement could not arouse again the extravagant hopes and rejoicings which had greeted Leo.   There were still indeed some solid prospects.   Machiavelli's hopes received significant encouragement from the new Pope ; Florentine finance continued to enjoy its opportunities at Rome ; and the inhabitants of the papal states were still made to groan under the subtle exactions of the Florentine administrators.[17]   At the same time, however, the pontificate of Leo had disillusioned the Florentines of their more dazzling expectations ; and the colder manners of the new Pope were suspected to harbour a disposition very unlike the popular character of his kinsman.   His position in Florence was therefore even at his election decidedly weaker than had been that of his predecessor.

In addition to this the virtual succession in the family of the highest dignity in Christendom had subtly altered its status in Florence.   Its interests and its position were no longer those of Florentine citizens ; its importance was become international, not communal ; its leading members had been allied to Royalty and elevated to positions of dignity and influence both within Italy and without.   As a result even in the days of Leo there could be discerned on the part of Lorenzino a growing disdain to rule the city under the pretext of equality, and a growing movement towards undisguised absolutism.   Clement as Cardinal had been careful to revert to the older forms and shows of liberty, but upon his elevation to the Papacy the change became undisguisable.   With Leo X had died the last of the legitimate descendants of Cosimo the Elder in the male line ;   the elevation of Clement removed from the city the last adult among his illegitimate descendants.   There were now left, besides himself, only two children, natural sons of Lorenzino and Giuliano respectively ; but the one, Alessandro, was only thirteen years old ; and the other, Ippolito, a year older or younger.[18]   There were indeed still representatives of the family in other of its branches.   The most prominent among these was the noted general, Giovanni delle Bande Nere, almost the only soldier of ability of his time who was an Italian.[19]   But it was necessary to go back for nearly a century and for four generations, to the father of Cosimo the Elder, before the family connection could be established : and above all there was a traditional enmity between the two branches, the younger of which had attached itself to the people, plainly traceable in the attitude of the two Medicean Popes towards their cousin. There were therefore reasonable hopes that, in the absence of any obvious heir to the family influence and aspirations, Florence would now be allowed to recover its liberty. Clement himself had almost deliberately fostered these expectations. Whether from an honest curiosity or with wholly provocative objects, it had been his custom to make inquiries of certain of the better-known Florentines as to how they would advise that the government should be established. Thus in 1518 Machiavelli produced at his request his discourse upon the Reform of the State of Florence in which he suggested a virtual return to the system of 1512, while securing to the two ecclesiastics who were at the head of the family a continued supremacy during their lifetime. At the same time other prominent Florentines, from wealthy aristocrats down to avowed Savonarolans, were asked for their opinions ; yet no change was made in the administration. Soon after the death of Leo X the comedy was repeated. Hopes were so raised that rumour fixed even the day upon which the reforms were to be carried out. But again there was no result, excepting for a conspiracy which was put down in blood. Still it could have been expected that on Clement's departure for Rome he would now at least take steps to make use of the advice which he had so sedulously collected. It soon appeared that he had his own views upon the future. Extracting from the majority of a Florentine deputation an opinion favourable to his plans, he sent to Florence as representatives of the family the two bastard children, with Silvio Passerini, cardinal of Cortona, to govern on their behalf.

By this measure, the whole aspect of the Medicean rule was changed. It ceased to be that of an eminent citizen whose ability and influence secured him a preponderating voice in the administration, and became patently that of a nominee appointed by a non-resident and responsible to him. Nominal authority lay with mere children ; ultimate authority with a single individual, whose own claims even by birth were questionable in the extreme. At the same time the hopes roused by Clement were finally disappointed. Never again could there be so apt an opportunity for the Medici to retire of themselves : and it was plain that there was in reality no such desire. The only way for the city to recover her liberty was obviously by force. The opposition to the Medicean rule was driven to abandon its constitutional methods in favour of conspiracy and plot. Even those who had hitherto acquiesced sufficiently willingly in the Medicean rule had now grounds for complaint. The very first acts of the government in Florence after the election of Clement showed that the hand of the Pope was heavier than that of the Cardinal, and that his new name did not symbolize any change of character. Eight days after the event, a reputable Florentine citizen was arrested and within two hours executed for refusing to pay a wager upon the result of the Conclave, on the ground that a bastard could not be canonically elected. A member of the Otto who had scrupled to assent to this judicial murder was persecuted for it, though Clement disclaimed responsibility. The archbishopric of Florence was conferred on the Pope's kinsman, the Cardinal Ridolfi, though no more than twenty-six years of age, in succession to himself. The Balia was instructed to confer full citizenship and to qualify for all the offices of state the two bastards sent to govern them—a bitter sign that it was now descent and not ability which gave the city her rulers. Ippolito received what had now become almost the hereditary title of " Magnificent," resided in the Medicean Palace in the city, and was made member of the Settanta, the Balia, and the board of Accoppiatori. Alessandro, whose lack of ability seems to have been notorious even at this early age, retired to the family villa at Poggio a Caiano, where he gave himself up to pleasure, and paid the city the compliment of being kept in touch with its affairs only in writing.[20] Meanwhile Ippolito within the city had not chosen the best way to ingratiate himself with the citizens. To add to their disdain at being ruled by a child, they found him putting on the airs of a prince, taking precedence of everybody and forcing all to uncover in his presence.[21]

The real governor of the city, however, was the cardinal of Cortona. The choice of a representative was a bad one. He had indeed represented Leo X in the city for two years at the close of that Pope's life, but not with such conspicuous success as to invite repetition. Quite apart from his meagre ability, his personality itself was inacceptable to the Florentines. The proudest citizens of Italy were subjected to the rule of a foreigner ; and not merely a foreigner, but a native of one of those subject towns of which they were so intolerant. It was necessary for him at the outset of his rule to be naturalized a Florentine citizen, together with his brothers and his nephews, to the general disdain. His rough manners, his unsympathetic outlook, and his great avarice combined with this to render him objectionable. Moreover, though a creature of Clement, he disregarded the example set by the kindly and sympathetic administration which had made his personal rule noteworthy for the greatest appearance of civil liberty since the rise of the Medici.[22] " Very avaricious,

like the generality of priests, he had neither the ability to understand the Florentine character nor the judgement to content it.
Not trusting any citizen nor taking advice about any matter, it
was enough for him to be obeyed and honoured by all."[23]

As a result, the tradition of permitting the maximum outward show of liberty so long as the actual authority remained
unimpaired became utterly neglected. Autocratic rule became
open and undisguised. All of the councils and consultations of
state were carried on, not in the official seat of government at the
Palazzo della Signoria, but in the palace of the Medici. Here
all decisions were made excepting in matters of minor importance.
Ordinary councils did not meet ; the functions of the magistrates
were curtailed ; treaties of alliance or of peace were concluded
without reference to the representatives of the city. Ambassadors, after their first formal audience with the Signoria, treated
directly with the Cardinal. Public letters were mostly directed
to him ; and all, excepting those on affairs of trivial importance,
were referred to him. Appointments to the greater offices of
state were too obviously confined to the Medicean faction. The
Balia of 1512 was constantly resorted to in cases of difficulty, and
taxation was frequently levied through its means. Continual
instructions from the Pope served as a perpetual reminder that
the city was being governed from Rome. Even the aristocratic
supporters of the Medici began to object to this regime in which
the influence of which they claimed a share was administered by
an alien who took pleasure in depriving them of even their
legitimate voice in the conduct of affairs.[24] They found themselves neglected too in what they had come to regard as their
privileged position in the partition of offices and the assessment
of taxation—' the Florentine equivalent to political assassination.'
It was an open complaint that whereas Lorenzo the Magnificent
gave his friends the sweets of office and his enemies the burden
of taxation, Cortona reversed the system. However much this
may have been exaggerated, there is no doubt that Cortona's
methods seemed to be almost a deliberate attempt to alienate
the old supporters of the house.[25]

Nor did this growing tyranny have the justification even of
efficiency. The Cardinal followed his master in slowness of
movement and lack of success. " By tardy councils he aimed
at acquiring a name for foolish gravity," says one who might be
expected to write as a friendly partisan.[26] Above all the misgovernment showed itself in the matter of finance. The importance of Florence at this time in international politics was largely
a question of its great wealth. The military enterprises of the
Medici Popes were in great part financed from the Florentine
treasury : the repeated payments which they continually

promised their allies were expected to come from the same scource. Thus in the treaty to which the Pope was forced after the Battle of Pavia, Florence was bound to pay the Emperor 100,000 ducats. Since this was virtually the only provision which was carried into effect, the heavy payment gained neither the Pope nor the city the slightest advantage. Toward the league of Cognac alone Florence was stipulated to pay 20,000 florins monthly ; and this in spite of the fact that during the preceding seven months she had already disbursed upwards of a quarter of a million.[27] Such immense sums could not be raised by the ordinary processes. Thus for example we are told of an *accatto*, or forced loan, of 100,000 ducats ordered to be levied in 1526. The total was actually brought up to 140,000 ducats : and owing to financial stress had to be paid over again. Such an extraordinary extortion, equivalent to a whole year's ordinary revenue, was too oppressive ; and the consequent financial crisis led to widespread unemployment.[28]

Nor was there, as in the days of Leo, any sort of recompense or advantage, however slight, for these excessive calls upon the Florentine treasury. Clement was as uniformly unsuccessful in his policy as Leo had been successful. Every step brought him into fresh disaster ; and from every disaster he looked to Florentine gold to extricate him. Where the city was herself most immediately concerned the failure was the most abject of all. An expedition made by their combined forces to overthrow the new hostile popular regime in Siena in 1526 resulted in one of the most ignoble reverses which Florence ever suffered, and the credit of papal rule suffered with it.

The growing maladministration and disappearance of even the forms of liberty rendered Florence ever riper for revolt during the pontificate of Clement VII. It was a peril, indeed, from which the Medici were never free. There were always discontented democrats within the city and intriguing exiles without it, waiting for their opportunity to overthrow their rule. In the year following their restoration, the sceptical Boscoli had paid with Capponi the penalty for the supposed conspiracy in which Machiavelli was implicated. The harsh and unjust rule of the Bishop of Fano during the absence of Lorenzino had caused great discontent, which had been suppressed by wholesale banishments before it was mollified by the mild interlude which followed under Clement.[29] Yet just before his elevation to the Papacy there was another conspiracy which had to be put down in blood.[30] With the more clumsy administration of Passerini the danger was increased. It was known that the city was ripe for insurrection. Just after the formation of the league of Cognac, Clement was with difficulty dissuaded from despatching an army of three thousand men to hold it down ; and smaller forces were nevertheless sent in continuously, so that the garrison rose gradually from 300 to nearly 2,000.[31]   Clement's enemies in 1526 were confident of their ability to embarrass him by raising Florence against his rule.[32]   The reverse of the papal forces at Borgoforte (February 1526-7) had actually been followed by a tumult in the city led by members of its noblest families.   There were slight collisions with the troops, not to the disadvantage of the rioters.   It was said that Cortona weakly prepared to abandon the city ; and the overthrow of the Medici was averted (according to his own not unbiassed opinion) only by the Venetian ambassador, who reassured the Cardinal and quietened the populace by promising the support of the forces of the Republic against the Imperialist menace.   The arrest of three conspirators of high family and the weakness of the remaining leaders ended the tumult.[33]   The spirit of discontent, however, still remained ; and Florentine exiles, scattered about in Italy and outside it, were waiting and working to overthrow the government and return.   Florence was thus fully ripe for an upheaval : but it was left for external events to provide the occasion.

(4) THE APPROACH OF THE ARMIES

At the very end of March, the Imperialists moved from their camp at S. Giovanni near Ferrara.   It was a foregone conclusion that they would march upon Florence.   The Venetian territory was strongly defended by the army of the Duke of Urbino, which made an attack upon Venice unlikely.   Of the two most attractive alternatives, Florence and Rome, the former was the nearer and the more wealthy.   The city was one of the commercial capitals of the world, and more might be extracted from it by extortion or plunder than from any other without exception ; and it was notorious that it was in no position to offer a strong defence. With an army which had no object but to secure its arrears of pay, the consideration was overwhelming.   If Lutheran fanaticism gave part of Bourbon's forces a predilection for Rome, Spanish greed counterbalanced it by a longing for the more immediate gains.   And there was no need for disagreement; for Florence lay on the way to Rome, and formed naturally the first objective. Already therefore at the close of the previous year the danger was patent.   Machiavelli had been sent to the papal camp to beg succour, as the city was in no position to look after itself [34] ; and it was known that Bourbon's troops were in the habit of swearing " by the glorious sack of Florence." [35]

Moreover, encouragement was received from without.   The Sienese, traditional enemies of Florence, had bitter recollections of the attempt of the previous year by Clement and the Florentines to overthrow their popular regime. Eager to be revenged, and to recover the territories filched from them at that time, they added their incitements to the soldiers' greed. As Bourbon advanced, they despatched envoys to the " liberator and ex- tirpator of tyrants." They attempted to gain an additional hold over him by winning over his captains. They offered to supply him with artillery and with provisions—these, owing to the rapidity of his movements, his greatest need.[36] On the other hand, the Florentine exiles hailed him as Dante did Henry VII, and began to resort to his camp with encouragements.

Still, in spite of these clear signs, the movements of the Im- perial armies appeared to give some hope that the safety of Florence was not immediately threatened. Prevented by the deep snows and strong fortresses from directly crossing the Apennines, they did not march immediately into the heart of Clement's territories, but moved slowly by way of Bologna, plundering and burning along the line of the ancient Æmilian road. Urbino, finding that no attack was meditated upon the Venetian territories, began to follow at a safe distance. Under this threat, Bourbon was forced to brave the inclement weather and crossed the Apennines near Meldola by way of the Val di Bagno, despite the swollen torrents and deep snows, with numbers ever growing through the greedy irregulars who attached them- selves to his standard.[37]

Meanwhile, the Medicean government in Florence had been alternating between an elastic optimism and the most abject despair : but in spite of the clearest indications no steps for the security of the city were taken. The regular confidential reports sent by Fabrizio Peregrino in Florence to the Duke Alessandro, pleasure-seeking at his villa at Poggio, may be taken to mirror the sentiments of the government. At the commencement of March, they had reason to anticipate a diversion in the direction of Tuscany. But the city was prepared and fortified : and with the lanzknechts opposed in front by the Marquis of Saluzzo and threatened in the rear by Urbino as well as by other forces, they had no opportunity for doing damage, " ill paid and worse fed " as they were. The news from Rome was good, and Andrea Doria (the famous Genoese admiral in the pay of France) was " playing the devil " at sea. There was indeed some ground for apprehen- sion owing to the uncertainty of the enemy's movements. Was it true, as an intercepted letter from Lannoy gave them to suppose, that orders had come from the Emperor to extort from Florence what they might, but on no account to sack her ; or were they marching on Siena, Naples, or Rome ? For himself, Peregrino could not believe that Florence was their true objective ; and even when their intentions were more plain he had hopes that they would turn back, perhaps even without payment, as a result of the agreement between Lannoy and the Pope, or through the defection of the Spanish troops.   But on 1 April news reached Florence that a definite move had at last been made in the direction of the city.   The receding optimism gave way to despair. The rulers of the city lost their heads.   " It seems to me," wrote his confidant to Alessandro, " that we are in worse tribulation than ever ; and if they come in this direction, I fear that we have no one to defend us."   " I fear that we have few friends," he added plaintively upon the next day.   The delay of the Imperialists to cross the Apennines restored his confidence, but only for a short time.   On 5 April he discounted the threats that they would enter into Tuscany, impeded as they would be by the snows and the armies of the league ; but by the next day he had already changed his mind.   Meanwhile, the advance continued.   On 16 April Bourbon reached Sta. Sofia in the Florentine territory, and the threat to the city became unveiled.   Peregrino now counted upon the wretched condition of the Imperialists to ensure their defeat.   " They have been for two days without bread ; they are without money, naked, barefoot."   But two days afterwards he lamented the foolish strategy of the generals of the league who counted upon starving their enemies out without fighting, by the aid merely of the peasants.   " We are making war to lose, not to win, to my mind . . . all appears to me lies and chatter."   The generals were hoping to come to some arrangement, but Fabrizio saw no sign of it in the continued advance.[38]

The city meanwhile was filled with misgiving.   Many citizens fled to Venice or to other places of security.   Others transported their treasures and their families into the monasteries and places of sanctuary.   Michelangelo, hard at work for the Pope in the Church of S. Lorenzo, was asked to give shelter to the goods of a friend in the sanctuary.[39]   In the midst of the general dismay, Cortona remained impotent.   His hands had been strengthened at the close of 1526 by Clement's sending to assist him the Cardinals Cibo and Ridolfi, kinsmen of the Medici by marriage ; but their presence did not give his policy any greater vigour or success.   He was now attempting to raise money to finance the troops of the league or to buy off the Imperialists.   The first act of the new Signoria which entered into office upon 1 March was to levy a forced loan of 60,000 ducats " to pay the soldiers and to liberate our country and our children, our own persons and substance " ; and fearing to trust even the Cento, the unconstitutional channel of the Balia was employed.[40]   Upon 20 April, a second payment was ordered, so that in the space of eight months a sum of no less than 220,000 ducats in gold was extracted from a minority of the citizens.[41] Even this not proving sufficient, the goods of the gilds, and especially of the Arte della Lana, were seized and sold ; church plate was confiscated and melted down, and recourse was had to other expedients no less desperate.[42] Still, no good seemed to be done with the money. Machiavelli had been repeatedly sent to the camp of the papal army to beg succour ; but it was not forthcoming in numbers anything like sufficient.[43] The strengthening of the fortifications entered upon in the previous years had barely commenced to be carried out, and the initial step—the reduction of the towers in accordance with the latest ideas of fortification—had only served to foster a suspicion that the city's safety as well as its beauty was being deliberately impaired.[44] It was notorious that in its present condition the city could not hope to offer any resistance to attack. The Imperial forces might indeed have been stopped as they crossed the pass of the Val di Bagno, but through over-credulous trust in the efficacy of the papal agreement they were allowed to pursue their way undisturbed.[45] All seemed to be done deliberately to the detriment of the city.

In consequence, the discontent within the walls rose hourly. Francesco Guicciardini, famous as a political thinker and as historian, gives personal testimony to the condition of the city. In January he had been confident that the Florentines would not revolt without outside help ; but on arriving in the city on 23 April he saw two reasons which threatened an outbreak. One was the economic drain, and the other the misgovernment of the " great oaf," Cortona, " who concerns himself about trifles and neglects matters of importance. He will not permit others to attend to them, and can do nothing himself. He thinks only of protecting the residence of the Medici and the Palace ; he neglects the government, and does not perceive the ruin he is causing." Long since, Guicciardini had recommended the Pope to lighten the burden on the city. Now he advised in addition a more open and liberal administration of affairs. But he was aware that it was late to put his counsel into execution. " Only one thing," he wrote, " keeps back a revolution : fear of the Spanish and of sack." [46]

But in fact it was precisely the approach of the Imperial army which made the rising the more likely. With the advance of Bourbon the hopes of the Florentine schemers began to rise. Once more, as in the age of Dante, it was hoped that the exiles would be restored by the forces of the Emperor. A wide-flung conspiracy seems to have been formed, within the city and without, to overthrow the Medicean government with foreign aid.[47] Already at the commencement of December the Spanish ambassador at Rome had learnt that the discontented party within the walls would appreciate the sending of an envoy through whom they could treat.[48]   Outside the city, the exiles composed their internal differences and commenced to intrigue with Don Ugo da Moncada, one of the Imperial generals in Naples.   At their head stood Zanobi Buondelmonti and Battista della Palla, with others of those exiled from the city for their share in the conspiracy of 1522.   They gained over to their side without difficulty Filippo Strozzi, in spite of his being closely related to the Pope and hostage for him in Naples, and he in turn used his influence to secure Francesco Vettori, prominent among the Medicophile party in Florence, who became the centre for the intrigues within the walls.[49]   Niccolò Capponi, himself a brother-in-law of Strozzi, had done his best to induce Clement to allow the city to secure itself by a separate accord with the Imperialists. Failing in this, he was now in secret and mysterious correspondence with the Viceroy.[50]   Meanwhile it was arranged for Strozzi himself to be released to take charge of affairs.   Bourbon was instructed to refrain from sacking or overthrowing the city when he arrived, though he was not to spare its treasury.[51]   Lorenzo Salviati, a member of one of the noblest Florentine families, was sent to his camp to instruct him whom to take as hostages [52]; and it was believed that his family had come to a formal arrangement with the Strozzi and the Soderini to drive out the ruling house.[53]   Suspicions within the city rose.   Spies were daily being caught.[54]   It was forbidden by proclamation for any citizen to absent himself more than sixteen miles from the walls.[55]

Connected with all this was supposed to be a subsidiary conspiracy to urge Bourbon to change the government in Florence, formed at this same time at Venice.   But it was discovered, its leader was imprisoned, and others implicated fled to join the Florentine exiles in the Imperialist camp.[56]

Most subtle of all were the intrigues carried on from Siena. Discontent within Florence had been heightened by the inadequate supply of food which the mismanagement of Cortona had occasioned.   She was never anything like self-supporting, growing sufficient to satisfy only a quarter or a third of her needs.   The balance was brought from Montepulciano, Arezzo, and especially Pisa.[57]   But without doubt the demands of her allies proved a great drain on her resources, and on the approach of the Imperialists the shortage was increased by the influx of the refugees from the countryside.   As a result, the price of grain rose to five lire a bushel—far above the ordinary level.[58]   Some trivial measures were taken to prevent the dearth.   Towards the end of April, the duty upon solid provisions entering the city was suspended, while that on oil and wine was halved.[59]   This alone however could not appreciably ameliorate the position.   At the same time therefore we find the government much concerned about the supply of grain for which Clement was in treaty with the Sienese [60] ; but apparently nothing came of the negotiations. Siena, hotly Imperialist, had no desire to assist either the Pope or Florence, both her avowed enemies. Yet their need could be taken advantage of more effectively than by a mere withholding of supplies. Upon 12 April the Sienese government publicly decreed that, in case of a spontaneous revolt in Florence, they would send thither immediately not less than 4,000 bushels of grain at the rate of 500 a week, to be sold at 30 soldi the bushel : nearly a quarter, that is, of the current price. Battista della Palla and Zanobi Buondelmonti, the prime movers in the intrigues of the exiles, wrote the good news to the Signoria of their native city and had their letter printed as a broadsheet for the popular information. The citizens were called upon to rise against the government. They were advised how they could recover " Welfare, Liberty and Plenty " by subduing the authority of a single prepotent family.[61] Another incitement was thus added for the Florentines to rebel. They waited only for the opportunity.

In the face of the pusillanimous conduct of the generals of the league, there was one means only open for defence. Immediately the news of the movement of the Imperial forces had been received in Rome, Lannoy had been urged by the Pope to go and attempt to stop their advance by the payment of some of their arrears. He left Rome, taking with him 20,000 ducats scraped together by Clement with authority to raise from the Florentines the 60,000 promised by the armistice. Arriving in Florence on 6 April, he held a conference with the envoys of Bourbon. It was arranged that the Imperial forces should be paid 150,000 ducats, upon receipt of the first instalment of which they should commence to retire. The government by extreme measures managed to raise the first 60,000 and promised to collect an equal amount during the month of May. Thus, with the ransom to be paid for the Florentine hostages given by the Pope in the previous autumn, the sum required could be made up. Lannoy accordingly left Florence on 15 April, taking with him the 80,000 ducats already collected. Bourbon received the news of the agreement at Sta. Sofia, but pressed on his advance, informing the other that he would meet him the next day at Sta. Maria in Bagno. As the Viceroy proceeded to keep the appointment, he received a startling lesson as to the state to which Bourbon's depredations had driven the peasantry. Seeing a high Spanish officer with a small train, they set upon him with such ferocity that he escaped with difficulty with his life. The money was left in the hands of the Florentine commissary, who put it into safe keeping. The Viceroy therefore arrived at the Imperial camp with empty hands. This did not make the soldiers any more willing to assent to the agreement which had been made. Bourbon and his captains professed their preparedness to comply with the terms, but only on the receipt of the enormous sum of 300,000 ducats. Lannoy immediately wrote to the Pope informing him of these conditions and offering to provide part of the money ; he himself, ashamed to return to Florence, withdrew to Siena.[62] It afterwards transpired that there had been an actual conspiracy to deceive the Florentine government by lulling it into security while the army advanced.[63] Whether Lannoy was implicated in it, or whether Bourbon—as seems more probable—was hoping by discrediting the Viceroy to succeed to his office, the circumstances seemed to show that the whole thing—down even to the assault by the peasants—had been prearranged.   In spite of the negotiations, Bourbon continued to press on. On the day following the interview, he wrote to the Imperial governor in Milan that his army was short of corn, but could bear anything, longing for the plunder of Florence.[64]

The military outlook was however by now brighter. Guicciardini, at the time Lieutenant-General with the papal forces in the Romagna, had brought with him when he arrived in the city on the 23rd all the forces which could be spared from the camp. In response to the entreaties of the Florentines, he and the Venetian envoys sent urgent messages to the French and Venetian forces to come to their defence.   In spite of the fact that, by the armistice of the Pope, the connection of Florence with the league had nominally come to an end, the generals acceded to the request in return for a promise of independent adhesion on the part of the Florentines. A race accordingly took place between the opposing armies.   The forces of the league won, but by a very short space.   On 26 April, Bourbon arrived at S. Giovanni in the Val d' Arno, only 20 miles from the city ; but on the same day the Marquis of Saluzzo, with 10,000 Swiss and French, reached Barberino, about 12 miles away ; while the Duke of Urbino, with a Venetian army of 11,000, was no more than 10 miles distant.[65]

(5) IL TUMULTO DEL VENERDÌ

The danger to the city had nevertheless not passed. The opposing forces were not unequal ; and in leadership the advantage was with the Imperialists.   Urbino's lack of vigour and decision were notorious. Jealousies, personal and political, were quite as likely to influence the operations of Italian armies of the sixteenth century as military requirements ; and strictly speaking, the league was no longer under obligation to defend the city. Granted, too, that they had the desire and the ability, the peril was not over ; .for the forces of the league showed themselves very little behind the lanzknechts in their treatment of the territories through which they passed. The unfortunate refugees, crowding into the city in utter destitution, and sleeping in all the open spaces, where some even died of hunger, showed Florence what she herself might suffer at the hands of her allies.[66] The prospect of their victory was to be dreaded nearly as much as that of their defeat. The only sure safeguard of the city from either peril lay in the Florentines themselves. It was safe enough, wrote the English envoy to Wolsey, " if they lack no stomachs." [67] But it had been part of the deliberate policy of the Medici to keep the Florentines without arms, for fear that they would be turned against themselves. The tumult of 1526 had been caused by the insistent demands of the youth of the city for the resuscitation of the old armed militia in its Gonfaloni, for defence against the Imperialist menace. Now it was repeated, headed as before by Piero Salviati, who was probably in touch with his kinsman with the army of Bourbon, and with the connivance of some of the older citizens. For some days after the news of Bourbon's crossing the Apennines arrived, the city was kept in disorder by their insistent clamour. Collisions between the troops of the Medici and the populace became frequent. In one, the young Giuliano de' Gondi was mortally wounded ; but on the other side, one of the Palace Guard was slain, and with impunity, by Ludovico Martelli the poet. The readiness to arms of the soldiers within the walls made the youths more insistent that they should be granted the means of self-defence. Cortona, asked for his assent, applied to Rome and continually procrastinated. The Gonfalonier in office, titular head of the state, was Luigi Guicciardini, brother of the historian and member of a well-known Medicophile family. Daring neither to grant the youths' demands for fear of Cortona, nor to refuse them for fear of more violent consequences, he feigned himself ill and held informal consultations on the matter in the privacy of his own apartments. But by himself he could do nothing ; and the only result was to arouse the suspicions of the Cardinal, who, as in all times of stress, was still unable to come to a decision. A public consultation was held in the Medici Palace to advise upon the subject. Niccolò Capponi, asked his opinion, said boldly that such deliberations should be carried on in the Palazzo della Signoria, the official seat of government.

In the meantime, the Gonfalonier had continued to yield to the popular tumult. As a preliminary step, a list of those desirous of bearing arms was drawn up according to the ancient organization in Gonfaloni ; and the result showed that the whole city was practically unanimous in its desire. Guicciardini, in alarm, promised the agitators that he would satisfy their demands, and applied to the Cardinal for permission. The only answer he could get was that he seemed more eager in the matter than the youths themselves. Upon Friday, 26 April, the agitators again came into the Piazza clamouring for the fulfilment of the pledge. The Gonfalonier and his colleagues tried to quieten the tumult by a hurried proclamation to the effect that they should assemble in their companies that same afternoon and march in an orderly manner to the Piazza, when finally they would receive arms for the defence of the state.[68]

While matters were in this condition, news came of the arrival of the armies of the league within reach of the city, and her salvation from the peril of assault by the lanzknechts. The generals came in advance of their forces in order to study the ground at Incisa, a strong position at which they desired to coalesce. The citizens as usual gathered together to discuss the important news, especially in the Piazza and the Mercato Nuovo. The atmosphere was tense, and little was needed to cause a conflagration. The dispute of a cap-maker with some soldiers over payment was sufficient to commence an uproar : a cart-driver, beating a recalcitrant mule, added to the confusion. The merchants for safety commenced to close their shops. At this stage a rumour began to spread, sedulously fostered by some of the leading citizens, that Cortona had abandoned the city in dismay at the temper of the inhabitants. The story was indeed in part correct. True to his policy of attempting to settle all difficulties by a salutary neglect, he had ridden out at about mid-day to meet the allied commanders, who had arrived at Castello, no more than four miles distant. With him he took almost all of the garrison, who were to join the forces of the league at Incisa. Only about 400 troops were left behind. There went with him, too, the Cardinals Cibo and Ridolfi, Ippolito, and the majority of the military officials. Such amazing procedure caused a not un-natural impression that he had abandoned the city for good to the disorderly mob on the Piazza. The populace, aroused by the tumult, began to assemble ; and the crowd outside the Palazzo increased. Matters reached their climax at about three o'clock, when the youths who had led in the demand for arms, and had proceeded in their Gonfaloni according to instructions to the Duomo, marched into the Piazza to the number of some hundreds,[69] each wearing a white device. Immediately a clamour arose, and the people were called upon to rise and take arms. This soon developed into the ancient cry, to which the streets of Florence had so often echoed, " Popolo e Libertà ! "

Half the city was by now assembled on the Piazza pressing towards the Palazzo, armed with any weapons that came to their hand. Niccolò Capponi took the lead among the older citizens, as

Piero Salviati had done among the younger. At a sign from him, the two hundred arquebusiers defending the Palazzo forbore to fire, and, raising their weapons, retired into the neighbouring church of S. Piero Scheraggio.[70] The Gonfalonier came down upon the Ringhiera to still the tumult, addressing himself to the citizens by name and professing himself ready to do whatever was required of him. But he met with no success, and turned back into the Palace, with the mob pressing on at his heels into the building and up the stairs. Some remained below to guard the gate, not so much so that none should enter, as so that none whose presence was required within should leave. The Gonfalonier showed or feigned unwillingness to do what was demanded of him, and rebuked the ringleaders; but he could not oppose himself to the general will. The Signoria, though like himself nominated by the Medici, was overawed by the mob; and some of its members showed themselves sympathetic if not implicated. They were called upon to assemble; and some were even hastened by blows. The chamber in which they met was crowded with armed men, continually increasing in number and uproariousness, with no settled order or objects, and " all shouting as though in that consisted the victory." Only the Gonfalonier kept his head; and, with the aid of Jacopo Nardi and others, some sort of order was at last re-established. Amid acclamation, it was proposed to banish the Medici. The balloting-box was passed round to collect the votes—black beans for assent: white for dissent. " All black, God be thanked ! " cried Francesco Martelli, insincerely it was thought, as he scrutinized the votes. The notary of the Signoria was not present, and another was introduced almost by force to draw up the formal resolution. " The second time," he said, turning to the bystanders; he had performed the same office in 1494. The Signoria descended to the Ringhiera at the foot of the Palace; and there the Medici were publicly exiled to the sound of trumpets. Only a single dissentient voice was raised—that of a citizen who called upon his fellows to beware the penalties of excommunication; but he was only laughed at for his scruples by the people, who gaily mimicked and repeated the raucous cries of the herald.

The measures forced upon the Signoria did not end with this. All state condemnations, imprisonments, and banishments were revoked; and the constitution of 1512 was restored. Then only was the Signoria permitted to withdraw to its own apartments within the Palace, to which it was confined during its term of office. Still it was not wholly secure. The Gonfalonier himself had been wounded slightly in the neck by the young Jacopo Alamanni, his godson, with a knife of his own gift, in the midst of the deliberations [71]; and the flinging of his state robes out of

the window gave rise even to a report that he had been assassin-
ated.   One of the Priori was hurt more severely in the head by
the same youth as he returned from the audience room [72];
another escaped only by stooping.   Even the veteran Nardi was
threatened as a result of his attempts at pacification by one of
the youths " better endowed by fortune than by nature."   Returned to their apartments, accompanied by some of the more
responsible citizens, the Signoria remained puzzled and inactive.
They could decide on nothing else to do but to send a tardy
message to the Duke of Urbino confirming the adherence of the
city to the league.   It was an obvious move.   Knowing of the
hatred borne by the Duke towards the Pope, they had hopes that he
would be glad of the pretext not to oppose the city in its revolt.

Meanwhile, without, the rioters had taken matters into their
own hands.   The keys of the belfry had been seized and, despite
the unwillingness of the Signoria, the great bell of the Palazzo
was sending out its metallic clangour over the whole city, summoning to the Piazza those who had not yet come.   Only a few
Mediceans kept in their homes, or on their arrival were forbidden
entry by the angry mob ; while the *popolo minuto*, the unprivileged inhabitants, always negligible in Florentine affairs, remained
unmoved.   The prisoners in the Bargello were released.   The
armoury was entered, and the arms there seized and distributed.
Some, more far-sighted, made themselves masters of the artillery ;
others went to take charge of the public granaries.   Several of
the mercenary captains, deceived by a false report of a resolution
of the Signoria, were persuaded to continue under the Republic
the service into which they had entered for the Medici.

In all this, however, the essential peril had been overlooked.
The Cardinals had by a coincidence met the Duke of Urbino on
the road before they arrived at Ancisa.   They were therefore not
two miles distant from the city when news of the outbreak
reached them.   Immediately they set about return, accompanied by the generals and by the troops withdrawn from the
city.   Arrived at the Porta di Faenza, they found it open to
receive them.   Although instructions had been given to close
the gate, it was nobody's special care, and by unpardonable
negligence the order had been left unobeyed.   Baccio Valori,
one of the strongest supporters of the Medici, had been repulsed
with blows on trying to enter the Palazzo, whither some of the
leaders had summoned him.   Considering it impossible to gain
the friendship of any new regime he determined not to forfeit
that of the old.   With the help therefore of Ottaviano de' Medici,
a distant kinsman of the ruling house, he set about reconverting
some of the captains to their old allegiance, and confirming
those who were vacillating.   As soon as possible he had sent a

force to make sure of this all-important gate, which was found open and unguarded. Thus the Cardinals found their entrance to the city easy and unopposed. Cortona, with more spirit than was consistent with his character and more activity than could be expected from his unwieldy person, struck spurs into his horse and darted forward, crying " To the Piazza ! To the Piazza ! " The others followed him with alacrity. It was an ill requital for this ardour that Cibo's steed fell on top of him, bruising one of his legs. Count Piero Nofri, captain of the infantry in the pay of the city, pressed on in advance with a thousand of his men. As he came towards the centre of the city, he ordered his troops to fire into the air. The operation had the desired effect. No sooner had the reports of the arquebuses been heard than the majority of the rioters dispersed to their homes, where they remained shut in anxiously awaiting the result. The republican fervour of the citizens melted into thin air ; and those who already had their mouths open to cry " Popolo," says Varchi, concluded the word as " Palle." As the troops entered the Piazza, the people who remained suddenly scattered, leaving it empty. Only a couple of hundred were left in the Palazzo, badly armed and without provisions ; though among these were included the majority of the aristocratic leaders of the revolt, and even a Canon who was prominent in the defence.[73] The great bell continued to sound over the city, but there was no further response to its call. Only in the Oltr' Arno, Palla Rucellai and one of the Ridolfi now plucked up courage to collect a couple of hundred of the populace of the neighbourhood, and to parade the streets as far as the Piazza [74] with shouts in favour of the Medici. First occupying the openings of the streets in order to prevent succour, Nofri's troops advanced to attack the Palazzo. With their seven arquebuses, the defenders succeeded in wounding several of their assailants and killing one ; but they could not prevent them from reaching the gates. These were locked and barred. The soldiers immediately set about prising the greater open with their pikes, and setting fire to another. No attempt was made to oppose this fatal operation excepting by throwing down light tiles from above, which generally fell too far out, and by ineffectual thrusts made through the interstices. At this juncture the veteran Nardi, who had more experience in such matters, recollected the provision made for similar emergencies in the old days. Going up to the roof, he found there some piles of heavy stones brought up for the purpose, which, neatly stacked together and outwardly cemented with mortar, appeared to be ordinary benches and so had hitherto escaped notice. With these they set about smashing the coverings of the machicolations, and dropped them down upon the heads of the assailants with such effect that they were forced to draw off, pursued with good effect by further arquebus shots. But the Florentines, too, suffered a serious casualty. One stone, falling upon Michelangelo's famous statue of David—the Giant of the Piazza, as it was unappreciatively called [75]—broke its arm into two pieces. It was several years before the precious fragments were restored.[76]

Meanwhile, the Cardinals had arrived with the commanders, and had taken up their station in one of the streets leading into the Piazza.[77] It was determined not to risk another assault without a preliminary bombardment. Though the approach of night was making the question immediate, operations ceased while artillery was being fetched from the Medici Palace, and Venetian troops were summoned from outside. During the pause, there was seen coming across the Piazza from the Palazzo Federigo da Bozzolo, an able captain in the French pay come to Florence a few days previously at the request of the Pope, but already well known and popular in the city. He had ridden out that day with the Cardinals; but immediately he heard of the occurrences of the afternoon had spurred back with only two grooms. With some difficulty he had obtained admission to the Palazzo at the height of the tumult, and endeavoured to pacify the rioters. He was met with refusal if not with threats; but on the arrival of the troops of the league was somehow left inside. Fearing the fury of the defenders as well as perhaps some error of the assailants, he had kept himself out of sight; but had taken advantage of the lull in the fighting to obtain permission to leave. This was possible only in one rôle, that of the peace-maker. To the surprise of the rioters, who had forgotten his presence, they heard him call up the stairs offering himself as an intermediary for accord. There was an immediate rush to accept the offer, says Nardi, each one fearing to be omitted. The ruse succeeded; and Bozzolo was allowed to leave. Once outside, he showed himself in his true colours. He crossed the Piazza burning with indignation and intending to advise the Cardinals to make a determined attack, which he was assured must succeed. In this mood he was accosted by Guicciardini, who came out to meet him.[78] The papal commissary was not destitute of the feelings of a Florentine, and was in addition concerned for the safety of his brother, the pliant Gonfalonier. He set himself to dissuade the fiery captain, pointing out to him the harm that would succeed from an assault, both to the Pope and to the confederates. Bozzolo allowed himself to be persuaded. Together they went to Cortona, who was obdurate, though they pointed out to him the fatal possibilities of the use of violence. But with the aid of the Cardinal Ridolfi, together with Urbino and the other commanders, his objections

were finally overcome. Guicciardini drew up a rough draft of
the terms, offering a free pardon in return for surrender, in a
shop upon a bench : and Bozzolo returned with him to the
Palazzo bearing them. Some of the defenders had already commenced to slink away through a side entrance. Those who
remained were appealed to by Bozzolo in the name of the King
of France, and of the exigencies of the city and the league. There
was indeed no alternative for them but surrender. Enormously
outnumbered by the attackers, and with the odds ever increasing,
there can be no doubt that their stronghold could easily have
been carried by assault and that its historic halls would have
run with the blood of some of the noblest of Florentine families ;
nor could the rest of the city be considered safe once the confederate army had whetted its appetite for slaughter and for
spoil. The terms were therefore accepted in an amended form
drawn up by Francesco Vettori, still among the defenders of the
Palace, and the third historian to be prominently connected with
the happenings of the day. Nevertheless, it had become almost
a maxim in Italy not to trust to the faith of a priest. It was
stipulated therefore that the articles of surrender should be
guaranteed also by Urbino and the other commanders. Bozzolo
again returned across the Piazza ; and there, in Or San Michele,
the document was formally signed by the Cardinals and the
generals of the league. The intermediary went back once more
to the Palazzo. At the gate he and Guicciardini gathered the
remaining defenders in a circle around them and ordered them
to go home, pledging their word of honour that they would not
be molested. The Signoria in a less uproarious session meekly
determined to consider as null all the resolutions which they had
passed earlier in the afternoon. The comic-opera revolution was
at an end.[79]

What might be facetiously called the Third Florentine Republic
had lasted for no more than a few hours.[80] In the course of a
single afternoon it had experienced all the vicissitudes of a state :
a revolution, a new constitution, a victory, a capitulation. It
could pride itself that it had inflicted more injury than it had
suffered. As many as twenty soldiers had fallen in the attack,[81]
but not one of the defenders ; and only four citizens were killed
in all. Elsewhere some troops, called in to defend the Palazzo
de' Gondi, had set about sacking it. They were induced to withdraw ; but not before their tumult had disturbed and perhaps
hastened the last hours of the youthful head of the house, who
was lying seriously wounded. Another citizen, returning home
wounded by a pike-thrust, met some soldiers before the church
of S. Pulinari, who ordered him to cry " Palle ! " He stoutly
refused and was stabbed to death with a cry of " Popolo ! " still

on his lips. Bernardo Ciacchi was remembered as the martyr of the day.[82]

The insurrection had proved a complete fiasco. Alessandro de' Medici had remained throughout undisturbed in his villa at Poggio, and the next day received an exuberant account from his faithful correspondent. Bozzolo had acted like a Cæsar : Nofri had been a very Paladin. But above all Cortona had displayed his greatness. He had saved all by his prudence and wisdom, and had shown his will and his ability to act.[83] As a matter of fact, this praise is not so out of place as might be thought. The rising had failed owing to Cortona's masterly inaction, though this was due to his stupidity rather than to his foresight. His amazing action in leaving the city to its tumult had paralysed his enemies. The revolt lost its purpose. The citizens could only clamour around the Palazzo and force resolutions through the Signoria. All those against whom they could have turned their arms had left. The organization and cohesion which could have come to them from fighting alone was thus lost ; and the forced diversion of their attention to the political side made them neglect even such a primary military necessity as making themselves masters of the city gates.

In another way, too, the insensate departure of the Cardinal was a lucky stroke. According to information later received, the web of intrigue which had been woven to overthrow the Medici with the aid of the Imperialist arms had fixed the revolt for the following day.[84] Bourbon had already reached Figline near Incisa : and on the Saturday he was to have approached the city and would have been aided by a simultaneous rising within the walls. The departure of the Cardinals had provoked a premature outbreak, unaided by outside assistance ; and now it was suppressed there was no fear of an immediate repetition. The rule of Cortona was to last for another few weeks.

NOTES TO CHAPTER I

[1] I.e. " The Balls "—an allusion to the famous coat of arms of the Medici, said to have left its trace even in the pawnbrokers' signs of the English streets.

[2] *Balia*—" an extraordinary commission with plenipotentiary powers." The word is allied to the French *bailli*, or the English *bailiff* ; and with the accent on the first syllable instead of on the second has the meaning of " nurse."

[3] For the Parlamento in theory and in practice as it appeared to a Venetian contemporary, cf. Foscari, *Relazione, apud* Albèri, *Relazioni degli Ambasciatori Veneti al Senato*, Ser. II, i, 45.

[4] Cf. Aristotle, *Politics*, IV (ix), § 4. " The appointment of magistrates by lot is democratical, and the election of them oligarchical."

[5] Hence the secondary name " *Imborsazione*."

[6] This system was called "*a mano*," or "*Le borse aperte*" as contrasted with "*Le borse serrate*."

[7] For a history and description of the Palazzo Medici, better known as the Palazzo Riccardi, cf. Reumont, *La Jeunesse de Catherine de Médicis*, pp. 75–9.

[8] Cf. especially Anzilotti, *La crisi costituzionale della Repubblica Fiorentina*, pp. 54–9, and Caggese, *Firenze dalla Decadenza di Roma al Risorgimento d'Italia*, II, 434–5.

[9] That this was not a matter of theory only is shown, for example, by a commission appointed in 1521 to suppress disorder in the contado and lighten its taxation (Anzilotti, p. 61). For the instructions of Leo X to Lorenzo, see *A.S.I.*, Ser. I, Appendix VIII, 299–306.

[10] Anzilotti, *ubi supra*.

[11] For all this, which makes no claim to originality, see the usual authorities, especially Perrens, *Histoire de Florence*, 1434–1531, Vol. III, cap. (i) ; Villari, *Life of Machiavelli*, Book I, caps. xv–xvi, and II, cap. vi ; and Caggese, op. cit., Vol. II, cap. v.

[12] Treaty of 1519 with Charles V *apud* Caggese, II, 438. Cf. also that with Francis I of the same year, *ibid.* ; and *State Papers, Venetian*, IV, 62. " With regard to the Florentines, the Nuncio promised their assent."

[13] In a letter to his mother, not in the traditional formula or manner ; cf. Villari, *Machiavelli*, II, 473, n. 2.

[14] This account of the foreign policy of Clement is taken from *Cambridge Modern History*, Vol. II, cap. 2 ; Pastor, *History of the Popes*, Vol. IX, caps. 7–9 ; and Creighton, *History of the Papacy*, Vol. V, caps. 8 and 9.

[15] Priorista di Ser Paolo Paoli in *Ricordi Storici di Filippo Rinuccini*, p. clxxxi.

[16] 350,000 ducats out of a total of 800,000.

[17] Benedetto Varchi, *Storia Fiorentina*, I, 96. (References are to the pagination of the edition of 1838–41, used by Arbib in his indices and set out by him marginally.)

For an evaluation of Varchi and the other historians of the period, cf. Lupo Gentile, *Storiografia alla Corte di Cosimo I*, in which he shows that Varchi's value is as a compiler rather than an original historian, as which *Nerli* is to be preferred. Cf. also *Sulle fonti inedite della Storia Fiorentina di Benedetto Varchi* by the same author in *Studi Storici*, XIV (Pisa, 1905), and *Sulle fonti della Storia Fiorentina di Benedetto Varchi* (Sarzana, Costa, 1906). It will be found convenient, nevertheless, to refer to Varchi instead of to his less comprehensive sources in many instances in the succeeding pages.

The *Vita di Niccolò Capponi*, attributed to Segni, whether by him or by Giannotti, as has been affirmed, is a primary authority for the history of this period, unlike Segni's *Storie Fiorentine*. The works of Giovio, Nerli, and Segni have been examined by G. Sanesi in *Alcune osservazioni su tre storici minori del Cinquecento*.

[18] Even this natural paternity was not unquestioned. Giuliano is said to have hesitated before recognizing Ippolito as his son : while Alessandro (later Duke of Florence) was reported to be child of Clement himself, born while he was a simple Knight of St. John. This seems, however, to be mere scandal : and an amazing begging letter of 1528, published by Ferrai (*Lorenzino de' Medici e la Società Cortigiana del Cinquecento*, Appendix II (ix)), confirms, if authentic, "Lorenzaccio's" account, that Alessandro was son of the Duke of Urbino and a half-caste servant named Simonetta, afterwards wife of a carter of Collevecchio. Cf. *infra*, p. 108. Which of the two youths was the senior is doubtful ; see *Varchi*, I, 68 and editor's note (i).

[19] Perrens, *Histoire de Florence*, III, 105–6, carried away by the prevailing illegitimacy among the Medici of the time, states incorrectly that Giovanni himself was a natural son. Was he misled into thinking of Bande Nere as equivalent to the bar sinister? Actually, Giovanni's mother was Caterina Sforza, who introduced a new and fresher strain into the breed.

[20] Paolo Paoli, p. clxxxi ; Rastrelli, *Storia d' Alessandro de' Medici*, I, 3–11.

[21] Foscari, *Relazione*, p. 74.

[22] *Ibid.*, p. 73.

[23] Varchi, I, 69.

[24] Foscari, *Relazione*, pp. 43–4.

[25] *Ibid.*, p. 74.

[26] *Storia di Paolo Giovio*, II, 22.

[27] Pastor, IX, 278–83 ; Varchi, I, 107.

[28] Foscari, *Relazione*, p. 31 ; *Relazione di Antonio Soriani, apud* Albèri, Ser. II, v, 415–16 ; Paolo Paoli, p. clxxxii.

[29] Perrens, III, 63–4.

[30] Villari, *Machiavelli*, II, 353–6 ; Hauvette, *Luigi Alamanni, sa vie et son œuvre*, pp. 29–39.

[31] Varchi, I, 99, 110.

[32] Pastor, IX, 283.

[33] Varchi, I, 104–5 ; Foscari, *Relazione*, p. 84 ; Nerli, *Commentarj*, p. 147

[34] .Villari, *Machiavelli*, II, 517.

[35] Letter to Capponi of 15 January 1526/7 in *Lettere di Principi*, II, 47.

[36] Pio Falletti Fossati, *Assedio di Firenze*, I, 273–86. Cf. also *Calendar of State Papers, Spanish*, III (ii), 58 (Prothonotary Caracciolo to Charles V, Milan, 28 April 1527). Similarly he was being encouraged by the Imperial Ambassador at Venice to restore the liberties of Florence, while obtaining at the same time a monetary payment. *Ibid.*, III (i), 626.

[37] Cf. V. G. Salvioli, *Nuovi studi . . . sulle vicende dell' esercito imperiale in Italia nel* 1526–7, in *Archivio Veneto*, Vol. XVIII, and Jacopo Buonaparte, *Sul sacco di Roma*, in *Chroniques et Mémoires sur l'histoire de France*, ed. J. A. C. Buchon, Vol. XI.

[38] Archivio Mediceo avanti il Principato (*R. Archivio di Stato di Firenze*), filz. 126 *passim*, January–April, 1527. Cf. also Ferrai, *op. cit.*, App. II, n. 6.

[39] Paolo Paoli, p. clxxxiii ; Varchi, I, 110–11 ; Michelangelo, *Lettere*, ed. Milanese, p. 598.

[40] *R. Archivio di Stato di Firenze*, Balie, Vol. XLIX, fo. 393.

[41] *Ibid.*, fo. 398 ; Ammirato, *Istorie Fiorentine*, VII, 28.

[42] Paolo Paoli, *ubi supra*. *R. Archivio di Stato di Firenze*, Deliberazioni de' Signori e Collegi (to be cited as " Signoria "), Vol. CXXIX, 14 April 1527. " Deliberaverunt et mandaverunt . . . locis piis & ecclesiasticis civitatis florentinæ quatenus per totam diem xv dictj presentis mensis debeant dedisse et cum effectu consigniasse prefatis excelsis dominis omnia eorum argenta cuiuscunque qualitatis existans. . . ."

[43] Villari, *Machiavelli*, II, 512–13.

[44] Varchi, I, 108. Cf. also *Cronica di Fra Giuliano Ughi*, in *A.S.I.*, 1st series, App. VII, p. 141, " e fu questa cosa una delle maggiore pazzie del mondo."

[45] In Foscari's opinion (*Relazione*, p. 15).

[46] Guicciardini, *Carteggio dal* 1527 *al* 1534, in *Opere Inedite*, Vol. V ; letters of 26 and 29 April.

[47] Slender indications of this intrigue are to be found only in Varchi, I, 111.

[48] *State Papers, Spanish*, III (i), 628. Perez to Charles, 4 December 1526.

[49] See Strozzi's letter of 18 January 1527/8 to Vettori in Bardi, *Filippo Strozzi da nuovi documenti*, in *A.S.I.*, Ser. V, Vol. xiv, p. 55. For further information as to his position, see *infra*, pp. 42–3, and the letter there cited.

[50] R. Bibliotheca Nazionale di Firenze, Strozziane, II (iii), v. 433, fo. 7:—

Honorando Niccolo. Io riceve la vostra Sabato a prima hore ; et domenica trovai qui elvice Re donde subito che avemo pranzato ripartimo et lo acconpagniamo poco dilà dalla vernia donde sene andò in campo et per la stremità del tempo et perchè staua anchora in collera del caso di venerdì non mi parse da parlare del negotio vostro. Chiamaci che andiamo a Cortona dove vuole he. re ancora sua ex. et la spero farmi conoscere che la antiqua affectione mia a le cose vostre non è diminuita et (. . . ?) la vostra buona gratia mi raccomando che dio vi contenti da poppi a li XXIIII. d' aprile 1527.

Deditiss⁰ fratello Rosso Ridolphi Comm.

(*Superscription*) Nobili dⁿᵒ Niccolò Capponi
Come Fʳᵉ honrᵈᵒ a Fiorenza.

Cf. also Capponi's correspondence with Pope in Ruscelli, *Lettere di Principi*, II, 46–9 and 51–3 (15 January and 7 February). It is impossible to interpret these, with Pitti in the *Apologia de' Cappucci*, as an attempt to persuade the Pope to accord the city a more liberal government. Capponi asked that the citizens should " govern themselves " and " have the rein " only with regard to pursuing a separate direction in foreign policy. He would not have dared to request more.

[51] Archivio Mediceo, *ubi supra*, 1 March . . . " Meglio intesa, la lettera del vicere intercetta ; scriveva a Borbon che venisse a Firenze et vedesse di entrarci senza saccheggiar nè rovinar la Città ; perchè così era la voluntà della Cesarea Maestà per esser devotissima sua : ma che vedesse di trarne più denari che'l posserà . . ."

[52] *Ibid.*, 3 March . . . " Lorenzo Salviati, figliuolo di Jacopo, è nel campo de' Lanzenech con alcuni altri fiorentini, banditi et confinati, et è quello che doveva dar l'ostaggi di questa Città a Borbon."

[53] British Museum, Bergenroth Transcripts of Spanish State Papers, Vol. VII (Add. MSS. 28,586), f. 187 (Perez to Charles, 2 May 1527 ; not in the printed *Calendar of Spanish State Papers*) . . . " Se junctaron los sarviatis y strocis y sederinos a una parte contra el presente govierno." This may be, however, a distorted account of the Tumulto del Venerdì. The same names appear in Agnello's account (Sanuto, *Diarii* XLIV, 583).

[54] Archivio Mediceo, *ubi supra*, 28 February, 1 March.

[55] Ammirato, VII, 29.

[56] Archivio Mediceo, *ubi supra*, 1 and 2 March. Varchi, I, 210. Cf. also Sanuto, XLV, 26.

[57] Foscari, *Relazione*, p. 25 *seqq.*

[58] Even at the time of the siege it was fixed at only 3 lire 15 soldii (*Diario di Luca Landucci*, 10 October 1529).

[59] Signoria, CXXIX, 20 April 1527.

[60] Archivio Mediceo, *ubi supra*, 2–15 April 1527.

[61] See the unique copy of the printed proclamation, signed by hand, in the R. Bibliotheca Nazionale di Firenze, Strozziane, II (iii), 433, f. 8. The text was printed by Rafaelli most inconsequentially in *Verse e Prose di Luigi Alamanni* (I, 347) without any suggestion of its provenance or

of its significance : and, what is of most importance, without even indicating that the original is in proclamation form.

⁶² The order of these transactions, confused and contradictory in the accounts of contemporary and subsequent historians, is cleared up by the Spanish despatches from the Bergenroth Transcripts, Vol. VII, in the *State Papers, Spanish.* Cf. especially III, ii, 54 (Lannoy to Lope de Soria, Siena, 25 April 1527), and 56 (Perez to Charles, 26 April). For other details, see Ammirato, VII, 30–1 ; Varchi, I, 116 ; and Sanuto, XLIV, 472, 498–9, 521, and XLV, 24.

⁶³ Rossi, I, 7. Cf. Sanuto, *ubi supra,* " Qui si dice pubblico che' l Vicerè ha intendimento nella città di Firenze."

⁶⁴ *Ibid.,* XLIV, 570–1.

⁶⁵ Ammirato, VII, 31 ; Foscari, *Relazione,* pp. 48–9.

⁶⁶ Cf. MS. Diary in Bibliotheca Nazionale di Firenze (Magl. XXV, 555), f. 12. " Ruborono e predorono ttutta il muglielo ell val darno e mesono an sanco ogni vjlla dove canpjtavano di Bestjame di robe eccosì pigliavano gliomjnj e ponevano tanglia sichè nocivi demonj comparē . . . in modo istabrò in firenze tutto il conttando anpreso a mjglia venti in modo che in firenze non si trovavon pane . . ." Cf. also Paolo Paoli, 184. " They sacked all of our contado worse than if they had been enemies in the cruelties which they did. And besides the goods they carried off, they took away girls, and laid levies on the men . . ."

⁶⁷ *Letters and Papers, Henry VIII,* IV, 3042.

⁶⁸ This is the most probable and consistent account of these transactions which can be made up from the tangled and contradictory narratives of the historians. Varchi, I, 116 ff. ; Ammirato, VII, 31–2 ; Nardi, *Historie,* p. 191, and *Lettera sopra la mutazione dello stato nel 1527,* in *Miscellanea Fiorentina,* I, 132–42. Perrens' brilliant account of this, as of succeeding events, is original only in its inaccuracies, which are legion. It is impossible to point them out as they occur. The order of events is put beyond doubt by the actual terms of the proclamation (Signoria, CXXIX, 26 April 1527).

Bamnum. Item dicti excelsi Domini & Vexillifer simul adunati ec. verbo buonominibus commiserunt micti Bamnum in Locis publicis per unum ex eorum Bamnitoribus quod omnes se congregent ad eorum Gonfalonem & veniant in eorum plateam pro defensione huius præsentis pacifice status ibique consummant arma Libere licite & inpuniter.

⁶⁹ 600, says Foscari in the *Relazione,* p. 49 ; 300, in his letter to his son of the same day (Sanuto, XLIV, 580–2) ; 1,000, reported Peregrino to Alexander (cf. his letter of 27 April in Appendix of Documents, no. I) ; 300–400, wrote Pazzi to Segni (latter of 4 May *apud* Lupo Gentile, *Storiografia,* Appendix V).

⁷⁰ Their commander was not unnaturally suspected of having been bribed : cf. letter of Peregrino, *ubi supra.*

⁷¹ In sport, according to Nardi. Nevertheless, a formal pardon to Jacopo and his father was considered necessary after the Revolution for their actions on this day: Signoria, *ibid.,* 18 May.

⁷² Sufficiently severely to be still unable to serve as " *Preposto* " (or chairman of the Signoria in rotation) two days later. *Ibid.,* 28 April.

⁷³ As one of the Buonuomini, in whose province the care of the Palazzo was.

⁷⁴ Cf. the resolution of the Balìa (*infra,* p. 41), " si trovò personalmente alla recuperatione della Piazza."

⁷⁵ " Et insino al povero Gingante di Piazza ha patito per lo stato de' Medici " (Peregrino to Alexander, 28 April, in Archivio Mediceo, *ubi supra*).

[76] Vasari, *Vita di Francesco Salviati*, in *Opere*, VIII, 8. The restoration took place only under Cosimo.

[77] At the Canto de' Banderai in the Via tra Farsettai, says Nardi ; nella Strada del Garbo, reports Guicciardini ; at the Canto degli Instaupatori, according to the MS. diarist :—an interesting insight into Florentine street nomenclature, if all are intended to refer to the same place. Passerini, in his notes to Ademollo's *Marietta de' Ricci*, I, 165, fixes the Cardinal's headquarters precisely at the shop under the Cerchi Palace.

[78] For the parts played by Bozzolo and Guicciardini in the negotiations, see Appendix A. The account here given differs in important particulars from the accepted story.

[79] In addition to the accounts cited above, cf. letters of Foscari, Agnello and Moro of same day in Sanuto, XLIV, 580–4 ; Paolo Giovio, II, 17–22 ; Segni, I, 8 ff. ; *Vita di Niccolò Capponi*, p. 913 ff. ; Foscari, *Relazione*, p. 50 ff. ; Guicciardini, *Storia d'Italia*, IV, 116–20 ; Letters of Paolo Pazzi to Bernardo Segni, in Appendix to Lupo Gentile, *Storiografia* ; and report of Peregrino to Alessandro (see Appendix of Documents, No. 1). The true part played by Luigi Guicciardini is in dispute. Both parties seem to have thought that he was tricking them. Pazzi suspected him of temporizing with the revolters while help was coming up ; Peregrino, of playing false to the government. The former had suspicions even of Capponi and the elder citizens.

The resolutions were not formally revoked, as is usually said, on the *same* day, but on the last day of the Signoria's term of office. See Signoria, CXXIX, 30 April 1527.

Revocatio partitorum rogatorum per S. Julianum de Ripa.   Item prefati Mag[d] et Ex[si] Domini et vexillifer simul adunati atteso che venerdì proximo passato che fummo addì XXVI del presente mese silevò uno tumulto nella città contro alpacifico stato di quella et assai numero di gente corso impalazzo de Signiori et quelli assaltorno al improviso et parte di quelli ferirno et tutti furno quasi constituiti in pericolo della vita ; et atteso che alhora constrecti da quello tumulto per evitare el pericolo della morte et perchè non seguisse maggiore scandolo feciono certi partiti rogati alhora per S. Giuliano di S. Domenico da Ripa e' quali partiti Benchè di sua natura sieno nulli et non vaglino sì per essere facti per forza et per paura sì per esser rogati da persona inhabile arogare partiti della Signoria Nondimancho per ogni abbundante cautela Servatis ec. Deliberorno et deliberando quelli et qualunque di quelli per questo presente partito annullorono cassorono et rivocorono et percassi et annullati havere uolsono et comandarono per ogni miglior modo che poterno. Mandantes ec.

[80] Five, according to Foscari (Sanuto, XLIV, 581).

[81] Accepting the estimate of Ammirato and Nardi, though others place it lower.

[82] Varchi, I, 128, 132–3.

[83] Letter of 27 April in Appendix of Documents, No. I.

[84] Letter of Peregrino of 28 April in Archivio Mediceo, *ubi supra*, . . . " Et la congiura si doveva scoprir hieri, et non l'altrieri . . ."

CHAPTER II

THE RESTORATION OF THE REPUBLIC

(I) THE EXPULSION OF THE MEDICI

" THE House of Medici now has it made clear who is its friend and who its foe," wrote Peregrino to Alessandro after the revolt, " and henceforth it knows what to do." [1] It was true : but the result was not a comforting one. It had found out that it had barely a single wholehearted supporter in the whole city. Baccio Valori and half-a-dozen others alone had dared to work in its favour during the temporary eclipse in its fortunes. The story went that the Pope, who in the space of four or six hours had received the news of the overthrow of his authority and of its restoration, wrote to Cortona instructing him to search out the authors of the tumult and to chastise them without respect of person. The Cardinal replied that in such a case it would be necessary to punish the whole city. [2] It is more probable that his abstention was due to the prospect of the opposition of the other signatories to the compact, especially the Duke of Urbino, who would respect his word of honour the more punctiliously in a matter whereby the Pope would be annoyed. Cortona refrained therefore from following the counsel of his intransigeant supporters, who advised him to take advantage of the presence of the doves in their cote to crush their heads. He sent a list of sixty of the greatest offenders to the Pope for his instructions, but was told to wait : " Now we must attend to the enemies without, and then to those within," wrote Peregrino. [3] For the moment, therefore, Cortona contented himself with punishing, and not too severely, some of the less important leaders. Antonio Nerli, the canon who had been among the first to raise the cry of " Popolo e Libertà " and had shown himself prominent in the defence of the Palazzo, was handed over to the dubious mercies of the spiritual arm and imprisoned in the Archbishop's palace ; the notary who drew up the resolution of exile was heavily fined ; and three or four others suffered similarly. [4]

Meanwhile the facile Florentines, pallid and shamefaced, had commenced to put in an appearance at the Palazzo de' Medici to excuse the part they had played in the revolt. On the very same evening Capponi and some others had set the example by going in a body from the scene of their insubordination to exculpate themselves. Even Piero Salviati, the leader of the youth, after keeping himself low for some days, finally followed the rest, and was to be seen continually in the ante-rooms of the Cardinal's lodgings. Some sixty others fled from the city. It seemed that the Medici were re-established more securely than ever ; and the cry of " Palle " was heard everywhere about the streets.[5]

Yet they did not have the hardihood to trust merely to an artificial revulsion of sentiment. The gates of the city were watched. The street corners and public squares were defended with artillery, and the citizens found difficulty in going about their private business. The entrances to the Piazza were barricaded and guarded day and night so that the young Giorgio Vasari, going with Francesco Salviati to search amid the debris for the precious fragments of Michelangelo's David, had to pass between the pickets.[6] The Palazzo was filled with troops more reliable than the suspected arquebusiers of Friday : and even the members of the Colleges had difficulty in obtaining admission. Ippolito went about with a bodyguard of two hundred.[7] A proclamation was made that all should lay down their arms with the exception of persons specially licensed to bear them ; while those seized from the armoury were to be immediately restored under the penalty of the strappado.[8] All citizens were forbidden to leave the city and those absent ordered to return. The Commissaries of Pisa and Poggibonsi, and the Captain of Volterra, who had acted equivocally on hearing the news of the revolt, were removed from their posts and replaced by others more reliable.[9] The fidelity of the troops was assured by securing their rations by a special distribution.[10] The term of office of the Signoria, which had begun on 1 March, was drawing to its close ; and the names of its successors had already been decided and put into the ballot bags for the formal extraction. The recent happenings had shown that a man's ancestral proclivities could no longer be counted on implicitly. The choice was accordingly revised. In particular the name of the chosen Gonfalonier was replaced by that of Francesco Antonio Nori, a partisan above suspicion, whose father had fallen with Giuliano de' Medici in the Conspiracy of the Pazzi. On the 28th, the solemn farce of the extraction was carried through ; and on 1 May, the new Signoria came into office.[11]

During their period of office, while the treasure in the Palazzo was being weighed, a great cross of silver that hung in the chapel proved too heavy for the chains and came crashing to the ground. It was noted as an omen to the Church and to the city : amply to be fulfilled before the term was ended.[12]

Meanwhile, the city had been adjusting itself in its external relations. By the Treaty of Cognac, Florence had been put under the protection of the league without formally joining it, and that only by a secret clause. Even this had been negotiated by the Pope without reference to the Florentines ; and the events of Friday had shown how little they could be considered bound by his influence. Moreover, the Pope had formally detached himself from the league by his truce with Lannoy, and thus this indirect connection was now at an end. These considerations greatly exercised the minds of the confederate generals and politicians ; and they took advantage of their presence in Florence and of their momentary importance to the government to press for a formal entry of the city into the alliance on its own behalf as a principal. Upon the Sunday the treaty was signed in the Palazzo de' Medici. Florence became a formal member of the league with the obligation to maintain in its armies a force of 5,000 foot with 250 men at arms and 500 light horse.[13] At the same time Urbino took the opportunity to secure the cession, refused by him a few days before for fear of an appearance of venality,[14] of the castle of St. Leo with the neighbouring Maiuolo, which had been filched from him and added to Florence after the iniquitous war of 1517.[15] It was noticed that this, too, was done unconstitutionally, without the cognizance of the magistracy in whose province it lay.[16] A review of the confederate troops in Florence upon 30 April, " *fiorita e bella gente*," showed the citizens the nature of the league into which they had entered, and conveyed a scarcely-veiled threat of the penalty for defection.[17]

Upon the day after the tumult, Bourbon, who had approached almost within sight of the city, inexplicably turned aside and, crossing the Arno, passed down the Val d' Ombra in the direction of Siena. Men hailed the deliverance as a veritable miracle of God.[18] The Signoria less optimistically feared that, hearing of the preparedness of the city, he had gone to avail himself of the offer of their enemies, the Sienese, and would return before long strengthened by their artillery.[19] Others, and with perhaps greater reason, thought his action due to the failure of the premature rising and to the consequent impossibility of support from within.[20] A contributory cause might be found in the counsels of the Duke of Ferrara, who had discouraged the enterprise ; and his envoy in Florence reported that he was regarded by the citizens as their deliverer, to such an extent that they spoke of erecting a statue to him as an expression of their gratitude.[21] However this may be, all apprehensions turned out in the event ungrounded. Under the stress of circumstances, Bourbon pushed on by forced marches to Rome, which he knew to be utterly unprepared and undefended. The army of the league, delayed about Florence by reason of the insurrection and the subsequent negotiations, was slow to follow him : though whether Urbino would have shown greater activity under any circumstances is to be questioned. The arrival of the news of the re-entry of the Pope into the league upon the 25th stimulated him to greater exertion. Count Guido Rangone was sent in advance by way of Perugia with 5,000 men to intercept the march of the Imperialists. Upon 1 May, the Duke himself tardily followed with the rest of his troops through Florence, succeeded on the following day by Saluzzo.[22] As the soldiers marched through the city, its quiet was again disturbed at the Mercato Nuovo and other places by peasants forced to follow the march who desired to escape with their cattle, and citizens who recognized their property among the booty which was being carried off by these questionable allies. The tumult was, however, quietened without incident.[23] Thus at last Florence was rid of the neighbourhood of the two forces the peril of which had so long disturbed her peace. They passed on their way to play their part in a greater tragedy ; and Florence was left for a few more days to experience Medicean rule.

Cortona was now attempting the expedient of intimidation, by flooding the city with troops, of whom more were continually arriving. " There were to be seen," writes Varchi, " more military cloaks than mantles, more soldiers than citizens, more arms than men." [24] There were constant reviews and parades ; and the roll of drums was continually to be heard in the streets. At the slightest noise of disturbance there would be a concourse of soldiers, swearing and threatening ; the shops would be closed ; and the inhabitants would shut themselves up for safety in their houses. Their pay was raised by melting down silver from the Palazzo and other public places.[25] " No one seemed to have the courage even to raise his eyes," says the historian ; and the timid began to seek safety from the storm which they felt to be imminent.[26] But on 11 May [27] Cortona received news which completely altered the aspect of affairs. The army of Bourbon, tardily pursued by the Confederates, had reached Rome and stormed the city almost without opposition on 6 May, though they lost their leader in the operation. The Pope was driven for refuge to the Castle of S. Angelo ; and the most venerable and magnificent city in Europe was sacked during eight days with a horror and mercilessness which shocked even that callous age. Men regarded it as a tardy manifestation of Divine Providence. " Never," wrote Varchi, " was punishment more cruel nor more deserved."[28] This was the epitaph of Renascence Rome.

The disaster which befell Clement left his lieutenant in

Florence in a position which was fundamentally changed. He could no longer count upon help or support from without ; in future, he had to rely upon his own resources. He called together the Balia and did what he could to strengthen his hands. A fresh imborsation was ordered to secure the Council of One Hundred. The officials of the *Monte di Pietà*, the public loan-bank " the heart of the city," were renewed. Money was raised by a series of desperate financial measures, of which the pardon of malefactors in return for payment was typical. Loyalty to the present regime was encouraged by a belated recognition of the harmless services of Luigi Ridolfi during the Tumulto del Venerdì. A tardy bid for popular support was made by an indemnity to twenty named persons in celebration of the suppression of the revolt. The customs officials were encouraged by a provision securing their salaries in spite of a decreased increment. Finally, a commencement was made to secure the city from attack by arrangements for the fortification of Empoli. [29]

These measures, however, were too late and insufficient to secure or to control the obedience of a disaffected people. Upon the next day the news of the disaster at Rome became known through the city. With Cortona, the citizens understood the import of the event to their present government. But to them there was in it a second side. The greatest importance to them of the connection of Florence with the Papacy had been financial. This was now destroyed. " Rome," wrote the Signoria to their envoy in Venice, " was the marrow and the heart of this city . . . lacking which we remain like a dead body." The Florentines in Rome had been among the wealthiest, and they had suffered proportionately in the sack. It was estimated that they had lost no less than a million in gold. [30] Their creditors and connections at home suffered correspondingly. Besides this, offices bought by the citizens to the estimated value of 350,000 ducats, and a weekly export trade amounting to 8,000 ducats, were nullified ; and widespread bankruptcy was dreaded. [31] The strongest solder of the papal connection was destroyed ; and with it, the force which had made that connection irrevocable. The Mediceans had no longer anything to hope for : the rest of the people, nothing more to dread. Under such circumstances, all the precautions of Cortona were useless.

Once again the citizens began to raise their heads and to assemble. The dread of punishment left the leaders of the Tumulto del Venerdì, who again fearlessly took the lead. Niccolò Capponi, in particular, went about inciting the citizens to action. This time there was something different from the disorderly tumult of the previous month. The shops were closed, the citizens gathered and surged through the streets in a temper uglier if less turbulent than ever before.   Cortona in an agony of despair was again unable to make up his mind to action.   Baccio Valori urged him to seize and execute Niccolò Capponi, and to crush the movement with its leader[32]; but the Cardinal could not bring himself to take such a decisive step.   The troops with which the town had been flooded had seen the ultimate guarantee of their pay cut off with the sack of Rome.   Deprived of encouragement from above, and fearing the temper of the populace, they therefore contented themselves with holding the Medicean Palace and the Piazza, with the Palazzo della Signoria and the adjacent Loggia.[33]   Their commander, Count Piero Nofri, offered to put down the movement if the Cardinal would allow him 20,000 ducats to satisfy their most instant claims.   His vacillation and his avarice combined to cause Cortona to delay.[34]   The only action he took was to send away secretly by night sixty mule-loads of the most valuable of the family possessions in preparation for flight.   It was obvious that he was beginning to fear the worst.[35]

The principal citizens now commenced to visit the Medicean palace, urging the Cardinals to renounce the government pacifically and to evacuate the city before violence ensued.   On 14 May, Cortona held a *consulta* of sixty or seventy of them, calling their attention to the good work he had done for Florence.   He received the reply that nevertheless it would at present be better to leave it to itself.   Even the Cardinals Cibo and Ridolfi, now by the ruin of Clement Florentines rather than Papalists, were inclined to agree.   Cortona, however, greedy of power, still hesitated. He was thought to be meditating a tardy display of severity : but it was by now too late.[36]   That evening in the Palazzo the Signoria met with seven citizens selected from each quarter, and deliberated till an advanced hour.   As a result, four representatives were sent on the next day to the Cardinal asking him point-blank how he desired that things should be settled.   Undecided as ever, he said that he remitted all to them ; and a special council of ninety was called to consider the situation.   The populace, seeing all this coming and going, had begun to get restive, and some uproar—perhaps fomented from above—succeeded the seditious whisperings of the past few days.   It was thought that the Medici had definitely agreed to renounce all power.   As yet, however, the news was premature.   Something more was needed to give the *coup de grâce*.[37]

Just as matters had reached this point, there arrived in Florence (14 May) Clarice, wife of Filippo Strozzi, and daughter of Piero, eldest son of Lorenzo the Magnificent.   Her husband was son of that magnificent builder of the same name who had erected for himself in Florence an immortal memorial of his race ; and he was thus, by birth, by marriage, and by wealth, one of the first of Florentine citizens. Still, he and his wife were not on good terms with the Medicean regime. They resented the diminution of their influence, which might have been expected to increase after the death of Lorenzino, Clarice's brother. They considered that the goods at least of the Medici were wrongfully withheld from them, the legitimate heirs, by the bastards. As a result of a promise from the Pope to raise their son Piero to the Cardinalate, they had kept him from childhood in the long robes of a priest ; and they were indignant at their disappointment.[38] Worst of all was the treatment of Filippo himself by Clement. He had been sent to Naples by Clement as a hostage for the fulfilment of the truce of the previous September, and left to his fate by its repudiation. This unpardonable treachery finally stirred up his enmity. " I have been played about with without any respect as though I were a slave," he wrote to the Florentine exiles who were endeavouring to secure his co-operation, " and I wish more than ever immediately to show him who has so valued me that I may be worth little, but not so little that I should be thus treated ; and [to show] my fellow-citizens that I know what mind and will every proper citizen should have."[39] With sentiments such as these he secured his release, for which his intrigues with the Imperialists combined with the efforts of his wife and the payment of a large ransom. He first went to Rome. Here Clarice feigned sickness ; and in consequence they obtained permission, unusual in those days of stress, to leave the city. This they did just in time to escape the sack, and proceeded by sea by way of Civita Vecchia and Pisa towards Florence.[40] Shortly after landing, on 11 May, he received two messages begging him to hasten his return. One was from Cortona, who appealed to him in the name of the Medici ; the other from Capponi, his brother-in-law, who summoned him on behalf of liberty. Filippo, eagerly availing himself of the opportunity to be avenged upon the Pope, had no difficulty in making up his mind. He pressed on to Florence. His wife, whose person was safer and whose eagerness perhaps greater, hastened on before him to spy out the land. Going on the next morning to the Palazzo de' Medici, she reproached Cortona with the manner of his rule, and urged her young kinsmen for their safety's sake to leave the city. The Cardinal rebuked her for her opposition to her own family. She replied insinuatingly that her family had been wont to enjoy only so much power as was freely conceded to them, having enough discernment to leave when the people wished it and to return when they wished it.[41] According to rumour, she added to this a blunt denial of the right of the provincial priest and the illegitimate youths to represent the family at all.[42]   At this stage, an arquebus was fired at some slight excuse at the entrance to the chamber where she was, by accident or by design.   Terrified, she escaped from the Palace through the garden into another house ; and sent to her husband to come immediately.   He pressed on, and lay that night at Legnaia, a villa of Capponi's just outside the gates. Here he was visited by many of the most prominent citizens, and commenced to detach to the popular side some of the most prominent among the Palleschi, such as his kinsman the Cardinal Ridolfi.   On the next morning (16 May), two hours after day-break, he entered the city, where he was informed that Cortona had at last agreed to come to terms and had appointed four citizens to treat on his behalf.[43]   With a number of citizens in his train, Strozzi went on to the Palace in the Via Larga.   He was received with an ill grace, being forced to pass between armed guards, and was appealed to by Ippolito in the name of kinship to exert his authority in restoring the authority of his house, which might even now be retrieved.   Strozzi proudly refused, and urged his relatives to accept the agreement which was under discussion.[44]   He had already taken a more practical step to frustrate the display of force to which Cortona was being urged and for which he was becoming more and more inclined. He had induced Francesco del Nero, the Treasurer, over whom he had a business hold, to send the funds in his charge into the house of his brother.   Cortona, on finally demanding the money to pay his soldiers, was told that the treasury was empty ; and Nero made his answer final by stealing away to Lucca.   It was to him especially that Cortona in after-years attributed his failure,[45] Further resistance was now impossible ; and the Medici yielded to Strozzi's representations.   He himself acted as an intermediary, passing to and from the Palazzo della Signoria and bringing back with him a draft of the arrangements for the future of the city as they had been outlined.   The Medici stipulated that there should be added provisions for their own safety and dignity. They were to continue to be regarded " deserving and good citizens " ; their adherents and servants, together with the rela-tives of Cortona, were to be free from persecution upon their account ; they were to be exempt from all extraordinary taxa-tion ; Ippolito was not to be deprived of his habilitation to all the offices of state, in spite of his being below the legal age ; and they were to be allowed entrance to the city and egress without hin-drance.[46]   When this was agreed to, they professed themselves ready to renounce the government and to leave.   In return for their safe departure, they were to consign to the popu-lar administration the citadels of Pisa and Livorno, held by foreign captains directly dependent upon them and in their name.[47]

The terms, haughty though they were, were accepted. Upon the next day (Friday, 17 May) Filippo came to request them to raise the guard from the Palazzo, and to disarm that in their own house. At the same time he suggested that they should immediately leave the city, at least for a while.[48] They meekly obeyed. With Cortona and the two youths went Count Piero Nofri, hated for his boast that with 300 men he had made 80,000 citizens " curdle," a conspiracy for whose assassination had become known.[49] Two Commissioners at the head of 300 troops were sent with them by request to protect them on their way, together with Filippo Strozzi, who, ostensibly on another mission, was to take over the two fortresses.[50] As they passed through the throngs of citizens in the Via Larga, some regret was expressed that they were allowed to leave thus unmolested ; and Dante da Castiglione, one of the republican hotheads in the company of Strozzi, was even suspected of trying to kill Ippolito by an arquebus shot. Nevertheless, they proceeded untouched through the Porta San Gallo to their magnificent villa at Poggio a Caiano.[51] After fourteen and a half years of subjection, and three weeks precisely after the suppression of the first tumult, Florence was free again. On the following night the arms of the Pope above the door of the Palazzo were replaced, amid great enthusiasm, by those of the people.[52]

The joy of the citizens knew no bounds. It seemed a veritable miracle of God that without violence and without bloodshed they had shaken off their servitude.[53] Every age, every rank, every profession, joined in the general rejoicing. The reputation of Savonarola as a prophet was rehabilitated among those who remembered his teachings of thirty years before and among the younger men who had been brought up in his traditions.[54] And if some staunch Medicean was seen weeping publicly at the ignominy with which his masters had left the city,[55] it was a rare exception and no disturbances followed to mar the general joy.

(2) THE RESETTLEMENT OF THE CONSTITUTION

The new form of government had been decided upon on the previous day by the Balia. Originally it had been intended that the Medicophile Signoria should resign its office in favour of a new magistracy more in sympathy with the people.[56] The bloodless course and the aristocratic bent which the Revolution had taken now decided it to retain its functions and to attempt to control the city under the very regime which it had been selected to oppose. Its intention was to remain in office until the close of their term and to induct the new constitution. Of this the essential part was to be the restoration of the *Consiglio Maggiore*—that most fundamental and most cherished of the Savonarolan innovations. This was to meet, however, only on 20 June, —over a month later. In the meantime the government was to be controlled by a council of one hundred and twenty—thirty from each quarter—nominated and elected by the existent boards, to last for the coming four months and to take the place of the Councils of Seventy and of One Hundred. Together with the present bodies, it was to elect a committee of twenty to control and organize the Consiglio Maggiore. The Balìa, however, was to end its existence. The effect of these provisions was to continue the power of the present Medicophile government virtually unimpaired, through a fresh council nominated by it, for the next five weeks; ensuring for it afterwards a continuation of its influence in the executive through the hundred and twenty, and in the Consiglio Maggiore itself through the twenty. It was no doubt hoped that the new government would retain the complexion thus given it during the first crucial weeks of its existence.[57]

Upon these provisions for the new constitution becoming better known or perhaps better appreciated, the joy of the people became more moderate. Its suspicions were increased by a variety of circumstances. It had been restrained from sacking the dwellings of the Medici after their departure. A well-founded rumour had circulated that they were returning to the city accompanied by a large force, whereas in fact they were pressing on their departure with unseemly haste on receiving the report that the hotheaded, Piero Salviati, was spurring at their heels with two hundred arquebusiers.[58] It was noticed with apprehension that the aristocratic leaders of the revolt, Niccolò Capponi and the rest, were still assiduously visiting the Palazzo Medici, where Clarice Strozzi had taken up her abode together with the Archbishop Ridolfi and other of her kinsfolk. Hither, too, she had conducted her little niece, Caterina, daughter of Lorenzo Duke of Urbino, just brought from Poggio a Caiano to the Convent of Sta. Lucia in the city by order of the government as a valuable hostage.[59] Disturbed by these incidents, the people took alarm, which was increased by a rumour that the Pope had been released from the Castle of S. Angelo. The more suspicious feared that they had been deceived and that the government was only playing with them until the Medici could return at the head of an army. The less credulous thought, with better reason, that the old Signoria had allied itself with the aristocratic revolutionaries and Medicophiles and aimed at a close oligarchy, hoping to avoid or at least to control the meeting of the Consiglio

Maggiore. These fears kept the city in disorder. The shops, only just reopened, were again closed—it had come to be a daily operation. The gates were guarded against attacks from without.[60] Niccolò Capponi, alarmed by the information of his friends and the frankness of his opponents, procured from the Signoria an order for all persons to leave the Palazzo Medici. Popular apprehensions were lulled by forbidding the soldiers still in the city to leave their billets after one hour from nightfall on the pain of hanging ; and the public security was furthered by ordering every citizen to keep a light burning in the window of his house after the same hour.[61] · This, however, was not sufficient. Upon the following day, the Saturday, the people were assembled before sunrise in the Piazza murmuring against the government and against the sham revolution.[62] The Signoria met in alarm and took measures to quieten them. As a preliminary, the *Otto di Guardia e Balia*—the body responsible for the maintenance of internal order—unpopular as the creatures of the Medici and as the instruments of their tyranny, were dismissed from their office.[63] This, however, did not succeed in quietening the populace. In the afternoon the tumult recommenced. Turning this time to stronger measures, the Signoria commanded all persons [64] to leave the Piazza and the shops to be reopened. This timid order met with no result, though it was accompanied by the long-desired licence for all Florentine citizens to bear arms. The commotion even increased, and for greater security more shops were closed. In the Piazza the mob remained as clamorous as ever.[65]

The more prominent citizens saw that some greater concession must be made. Niccolò Capponi had taken the most important part in the Revolution, together with Strozzi, and was generally regarded and saluted, owing to the other's absence, as the saviour of the city. Mounting the Ringhiera he endeavoured to quieten the popular apprehensions by denying the rumour that the Medici were returning and begged the people to have regard for the perils which were menacing the city and not to hamper the hands of the government. His words apparently had no marked effect, and he was forced finally to promise his advocacy to hasten the meeting of the Consiglio Maggiore. Within the palace a consultation was held. The Signoria at last agreed to bow before the storm. By a public proclamation, the meeting of the Council was ordered for the following Tuesday, a whole month before the time originally fixed.[66]

The Consiglio Maggiore had been the great innovation of the Savonarolan regime. In the traditional Florentine system the supreme authority had been variously distributed. Elections were supposed to be left to the chances of lot ; legislative power resided in the nominally representative Councils of the People and of the Commune, the one admitting and the other excluding the old nobility, the division corresponding to a condition of affairs in the city which had long ceased to exist. Ultimate authority in all matters was supposed to be left to the populace assembled in their Parlamento at times of emergency. This nominal state of affairs had long ceased to correspond to the facts, as has been shown above, and had become completely amenable to the control of any influential individual or faction. In form it was obsolete ; in practice, tyrannic ; in theory, ultra-democratic. All combined to render it distasteful in an era of reform, when the reaction from absolutism was at its height while full democracy was hardly dreamed of. Accordingly in 1495, upon the proposal of Paolo Antonio Soderini, aided by the powerful support of Savonarola himself, there was instituted a new popular council which should combine all the authorities ordinary and extraordinary, nominal and real. This was composed of virtually all citizens above the lowest class. The minimum age for membership was 29 ; the qualification, to enjoy the benefit of the state—that is, to belong to a family which had shown its qualification to serve on the highest executive bodies [67] within the past three generations. Should those with this qualification exceed 1,500 in number, a third should serve at a time, changing every six months. To its number were admitted every three years sixty non-beneficed citizens, thus modifying its exclusiveness ; and twenty-four full citizens below the legal age, who thus obtained experience and encouragement.[68] The chief function of the Consiglio Maggiore was the election of magistrates—the safest guarantee of liberty, hitherto the merest farce. Besides this it possessed the legislative power by its right of voting, though not of discussing, new legislation. Every six months it elected from citizens of above forty years a council of eighty (*Ottanta*), which sat once a week to deliberate in conjunction with the Signoria on more intimate and delicate questions which could not be communicated to the larger assembly. The higher officers of state and more important ex-dignitaries had the right to attend its meetings, and the body was joined with the Colleges for the nomination of ambassadors or the appointment of captains.[69]

It is important to note that this system was, despite all that has been said and thought about it, no democracy in the modern sense. Theoretically there was an actual diminution of popular rights by the abolition of the Parlamento. In practice, authority was strengthened and given a more uninterrupted course in the same classes who had been supposed previously to enjoy office and control. Out of a total population of about 90,000, only about 3,200 were found to answer the qualifications for membership. The Savonarolan democracy thus differed very little in fact from the so-called oligarchy of the Venetian council of the same name from which it had been copied. This was the nature of the institution in which the hopes of the Florentines were centred and which was now to meet again after a suppression of fifteen years.

Some minor adjustments were necessary before the first session could take place. Upon the day previous, the Council of *Arroti* (as the new body of a hundred and twenty was called) met in conjunction with the Signoria and the Colleges to determine these points. A few minor changes were made in its constitution. The previous experience had given some idea of the number of the qualified citizens ; and it was now determined that the maximum of the full Council should be 2,400 instead of 1,500, being divided up only when those eligible exceeded that total. On the occasion of the first meeting there were to be admitted even such as were in arrears with their taxation—normally a disqualification, but now become almost a recommendation since it had been in despite of the Medici ; and they were even declared eligible for election to any office provided that their indebtedness were cleared up within twenty days. On this occasion, too, the normal minimum age of 29 was lowered to 24—perhaps in gratitude to the youths who had taken so prominent a part in the revolutionary movement.[70] At the same time, those creatures of the Medici who had been raised by them to high office were not allowed to take advantage of this and to sit in the Council excepting if they belonged to a family previously qualified. The functions and constitution of the body were otherwise confirmed as they had existed previous to 1512.[71]

Upon the original institution of the Council, a stately hall had been constructed for its meetings by Cronaca upon the first floor of the Palazzo della Signoria,[72] called the Sala dei Cinquecento, or Hall of the Five Hundred—the minimum number of which the Council could then consist. The Medici upon their restoration had naturally, and probably with deliberate intent, put the apartment to other uses. The shrine of Florentine liberty had been adapted to house the instrument of Medicean oppression ; and, partitioned up into small compartments, had been used as a barracks for the Swiss and other mercenaries employed to keep the city down. The condition of the hall had been one of the excuses for the postponement of the meeting of the Council. Now it was ordered that it should be cleared. The enthusiastic youth of the city set themselves to the task by the side of the ordinary workmen, considering it an honour to assist. Members of the highest families vied with one another in the noble labour, which was regarded as a distinction. Commencing at the dawn of Monday, it continued all day and all night, and thus by the Tuesday morning, after it had been re-consecrated and sprinkled with holy water, all was ready for the meeting.[73]

It was commenced under the best of auspices. Nineteen condemned prisoners had been reprieved from capital punishment, and in their pardon were of course associated those who had been sentenced for their share in the Tumulto del Venerdì.[74] A general amnesty had been proclaimed for all political offences. A hundred bushels of grain were distributed in alms to the poor of the city.[75] At last upon the Tuesday the great bell of the Palazzo began to toll, summoning the people to the meeting of the Council as it had done fifteen years before. Each man as he entered the hall gave in a slip of paper bearing his name and gonfalone or " standard " under which he was formally enrolled ; for there had been no time to make up detailed lists of those qualified to sit.[76] The numbers assembled were unprecedented. Many could find no seats or had to stand in the doorway. Over four hundred late-comers were unable to get into the hall at all and were forced to leave.[77] Altogether, no less than 2,272 persons were counted[78] ; though the requisite quota for division was not quite reached and the whole body therefore sat together. The proceedings were opened by a solemn celebration of the Mass to invoke the Divine benediction ; and tears of gratitude were shed as the Host was elevated.[79] This was followed by the elections to replace two of the more important governmental boards. The Otto di Guardia e Balia, the commission for the public police recently quashed, was reappointed from adherents of the new regime.[80] The *Otto di Pratica* had been instituted by Lorenzo the Magnificent as a committee of the Settanta to deal with foreign and military affairs and so had come to be a symbol of the despotic government. Accordingly, though without real significance, it had been swept away with the Medici and reappeared with them. In its stead there was now again elected the old body of ten—the Dieci di Guerra—to fulfil precisely the same functions ; though it entered into office only three weeks later.[81] With this, the session of the day finished amid another manifestation of popular joy that the old liberty was indeed regained.[82]

A letter from an old friend to Bernardo Segni, the future historian then studying at Venice, gives a striking insight into the new spirit. " I must confess," he wrote, " that I find much pleasure in hearing the great bell toll, and the deliberations and adjournments of the Council, and in seeing and hearing all the other proceedings of the Republic." The old man, in the ardour of his return from exile, eagerly availed himself of the opportunity to practise the use of arms : " And as for what you say, that you advise me to help the Republic with counsel rather than with weapons . . . none the less, in order not to be a wholly useless member of the state, I will persevere in this in which, though I can perhaps help little, I can at least do no harm . . . and if the spirit fail me, I will wait on to encourage those more spirited than myself.[83]

This ebullience of joy was soon modified by the arrival of news which turned the attention of the citizens to the state of affairs outside the city, which was still one of extreme peril. The military disturbances had left only one direction open to the Medici after they left the city—that to the north. Hastened by the fear of pursuit, they had gone by forced stages through Poggio a Caiano and Pistoia to Lucca. Here, an independent city as it remained till the nineteenth century, they were magnificently received and entertained, as the Marquis of Massa refused them permission to continue their journey through his territories.[84] Filippo Strozzi, having fulfilled one part of his task by seeing them into safety, now turned to the other—the receipt of the citadels of Pisa and Livorno from the hands of their captains. He had received from the Medici as price for their safe departure an order for the surrender of the fortresses signed by both the Cardinal and Ippolito. The two captains refused however to obey it on the grounds that they held their charges from the Pope and could not yield without the countersign given by him. Strozzi received this news before he left Lucca,[85] and promptly made representations to have the matter rectified. As a result, Ippolito set out in his company, ostensibly to enforce obedience. Arrived at Pisa, he went in to the citadel alone and spoke for some time to the Constable. At length he came out and told Filippo that the other persisted in his refusal and would not surrender without first receiving the countersign, known only to the Pope and to one of his confidants at Lucca. To prove his sincerity, the young man immediately wrote to Cortona begging him to secure it. This, however, was a mere feint. While Filippo, fearing deception, was deliberating as to whether he should be kept under restraint, Ippolito slipped out of the house by an unguarded door and returned to Lucca. Cortona immediately wrote deprecating the hot-headedness of his young ward and promising to do what he could to secure the precious countersign. Almost at the same instant he showed his sincerity by sending a party of reinforcements to assist to hold the citadel. These were luckily intercepted on their way. Nevertheless, minor succours succeeded in entering and the two fortresses still held out, marring the even course of the change of government.[86]

The receipt of the news in Florence damped the unmeasured optimism which had hitherto prevailed. The two places were of immense importance to her, controlling as they did her outlet to the sea. The first business of the Ottanta elected by the Consiglio Maggiore in its second meeting was to consider this urgent matter. The Medicean partisans were suspected of complicity, and mutual distrust again became rife. The suspicious circumstances were enhanced by the release without punishment, owing to the insistence of the Florentine captains, of the intercepted relieving forces, who were expected to have been hanged. Filippo Strozzi, after having been for a few days the popular idol and leader of the revolutionary movement, now lost in a moment all his credit. He was thought to have beguiled the city on behalf of his relatives rather than to have been beguiled himself ; and an explanation even more scandalous was whispered. From very shame he withdrew to his country villa, the famous Orti Rucellai near Ripoli, immortalized through the brilliant society which once met in its shades, and henceforth he hardly dared to show his face within the walls.[87]

All this had been carried out under the auspices of the old Signoria. That body had by now, however, outlived its usefulness. Nominated originally from among the most intransigeant supporters of the Medici, they had bent before the Revolution only with the greatest unwillingness, and endeavoured to restrict it to the establishment of an oligarchic government. Now that the wheel had turned full circle, they found themselves out of place in the new atmosphere of democracy. Nevertheless they clung to their office, of which they had as yet enjoyed only one-half of the legal term of two months. Their hesitating compliance with the popular will and the fiasco at Pisa had combined to exasperate the minds of the citizens. Antonfrancesco degli Albizzi, who fifteen years before had led in the acts of violence which forced the resignation of Soderini, now attempted to rehabilitate his reputation by showing how the *coup* could be repeated.[88] At his instigation, the same body of hot-headed youths who had led in the previous outbreaks again raised a clamour and threatened to throw the Signoria down from the windows of the Palazzo into the Piazza below.[89] Fra Bartolommeo da Faenza, who held Savonarola's position at San Marco and desired to fill it in the city as well, demonstrated his practical sympathy by attempting to draw over to the popular side the captain of the Palace Guard.[90] Niccolò Capponi, moderate as usual, intervened to prevent violence. First addressing and calming the mob, he then went into the Palazzo to intercede with the Signoria. Tardily, they resolved to yield. Upon 28 May the Gonfalonier called together the Ottanta and proposed in the name of his colleagues that they should all retire from office for the good of the Republic. The offer was unanimously accepted, and three days later, a fresh election took place.[91]

A day or two before there had been chosen in the Consiglio Maggiore the body of twenty which was to regulate the meetings of the Council.[92]   Among its functions was to decide the methods and conditions for the election of the Gonfalonier.   This was a matter of some uncertainty.   Under the traditional arrangement, retained by the Medici, the Gonfalonier was appointed for two months, thus satisfying the Florentine passion for equality by the rapid rotation of office.   The abuses of the system were notorious ; for the constant change had either made for instability of policy or had tended to concentrate the real power in the hands of some unseen force behind the government.   As a result a change was made after Savonarola's death.   Admiration for the Venetian model of the Dogeship combined with a doctrinaire belief in the efficacy of an admixture of the principle of monarchy with the democratic forms of the Consiglio Grande ; and Piero Soderini was elected Gonfalonier for life.   On his abdication and flight in 1512 a change was made, and the tenure of the office was reduced to one year.   Though a partisan of the Medici was chosen to fill it, they themselves preferred to sweep away this innovation with all the other reforms, and to revert to the traditional system of a two-month tenure.   Now, after the Revolution, the Twenty, distrusting the excessive power given by the life appointment of one man, reverted to the system which had obtained for a few weeks in 1512.   The Gonfalonier was to be elected for one year, though eligible for re-election at its close.   This decision seems to have had some deeper significance.   As has been seen, the Medici had reconsolidated their position by the employment of the Parlamento, though it had been abolished formally in 1494. Thus all of their measures might be considered in a constitutional sense illegal.   The Revolution of 1527 had been accomplished without the employment of this obsolete device, and the general abhorrence of it soon found expression by the re-inscription of Savonarola's old verses on the walls of the Sala dei Cinquecento.[93] The revised system was therefore not so much in the nature of an innovation as of a simple reversion to the system of the Second Republic, of which the establishment of the annual Gonfalonierate had been the last constitutional measure.   The essential continuity of the last Florentine Republic with its predecessor was thus accentuated.   On this solitary occasion, however, the office was to be held for thirteen months so as to complete the truncated term of the retiring Gonfalonier ; and similarly the Signoria, the constitution of which was unchanged, was to serve in the first instance for three months instead of for two.[94]

Upon the last day of May, the Consiglio Grande met to proceed to the election according to the recently sanctioned forms. Sixty citizens were drawn by lot, each of whom made his nomination for the supreme office, a minimum age of 50 years being the only restriction. The sixty thus proposed were balloted upon one by one : and of those whose nomination secured the approval of an absolute majority, the six who obtained most votes were sent again to the ballot. The final competitors included Niccolò Capponi, a leader in the recent proceedings ; Alfonso Strozzi, brother of Filippo and a hot democrat in spite of his aristocratic connections ; Tommaso Soderini, a nephew of the old life Gonfalonier ; and Baldassare Carducci, Reader in Jurisprudence at Padua, whose recent imprisonment by the Venetians for intrigues against the Medici and for calling the Pope " bastardaccio " had rendered him a popular favourite.[95] Again the Secretary proclaimed the name of the competitor under consideration, and those of his family left the hall. Again the ushers passed along the crowded benches, receiving from the citizens in the right hand the beans, white or black, which they put into the boxes they bore in the left.[96] Again the votes were taken up to the tribunal to be counted. Strozzi had been discredited by the recent fiasco of his brother at Pisa, and was suspect by reason of his family connections. Soderini lost votes by the recollection of his uncle's weak rule and through the fear of the Florentines to seem to alternate between the hegemony of two over-mighty families. Carducci was hot on his way from Venice, the demand for his release having been one of the first cares of the government after the departure of the Medici [97] ; but he had not yet arrived, and his absence told against him. Capponi alone suffered from no insuperable objection and was acceptable to all parties of whatever complexion from some recommendation in his character, his personal record, or his ancestry. It was found therefore that he was elected 1,360th Gonfalonier of Justice of the Florentine Republic.

NOTES TO CHAPTER II

[1] Archivio Mediceo, *ubi supra*.

[2] Baccio Carnesecchi, *Ragguaglio* (published by Lupo Gentile in *Studi Storici*, XIV, 445–71 (Pisa, 1905).

[3] Archivio Mediceo, *ubi supra*.

[4] Signoria, CXXIX, 19 April, cf. Nardi, *Lettera sopra la mutazione dello stato nel* 1527, *ubi supra*; and Bernardo . . . . . to Alessandro, 2 May, in Archivio Mediceo, *ubi supra*: " Messer Antonio Nerli Canonico fiorentino, quale fu de' primi gridasse populo e libertà et sonassi la compana è sostenuto in veschovado : credo là farà male. . . ."

[5] Nardi, p. 194 : letter of Pazzi of 4 May, *ubi supra*; letter of Pere-

grino of 28 April in Archivio Mediceo, *ubi supra* : despatches of Foscari and Agnello in Sanuto, XLV, 9, 28.

[6] Nardi, p. 194 ; Archivio Mediceo, *ubi supra* ; Vasari, *Opere,* VIII, 8.

[7] Nardi, *ibid.* : letter of Pazzi, *ubi supra.*

[8] Cf. letter of Peregrino of 27 April in Appendix of Documents, No. I.

[9] Signoria, CXXIX, 27–8 April ; Varchi, I, 144–5.

[10] Anonymous MS. Diary above cited in Magl. XXV, 555, fo. 19.

[11] Paolo Giovio, II, 23 ; Signoria, CXXIX, *ad diem.*

[12] Anonymous MS. diary, *ubi supra.*

[13] Varchi, I, 145–6 ; Foscari (who prides himself for the principal share in bringing it about) in *Relazione,* pp. 54, 86, and Antonio Bolani *apud* Sanuto, XLV, 16–17. For the text of the treaty see *ibid.* 17–20 (abstract in *State Papers, Spanish,* III, ii, 57).

[14] Varchi, I, 49.

[15] In part recompense for the enormous expense of the campaign, of which the Florentines had borne the major part.

[16] Varchi, I, 147 ; Nardi, p. 195.

[17] Paolo Paoli, p. CLXXXIV.

[18] *Ibid.,* p. CLXXXIII.

[19] Cf. their despatch of 29 April *apud* Rossi, I, 17.

[20] *State Papers, Spanish,* III, ii, 60.

[21] Salvioli, *ubi supra,* p. 26.

[22] *Ibid.*

[23] Letter of Bernardo . . . to Alessandro of 2 May in Archivio Mediceo, *ubi supra* : " Stamattina s'è partito il marchese di Saluzi et il Sʳ Federigo e assai fanteria e nel passare per voler assai contadini menati da loro fuggire et salvare il suo come asini boj et altre baggaglie è suto per esserci qualche romore : pure dei gratia non è seguito altro. In Palazzo si fa buona guardia. . . ." Cf. Varchi, I, 147–8.

[24] *Ibid.* I, 148.

[25] Signoria, CXXIX, 30 April.

[26] Varchi, *ubi supra.*

[27] Varchi says that the news was generally known only on the 12th ; Ammirato and Vettori, on the 11th. Considering the wonderful outburst of activity on the part of the Balia on that day after a silence of three weeks, the second date is certainly correct, though perhaps Cortona received the news a little earlier than the city. In any case, the tale of Nerli (p. 151), followed by most recent historians, that the news was brought by Filippo Strozzi, is quite inconsistent with the facts.

[28] Varchi, *ubi supra.*

[29] Balie, XLIV, 339–47 (11 April 1527).

[30] Despatch of 13 May *apud* Rossi, I, 21.

[31] Soriani, *Relazione,* p. 420. Cf. also Paolo Paoli, p. clxxxiv.

[32] *Vita di Niccolò Capponi,* p. 916.

[33] MS. Diary in Magl. XXV, 555, f. 19.

[34] *Vita di Niccolò Capponi,* p. 917.

[35] Foscari, *Relazione,* pp. 55–6, and letter of 15 May in Sanuto, XLV, 138–9.

[36] *Ibid.* These contemporary accounts uniformly give the most reliable though not always the most important details of these events. Cf. also Nardi, p. 195, with his *Lettera sopra la mutazione dello stato, ubi supra* : and Giovio, II, 25–6.

[37] Letters of Foscari of 15–16 May in Sanuto, XLV, 138–9 and 153–5.

[38] Varchi, I, 149–50.

[39] Letter of 30 January 1526/7 to Battista della Palla and Zanobi Buondelmonti *apud* Rossi, I, 22.

[40] *Vita di Filippo Strozzi, scritta di Lorenzo suo fratello*, in *Uomini Illustri di Casa Strozzi*, pp. 122–3. (Also in *Thesaurus Antiquitatum et Historiarum Italiæ*, ed. Grævius, vol. VIII, pt. (i).) This is the most reliable clue to the involved history of these events, being (though at times misunderstood) one of Varchi's main sources. Cf. also the letters published by Bardi in *Filippo Strozzi da nuovi documenti* in *A.S.I.* ser. V, vol. XIV.

[41] Nardi, *Lettera sopra la mutazione del governo, ubi supra*.

[42] "Shameful words . . . a peasant would not have used," says Giovio (II, 27). Cf. also Busini, *Lettere sopra l'assedio di Firenze*, p. 7; *Vita di N. Capponi*, p. 192.

[43] *Ibid.* Strozzi, *Vita*, p. 123 *seqq.*, is still the best guide. Even Nardi, a contemporary and participant, is not always consistent or correct in his account.

[44] *Vita di F. Strozzi*, pp. 126–7.

[45] Busini, pp. 8, 21–2.

[46] Provision of Balia of 16 May (see Appendix of Documents, No. II); Varchi, I, 158.

[47] *Vita di F. Strozzi*, pp. 129–30.

[48] Letter of Borromei of 17 May in Sanuto, XLV, 455–6.

[49] MS. Diary in Magl. XXV, 555, f. 19.

[50] *Vita di F. Strozzi, ibid.*; Varchi, I, 159–60.

[51] *Ibid.*; Giovio, II, 27.

[52] Ammirato, VII, 36–7. G. Thomas, *Les Revolutions Politiques de Florence* 1177–1530, gives no fresh information about this change of government.

[53] Paolo Paoli, p. clxxxv; Cambi, *Istorie*, vol. III (*apud* Ildefonso, *Delizie degli eruditi toscani*, vol. XXII), p. 316; anonymous diary *apud* Gentile, *Storiografia*, Appendix; *Vita di N. Capponi*, pp. 920–1.

[54] Varchi, I, 158–9. Cambi, the chronicler, is a typical instance of this spirit. He refers (IV, 3) to him as "Profeta Ieronimo"; and (5) to the Medici as "Chacciati da Christo." Cf. also pp. 61–2.

[55] Busini, *Lettere*, p. 8. The popularity of Ippolito among some sections is attested by Foscari in his letter of 16 May (Sanuto, XLV, 139–41); and the tender and tearful leave-taking is described by Borromei in his of 17th (*ibid.* 155–6).

[56] The commencement of a provision for the "deputation" of a new Signoria and Gonfalonier of Justice under the date of 16 May is struck out; under it follow the provisions for the new government. See Appendix of Documents, No. II.

[57] See provision of Balia in full, *ibid.*

[58] Varchi, I, 161–2.

[59] Reumont, *La jeunesse de Catherine de Médicis*, pp. 85–7; Varchi, I, 165.

[60] *Ibid.* p. 167.

[61] Signoria, CXXIX, 17 May 1527.

[62] Letter of Foscari of 18 May in Sanuto, XLV, 170; Varchi, I, 166.

[63] Signoria, CXXIX, 18 May 1527. "Cassatio Otto custodiæ et Baliæ."

[64] Only non-citizens, says Varchi; but the actual provision applies to "qualunque persona di . . . qualunque stato si sia, così cittadino come soldato o forestiere. . . ."

[65] Varchi, I, 166–7.

[66] *Ibid., Vita di N. Capponi*, p. 923. For text of proclamation see Signoria, CXXIX, 18 May 1527.

E' Mag^{d} et ex^{si} Signori Signori di L. e Gonf: di Giust: del popolo fiorentino insieme ragunati per virtù di qualunque loro auctorità et per juste et ragionevoli cagioni mossi fanno publicamente bandire notificare et commandare a ogni et qualunche cittadino habile al consiglio maggiore come si faceva inanzi al 1512 che martedì matina proximo futuro al suono della campana che sonerà a dicto consiglio maggiore si ragugino personalmente in sulla sala di tal consiglio per fare li uffizii et l'altre cose necessarie per la città et per mantinamento del presente governo ; non obstante la provisione ultimamente facta che dovressi cominciare a dì XX. di giugno proximo futuro nè alchuna altra cosa incontrario non obstante.

[67] i.e. as one of *Signori, Gonfalonieri delle Compagnie*, or *Buonvomini*.

[68] For instances of such extension under the last Republic see Cambi, XXXIII, pp. 23–5, 28–31, 38–9.

[69] Cf. Villari, *Machiavelli*, I, 219–21.

[70] This privilege was extended by a majority on 12 June 1527 (Signoria, CXXIX, *ad diem*), lasting apparently in all for just over a year (see *infra*, pp. 106–7).

[71] Cf. provision of Balia of 20 May in Appendix of Documents, No. III.

[72] There is an interesting account of the original consecration in the Ricordanze di Stª Maria del Carmine, vol. XIX, in the R. Archivio di Stato di Firenze, its friars having officiated.

[73] Nardi, p. 196 ; Varchi, I, 170.

[74] Signoria, CXXIX, 18 May 1527. Pardons continue to be granted during the next ten days.

[75] Cf. the provision of 20 May in Appendix of Documents, No. III.

[76] Anonymous diary *apud* Lupo Gentile, *Storiografia*, Appendix.

[77] *Ibid.*

[78] So the anonymous MS. diary and that of Giambattista Betti in the same codex (Magl. XXV, 555). Ammirato says, 2,270 ; the anonymous diary printed by Lupo Gentile, 2,362. Varchi inexplicably asserts, more than 2,500—an obviously impossible number, as in that case the Council would have passed the limit for subdivision. The number rose again to 2,006 in July, 1528 (Cambi, IV, 38).

[79] Anonymous diary *apud* Lupo Gentile, *ubi supra*.

[80] Signoria, CXXIX, 22 May.

[81] Varchi, I, 241

[82] *Ibid*, pp. 170–1.

[83] Letter of Pazzi to Segni, September 1527, *apud* Gentile, *Storiografia*, Appendix VII.

[84] Sanuto, XLV, 301.

[85] *Vita di F. Strozzi*, pp. 129–30—an important detail which clears up the contradictions on this matter in the other accounts.

[86] *Ibid.* 130–1 ; Sanuto, XLV, 227.

[87] Varchi, I, 174–5 ; *Vita di Filippo Strozzi*, pp. 131–2 ; Segni, I, 29.

[88] Nardi, p. 196 ; Varchi, I, 215–16.

[89] Foscari, *Relazione*, pp. 57, 71–2.

[90] Nerli, p. 157.

[91] Varchi, I, 188–9.

[92] This was itself a concession on the part of the Council of 120, as this body was originally to have been elected by the existing Medicean councils.

[93] The last couplet ran :

" E sappi che chi vuol far Parlamento,
Cerca torti di mano il reggimento."

(Varchi, I, 330).

[94] *Ibid.* 189–91.

[95] Busini, pp. 11, 80 ; Nerli, pp. 163-4.

[96] They were not put in directly by the voters as a precaution against any irregularity.   For this ceremonial see Donato Giannotti, *Della Repubblica Fiorentina*, in *Opere*, I, 22-4.

[97] Despatch of 22 May in Sanuto, XLV, 120.

CHAPTER III

ACTION AND REACTION (I)

NICCOLÒ CAPPONI was a member of one of the most illustrious Florentine houses. His great-great-grandfather was the chronicler of the first capture of Pisa, who served in the camp as Florentine Commissary during the siege. His father was that gallant soldier who earned immortality in one moment for his bold reply to Charles VIII's threat that the French would sound their trumpets :—" Then we shall sound our bells." He had enjoyed the usual training, both at home and abroad, of a Florentine merchant citizen. He had his earliest experience of foreign matters working in the bank of an uncle at Lyons ; and he obtained his first introduction to public affairs under the Second Republic, when he accompanied his father on a mission to the French court. A youth of exemplary virtue is celebrated in the biography of his nephew ; and he obtained wealth and honour in his native city. He passed through all the normal stages of Florentine public life—vice-ambassador at Venice, Prior at the minimum age of 29, Commissary at the close of the second Pisan war, in the early stages of which his father had met his death. Just before the fall of the Republic he had been on a mission to Gaston de Foix and had witnessed the catastrophic French victory at Ravenna. He had married a sister of Filippo Strozzi, whose match with Clarice de' Medici thus brought Capponi into the orbit of the family alliances of the dominant house. Nevertheless, he did not at the first favour their rule, and is said even to have refused to salute them in the street. The favour of Lorenzino in securing the hand of Buonaccorso Pitti for one of his daughters mollified his opposition ; and he became henceforth one of the strongest adherents of the house. Under the Cardinal Giulio he served as Gonfalonier as well as in minor offices ; he had been chosen for an embassy of congratulation to Pope Adrian ; and he was reckoned by Cortona according to report as his closest friend, with Francesco Vettori. Nevertheless, by the close of the Cardinal's rule Capponi had turned against him. He was considered head of the band of discontented aristocrats and connections, and was the first to speak openly against their rule when, in a consultation, he recommended that they should cease to worry about the Pope's affairs and look to those of their country. A friend warned him of the danger of his outspokenness. " I am the son of Piero Capponi " was the gist of his reply. We have seen him intriguing with the exiles and Imperialists for the expulsion of the Medici, and rebuking the Cardinal for his unconstitutional rule. In the Tumulto del Venerdì, he had taken the leading part among the older men. In the final expulsion of the Medici, he was no less prominent ; and his refusal to follow the method of the ancient Florentine civic upheavals by " coursing the streets " with cavalry had secured the revolution its bloodless triumph. As an orator he did not excel, though a fine presence and a stately manner palliated the heaviness of his speech, which itself improved with time.[1] All this combined with his reputation for virtue, his ripe experience, and his noble lineage to recommend him to the affections of the people. His popularity had already been shown by the fact that at the first meeting of the Consiglio Grande he had been elected to the Dieci with an almost unanimous voice.[2] This was the man who now, at the age of fifty-three, was elevated to the highest office of the state.[3]

When the first outbursts of revolutionary ardour had passed, it was found that the citizens ranged themselves swiftly into parties—a plague to which Florence was considered subject even according to the exaggerated Italian norm. The most powerful section was found to be that inspired by the memories of the Second Republic. The influence of Savonarola was still strong ; his memory was cherished as that of a martyr ; and even during the siege a formal proposal was made for the reversion of his process. His followers, who advocated a republic upon a religious basis, had been given the name of *Piagnoni*, or the Weepers,[4] in which was included more than a suggestion of hypocrisy. The party was strongest among the burgher class, the backbone of the city. In it were reckoned most of those who were foremost for ability, lineage, or wealth. They were strong in numbers, though they did not enjoy an absolute majority ; but they were stronger still in their cohesion, all being inspired by the positive ideals of the Second Republic. In the old days, their strongest opponents had been christened the *Arrabbiati*,[5] as being " enraged " against the authority of the Friar. But similar hot spirits had revolted against the authority of the Medici ; and the name was now given to the body led by that band of fiery youths who had been first in all the more violent episodes of the revolution. They were the extremer democrats, very jealous for independence, and impatient of the caution and conservatism of the Piagnoni. Their number was estimated at about 800 ; but their violence gave them an exaggerated prominence. They were drawn, naturally, from the lower classes of the population—from its dregs, thought even the judicious Foscari.   The body came from the Arti Minori, but there was more than a sprinkling of unruly or reduced members of the upper classes—many, as their enemies asserted, bankrupts.   There was united with them, too, a minority of the Piagnoni who fell in with their more extreme political programme.   To them, also, a few of the older men attached themselves, whose ambitions might be furthered by their support ; while other pushing politicians such as Alfonso Strozzi or Tommaso Soderini courted their favour without formally joining their numbers.   At their head stood Baldassare Carducci, the hotheaded septuagenarian whose outspokenness and whose punishment had made him the idol of all those who most detested the Medici.

The party of the *Ottimati*, or Aristocrats,[6] was in every way the opposite of these.   In numbers, indeed, it was of no great importance ; but it comprised the members of the noblest and most experienced of the Florentine families.   It was they who had negotiated the pacific departure of the Medici, and they gave themselves all credit for it.   While eager for independence, however, they had no leanings towards democracy even of the qualified Florentine type.   As members of the oligarchy through which the earlier Medici had ruled the city, they had resented their loss of power under Cortona.   The alienation of their affections had transformed them into patriots ; but it was in their own favour that they had accomplished the revolution.   The abortive oligarchic constitution of 16 May had been designed by and for themselves.   Now, with their hopes in this frustrated, they stood jealously watching the encroachments of the democrats.   Distrusting the violence of the Arrabbiati, they favoured accord with their kinsmen the Medici as the surest safeguard of independence and of their own position.   With them stood also the remnant of the Medicean partisans, the *Palleschi*, called after the *Palle* or Balls from which the Medici had derived their badge and their cry.   At the moment, they did not dare to proclaim themselves openly and remained concealed under the title of *Bigi*— the Greys, or neutrals.   Still, they were an influential body, strong in the support of the populace and of the dominion[7] ; and a little later when consolidated they were reckoned to control as many as 400 voices in the Consiglio Maggiore.   For the moment, however, unable to declare themselves publicly, they remained in the background, ranging themselves among the supporters of moderation.[8]

From all of these parties, excepting the Arrabbiati, Niccolò Capponi could hope for support.   The Palleschi knew him as one closely connected with the Medici who had served under them ; and they saw in this a guarantee of toleration at least.

The Ottimati regarded him as one of themselves, certainly by birth and, as they hoped, also in opinion.   With the Piagnoni his connections were more slight ; yet here he was helped by the memory of his father and by his own somewhat ostentatious virtue and piety.   It was the coalition of all these which had secured his election to the highest dignity.   Originally, the revolution had been secured by a combination of all, headed by the disappointed Ottimati, against the Medici ; the demo-cratic constitution had been ensured by the alliance of the Piagnoni and Arrabbiati against the Ottimati ; but in the election the moderate parties joined in fear of the excesses of the Arrab-biati.   It was natural for this coalition to continue, especially in view of its greater homogeneity of blood.   It became dominated by the Piagnoni, the strong centre party, whose numbers were sufficient to secure the supremacy of whichever side they joined. The coalition to which he owed his election was thus the best basis for Capponi's influence ; and his policy was consistently directed throughout his term of office to securing its continuance and thereby his own re-election.   So strong did the fusion become that Varchi reckons the moderate parties as one under the title of " The Party of Niccolò, or of Capponi."   As a result, the Arrabbiati under the leadership of Baldassare Carducci became the party of opposition, making up in violence what they lacked in numbers, and continuing to rely more upon tumults in the Piazza than upon deliberations in the Council.   Capponi was forced to mould his policy in accordance with the sentiments of the section which controlled the balance of power in the state ; and indeed the somewhat ostentatious virtue of his private life gives ground to believe that his own inclinations tended in the same direction.[9]   The government of Florence therefore received a theocratic tinge which brought to mind the heyday of the Savonarolan rule.   Indeed, even while the old Signoria was still in office the new spirit had begun to manifest itself.   Only four days after the departure of the Medici, a letter had been addressed to Fra Bernardino da Vicenza begging him in the most pressing terms to come to Florence that there by his preaching " some worthy fruit of penitence be wrought in the present most troublous times." [10]   Immediately after the revolution, too, San Marco sprang once more into the reputation which it had lost since the days of its great Prior.   The citizens began to flock to it again ; Capponi himself frequently displayed himself in the company of its friars ; and Fra Bartolommeo da Faenza, though a man of a much lesser mould, began to be considered the successor to the mantle of Savonarola even as he was to his office and to his ideas.[11]

The day after the election of Capponi, upon the first Sunday in June, a solemn religious procession (originally fixed for 23 May, but postponed lest the unpopularity of the old Signoria should raise some disturbance on its public appearance[12]) inaugurated the new regime. The miraculous picture of the Annunciation attributed by the admiring to Giotto and by the credulous to St. Luke himself,[13] was uncovered and left to the public adoration —an unprecedented event—in the Church of the Servite Friars which took its name from this most precious of its adornments. The crowds of the faithful who thronged to see it, more even from outside the city than from within, made a gratifying show of public devotion even though entrance into the church was impeded by their very numbers. Meanwhile, a procession of all the religious companies and orders of Florence started out from the Duomo bearing the head of S. Zanobi, and followed by all of the magistrates and priors of the arts as well as by a multitude of private persons. At the Palazzo it was joined by the Gonfalonier and the Signoria in robes of state. Thence it made the complete circuit of the city, passing through the Church of S. Marco, and then through that of the Annunziata in homage to the miraculous picture. It ended, as it had started, at the Duomo, where a solemn mass was chanted by the Bishop of Fiesole. The concourse of spectators and participants, both from the city and from the contado, was such as the rarity of the occasion merited. Never, it was thought, had such a procession been seen in Florence. Still, it did not redound wholly to Capponi's credit. His critics thought that at a time of such instability it gave opportunities for further tumults ; and it was true that some slight disorder disturbed the progress of the procession itself, and caused the sacred picture to be for a time covered. A more serious allegation was that the great concourse of people prepared the ground for the pestilence which was shortly to break out in all its terror.[14]

The renewed spirit of religion in the administration of the state next manifested itself in the treatment of the Jews. The position of that unfortunate people in Florence formed a sort of barometer by which the character of the government could be gauged. Excluded by the narrow piety and commercial intolerance of the early Republic, they had been first summoned in 1437 to open loan-banks ; four years, it is to be noted, after the recall of Cosimo de' Medici and the commencement of his hegemony. They had taken a notable share in the philosophical interests and discussions of the Medicean circle. But the provisions of 1495–6, through which had been set up the Monte di Pietà—the *public* loan-bank—had cancelled their concessions ; and their efforts could succeed only in postponing, and not in evading, the expulsion decreed. Nevertheless, within four years of the fall of Soderini the Jews were again admitted to the city on the old terms, and were protected by the rulers even though their lives were at times in danger from the mob. One of the first acts of the new regime was to restore in this respect as well the position previous to 1512. Their loan-banks were closed ; the owners were given twelve months to settle their affairs and to leave the Florentine dominion ; and if a few continued to remain, they fared ill without the solitary means of subsistence vouchsafed to them by the law. It was not until the re-establishment of Medicean rule that a permanent settlement could be formed.[15]

A number of further provisions marked the return to the days of the Theocracy. Detailed sumptuary laws were passed which closely regulated the attire and adornments of men as well as of women. The penalties against unnatural vice were confirmed. Some poison-spots in the city were purged. It was prohibited for any but clerics to argue upon matters of faith. Blasphemy was proceeded against with rigour. Gambling was prohibited. The size of dowries, now grown immense, was limited. Even the taverns were regulated. By a provision more modern in idea and requirements, it was prohibited to walk about the churches during divine service.[16] Even such harmless amusement as the Bravia, or traditional races, sometimes called Palio, were continually forbidden and the money thus saved devoted to pious ends.[17] A censorship of books was set up.[18] Instead of the licentious Carnival observances of St. Matthias' Day (25 February) a religious procession was held. Capponi's critics objected that such regulations, however good in intention, were extremely ill-timed. Nevertheless, they were approved of by the people with a surprising unanimity. The sumptuary laws, which must have been as unpalatable as any, passed through the Ottanta by 72 votes to 18, and through the Consiglio Maggiore by 1,017 to 344 ; and in this case the strength of the minority was exceptional. The theocracy did not exist on paper only, as many found to their cost. Some suffered for crimes which they had committed with impunity under the Medici. In a fit of anger through losing at play, one citizen threw a crucifix into a well. He expiated the crime with his life ; nor was he the only one to suffer so severely for more venial faults.[19]

This attempt to conciliate the support of the Piagnoni had to be balanced by some concessions to the Arrabbiati. The pressure of extremist opinion led to the introduction of a series of measures directed against the Medicean partisans which could not have been welcome to Capponi's conciliatory spirit. As expedients for raising money, however, they could not but find a general support in the precarious condition of the public finances. The first measure of ordinary business brought before the Consiglio Grande was one for the election of a special commission of five to audit the accounts since 1512, with full power over the possessions of any whom they found to be through fraud or favour in debt to the state.[20] This measure virtually gave the Palleschi over into the hands of their enemies, and was a manifest infraction of the agreement under which the Medici had agreed to leave the city, which provided that there should be no proceedings taken against their adherents for deeds committed since 1512. The five commissioners came to be known as the *Tribolanti* or Tormentors owing to the severity of their measures.[21] Naturally, they were chosen from the numbers of the Republicans, and the partisans of the old regime, whether guilty or innocent, had good reason for apprehension. Nor was it this only that they had to fear. The legitimate, and even essential, requirements of the Republic were such as to strike principally at the same class of the population. Within a few days, a further commission of five was appointed by a complicated system of election to assess a *balzello* or extraordinary tax of from 70,000 to 80,000 ducats upon the wealthier citizens, to be paid within four months. It is true that a provision was inserted that no single assessment should be of more than 300 ducats or less than 60, which prevented any extravagant abuse ; but it was natural that at the full flood of the Revolution the assessors should not spare the opulent who had been the strongest partisans of the Medici.[22] A day or two later, in view of the pressing requirements of the Commune, twenty citizens were selected out of a number nominated in closest secrecy by the Signori and Colleges who were to make a forced loan of 1,500 ducats each, to be reimbursed from the first receipts of the new taxation.[23] Again, there could be no doubt upon what section of the population this unwelcome privilege would fall ; and these impositions were the first of a long series. A typical example was that of the historian, Guicciardini, notorious as owing all his advancement to the late ruling house. He could hardly have been expected to evade the balzello ; and he was of the number chosen to contribute to the forced loan. He again had to lend in October ; in the following May he was fearing another call upon his purse ; while in the next year he had to run into debt in order to satisfy the demands of the treasury.[24] Similarly Roberto Acciaiuoli, recently returned from an embassy in France, was assessed beyond his means for the balzello and was imprisoned on his failure to pay.[25] " Appeals and complaints were heard to the very heavens," writes the Venetian ambassador ; " for the taxation was piled upon those who could not bear it, and particularly the partisans of the Medici."[26]

A yet stronger weapon in the hands of the extremists was the institution of a special tribunal to deal with cases for which the normal judicial system was considered inadequate. The ordinary courts for criminal matters were the Otto di Guardia e Balia and the Conservadori delle Leggi ; but the numbers of each body were small, and they were thought to be amenable to intimidation and partiality, even if not to actual corruption. The possibility was greatest precisely in those state cases in which danger was most imminent. Under Soderini, therefore, an attempt had been made to combat this by the institution of a larger tribunal of forty drawn by lot from the Ottanta.[27] It was this institution which was now revived and reorganized under Capponi.[28] Provision was made in the first place under the most severe penalties for the registration of all criminal complaints and accusations. As a result of this, it was possible to ensure the proper prosecution of all those against whom some charge was made, without any opportunity of evasion. In the event of the judiciary considering itself too weak to give judgment or to pronounce adequate sentence, or of any of its members being dissatisfied with the result, notice was to be given to the Signoria and the case came under the cognisance of the new board. Similarly—and this was of paramount importance—in any case which could be considered an affair of state, all power of decision was taken away from the Otto, with whom alone cognisance had previously rested. They now retained only the duty of making a preliminary inquiry into the case and reporting it to the Signoria, which referred it to the new tribunal. This was now wholly reconstituted. Forty names were drawn by ballot from the Ottanta. To these were added representatives of all the principal councils and magistracies to the number of nineteen, together with the whole of the tribunal from which the case had been reserved.[29] This composite council, deliberating in closest secrecy, deciding its sentence by ballot,[30] and presided over by the Gonfalonier himself, was considered sufficiently strong, both in numbers and in standing, to deal fearlessly and adequately within a fortnight with any case, however delicate. Further precautions were taken to ensure the recording and executing of the sentence. Appeal was indeed allowed to the Consiglio Maggiore ; but even so the sentence of the Quarantia could be quashed only by a two-thirds majority.[31] Its critics thought that the new procedure left much to be desired. In particular, it was considered that its dependence upon the minor judicial bodies sapped it of its force and strength. There was nothing to ensure its cognisance of all these cases for which it was intended. The criminal tribunals might not refer cases to it, or, more perilously, the Otto might keep state cases to themselves merely by registering them as criminal. In addition, the composition of the Quarantia as reconstituted was feared to be too amenable to aristocratic control owing to the excessive representation upon it of the higher officers of state.[32]   In spite of this, however, the new tribunal showed itself on occasion to be terrible in its efficiency.

Its first victim was Benedetto Buondelmonti, remembered for his pride and his excessive partisanship of the Medici,[33] who had come to Florence after the sack of Rome at the invitation of Filippo Strozzi and of his republican cousin Zanobi.   The newly appointed Auditors of Accounts asserted that he was in debt to the State to the extent of 1,000 crowns ; and, taking full advantage of their statutory powers, sent to his country estate where he was staying, to distrain upon his goods.   It was not unnatural that commotion was raised among his men, who even offered some opposition. It was even proposed to give the alarm by sounding the church bells.   The pretext was sufficient.   Buondelmonti was arrested, and arraigned for attempting to raise the countryside and for opposing the execution of justice.   To this were added accusations of practices against the Republic and an ancient charge dating back to the Medicean times.   The Otto certified it as an affair of state, and referred it to the Quarantia.   Buondelmonti defended himself not unconvincingly against the charges ; but his friends acquiesced in a sentence of close imprisonment for four years in order to avoid worse punishment.[34]

While these things were going on inside the city, the attention of the government was being turned to more unexceptionable matters outside it.   The recovery of the fortresses of Pisa and Livorno was the most essential requirement for ensuring the security of the state.   The treacherous conduct of Cortona in withholding them had been condemned even by the Palleschi, in spite of the Cardinal's specious excuse that he could not extract the countersign from its keeper.   Guicciardini himself professed to be confident that the Pope, if he knew, would give an order for their surrender and that he was displeased at the event.[35]   Meanwhile, stronger measures were resorted to, and Antonfrancesco degli Albizzi, whose *volte-face* had secured his position under the new regime, was sent with a sufficient force to recover the fortresses.   He prepared to make a vigorous and destructive bombardment, and artillery was sent up in his support.[36]   But both the example and the expense of such violent measures were feared at Florence.   Zanobi Buondelmonti was therefore sent to Pisa with a superior authority and under instructions to seek for surrender by agreement.   The Medici, seeing that their day was over and threatened with outlawry for their ill-faith,[37] determined to obtain the best possible price.   By a private agreement they secured a promise that they should be allowed to live in the city and enjoy their property, with the observance of their privileges, if the fortresses were restored ; and they took the precaution of securing the oath of some of the foremost citizens—among them the Gonfalonier—to the agreement.[38] The captain of Pisa, despairing of succour, appealed to in the name of loyalty, and tempted by a large bribe, agreed to surrender his charge on this understanding (9 June). A week later, the captain of Livorno drove a similar but harder bargain.[39] Over 12,000 ducats and many heartburnings were the price of the faithlessness of the Cardinal. In recompense, envoys had been sent to Lucca to induce that Republic to expel the exiles from their territory. The surrender gave an opportunity to abandon this hopeless task with a good grace.[40]

While the internal position of the Florentine dominion was thus being secured, the external policy had to be decided. The city had been at the time of the Revolution one of the members of the league of Cognac, under obligation to maintain a force of about 6,000 in its army.[41] This was under the control of Francesco Guicciardini, Lieutenant-General[42] for the Pope at the camp. After the Revolution, the Otto di Pratica—the body responsible for foreign affairs—had hastened to reassure the league of their continued adhesion, and to insist that the change of government had only been for the better defence of their own liberty and that of Italy.[43] Their assurances were for the time accepted ; but the continued delay of the Florentines in forwarding their contribution for the upkeep of the troops in their pay began to rouse suspicion.[44] Guicciardini was continually pressing ; the Otto continually procrastinating or excusing themselves on the ground of economic stress, or of their need of the money to recover the fortresses of Pisa and Livorno, or to defend their frontier against the Imperialist Sienese.[45] At last Guicciardini's warnings that the delay was alienating their allies and causing their troops to desert had some effect. The driblets which were forthcoming were, however, wholly inadequate, and nothing was done to substantiate their protestations of loyalty.

There was indeed good reason. No change in sentiment was necessary in order to procure a reversal in the Florentine policy. The immediate question to be solved was how to avert the imminent peril that the all-conquering lanzknechts would return and treat Florence as they had treated Rome, even as they were boasting that they would do.[46] In his official capacity, Guicciardini was continually urging that the city should secure the protection of the league by a prompt fulfilment of her engagements. Yet even he confessed that the support of the allies was not to be relied upon. The Venetians were slow and selfish ; the French insubordinate and ill led ; while the Imperialists seemed to be favoured by God Himself. Under these circumstances, the Lieutenant-General in his private capacity recommended an accord with the Emperor, and even offered his own services as intermediary.[47]

It must be remembered in addition that the revolutionary movement in Florence had been in its inception closely bound up with hopes of Imperialist aid, and that its leaders had been in close touch with Bourbon's forces. Even after the failure of the first revolt the practices had continued, and Capponi with Alfonso Strozzi had continued to seek for accord through the medium of the Duke of Ferrara.[48] The expulsion of the Medici had been hailed by the Imperialists as a triumph for their cause.[49] Almost immediately afterwards, even as the Florentine government was reiterating its loyalty to the league, direct negotiations were opened up with the Emperor. Secret instructions were sent to the Florentine envoy in Spain to implore the protection of Charles V. He was, however, ordered to keep to generalities without making any definite promises. For the moment they could not take any obligation upon themselves ; what they craved was an order to the Imperialist commanders in Italy not to molest their city.[50] Thus it was hoped to escape both the perils and the expenses of war. But Spain was distant and the danger was pressing ; and so at the same time negotiations were opened directly with Charles's representative in the country through the agents of his ally, the Duke of Ferrara, in the city and the camp. A third channel lay through Siena, both immediately and through the medium of the Ferraran envoys. It was natural that on the fall of the Medici the two neighbouring republics, united by their common hatred, should draw closer together. Both sides favoured the idea—the Imperialists, as a step to win over Florence ; the League, as likely to cause the adhesion of Siena. There too was residing Lannoy, the Imperial Viceroy, with whom direct communications were opened. But he had experienced the extent of his control over the troops, and admitted frankly that he could not bind them. The decision therefore lay with the military leaders, to whom Lannoy referred his petitioners.[51]

The object of the Florentines in initiating these negotiations had been not only to secure their safety, but to secure their safety with the greatest possible economy. They had informed the Emperor that they could for the moment at least provide him with no funds in return for his ordering that the city should be spared. The military leaders, however, to whom they were now referred, thought of politics and treaties in terms of money only. The Florentines were offered much the same conditions as the Pope had received : the payment of 300,000 ducats within one month, and of an additional 20,000 monthly for the duration

of the war.   In addition they were to repay the Duke of Ferrara
for his trouble by the expensive compliment of taking his son
into their service as their Captain-General.   These demands
were put forward as a minimum, in spite of the attempts of
Ferrara to get the capital sum reduced by one-third.   Through
this extravagance, the negotiations with the Imperialists in
Italy failed.   Nevertheless, it was generally believed that had
the Emperor been closer at hand an agreement would have been
concluded.[52]

Meanwhile, relations with the league were no easier. Supplies of money were indeed sent to Guicciardini, but in inadequate amounts, and continually accompanied by protestations of
the poverty or the exhaustion of the city. The confederate
generals avowed their readiness to protect her, but suspiciously
added "only if the government showed that it wished to be
defended." When pressed by the English ambassador to put
their promises into writing, such equivocal conditions were added
as to make the assurance practically valueless. At the same
time the growing suspicions resulted in a formal demand that
Florence should confirm the fact of alliance concluded after the
Tumulto del Venerdì. The request was refused, but in a non-
committal manner, on the ground that it was considered unnecessary. Nevertheless, the allies continued to press under the pretext that the King of France himself desired it. The Venetian
envoy used alternately arguments and menaces to secure his
end, threatening the complete withdrawal of all protection and
the abandonment of the city to the lanzknechts. Guicciardini
continued from the camp to point out the dangers of delay.[53]
At last, therefore, some open decision had to be made. The
Ottanta was called together to consider the question, and a
vigorous discussion took place. Tommaso Soderini pleaded for
the traditional policy, by which his uncle had fallen, of alliance
with France. He appealed to the city to maintain its good faith
and to secure its safety by a continued adherence to the league.
Capponi, with Zanobi Buondelmonti, led the party of those who
had intrigued with the Imperialists before the revolution and
now favoured alliance with the victors as a greater security for
the city than that with the allies of her late tyrants. Yet the
difficulties found in the conduct of negotiations formed an insuperable obstacle ; and the powerful section by which the
memory of Savonarola was still held sacred remembered his
political teaching, summed up in the recommendation that "lilies
should bloom with lilies "—those of Florence, that is, with those
of France. The stronger party was accordingly found to be that
to which the traditional Guelph sentiment had the stronger
appeal. A commission was appointed with Baldassare Carducci

at its head to negotiate the form of the new treaty. It was agreed to maintain 4,000 foot and 400 horse with the army of the league ; and under these modified conditions the arrangement was finally concluded (22 June).[54]

Even now, however, the mutual relations did not work wholly smoothly. The negotiations with the Emperor continued uninterrupted, an excuse for them not being difficult to find.[55] To the disgust of the confederates, a safe conduct through Florentine territory was given to the Imperial envoys sent to take over Parma and Piacenza, in consequence of the recent agreement with the Pope ; and its sincerity was proved by the sharp punishment meted out to those who had the hardihood to disregard it.[56] At the same time, the Florentines regarded with suspicion only too well founded the occupation of Ravenna by Venetian troops " to guard it for the Church," and intrigued with the other confederates, though without success, for the Papal Romagna to be occupied by their own troops instead.[57] The Venetians must have thought similarly of the attempt by Florence to induce Faenza to put herself again under her protection, as during the previous century.[58] The Ferrarese ambassador was informed by some of the leading citizens that a more than legitimate pretext was not lacking to break with the league.[59] The inadequacy of its forces was in itself sufficient. Instead of the agreed minimum of 20,000, they barely reached half that number ; and they were daily losing in credit through inaction and in numbers through desertion. Its commanders were continually at cross-purposes with one another.[60] A minor encounter near Terni, in which no more than 2,000 men were engaged all told, was the only action of any importance during the whole course of the campaign.[61]

A further subject of dispute with the allies came up when at last the question of the movement of the confederate army was raised. The Florentines had urged that on its retirement from the ineffectual campaign to relieve the Pope it should neither withdraw upon Florentine territory nor yet make an incursion upon Imperialist Siena. The first they dreaded, since " the losses we have already suffered from the allied soldiery cannot be related "[62]; the second, because it would disturb the possibility of amicable relations with the neighbouring Republic and still more since it might have the perilous effect of drawing the Imperialist forces after them into Tuscany.[63] The same considerations were impelling them to content themselves with peaceful remonstrations for the predatory raids of Sienese subjects over the border, and even to reprimand retaliation.[64] It was true that the traditional Florentine policy was followed in harbouring the refugees after one of the periodic Sienese revolu-

tions which occurred at about this time,[65] and in giving the exiles
aid in a surprise attack upon their native city. But the assistance
was kept secret, and the refugees were refused safe-conducts ;
while upon the failure of the attack the booty seized by the
assailants was ordered to be returned and they were commanded
to withdraw from the immediate border.[66] But in spite of these
preoccupations on the part of the Florentines, their representations were without effect upon their allies. Part at least of
the army of the league retired through Tuscany with the usual
results. So equivocal were the relations with the French forces
that it was possible to excuse depredations and even fatal assaults
directed against them under the plea that they were justified by
official licence.[67] The conduct of Andrea Doria, the great Genoese
sea-captain in the service of the French, was of a piece with this
upon his arrival at about this time in the neighbourhood of
Livorno to support the campaign of the league in the South.
Instructions were given that his men should be amicably and
hospitably entertained, but yet with all proper precaution, Luigi
Alamanni being sent as Commissary-General to receive him.[68] How
far this prudence was justified was shown by the action of Doria
in forming a close blockade of the port—presumably in order to
prevent supplies from reaching the Imperialists—allowing nothing
to enter but food. Representations to the French commanders
proved useless.[69] Such were the equivocal relations between the
Florentines and their nominal allies in the first months after the
revolution. Only with the approaching revival of the league
in Italy, with the progressive dwindling of the Imperialist forces,
did they become more consistently and sincerely friendly.

   With allies so unreliable and so dangerous, the Florentines had
to look to their own resources. These were at the commencement
none too great. Before the revolution they had borne the
expenses for over 7,500 foot with the forces of the league besides
cavalry [70] ; but this must have included also the troops serving
in the name of the Pope, for the payment of whom Guicciardini
was drawing irregularly upon the city.[71] Actually, they were
supposed to be maintaining about 5,000 foot [72] ; but in fact they
did not amount to more than 3,000 owing to losses from sickness
and desertion (for from action they had little to fear).[73] These,
with a few cavalry proportionately fallen from strength, were
all the troops upon which the Florentines could count in case
of the emergency, of which they stood in perpetual apprehension,
of an attack by the Imperialist forces. If the warnings of Guicciardini and of the other representatives were not enough, a
savage attack of the lanzknechts upon the little Umbrian town
of Narni,[74] and a flying visit of one of the Imperial commanders
to Siena,[75] were sufficient to confirm their fears and to hasten

their preparations.   The first step in the reorganization was to appoint a fresh Commissary as civil representative for the control of their forces.   A more able man than Francesco Guicciardini it would have been almost impossible to find ; yet he himself recognized that after the revolution his position was impossible. He had owed all of his advancement to the Medici, and though he had accepted the new government, he did not scruple to continue to correspond with the Pope and even to profess a certain loyalty to him.[76]   He was suspected therefore by the allies as well as by his fellow-citizens ;   and in particular was notoriously on the worst of terms with Urbino, the commander-in-chief.   He was cordially disliked even by the captains nominally under his control, whose violence he feared with good reason, as a recent event had shown.   His lack of tact in giving exaggerated promises of promotion as commander of the Florentine forces to one of these officers had led to the estrangement of his patron, the Duke of Mantua, and to his own withdrawal from the camp with all the cavalry under his command.   As a result of all this, and still more of his political record, Guicciardini's repeated requests were at last granted and he was allowed to retire.[77]   His successor was Raffaello Girolami, who had been removed by the Medici from his post as Commissary of Poggibonsi for his suspected sympathy with the Tumulto del Venerdì.[78]

Under Girolami, the Florentine forces began to be reinforced ; and the city had the good fortune to be able to reconstitute in its service the body of troops upon which Italy had most reason to pride herself.   Giovanni de' Medici, a member of the cadet branch of the family and father of the young Cosimo who was to become the first Grand Duke of Tuscany, had first instituted that force of mercenaries which later became known as the Bande Nere, after the " Black Bands " which they wore in mourning for his untimely death ; the name being afterwards anachronistically applied to their dead leader.[79]   The loss of their founder at Borgoforte and the parsimony of the Pope, in whose service they were serving, had led to the disintegration of the force, but a compact body remained in Florentine pay.[80]   They laboured, indeed, under the serious disadvantage of being " the most insolent, troublesome, and rapacious " infantry of the time.[81]   At the same time, however, they were generally considered to be the best and most capable, fully qualified to compete with the famous Spanish and German infantry [82] ; and they had the additional advantage of being in great part Florentine subjects by birth. To that section which had remained in the service of the city there was now added the majority of the remaining companies, until the force was almost entirely reconstituted.   As their Captain-General was appointed Orazio Baglione, head of the family which ruled Perugia and which was destined to be bound up with the darkest memories in Florentine annals. At the same time a large force of cavalry was engaged ; the border-fortresses were strengthened or restored ; and the care of them was entrusted to more reliable representatives.[83]   Upon the arrival of the news of the sack of Narni, it was formally forbidden for any Florentine subject to take service under a foreign captain excepting in the service of the league ; and all those already so engaged were ordered to return.   From them, additional forces were recruited for the defence of the city.[84]   In addition, there was reorganized under the Nove della Milizia (a board in abeyance under the Medici) the old militia which Machiavelli had founded and which had been renewed in 1514.   The force was recruited from the Florentine dominion from those between eighteen and thirty-six ; though only 10,000 were to serve at a time for fear of detriment to agriculture.   It was divided into thirty " ordinances " under two commanders, with four Commissaries in the provincial centres to supervise the arrangements.   Arms were imported from Germany for their use.[85]   Thus prepared, Florence had little to fear from surprise attack.

Meanwhile, however, the attention of the citizens had been diverted from politics by a great public calamity.   Plague broke out in Italy with greater force than ever before, perhaps, since the Black Death.   Commencing in Lombardy, it spread rapidly from town to town.   Rome, weakened by its sufferings, fell an easy victim to its ravages.   The licentious armies of either side suffered terribly ; and it was noted with superstitious reverence that of the troops which had sacked the Holy City few survived to tell the tale.[86]   In Florence it had appeared as early as 1522, and had returned later after a brief intermission ; but now, as was thought, it was ended.   Some lingering vestiges, however, still remained, and these, fostered perhaps by the crowds who thronged the streets during the great procession of 2 June, burst forth anew with terrible violence.   During the course of the next month, it rapidly spread,[87] so that two hundred persons were reckoned to die each day.   In August the number increased to three or even four hundred, and for three terrible days in succession, it reached the appalling total of five hundred.   Michelangelo had the grief of watching his brother Buonarotto die in his arms.[88] All of the citizens who could left for their villas or elsewhere, and Prato in particular became filled with the refugees.   It was computed that no less than seven-eighths of the better class sought refuge outside the walls.[89]   Even here they were not safe, for the young Giorgio Vasari, whose Medicophile family had retired to Arezzo at the revolution, lost his father and the most part of his kin.[90]   An attempt was made to restore confidence and to

secure the conduct of public business by ordering all the heads of
families to return and attend to their duties under pain of fine ;
or by continual proclamations to office-holders and members of
the councils to return to their posts.[91] All this had little effect.
The city seemed to be deserted. " All the houses and shops were
shut," wrote the Venetian ambassador, who prided himself upon
his courage in remaining. " No persons were to be met with who
had the form of human beings ; one saw only the ministers of the
churches and spectacles of horror and scenes which I tremble to
relate." [92] Wills, and even confessions, were made in the streets
or on the house-tops, and the dead were carried to burial in carts,
without following or ceremony. The Great Council could not
function as before. The number of its meetings was fixed at only
two each week, and the minimum attendance for ordinary business was reduced from eight to four hundred. Such was the zeal
of a section of the citizens that this number was always reached,
and at the peril of their lives many used to enter the city from
their safe retreats outside the walls when the great bell of
the Palazzo tolled out its summons. This, it was thought, led to
the spread of the disease in the contado. In the Council Hall
itself, those who assembled appeared a mere handful, with ample
room to keep aloof from one another in order to avoid contagion.
In spite of special precautions,[93] two-thirds of the staff of the
Palazzo were reckoned to have died ; but it was noted with
amazement that not one of the Signoria was among the number.
For the other magistracies, however, despite insistent orders and
sharp punishments,[94] it was difficult to get a quorum, and the
Signoria was authorized to take all necessary measures for the
government of the city without further reference and even to
appoint their successors without the normal quota being
present,[95] under the understanding that all their provisions would
be subsequently legalized. Capponi remained at his post in the
city during the whole period, carrying out his duties and super-
vising the arrangements for relief. These were organized under
a special magistracy, serving without salary in this pious office.
Salt was regularly distributed to the sick without payment.[96]
Churches and convents were commandeered to house the infected,[97] in addition to 600 huts erected outside the walls ; and
two new prisons had to be opened and even a new gallows erected
for the ghouls who preyed upon the impotence of their fellows.
Naturally, prices rose to extreme heights. The horrors of famine
were added to those of plague, and continued when they had
passed. The Uffiziali dell' Abundanzia were invested with extraordinary powers which had to be protracted long after the plague
had subsided.[98] The Cardinal Archbishop ordered, and the
Signoria repeated, that all should kneel in prayer at the sounding

of the Ave Maria.[99] The measure of the calamity was marked by recourse to what was almost the argument of despair in Florence. On 18 August, when the disease was at its height, the miraculous picture of the Madonna was sent for from Imprunetta. At the city gates it was solemnly met by the Signoria, in robes of state but barefoot, who accompanied it to the Church of the Annunziata, where it remained for two days.[100] From this date, it was thought, there was some relaxation ; but an excess of optimism authorized the resumption of preaching, and the assemblies of people gave the disease a fresh hold. Not till the autumn was there any appreciable diminution, and only in November could it be said that the worst was over.[101] Still, however, the sickness continued sufficiently for the minimum for the Council to be continued at 400 for another twelve months.[102] There was a recrudescence from February ; and during the Lent of 1528 preaching was again suspended, to the horror of the pious.[103] In May the mortality still gave rise to considerable apprehensions [104]; and not till the close of the year could it be reckoned at an end. Its ravages had been terrible. As many as 30,000 died in the city and suburbs—no less than a quarter of the population : and over twice as many in the Florentine territories.[105] Such a terrible loss could not be without results. The manufactures of the city suffered a terrible diminution, and Florence never completely recovered either in population or in wealth.[106]

The Great Pest of 1348 had been celebrated in Florence by the meetings of the happy band whose conversation Boccaccio has immortalized. The close of that of 1527 was signalized in a manner absolutely opposite, yet no less typically Florentine. By the following February the scourge had gone far towards abating and the refugee citizens had commenced to return. The Gonfalonier seized the occasion of a meeting of the Great Council (Sunday, 9 February 1527/8) to make a speech partaking more of the nature of a sermon than of an oration and showing obvious echoes of Girolamo Savonarola.[107] He enlarged at length upon the tribulations of the city and upon the majesty of God. Finally he threw himself upon his knees, crying " Mercy ! " and the responsive people followed him in both his action and his exclamation. Then, rising, he solemnly proposed that Jesus Christ should be elected King of Florence. Only eighteen votes were cast against the motion in an assembly of 1,100. A special register was prepared in which all the citizens were made to sign their allegiance, quarter by quarter, promising never to cede the government of the city to any other sovereign. Above the portals of the Palace an inscription was placed in eternal remembrance of the fact that Christ was King of the Florentine people.[108] The later Medici, hardly daring to abolish the tablet, altered it so as to express a more remote lordship : " King of Kings and Ruler of Rulers." [109]

During the course of the pest, though not as a result of it, there died one, who if not the most distinguished citizen of Florence, yielded that place only to Michelangelo Buonarotti. Niccolò Machiavelli had been forced into an unwelcome retirement by the downfall of the Second Republic. From the Medici, from whom he had hoped to see some benefit to Italy as a whole, he had succeeded at last in obtaining with difficulty a series of minor employments. During the revolution he had been on a mission from Cortona to Guicciardini, to urge his fellow-historian to do something to save the Pope. The events in Florence reduced him to the most unhappy of positions. All possibilities of advancement from his new employers was over, even though at last they should have decided really to trust him ; and the sole result of his labours was to discredit him in the eyes of his old masters who were now again to the fore. Sadly and with many sighs he returned to Florence,[110] worn out by his years, his labours, and his disappointments. Nobody took any account of the old and discredited patriot. On 10 June the Dieci di Guerra was reconstituted. Machiavelli had some hopes of regaining the office of Secretary, which he had held for fourteen years under Soderini, and made all efforts to be reappointed to the post. But his record told against him. " The generality hated him on account of *The Prince*. The rich thought this *Prince* of his a document to teach the Duke to take away their property ; the poor, to take away their liberty. The Piagnoni thought him a heretic, the good thought him immoral, and the bad either worse or else more capable than themselves, so that everybody hated him." [111] One Francesco Tarugi was appointed to the post which Machiavelli regarded as his own.[112] The blow was fatal. Whether the digestive ailments from which he had long suffered were a contributory cause or no, within ten days he fell dangerously ill and in two more he was dead.[113] In the dark times that were to come Florence had reason to miss his wide experience and sage counsel, and to regret her neglect of his advice.

NOTES TO CHAPTER III

[1] Jacopo Pitti, *Apologia de' Cappucci* (*A.S.I.*, ser. I, vol. IV, pt. 2), p. 340, *n*. I.

[2] MS. diary in Magl. XXV, 555, f. 20. " Et fucci due cittadinj ch' ebboron piue di dumiglia diucentto faue nere, l' uno fue njcholoe din piero champonj, l' anltro tthomaso ttosinghi."

[3] *Vita di N. Capponi*, p. 887 *seqq*. His age may be deduced from p. 980.

[4] Or *Frateschi*, after *Frate*, the Friar. For these cf. also *infra*, p. 368, and for their character Giannotti, *Opere*, I, 232 *seqq*.

[5] Or *Adirati* with the same meaning ; or *Compagnacci*, in memory of the " ill companions " against Savonarola ; or *Popolani, Ciompi, Poveri,* or *Plebe,* by enemies who accentuated their lowly origin.

[6] Or *pochi, ricchi, nobili, grandi.*

[7] " Il popolo minuto è tutto pallesco " (Foscari, *Relazione,* p. 75).

[8] The best and most impartial accounts of these factions are to be found in the judicious reports of the Venetian observers—*Relazioni* of Foscari, pp. 69–73 ; and Soriani, p. 412. Cf. also Varchi, I, 207–15.

[9] " Come idiota," observes Varchi maliciously in mentioning the conceivability (I, 212). His partisan, however, Baccio Carnesecchi, approves of these " bellissimi ordini " in the strongest terms, " considering that it is always necessary to hold a state in one of two ways—eith.er by force or by religion " (*Ragguaglio di Baccio Carnesecchi, ubi supra*)

[10] Letter of Signoria of 21 May 1527, in *R. Arch., di Stato di Firenze :* Signori Missive Minutari 1° Canc.

Frd Bernardino de Vicentia : die 21 euisd.

Rvd* Pr ; Essendo desiderosi che in questa nostra città si viva col timore di dio et in questi pericolissimi tempi si facci qualche degno fructo di penitentia, sappiendo ad questo effecto esser necessaria la exortatione delli huomini religionis et de' servi di Dio : preghiamo con ogni possibile effichaccia la Patᵓᵃ vostra, et per viscera misericordiæ dei la exortiamo ; che non li sia grave subito subito alla ricevuta di questa trasferirsi insino quà : secondo anchora ne faranno intendere li sui superiorj, per fare qualche predicationi secondo quella giudicherà ad proposito et conveniente ; perchè speriamo la venuta sua havere ad essere con universale satisfactione di tutto questo popolo ; et havere mediante la gratia dello omnipotente dio ad fare tale fructo, che ne sia per resultare, prima l' honore di Dio, dipoi la salute delle anime nostre ; il che debba essere la principale intentione di chi è proposto al ghoverno d' altri. Et pertanto la preghiamo stretissimamente, che ne vogli pigliare per noi questa faticha ; aspetandone da Dio merito et da noi perpetua obligatione. Bene vale.

He was selected as preacher to the Signoria a year and a half later (Signoria, CXXX, 4 October 1528).

[11] In spite of the failure of his first attempt—to induce the Gonfalonier Nori to retire and to detach the Captain of the Guard to the popular cause. Varchi, I, 216 ; Nerli, p. 157.

[12] According to Nerli, p. 160, the object was precisely this—to draw the Signoria away from the security of the Palace and then assail them.

[13] Vasari, however, attributed it to Giotto's disciple, Cavallini (*Opere,* I 539).

[14] *Ragguaglio di Baccio Carnesecchi, ubi supra* ; MS. diary in Magl. XXV, 555, fo. 20 ; anonymous diary, *apud* Lupo Gentile, *Storiografia,* Appendix. This last is the main source of Varchi's account, I, 217–18.

[15] See my study, *Gli Ebrei a Firenze sotto l' Ultima Repubblica* in *Israel* of Florence (Disp. 15–16 and 17 of 17 April and 1 May 1924) ; reprinted separately with additional detail and full references, Florence, 1924. In this it is shown that in spite of the edict of expulsion individual Jews, if not a settled community, continued in Florence during almost the whole course of the last Republic.

[16] Provisioni (Consigli Maggiori), v. CCVI, 17 June *seqq.* Signoria, CXXIX, 25 May, 17 June. Cambi, IV, 12, 17–18 expresses the wholehearted approval of a " Piagnone." Cf. also Varchi, I, 223–4 ; *Vita di N. Capponi,* p. 928–9.

[17] Signoria, CXXIX, 4, 6 June, where the Palii of S. Lorenzo and S. Vettorio, organized by the Captains of the Guelph Party, are specified.

[18] *Ibid.,* 17 June 1527.

Preceptum librarijs et Stampatoribus quod non stampent opera Nova sine licentia.

Item dicti excelsi dominj et Vexillifer ut supra adunatj et Justis causis motj ut dixerunt et servatis servandis ec. deliberaverunt fieri preceptum et precipi

Giamstephano
Michelangelo
S. Antonio Jubini
Bernardo Zuchetto
et
Bernardo Gunente

librarijs et stampatoribus librorum et aliorum operum et omnibus alijs librarijs et stampatoribus librorum et aliorum operum et cuilibet eorum quatenus deinceps non audeant modo aliquo stampare nec stamparj

facere aliquem librum novum nec aliquam aliam nouam operam alicuius matherie sine licentia et partito dictorum excelsorum Dominorum sub pena eorum indignationis et arbitrij Mandantes ec.

Notificatus dicta die dictis S. nominatis et cuilibet eorum pro famulum rotelinj cum copia precepti prout ipse retulit.

[19] Cf. Giuseppe Rondoni, *I Giustiziati a Firenze*, in *A.S.I.* ser. V, v. 28 (1901), where the notable increase in condemnations after 1526 may be noted. For instances, see Busini, *Lettere*, pp. 35-6, and Varchi, II, 259, *n.* 1.

[20] Consiglio Maggiore, Provisioni, CCVI, 4 June 1527.

[21] Busini, *Lettere*, p. 69.

[22] Provisioni, CCVI, 11 June. The strength of the minority in the Council—418 to 812—is noteworthy ; though the more responsible Ottanta passed the measure by an unusually large majority—91 to 5.

[23] *Ibid.* 19 June. In that they were ultimately repaid, the forced loans of Florence differed radically from those of the contemporary England.

[24] Rossi, I, 94-6 ; Guicciardini, *Lettere* (*Opere*, Vol. IX), p. 134 ff.

[25] Varchi, I, 255 ; Nerli, p. 167.

[26] Soriani, *Relazione*, p. 418. A striking illustration of the way the incidence of taxation was regarded is provided by a case in Otto di Guardia, v. CCII, f. 54—a trial for assault, the attackers crying meanwhile, " Voi ci avete posto el balzello ! "

[27] Busini, p. 143.

[28] The actual author, according to Busini (*ibid.*), was Antonio Alamanni.

[29] Thus the minimum membership of the Quarantia (i.e. Forty) was actually 59 ! The titles of the chief Florentine boards were almost always numerical, but the number rarely corresponded with the fact.

[30] By ballot—but in a most complicated fashion. The sentence had to be agreed upon by at least two-thirds of the votes. If after three ballots the requisite majority was not attained, a fourth was taken and the total of votes cast on all four occasions for each sentence was ascertained. In this case, only a bare absolute majority was needed. If this were still not forthcoming, the most precise regulations were laid down for subsequent procedure until a majority was secured.

[31] Provisioni, CCVI, 17 June ; resumed in Varchi, I, pp. 247-55 ; and its working examined by Giannotti, *Opere*, I, 41-2, 204-10 (with suggestions for amelioration).

[32] Busini, pp. 144-5 ; Varchi, I, 255-7 ; Anzilotti, *op. cit.* p. 74.

[33] See Varchi, I, 67.

[34] Ragguaglio del caso di Benedetto Buondelmonti, per Messer Fillipo suo figliuolo, in Bib. Nat. di Firenze, Magl. II, iii, 433, f. 161 ff. This account, written for Varchi, is closely followed by him, I, pp. 254-5. Cf. also Busini, pp. 14, 145. The case is to be found in Signoria, CXXIX, 25 November, 1 and 10 December 1527.

[35] Letters to Otto di Pratica and to Niccolò Capponi of 30 May in *Opere*, IX, 36–44.

[36] Cf. instructions of Dieci of 2 June to the Captain of the Town of Pisa, in Bib. Nat. di Firenze, Magl. II (iii), 433. " Per la tua del 25 s'intende li bombardieri condotti esser comminciati a giungere costì."

[37] Letter of Branchi of 20 May in Sanuto, XLV, 227.

[38] Letter of 8 September, *Ibid.* 301. Cf. also terms of the absolution of 26 November (App. of Docs. IV(i)).

[39] Varchi, I, 234–7.

[40] *Ibid.* pp. 237–8. Dieci, Carteggio Missive, vol. XLII, f. 7 (16 June) : " Et quanto a concederlo (*sc.* salvocondocto) a M. Nofri et alli R^{mo} del Cortona e Cibo non occorre parlare, perchè sendo cassata la causa per la quale lo desideravamo con la restituzione della fortezza di livorno. . . ." A week later, however, a further vigorous complaint was made to Lucca because of the " violentia facta a Franc° di Girolamo da filicaia del R^{mo} di Cortona et sui ministrj " (*Ibid.* f. 10–11, 24 June).

[41] Guicciardini gives a total of 7,700 infantry, besides cavalry (*Opere*, IX, 7). This must have included the remnants of the papal contingent.

[42] An essentially civil, not military, post : equivalent to the Commissary. Cf. the correspondence in Dieci, Missive, vol. XLII, for further illustrative details.

[43] Guicciardini, Letter to Otto di Pratica, 21 May (*Opere*, IX, 11–15) : " Forcing myself to persuade them that the city would not only not turn from the league through this, but would be more ready than before."

[44] *Ibid.* : ". . . I cannot tell how discontented they are commencing to be."

[45] To Gambara, 29 May, *Ibid.* pp. 33–5.

[46] Letters of 26–30 May, *Ibid.* 18–44, cf. especially that to Niccolò Capponi, 30 May (p. 43) : " They do not speak of anything else but sacking Florence." Perez in a despatch to Charles of 18 May speaks of a more statesmanlike plan of depriving Florence of Pisa and Livorno, and raising a levy from her (*State Papers, Spanish*, III, ii, 71).

[47] To Luigi Guicciardini, 26 May (*Opere*, IX, 18–20). For these transactions, see Rossi, *op. cit.* I, 23–37.

[48] Salvioli, *ubi supra*, p. 26 ; yet this seems doubtful. Is the date perhaps wrong ?

[49] Abbot of Najera (the Proveditor-General) to Charles, 27 May (Bergenroth Transcripts, vol. VII, f. 212) : " A loz 24 del presente vino aviso . . . como Florencia . . . habian pueste se in su libertad a la devocion y servicio de V. M." Similarly Perez to Charles, *ibid.* f. 240, 11 June : " Ha venido nueva que en florencia han levantado vanderas por V.M. y hechado fuera a los que governaran por el papa " (cf. *State Papers, Spanish*, III, ii, 78).

[50] Rossi, I, 39–40 ; cf. Sanuto, XLV, 305.

[51] Rossi, I, 40–46.

[52] *Ibid.* Bardi, *Carlo V e l'Assedio di Firenze* in A.S.I. ser. V, vol. II, pp. 8–13. Cf. also despatch of Najera of 23 June, 1527, in *State Papers, Spanish*, III, ii, 93.

[53] Letters of May and June 1527 in *Opere*, vol. IX, *passim*. Rossi, I, 48–52. Cf. also Sanuto, XLV, 250, 315, 336, 339–40.

[54] Rossi, I, 52–4 ; Foscari, *Relazione*, p. 88 ; Sanuto, XLV, 385 ; Segni, I, 34–5 ; *Vita di N. Capponi*, pp. 924–5. Varchi, I, pp. 176–189, confuses the account by describing the event as taking place under the old Signoria ; though he is probably right that a discussion about it took place then. His orations, though artificial, must represent faithfully enough the arguments which were brought up.

[55] Dieci, Missive, vol. XLII, 3, 9–10 (11 and 23 June), to the envoy in Spain. Cf. Rossi, I, 55–6.

[56] Varchi, I, 259–60 ; Dieci, Missive, XLII, 16, 18–19 (3, 7 June 1527), to envoy at Venice.

[57] Varchi, I, 261–2.

[58] *Ibid.* p. 305.

[59] Rossi, I, 55.

[60] Guicciardini, letters of June, 1527, *passim* ; Varchi, I, 267.

[61] Guicciardini, *Storia d'Italia*, IV, 139 ; Varchi, I, 282–4.

[62] Even so late as in October 1527, relief from taxation had to be accorded to the inhabitants of the country desolated by the armies in April (Varchi, I, 311).

[63] Rossi, I, 53–9.

[64] Varchi, I, 253–4.

[65] *Ibid.* p. 265.

[66] *Ibid.* p. 312 ; Segni, I, 39.

[67] Bib. Nat. di Firenze, *Carte Strozziane*, filz. G.O., f. 138 : letter to Otto di Pratica of 6 March 1528. ". . . Nel transito dele gente del S^re Marchese Saluzzo per el Cortonense neli proximi mesi passati fu facto edicto o vero bandimento dala S. del Comiss. del medesimo loco, secundo mi è stato relato, che a chiasduno fosse lecito svaligiare la nation francese come quella che multo danificiare el dominio di V.M. S^rie et . . . per vigor di tale lic^a et auct^a data multi furono perseguitati et interfecti in quello acto . . . trovandose allora uno Heron^o di p^o paulo perusino et volendo svaliciar uno deli prædicti francesi nela pugna facendose da ipso francese resistentia fu dal prædicto Hieronimo interfecto . . ," the assassin being thereupon imprisoned. His release is begged for !

[68] Hauvette, *Luigi Alamanni, sa vie et son œuvre*, pp. 167–8.

[69] MS. diary in Magl. XXV, 555, f. 21 : " Et perchè Andrea Doria era intorno a Livorno e vi lasciasse entrare niente, et venutoci Lautrecha vi si mandò a dirgli che fussi chonvinto a volere lasciarci venire chose nela città ; e lui dise che da mangiare in fuore non vi lasciarebbe venire niente : anzi aveva preso una nave di cjbo, e quela rende andretto. . . ."

[70] Guicciardini, Letter to Otto di Pratica, 16 May 1527, in *Opere*, IX, p. 7.

[71] Rossi, I, 85–6.

[72] By the pact of April ; reduced to 4,000 by that of June.

[73] Varchi, I, 267.

[74] *Ibid.* p. 257.

[75] *Ibid.* p. 265.

[76] Cf. letters in *Opere*, IX, 80, 104.

[77] Rossi, I, 59–66.

[78] Dieci, Missive, XLII, 4 (11 June 1527). Cf. Varchi, I, 109, 205.

[79] *Ibid.* p. 112 ; Ammirato, VII, 39.

[80] 3377, on 16 May 1527, according to Guicciardini (*Opere* IX, 7).

[81] Varchi, I, 245.

[82] Their fame penetrated even to the ears of that ardent amateur, Henry VIII of England. See my article, " *England and the last Florentine Republic,*" in *English Historical Review*, vol. XL (1925), pp. 174–195.

[83] Varchi, I, 245–8 ; Segni, *Storia*, I, 32–5 and *Vita*, p. 931 ; Bardi, *ubi supra*, p. 13 ; Sanuto, *Diarii*, XLV, 437, 568.

[84] Varchi, I, 258.

[85] Canestrini, Introduction to A.S.I., ser. I, vol. XV ; Varchi, I, 401–2 ; Segni, I, 38 ; cf. Signoria, v. CXIX, 16 June 1527, " licentia Novem ordinantie quod possint descrivere & ordinare homines intus in civitate " ; and 29 June, " auctoritas puniendi usque ad mortem."

[86] *Ragguaglio di Baccio Carnesecchi, ubi supra.*

[87] Cf. Sanuto, XLV, 386, 459, 504, 530.

[88] J. A. Symonds, *Life of Michelangelo Buonarroti*, I, 405.

[89] Pazzi to Segni, *apud* Lupo Gentile, *Storiografia*, App. VII.

[90] Vasari, *Opere*, VII, 9.

[91] Signoria, CXXIX, 8 July: "Quod absentes a consilio 80 et collegiis incamerentur." *Ibid.* 20: "Bamnum quod cives habentes officium & capita domorum revertantur Florentie." *Ibid.* 4 August: "Quod absentes a Consilio Maiore incamerentur." See also *ibid.*, 2 November, etc.

[92] Foscari, *Relazione*, p. 29.

[93] E.g. Signoria, v. CXXIX, 23 June: "Quod Pars familie Dominorum non descendant Catenam . . . attento qualiter pestis epidemie in dies inmalescit in civitate."

[94] *Ibid.* 7 September: "Confinatio duorum Coll." who "speverunt Bamnum & preceptum Dictorum Dominorum in se congregando hoc mane in maiore consilio . . . et quod eorum causa fieri non potuit numerus perfectus collegiorum. . . ." Same on 12th for two of Gonfalonieri, *ibid.*

[95] *Ibid.* 22 August, 12, 20 September ("Præceptum S. Ant° de vespuccis quod extrahat officia non obstante quod numerus collegiorum non fuit") and 11 October.

[96] *Ibid.* 1, 22, etc. July.

[97] Cf. *Ibid.* 22 July: "Præceptum Cap[is] societatis Templi quod concedent eorum hospitalem pro infermis peste. . . ."

[98] For all the above cf. Varchi, I, 319–24.

[99] Signoria, *ibid.*, 13 August.

[100] A few days later a further intercessory procession took place, with the miraculous crucifix of S. Piero del Murone (*ibid.*, 23 August).

[101] Cf. Guicciardini, letters of 22 October and 24 November in *Opere*, IX, 124, 127, where he describes how he disinfected his house.

[102] Varchi, I, 308, 350.

[103] See Cambi, to whom this precaution seemed to betoken a lamentable lack of faith.

[104] Cf. British Museum (Pandolfini Papers). Add. MSS. 28,272, f. 93. Giovambattista Pandolfini to Giovanni Pandolfini Potestà di Terranuova, 29 May 1528: ". . . Et qui ancora fu [*sc.* la peste] male, ch' ogni dì venne 6. 8. casa et tocha qualche d' huomini da bene. Se va seguitando la fareno male. . . ." Cf. also Guicciardini, letters of 8 May 1528 (four houses infected daily); and 13 (five or six) in *Opere*, IX, 128, 132; and Sanuto, XLVII, 28, 47, 75, 116, etc.—reports of Soriani of February–April 1528.

[105] G. Pardi, *Disegno della storia demografica di Firenze*, in *A.S.I.* ser. V, vol. 1916, where the figures of contemporaries are compared.

[106] For general story of the pest, see especially Varchi, I, 256–7 and 464–72; Segni, I, 43–4; Nardi, pp. 201–2. Among the dead was Zanobi Buondelmonti, whom we have sèen intriguing for the restoration of the Republic and working for it when restored. In his memory his friend Luigi Alamanni wrote some of his finest verses (*Selvæ*, XI, XII, and especially VIII). The extent of the ravages may be realized from Cambi's lists, presumably of personal acquaintances, IV, 12–15.

[107] Actually one of his, says the cynical Nerli.

[108] Cambi, IV, 5–11, gives a detailed and delighted account of the proceedings: cf. Ammirato, VII, 40–2; Nerli, p. 170; Nardi, p. 202; Segni, I, p. 71; Varchi, 329–31, and *Ragguaglio di Baccio Carnesecchi, ubi supra*, in which the tablet is mentioned as remaining unaltered. It was unveiled after a religious service, on 10 June (Cambi, IV, 35).

[109] It is this, of course, which still remains; but there has been much

dispute about the original form.   Segni gives two different inscriptions in the *Storia* and the *Vita* ; and Varchi, yet a third.   Perhaps one was a temporary and another the final form.   In the Sala del Udienza of the Palazzo Vecchio there is a tablet which may perhaps bear some relation :

Y.H.S.
Sol Justitiæ
Christus Deus Noster
Regnat in Æternum

[110] Busini, *Lettere*, p. 85.   It is only with the most extreme diffidence that one can venture to call attention to a slip of Villari's, *Life of Machiavelli*, II, 533.   Still, his unfairness to Busini is too great to be passed over. " Certainly, however, his sighs were not caused, *as Busini ill-naturedly supposes*, by regret for the revival of freedom, but on the contrary by grief that he should be regarded as its opponent."   Busini actually says precisely the reverse.   " I believe that he was grieving of his practices, because in fact he loved liberty most surpassingly ; but he was grieving that he had embroiled himself with Pope Clement."

[111] *Ibid.* p. 84.

[112] 22 June 1527.   It is a common error, originating in Busini (*ibid.*), that Machiavelli died of disappointment at the election of Donato Giannotti, " heir to his office and to his thought."   Actually, however, the first Secretary to the Dieci under the Republic was Tarugi, Giannotti only being appointed in October, after the death of the other and long after that of Machiavelli.   See Villari, *Machiavelli*, Appendix 20 (Italian Edition).

[113] *Ibid.* pp. 533-4.

CHAPTER IV

ACTION AND REACTION (II)

MEANWHILE events in Rome had been slowly moving. During the sack of the city and after, Clement had remained shut up in the Castle of S. Angelo, secure from the violence of the Imperialist soldiery and hoping for relief. But on 2 June the army of the league which had approached within nine miles of the city was pusillanimously withdrawn, and preparations were made by the enemy to assault the Pope's stronghold. This brought him at last to his knees. By an agreement concluded on 5 June, after a siege of one month, he surrendered himself to his enemies. He agreed to make a payment of 400,000 ducats, and to surrender six of the most important strongholds and castles in the papal states. On this occasion no opportunity was left him to evade his promise. A number of hostages were given from among the most prominent ecclesiastics and relatives of the Pope ; and he himself was to remain under surveillance in S. Angelo until the major part of the terms were carried out, when he would be allowed to withdraw—but only to Naples even then. The Imperial troops replaced the papal garrison in the castle ; and Clement's hopes seemed finally dashed to the ground. Yet thereby Rome at last felt some relief. About the middle of June the Spanish and Italian troops left the city. With infinitely more trouble the lanzknechts were induced to follow about a month later, and marched northwards, still mutinous as before, and showing by their unspeakable brutality upon the route that their passions had not been glutted by the sack of Rome.

The news of events in Italy had far-reaching repercussions throughout Christendom. The sack of Rome provided at least a pretext for the jealous princes of Europe to act against Charles. Francis I still longed to reverse the Treaty of Madrid, and above all to secure the liberation of the two sons whom he had pledged as hostages for its fulfilment. Henry VIII, for whose projected divorce the captivity of the Pope in the hands of the nephew of his unfortunate queen spelt disaster, could deplore the recent events with greater sincerity if with no more ultruism. At the end of May an alliance was concluded between the two sovereigns by which the English king promised to support by subsidies the steps to be taken by the armies in Italy for the release of the Supreme Pontiff. Vigorous preparations were immediately commenced. Andrea Doria, the famous Genoese naval captain, was taken into French service and secured the command of the Mediterranean. A great army was assembled in the neighbourhood of Asti under the command of Odet de Foix, Vicomte de Lautrec. New life was infused into the league of Cognac. The greater part of the Milanese was secured again for Francesco Sforza by a prompt assault, though the capital under Da Leyva still held out for the Emperor. Without stopping to complete the conquest, Lautrec began to march south to release the Pope. By now, however, he had succeeded in releasing himself. After months of protracted imprisonment and ignominy, during which the perils of the plague had been added to the violence of the returned Lanzi, and Rome had suffered another pillage barely less terrible than the first, a peace had at last been negotiated between the captive Pope and the Emperor (26 November). The principal clauses related as usual to the payment of money and the cession of hostages and securities. Excepting for a promise to convoke a General Council to deal with the Lutheran heresy—important to Charles in his capacity of Emperor— the Pope seemed to be treated merely as a vanquished civil enemy. However, before the day fixed for his release the Pope fled from his gaolers and sought refuge in Orvieto (6 December).

When, early in the following year, war was resumed between the league and the Emperor, the Pope maintained himself in neutrality, intermittently benevolent on the side of France. To declare himself formally a member of the league was too much. On the one hand he still had good reason to fear the resentment of the Emperor, who was in addition commencing to make overtures for an understanding. On the other, he recognized among the members of the league some of his own most determined enemies. During the tribulations which had beset him, Venice, in spite of her alliance, had occupied Ravenna and Cervia. With as little pretext, though with less ingratitude, the Duke of Ferrara had seized upon Modena and Reggio. Both were now members of the resuscitated league, Ferrara having made a dexterous change of front, and neither showed any disposition to renounce an inch of their recent gains for the general good. It could not, therefore, be expected that Clement should join himself with his plunderers excepting after restitution. Nor, indeed, was it easy for him to bend to ally himself with the revolted city of which he considered himself the lord.[1]

The news of the escape of the Pope changed the face of affairs at Florence. The devil was for them indeed let loose. It could never be expected that Clement would tamely acquiesce in the loss of the city. Not only was his personal pride touched by the secession. He resented the blow all the more because of the time when it had been struck. When he was impotent and his life was in peril ; at the hour of his very greatest tribulation, when the whole of Christendom was shocked by his treatment—this was the moment which had been chosen by the Florentines to add to his cup of bitterness so that it overflowed. A fierce resentment was added to his natural desire to come into his own. In addition he felt the need now more than ever for the golden eggs which had always been forthcoming from his native city. Until he could again dispose of the Florentine wealth, his power was crippled.

At the same time circumstances forced him to be amenable to conciliation. There can be no doubt that had he an army at his disposal it would have been used in chastising and reducing the rebellious city. Luckily he had none. There were therefore two courses open to him. One was to find himself allies who would help him in this task. For the league of Cognac to do it was unimaginable. Florence was the traditional ally of France, which was at the head of the league ; and was itself a member of it. The peril would come if ever there were a *rapprochement* between Pope and Emperor. Restrained by no alliances and by no memories the Imperial forces might show themselves very ready to assist in the subjection of a city from which such plunder was to be expected. But the idea of such a *rapprochement* was very remote after the treatment which the Pope had undergone. It seemed more profitable for him to acquiesce, for the moment at least, in the revolution which had taken place. By it, the Medici had lost more than political influence ; for they had left behind them in the city the best part of their property, which they were now unable to enjoy. Though it was not formally confiscated, arrears of duties and taxation which had not been paid gave the treasury a strong hold over it.[2] The mother of Alessandro had to write imploring him to save her family from starvation.[3] His kinswoman, Lucrezia Salviati, from whom he himself had been wont to borrow,[4] was now staying at Venice in actual want.[5] The distant prospects of lordship were counterbalanced by the more immediate possibility of re-entering into the administration of their legitimate property, which was the least to be expected from an agreement. The family might even hope to be allowed to return to Florence as private citizens, and to enjoy their immense possessions in the city in person and undisturbed. Thus they might expect to exercise again the influence natural to a family of such wealth and such connections, and in the end to climb again insensibly into the position from which they had been ousted.

For Clement himself, there was one advantage especially which might be immediately derived from an agreement. He could not perhaps hope for a restitution of his temporal revenues ; but the ecclesiastical revenues alone from one of the foremost Italian states were not to be despised. By peace, he could secure the uninterrupted enjoyment of these at least. The republican government in Florence had brought this home to him by more than one practical example. A short time before the revolution Clement had authorized the sale, for his own benefit, of one-tenth of the property of all the pious and ecclesiastical foundations of the city. Almost immediately after it, the Great Council, by an overwhelming majority, had passed an audacious measure whereby the sale was ordered to be proceeded with for the benefit of the Republic by virtue of the old papal licence.[6] Thus the measure which he had authorized for his own benefit was carried out for use against him. Similarly in October, a forced loan upon the ecclesiastical foundations of the city had been proposed. The Pope, hoping by graciously yielding to circumstances to keep it within small bounds as well as perhaps to ingratiate himself with the city, had sent an envoy to authorize one of 20,000 ducats.[7] This, however, was not sufficient for requirements ; and so, without waiting for further negotiations, it was summarily levied even upon the establishments usually exempted (excepting nunneries alone), to the amount of 100,000 florins to be paid within the year. Resistance was dealt with by an authorization to seize and sell goods to the required sum ; religious scruples, by the power to enforce purchase and, on the other hand, by special exemptions from taxation. Exile and confiscation, as though for treason, were decreed against any who protested that the sacrilegious provision was invalid ; and the high officers of the Republic were ordered to swear obedience to it.[8] It is small wonder that Clement showed especial displeasure at such news [9] ; yet at the same time these episodes brought home to him the fact that the minor profits which he drew from the city were worth while taking into account. He could hope from peace at least the enjoyment of the ecclesiastical prerogatives now usurped by the city. This was only one of the advantages which could be expected. He had to consider the position of the few of his kindred left in Florence, of whose property the Signoria had appointed Ottaviano de' Medici trustee.[10] Nearest of these was the young Caterina, daughter of Lorenzo, Duke of Urbino, and half-sister of Alessandro. The " Duchessina," as she was called, was, with Lucrezia Salviati, the only legitimate representative of the line of Cosimo [11] ; and she was thus regarded as a great prize which nothing could tear from the hands of the Florentines. The poor child, only eight years old, was kept almost as a hostage in the nunnery of Sta. Lucia near the Piazza S. Marco ; until removed through the intervention of the French envoy, to avoid the Pest, to the Convent of the Murate in the Via Ghibellina.[12] Yet if there she learnt any bitterness of spirit, it was the Huguenots of France who forty years later felt its effects. These considerations forced the Pope to modify his attitude. He protested to foreign powers, with whatever mental reservations, that he was willing for Florence to remain as she was. Only he insisted that he should be recognized as Pope if not as citizen ; and that his supporters and kinsmen should escape from the persecutions to which they were subjected.[13]

On the side of the city, similar considerations came into play. It was impossible to neglect the fact that, however impoverished, Clement was yet Pope. His enmity would tell fatally against the city in the eyes of every European power. Antagonism to him was directed against the supreme head of the Catholic Church ; and this could not but be unwelcome to the body of the faithful within the city, however staunch upholders of liberty. As his material position gradually improved, there began to be opportunities of making good some, at least, of the losses which the Florentines had experienced in the sack of Rome, and of re-opening commercial relations with the papal states. Above all it was to be dreaded that in case of a factious opposition towards Clement and of a refusal of all minor concessions, he would be driven to seek alliances and to reinstate his family as in 1512 by sheer force of arms. To refuse to admit them as private citizens might lead to a violent restoration of their autocracy. But in order to bring about an understanding with the Pope it was necessary to make some alteration in the treatment of the Palleschi within the city. It was impossible to expect any concord with the head of the Medici while his supporters were being kept depressed, if not actually persecuted. There was, too, another reason why they should be admitted to a larger share in the public councils. However unpopular their views, they represented the noblest and wealthiest and most influential class among the citizens, and they could not therefore be neglected. In addition, they had monopolized office for the past fifteen years, and thus they were the only class with any knowledge or practice in the conduct of public affairs. They counted among their numbers the majority of those who had adminis-trative and diplomatic experience ; and it was absurd to neglect the views of precisely that class most qualified to give an opinion. Side by side, therefore, with the movement for external understanding, there was another for an internal accommodation.

This was the line of thought which Niccolò Capponi had begun to follow at the time of the Pope's liberation.   In it he was supported naturally by the Palleschi themselves and by the Ottimati, together with a large number of the Piagnoni.   The Arrabbiati, on the other hand, were intransigeantly opposed to any sort of understanding with the Pope.   They feared, and with reason, that if the Medici obtained the least hold in the city they would end by becoming its masters.   They remembered that Cosimo de' Medici had returned to Florence as a private citizen in 1434, and that his descendants had been pledged to similar moderation in 1512 ; and they feared that any similar concession would lead to a similar conclusion.   They refused to trust the Palleschi with any share in the government lest they should betray the city to the Pope.   They watched the actions of the Gonfalonier with suspicious apprehension ; and he was forced on more than one occasion to yield to their violence or to acquiesce in their headstrong action.

The growing ill-feeling was increased by reports, probably exaggerated, of the careless and boastful conversation of prominent Palleschi.   Thus Chiarissimo de' Medici was ordered to be arrested at Pisa for " having dared to say to several persons how within a short time he would return to that place more master than ever and such that he would be able to chastise his enemies and those who had done him harm."[14]   His son Jacopo, who had held minor office under the previous administration,[15] was similarly detained[16] ; and it was some little time before either was set free.[17]   Francesco Guicciardini also was repeatedly cited to appear and justify his conduct.[18]

The violence of the extremists came to a head in November 1527, in an attack upon the late rulers of the city themselves, strangely neglected by all the historians of the period.   By the terms of the agreement made with them on their relinquishing the government, and confirmed at the surrender of Pisa, it had been agreed that neither they nor their adherents should be specially taxed or proceeded against for any action committed during their period of rule.   This, however, had been cleverly evaded by levying charges on their property on the pretext of their having been debtors to the city already at the time when they assumed the government.[19]   Nor did the matter rest with this.   On 4 November, Ippolito and Alessandro together with the Cardinal of Cortona were formally denounced to the Otto. This body was actuated by extreme views and cited them to appear within three days.[20]   Some little delay was caused by a mistake in the Christian name of the Cardinal's brother, upon whom his writ, presented at his palace at Cortona, was served.[21] The summons on the Medici remained unanswered and was repeated on the 19th [22]; and apparently they deputed Chiarissimo de' Medici their kinsman to appear on their behalf. Meanwhile, however, a general commotion had been caused ; and not only in the city. It was at the time of the Pope's captivity ; but four Cardinals took it upon themselves to address to the Signoria a letter of remonstrance on behalf of their fellow Prince of the Church.[23] Their appeal was not without effect upon the more moderate elements in the government. Not only the Signoria, closely under the influence of Capponi, but also the Dieci, usually more extreme, joined in an appeal to their colleagues of the Otto to show prudence. Finally, though apparently somewhat unwillingly, the latter body allowed itself to be persuaded by the sacred rights of treaty, the intercession of its colleagues, and especially " since the times do not require to raise up the enmity of the accused. . . ." On 25 November they were formally absolved [24]—it is probable not wholly by coincidence upon the eve of the treaty which arranged for the Pope's liberation. The Signoria had lost no time in conveying the news to the reverend intercessors. The devotion of the city towards the Apostolic See and the College of Cardinals was affirmed ; but it was added in dignified language that in a republic, unlike a principality, all are subject to the laws and that the magistrates had no alternative before them but to cite the Cardinal. Nevertheless, upon the main point they yielded. The accusation had been silenced ; not (of course !) out of favour, but out of regard for justice. The result was, however, the same ; and it was in a way an olive-branch proffered to the Pope.[25]

This mitigatory policy of Capponi aroused the fierce antagonism of the party of the Arrabbiati. Already there had been suspicions of the purity of his republicanism ; now he began to be suspected of an actual desire to restore Medicean rule. Every circumstance went to feed the flames : his birth, his record, and his connections ; his Imperialist preferences in foreign affairs ; the personal influence he had acquired among the citizens during the plague ; his close councils with the ancient servants of the Medici, whose ripe experience it was preferred to forget.[26] Even the theatrical appointment of Christ as King of Florence came to be regarded as a preliminary to submitting the city to the government of the Pope, as Viceroy of Christ upon earth.[27] In proportion with the suspicion, the violence of the opposing party increased. Baldassare Carducci, seen one day coming into the Piazza with a short sword under his cloak, received the nickname of Ser Scimitarra ; and the title accorded well with the violence of his followers.[28] Capponi's task of reconciliation became more and more difficult with the growing bitterness of the most vociferous and active, if not the most numerous, party within the city.

These political differences had become exacerbated by family rivalries. Niccolò Capponi and Tommaso Soderini had become rivals, not for the hand of the same lady, but, less romantically, for the hand of the same man for their respective daughters ; though the prospective bridegroom preferred in the event to remain unmarried. The ill-blood thus engendered might have been removed by a marriage between Capponi's eldest son and Soderini's daughter ; but the Gonfalonier preferred a family alliance with Francesco Guicciardini. Thus the ill-feeling was embittered ; and Soderini was driven to cement his political amity with Alfonso Strozzi by a family union.[29]

Capponi's choice was, however, tactless. Though as a matter of fact the marriage between his son and Guicciardini's daughter did not take place till after the Gonfalonier's death, the conversations on the subject were already commenced and generally known.[30] It is not to be wondered at that they were regarded with suspicion. Guicciardini was more, perhaps, than any other of those who had served under their regime, a creature of the Medici ; and his part in suppressing the Tumulto del Venerdì had given concrete expression to his sympathy, if also to his humanity. He had indeed accepted the revolution and paid lip-service to its principles ; but he had continued his correspondence with Clement and his protestations of fidelity, even though this was in his capacity as Pope, and not as lord of Florence.[31] On his retirement from being Commissary-General of the Florentine contingent with the forces of the league, he fell peculiarly under popular suspicion. Though he could clear himself of any specific charges, he was not able to evade the heavy taxation which fell upon the late Medicean partisans with especial weight.[32] A few months later he was drawn as one of the two Provedittori of the Hospital of S. Bonifazio, but was charged with peculation. The petty nature of the accusation and the personality of the accuser—the demagogue, Alfonso Strozzi—indicate the political venom which inspired the attack.[33] Nor could the great abilities and experience of Guicciardini even secure his election as an Advocate of the Arte della Calimala.[34] This was the man, or rather, this was the popular impression of the man, with whom Capponi chose to ally himself. The especial importance which he attached to his counsels, with those of Roberto Acciaiuoli, Francesco Vettori, and Filippo Strozzi on his infrequent visits to the city,[35] enhanced the suspicions of partisans to whom politics had become a question of personalities and to whom no breadth of experience or height of intellect could excuse the past record of a servant of the Medici. That such relations were natural between two old acquaintances and familiar correspondents was overlooked[36] ; it was only noted that they would secure the Gonfalonier the support of the four hundred Palleschi. In January, Capponi made in the Consiglio Grande a public appeal for a cessation of these civic bitternesses and persecutions. If the moderate applauded his sentiments, the extremists only found in them confirmation of their suspicions.[37]

A result of these apprehensions was that they began to have some foundation in fact. It was the meaner of the citizens who formed the majority of the party of the Arrabbiati and whose suspicions, after frequently forcing the hand of the government, now began to be directed against the government itself. It was they who prevented every attempt to introduce any sort of peace into the internal or external affairs of the city. An endeavour had been made to placate them by concessions ; but with them the clamour had only grown greater and had begun to imperil any chances of accord that might previously have existed. It was amongst the more aristocratic and wealthy of the citizens, the Ottimati and the Piagnoni, that the desire for peace was to be found : and it was through them only that the desire could be brought to fruition. Capponi came therefore to take up gradually, for practical reasons, if not for theoretical, a position of antagonism to the democracy ; for it was not until the upper classes had the predominant voice that he could hope for his policy to triumph. His birth and connections urged him in the same direction ; and in this he was at one with the large section who had desired to replace the absolutism of the Medici by an aristocracy. This was indeed probably at this time the desire of the majority of the upper classes, including even the Palleschi ; for with the total debacle of the Pope and of his house even he barely hoped for a return of his supremacy.[38] Guicciardini himself, in his *Dialogo sul Reggimento di Firenze*, had put in the mouth of Bernardo del Nero (Savonarola's victim) his ideal of a free government in which the wiser and better citizens should have the most authority.[39] It was a similar position, as a stage towards his ideal of peace, that the opposition of the Arrabbiati drove Capponi to adopt.

For such a programme, Italy was not lacking in examples nor the city of Machiavelli in exponents. Francesco Zeffi, tutor to the children of Filippo Strozzi,[40] possibly acting as the mouthpiece of his employer and expressing the views of the Ottimati as a whole, recommended the adoption of the Venetian model—always the admiration of Florentine theorists—especially in the matter of the Great Council.[41] This does not seem to have been an isolated case. Capponi himself turned, in particular, to a theorist of greater note. Donato Giannotti, who had recently succeeded to the post of Machiavelli as Secretary to the Dieci upon the death in the pest of the intervening incumbent, was

considered heir in some measure to the spirit as well as to the
office of his greater predecessor. He combined with the greatest
erudition and experience a patriotism and love of liberty which
even his enemies could not impeach ; though they regarded
him as too ambitious and too obsequious to wealth and birth.[42]
In the year before the revolution he had composed a dialogue
upon the Venetian Republic, in connection with which he became known as an admirer and an expert.[43] Now, at the
Gonfalonier's express invitation, he wrote a discourse upon
the settlement of the constitution.[44] His ideas were fettered
by Aristotelian theories and current doctrines of a system
of carefully regulated balances which should satisfy and check
all political ambitions. The basis of his reforms was therefore a mixed constitution in which democracy, aristocracy,
and monarchy should all have a share. The constitution and
powers of the Gonfalonierate were to remain virtually unchanged ; but in order to satisfy the ambitions of those foremost
citizens who might have hoped for election to the office, he recommended the replacement of the Signoria by twelve *Procuratori*
appointed for life who were to be nearly equal to the Chief of the
State in dignity and influence. As a body, these were to have
the initiative in legislation and taxation ; and they were in
addition to be represented in all the more important business
of government. The Ottanta was to be replaced by a senate of
one hundred, which was to approve of measures initiated by the
Procuratori, and to have the power of decision also in foreign and
military affairs. This was thus to be taken away from the
cognisance of the Dieci—a most oligarchic body according to
Giannotti, endowed with an importance out of proportion to its
size and over-amenable to the influence of a single individual.
They were therefore to be left with only the functions of initiation
and execution. The ultimate sovereignty was to rest with the
Consiglio Grande. This was to have control of the election of all
the civic officers, by a simple vote instead of the complicated
system in vogue of vote and ballot. It was also to have the final
decision upon new laws, with the exception of financial measures,
which were to receive their final sanction from the senate. In
addition, a new court of final appeal from the sentence of any
tribunal was to be set up on the confessed model of the Venetian
Quarantia. Antiquated magistracies would either have been
adapted to new needs, or, like the Captains of the Parte Guelfa,
wholly swept away. Together with this there were to be some
striking practical reforms of considerable moment which seem
almost out of place among such academic speculations. The
constitution of Florence, still based upon its ancient mediæval
system, gave an exaggerated place to the members of the seven

greater gilds, engaged in the most important occupations. To these, three places in every magistracy were assigned to every one given to the fourteen lesser gilds occupied in the more petty operations of trade. This distinction Giannotti would have abolished, throwing all offices open equally to all. Again he would have done away with the arbitrary distinction between citizens with and without the " benefice " of having had an immediate ancestor serving upon one of the higher magistracies—the essential condition for membership of the Consiglio Grande. These measures would have been a great step towards a real democracy ; yet it seems that for the great mass of the people, excluded even from the minor gilds, Giannotti had no sympathy or consideration.

Such were the essential parts of the system, compounded of Monarchy, Aristocracy, and Democracy, the adoption of which was recommended as a cure for the ills from which Florence was suffering ; and we have the word of the author that the Gonfalonier would have adopted it had he found the opportunity.[45] That he was in complete agreement with a system which would have circumscribed his own powers one may well doubt. Yet this proposed *rifacimento* of the constitution, giving an increased stability and influence to the aristocratic element, is certainly typical of the ideas to which the violence of the Arrabbiati was driving him, together with other Piagnoni, to incline. The practised eye of the Venetian envoy remarked upon the opposition of the better class of citizen to the frenzied violence of the extremists, and as a consequence even to the Consiglio Grande itself ; and he gave it as his considered opinion that a few months would see an understanding with the Pope and a revolution in favour of an aristocracy.[46] The events of the succeeding period strengthened this possibility.

This was the state of affairs when the Pope actually regained his liberty (7 December 1527). In his helpless condition, he could not even think of revenge or reinstatement, and the friendship of the city with its immediate advantages became of more importance to him than any distant prospects of lordship. The English envoy was urging Florence to open negotiations, and not without hope of success.[47] With the strong support of the Gonfalonier and through the mediation of Vincenzio Duranti, later Bishop of Orvieto and major-domo of the Cardinal Ridolfi, through whom the Gonfalonier was in communication with the Pope, an envoy was sent almost immediately to treat for reconciliation. Admitted to the audience of the Signoria, he disclosed his mission. He complained of the conduct of the Florentine troops in the States of the Church, and of the hostile behaviour of their Commissary, especially in the matter of hostages. He attempted to show how the Pope had drawn all his sufferings

upon himself in order to save the city, quoting almost blas-
phemously the passage " He bare our wounds, and with His
stripes we are healed." He reproved them gently for their
precipitancy in exacting from the clergy the subsidy which he
was willing to grant ; and he appealed for an understanding.
The Signoria made their excuses ; the Gonfalonier privately
promised to do his best to procure the sending of representatives to the Pope. He assured him that if he manifested a
genuine desire for amity and was willing to leave the matter
in the hands of the Ottimati, all would be well. Everything
seemed to promise well for an accord ; and the envoy went
away quite contented.[48]

But Capponi had misunderstood the temper of the people.
The news of the Pope's approaching liberation and then of his
escape had been received in Florence with apprehension, and the
whole city dreaded the possibility of a renewed subjection.[49]
These suspicions were confirmed by the untimely conduct, and
perhaps by the tactless words, of the Pope, who had naturally
seized this first opportunity to send agents to report upon the
state of the city and its disposition towards him. One of these
was immediately escorted outside the Florentine territory ; and
the others effected no result other than adding to the fears already
rife.[50] Reports were current that the Pope was persisting in his
hostile intentions against Florence, and purposed to make a
sinister departure from the methods of his predecessors by
executing his opponents ; or that he proposed to sack the city,
using the money to recover Cervia and Ravenna.[51] Rumours of
a colloquy of the Pope with a Florentine at Viterbo, and of an
approaching agreement with the Emperor, caused especially widespread alarm.[52] An intercepted letter from the Florentine envoy
in Spain, who had been appointed under the old regime, showed
that he still considered it his duty to send reports to the Pope as
well as to his actual employers.[53] It was certain that he was
continually voicing his complaints to foreign Powers, particularly
France and England.[54] The new Dieci of 10 December comprised
some of the most violent anti-Capponists, including members of
the immediate families of both Soderini and Carducci. As a
result, the promising schemes of the Gonfalonier utterly failed,
and the hopes of peace were completely cut off. The Dieci, at
whose sittings he could not intervene, decided not to send Orators
to the Pope until he made the first advances, and certainly not
until he joined the league.[55] A dangerous reaction even set in.
The border fortresses were put in a state of preparation.[56]
The part of Duranti in the negotiations led naturally to suspicions of his master, the Cardinal Ridolfi. He was among
those influenced by Filippo Strozzi to whom the city owed the

tranquil recovery of its liberty. But he was a Prince of the
Church and a cousin of the Pope. By the fact, he stood condemned to minds made suspicious by fear ; and he was summarily escorted outside Florentine territory.[57] When Messer
Antonio Pucci desired passage through the city on his way to
France and England as Papal Legate, he was sternly excluded
on the grounds that it was through a Pucci, Messer Lorenzo, that
the Republic had fallen in 1512.[58]

The Gonfalonier's advocacy of the Pope's cause greatly
enhanced the distrust which had commenced to grow up against
himself. While it was impossible to aim at him directly, advantage could be taken of the rumours and suspicions of treason which
had become more and more rife about the city. The Pope was
reported to be concentrating forces towards the Florentine
border [59] ; and Capponi's political opponents diligently fomented
the fear that a counter-revolution was about to be attempted in
favour of the Medici by the old method of a Florentine *coup
d'état*—the armed seizure of the Palazzo della Signoria. The
youths who had led in all the more violent episodes of the revolution began to become clamorous that one hundred of them should
be allowed to form themselves into a regular guard to protect
the building. Some of the more responsible statesmen tried to
dissuade them ; but the request was taken up by the opposition
party in the Signoria and forced through. Capponi was only able
to procure that the number should be three hundred, amongst
whom he could hope to have more of his own faction. The
guard was instituted—twelve for the Palace, and fifty for the
Piazza, with a detachment patrolling through the streets. It
served day and night, voluntarily and gratuitously, under the
command of one of the Buonuomini, and in reliefs changing every
three days.[60] Thus the Palace was certainly safe against surprise ; but it was not against those without that the precaution
was directed so much as against those within. If Capponi's
opponents should attempt a *coup* themselves, they would find
an armed force in which their supporters predominated continually on guard within the Palace, while the object of their attack
would be left defenceless.[61] It was a fact, too, that the assault
was seriously proposed and discussed in the house of Dante da
Castiglione, and that the Signoria had been solemnly warned to
be on their guard.[62] Capponi found himself almost a prisoner
in the building which was supposed to be the seat of his administration.

The increasing turbulence of those emboldened by this
success made more and more difficult his self-imposed task of
conciliation. The most pointless and wanton manifestations of
this were directed against the symbols of the Medici which were

still to be found in the city. It was the custom in Florence to display hung up against the walls of the Church of the Annunziata images in wax of prominent citizens and others clad in rich costumes.[63] One morning a band of riotous youths, led as usual by Dante da Castiglione and Piero Salviati, entered masked into the church. Regardless of the sanctity of the spot, they began to strike at the representations of the two Medicean Popes, Clement and Leo, as well as at those of Lorenzo the Magnificent and all the other prominent members of the house, until they came crashing to the floor, when the fragments were dragged away with ignominy.[64] It was a fashion which had been set at the downfall of Piero Soderini ; and the example now renewed was promptly followed. A little later, a similar fate befell a statue of Clement's in another church, though the presence of an artist among the perpetrators might have explained an ardour perhaps as much professional as revolutionary. The Otto di Guardia, instead of punishing the culprits, showed their approval by consenting to issue instructions for the obliteration of all the representations of the Medicean arms by which any place under Florentine rule had been adorned since the Restoration of 1512. The turbulent zeal of the youth of the city saw to it that the order was thoroughly carried out, whether in private buildings or in public, within the city or without. Even in churches which owed so much to the munificence of the house as S. Lorenzo or S. Marco, the instructions were ruthlessly executed, and all signs of their benefactors were removed.[65] Demands were even made, and more than once, to erase the well-known epitaph of Cosimo " Pater Patriæ " on the grounds that " he was no father of his country, but tyrant of his country," and that the inscription was " to the dishonour of this liberty." [66] The epitaphs in the Duomo of Marsilio Ficino, the greatest of Florentine humanists, and of Antonio Squarcialupi the organist, were similarly denounced and were ordered to be deleted of phrasing too complimentary to the former ruling family.[67] Another suggestion even more militant was said to emanate from the great Michelangelo himself. It was proposed to follow the example of past history in Florence and of contemporary events in Bologna by razing to the ground the palace of the Medici, and to create on its site a " Piazza de' Muli " in indelicate allusion to the Pope's birth.[68] The building escaped this fate ; but it was nevertheless appropriated for the use of the Trustees of Minors, whose work had become increased as a result of the plague.[69] The wish was father to the thought in the insistent rumours of the Pope's death which were continually afloat.[70]

Meanwhile the financial requirements of the city led to the passing of a series of measures which, if not actually aimed at the Palleschi, certainly affected them most. Forced loans and balzelli had followed one another in rapid succession since the revolution,[71] and sharp measures were now taken to secure the payment of arrears by investing the officials over such matters with extraordinary authority to enforce payment.[72] A further commission was appointed to raise a fresh accatto of 70,000– 72,000 florins ; and the religious bent of the Republic appeared in the important share assigned to friars in the assessment.[73] A further provision, more patently and exclusively aimed against the Palleschi, submitted to review all accounts as far back as the expulsion of the Medici in 1494, ordering payment as before to the " Tribolanti." Even stern republicans admitted that this was in flat contravention of the agreement of the previous year.[74] Most symptomatic, though of minor import- ance, was the revocation of the sale of the Lake of Fucecchio to the widow of Piero de' Medici on the ground that payment had not been made.[75]

These enactments, however, reflected only mildly the state of the mind of the people. Suspicions against the Palleschi were growing every day. If an impartial observer was to be believed, they had full grounds. The people (by which he meant the aristocrats) of Florence were commencing to murmur that they were at war, and that when they were under the Medici they were in peace without paying this oppressive taxation ; and had there been any representative of that house in the city, there would have been danger of revolt.[76] The reported move- ments of Ippolito de' Medici about the Florentine border caused increasing alarm, and the city was full of rumours and accusations about the traffic and communications of indi- viduals in the city with the Pope and his kinsmen.[77] A veritable reign of terror had commenced for the Medicean partisans, whose opponents seemed now to be officially recognized and encouraged. They were publicly insulted and threatened in the streets ; they barely dared to show their faces out of doors, much less to visit churches or to attend meetings of the Council. Even murders were known to take place.[78] " He is a Pallesco " became a stereotyped yet dangerous accusation, to be bandied about irresponsibly.[79] Roberto Acciaiuoli scarcely ventured to show himself at his windows from fear of a neighbour. Ottaviano de' Medici, openly threatened by the hot-headed young Jacopo Alamanni, did not scruple to complain to the Signoria ; but his complaints did not save him from an attempt at assassination which was nearly successful, and he was removed from a minor office which he held.[80] A victim even more distinguished was Filippo Strozzi, who had lived in shamefaced retirement since his suspicious failure at Pisa. His continued intimacy with the Gonfalonier had heightened the feeling against both, and it was even reported that Capponi had secured the burning of a book of public accounts by which his brother-in-law would have stood condemned.[81]   Not long after, Filippo left the city, ostensibly to look to his private affairs at Lyons ; for the most aristocratic and wealthy of the Florentines were still not ashamed to continue their business operations.   The Arrabbiati could insinuate that his real desire was to regain the favour of the Pope.   It was notorious, however, that the same Alamanni, passing one day his country seat at the Orti Rucellai, had signified without any mincing of words the popular feeling : " Can you not see that we do not want you here ? " [82]   It was not a question only of popular violence.   The virtual revolutionary tribunal in this outburst of vindictiveness was the newly established Quarantia, which had hitherto remained comparatively quiescent.   After the liberation of the Pope it became increasingly active and severe.   Michael de' Modesti, son of Jacopo, chancellor of the *riformagioni* under Medicean rule, was examined under torture for blasphemy and " words against the present pacific state."   His punishment was to have his tongue publicly pierced and to be imprisoned for four years.[83]   Carolo de' Medici, not an immediate kinsman of the late ruling house, was charged with " words spoken against the present popular pacific state," to which were added the more tangible accusations of bigamy and usury ; but it being impossible to substantiate them he was acquitted.   A similar accusation of treasonable talk was brought against Girolamo degli Albizzi, and on his failing to appear to answer the charge he was condemned in his absence.[84]   Francesco del Nero, late Treasurer, was condemned to a payment of nearly 3,000 ducats to the Commune, though this sum was reduced on appeal [85] ; yet even afterwards he was not free from prosecution.[86]   The ordinary tribunals were kept busy going into denunciations which had been sent to them.   The Castellan of Volterra was accused of not keeping sufficiently strictly in his dungeons the prisoners of state, Bendetto Buondelmonti and Giuliano de' Medici, entrusted to his care, and was ordered to see that they were more closely confined.[87]   The Rector of the church of S. Giovanni in Soana was condemned for having kept the Medicean coat of arms above the high altar of his church.[88]   Bivigliano de' Medici, once a friar, but who had now " denied Christ," had taken the order of the Otto somewhat sarcastically and displayed the golden balls together with the cross of the people and the lily of Florence upon his house in the Via del Cocomero ; and he was denounced for it.[89]

But above all the air was full of alarms and excursions about negotiations of individuals with the Pope and the return of the

Medici. The same Bivigliano was accused of most treasonable talk, that " these *arrabbiati* wish to draw the arquebus so much that they will break it " ; and he swore by the body of Christ that they " would see more vengeance than they willed if God gave grace to the Pope to live for some months." [90]   A woman of the town was the authority for saying that one of her clients made her long promises on the score of a letter which he was bearing to the Pope, in which Filippo Strozzi, Francesco Vettori, and Roberto Acciauioli were implicated.[91]   Others, including a friar of Sta. Croce, were charged with sending letters with information to the Pope at Viterbo.[92]   A native of Pistoia was exiled for continual journeys between the Pope at Viterbo and his nephews at Parma.[93]

This was the heated atmosphere in which Capponi was striving to bring about peace for the city within and security from without. For himself, there can be little doubt that he would still have preferred alliance with the triumphant Emperor as the surest of all safeguards.   He had seen the French in peace and war ; yet (perhaps as a result) had been consistently in favour of the Imperialists in his public life.   Repeated experiment, however, had shown that the traditional inclination of Florence towards France was not to be overcome by his influence.   The body of citizens still vigorously upheld the traditional alliance ; and at their head, Tommaso Soderini effectively championed the policy by which his uncle had fallen.   He had secured the appointment of his own brother, Giuliano, Bishop of Santes, as ambassador in France ; he had prevented one of the family of the Gonfalonier from taking up similar office in Spain though elected to it ; and another brother, Giovanbattista, in exile at Vicenza till the Revolution, was later made Commissary in the army of the league.[94]   At one point indeed it had seemed that his success would be broken.   Through Filippo Strozzi, the Imperialists made overtures for an alliance, professing that they would be contented even with neutrality.   Battista della Palla was even appointed to carry on the negotiations on the part of the city. At a final consultation, however, Soderini's measured appeal to honour and to sentiment had its usual effect and instructions were sent for the league to be confirmed.[95]   Capponi loyally accepted this clear expression of the will of his fellow-citizens, so often reiterated, and instead of continuing to attempt to sway their opinions, he tried to avert the perils to which in his opinion their policy was exposing the city.   The position of the Pope had to be considered dispassionately.   Florence had recovered her liberty and was oppressing his friends.   Venice at the commencement of his captivity had seized on Cervia and Ravenna, while the Duke of Ferrara had occupied Modena.   Of course, this had only been, as they professed, to save them for the States of the Church from the hands of the Imperialists ; yet now, after the Pope's liberation, they did not seem disposed to give up their spoil. Venice and Ferrara, like Florence, were members of the league of Cognac. The French king naturally could not be expected to put serious pressure upon his allies to disgorge. If they remained obdurate, therefore, only one way was left, for Clement to recover his own. This was, by agreement with Charles V, who was coming to consider his aid essential to combat the Lutheran heresy in Germany and the Royal Divorce in England. This was the step which Capponi dreaded. He saw clearly that the alliance between the Pope's hostile intentions and the Emperor's over-whelming forces would spell disaster to Florence ; and he felt that the arms of the league would not suffice to save her, even if they were employed on her behalf. At all costs, Clement must be placated, and spontaneously. To this, Capponi devoted all of his powers. On the one hand, he was attempting to mollify the Pope's opposition by a more liberal policy to his adherents and by trying to conclude an agreement which should secure his ecclesiastical and family revenues within the city. On the other, he was attempting to strengthen the bonds which still connected the Pope with the league. It was his aim to accommodate the territorial dispute with the Duke of Ferrara and thereby to induce Venice, thus isolated, to give up her spoil either by per-suasion or by force. Thus Clement would have little to gain by joining the Imperialists, and Florence would be saved. At the same time, Capponi was pointing out to the Pope that in the event of the victory of Charles he would be left in a state of utter subjection to the Empire ; and that his interest clearly lay in throwing his weight upon the side of the French and preserving the balance of power. Otherwise, all would end ill, and Florence worst of all.[96]

There was another aspect of the affair. The extraordinary expenses of the last years had taxed the financial resources of the city to the utmost, and she still had to supply 30,000 ducats monthly for the support of her troops with the armies of the league. Other extraordinary expenses were thrown on her to provide for the dangerous shortage of corn and the 4,000 inhabitants out of employment, together with other matters occasioned by the war and the pest.[97] The clergy of the city had disbursed with the rest —first through the audacious employment of the Pope's own licence, then by contribution to the forced loan in October ; and it was already intended to raise another.[98] The lot of the Convent of S. Maria del Carmine was no doubt typical. " I record how from November (1527) the commune of Florence laid upon us an accatto of which 300 ducats fell to us to pay in four instalments

. . . whence we friars . . . drew ourselves together not having money and the convent being half undone by the soldiers, and the Arno having taken from us more than one-third our income of grain and having had Pest in the convent, wherefore it was in very great disorder ; " and in order to pay they were forced to raise an internal loan.[99]   Clement had ample cause for protest ; and he launched at Florence the threat of excommunication. Capponi was able to overcome the prejudices of his colleagues of the Signoria, and a humble letter was addressed to him interceding for pardon.   There was of course no officially accredited Florentine agent about the papal court ; but representations were made to certain churchmen of the Curia asking for their support. In particular use was made as intermediary of the Dominican Tommaso da Caiano, in whom it was hoped that a sentiment of patriotism would support the spirit of religion.[100]   This was a preliminary triumph for the Pope ; and he was so far mollified as to suspend the bull of excommunication.   The Signoria replied in the most cordial terms, expressing its warmest gratitude, and begging him to alter the suspension into a withdrawal.[101]

This relief however, grateful though it was, did not solve the difficulty.   Extraordinary taxation to the amount of 40,000 ducats was not enough.   It was necessary to explore every channel for raising funds.   How could the vast wealth of the clergy be suffered to remain untapped ?   Yet to touch it would be to stir up again the wrath of the Pope, to alienate him yet further, to secure infallibly the launching of the suspended bull of excommunication.   It was a responsibility which Capponi could not bring himself to assume.   In vain it was pointed out to him that even the excommunicated could eat and drink.[102]   It was not the spiritual consequences only that he feared, but also the temporal—that the challenge would drive the Pope into the arms of the Imperialists.   Only by concord could the city secure its safety.   Once again the Pope was approached for a licence to raise from the clergy a levy of four or five " tenths." [103] The Pope in response sent a bull conceding only two tenths, but under conditions.   He insisted that arrears of clerical taxation should be remitted, that the Medicean arms should be restored where they had been destroyed ; and that the exiles should be allowed to come freely to the city and enjoy their property undisturbed.   The terms were not such as the Florentines were likely to accept.   The envoy bearing the bull was not so much as allowed to enter the city, and the collection of arrears went on undisturbed, with the threat of imposing a fresh tax.[104]   Capponi had to set to work through different channels.

The natural intermediaries to use in these transactions were the Florentines about the papal court, and especially Jacopo

Salviati.   He was recommended to the city in the first place as
having been originally a hot supporter of freedom, and as such
had been driven to seek refuge at Rome during the rule of
Lorenzino.   But he had married Lucrezia de' Medici, " the lady
of most worth and dignity who might be met," a sister of Leo X.
Thus attached to the ruling house, he had entered the service of
Clement, to whom he was now confidential secretary.   It was
well known that he was almost omnipotent at the papal court,
and through his means Capponi hoped to bring about the understanding he required.   Since direct correspondence contained
some element of danger, a go-between was found in the person
of Giachinotto Serragli, a minor satellite at the papal court, also
a Florentine.   It was their function to attempt to rouse in Clement
that spirit of patriotism which should save their common city.
Capponi's letters to them breathed an elevated but impatient
love for Florence which he attempted in vain to instil into the
cold politicians of the Curia.   "Are you all ill disposed," he
wrote, " or are you asleep ? . . . For the love of God, draw
yourselves together and force His Holiness to do something
useful. . . . You also are citizens of this city.   If you cannot
help us, you should desist rather than be the cause of our ruin. " [105]
It was no occasion to dissimulate or to delay—they must decide ;
and if they decided wisely, the conclusion could not be other
than to join with the French and to assist the city.   " For
the love of God, do something without waiting for us to be
the first. . . . You must be suffering from obstinacy, or hatred,
or blindness."   The Papacy was on good terms with no power,
Italian or European.   It should at least win over Florence to
its side.   " Why do you still wait ?   Had you been as tardy to
make the city spend as you are at present to do it a benefit, it
would not now be in such straits. . . . I should like to see something besides words . . . [106] "   " . . . I tell you that this is as
necessary to the city as bread is necessary to live. . . ."   " Can
they not understand," he cries again in requesting the release of
a son of Ludovico Martelli, no doubt as an earnest of good intentions, " that it is a baseness not to be liberal ? " [107]   The Pope
too came in for his share.   Capponi implored him in the name
of devotion to his native city, and of the perils which she was
undergoing through his action ; he invoked the example of the
patriotic Camillus, and the memories of what the city had done
for the Holy See. [108]   The need must indeed have been urgent
to have been pressed with such insistency, and apparently the idea
was seriously entertained at the Curia.   For at one time it
seemed as though Capponi's efforts were to be blessed with success.
The Abbot of Negro was received by the Signoria in April
with a mission to treat of " certain matters with the Pope " ; and

in the middle of July responsible observers believed that within a fortnight the accord would be finally concluded.[109]   There was, however, one great difference of opinion.   It seems that Capponi himself was begging for an immediate concession to satisfy the city's pressing needs, which he could present to the people as an earnest of the Pope's good will in order to further the mutual agreement.   Clement, on the other hand, demurred, regarding the grant as a price to be paid only after a concession had been made to himself, and demanding a preliminary declaration from the other side before taking steps.[110]   As a result, the negotiations fell through when they seemed on the brink of success.   On the pretext of referring the matter to a Consistory, it was deferred until the result of the Neapolitan campaign showed the Pope on which side his interest lay ; and Capponi's hopes faded away into nothingness with the triumph of the Emperor.

Lautrec had remained inactive at Bologna when, after securing the Milanese, the escape of the Pope had deprived him of his immediate objective.   Early in January, Charles rejected the terms which had been offered to him on behalf of the league, and war was solemnly declared by France and England, the Florentine ambassador in Spain being arrested in consequence with the others.[111]   At the same time, Lautrec left Bologna and began to press southwards.   His objective was Naples—the base for the Imperialist activities in Italy and the original bone of contention between Spain and France.   The Pope maintained an outward neutrality, but secretly favoured Lautrec, through whom he was enabled to recover Imola and Rimini and who promised to release the papal states after reducing Naples.   A little later he received a yet greater benefit ; for the lanzknechts, on hearing that the enemy had actually entered into the kingdom of Naples, were finally induced to evacuate Rome and to throw themselves in their way.   By greater promptness, Lautrec might have achieved an immediate victory; but despite his dilatoriness, it seemed as though all was over with the Imperial cause in Italy.   While the Venetians followed their usual practice of occupying the cities on the Adriatic coast and the Genoese fleet intercepted supplies, the French easily overran Apulia.   At the end of April, perhaps tardily, the siege of Naples was formed by the combined forces, naval and military ; while a German diversion in the north, under the Duke of Brunswick, came to utter failure.[112]

The part of the Florentine forces in these operations had been notable if not glorious.   Upon his arrival at Bologna, Lautrec had requested the fulfilment of their treaty obligations, and the English envoy, then in the city, supported his demands.[113] With such an army on their borders, a refusal was out of the question, and the method of compliance only was in dispute.   The

Ghibelline party supported a less committal and more economic adhesion by sending money for the upkeep of their 4,000 troops, as the terms of the treaty allowed them. Soderini, as usual, pleaded for a wholehearted adhesion by sending and maintaining their actual troops. As before, his followers gained the day, and he was himself sent as one of the envoys to Lautrec.[114] The French commander, rejoiced by this decision and by the provisions sent for his army, consented to be dissuaded from leading his troops through Tuscany, on the specious pretext of the pest which was still raging there. While, therefore, the main forces penetrated through the Romagna, Orazio Baglione led the Bande Nere by way of the Campagna to join them near Lucera. On their march, they sacked Aquila, which had capitulated to Lautrec, with a cruelty which rivalled their insubordination, for which three of their captains were made to atone with their lives. With the aid of the Gascons, they stormed Melfi after an unsuccessful attack ; and the addition of their numbers and reputation to the forces of the league led the Prince of Orange to withdraw without a fight from his strong position at Troja.[115]

The fall of Naples and, with it, of the Imperial hopes in Italy seemed imminent when at the commencement of July an estrangement which widened into a breach led to the withdrawal of the Genoese fleet from the city. Nevertheless, the result might have been unaltered but for the outbreak of the plague among the besieging forces. More than half of their number fell victims to its ravages, together with the commander-in-chief himself ; and the debacle became inevitable. At the end of August, the remnant withdrew under the Marquis of Saluzzo, but they were forced to capitulate at Aversa. The Florentine forces suffered with the rest. Their commander, Orazio Baglione, had fallen in a skirmish, early in the siege ; his successor, Count Ugo de' Pepoli, died in prison. The Bande Nere, reduced almost to nothing by fighting, sickness, and capture, broke up entirely and never again figured as a whole in Italian history. This was the end of the most promising campaign which ever fell to the lot of the league of Cognac.[116]

Meanwhile, in Florence, a series of reforms had been commenced. The notaries were put under control by being ordered to keep a proper record in the vernacular of all legal instruments which they drew up, and their fees were limited.[117] The proper registration of marriage and other contracts was extended to the contado.[118] The status and powers of the Conservadori di Legge were defined and enhanced, so as to increase the authority of that important tribunal. Four of their representatives were introduced to maintain the decorum of the Consiglio Grande, which was to be purged by them of all unauthorized persons—both minors under twenty-four years of age, and (under more severe penalties) those " non-statuali " of full age who had introduced themselves into it without right.[119]   Corruption and reciprocal understandings in nominations to offices or to membership of the Council were to be severely checked.   Descending to more minute detail, the very costume in which the citizens were to attend its meetings was defined with penalties for disobedience heavy out of all proportion to the offence.[120]   The Ruota, the first judicial tribunal, was thoroughly reformed.[121]   The wide-felt sympathy for Pandolfo Paccione, a popular captain in the Florentine pay who had been condemned to death by the Quarantia for homicide and mutiny, had given rise to some fear that his sentence would be reversed by the Consiglio Grande, to which he made the first, and only, appeal.   Upon this occasion, the apprehension was unfounded ; but nevertheless, it led to the immediate abrogation of the right of appeal from the sentence of the new tribunal, thus converting it more than ever into a potential instrument of oppression.[122]

Even in these crowded and troublous times, that which was best and most characteristic in Florentine life was not forgotten ; and the humanities intermingled with politics in the old inimitable manner.   Michelangelo Buonarotti was still working away in Florence, and patronized by the government.   In August 1528 he was assigned by the Signoria a great block of Carrara marble from which he proposed to make a statue of Samson the deliverer smiting a Philistine, in commemoration of the recovery of the liberty of Florence, " to be erected in a public place for the ornament of the city."   It was this block which had been originally intended for Baccio Bandinelli, now in refuge at Lucca, and which was ultimately used by him for the Hercules and Cacus which still disfigures the Piazza della Signoria.   Though Michelangelo never actually commenced work on this, he painted at this period his " Leda " for the Duke of Ferrara.   Perhaps, too, he was working away in stealth at the Medici monuments in S. Lorenzo.[123] Benvenuto Cellini, who had returned to his birthplace after the sack of Rome, was industriously engaged in a shop he had opened in the Mercato Nuovo, where he enjoyed the patronage and encouragement of the more distinguished artist.[124]   Andrea del Sarto was kept busy painting for Ottaviano de' Medici, for Sarzana, and for Vallombrosa.[125]   A most interesting instance of the Florentine spirit may be seen in two successive decisions made by the Signoria in the midst of the round of ordinary business. The famous book of Pandects, now in the Laurentian Library, was ordered to be left open for public inspection—a most significant token of popular interest which would assuredly not have been met with elsewhere.[126]   The great picture originally painted by Fra Bartolommeo for the Hall of the Great Council was ordered to be brought from S. Marco and put in the place for which it was originally intended.[127] Even in the middle of the siege, time could be spared to give Giovanni Matteo Bembo an exclusive licence to print the works of his kinsman, the great humanist Petro Bembo, which had of late been pirated at Venice.[128] In a different sphere, it was attempted to detach the Franciscan houses of Pietrasanta and adjoining places from the interloping chapter of Lucca.[129]

In the midst of such preoccupations, the thirteen months for which the Gonfalonier had been appointed drew to their close, and the time was now ripe for a fresh election. Under the terms of the constitution, however, re-appointment to the office was permissible ; and it had been maliciously said that to secure this had been Capponi's prime object during the whole of his term. It had seemed, indeed, that with the increasing fury against the Medici and suspicion against himself, it had become highly improbable. Capponi himself, feeling this, had attempted to get the minimum age for Gonfalonier reduced to forty-five, so that he could throw his own influence on the side of Marco del Nero, upon whom he could rely to continue his policy; but even in this he was unsuccessful.[130] In addition, the Ottanta elected in the previous month had been decidedly of the adverse faction, hardly containing a member of the more aristocratic sections.[131] Events showed, however, that the Arrabbiati had reached the height of their power with the authorization of the Palace Guard ; and their violence had resulted in the union in a single block with the Palleschi and Ottimati of all the republicans who favoured a more moderate policy. Capponi had in addition the advantage of being faced with a party weakened by internal divisions. Two of the Soderini family—Tommaso and an uncle—split up the family following among themselves, and weakened Carducci, the strongest competitor, who was generally thought to have the best chances for the office.[132] Moreover, this was an occasion when there was a real numerical trial of strength. The cohesion and assiduous interest of the Arrabbiati might secure the appointments to minor offices, or carry a provision through the Council ; their vociferous clamour might force a measure upon the Signoria. They were even thought capable of causing bloodshed at the time of the election.[133] At this juncture, however, the most important of all, the whole city was equally keen, and nearly every citizen was expected to register his vote. Carducci himself had recognized this, and had attempted by a change of attitude to placate and attach to his own cause with soft words and promises some even of the Palleschi. But his patent ambition to succeed to the office, too openly pursued, told heavily against him, and Capponi was aided rather than hampered by the very violence of an anonymous and misunderstood satire which had been published against him.[134] Nevertheless, the voting was very close in a Council of very nearly 2,000. As on the former occasion, both were selected in the first ballot, together with the two Soderinis ; and Capponi polled only fourteen votes more than his rival. In the second division, however, he once more secured the requisite majority and his tenure of office was extended for another year (10 June 1528).[135]

NOTES TO CHAPTER IV

[1] For the consequences of the sack of Rome and the imprisonment of the Pope see *Cambridge Modern History*, II, i ; and Pastor, Vol. IX, cap. 12.

[2] Foscari, *Relazione*, p. 76.

[3] See the remarkable begging letter of 12 February 1527/8 of " Your loving mother, Simunetta," printed by Ferrai in *Lorenzino de' Medici*, Appendix II (ix) (cf. *supra*, cap. I, note 18)—a most curious human document if authentic. She actually sends her lawful husband to take the letter to her illegitimate son !

[4] MSS. index to Carte Strozziane, in R. Arch. di Stato di Firenze, s.v. Alessandro. " Lettera . . . la quale la prega a volerli mandari de' denari," 27 April 1527 ; receipt for 300 ducats, 2 May. The actual documents cannot be traced. Cf. Ferrai, *Lorenzino de' Medici*, App. II (iv) and (v).

[5] Letter of 28 June, 1527, to Jacopo Salviati (Bib. Nat. di Fir. Carte Strozziane, filz. G.O., f. 29) " . . . con poca roba e manco danari, che ci partimo di Firenze senza uno ordine al mondo et con paura . . ."

[6] Provisioni, CCVI, 11 June. The figures were 86 to 14 in the Ottanta, and 1,120 to 190 in the Great Council.

[7] See Appendix of Documents, No. 5.

[8] Varchi, I, 306–9.

[9] *Ibid.* 222–3.

[10] Signoria, CXXIX, 27 June 1527. " Quod Ottaviano de Medicis curet bona illorum de Medicis."

[11] Soriani, *Relazione*, p. 410.

[12] Reumont, *La Jeunesse de Catherine de Médicis*, caps. IX and X. Her maintenance was provided for, out of her own property, by the Sindaci del Commune. (Signoria, CXIX, 19 December 1527 and 11 January 1528–9.) Cf. *infra*, p. 155 *n.* 25, and p. 195 *n.* 98.

[13] Varchi, I, 433.

[14] O.G., CC, 5a, 24b, 36a (4–21 September 1527).

[15] Varchi, I, 147.

[16] O.G, CC, 28b, 45a (18–25 September).

[17] *Ibid.* f. 40a, 47a, 54b, 56a (23–28 September).

[18] *Ibid.* f. 99 (16 October).

[19] Sanuto, XLVI, 472. Cf. Dieci, Missive, XLIII, 6 March 1527/8. Instructions to Battista della Palla. . . " Et se la casa de' Medici è stata chiarita debitrice di qualche somma grande di danarj alla città, è segno che se n'era servita."

[20] O.G., CC, 160 (11 November).

²¹ *Ibid.* f. 171 (14 November).

²² *Ibid.* ad diem.

²³ Index to Carte Strozziane, f. 211. " Lettera scritta di P. Partita (?) da Cardinali Farnese, Cibo, Ridolfi e Gonzaga alla Signoria di Firenze dolendosi degli Otto di Guardia e Balia della detta Città che havessino vituperosamente fatto citare il Cardinale di Cortona . . . che in termine di tre giorni dovesse comparire dinanzi al Magistrato loro a rispondere una querela exhibita contro a lui 1527 : *T.T.* 328." Unfortunately this, like other of the more interesting of the Carte Strozziane relating to the last Republic, seems to have disappeared and the volume cannot be traced.

²⁴ See Appendix of Documents, No. 4 (i).

²⁵ Signori, Carteggio, 1st Canc. XXI, 27 November 1525 (see Appendix of Documents, No. 4 (ii.). In the next month there were further friendly advances. Cf. Signoria, CXIX, 19 December, " *Preceptum pro Filia Laurentij de Medicis* " (for whose upkeep the Syndics of the Commune were to pay a regular contribution) and 31st Id., " *Approvatio gratie illorum de Medicis* (facta per sples. officiales venditionum). "

²⁶ Varchi, I, 257.

²⁷ *Ibid.* 329 ; editor's note A.

²⁸ *Ibid.* 212.

²⁹ *Ibid.* 397 ; Nerli, p. 171 ; *Vita di Niccolò Capponi*, pp. 942–9.

³⁰ Rossi, I, 37.

³¹ *Ibid.* 67–8.

³² *Ibid.* 82–6.

³³ *Ibid.* 90–3 ; cf. letter of 8 May 1528 in *Opere*, IX, 129.

³⁴ Rossi, I, 93–4.

³⁵ *Vita di Niccolò Capponi*, p. 927.

³⁶ Capponi (before his election) is almost the only non-official person to whom Guicciardini's correspondence, at the time of the Revolution, was addressed. See *Opere*, IX, pp. 42, 53, 61.

³⁷ Segni (I), 67–70 ; *Ragguaglio di B. Carnesecchi, ubi supra*, where the oration is very similar to the other. Does this indicate a common and reliable tradition or mere plagiarism ?

³⁸ Cf. letter of Guicciardini of 21 June 1527 in *Opere*, IX, 101.

³⁹ *Opere*, II, 28 seqq. Cf. Rossi, I, 71–3.

⁴⁰ For Francesco Zeffi, who was also biographer of Lorenzo Strozzi and censor of the Florentine Academy 1542–4, cf. Ferrai, *Lorenzino de' Medici*, p. 20, *n.* 1, and *Vita di Filippo Strozzi*, p. 124. He is to be carefully distinguished from his contemporary of the same name.

⁴¹ Index to Carte Strozziane, " Due Lettere di Gio : Francesco Zeffi del Governo della Republica di Venezia, et in particulare del Consiglio Grande, mettendo in consideratione se poteva introdursi in Firenze, 1527. LLL. 16–22." The treatise could not be traced. Another, similarly lost, " sopra il riordire il Governo, a Niccolò Capponi," is referred to *ibid.* f. 214.

⁴² Varchi, I, 241.

⁴³ *Opere*, vol. II, 1–173 ; published indeed only in 1540 ; *Ibid.* p. xlii.

⁴⁴ *Discorso sopra il Fermare il Governo di Firenze l'anno*, 1527 : *indiritto al Magnifico Gonfaloniere di Giustizia Niccolò di Piero Capponi*. *Ibid.* vol. I, pp. 1–15. In spite of the testimony of the MSS. the year, it seems, must be postponed. He refers, p. 7, to Doria's invitation to the city to leave France for the Emperor, which must have been after June 1528 ; and p. 15 to "La Milizia nuovamente ordinata "—indicating a date later than November 1528. Perrens' summary (III, pp. 162–4) is both inaccurate and unjust. Through a misreading of Falletti Fossati

(*op cit.* I, 44–6) and a neglect of the actual sources, he confuses it with the " *Discorso* " of 1531, and uses his blunders to give weight to his malice.

[45] *Lettera a Zanobi Bartolini* prefixed to the " *Discorso* " ; *Opere*, I, p. 1. This is supported by Nardi, who mentions (*Historie*, p. 200) precisely reforms like these last as having been brought up for consideration. Similarly Busini, p. 45.

[46] Foscari, *Relazione*, pp. 73–6, analyses the situation, showing how the popular extremists were in his opinion playing into the hands of the Pope.

[47] *Letters and Papers, Henry VIII*, IV, 3672, 3758.

[48] Reports to Pope of 23 and 25 December 1527 in Appendix of Documents, No. 5—apparently the only authority for these negotiations.

[49] Cf. Dieci, Missive XLIII, 10 December 1527 ; to Antonfrancesco degli Albizzi, Orator with Lautrec : " Per questa nuova tutta la città si truova sollevata perchè ciascuno guidicha che tale venuta non possa partorire altro che noia & travaglio . . . et è tanto in ciaschuno il sospetto grande, che niuno si persuade, che da sua Sta possiamo maj havere pace e riposo."

[50] Varchi, I, 331–2.

[51] Soriani, *Relazione*, p. 427.

[52] Sanuto, XLVI, 419.

[53] Varchi, I, 429–30.

[54] Dieci, Missive, *passim* at this period.

[55] Dieci, Missive, XLIII. Cf. Giannotti, *Opere*, I, 146–7, for a project of Capponi's to alter the method of election to the Dieci in hope of securing a membership more favourable to himself.

[56] Cf. Gaye, *Carteggio Inedito d' Artisti*, (II) CVII, *seqq.* Giovanfrancesco da San Gallo sent to inspect and put in order fortifications of Montepulciano, Livorno, Cortona, Pisa, Pistoia, S. Gimignano, and Prato, commencing 24 December 1527.

[57] Varchi, I, 324. Cf. also report of Soriani of 26/7 February in Sanuto, XLVII, 28.

[58] See explanation sent to Portinari for transmission to Henry VIII in Dieci, Missive, XLIII, 12 February 1527/8.

[59] Sanuto, XLVII, 49 (26 February 1527/8).

[60] *Vita di N. Capponi*, 939 ; Varchi, I, 325–7 ; Signoria, CXIX, 13 December 1527. Its organization was modified on 25 May and 25 September (*ibid. ad dies*).

[61] Soriani, *Relazione*, pp. 426–8.

[62] Busini, p. 28. He was himself present at the meeting and advised against action.

[63] Cf. Ademollo, *Marietta de' Ricci*, I, 11–12, and Passerini's erudite note.

[64] Fullest account in Pitti, *Apologia de' Cappucci*, 148–9.

[65] Varchi, I, 317–9.

[66] Cf. O.G., CCI, 12B.

Addì 8 di gennaio 1527
Mag^{d} S. octo, Fassi intendere a V.S. come
Nella chiesa di S^{to} Lorenzo è scripto nella sepultura di Cosimo de Medici questo epitaphio, nel quale sono queste parole.

Cosmus medices hic situs est, Decreto pub^{co} Pater Patrie laqual cosa non sta bene, ne si debbe Patire, perche non è vero che lui fussi Pater patrie ma Tyrannus patrie, per tanto V.S. faccino redurre tale epitaphio al suo dovere come si è facto a M^o Ficino & Antonio delli orghani & come di questo et altra volta fu facto,

Dicta die data notitia Dominis octo.

---

f. 47B.

Addì p° di febraio 1527

Epitaphio. Avoi Mag^ci S. octo di guardia e conservatorj della libertà del popolo fiorentino si fa questa querela come egli è uno epitaphio in S^to Lor° che dice p^r patrie, & indebitamente & con dishonore di questa libertà, perche sono stati sempre tiranni, & hanno sempre vituperato questa Città tagliato capi a v^ri Cittadinj & rubato e' danarij del comune & lo honor diviver da hom^i nobili et meritato esser decti pater patrie quelli che hanno sempre tenuta in servitù la cosa di prato si ricorda a V.S. meritano di esser corsi in casa & dati a Cani, quelli non vogliono che questo partito si vinca vogliono tenere el pie in dua staffe voglionsi salvare a tucti e' tempi & aspetano la tornata di questi trannj

expedita die xx februarij

[67] *Ibid.* CC, 146B (4 November 1527) :

Item adunati ut supra visa quadam querela seu notificatione coram eorum offitij exibita et mota et in tamburis eorum offitij reperta sub die 16 mensis ottobris proxime preteritj continente in effectu qualiter epitaffium dominj marsilij ficinj respublica tamen scriptum est in laudem cosimj et laurenzij de medicis tum sit in eclesia cathedralis eclesie debet reddere honorem reipublice q^a pestifera domus sempre conculcavit honorem publicam et erepta libertatem facit reattare epitaffium istum et illum m' ant. de organis et visa et considerata dicta tanburatione et querela et que in predicta consideranda fuerint pro expeditione eiusdem obtempto partito secundum ordinem deliberaverunt quod fiat preceptum

Provisorj opere sive operanorum sante marie floris de florentia quatenus hinc ad per totam diem veneris proxime futurj debet fecisse delere ex epitaffio dominj marsilij ficinj posito in santa maria floris de florentia haec verba viz ante cosmj munere laurentique medicis numc (*sic*) revixit publico et quod similiter infra otto dies ab hodie debeat fecisse amovere et removere de dicta eclesia et de loco ubi est inmaginem marmoream m' ant' squartalupj cum eius epitaffio et talem inmaginem reponj faciat in sacrestia ubi jam erat cum verso ad prd. vulgarj vel latino infrq. tenoris m° ant° squarcalupj degliorganj et omnia exequat et executionj mistat nocturno tempore et sub pena fl. centum.

Ibid. f. 213 (3 December).

Super . . . Querela non esse procedendum.

All these inscriptions, if ever actually erased, have now been restored.

[68] Varchi, I, 403 ; Foscari, *Relazione*, p. 73. That the proposal emanated from Michelangelo is improbable to a degree. It is more likely that he had some suggestions to make for reconstruction from the purely architectural point of view. A similar proposal was brought up formally during the Siege (*infra*, pp. 201–2).

[69] Signoria, CXXIX, 3 March 1527–8.

[70] Cf. Sanuto, LI, 375 ; *Letters and Papers, Henry VIII*, IV, 5230, 5261.

[71] E.g. Varchi, I, 350, 405 ; Cambi, IV, 1, 2, 36–8. The burden on the city was enhanced by the continued inability of the contado to pay taxes owing to the ravages of war and pestilence. Cf. Signoria, CXXIX, 23 January 1527/8, for a typical remission.

[72] Varchi, I, 373.

[73] *Ibid.* 374–6.

[74] *Ibid.* 379.

[75] *Ibid.* Ammirato, VII, 43 ; Cambi, IV, 28.

[76] Sanuto, XLVII, 156–7.

[77] *Ibid.* 94.   A letter is cited by Gauthiez, *Lorenzaccio*, p. 62, from the Autografi di Principi in the Milanese Archives as written by Alessandro from Florence on 18 September 1528.   Without corroborative evidence it is difficult to admit this as authentic, as his presence at that time could not have escaped notice in other sources.

[78] *Vita di N. Capponi*, p. 926 ; *Ragguaglio di Baccio Carnesecchi, ubi supra.*

[79] Cf. Strozziane, filz.   G.O. f. 136 in Bib. Nat. di Firenze ; letter of 28 December 1527 to Cecotto Tosinghi recommending to his protection one who has been falsely accused by his enemies as being Medicophile. It is of themselves that the charge is actually true !

[80] Signoria, CXXIX, 6 March 1527/8.   Busini, p. 18 ; Varchi, I, 253–4, hopelessly antedates these events, which his informant distinctly states to have been " dopo la peste."

[81] *Vita di Niccolò Capponi*, p. 927 ; *Ragguaglio di Baccio Carnesecchi, ubi supra.*

[82] *Ibid.* and Varchi, I, p. 392.   Clarice died on 3 May 1528.

[83] Signoria, CXXIX, 3 February 1527/8.   Varchi (II, 188) wholly misdates this occurrence.

[84] Signoria, CXXIX, 3 May 1527.

[85] *Ibid.* 23 May.

[86] *Ibid.* 5, 8 August.

[87] O.G., CCI, 103b ; CCII, 104b.   Buondelmonti's confinement was, however, made less rigorous owing to his ill-health at the commencement of the Siege.   Signoria, CXXXI, f. 201–2, 6 October 1529.

[88] O.G., CCIII, 33.   For a similar charge, see *ibid.* f. 100.

[89] *Ibid.* f. 106, 107.

[90] *Ibid.* f. 51–2.

[91] *Ibid.* f. 58.

[92] *Ibid.* f. 89, 93 ; *ibid.* CCII, f. 120–1.

[93] *Ibid.* CCIII, f. 85–6.

[94] Varchi, I, 249–52.   For the Soderini family, see Ferrai, *Lorenzino de' Medici*, cap. II, pp. 39–64.

[95] Ammirato, VII, p. 39.   Varchi, I, 293–304, is obviously confusing these with the deliberations of the summer of 1528, at which Luigi Alamanni spoke to further the negotiations initiated by his patron, Andrea Doria.   See below, p. 122.

[96] See letters of May and June 1528 in Sanesi ; *La Politica di Niccolò Capponi dessunta di quattro sue lettere inedite* in *A.S.I.*, ser. V, vol. 21 ; and despatches of Guarini to Duke of Ferrara, in Rossi, *op. cit.*, Appendices 1 and 2.

[97] *Ibid.* App. I, despatch of 8 July 1528.

[98] Sanuto, XLI, 201 (Report of Soriano, 1–2 April).

[99] MS. Ricordanze di Santa Maria del Carmine (*R. Archivio di Stato di Firenze*), Vol. XX, 1517–31.

[100] See Appendix of Documents, No. 6 (i) (letter to Tommaso da Caiano of 4 April 1528).   These transactions are ignored by the contemporary historians, save for a bare reference in *Vita di N. Capponi*, p. 951.

[101] Appendix of Documents, 6, ii and iii (letter to same of 6 May and to Pope of 5 May).   The report of Soriani (Sanuto, XLVII, 260) seems to be a confused version of this.

[102] Guarini to Duke of Ferrara, *apud* Rossi, App. I.

[103] The official request of the Signoria was addressed only on 28 June 1528, with a covering letter to Serragli (Appendix of Documents, 6 (iv) and (v)).   From the correspondence published by Sanesi, however, it is obvious that negotiations had been going on for some time previous.

[104] Letter of Soriani of 18 July in Sanuto, XLVIII, 294.

[105] Sanesi, *ubi supra*, letter ii.

[106] *Ibid.* letter iii.

[107] *Ibid.* letter iv.

[108] *Ibid.* letter i.

[109] Falletti, I, 229–30.

[110] Sanesi, *ubi supra*, letter i : " Intendo quanto mi di' circha la declaration, che dichi bisogniava farla prima."

[111] *State Papers, Venetian*, IV, 234, 290–1 ; Sanuto, XLVI, 472.

[112] Vito Vitale, *L'Impresa di Puglia* in *Nuovo Archivio Veneto*, N.S. VII, v. 13, p. 5 *seqq* ; Robert, *Philibert d'Orange*, caps. 10–12 ; H. Omont, *Les suites du sac de Rome par les impériaux et la campagne de Lautrec en Italie* in *Mélanges d'archéologie et d'histoire*, XVI (1896), p. 35 *seqq*.

[113] *State Papers, Henry VIII*, IV, 3672.

[114] Segni, I, 48–9. Cf. the correspondence in Dieci, Missive, XLII and XLIII.

[115] Segni, I, 49–52 ; *Vita di N. Capponi*, p. 931–2 ; Varchi, I, 381 *seqq.* ; Robert, cap. VIII. The victory at Aquila was celebrated at Florence in some pomp, with a state service and a sermon by Fra Bonaventura at S. Marco (Sanuto, XLVII, 213).

[116] Robert, caps. X–XII.

[117] Varchi, I, 367–8, 372.

[118] *Ibid.* 369.

[119] Signoria, CXXX, 9 June 1528.

[120] Varchi, I, 376–9.

[121] *Ibid.* 380.

[122] *Ibid.* 351–66 ; Ammirato, VII, p. 43 ; Cambi, IV, 19–22. Cf. letter of Guicciardini in *Opere*, IX, 129.

[123] Symonds, I, 439 *seqq*. There is no reason to disbelieve the tradition that Michelangelo continued to work at S. Lorenzo during the Republican *régime*. His artistic feelings were not affected by political conditions ; and the work in question is assuredly something more than a merely glorificatory monument.

[124] *Memorie*, I, c. 41.

[125] Vasari, V, 51–2, 71.

[126] Signoria, CXXX, 29 March 1529–30. " *Quod Pandecte Ostendantur* Item per eisdem simul adunati & servatis servandis ec. Deliberaverunt Quod librj pandectarum qui sunt clausi in dicto eorum palatio hodie aperiantur & ostendantur."

[127] *Ibid.* " *Quod Tabula consilij ponatur in dicto consilio* . . . deliberaverunt quod egregia tabula consilij maioris picta per olim Fratrem Bartholomeum fratrem sanctj Marci que hodie reperitur in convenctu Sancti Marii predictj hinc ad per totam diem Sabati que erit dies iij mensis Aprilis proxime future ponatur in sala consilij maioris in capella & loco . . . ordinato in dicta sala per eos ad quos pertinet sub pena eorum indignationis. . . ." For this picture, now in the Uffizzi, cf. Vasari, IV, 198.

·[128] Signoria, Carteggio: Missive, Minutari, XXI, 31 December 1530.

[129] Signoria, Carteggio: Missive, Registri, LVIII. To General Chapter of Minor Friars, 1 May 1529.

[130] *Vita di N. Capponi*, p. 949.

[131] Letter of Guicciardini of 8 May, 1528 in *Opere*, IX, 128.

[132] Letter of Giovambattista Pandolfini to Giovanni Pandolfini, 29 May, 1528 (B.M., Add. MSS. 28,272, f. 93). " Del Gonfaloniere si crede indugeranno all' ultimo, et ogni uno crede sarà Messer Baldassare Carducci, non altro." The postponement of the election here referred to (it took

place on 10 instead of 1 June) was owing to the threatening proximity of Brunswick's lanzknechts.

[133] Guarini to Duke of Ferrara, 21 May, 1528 (*apud* Rossi, I, 96–7).

[134] Actually by Pierfilippo Pandolfini—an ascription confirmed by the fact that an MS. copy of the text is preserved in the Pandolfini Papers (British Museum, Add. MSS. 28,272, f. 106 *seqq.*). Cardinale Rucellai was, however, punished for it, being banished by the Otto for unlicensed publication and unauthorized absence in Siena, in spite of the acquittal of the case by the Quarantia (O.G., CCII, 57, 62, 74–5).

[135] Cf. Ammirato, VII, 44 ; Nerli, 172–3 ; *Vita di N. Capponi*, 932–3 ; Varchi, I, 398–400.

CHAPTER V

THE FALL OF NICCOLÒ CAPPONI

THE first days of Capponi's second tenure of office were marked by the dramatic episodes of the Neapolitan campaign. During their course, he did not cease in his efforts to bring about an understanding with the Pope. The correspondence with Salviati continued uninterrupted. Giachinotto Serragli was continually in Florence, paying secret visits to the Gonfalonier's private apartments at unusual hours of day and night.[1] The Arrabbiati, whose suspicions were newly aroused by the report that Brunswick's lanzknechts had been brought to Italy by agreement with the Pope to be directed against Florence,[2] got wind of the negotiations. One day Jacopo Alamanni caught sight of Serragli himself entering the city in disguise, bound on his usual mission, though sent for, as he said, by the Dieci. The young hothead immediately seized him and took him by force to the house of Baldassare Carducci, where he was interrogated but set free.[3] At about the same time there was found by chance a letter to the Gonfalonier from Jacopo Salviati. It disclosed indeed nothing incriminating besides the fact that he was in correspondence with persons about the Curia. This was, however, in itself highly irregular, and Capponi was forbidden to send to Viterbo any letters in his own name. Regretfully, he instructed Serragli that in future all letters should be addressed to the Dieci and not to himself.[4]

This was followed almost immediately by a fresh limitation. In treating of these matters, Capponi had not acted entirely alone. Associated with him had been at least those of his colleagues of the Signoria and the Dieci whom he knew to be in sympathy with his ideas.[5] He continued to be also in close communication with some of the leading Palleschi within the walls, and complaint was still vociferous at his over-great intimacy with such men as Vettori, Guicciardini, and Acciaiuoli. The Florentine constitution indeed gave openings for a certain amount of independent and uncontrolled action on the part of the Gonfalonier. The Dieci was supposed to be assisted in its deliberations upon foreign affairs by the Council of Ottanta, elected every six months. This was, however, too large and unwieldy to be consulted on all occasions, and usually met only once a week to decide in matters of major importance or of dispute. Other points were discussed in a smaller " Pratica " summoned at will by the Gonfalonier from among the number of the more experienced citizens. With full control over the composition and scope of this body, he was rendered to a certain extent independent of all restraint, inviting only his friends or even relatives and obtaining from them what conclusion he pleased ; though indeed their advice was not binding. There was always in the city a certain dislike of this excessive power. This now combined with the newly confirmed suspicions of the Gonfalonier to bring about a measure to take it out of his hands. It was enacted that a board of twenty " *Arroti* " should be elected bi-yearly in the Consiglio Maggiore which, together with the present and the past Dieci, should form the Pratica to deal with ordinary business as it arose.[6]

While the Gonfalonier's power was being thus hedged in by his political opponents, there occurred the tragical debacle of the confederate forces before Naples. It must be imagined that this striking confirmation of his political sagacity in preferring the Imperial alliance and supporting a less lavish expenditure on behalf of the league must have gone far to strengthen his position within the city, and proportionately to discredit the adverse faction. He therefore began almost immediately after these setbacks to make headway against his opponents. There remained, however, one perpetual reminder of his position. The Palace guard continued on duty, at once a warning and a threat, and with its members standing vigilant in the courtyard below, he could never feel secure in the State apartments above. By gradually diluting its composition with its own adherents, he had done something to relieve his position ; but nevertheless he had every reason to feel some apprehension at the mere thought of the origin of the institution, let alone its *personnel*. Recently, too, he had received a sharp reminder of its temper. Some of the ringleaders, headed by his opponent, Pierfilippo Pandolfini, had obtained from the Signoria, almost by threats, permission to bear a standard inscribed with the name of Jesus and the word " Liberty." Thus his enemies were given a rallying-point.[7] These apprehensions drove him to the most memorable measure of his administration.

The disaster in Naples had virtually destroyed the military forces of the Florentines, so that only six companies of the Bande Nere were still attached to their flag.[8] Immediately the news reached Florence the city set indefatigably about making good her losses, engaging any fugitives from Naples who passed through her territory. Before long she again had twenty-two captains of foot serving in her pay, together with about 400 light horse. Part of these were, however, still employed in the last phases of the campaign, in which Renzo da Ceri was making some headway for the King of France around Barletta, in conjunction with the Venetians who still retained their hold upon the coastal towns. The Florentines, in the hope of keeping the war away from their own borders, had again consented to help and were undergoing one-third of the expense.[9] In the case of eventualities nearer home, there were the thirty companies of the Battaglie Florentine centred upon the more important spots in the Florentine territory. This, however, would be nothing like adequate in the case of real emergency, and some further provision was thought necessary. In addition, the fate of Pandolfo Puccini and the conduct of the Bande Nere in the present war had shown that not even the most faithful paymasters in Italy [10] could be assured of the fidelity of their mercenaries. It had therefore come to be felt that it was necessary to train and arm all of the citizens, a thing which had not been known since the days of Cosimo, from which time the old Militia had been in abeyance. At present, all had the option to bear arms; it was now suggested that they should have the obligation. Thus there would be extended and applied to the city the system which Machiavelli had originally instituted in a minor degree for the Florentine territory as a whole, and from which he had actually excepted for the sake of security the inhabitants of walled towns.[11] The idea originally aroused great opposition. On the one hand, it was remembered how ludicrously Machiavelli's militia had failed when it was put to the test at the Siege of Prato ; and in the official view all Italian soldiers, even professional, were regarded with some contempt.[12] On the other hand, the possibility of success was viewed with apprehension. More than one Italian tyrant had climbed to a throne upon the shields of the soldiers under his command. " I fear a Caesar," pithily said Filippo de' Nerli, the Medicophile historian of the Siege.[13] Nor were the feelings of the unwarlike burghers, long unused to arms, to be disregarded.

Capponi, with his pacific and somewhat opportunist nature, had originally found so warlike a measure little to his liking, and all the more so since it breathed defiance precisely against those whom he was endeavouring to placate. He had therefore been at the outset among its foremost opponents, and had even demeaned himself to canvass against it.[14] The growing necessity, however, became reinforced by the threatening attitude of the Palace guard, from whom he felt that his position if not his life was in danger. It was known that some of them had formally deliberated the assault of the Palace, while they were beginning to demand the disarmament of the rest of the city. These considerations changed his attitude. If Florence were defended by a militia chosen from all citizens, Capponi would have on his side strong forces to use in the defence of law and order—that is, of his own position ; and the strength in it of his opponents would certainly be no more than proportionate to their numbers in the city. Most important perhaps of all, with the whole population thus armed and prepared, it stood to reason that the petty guard of the Palazzo would have its power restricted and might even be dispensed with, while he himself would be rid of its uncomfortable vicinity.[15]

Backed up by his encouragement, the measure went rapidly forward. Donato Giannotti, one of the foremost supporters, had adumbrated a scheme which was accepted in all of its essentials.[16] All full citizens from eighteen to forty, whether qualified to sit in the Consiglio Maggiore or no, were ordered to be inscribed in the new militia, part of which was to act as the guard of the Palace. The ancient framework of the sixteen Gonfaloni was used as the basis for their organization, each quarter being composed of four of these and furnishing one company. Each Gonfalone was to elect its own officers, subject to the approval of the Ottanta, while four Sergeants-Major, all experienced soldiers, were to be appointed to give instruction. Detailed directions were added for regular parades and reviews, and penalties were laid down for evasion.[17]

During the passage of the measure through the various Councils, the leaders of the Arrabbiati, who fully appreciated the standpoint of the Gonfalonier, maintained a factious opposition. This was, however, in contradiction to their usual gospel of preparedness, and their efforts met with no success. The only result of their violence was to play into the hands of Capponi, who was given an opportunity to make a signal example. Upon 6 November, as the Great Council broke up after passing the new ordinance, some of its members were passing through the gate-way where the doomed guard was stationed. " Thank God that this child's play will now be removed," cried Jacopo Capponi, son of the Gonfalonier. It happened that there was on service that day the turbulent young Jacopo Alamanni, the same who had shed blood in the Palazzo on the occasion of the Tumulto del Venerdì, and had driven Filippo Strozzi into exile by his threats. " You will be hanged before that," he replied, hotly. Lionardo Ginori, whose uncle had just married Capponi's daughter, took up the part of his new kinsman, and hot words followed. Blind with passion, Alamanni fell upon the other with repeated blows of his dagger. Seeing him fall (as a matter of fact unhurt and merely tripped up in his cloak), he commenced to flee, with Ginori's uncle and the officials of the Otto at his heels. There was only one way to avoid, as he thought, trial for homicide. As he reached the Piazza and was overtaken, he commenced to call upon the people and the guard to rise in his defence. Only one of his comrades in arms, however, made any move, and so he was easily arrested and taken into the Palace, the gates of which were closed without resistance. At the tumult, slight though it was, the shops had been closed as in the old days of unrest ; and spite added that the Gonfalonier had swooned in his alarm. However that may be, he had the opportunity of trying the ringleader of his enemies upon a clear charge of treason. It so happened that in the alarm caused by the case of Paccione, a provision had been passed enabling the members of five of the greater magistracies to form a special tribunal for dealing immediately with urgent state charges.[18] Alamanni, a friend of Paccione,[19] was the first victim. The magistrates, not yet issued from the Council Chamber, resolved themselves into the Court. The efforts of Baldassare Carducci were of no avail to save him excepting from torture ; and it was disputed whether it was the sympathetic partisan, or the tender-hearted Gonfalonier himself, who cast the solitary vote for acquittal.[20] Within four hours of the offence, before even the Compagnia di Sta. Maria could be called to adminster the last solaces,[21] Alamanni was beheaded upon a balustrade of the Palazzo " for having wished to raise the people, for calling the guard, and for being Jacopo Alamanni." He met his death calmly, and with a sentence on his lips which deserved to be remembered. " If the people of Florence deals out justice thus sharply to every one, I am sure that it will retain its liberty." [22]

Capponi was thus rid of the ringleader of his opponents. He lost no time in following up his advantage. Two days after this event, it was prohibited to carry arms in the Consiglio Grande. On the next, the Palace guard was deprived of part of its recently won advantage by being forbidden to carry its banner outside the Palazzo, and they were submitted to a more rigorous discipline.[23] Before long, he was rid of a more dangerous enemy. Baldassare Carducci had recently refused the post of envoy to Venice, but a little later, Capponi procured his election to that of ambassador to France. He could not refuse a second time without incurring a very heavy fine and the reproach of a lack of public spirit. Neglecting therefore his advancing years, his gains as advocate, and the daughter he had to marry, he accepted the post. He had continually delayed his departure, but at the commencement of December he was peremptorily ordered to leave within the week.[24] In the height of winter, he was forced to make the long journey into the exile where he died. Thus Capponi was rid of his worst rival; but shortly after an indirect censure was passed upon his action by a provision which exempted those over seventy from taking up such offices.[25] Deprived of their leaders, the party of the Arrabbiati became somewhat subdued. The tide of popular favour had receded from Alfonso Strozzi and Tommaso Soderini, men recommended by their families rather than by their abilities [26]; and Capponi was able to secure his position by milder proceedings with varying success against some of the secondary leaders of the party.[27] Thus he was enabled to pursue again with less apprehension the policy on which he had set his heart : to secure the safety and tranquillity of the city by an accord with the Pope and co-operation with the Palleschi.

In November, his triumph was followed by the election of a new Dieci of a more moderate complexion.[28] This gave Capponi an opportunity to evade the restrictions to which he had recently been subjected. The composition of the Pratica which was to discuss foreign affairs was indeed laid down, but there was nothing to ensure that he should consult it. He therefore commenced to treat it with a studied neglect. The matters most dear to his heart were treated of as usual at informal gatherings of a very few of his confidants ; while the meetings of the important body whose true function it was were restricted both in scope and in frequency.[29] At the same time he began to neglect the Priors of Liberty, his colleagues upon the Signoria, whose less expert functions and frequent changes rendered them more sensitive and more responsible to public opinion, and thus to his mind doubly unsuited for a knowledge of state secrets. The gradual diminution of their responsibilities made them all the more jealous of those which remained. It was usual for envoys from foreign powers only to present their credentials and instructions before them, conducting all further negotiations with the Dieci. Capponi commenced to neglect even this slender relic. At the end of 1528, when the English ambassadors passed through Florence on their way to Rome to treat for the Royal Divorce, Capponi went so far as to interview them alone as if he were an absolute monarch ; and such action was not isolated. As a result of this and similar neglect, the Priors carried a resolution by a majority of seven to two that they should all be present on the occasion of any sort of Pratica. This, virtually a vote of censure upon the Gonfalonier, was taken by the newly elected Arroti of whom the Pratica was formed in a very different sense. They suspected that they saw in it the finger of Capponi himself. The inexpert Priors, who were not permitted to leave the Palace during their two months of office, were liable to come unduly under the influence of the Gonfalonier in whose company they were thrown, and would thus merely serve to propagate his views. This usurpation of prerogative on their part was accordingly all the more resented. Hence the Pratica passed an utterly con-tradictory measure, whereby the Priors were expressly excluded from its meetings. In this conflict of powers, Capponi was able to escape virtually all restriction.[30]

Nevertheless, he was unable to carry his policy into practice in its main issues. In minor matters, indeed, he could bring about a certain ill-feeling with the Duke of Ferrara, whose son Ercole with 200 men-at-arms the city had recently taken into its pay as Captain-General, so that he sent a lieutenant to represent him instead of coming in person [31]; or he could attempt to revive the trade with Rome, as a first step to a return to better relations [32]; or his distrust of warlike preparations could put obstacles in the way of the defence works of Michelangelo, whose versatility could turn with ease to the occupation of military engineer.[33] On matters of greater importance, however, he could not succeed in overcoming the opposition of his countrymen. England [34] and France [35] had both urged them to take the initial steps to placate the Pope by sending him an ambassador. In addition to this sign of honour, Clement demanded the surrender of his niece, the restitution of the family possessions, and the restoration of the Medici arms upon the churches built by Cosimo.[36] While the city was demurring about these concessions, the external situation was becoming more and more difficult. The Pope was now in a stronger and more threatening position than he had ever been before. In October he had returned to Rome, and was thus no longer an exile but an independent prince once more. With the triumph of the Imperialists in Naples, he had begun to put an end to his long period of watchful neutrality. The obduracy of the members of the league over the matters which touched him most closely was determining him upon the other side. Ever since January 1528, he had been threatening to declare for the Emperor [37]; and in April he told the English ambassador with tears that therein lay his only hope.[38] " These people wish me to make the Emperor master of Italy," he cried to the Sienese envoy, " and I shall do it." [39] From the commencement of 1529, the *rapprochement* became more and more pronounced, and every act of violence or obduracy on the part of the members of the league only served to strengthen and hasten it.

Capponi's fears were thus realized. In the event of an alliance between Pope and Emperor, Florence would stand in the most extreme peril. His policy was admittedly opportunist, based on no general principle but to secure peace. " I am neither Spanish nor French," he wrote to Carducci, " but I only wish the safety of the city" [40]; and while admitting that Florence might fear less ill from the French king than from the Emperor he doubted with good reason his reliability. " In him," he wrote, " is confirmed the passage, that the spirit is willing but the flesh is weak." [41]   The only security which he could see for the city, if it persisted in its refusal to come to some arrangement with the Pope, was to ally itself with whatever side the Pope supported. Thus and thus alone there would be some sort of surety that the hatred of Clement would not direct the military strength of his ally and overwhelm Florence. Capponi's correspondents at the papal court kept him informed of what was going on, and he was by now well aware of the imminence of the alliance. The Spanish forces in Naples were preparing to advance. " If you make up this difference with the Pope," wrote Serragli, " this army will advance upon the Venetian territory. . . . Now is the time to show yourself to be a good protector of your country." [42]

This, however, was a peril which he could not make his fellow-citizens appreciate ; and they were still obstinate in their attachment to the French alliance. Baldassare Carducci, on his way to France, and Pierfrancesco Portinari on his return from England, had been formally requested by Andrea Doria to invite the city to follow his example in changing sides. When the matter was discussed, Luigi Alamanni, the poet, lavished his eloquence on the proposal, but without any result save that of having his patriotism suspected. [43] At about the same time the Sienese, acting under instructions from the Imperialists, and possibly in order to force the Pope to disclose his hand, offered to reconcile Florence with the Emperor upon favourable conditions. Capponi pushed the matter with all the insistence in his power in the Pratica, where it was discussed for three days in succession. But his efforts were without avail, and the Soderini policy of trust in the support of France was still adhered to. [44]

Capponi was desperate at the result ; and the contemporary who thought him half-mad does not seem to exaggerate. His warnings to save his beloved city from the ruin to which he saw it drifting brought about only suspicion of himself and a growing disfavour with the public. He had come to be called " the Doge " with reference to his absolutist methods. [45] An impertinent attack had been made on him by Pierfilippo Pandolfini from the pulpit of S. Lorenzo, where he had been entrusted with the statutory harangue in honour of the Militia. [46] Worse still, nothing had come of prosecuting him together with two other members of a so-called Society of the Faithful. [47] A law was even proposed to prevent a Gonfalonier being elected for the third time. [48] This unpopularity was increased by Capponi's scruples, political as well as religious, against taxing the clergy without the Pope's consent. He could pride himself, indeed, that he had succeeded in obtaining the suspension of the edict of excommunication against the city. The citizens, however, only saw that the sparing of the clergy led to an extra burden upon themselves and an increase in ordinary taxation.[49] A graduated income-tax was introduced ; forced loans were again resorted to with increasing severity; a levy was made upon the suburbs and the contado ; and a committee was appointed to consider ways and means of raising new taxation. Human nature has strangely altered if this additional call upon the public purse, whether right or wrong, did not cost Capponi some additional popularity. He was generally distrusted and publicly criticized. He became utterly overwhelmed and weakened. His sleep was disturbed, and he found himself in consequence unable to keep awake while transacting his official duties during the day. His speech tended to become apologetic and moralizing, and he would repeat the same words three or four times over. The general impression was that of a man who had lost his spirit.[50] Away from the city there were already reports of uprising and bloodshed, with the death of the Gonfalonier's son.[51]

On 18 February, the Great Council met for the purpose of electing the new Signoria. When the ordinary business was over, Capponi rose to his feet. He was aware, he said, of what was publicly spoken of him, and wished to resign his office there and then in favour of some other person who was more trusted. A general commotion ensued. The magistrates intervened, saying that such procedure was unrecognized by law.[52] His term of office was to continue for another four months, and to resign it was equivalent to calling a Parlamento. The only constitutional practice was to consult the Pratica. The Gonfalonier's enemies asserted that this foiled attempt at resignation was the merest gesture. The known state of his mind, however, renders it probable that it was meant in all seriousness. He retained the office, making last despairing efforts to secure the object nearest to his heart.

He was however getting more and more out of sympathy with the city. It was not altogether his fault. There was a period of economic depression and of famine—" unusual penury and scarcity, which continually increase the one more than the other, so that it is a miserable and cruel thing to see and hear all day the complaints and stories of those in the city who perish from famine."[53] The usual methods of prohibiting the export of currency [54] and local remission of taxation [55] were not likely to give any substantial relief ; and a commission of five was appointed with power to deal with the destitute, sending them to hospital or requisitioning lodgings for them.[56] One of the places occupied for this purpose was the Sala del Papa, traditionally employed to receive the Pope during his visits to Florence.[57] At the same time the Signoria committed the strategic error of putting itself out of touch with the people by deciding, owing to pressure of

work, not to hear civil cases.[58]   In another direction the Pope
cut off all hopes by issuing an indulgence to the convent of the
Murate, where his niece was detained, for the absolution of all
sins, excepting that of the taxation of the clergy.   The Dieci
promptly sent to confiscate the bull, not allowing it to be published and ordering the convent to be reimbursed out of the public
funds.[59]   The flood of accusations against the Medicophiles had
virtually ceased after the spring of 1528.   Now, after the lapse
of nearly a year, it recommenced.   The new Otto tended as
frequently towards the Arrabbiati, and sent case after case to be
decided by the special tribunal as " an affair of state."   Yet
apparently the more moderate Signoria under the influence of
Capponi was powerful enough to prevail over the prejudices and
alarms of their colleagues, as the cases were referred back to the
Otto with the utmost regularity.[60]   Lucrezia Salviati was, as we
have seen, one of the closest relatives of the Pope, as well as wife
of one of the most distinguished Florentines.   Her rank and sex,
however, did not save her from prosecution.   But the Quarantia
allowed her to plead through a procurator, and her case was
virtually absolved by being referred back to the Otto.[61]   Priests
were not exempt : and three " presbyters " once connected with
the household of the Medici were brought for trial.[62]   Within
the space of a few days, one after the other of the aristocratic
leaders of the revolution were accused : Rafaello Girolami,[63]
Tommaso Soderini, Alfonso Strozzi, and Antonfrancesco degli
Albizzi.[64]   There was only one point higher at which fanaticism
could aim.

In April 1529 a new Signoria entered into office, comprising
some of Capponi's most determined opponents.   In addition to
Francesco Valori, nephew of Baccio, there was Jacopo Gherardi,
a man whose dissolute life ill accorded with his years, and who in
spite of them had become leader of the younger extremists by
reason of his ardent if jealous love for the Republic.   Entertaining
suspicions of everything, he soon made himself ridiculous by
scenting treason in a chance sketch of a man's head encircled with
a crown which he found scrawled up on one of the walls of the
Palazzo.[65]   Nevertheless he continued vigilant.   Upon the evening of Thursday, 15 April, Capponi had received a batch of letters
which he read in the audience chamber.   In the morning, shortly
after dawn, when he began his day's business, he noticed that one
was missing, and sent one of his servitors to look for it.   He found
it lying where it had been dropped, and picked it up to take back.
While doing this he was noticed by the suspicious Gherardi.   His
curiosity was aroused to know what the letter could contain, and
he succeeded in obtaining it from the servitor.[66]   Its tenor
was suspicious, but barely incriminating.   It was addressed to

Capponi from Rome by Giachonotto Serragli, though not in the invisible script which he had recently advised him to use.[67]   He deplored the loss of two preceding letters, though positive that nothing could be found in them which was not for the good and freedom of the city.   He requested an immediate note from the Gonfalonier through the medium of his son Piero.   He gave the latest news of the Pope and the Imperialists, rapidly advancing to concord.   In cipher, already decoded by Capponi, follows what was of greater importance.   He reported on the excellent progress of the negotiations with the Pope and the " Friend " for the benefit of the city ;   and he requested Capponi, if he desired to free the city from the " barbarians," to send his eldest son Piero to speak with him outside the walls—secretly, lest " seeking to do good, evil be thought,"—in confidence that this would be of avail.[68]

In this letter, Gherardi saw the opportunity for which he and others of his party had been waiting.   Secretly, he commenced preparations to make use of his discovery.   He communicated the letter to Francesco Valori, another of the Signoria whose hatred to Capponi he knew.   He sent a copy—rumour said, vitiated—to the leaders of the Arrabbiati, whom he asked to assemble in the Gild Hall of the Money Changers opposite the Palace, depicting it as blackest treason.   For the moment, however, he took no open steps, and went in to dine with his colleagues. Preoccupied with his thoughts, he turned back his sleeves more than was ordinary to wash his hands.   Capponi unsuspectingly chaffed him that he seemed to be stripping for a fight.   " Aye, for a fight with you, with the ways you are keeping," retorted the other fiercely.[69]

By now, Gherardi's friends outside were prepared and began to assemble in arms.   It was therefore possible to commence to act.   Assembling his colleagues of the Signoria, he showed them the letter.   They were sufficiently in sympathy with his view to recommend that the Pratica should be called together.   After a long session, it in its turn recommended that the question should be referred to the more numerous and representative body of the Ottanta.   Meanwhile, the whole city had been aroused.   The partisans of either side were commencing to assemble, but the Arrabbiati, who were the better prepared, were able to exclude the opposing faction from the Palazzo.   In fear of an armed rising, the militia was called out.   Capponi himself had remained cowed in his apartments, excluded from the meeting of his colleagues, whose first care was to have him and Piero, his son, put under guard.

After a night of excitement, the Ottanta met, upon the Saturday morning.   Capponi was cited to appear before it ; but,

absolutely overwhelmed by the event, he barely attempted even
to exculpate himself.   Only he tried to clear the innocence of his
son.   He was taken away and kept under guard, while the case
was being discussed.   His enemies were desirous of taking summary vengeance from him for the fate of Jacopo Alamanni ; and
unsuccessfully urged a death sentence.[70]   His friends contended
that he had done nothing deserving of serious censure.   It was
proposed that he should be put to the torture, but Tommaso
Soderini strenuously opposed himself to it, his natural kindliness
combining with a desire to conciliate Capponi's followers.   One
of the opposing faction expostulated with him privately, in the
name of the infuriated mob below.   He fearlessly retorted in a
public protest against such intimidation.   The deliberations
were prolonged and tumultuous, and daggers were drawn in the
Council Chamber itself.   During their course, the disorder outside
increased.   The supporters of Capponi, numbering many of the
noblest Florentine families, commenced in their turn to assemble
armed in several of their houses, whether in fear of attack or in
preparation for assuming the offensive.   While the fate of the
Gonfalonier was being discussed, a number of them, led by Piero
Salviati, came into the Piazza in arms with the intention of forcing
an entry into the Palazzo, to ensure, as they said, fair play.   The
temper of the people whom they found assembled was however
against them.   " If you come forward, I will be the first to break
my halbard on your head," said Lionardo Bartolini to his brother
Cerotta who led them.   The assailants were discouraged ; the
guard was put in readiness ; and the Otto sent ordering all persons
in arms to leave the Piazza upon pain of death.   Capponi's friends
withdrew, but remained in readiness.   In the disorder it had been
demanded that he himself should be hurled down from the windows.   This uproar led the Ottanta to hasten its decision.   All
were afraid that further delay would result in riot ; and Capponi's
friends dreaded for his security if the enraged populace met with
further obstacles.   They therefore commenced to acquiesce in
the proposal which had been made for his deposition, in order to
avert worse consequences.   It was ordered that on the following
day a fresh Gonfalonier should be elected, and a proclamation
was immediately made to the city to that effect.[71]

Upon the Sunday, in accordance with this decision, the Consiglio Grande met to approve of the conditions for the election of
Capponi's successor.   The recent events resulted in a series of
limitations which should prevent their recurrence.   In future,
the Gonfalonier (appointed on this occasion for eight months only)
was not to give audience to the diplomatic representatives of
foreign powers or to any other foreigner, or even to open letters
from them, excepting in the presence of the Preposto of the

Signoria or one of his colleagues ; he could not maintain private correspondence, either by envoy or in writing, with any foreign power, nor could he give instructions in his own name to any Florentine envoy. He was not to visit any quarters in the Palazzo but his own ; and the acme of suspicion was reached when it was ordered for the separate entrance to his apartments to be walled up, so that he could not hold any communication with the outside world excepting through the common lodging of the Signoria. Non-observance of any of these conditions was to be punished by the Quarantia within an interval of five years and by a fine of 1,000 florins for each offence. These provisions were carried by a majority of a little over 300 in a total attendance of 1707.[72]

The Council went on immediately to elect the Gonfalonier who was to hold office under these conditions. The result was surprising. So aroused were popular suspicions that none of the prominent aristocratic leaders who had previously disputed the post with Capponi was chosen even at the preliminary ballot. At the second, it was found that the popular choice had fallen upon Francesco, kinsman of Baldassare Carducci.

It still remained to be decided how Capponi should be proceeded against. Thinking that with the election of his successor he was set free, he had called for his mantle ; but it was ordered that he should be kept confined to the Palazzo.[73] The Signoria had favoured condign and probably capital punishment, and indeed they would have wished to administer it from the first without the co-operation of the other boards.[74] Two of their number, however, to some extent implicated with Capponi and to whom he had previously shown the letter,[75] refused to attend their meeting upon the plea of ill-health, and so prevented the necessary quorum from being attained.[76] The matter was, therefore, referred upon the Monday to a further meeting of the Ottanta. The same dispute took place between those inclined to severity and to leniency. Many of the bodies represented pleaded that he should be liberated and sent home ; but a majority advised that he should be dealt with in accordance with the law.[77] This was contained in the ordinance made at the creation of Piero Soderini, which ordered delinquencies on the part of the Gonfalonier to be dealt with by a special tribunal composed of the members of all the higher magistracies. A preliminary meeting was held the same evening, at which Capponi appeared and spoke in his justification. The main proceedings followed upon the Wednesday.

The day that intervened was occupied by a feverish canvass upon both sides. The intransigeant Arrabbiati, headed by Gherardi, continued to demand an exemplary punishment.

Francesco Carducci, however, was sobered already by the responsibilities of office, and by a natural desire to conciliate Capponi's personal following. Soderini and Strozzi, the disappointed candidates, began to regret the fall of their old rival. The more responsible statesmen feared to set an example of violence. In addition, upon more mature consideration, the letter did not seem so terrible as initial alarm may have depicted it. As a result, the temper of the tribunal was more favourable than Capponi might have expected. In the days that had elapsed his supporters had taken heart and a number of them were now present in the Palazzo to give him encouragement. One of them, in addition, had removed from among his papers all the more incriminating documents.[78] Thus strengthened, he had time to recover from his original shock and to collect his thoughts ; and he was now able to make a calm and dignified defence of his conduct. He protested the uprightness and purity of his intentions—to reunite the city, mollify the Pope, and thereby avert the dangers of an Imperialist attack ; he reproved the subtle practices of Gherardi and the tumult which he had caused. The defence, coupled with the altered spirit of the magistrates, was effective. The discussion showed that Capponi was absolved from all suspicion of treachery. " It is supreme goodness of the Gonfalonier, and no craft," [79] said Soderini, referring to the letter. Gherardi, by chance drawn as Preposto for that day,[80] rose and attempted to reply to the charge brought against him, but was forbidden by the Dieci. Then, in rage, he proposed that Capponi should be put to the torture so as to disclose his plottings, but the motion did not receive sufficient support. Next he suggested a punishment of banishment for two years, but even this was turned down. It could not, however, be denied that Capponi had carried on a correspondence with persons about the Curia in direct contravention of the express prohibition of the Pratica six months previously ; and it was feared in addition that an over-great leniency might result in a fatal outburst of popular rage. Finally, therefore, it was decided on the one hand that he should be absolved from all the suspicion into which he had fallen ; but on the other it was agreed again on Gherardi's motion that he should give bail for 30,000 florins to appear when called upon and should not leave the Florentine dominion within five years.[81]

The number of guarantors who offered themselves was so great that the formalities were delayed by the confusion. By nightfall, all were concluded, and Capponi was released. He left the Palace in private garb, but he was received with more deference than he had known when in office. A large band of his supporters waited below to do him honour, and they formed up behind him as he went to his home through the crowded streets.

So long was the train that by the time Capponi ha reached his
house the other end had not yet moved from the Piazza. It did
not take him long to accommodate himself to civic life. On the
very next day he was seen attending to his business in the Mercato
Nuovo, and justifying his conduct to his acquaintance. A week
later, to put an end to all suspicion, he yielded to the advice of
his friends and went, with his wife and a single servant, to stay at
his country villa.[82] In the Pratica of 4 May a committee was
appointed to examine those of his letters which remained in the
Palace, but nothing incriminating was to be found in them.[83] It
was not long before he commenced to regain confidence, and
though he left the Florentine dominion before the five years
were elapsed, it was on a mission for the state. Time indeed fulfilled all his apprehensions and justified all his aims. Posterity
can condemn only his methods.

NOTES TO CHAPTER V

[1] *Vita di F. Strozzi*, p. 136.
[2] Despatch of Guarini to Duke of Ferrara, *apud* Rossi, App. I; Sanuto,
XLVII, 196, 219.
[3] Nerli, p. 173.
[4] Rossi, I, 126–7; Busini, p. 44. Segni, in the *Vita di N. Capponi*,
p. 952, writing as an apologist for his uncle, pretends that this solitary
correspondence was actually authorized by the Dieci.
[5] Nerli, p. 173. Segni, however, states (*ibid.* p. 936) that it was known
to all, and approved of privately even by those who attacked him for it
in public.
[6] Signoria, CXXX, 18–19 August 1528. The first election took place
on 28 August (*ibid. ad diem*). Cf. Pitti, I, 157; Varchi, I, 486–7; Soriani,
Relazione, p. 415; Nerli, pp. 186–7.
[7] Signoria, CXXX, 28 October 1528. Segni, I, 76–80. The oration
he ascribes to Pandolfini is in verbal agreement with that preserved in
the Pandolfini Papers (British Museum, Add. MSS. 28,272).
[8] Soriani, *Relazione*, p. 425.
[9] Varchi, I, 447–50; *State Papers, Spanish*, III, ii, 564.
[10] As Soriani calls them, by the testimony of those in their employment.
[11] It is most important to observe that the militia of 1528 was *not*
a revival of Machiavelli's, which had continued an almost unbroken existence, but something quite different. See Canestrini, Introduction to
A.S.I., vol. XV, pp. cxvii–cxx.
[12] Cf. letter of the Dieci to Bartolomeo Gualterotti, ambassador at
Venice, 8 May 1528 (B.N. di F., Magl. II (ii), 147, f. 28): " Et volendosi
opporre loro (*sc.* ai lanzi) non giudichiamo bene che le fanterie Italiane
siano al proposito, ma che bisogni servirsi di genti simile a loro, et che
habbia le medesime ordinanze, et perciò giudichiamo sia necessario far
calare Svizzeri o valersi di Lanzi, li quali solo possono fare tale oppositione."
[13] Varchi, I, 451.
[14] *Ibid.* Cf. Giannotti, *Opere*, I, 133.
[15] *Vita di N. Capponi*, pp. 939–40.

[16] Cf. G. R. Sanesi, *Un Discorso Sconosciuto di Donato Giannotti, intorno alla Milizia,* in *A.S.I.,* ser. V, vol. 8 (1891), pp. 1–27.

[17] Text in *A.S.I.,* vol. XV. Cf. also *Signoria,* CXXX, 12 October 1528 (an experimental enrolment from 15 to 50) and 7 November. There were *sworn to arms* only those from 18 to 36 (*ibid.* CXXXI, 16 January 1528/9), the others being merely *enrolled.* Hence the remarkable confusion on this point among the historians.

[18] Varchi, I, p. 367.

[19] Busini, *Lettere,* p. 57. It was perhaps a suspected complicity with the Arrabbiati which explains the great alarm which Paccione's case had caused.

[20] Segni, I, 83.

[21] Rondoni, *I Giustiziati a Firenze* in *A.S.I.,* ser. V, vol. 28 (1901) ; Signoria, CXXIX, *ad diem.*

[22] *Account of L. Ginori,* written for Varchi, who has copied it almost verbally (B.N. d. F., Strozziane, filz. G.O., p. 159) ; Busini, pp. 26–7, 69 ; Segni, I, 80–83.

[23] Signoria, CXXX, 8, 9, 30 November 1528.

[24] *Ibid.* 2 December.

[25] Busini, p. 32.

[26] Varchi, I, 486 ; Nerli, p. 177.

[27] Busini, pp. 27–8.

[28] *Vita di N. Capponi,* 942 ; Rossi, I, 101.

[29] *Ibid.*

[30] *Ibid.* ; Soriani, *Relazione,* p. 415. Bryan, the English envoy, dates a letter from Florence on 9 January 1528/9 (*State Papers, Henry VIII,* VII, 229).

[31] Soriani, *Relazione,* p. 423.

[32] *Ibid.* p. 421.

[33] Symonds, *Life of Michelangelo Buonarotti,* I, 412–13.

[34] *Letters and Papers, Henry VIII,* IV, 3758.

[35] *Vita di N. Capponi,* p. 945.

[36] *Ibid.* 935.

[37] *Letters and Papers, Henry VIII,* IV, 3829.

[38] *Ibid.* 4168.

[39] Falletti, I, 208.

[40] Desjardins, *Négociations Diplomatiques de la Toscane,* II, 1026–7, and the letters which follow. As will be seen, this collection is ridiculously incomplete for the present period.

[41] *Ibid.* p. 1004.

[42] Sanesi, *ubi supra,* letter v.

[43] Donato Giannotti, *Opere,* I, 7, 127–8 ; *Vita di N. Capponi,* 946–7 ; Hauvette, pp. 73–4, dates Alamanni's intervention somewhat earlier.

[44] Falletti, I, 301–4, in Bergenroth Transcripts, IX, f. 75. (cf. *State Papers, Spanish,* III, ii, 639). According to a despatch of Doria to Charles of 3 March a secret envoy was actually sent to inquire into the possibilities of peace ; cf. also letter of Charles of 15 February in Bardi, *Carlo V e l'Assedio di Firenze, ubi supra,* p. 81. Negotiations were similarly reported to be in progress through the medium of the Bishop of Pistoia (*State Papers, Henry VIII,* VII, 190, 13 March 1528/9). It is likely enough, however, that all this was merely unofficial sounding, promoted most probably by Capponi. Alamanni cannot have left the city finally in consequence of this debate, as the historians allege, since he received a safe-conduct to go to Genoa for ten days only on 4 March 1528/9 (O.G., CCIV, f. 64)—possibly on this same business.

[45] Guarini, *apud* Rossi, App. ii.

[46] Printed in *A.S.I.*, ser. I, vol. XV.

[47] Pitti, I, 168–71. Cf. Signoria, CXXXI, 26 February, 1–5 March 1528/9; Quarantia on Pierfilippo Pandolfini, Jacopo Ringhiardori, and Battista del Bene, referred back to Otto, by whom absolved (O.G., CCIV, 93). Pandolfini was almost immediately arraigned again with Braccio Guicciardini and Dante da Castiglione (*ibid.*, f. 53, 23 February 1528/9).

[48] Pitti, I, 173.

[49] Yet apparently the clergy granted a free-will offering for charitable purposes (cf. Signoria, CXXX, 7 September and 17 October 1528, and CXXXI, 27 January 1528/9). The result, however, was for them identical. See MS. Ricordanze di S. Maria del Carmine, *ubi supra*, " Ricordo come oggi questo dì 29 di novembre 1528 ragunati tutti e' frati cap° convento considerando nostra grandissima necessità come paghare al commune di firenze per resto dello accatto di questo anno."

[50] Letter of Guarini of 6 March 1528/9 (Rossi, App. II).

[51] Micer Mai to Charles, 6 March 1528/9 (*State Papers, Spanish*, III, ii, 643).

[52] Varchi, I, 487–8; *Vita di N. Capponi*, 950–1; Sanuto, XLIX, 504; MS. diary in Magl. XXV, 555, f. 23.
". . . E' gonfalonieri non volorono che si ci mettansi quell partito, perchè dicevano che se si vincenva che fusi rinfatto chonfaloniere che gli era chome a uno parlanmentto, e che se luj non voleva esere più chonfaloniere, che si fanciesi pranticha. . . ."

[53] Signoria, CXXXI, 27 February 1528/9. Cf. Cambi, IV, 35–6.

[54] Signoria, CXXXI, 20 February 1528/9.

[55] *Ibid.* 1 March.

[56] *Ibid.* 27 February.

[57] Varchi, I, 474; II, 103.

[58] Signoria, CXXXI, 1 March.

[59] Letter of Soriani of April 5 1528 in Sanuto, L, 137.

[60] An exception was the condemnation of Giuliano Strozzi, but though his lineage may have had something to do with the accusation, it was for moral crimes ('de neglecta religione de statu homicidio & sogdomia') that he was punished and exiled (Signoria, CXXXI, 4 February 1528/9).

[61] O.G., CCIV, 10, 29, 47, 57–8; Signoria, CXXXI, 26 February, 4, 8, 17 March. The details of this charge, as of the following, are lacking.

[62] ". . . Aliam contra S. Johannembattistam iam magistratum paggiorum ducis Laurentij et postea cappellaneum yppolitj quando erat florentie & contra Jacopum fratrem dicti S. Joh. bap[te] & S. Gherardum capellaneum in ecclesia S[te] Marie de Ughis." In the *Extractio Quarantie* (*ibid.*, 10th Id.) the last named is referred to as " S. Gherardum Giuchatore di palla " —a strange and unpriestly profession! The case was referred back to the Otto on the 24th Id.

[63] *Ibid.* 17th Id. ("notificationem . . . repertam in eorum tamburis ") and 21st; referred back on 24th.

[64] *Ibid.* 24, 28 March (when Michelangelo Buonarotti was drawn to serve on the Quarantia for the Nove) 1, 3 April (Acquittal), O.G., CCIV, 59, 75, 87–8. It is possible however that the Gonfalonier's finger was in this pie. An injunction ordering him to evacuate a house to Filippo Pugliesa was obtained at about this time against Francesco Guicciardini (O.G. *ibid.* ff. 53–6–8), who had been refused permission to leave the city to join the Pope (Sanuto, XLVII, 613; Rossi, I, 132–3).

[65] *Vita di N. Capponi*, 945–6.

[66] It seems impossible to believe, in spite of the authority of Niccolò Carducci, son of Francesco, that Gherardi picked up the letter the evening before, spent all night making exaggerated copies of it to rouse his friends,

and replaced it in the morning, or in the even more Machiavellian operations reported by Segni (*Vita*, 956–7).   The latter asserts (*ibid.* 957–8)
that the letter was not kept secret by Capponi, who showed it to a couple
of his colleagues.

⁶⁷ Cf. letter in *A.S.I.*, ser. I ; App. VII, p. 261.

⁶⁸ See text from official copy in Signoria, CXXXI, *ad diem* in *A.S.I.*,
ibid., and in Falletti, I, 232–3.   Varchi's version (I, 498–9) is sufficiently
faithful, and seems to be taken from the official abstract sent to
ambassadors.   The version of Capponi's apologists—Giovio, II, 109,
approved by Segni, *Vita*, p. 955, and followed by other historians, is
infinitely more incriminating.   One wonders whether this form was set in
circulation by Capponi's opponents to justify his deposition.

⁶⁹ Busini, pp. 45–6 ; Nerli, 179–80.

⁷⁰ Only one vote was cast for it, according to the anonymous author
of the MS. diary in Magl. XXX, 555, *ubi supra*—that of Francesco Bramanti.

⁷¹ For these events, cf. especially the records of the Signoria, CXXXI,
for these days and the identical official despatches to ambassadors abroad
in Dieci, Missive XLVI, of 23 April, 1529 (cf. that to Gualterotti at
Venice in Sanuto, XL).   See, also, besides the usual authorities hereafter
cited, the letter of R. Girolami in *A.S.I.*, *ubi supra*, pp. 256–8.

⁷² Provisioni, CCVIII, f. 5–6 (18 April 1529).   Cf. Arzilotti, *op.
cit.* pp. 75–6, and letter of R. Girolami, *ubi supra*.

⁷³ *Vita di N. Capponi*, p. 961.

⁷⁴ *Scrittura di N. Carducci*, in *A.S.I.*, *ubi supra*, 262–5.

⁷⁵ The letter of R. Girolami, *ubi supra*, bears out on this point the
Vita di N. Capponi, p. 956, where it is added that the two to whom the
letter was shown advised the Gonfalonier to tear it up.

⁷⁶ Cf. Signoria, CXXXI, 20 April 1529: " Commissio fabe unius ex-
dominis "—i.e. appointment of proxy—for Giovanni Bramanti.   This
explains the quiescence of the Signoria on the previous day.

⁷⁷ Abstract of Pratica of 19 April 1529 in *A.S.I.*, *ubi supra*, p. 265.

⁷⁸ Not *all*, as some remained to be examined by order of the Pratica
of 4 May.   They had been sequestered on 20 April (Signoria, CXXXI,
ad diem).

⁷⁹ Sanesi, *ubi supra*.

⁸⁰ Signoria, CXXXI, *ad diem*.

⁸¹ *Ibid.*   The general story of the deposition of Capponi is told, with
the inevitable contradictions, by Varchi, I, 498–524 ; Cambi, IV, 40–4 ;
Giovio, II, 108–14 ; *Vita di Niccolò Capponi*, 956–63 ; Nerli, 179–82 ;
Busini, Letter VI, pp. 42–50, etc.   The above is an attempt at a consistent
account in accordance with the records of the Signoria *ad dies*.

⁸² *Vita di N. Capponi*, p. 964 ; *Ragguaglio di Baccio Carnesecchi*,
ubi supra.

⁸³ Pratiche, *ad diem* (see *infra*, cap. VI, *n.* 17 and 100).

CHAPTER VI

THE GATHERING OF THE STORM

THE new Gonfalonier was of a type altogether different from his predecessor. He had come into prominence only since the revolution of 1527, and even so largely through the magic of the name of his more distinguished kinsman. He first gave proof of his political ability in a mission to Siena, on his return from which he had been elected to some of the higher and more responsible magistracies.[1] Nevertheless, his sudden rise to power, and the preference shown to him rather than to his better-known rivals, came as a general surprise; and it is hardly to be doubted that he owed his election largely to the absence in France of Baldassare, whose party supported him wholeheartedly. His victory signified the eclipse of the great magnates, connected with the Medici by marriage and interest, who dominated Florentine society and commerce, and their supersession by something more approaching a true democracy. He himself was of lowly parentage and had always been occupied in trade, mostly in a subordinate capacity. Rumour or malice added that when he set up on his own account he had twice become bankrupt. The basis of this report apparently was that the great commercial house of the Nasi had failed during the period he was acting as its representative in Spain.[2] In any case this was not the reproach in sixteenth-century Florence that it might have been in another place and age; and his very antecedents secured him the enthusiastic support of the lower classes, amply compensating for the disdain of the aristocrats, who forgot that it was precisely against themselves that the office of Gonfalonier had been originally instituted. Pallid and wild-eyed, a fiery speaker without pretence to elegance, he was physically almost the type of the revolutionary leader. He had in addition a fixity of purpose and firmness of character which give his career and administration a consistency and nobility lacking in the rather pathetic figure of his predecessor.[3]

The circumstances of his personality and election made his policy to a certain extent a reaction. Capponi had set himself to narrow and restrict the constitution; Carducci commenced to enlarge it. Thus, for example, the Consulta, which had tended under the former regime to be a small body merely endorsing the decisions of the Gonfalonier, was now thrown open to members of all the magistracies, to the detriment of efficiency as well as of secrecy. In other spheres of government a similar policy obtained, and ruder opinions and actions began to prevail.[4] The reaction from Capponi's moderate principles led to a change in the composition of the magistracies. Republican extremists were almost invariably elected ; and the names of popular families became increasingly frequent in the public records.[5] The Palleschi, whose hope of reconciliation was now gone, were said to cast their votes cynically for the worst candidates.[6]

Carducci himself, however, was sobered by the responsibilities of office. Already in the delicate task of settling the affairs of his predecessor he had shown signs of this ; and in returning thanks before the Great Council for his election he spoke with the utmost moderation, and promised to shed his old animosities with his old costume. Critics suggested that already he was commencing to sacrifice his principles and to conciliate his opponents in the hope of securing re-election when his eight months should be at an end.[7] Certain much-needed reforms, however, could be carried by a general consensus of opinion. The *Specchio* or " looking-glass " of the Commune, in which were inscribed the names of those in arrears with their taxation, and thus ineligible for office, was taken from the hands of corrupt or corruptible notaries and given in charge of a commission of private citizens.[8] A further board was appointed to suppress the evasion of taxes on property once held by religious or charitable bodies, but now alienated.[9] Another important measure of a slightly later date co-ordinated and regulated the rules for the election and conduct of ambassadors. In this the most interesting innovation was the appointment in each case of an under-ambassador, who should at the same time gain experience of the conduct of affairs and provide a check upon his principal.[10]

The fall of Capponi, however, could not be an isolated event. The suspicions which had caused it and which had in turn been fostered by it continued to manifest themselves. The younger citizens were still encouraged to come at all hours of the day to defend the Palazzo against the eventualities which might still arise.[11] Assemblies of more than ten persons, excepting for religious purposes, were prohibited.[12] The Bishop of Balnei was tried for " thinking of nothing but to restore the family of the Medici into the city of Florence," and for having conspired with the Pope through the medium of the Eremite Friars of Camaldoli.[13] A humble brother of S. Marco was committed to prison for having asserted that if Clement came to Florence the present

state could not continue.[14]   Alamanno de' Pazzi was accused of
saying that Florence would not have rest until there was a man
at the head of affairs like the one who had just been driven out
of the Palazzo.[15]   Antonio Brucioli, in the old days friend and
fellow-conspirator of Luigi Alamanni, was exiled for having used
in a letter written to France words derogatory to the present
government.[16]   A plot on behalf of the Medici was thought to
have been discovered among Florentine citizens living at Venice.[17]
Alessandro de' Pazzi, head of one of the most wealthy Florentine
houses, who had a lawsuit on at Rome with the Cardinal Cibo
over some Florentine affair, was repeatedly refused permission
to leave the city for fear of some ulterior motive.[18]   It was twice
proposed to declare Jacopo Salviati a " rubello " and to confiscate his goods for the manner in which he was working for the
Pope and, therefore, against the city.[19]

But above all the spirit of alarm showed itself in military
preparations.   It was feared now more than ever that the Pope
intended a *coup de main* : and there could be no doubt that he
would attempt one willingly had he the forces at his disposal.
There was, however, an army at large in Italy, the movements
of which were raising the greatest apprehensions throughout the
whole peninsula.   Ever since the disaster at Naples, the Florentines had been speculating nervously upon the intentions of the
Imperial forces which the scattered embers still smouldering in
Apulia were insufficient to retain.   Since the autumn, rumours
had been current on all sides to the effect that Orange was pro-
posing to march upon Florence, the nearest active member of
the league, in conjunction with the Pope or otherwise.[20]   The
fall of Amatrice in particular, laying open the road to the north,
had increased these fears and had been followed by active military
preparations—the solicitation of allied aid, the collection of
money, the hiring of mercenaries, and the concentration of
troops at Cortona and Arezzo.[21]   With the accession to power
of Carducci, the preparations were intensified, and a new tax of
general incidence was levied for the purpose of defraying the
cost of new fortifications.[22]   But above all it was necessary to
secure an efficient military force and a reliable commander.   Don
Ercole, son of the Duke of Ferrara, had received some time previously the bâton of Captain-General of the forces of the Republic.
But the lukewarmness of his father, seconded by the reluctance
of Capponi to become even more closely allied with the Pope's
most bitter enemy, had made the appointment remain almost
nominal ; and the Republic's alarmed summons for his presence
had been unanswered.[23]   In any case, Ercole was too young to
take command in person ; and it was necessary to look round
for some more effective if less ornamental general.

The Baglione family had been connected with Florence as stipendiaries for some considerable time. It was a house typical of the worst aspects of the Italian renaissance.[24] Men of great culture, appreciating the arts and patronizing Raphael and Perugino : endowed as an hereditary trait with an heroic beauty : they combined with all this an utter absence of morality which shocked even the age of the Borgias. They had risen to power during the fifteenth century as the dominating family in their native city of Perugia ; but internecine strife had prevented their rule from developing in anything like a normal fashion. Hardly a member of the family survived middle age if he reached it ; few died in their beds ; and the majority met their deaths at the hands of their own kinsmen, later to be slain in their turn. The climax came in 1500 with the Great Betrayal and its avenging, which almost wiped out the family, and left sway in the hands of the well-known condottiere, Giampaolo Baglione.[25] At this period Perugia came into the pathway of the extending power of the Borgias, and the Baglioni were brought into collision with the successive holders of the Papacy. Giampaolo, after escaping the massacre of Senigallia, was forced to abandon his city. Returning on the death of Alexander VI, he had to submit to Julius II, regained power at the close of his pontificate, and was finally lured to execution at Rome by Leo X. He left two sons, Orazio and Malatesta, both of whom followed the family tradition in their choice of profession as well as in their morality and methods. On the death of Leo they returned to their native place, until the accession to the Papal throne of Clement, who re-established papal influence. Malatesta, the elder brother, went to fight in Lombardy in the pay of the Venetians : Orazio, the intimate of Benvenuto Cellini, was imprisoned in the Castle of S. Angelo until on the approach of the Imperial armies the Pope did homage to his military abilities by releasing him to defend Rome. After the sack he returned to Perugia, where he made a solemn oath of peace with his cousin of the elder branch, Gentile, ex-Bishop of Orvieto, who had been governing for the Pope. In little more than six weeks, Orazio had him murdered with his two nephews. A short time afterwards, he completed his vengeance by assassinating with his own hands his cousin Galeotto.[26] Such actions, however, were not an adverse consideration in the career of a condottiere, especially when his anti-papal prejudices were shared by his employers ; and Orazio's reputation did not prevent him from being appointed by the Florentines to the command of the Bande Nere. During the Neapolitan campaign he was mortally wounded.[27] Shortly before his death, however, his brother Malatesta had suddenly returned from Lombardy to exercise the family influence in his

native place.[28] It was natural for the mind of the Florentines
to turn to him in this juncture. His family had been connected
with Florence since the commencement of the century. In an
age deficient in military talent, he had a name as condottiere
second to none in Italy. He could provide in his dependency a
useful alliance, too strong to be neglected and sufficiently weak
to be safe. His branch of the family was traditionally in deadly
enmity with the Pope, who even now was supporting and encouraging his cousins Braccio and Sforza Baglione in their claims
on Perugia.[29] He himself had recently shown his attachment
to his family policy by attempting to murder the bearer of a
papal brief which appointed Ippolito de' Medici papal legate in
his city, and by soliciting and receiving Florentine support.[30]
His fidelity therefore seemed assured. Above all, with him in
their service, the Florentines would have a very strong outpost
to the south, newly put into a state of defence and garrisoned
by faithful allies,[31] which might be expected to keep the war
away from their own territories. It was natural, therefore, that
for some considerable time an attempt had been made to get
him into the Florentine employ.[32] There were, however, serious
obstacles in the path. The Duke of Ferrara objected to his son
being assigned such an overshadowing second in command.[33]
Baglione on his side resented the idea of being put in nominal
subordination to another. In addition, he insisted, for his own
security and dignity, that he should receive his commission in
part from France. Above all, Clement, who was fully aware of
the negotiations, put forward all the difficulties and counter-
attractions which lay in his power, and for some time succeeded
in postponing a conclusion. When Baglione, as a subject of
the Holy See, applied for formal consent to the proposed arrangement, he attempted to dissuade him, alleging an existing contract of the previous year with himself. Malatesta replied that
this had been for twelve months only, already at an end, and
with option to withdraw ; and he begged permission to carry on
with the arrangement, professing that it might at some time
serve the Pope in good stead. Clement, however, continued
to demur. Finally on 18 April he issued an edict prohibiting
any subject of the papal states, in which Perugia was included,
from taking foreign service without authorization ; and this was
followed a few days later by a further personal remonstrance.[34]
Already, however, on 15 April, Malatesta had been unanimously
elected by the Dieci as " Governor-General of all the Florentine
forces, horse and foot "—a rank subordinate to that of Captain-
General—subject to the approval of the King of France. On the
next day it was confirmed by the Ottanta, and on the 20th by
Malatesta—of the approval of Francis there was not much

doubt.[35] The " Condotta " was to last for one year from 1 June 1529, at a salary of 2,000 gold florins, with 100 ducats monthly for the retention of ten captains. The commander was to have immediate command of 1,000 foot, with 2,000 more on behalf of the King of France in time of war. Minor commands were given to his son and nephew in spite of their being too young to exercise them in person. In addition, the Florentines took him under their protection and were bound to succour him in case of attack.[36]

About this same time, the city took into its pay another sworn enemy of the Pope. Napoleone Orsini belonged to one of the greatest and most turbulent of Roman houses, and having among his possessions the Abbey of Farfa was usually called by the title of " Abbate." [37] His ecclesiastical appellation notwith-standing, he had adopted the career of condottiere, and even for that was considered " marvellously unreliable and of bad faith." He had once suffered imprisonment for a plot to kill the Pope ; and on the evacuation of Rome by the Imperialists he had avenged himself by submitting it without pity to the horrors of a second sack at the hands of the riff-raff of the various armies. More recently he had recovered, in the teeth of the rival family of the Colonna, the castles of his house occupied by Clement, and was still infesting the Campagna. It was not calculated to propitiate the Pope that this ecclesiastical bandit was taken into their pay by the Florentines as one of their principal cap-tains at the head of a thousand men.[38]

For some time past Clement had been inclining towards an agreement with the Imperialists ; and as early as February, Charles had written him a most conciliatory personal letter.[39] The desultory warfare kept up by the few remaining French forces in Italy gave him no cause to change his mind ; and the obduracy of Ferrara and Venice in refusing to disgorge their spoils did not increase his benevolence towards the league. It was reported, and it was not unlikely, that definite arrangements for his inclusion had been prevented through the obstinacy of the Florentines.[40] In the midst of this there came the news, exaggerated in the transmission,[41] of the fall of Capponi, with the ruin of any possibility of arriving at some sort of pacific agreement and accentuated by an increased bitterness against his house. This virtually determined the question. " I have persuaded myself, and have been assured by Salviati a thousand times, that the Pope would never join the Emperor," wrote a correspondent to Wolsey in reporting these events. " Now, I should not be surprised if he did, for the persecution of his rela-tives and friends will be a great incitement to him. The French ought to prevail upon the Florentines to restrain themselves." [42]

Affairs were in this condition when there arrived the news of the crowning insult, the engagement of Farfa and of Malatesta Baglione in spite of his express prohibition. The Pope's anger knew no bounds. He professed to believe that the Florentines wished to take him prisoner to their city, and that commissaries had already been appointed to govern the states of the Church. He told the English envoys with tears in his eyes that he would avenge this boldness, and that he would rather serve in the Emperor's stable than endure any longer the insults of his subjects and vassals. Finally he exclaimed that he was not God but man, and would use every means, force or fraud, to defend his own and to recover what he had lost.[43]

By the time that this indignant outburst took place the die was already cast. On 7 May the Pope had sent Charles an autograph letter of thanks ; two days later the Bishop of Vaison left Rome for Spain with further marks of his favour and a commission to come to an arrangement ; and on 29 June a solemn treaty of alliance was concluded at Barcelona. Charles, to whom the friendship of the Pope was essential to safeguard his interests in Northern Europe, as well as to secure his position in Italy, conceded to his vanquished but still powerful foe almost all of his demands. The fatal article was the ninth clause. The Emperor expressed his regret at the exclusion of the Pope's kinsmen from their native city at his hour of stress, and undertook to use all of his resources to restore them to the state which they had previously enjoyed. At the same time a match was arranged between the lay representative of the exiled house, Alessandro de' Medici, and Margaret, the Emperor's natural daughter. This formed the guarantee that the arrangement would be carried out, and indicated very clearly the object in view. The Pope solemnly ratified the treaty on 24 July ; and on 1 August he assisted in person at the Te Deum at St. Peter's upon the conclusion of peace.[44]

While the fate of Florence was thus being decided in Spain, matters were rapidly becoming more threatening nearer home. Hitherto the alarms of war had been at a distance. The city could afford to reply with diplomatic evasions to the Venetian requests for help in an enterprise in Lombardy or elsewhere : or to the French suggestion to assist the Sienese exiles against their native place. It could send almost negligible aid in the shape of bales of cloth to Renzo da Ceri, who was still making some headway on behalf of the league in Apulia, or solicit French aid on his behalf. It could attempt, in conjunction with Venice and France, to seduce a number of lanzknechts away from the Imperial service in Southern Italy.[45] But from the end of May

more immediate alarms arose. The restless cousins of Malatesta Baglione were supposed to be preparing an attack under
the auspices of Siena, and a concentration for that purpose was
reported at Norcia, which might be the prelude to a general war.
At the same time preparations were reported on the other flank
at Bologna and in the Romagna. Counter-preparations were
made by the city. It was unanimously agreed that Malatesta
should be given the help which he asked to keep operations from
the border.[46] Wood was brought in as material of war ; fresh
taxes were proposed and payments authorized for the construction of fortifications ; S. Gimignano was reinforced according to its request ; and demands for assistance to the French
and Venetians were reiterated.[47] Special precautions were
taken for the guarding of the Palazzo.[48] On 24 June, instead of
the customary races in honour of the patron of the city—the
Palio di S. Giovanni—a review of the new militia was held on
the fields of Ognissanti.[49] As if to point the moral, on the previous
day arrived the news of the overwhelming victory of Da Leyva
over St. Pol, in command of the last considerable body of French
troops in Italy, at Landriano, which made Charles master of
Lombardy and freed his forces under Orange from all diversion.[50]
The war clouds were rapidly gathering about Florence ; and it
was necessary to make all preparations before the storm should
burst.

This had already been commenced in a manner peculiarly
Florentine. The fall of Capponi had been in effect the reiteration of the original principles of the revolution in their extremer
forms. It is natural therefore to find accompanying the political
movement a fresh outburst of that religious feeling which was
one of the most typical if most paradoxical phenomena in Florentine life from S. Giovanni Gualberto onwards. It goes far to
prove the essential orthodoxy of the Tuscan spirit that even at
this moment, when the opposition to the Pope was so extreme
and so outspoken, there was never the slightest movement in the
direction of Reform. Any disrespect to the Catholic faith was
ruthlessly punished. The conviction of Antonio Brucioli was
perhaps due more to his audacious opinions in matters of religion
and attacks upon the excessive influence of the priesthood than
to his political views.[51] It was followed by an unusual number
of condemnations for moral crimes and blasphemy.[52] The
miraculous picture of the Virgin was again brought from
Impruneta into the city and there exposed, " considering the
perils which overhang all Italy, of famine, pest, and war." [53]
But the climax came after the receipt of the news of Landriano
and the imminent peril of war. On 25 June one of the most
typical of all Florentine measures was passed through the Great

Council, its clauses coming in a continual crescendo. The penalties for blasphemy and murder were restated and increased. The citizens were enjoined to pardon one another for all injuries received until that day. Finally, Jesus Christ was solemnly reaffirmed King of Florence. " It was right and proper that, on 26 June 1529, there should have been present in the Hall of the Great Council the spirit of Savonarola, the unintimidated and uncorrupted counsellor of the democracy. That day there seemed to be enacted one of those scenes so frequent during the apostolate of the Friar ; for Christ alone was desired as Lord and King . . . and before the majesty of so great and noble a sovereign should fail all partisan angers, all class hatreds, personal ambitions and malicious instincts. . . . The thought of the people goes back to the teachings of its unhappy martyr, and the hope that religious sentiment would fulfil the miracle which no other force could bring about illuminates these last moments of the Republic."[54] There were some citizens who raised objections to a proposal fitted, as they said, only for a monastery, and who wished to vote on the proposals separately ; but they were overruled. Two days later, registers were laid open upon the altar of the Sala dei Cinquecento, in which every citizen appended his signature to a solemn oath of fealty to Christ and to the popular regime. It was the acme of the Theocracy.[55]

The feeling against the Pope, however, continued to increase almost in proportion to the growth in religious sentiment. Neither side went out of its way to show the sightest tact ; and there ensued a dispute which might in a less orthodox atmosphere well have led to a religious rupture. The Pope's conciliatory attitude in the matter of ecclesiastical taxation during Capponi's administration had been without result ; and he now determined to show a stiffer front. He prohibited the clergy of Florence from making any payments to the civil authorities, and at the same time imposed upon them a tax of two " tenths " for his own purposes, to be paid under penalty of excommunication and deprivation. The person to whom the brief was sent, knowing the temper of the city, did not have the courage to publish it ; but proceedings could still have been taken in secret. This, however, was not the Pope's intention. One morning Castrocaro, the capital of the Florentine Romagna and near the Papal states, awoke to find that a proclamation to the same effect had been affixed to the city gates. Florence was stirred to defiance by the discovery. It was determined that in the event of the culprit being found, he should be hanged without trial. So that the pain of excommunication should not be incurred, the tax indicated was to be raised ; but it was to be paid into the public treasury on account of what the Medici were alleged to owe to the city. It was thus that any whispers of mediation were met.[56]

The foreign situation was meanwhile becoming more and more threatening. On 12 July the news of the match arranged between Alessandro and Margaret reached the city, and the menace which it implied was immediately understood. Reports of a *rapprochement* between the Pope and Siena concealed another threat.[57] Rumours began to trickle through of an agreement between France and the Emperor, in which the city could not be sure that its interests would be considered.[58] Finally on 16 July became known the news of the Treaty of Barcelona and the imminent embarkation of Charles for Italy. The information caused general consternation, as well it might.[59] The Pratica, hurriedly called together with the Ottanta, was unanimous in making the recommendation—common in these and the following days—that recourse should be made to God.[60] The French and Venetians were insistently pressed to convert their promises into deeds, and to give help instead of demanding it.[61] To oppose the forces which might be expected to march on Florence—Orange's army of 12,000 with what the Pope could raise—an attempt was made to get a similar number in the pay of the city, and captains of the Bande Nere were sent to raise men.[62] The fortresses of the dominion were put into a state of defence. Preparations began to be made against a siege ; fortifications were pressed on ; and the custody of the Palazzo was again revised.[63]

In France, too, the news of the Treaty of Barcelona made an immediate impression. Hitherto Francis had fluctuated irregularly between one policy and another : yet he had consistently promised to make no peace without consulting the fullest interests of his Italian allies ; and he was continually bringing forward far-reaching plans of campaign for which their aid was solicited—attacking the Emperor in Spain, or leading in person a great army into Italy. Capponi had doubted his sincerity ; but Florence, in spite of warnings from every direction, persisted in believing in the honesty of his intentions.[64] His kingdom, however, was worn out by a series of expensive wars and was incapable of sustaining further burdens. Of his allies, England was distant and lukewarm as ever, and the definite defection of the Pope virtually settled the course of events in Italy. There was a powerful peace party at the French court, headed by the Queen Mother, Louisa of Savoy. For some time past she had been in communication with the aunt of the Emperor, Margaret of Austria. These negotiations became gradually more decisive ; and early in July the two women came together at Cambrai. In the face of this, Florence was compelled to abandon its uncompromising attitude and signified its willingness to be included in the peace even at the price of some money payment. Bartolommeo Cavalcanti, who had been sent to France to strengthen Carducci's hands in the event of a treaty, went to Cambrai to watch events on behalf of the city.[65] Francis, however, had concealed the negotiations from the knowledge of his allies as long as he could, and when that was no longer possible sedulously dissembled their nature. Up to the commencement of July he declared repeatedly that he would sacrifice his own life and his children's in order to save the other members of the league, and swore that Florence would be included in any peace which might be made. His queen spoke to the same effect; and the Admiral, Anne de Montmorency, affirmed that if any agreement were made without safeguarding Florence, they might call him a traitor.[66] Carducci allowed himself to be duped, and contradicted the less optimistic reports of his better-informed colleague. He had sent home for a mandate empowering him to treat for inclusion in a general peace, which he was given to understand would be easy on condition of a money payment; and his request was granted on the understanding that " the sum should be small and the time long."[67] Yet to get back his sons, as his mother herself declared, Francis would have sacrificed a thousand Florences,[68] and the whole thing had been a deceit. On 3 August he again affirmed that nothing would be determined without the Florentines' assent.[69] Two days later, the " Ladies' Peace " (as it was called after its authors) had been concluded.

The Treaty of Cambrai was for Francis anything but a triumph. Excepting that he secured on the whole the integrity of his territories, it was a mere recapitulation of the Treaty of Madrid. As an indemnity for the war and for the ransom of his sons he was to pay two million crowns. He had to promise that henceforth he would abstain from all interference in Italian and German affairs; he was to renounce all his rights in Italy, to surrender the places in it still under his control, and to withdraw all his troops from the Peninsula within six months. His Italian allies were left at the Emperor's mercy, and he pledged himself to do all in his power to make them come to an agreement—i.e. to capitulate—within four months. It was under these conditions that he bartered away his honour. For some days, it is said, he avoided the Italians about his court and was heard to cry out in his mental anguish, " I wanted to have back my sons ! "[70]

The city was informed of its abandonment in a despairing letter from Baldassare Carducci. Italy was sacrificed, he wrote, to the desire of recovering the French princes ; and nothing was left but to come to terms with the Emperor.[71]   Though not unexpected, it was the bitterest news which could have been received.   It was upon France that Florence had throughout relied blindly, for her sake that she had neglected the opportunities of a separate agreement, and through her therefore that she found herself in her present quandary of having to face the combined attack of her powerful opponents alone.   There was only one avenue of escape.   Abandoned by her friends, she could only hope to mollify her enemies.

After the recent events, there could be small hope in approaching the Pope, the more so now that his expectations had been sharpened by the arrangements made at Barcelona.   Nevertheless, it was not too late to adjust matters.   The expedition against the city was not irrevocable.   Even after the Treaty of Barcelona, the Emperor in a despatch to the Prince of Orange had envisaged a monetary accommodation with Florence.[72]   At the Papal curia, too, Clement's most influential advisers, all Florentines—Salviati, Ruberto Pucci, and Sanga—were aghast at the idea of turning against their native city an ill-disciplined army composed of so many different nationalities.[73]   Other obstacles   stood   in   the   way   before   the   expedition   could   be commenced—financial, political, and sentimental ; and while events were maturing at Cambrai, it might easily have been averted before it was too late.   However, this last chance was deliberately thrown away.   The Cardinal Salviati, Papal envoy in France, had amicably suggested to the Florentine representatives some mutual association for the common good in the forthcoming treaty ; but his sincerity was questioned, and his advances brusquely rejected.[74]   In Italy, the closest connection was maintained with Malatesta Baglione and Napoleone Orsini, who had recently performed a characteristic exploit in kidnapping some Franciscan friars.   The Florentines had just sent him the sum of 3,000 ducats for the recruiting of troops.   This had been intercepted and withheld on behalf of the Pope ; but the " Abbatino " was not long in avenging himself.   The Cardinal of Santa Croce, going to greet the Emperor at Genoa, was set upon in the woods in the neighbourhood of Viterbo, and held to ransom until the intercepted sum was repaid.[75]   The Florentines on their side disclaimed responsibility but would not interfere.   This was one of the deepest humiliations which the Pope could have suffered ; and his intense resentment may be imagined.   He had recently been again extremely ill, and the Florentines had been accused of poisoning him.   The accusation was the product of an embittered brain ; but his enemies did nothing to make it seem improbable.[76]

Meanwhile, Florence's opportunity was passing.   Directly after the conclusion of the Treaty of Barcelona, Lewis de Praet, one of Charles' confidential advisers and plenipotentiary at the treaty, was sent to Rome to procure its ratification and execution.   He became immediately a champion of the clause directed against Florence, which he saw to be the best method of retaining the friendship of Clement, in addition, as he thought, to acquiring reputation, gaining money, and setting an example to the rest of Italy.   His support resolved any hesitation which the Pope might still have felt, and confirmed the Emperor in his decision. He continually pointed out the justice of the cause and the inevitability of the course which was being pursued.   Though he did not minimize the resistance which might conceivably be offered, he was of the opinion that in all probability a firm front would result in immediate capitulation.   His reports to Charles were filled with encouragements to persevere in the enterprise and even to lead it in person.[77]

The final decision, however, still lay with the Emperor himself, the central figure of the whole of Europe.   For a long time his movements had been nervously discussed in Italy, and an approaching visit had been rumoured ever since February.[78] With the passage of time these reports had become more and more insistent, and it seemed that Charles was awaiting only the calmer weather of spring.[79]   His coming could only mean that Italy would become the scene of events of the first magnitude ; but in what direction ?   Some thought that he was going direct to Naples to unite his fresh forces with Orange's veterans and to give the final blow to the hopes of the league in the south ; others, that his real objective was Flanders and Germany, and that he intended to suppress Lutheranism, drive out the Turk, and only then turn his attention to Italy from the north ; others, that the whole rumour was a false one deliberately raised in order to terrify the Italian powers and detach them from France.[80] The danger to Florence was recognized ; but there it was optimistically hoped, under the encouragements of the vaticinations of a popular oracle, that the Emperor would never leave Spain, and that even if he did his difficulties would prove too great for him to have energy to spare in that direction.[81]   As the reports gained strength, the French king promised his assistance and asked for co-operation to oppose him personally.[82]   Finally Luigi Alamanni, the patriot poet who was living with Andrea Doria at Genoa, wrote of the thing as a certainty, and at the suggestion of his patron asked permission to go over to Spain with him to meet the Emperor in the name of the city.   The Pratica hesitated to comply for fear of appearing unfaithful to the league and to France, whose fickleness was not yet become apparent ; yet they did not wish to refuse, so as not to seem lacking in respect for the Emperor. It was resolved accordingly to cut the Gordian knot by not replying at all—on the understanding that in such event he would go ! [83]   The poet, however, repeated his request insistently ; and finally he was ordered to return to Florence for a consultation. A special courier made the journey to Genoa in the record time of twenty-six hours ; but whether by design or by accident, he arrived too late. On 9 June, just before day-break, Alamanni had left on his irregular mission. [84]   Neverthe-less, without any official authority, his presence in Spain was useless. He could only keep the home government informed from time to time of the momentous events which were going on in Barcelona ; and without waiting for the actual departure of Charles he returned to Genoa. [85]

With the approach of the visit, however, and the gathering of the storm, the Ghibelline, or pro-Imperial, party among the citizens had again begun to gather strength, and a change of attitude commenced to be discussed. [86]   Tommaso Soderini him-self, who had effectively opposed Niccolò Capponi upon this same question of policy, changed his opinions. On 30 June, when doubts as to the French attitude first arose, he broached in the Pratica the idea of sending an envoy to the Emperor ; and the proposal was favoured by the Dieci. [87]   On 13 July, when definite news of the negotiations at Cambrai arrived, he returned to the charge ; but his colleagues, still confident in their French allies, rejected the suggestion, and were content to employ the ever-willing medium of Luigi Alamanni merely to give information as to the Emperor's movements. [88]   But every day reports became more threatening, till real consternation was caused in the city. [89] On 18 July, certain information as to the approaching voyage of the Emperor was at last received. On the following morning the Pratica was summoned, and after a general debate it was adjourned till the evening of the same day. Antonfrancesco degli Albizzi came back with a long prepared oration in which he closely argued every aspect of the situation. He spoke of the hopelessness of a struggle with the Empire, pointed out the virtual unpreparedness of the city, and insisted that it was suicidal to enter into war if their liberty would be respected without. It was determined, however, to wait for more precise information from France. [90]   Yet if the proposal that Charles should be treated as an enemy was brought forward, it was rejected with virtual unanimity. [91]   A week later, the question of sending ambassadors was again brought up, but still no decision was arrived at in spite of the increasing indications of the default of the French and the growing indications that little faith could be placed in the remaining allies. [92]   A trusted authority in the city wrote, apparently by request, a recommendation as to the conduct which should be adopted with regard to Charles, attempting to show how the city had always favoured the Emperor, and strongly advising the delegation of an embassy.[93] On 7 August, news was received from Alamanni that the Emperor was expected in two days' time. An immediate decision was now necessary; but still—for the news of Cambrai was not yet known—it was not desired to raise suspicion in the mind of the allies, in view of the opposition which the orators of France, Ferrara and Venice had shown. The Gonfalonier accordingly proposed in guarded terms that ambassadors should be sent to welcome the Emperor, " as has always been the custom of the city."[94] The proposal was generally approved; and letters were sent explaining and justifying this procedure to the other members of the league.[95] Nevertheless, there was no hurry to carry the resolution into practice; and all that was done immediately was to appoint Alamanni to act as envoy until the arrival of the delegation.[96]

On 12 August the Emperor landed at Genoa, accompanied by a stately retinue of Spanish grandees and a powerful following of troops. Two days previously Alamanni had approached him at Savona, congratulating him on his coming on behalf of the city and intimating the appointment of the embassy, for which a safe conduct was requested. At the same time he asked that the expedition directed against Florence should be ordered to suspend operations and postpone entry into its territories. Charles did not reply until he had communicated with the papal nuncio. Finally he sent word that the embassy might come without fear, but indicated that, as far as Orange went, he must await more exact information. A " great personage "—probably the Chancellor Gattinara—added in a private colloquy that the army was acting on behalf of the Pope and could not be interfered with.[97] In the meanwhile, the arrangements for the despatch of the embassy were only slowly being determined in Florence. On the morrow of the Emperor's disembarkation, spurred on by Alamanni's information and the insistent reports from France, the Dieci decided upon its instructions. Still, however, matters were not pressed on with the requisite speed. The Bishop of Tarbes had just arrived in the city on a mission from Francis, and insisted that they should await more detailed accounts of the proceedings at Cambrai, the reports of which he did not believe; and he undertook to persuade the Pope to suspend the advance of the armies. Not quite convinced, but not wishing to reject the possibility, the Pratica suggested the compromise of despatching the embassy, but instructing it to take as long over the journey as possible. It was held, however, that "all practices with the Pope, whoever be the mediator, only serve to waste time."[98]   On the next day, therefore, the instructions and *personnel* of the embassy were decided, though it did not set out. The expected information from France did not arrive ; and on 17 August it was ultimately determined that the embassy should leave.[99]   Its most prominent member was none other than Niccolò Capponi, the ex-Gonfalonier. His reputation had already been in part rehabilitated by his trial ; and a commission appointed to examine his correspondence had failed to discover anything to incriminate him.[100]   The recent proofs of his insight into foreign affairs had assisted him to recover from his temporary eclipse : and already in July he had been summoned again to the meetings of the Pratica, where he had expressed his opinions in the old strain.[101]   His colleagues were Tommaso Soderini, Matteo Strozzi, and Rafaello Girolami.[102]

These protracted delays had done the city much harm, and barely had the delegation left than it was definitely ascertained that the apprehensions of the past days had been well founded. The Italian powers had been abandoned by their French ally, and had no hope left excepting in the benevolence of the Emperor.[103]   The ambassadors arrived at Genoa only on 23 August—not indeed latest of the Italian delegations, but near it. Even the sympathetic Andrea Doria rated them for their foolhardy delay. He had reason. By this time there was already present the papal commission of welcome, which had been escorted with some ceremony and much suspicion through the Florentine territories. It brought him the tale how one of its members, a Spaniard, had been waylaid by the Abbot of Farfa ; it included—ominous selection—Ippolito de' Medici, raised to the Cardinalate at a low ebb in the Pope's political fortunes ; and it was accompanied by his cousin Alessandro, come to make the acquaintance of his intended father-in-law.[104] Finally, in reply to Charles's report of his transactions with Alamanni, an additional envoy had been sent after them to urge him not to receive the embassy at all. Under their combined influence, the Emperor determined to entrust all negotiations to his Grand Chancellor. It was all that Doria could do, at Alamanni's request, to induce him to accord a preliminary interview on the day following their arrival.[105]   They were admitted to audience in the embarrassing presence of the papal envoy. Soderini with all humility exposed their mission in Latin : and he was followed by Girolami in Spanish, which he had learned while on a mission to the court of Charles some years previously on behalf of the Medici.[106]   They commenced by formally congratulating him on his coming, and justifying the course of conduct which the city had previously pursued.   They commended its cause to his clemency and justice, accentuating the invariable good faith for which (they said) Florence had always been noted, and promising its fullest co-operation in the Imperial mission " to put all Christendom at peace."   Yet they protested against the papal designs upon their liberty, attempting to show that Charles's worst enemy was Clement himself, and begging finally that the advance of the Imperial forces should be arrested.   In return for this concession and for an amicable agreement, the city was ready and willing to pay.   Only it refused to receive the Pope or anybody on his behalf, though prepared to restore the Medici to the full enjoyment of their possessions ; and it insisted that the integrity of its territories should be respected.[107]   Some days before, these representations might have been accepted. But in the meantime the news had arrived of the signing of peace at Cambrai, and there was no longer the slightest reason to conciliate a minor power.   Acting always in close consultation with the papal nuncio, Charles replied firmly, though in a not unfriendly tone, that he could have nothing to do with them until they showed honour to the Pope his ally : and he told them to send home for a mandate to treat for an agreement with him, for which he offered his own services as mediator.   The Grand Chancellor was even more uncompromising in his reply in a subsequent interview—he was even then expecting a Cardinal's hat—asserting that by the help Florence had given in Lautrec's expedition it had forfeited its privileges and even its independence. Nothing was left for the envoys but to follow the Emperor's recommendation.[108]

Even in this, however, there was difficulty.   The embassy itself was chosen—perhaps deliberately—from conflicting elements.   Capponi wrote home private letters to the effect that the sole hope of the city lay in coming to terms, even the worst of which need not survive the lifetime of the Pope ; and the aristocratic Matteo Strozzi agreed with him.   Soderini and Girolami, on the other hand, still had faith in the allies of Cognac and in the diversions with which the Emperor would be faced elsewhere. Anxious, too, to impress all with the independence and resources of the Republic, they kept splendid table and open hospitality at Genoa, in contrast to their colleagues (it was recounted that the parsimonious Strozzi kept his wine in his bed-chamber). The four could never be in agreement in the writing of despatches, and by the terms of the new regulations for ambassadors, they might not write separately.   Nevertheless, by dint of the tears and entreaties of Capponi, the Emperor's wishes were conveyed to Florence where, in the meantime, definite news of the Treaty of Barcelona had arrived.[109]   On the motion of Antonfrancesco degli Albizzi, it was determined, almost unanimously, to accord the envoys the full powers for which they asked. They were instructed, however, to make no concession on point of principle, and they were authorized to treat only through the medium of the Emperor, all direct negotiations with the Pope being prohibited.[110]

By the time that this second mandate arrived, the Emperor had left Genoa on his way for Piacenza (30 August). Before his departure, he sent for the envoys and reiterated his encouragement to the city to come to terms and thus save itself from the fate of Rome.[111] On the arrival of their instructions, accordingly, Rafaello Girolami and Luigi Alamanni were sent post-haste after him to explain how matters stood. In spite of their insistent pleadings, Charles refused to carry the matter further under such conditions as were proposed. In consultation as always with the Nuncio, he said that immediately the city authorized them to treat with the Pope, and to allow him to re-enter into his old rights, he was willing to open negotiations ; and so as to save them time and trouble, the Prince of Orange might act in such an event on his behalf. Without such authority, however, he would do nothing with them and there was no purpose in their remaining.[112] The two returned to Genoa and reported to their colleagues the hopelessness of their mission and implacability of the Emperor. Nevertheless, hoping that this might be after all a pretence, the ambassadors determined to follow him together to Piacenza, leaving Alamanni behind to act as agent at Genoa. With them went an envoy of Malatesta Baglione to see that his master's interests should not be neglected. Arrived near the city, they sent to Charles to inform him of their coming. The Pope, whose delight at the Emperor's attitude was changed to alarm by the reception of the embassy at Genoa, had despatched a further emissary in protest.[113] On this occasion, therefore, Charles left the matter to the Nuncio, whose reply was a foregone conclusion. They were told that nothing could be done without reinstating the Pope, with whom and the Prince of Orange all negotiations must be carried on : and they were refused permission to enter the city.[114] They went on together to Modena, but here the embassy broke up. Girolami posted home to Florence, where immediately on his arrival he went booted and spurred and covered with the dust of the road into the presence of the Signoria, speaking contemptuously about the forces of the Emperor and urging them to prepare for resistance without fear or doubt. Soderini, more timidly, delayed at Lucca under the pretext of being ill ; whilst Strozzi ultimately made his way to Venice. He rode, however, the first part of the homeward journey with Niccolò Capponi. Arrived at Castelnuovo da

Garfagnana, report says that they were met by Michelangelo Buonarotti, flying in a sudden panic from Florence, who informed them of the imminent peril of the city.   Capponi's intense commotion, added to his exertions in travelling in the height of summer, brought on a violent fever ; and eight days later he died, crying, " To what a pass have we brought this unhappy country ! " (18 October 1529).   He had lived just long enough to see what he had dreaded come to pass.[115]

NOTES TO CHAPTER VI

[1] Busini, *Lettere*, pp. 16, 17.

[2] Varchi, I, 504–5.   A later witticism said that it was natural for the Republic to fail when put into the charge of a bankrupt.   This was reported by Giovio and Segni in all seriousness.   See *Errori di Paolo Giovio*, p. 119, and Gentile, *op. cit.* pp. 56–7.

[3] Paolo Giovio, II, 109 ; Varchi, I, 525.   " A mad, scandalous and wretched creature " (loco, escandoloso, y mal fortunato) was the verdict of the Spanish ambassador at Rome (*State Papers, Spanish*, IV (i), 5).

[4] *Vita di N. Capponi*, p. 565 ; Giannotti, *Della Repubblica Fiorentina* in *Opere*, I, 123.   Nerli, p. 187, attempts to show how some of the party opposed to Carducci were irregularly excluded from the Consulta.

[5] Anzilotti, *op. cit.* p. 75.

[6] *Vita di N. Capponi, ubi supra.*

[7] *Ibid.* p. 961 ; Busini, p. 50 ; Varchi, I, 525–8.

[8] *Ibid.* p. 529.

[9] *Ibid.* p. 530.

[10] The text of this *Costituzione per gli ambasciadori* of 23 July 1529 is printed by Falletti, *op. cit.* I, 58–66 *f.n.*

[11] Signoria, CXXXI, f. 69 (24 April), " Pro cittadini e Giovanni che vennono al Palazzo."

[12] O.G., CCV, f. 2 (2 May).

[13] The more responsible Quarantia, however, did not accept the charge as an affair of state (Signoria, *ibid.*, ff. 77–8 (3 May), 91–2 (10 May)) ; and he was in consequence absolved by the Otto (O.G., CCV, ff. 15–16, 15 May).

[14] Though the Quarantia, as before, did not proceed in the matter (Signoria, *ibid.*, f. 72, 27 April), he was punished by the Otto (O.G., *ibid.* f. 6, 7 May).

[15] The accusation was proved false (O.G., *ibid.* f. 38, 9 May) ; but it illustrates the temper of the population.   Nerli, p. 190, asserts that it was instigated, with other charges, by the Gonfalonier himself.   His testimony is, however, biased in the extreme.

[16] Varchi, I, 530–4.   Cf. letter of Marcantonio Cartolaio of 29 May 1529, in *Carte Strozziane, Inventario*, I, 368.

[17] Consulte e Pratiche (*R. Archivio di Stato di Firenze*), LXXI, 3 May 1529.   This volume, which with the succeeding is the only one which exists for our period, was saved by the Bishop of Assisi from the fate which overtook a large part of the archives of the last Republic.   On the flyleaf we read : " Relationi della Pratica : questo libro si è tenuto secreto e tiene per me Agnolo Marsi vescovo di Ascesi per non dare materia di

offentione ad chi haveva in quel tempo consigliato con diffamationj et iniuriosi improprerii come si costuma di chi si è aquietato et adherito allo stato et governo della Illma et felicissima casa de S^ri Medici che a nostro S^re Dio usque ad finem seculi piaccia conservarla."

[18] *Ibid.* 4, 6, 10 May.

[19] *Lettere alla Repubblica di Venezia del Cav : Carlo Capello, apud* Albèri, *L'Assedio di Firenze illustrato con inediti documenti* (Firenze, 1840), letter 12.

[20] Letter to Santes of 8 September 1528, in Dieci, Missive, XLV. . . . "Et vi sono anchora nuove benchè non certe come il principe d'oranges già si trovava in Roma, et si è sparsa voce che vengono per rimettere i medici in Firenze, di che anchora sene vede qualche altra dimostrazione. . . ." Cf. also Sanuto, *Diarii*, XLIX, 68, 505 (14 Oct., 24 Feb.); and L, 10 (24–5 Feb.); report of Salimbene of 22 September 1528 in Falletti, *op. cit.* I, 226; and *Letters and Papers, Henry VIII, u.s., n.* 5344, 5380 (3–15 March).

[21] Dieci, Missive, XLVI, to Gualterotti at Venice, 27 February 1528/9. Cf. *ibid.*, to Pandolfini at Ferrara, 21–2 February; and to Martelli with St. Pol, *idem*; and Sanuto, *ubi supra*, p. 38 (2 March). Friendly intercourse still continued, however, with Orange; cf. recommendation for Bernardo da Sommaio of 1 May 1529, in Signoria, Carteggio, Missive Registri, 1º Canc., LVIII.

[22] Pratiche, *ibid.* 3 June; Varchi, I, 530.

[23] Soriano, *Relazione*, p. 425.

[24] Cf. William Heywood, *A History of Perugia*, London, 1910.

[25] See J. A. Symonds' amazing description in his essay " Perugia," in *Sketches in Italy and Greece.*

[26] Cf. Varchi, I, 272–7.

[27] *Ibid.* and pp. 246, 289.

[28] *Ibid.* 284. For Malatesta Baglione see the biography by G. B. Vermiglioli, *Vita e imprese militari di Malatesta IV Baglioni*, Perugia, 1839. The favourable, not to say fulsome, tone of this work caused an exaggerated commotion among the violent passions of the Risorgimento.

[29] Varchi, I, 435.

[30] Pastor, X, 51.

[31] Varchi, I, 434–5.

[32] Dieci, Missive, XLVI. Letter to G. Pandolfini, Orator at Ferrara of 21 February 1528/9. ". . . Noi siamo in stretta Pratica con Malatesta Baglione che esso si conduca alli stipendij del Christianissimo. Ma desidera da noi il titolo di Governatore Generale delle nostre genti. . . ." Cf. Varchi, I, 304.

[33] Cf. Pratiche, *ibid.* 3 May. (Item III) . . . " Questa condotta non quadrar molto al Duce e a Do' Hercole. . . ."

[34] Cf. letter of 2 May in *Lettere de Principi*, II, 158; and Capello, letter 12.

[35] For these negotiations, see Falletti, I, 97–8; Pastor, X, 54; and Varchi, I, 492–4. The Pratica of 3 May resolved to disregard the Duke of Ferrara's protest, as " more fruit may be expected from an expert and practised Governor, as is Malatesta Baglione, than from a young and inexpert Captain " (Pratiche, *ad diem*).

[36] Text in Vermiglioli, App. XII; and substance in Falletti, I, 95–6. The French confirmation, in spite of the papal attitude, was not withheld, and the Order of St. Michael was even promised to the condottiere, though it never arrived. Capello, letter 20; Guicciardini, *Storia d' Italia*, IV, 222.

[37] Frequently by its diminutive " Abbatino."

[38] Pastor, IX, 367 ; Varchi, I, 98–9, 329, 431–2 ; Capello, letter 3 ; cf. *State Papers, Spanish*, IV (i), 5 (Mai to Charles, 11 May 1529). He had offered his services to Florence as early as the preceding March ; see despatch to B. Carducci of 8 March in Dieci, Missive, XLVI.

[39] Pastor, X, 49.

[40] Varchi, I, 323–4.

[41] *Ibid.* pp. 523–4.

[42] *Letters and Papers, Henry VIII*, IV, 5478 (21 April). Cf. also *ibid.* No. 5640.

[43] *Ibid.* No. 5676 (Casale and Vannes to Wolsey, 13 June). Cf. also Dieci, Missive, XLVI, to R. Girolami, 31 May, and Capello, letter 19.

[44] Pastor, X, 55–6. The text of the treaty may be found in Lunig, IV, 240, and Dumont, IV, 2, 1–7. The "Articuli matrimoniales inter nepotis Ponteficis et filiam naturalem Caesaris " (23 June 1529) are to be found in Bergenroth Transcripts, IX, f. 373 ; and Margaret's legitimization of a few days later, *ibid.* f. 386.

[45] Cf. the earlier letters of Carlo Capello and the Pratiche for the month of May *passim.*

[46] Pratiche, *ibid.* 6, 14, 31 May (when alarm first manifests itself), 21 June. Capello, letters 19, 20. There had been rumours in the latter direction for some time past. See *ibid.* No. 3.

[47] Pratiche, 31 May (2nd Meeting) and 3 June ; Capello, *ibid.* ; Signoria, *ibid.* ff. 111–15.

[48] Signoria, *ibid.* ff. 127, 153.

[49] *Ibid.* p. 98. See description from a letter in the Carte Strozziane, cited by Falletti, I, 347: 2,800 youths in uniform, with twelve pieces of artillery, paraded at Sta. Maria Novella and marched through the town to the Piazza, thence to the Oltr' Arno, where there was a discharge of arquebuses, and so to a mock fight on the Prato. There was one serious casualty.

[50] For the battle of Landriano, see de Leva, *Storia Documentata di Carlo V*, II, 517–20. The news, *pace* Varchi (I, 536) arrived in Florence on 23 June. Cf. Pratiche *ad diem* and letters of that date in Dieci, *Missive*, XLVI.

[51] *Vide supra.*

[52] Cf. O.G., CCV, ff. 77–8, 94, 98–9, etc. ; Varchi, I, 534.

[53] Pratiche, 9 May. "Item andando el tempo sinistro per le ricolte, pensassimo se fusse da fare venir la tavola della Impruneta o farla andare supra li monti." The decision was in favour of the former (Signoria, *ibid.*, f. 81 (10 May)).

[54] Caggese, II, 505–6. For text cf. Provisioni, v. CCVIII, ff. 24 *seqq.*

[55] Varchi, I, 543–4 ; Pitti, I, 183–4 ; Nerli, 189. Anonymous diary *apud* Lupo Gentile, *ubi supra.*

[56] Capello, letter 15. Pratiche, 4, 6, 16 June. Cf. Ricordanze di S. Maria del Carmine, XX (*R. Archivio di Stato di Firenze*). "Ricordo come questo oggi dì 3° dagosto 1529 pagano alli officiali della decima . . ."

[57] Dieci, Missive, XLVII, 12 July, to B. Carducci.

[58] Pratiche, *ibid.* 13 July.

[59] Dieci, *ibid.* 18 July, to B. Carducci.

[60] Pratiche, *ad diem.*

[61] Dieci, *ibid.* and Sanuto, LI, *passim*, for the second half of July.

[62] Dieci, *ibid.* 28 July.

[63] Cf. the usual authorities almost daily for the latter part of the month—Capello, letter 19 *seqq.* ; despatches of the Dieci ; deliberations of the Signoria ; and reports of the Pratiche.

[64] See despatches of Carducci in Desjardins, *Négociations Diplomatiques de la Toscane*, II, and the replies to him in Dieci, Missive, XLVI, 5 May, etc. Cf. also Pratiche of 3 May *seqq.* and Capello, letters 6, 10 *seqq.* For the relations between Florence and France, see Falletti, I, 249–62.

[65] See his instructions of 25 June in Dieci, Missive, XLVII.

[66] Cf. despatches of Carducci of 23 to 26 June, 9, 10, and 22 July, in Desjardins, II, 1064 *seq.*, 1078 *seqq.*, 1081 *seq.* ; and report in Capello, letter 10.

[67] Pratiche, 13 July ; Dieci, Missive, XLVI, to Carducci, 22 July ; Capello, letter 13 ; Nerli, p. 186 ; Segni, II, 173.

[68] Varchi, II, 27.

[69] Despatch of Carducci in Desjardins, II, 1098 *seqq.*

[70] Michelet *apud* Falletti, I, 258. Text of the treaty in Rymer, *Acta Publica*, VI (ii), 135. For the preliminaries see Lavisse, *Histoire de France*, V (ii), 61 *seqq.*, and authorities there cited. Even Charles himself condemned Francis's conduct. " I wish," he said at a later date to the Ferraran envoy, " to have regard for my allies and not to act like the Most Christian King." Perrens, *Histoire de Florence*, III, 216–7, naturally attempts to palliate his conduct. Bartolommeo Cavalcanti, the Florentine vice-ambassador, was among those who were refused an audience by the shame-stricken monarch on the pretext that he was out hunting. See his despatch of 19 August to Carducci in Desjardins, II, p. 1111.

[71] Desjardins, II, 1102 *seqq.*

[72] Bardi, *Carlo V e l'Assedio di Firenze*, pp. 26–7.

[73] Pastor, X, 64 ; Varchi, II, 49.

[74] Pratiche, 27 June ; Nerli, *Commentarij*, p. 186.

[75] Pastor, X, 64–6 ; *Letters and Papers, ibid.* 5841, and *State Papers, Spanish, ibid.* 106, 121, 134 ; Capello, letters 39, 41. The Florentines excused themselves to the Emperor through Alamanni. See Hauvette, *op. cit.*, App. III, 8.

[76] Varchi, II, 42. Falletti, I, 315–16, judges from the known symptoms that the complaint was not due to the poisoning alleged by Clement's friends nor to the disease suggested by his enemies, but to an intermittent rheumatic fever.

[77] See Bardi, *ubi supra*, section (ii), " Missione di Luigi di Praet a Roma."

[78] *Ibid.* p. 22 *seqq.* Pastor, X, 43. The visit had been determined upon since the debacle of the expedition of Lautrec in the previous year.

[79] Cf. Bardi, p. 28 ; letter of Orange of 28 April. " . . . Toute la chrétienté était informée de son allée en Italie . . ." Cf. also Capello, letter 3 *seqq.*

[80] Falletti, I, 23–5. Cf. Capello, letters 14, 15.

[81] Cf. *State Papers, Spanish*, IV (ii), 651 ; Capello, letters 6, 15, etc. ; Varchi, II, 19 ; Nerli, p. 188 ; Segni, I, 163.

[82] Pratiche, 3 May.

[83] Pratiche, 9 May ; Busini, pp. 34–5 ; Hauvette, pp. 76–7 ; Capello, letter 7.

[84] Busini, p. 69, and Hauvette, p. 77 (with documentation in App. III, No. 5) ; Capello, I, 13, 15. Segni's and Varchi's accounts of the movements of Luigi Alamanni are misleading to a degree.

[85] Hauvette, p. 78, and documentation.

[86] Pratiche, 13 June ; Capello, letters 17, 19 ; Nerli, p. 188.

[87] Pratiche, *ad diem* ; Dieci, Missive, XLVII, 3 July (to Carducci). Later, however, Soderini changed his mind again about treating with the enemy ; and it is on record that on one occasion he spoke for two

hours against it. (Capello, letter 33.   Cf. Nerli, p. 188, and Pratiche, *passim*.)

[88] Pratiche, *ad diem* (not 14 July, as Falletti (I, p. 360) says) ; and Capello, letter 17.   Paolo Giovio, II, 115, asserts that Carducci withheld or altered the despatches of his kinsman from France so as to foster the determination for defence.   This, improbable in itself, is contradicted even by the papal pensioner, Cosimo Bartolini, the litterateur.   See study on him by Mancini in *A.S.I.*, Ser. V, v. 38, p. 130.

[89] Paolo Paoli, p. clxxxvi.

[90] Pratiche, *ad diem*.   The speech of Albizzi, which is analysed by Falletti, I, pp. 55–7, enjoys the unique distinction of being preserved in full in a fair copy, together with the report of the discussion.   It earned him apparently the ridicule of his colleagues, especially of Soderini (Nerli, pp. 187–8).   Cf. also Capello, letter 31, and letter of Praet in Bardi, p. 45.

[91] *State Papers, Spanish*, IV (ii), 106.

[92] Pratiche, 27 July.

[93] *Monitorio di Anonimo alla Signoria per la venuta dell' Esercito di Carlo V*, in Rastrelli, I, 128–37.   The tone and circumstances, though not the style, would make one inclined to ascribe it to Giannotti.

[94] Pratiche, *ad diem*. Cf. Capello, letter 38 *seqq.*, for his efforts to prevent this, with the other ambassadors at Florence.

[95] Sanuto, LI, 307–8.

[96] See Hauvette, p. 79 and App. III, Doc. 7, of 10 August. Cf. also Signoria, Carteggio M.R. (58) and M.M. (21) under the date of 7 August : " Carolo Imperatori, die VII eiusdem.   Gloriosiss[e] ac Ser[me] Imperator et Rex Pater ac Benefactor noster singularissime.   Quanta sit nostra erga Ser[mam] ac Ces[am] M[tem] V. devotio atque observantia simul ac nonnulla alia, exponet nostro nomine latius Aloysius Alamannus civis noster optimus nobilis ac sua   virtute cariss[us] .   Precamur sereniss[am] M[tem] V[am] ne dedignetur integram suis verbis fidem ac Civit[em] nostram sui nominis observantissimam commendatam habere."

[97] See letter of Charles to ambassadors at Rome of 14 August in *State Papers, Spanish*, IV (i), 110, and his letter to Orange of same date in Robert, II, 183. See also Hauvette, *ubi supra*, and Capello, letter 39.

[98] Pratiche, 15 August. Cf. Capello, letter 40. From the trend of the discussion it seems very probable that the ulterior motive of Tarbes was to get possession on behalf of Francis of the " Duchessina " —his kinswoman through her mother, the unfortunate Madeleine de la Tour d'Auvergne, Duchess of Urbino. He had long shown his interest in this valuable pawn of international politics, whom he had not wished to remain in Florence for fear, among other things, that the Pope might dispose of her against his will (Desjardins, II, 1044, 1068). He had succeeded in addition in getting her monthly allowance increased from 30 to 40 ducats monthly (Pratiche, 4 May 1529, and Signoria, CXXXI, f. 96, 10 June) ; and on the success of this had requested her surrender to him " to marry her in France " (Pratiche, 3 July). The Florentine government, however, while rebutting accusations of ill-treatment (Dieci, Missive, XLII, to Santes, 19 August 1527), professing their obedience to Francis in the matter (*ibid.* 23 November 1527 : ". . . Quanto alla figlia, la città per questo appartiene allei, e disposta di fare tutto quello che è l'intentione del X[mo] . . ."), and even professing to prefer that she should be sent to France rather than surrendered to the Pope, as they heard that the Viscomte de Turenne, the French envoy, was to request (*ibid.*, Missive, XLV, to L. Martelli, 24 and 25 September 1528), finally

determined to keep the valuable hostage in their own hands (*ibid*. XLVII, to B. Carducci, 3 July : " . . . Quanto alla Duchessina, noi guidichamo che e' non sia male haverla nella terra nostra . . ."). All this is of interest when it is remembered what figure Catherine de Médicis plays in French history.

[99] Pratiche, *ad diem*.

[100] *Ibid.* 3 May, 10 June.   From Busini, pp. 48–9, it appears, however, that Lorenzo Berardi had removed at least the incriminating letters already.

[101] Capello, letter 31 ; Pratiche, 15 August.

[102] See in Signoria, Carteggio, Missive, Registri, LVIII, their credentials to Charles, dated 16 August, with recommendations to Andrea Doria, the Grand Chancellor, the Lucchese (through whose territory they were to pass) and others.

[103] Pratiche, 20 August.

[104] Varchi, II, 47.   The other member of the delegation was the Cardinal Farnese, later Pope as Paul III.

[105] Bardi, p. 44 *seqq*. ; Hauvette, p. 80 *seqq*., and Appendices.

[106] *Vita di N. Capponi*, pp. 973–4.

[107] The test of these instructions of 16 August from the Liber Legationum ad Esteros, *n*. 100, is printed in full by Desjardins, II, 1119 *seqq*., and in part by Falletti, 363–66.

[108] See letters of Emperor to Orange of 31 August in Robert, II, *n*. 187 ; Bardi, 52–3 ; and of 30 August to Empress in Bergenroth Transcripts, VIII, 93 (passed over in *State Papers, Spanish*, IV (i), 126). (*Cypher*) " Tambien llegaron los quatro embaxadores de florencia y auorque su embaxada es querer venir a nuestro servicio, porque en todo se ha de guardarlo que con Su S^d tengo asentado y capitulado tratarsea con ellos con intervencion y voluntad de Su S^d . . ."   Cf. also Varchi, II, 36–7.

[109] Busini, p. 76 *seq*. ;   *Vita di N. Capponi*, 973–5 ;   and Segni, I, 173–5 (where he gives the tenor of a letter of Capponi's to Lorenzo Strozzi) ; Nerli, 191 ; Capello, letters 41, 44.

[110] Pratiche, 29 August ; Capello, letter 44 ; Capponi, II, p. 210, prints part of these instructions.

[111] See despatch of envoys to Florence of 30 August, in Rastrelli, I, 138–40.

[112] See letters of Charles to Orange of 5 September in Rober., II, *n*. 190, and to Gattinara in Appendix of Documents, No. 7, and the despatch of the ambassadors of 3 September in Rastrelli, I, 141–50.   That to Gattinara should be dated 2 September instead of 2 August—a date impossible through internal evidence, especially as information of 27 August is cited (cf. Gayangos' note in *State Papers, Spanish*, IV (i), 130, where he says, however, that the letter is in Spanish, instead of French).   It is noteworthy that Charles mentions only Alamanni, with whom alone he apparently treated.   Cf. also Pratica of 7 September.   Capello's statement (letter 46) that, on the receipt of this information, the Ottanta sent instructing their representatives to conclude peace under any conditions without reservation, is certainly based on mere rumour.

[113] Bardi, pp. 41–4.

[114] See their despatch of 13 September *apud* Rastrelli, I, 156–64, and that of the Sienese orators at Piacenza of 6 September in Falletti, I, 368. The despatches of the ambassadors make their movements plain.   The contemporary historians (e.g. Varchi, II, 37–9) confusing this with the previous errand of Alamanni and Girolami, state that only some of them went on to Piacenza.

[115] *Vita di N. Capponi*, pp. 979–80 ; Busini, p. 105 ; Nerli, p. 196 ; Nardi, p. 211 ; Giovio, II, 120–1 ; Varchi, II, 38 (the reading of the older editions, *Lucca* instead of *Pisa* for Soderini's halting-place, is borne out by the official records. See below, p. 205). Cf. also Strozzi, *Vite*, p. xxiv. Capello, letter 58, postscript, confirms Varchi's date for the demise of Capponi (18 October), as against Segni's.

CHAPTER VII

THE OPENING OF THE CAMPAIGN

PHILIBERT DE CHALON, Prince of Orange, was at this time in his twenty-seventh year. The tiny principality from which he took his title was a curious survival of the old Middle Kingdom wedged in between the Pope's territories of the Comtat Venaissin and France proper. Like the Constable of Bourbon, he had been deliberately alienated by the foolhardy tactlessness of Francis I, who had designs on his territories, and was imprisoned by him on attempting to leave the country. Released after the Treaty of Madrid, he made his way to join his fellow-sufferer Bourbon, in command of the Imperial forces in Italy, from whom he received the charge of the advance guard and light horse. On the death of the other at the sack of Rome, he succeeded him in the supreme command, conducted the operations against the Pope, and became, in spite of his youth, Captain-General of the Imperial forces. In the campaign of Naples, he had the credit for the debacle of Lautrec, though disease had played in it a greater part than defeat ; and he succeeded Ugo da Moncada, who died of the plague, in the additional post of Viceroy of Naples. He was tall, fair-haired and blue-eyed ; but his appearance was marred by a scar on the left cheek, the result of an arquebus shot from the Castle of S. Angelo. He was of extreme irascibility, " raging like the great devil," wrote one who had reason to experience his anger ; but his character was pleasant excepting for this and for an incurable love of gaming. As a military commander he was efficient but without genius. It was to this man, raised by a series of lucky chances to be representative of the Emperor in Italy and commander of his forces, that it fell to conduct the campaign against Florence.[1]

The expedition was, by the time of the arrival of the Emperor, a foregone conclusion. Even before leaving Spain, he had sent ordering his commander-in-chief to put himself at the disposal of the Pope ; and on his delay, due to personal reasons, sent a special envoy to hasten him.[2] " Florence is of much importance," reported the ambassador at Rome, " both for its situation and for the money which it can, and did, contribute in time of war ; and therefore it seems necessary not only to detach it from the enemy but also to gain it over to the devotion of Your Majesty." [3]

With the Spaniards installed in Naples and Lombardy and dominant in the papal states the possession or friendship of Florence was essential to safeguard the line of communications. So much was this so that the Imperial Master of the Posts had recently made application to establish his couriers and transmit letters free from examination on Florentine territory; for, as the Emperor's agents were continually complaining, their mails were regularly intercepted and opened.[4] Even to this reasonable request, objections had been raised, and the fact can only have served to point the moral.[5] " The position of Florence," wrote the Venetian envoy, "is of the utmost importance; for, with Caesar commanding the roads through Tuscany and drawing funds from the city, Venice would be in the utmost peril." It would mean the undisputed command of the whole peninsula by the Spanish.[6]

Above all, it was from the financial point of view that the enterprise made appeal. We can to-day see that the decline of Florence had set in; but in that age it was still the proverbial centre of wealth, which could satisfy without difficulty any demand made upon it. " If the army had left Rome with the proper celerity," Moncada had written two years previously, " he (the Emperor) would be master of all Tuscany and would have settled the affairs of Florence, *where he would have found money to pay the army*, and would be marching on the Venetian territories."[7] " The first thing that the Prince of Orange would tell him on his arrival," wrote de Praet, " *especially if he did not oblige the Florentines to compound*, would be to have money to pay the troops."[8] With a treasury as invariably empty as the Spanish, with generals as regularly penurious, and with forces as perennially unpaid, no further attraction was needed; and the more they floundered in the slough of financial despond, the more longingly they looked upon the glittering prize which would resolve all their difficulties. The rank and file, promising themselves another sack like that of Rome, needed nothing more to stimulate their cupidity; and the assurance that the Florentines would not dare to withstand them and in any case could be overcome without difficulty, whetted their appetites.

Accordingly, it had been envisaged for some time, even before the transactions which led up to the Treaty of Barcelona, that the Prince of Orange should reduce Florence to the obedience of the Pope; or, if the expected agreement did not substantiate, that he should exact some sum of money from the city—two or three hundred thousand ducats is the amount mentioned— leaving its liberty untouched and even protected. Better still, he should persuade it to receive an Imperial garrison like Siena. But Clement's unquestioning acceptance put an end to all doubts;

and the accord which was being arrived at in France, isolating the Italian powers, rendered a policy of moderation all the more improbable. Leaving Giovanni d' Urbina as his lieutenant in the south, Orange pressed on with a nucleus of 1,500 men to Rome, where he made his entry at the end of July.[9]

Everything pointed to an immediate advance on Perugia, which all interests combined to recommend. As early as March, before the accord with Clement had become a reality, Orange had been meditating an attack upon his own account.[10] To military policy was now added the animosity of the Pope and the pretensions of the exiled Baglioni ; and above all the fact that Perugia had become the outward bastion for the defence of Florence. In June, Charles expressed his approval of the Pope's determination to chastise Malatesta, as well as to refuse compromise with Florence.[11] In this enterprise, Florence was herself immediately concerned both for her own sake and by the terms of her agreement ; though this, until the arrival of its ratification by Francis, was not yet legally binding. The condottiere's fears had become aroused during May by the activities of his cousins and by the suspicious movements of the lanzknechts upon his borders ; and he had continually solicited help from his employers. This they professed themselves ready to give, but, fearing that these preparations were a feint to distract their attention from the real direction of the attack, they contented themselves with asking help from their allies, putting their border fortresses in a state of preparation, and sending a couple of hundred soldiers as reinforcement. Hoping against hope for peace, they refused to acquiesce in their condottiere's more adventurous plan of a combined attack to be delivered before the enemy had time to concentrate. Meanwhile rumours came through insistently of preparations for war west and south, of agreement between Emperor and Pope, of the equivocal attitude of France. Again it was decided in general terms to succour Malatesta, but again and again his suggestions for taking the offensive were rejected. From the military point of view this was a capital error, as the Imperial forces were concentrating very slowly and could easily have been overwhelmed piecemeal ; but the decision was dictated by political considerations. Accordingly the idea was dropped, and Malatesta contented himself with requesting reinforcements. In July there came the news that the main body of the army had commenced to move from Apulia. The danger was seen to be imminent. It was the obvious policy, if war was inevitable, at least to keep it away from the Florentine borders, and for this purpose Perugia was of primary importance. " Its festival will be the vigil of ours," apprehensively wrote a contemporary. It was therefore unanimously agreed to do everything possible to help.[12]   Florentine captains were sent to assist in the defence : reinforcements were marched south, to the number ultimately of 3,000 men, and money was advanced for some hundreds more.[13]   Nevertheless, this enthusiasm was qualified by a fear that this menace was a mere feint, and that it was intended to pass Perugia by and march direct on Florence, taking it unprepared.[14]   At the same time, there was some nervousness lest the Pope, who was still straining every nerve to gain over Malatesta, would at last succeed in his object, and the Florentine representative at Perugia was especially charged to keep his eye on the negotiations.[15]

By now, however, the Pope had abandoned cajolery in favour of intimidation.   On 11 July an ultimatum had been sent to Perugia ordering the withdrawal of all hostile troops from the city and threatening the advance of the Imperial forces in case of disobedience.   This was repeated in a brief of 24 July calling on it to return to fealty.   Yet another, of 5 August, complained at the conduct of the Perugians in submitting to the rule of Malatesta after his fickle and unceremonious desertion of the papal service, and in accepting the military support of the French and the Florentines without the Pope's leave.   Up to the present he had shown leniency, but in the end he would be forced to treat such contumacy as it deserved.[16]   Indeed, two envoys of Malatesta on their way to the court of France were seized, put to the torture, and imprisoned.[17]   The Council of Perugia, assembled as a matter of form, gave a temporizing answer to the Papal menaces, but refused to change its policy.[18]   Both sides made ready for war.

A breathing-space was afforded by the question of finance, which had been a fruitful source of dispute and delay upon the papal side.   The treaty of Barcelona had contained no provision as to the division of expenditure.   Both sides were poor, and the Pope in addition avaricious : prolonged discussions ensued, and matters were said to have thrice reached a breaking-point.   At last a temporary agreement was reached through the mediation of Cardinal Pucci, who from his own resources advanced a considerable sum.   Clement was thus enabled to come to terms with Orange.   He agreed to supply him with 15,000 ducats down, 50,000 more in three weeks' time, and, if resistance were encountered, with 30,000 more for September.   Further very heavy contributions amounting to 200,000 ducats, of which 50,000 were to go to reimburse the Pope, were to be levied from the city on its capitulation as the price of an alliance.   He was moreover to supply Orange with considerable military supplies—four cannon with munitions, 4,500 infantry, and 1,000 pioneers.[19] Once more the papal territories became the scene of active military preparations.   " In those days," writes Varchi, " nothing

was seen about Rome but plumes, nothing heard but drums.   It
seemed that all Italy was to be filled with arms and soldiers and
turned into confusion, so great was the cupidity that was to be
found in those troops, and especially in the Spaniards, to sack
Florence. . . ." [20]

Meanwhile, in Florence, the preparations for defence were
being pressed on.   The uncompromising republicans had developed into a war party, most steadfast against compromise
and determined for resistance.   " We are ready not only to
expose our wealth," the Signoria had declared to Carlo Capello,
the Venetian orator, " but also to die, old as we are, sword in hand
upon the walls, to defend this our native city." [21]   At the
head of this party stood the Gonfalonier himself, and with him
half a dozen others whose names are foremost in the consultations
of the time—Jacopo Gherardi, Andreuolo Niccolini, Luigi
Soderini, Bernardo da Castiglione, Giambattista Cei, and Niccolò
Guicciardini. [22]   All were to pay for their steadfastness with their
lives.   As the usual measure of alarm, the tabernacle of the
Virgin was again sent for from Impruneta and conducted to
Florence with all solemnity. [23]   The Signoria, occupied with
graver matters, ceased to hear private disputes so as to devote
all of its attention to the serious business of defence. [24]   As an
immediate provision, 80,000 ducats were raised by a forced loan ;
and a commission was appointed for the collection of arrears
of taxation.   A proclamation was made for provisions of all
sorts to be collected in Florence and other fortified places, and in
a year of unusual abundance, immense quantities were brought
together.   As a further encouragement, the tolls on flour and
provisions were repeatedly suspended. [25]   The fortresses of the
dominion to the south and the west were inspected, put into a
state of defence, and reinforced ; and troops were continually
sent south to oppose the enemy's advance.   From the subject
towns, whose fidelity were not above suspicion, hostages were
ordered.   Commissaries were elected and sent to supervise at
various points, and certain ambassadors were replaced.   An
envoy was sent as far as Lombardy to seek help and to raise
troops. [26]   Finally a sort of directory of seven was appointed to
superintend and co-ordinate the whole work of defence—not with
conspicuous success, as, chosen without special qualification, it
was hampered by its own inexperience and timidity. [27]   One tactical error of the gravest sort was made in these preparations.
Owing to the recent suspicious conduct of the Duke of Amalfi in
command of the Imperial forces garrisoning Siena, it was imagined
that the menace to Perugia was a feint, and that the main enemy
advance would be not from this direction up the valley of the
Upper Arno, but along the Valdelsa.   Accordingly, forces had

been concentrated at the important fortress of Poggio Imperiale on the Sienese border, weakening those on the crucial line of advance.[28]

The resources of diplomacy, also, were not neglected. Though abandoned by its principal component, the league of Cognac still existed in Italy at least in name ; and the common peril might have been expected to make it more of a reality. The Venetians were persistently begged to fulfil their treaty obligations, and though they did nothing they were lavish in promises and always gave it to be understood that they would comply.[29] The relations between the two powers were, however, on an unsound basis. Both were very ready to protest their friendliness, but most unwilling to show it. Again and again the Florentines had replied to Venetian requests for assistance by " giving good words " and nothing more, excepting perhaps approaching France for vicarious assistance. In Apulia her help had been negligible, for the aggrandisement of Venice was no interest of hers.[30] Even in a matter of such vital interest to herself as the advance of the lanzknechts under Brunswick, she had been inclined to leave action to France, and there had been difficulties in working in co-operation.[31] On the loss of Amatrice, the final blow to the hopes of the league in the south, the Doge had told her ambassador without mincing words, " The poltroonery of the Florentines has done this, for if they had sent infantry to the aid of Aquila it would never have fallen, and the Spaniards would not have been able to go to Tuscany." [32] In addition, the recent delegation of envoys to the Emperor, against the advice of the Venetian orator, was ill advised unless they were willing to prosecute the matter to its logical conclusion. As it was, they alienated their old friends without conciliating their enemies. It was said openly in Venice that since they had abandoned the league, the league should abandon them. This, in spite of the specious promises which they continued to lavish, became the policy of the Venetian government.[33] An envoy was similarly sent to the camp of the Duke of Urbino to keep him informed of the state of affairs and to solicit his counsel and aid. But he was under the wing of the Venetians, and naturally nothing more substantial than counsel came of it. On the contrary, the apprehensions of the Imperialists in that direction were relieved by an undertaking that not only would the Florentines be given no assistance, but free passage would be accorded to their own troops through his territories.[35] More could have been hoped from the Duke of Ferrara, who, besides being included in the league and in the common peril, had engaged his son, Don Ercole, to the Florentine service as Captain-General for precisely such an eventuality. From the time of the defeat of St. Pol, the

Florentines had repeatedly summoned him to fulfil his obligations with the two thousand soldiers he had undertaken to provide.[36] The Duke, who had professed himself ready not only to send his son but also to come in person to defend his ally, was in a similar position to the Venetians, and was alienated also by the engagement of Malatesta Baglione. By now, too, his shrewd political sense had perceived that safety could lie only in conciliating Pope and Emperor. He temporized, therefore, doing nothing excepting to draw his salary and waiting for a lead from France; though his son wished to pay his debt of honour by escaping alone to Florence. Nothing remained for the city but to cancel its agreement.[37] It was left to bear the brunt of the attack alone.

On 16 August Orange at length left Rome, returning to Aquila to fetch his troops. On the 19th he arrived at Terni with Giovanni d' Urbina, his Lieutenant-General, and the bulk of his forces, and continued to pursue the easy road up the Tiber Valley. At the pleasant, but unruly, hill-town of Spoleto he was received honourably by the inhabitants, but with such a show of military preparation that he hesitated to remain. He concentrated his forces, therefore, in the flat country between Foligno and Spello on the borders of the Perugian territory. These comprised as yet some 3,000 German lanzknechts—the remnant of Frundsberg's army—with 4,000 Italian mercenaries under Pierluigi Farnese (later Duke of Parma), Camillo Marzio, Sciarra Colonna, and Giambattista Savelli. These were all seasoned and disciplined veterans of the Italian wars; and further detachments were continually arriving to swell his numbers. In addition, Malatesta Baglione's cousins, Braccio and Sforza, had joined his standard. The Spanish infantry, which formed the backbone of the army, was to be brought up from Apulia by Alfonso d'Avalos, Marquis del Vasto and nephew of the great Pescara, together with the light horse under Don Ferrante Gonzaga, brother of the Marquis of Mantua.[38] The preliminary campaign was short. Assisi, then in obedience to Perugia, was captured after a sharp defence protracted from the hallowed shrine of St. Francis itself. Less difficulty was found in occupying Montefalco and Bevagna, the captains in Florentine pay in charge retiring upon Spello. Here preparations had been made by improving the defence works and concentrating troops to put up a stronger resistance so as to provide a breathing-space for Perugia, as for Florence, to put herself into a state of readiness and to gather in the harvest. Malatesta had placed his natural brother, Leone, an ecclesiastic, in command. At the end of August, tired of waiting for the Spanish troops, Orange made ready to advance on this place. His Lieutenant-General, Giovanni d' Urbina, was mortally wounded while reconnoitring the walls, and a preliminary assault was repulsed with ease. Nevertheless, upon the commencement of a bombardment the city surrendered—not without some suspicion of treachery—and was sacked with great cruelty, against the terms of the capitulation and the will of the general (1 September). The way was now open to march on Perugia.[39]

The Marquis del Vasto was daily expected, having left Rome at the commencement of the month; and on 8 September the army crossed the Tiber and pitched camp before Perugia. In spite of their numbers, by now increased to something more than 10,000, the siege of this place would have been long and troublesome. It was peculiarly strong by natural position as well as through its fortifications, and it was defended by nearly 3,000 Florentine mercenaries as well as Malatesta's own troops—a force too strong to leave on the lines of communication. Other means were therefore tried. Before the advance had commenced, Malatesta, who saw no prospects of a successful defence, had already informed the Prince of his readiness in his personal capacity to come to terms; and his offer had been welcomed as laying open the path to Florence without loss of time.[40] Nothing had apparently come of it at the time, but negotiations were now reopened under the most favourable conditions.[41] Malatesta hesitated, and seemed to be attempting to gain time. Finally, not receiving such reinforcements as he desired, he came to terms. The Dieci, informed by their representative of what was going on, hurried down a couple of thousand men to secure better conditions and to safeguard the retirement of their troops. They found the capitulation already signed. Malatesta had received most honourable treatment. He was allowed to leave the city freely with his full forces and supplies, and was permitted to continue in the service of Florence. The Pope granted him a free pardon and the enjoyment of his possessions. Perugia was to return to its former relations with the Holy See, but at the same time Malatesta's cousins were to receive no encouragement. On the evening of 11 September, the Cardinal del Monte took possession of the city in the Pope's name.[42]

The terms were suspiciously favourable: and in the light of later events it is easy to read into them actual treachery. The matter must, however, be considered dispassionately. Florence had been informed of the terms directly as well as through her envoys, and had not disapproved. Official opinion could see nothing blameworthy in Malatesta's conduct, though it might have desired a greater steadfastness; nor was anything more known on the Imperial side. The whole position seems easy enough to explain. The central government was now converting its military policy to one of concentration instead of diffusion of resources. It was anything but unwelcome to them that their captain should be able to withdraw without molestation and with his forces untouched (including 3,000 of their own men) to defend the capital, instead of being shut up in an outlying fortress or having to fight his way against superior odds. The Imperialists, on the other hand, were faced with the alternatives of wasting their time and efforts in the siege of a minor position of great strength, or of leaving a standing menace upon their principal line of communications ; and it was peculiarly to their interest that it should be evacuated to them on whatever conditions. Between the one side and the other Malatesta was free to make the best terms he could, and he did not waste his opportunity.[43]

Upon the fall of Perugia, the Prince of Orange set about following up his advantage and carrying the war into Florentine territory proper. On Holy Cross Day (14 September) he crossed the Florentine border and arrived at Cortona. At this place of peculiar natural strength [44] it might have been expected that a stand would be made. Malatesta, however, retiring hurriedly by a mountain path, had pressed on northwards. Owing to the unfortunate diversion towards the Sienese territory, Cortona was defended by no more than 500 men. These, however, put up a sharp resistance, and repulsed with considerable loss an assault by the Marquis of Vasto, who was wounded together with a nephew of Orange himself. A bombardment was accordingly commenced and all preparations made for systematic operations. The townspeople, however, aware of the shortness of supplies and the small probability of being relieved, sent a delegation to ask for terms. It was agreed to surrender, making a payment of 20,000 ducats for the immunity of their lives and possessions. The Florentine captains were inveigled to put themselves in the hands of Orange and their troops were disarmed. A reinforcement of 500 men arrived just in time to find the town in the hands of the enemy. The next place to fall was Castiglione Fiorentino, which had in vain demanded help from Florence and was stormed just as it was on the point of opening negotiations. The way was now open to march on Arezzo.[45]

This city was the centre of the Florentine system of defence towards the south, and seat, at the moment, of the Commissary-General, who represented the city in the command of the mercenary troops. This position had been submitted to a rapid succession of changes. Rafaello Girolami, retired through ill-health, had been succeeded in July by Tommaso Soderini. After a short tenure of office the latter, too long accustomed to be at the centre of affairs, was recalled to serve on the embassy to Genoa, and Zanobi Bartolini was sent to take his place. His excessive corpulence and somnolescence, however, rendered him unsuitable for a quasi-military office, and he was succeeded in his turn by Antonfrancesco degli Albizzi.[46] When Malatesta, after passing through Cortona, arrived at Arezzo (18 September) he found him there with a force of a couple of thousand or more— a reinforcement sufficient to have enabled a stand to be made at this crucial spot. The instructions of the Commissary had been to remain defending the city if the enemy halted there, but otherwise to retire on Florence with the main body, leaving behind a sufficient garrison.[47] To the general surprise, however, Orange was not given the time to show his intentions. On the arrival of Malatesta, Albizzi joined forces with him and the two withdrew together on the next day to Montevarchi and thence, after a wait of two days for the baggage, to Figline and so to Florence (16 September). Arezzo was left to its fate with a handful of 700 troops—barely half the minimum number required for its defence. A thousand more, sent back in response to the appeals that it should not be abandoned, reconnoitred the situation and returned without doing anything.[48] The curious tactics of abandoning without a blow one of the strongest and most vital positions in the Florentine territory aroused general astonishment which ripened into suspicion. It appears, however, that this also was merely the result of the new policy of the central government. Machiavelli had himself pointed out how little reliable were the fortresses of the dominion, whose military strength was sapped through the disaffection of the population. Even more important was the consideration that the enemy might come upon the capital by a sudden march and find it almost defenceless with the major part of its forces isolated in outlying positions. To this was added the influence of some of the intransigeants, who wished to see the city irrevocably committed to the war, with the enemy beneath the walls. Accordingly, in spite of previous resolutions, it was ultimately determined, as it seems, to evacuate all but a few of the most essential fortresses, and to concentrate all military forces in the capital. From his first day of office, Albizzi had authority to abandon Arezzo; and he can be accused at the most of having done so without further reference to the central government, if indeed he had not already received secret instructions. Whosoever the blame, however, it was a strategic blunder of the first importance. The place should have been considered among the vital fortresses to be defended to the last. By its evacuation, there was surrendered completely the possession of the Valdichiana and the upper valley of the Arno—the natural highway from Florence southwards. Orange was able to secure his communications and supplies from the papal states on the one side and from Siena on the other; and he could now concentrate his forces upon Florence without fear of local distractions.

To public opinion this deliberate surrender was incomprehensible. It could have only one explanation ; and in the whispers of treachery was included the name of the Gonfalonier himself as the author of the new policy or perhaps even the secret instigator of the withdrawal, without the knowledge of his colleagues and against their orders.[49]   Albizzi, on his return to Florence, was greeted with a general suspicion, to which his past record gave probability.   It was broadly hinted that he was once more veering round like a weathercock, and that just as he had gained pardon from the Medici seventeen years before by the expulsion of Piero Soderini, so now he was seeking to buy their favour again at the price of his fidelity to the Republic.   He was summoned before the Dieci to explain his conduct and deprived of office ; while a further attempt to justify himself before the Pratica had no result.   The popular attitude towards him was unmistakable, and he paid for permission to leave the city.[50] During his exile, he was tried by the Quarantia but was acquitted.[51]   Notwithstanding this, on the return of the Medici he suffered for his part in the revolution, and his unquiet spirit continued to be prominent in the intrigues of the exiles.   But as a citizen of Florence his career was at an end.[52]

Arezzo, left to its own devices, lost no time in coming to terms.   Envoys were sent to greet Orange, bearing the keys in a silver basin.   In return for a payment of 30,000 ducats and supplies of provisions, he allowed the city to make a partial re-affirmation of its ancient liberty, the memories of which had not been blotted out by a century and a half of Florentine rule (18 September).   The garrison, however, remained faithful and continued besieged in the citadel.[53]   The way now lay virtually open to Florence, which could have been reached in no more than a couple of days.   To the general surprise, however, the further advance up the valley of the Arno was very slow.   This was partly explained by the bad condition of the roads owing to the unusually heavy and early rains and by the fact that Orange was awaiting the arrival of the artillery promised by Siena.   On the other hand, it was suggested that he was acting with an ostentatious independence and for his own interests rather than for those of the Pope : and the rumour suggested even that he proposed to marry the " Duchessina " and become master of Florence, lord of Tuscany, and—who knows ?—of the whole of Northern Italy.[54]   Whatever foundation there may have been for these reports, the reasons for his delay were to be looked for in a wholly different direction.   The Emperor had never been fond of war for its own sake, nor had he special reasons for desiring to press on the present one.   It is not improbable that he had been impressed to some extent by the Florentine envoys who had been sent to him ; while finally he was sufficiently sagacious to wish to avoid the ruin of the city which he could hope to serve as his pay-chest. Though at a council at Piacenza on 11 September he had decided, on the advice of Da Leyva, to persevere in the enterprise, he almost immediately commenced to think of conciliation as a better means. Accordingly he had signified to Orange his desire for a protracted advance which should allow time for a pacific agreement to be reached between his ally and the refractory citizens. Only in the case of this proving an utter impossibility did he desire to submit the matter to the arbitrament of arms, and even so merely for the sake of Clement's friendship.[55] In this lay the real reason for Orange's delays, which became continually more accentuated and proved the salvation of the Florentines, who had been expecting him hourly beneath the walls.[56] Advancing slowly by short stages through Terranuova, Laterina, and Ponte Levana, he arrived at Montevarchi only on 22 September [57] ; and from this point his inaction became all the more pronounced. It is true that his cavalry made incursions as far as Ricorboli, at the very gates of Florence, and caused panic in the city ; yet he did not fulfil expectations by following at their heels, although in that case he might have entered virtually unopposed.[58] He himself once pushed on to reconnoitre at Rovezzano, where his dinner was disturbed by a skirmish of the light horse. Similar minor engagements were taking place almost daily.[59] His forces meanwhile wrought unheard-of devastation in the surrounding territories. The miserable inhabitants, abandoning all their property, fled to the mountains and woods in fear of violence or worse, and one woman of Incisa emulated the fame of Camilla.[60] Other forces, largely irregular, moved down from the Romagna, committing even worse depredations. Among them were men of the character of Antonio Taddei, exiled from Florence many years before for his evil life, who was reported to have declared, " Any who do not wish to do the worst that can be done need not come with me." Another who peculiarly distinguished himself was Giovanni da Sassatello, known by the uncomplimentary sobriquet of Cagnaccio, who, not content with deserting the Florentine service for the Pope's without even returning his advances of pay, led from Bologna to join Orange a force of 3,000 men, robbing and pillaging wherever they could. Other leaders of similar character continued to swell the Imperial forces. In the words of the monastic chronicler, " there were never Turks or other nation who did worse to their enemies than did they, . . . burning houses, seizing captives, sacking and ruining the neighbourhood." [61]

As war had approached nearer to their borders, the desires of the Florentines to find a peaceful solution had increased. At the same time there had arrived the letters reporting that the Prince of Orange was empowered to treat on behalf of the Emperor. On 7 September, therefore, the day following the arrival of the Imperialists before Perugia, it was determined by the Ottanta to " send some one qualified to the Prince to mollify him and work upon him in favour of the city." It was understood moreover that he should dally with him and attempt at the least to delay his advance. No attention was paid to the admonitions that nothing could be done without coming to terms with the Pope, for, as Battista della Palla pithily put it, " he who goes down one step of a ladder must go down all."[62] After a further delay, Rosso Buondelmonti, who could claim some acquaintance with the Prince from intercourse in France in happier days, was chosen to carry out the mission.[63] At Arezzo he came into contact with Malatesta Baglioni and Antonfrancesco degli Albizzi, whose ill-advised retreat he attempted to delay. On 15 September he reached the camp before Cortona, where Orange had arrived on the previous day. He was immediately admitted to audience and unfolded his mission, couched in very general terms, insisting on the affection and obedience of the city towards the Emperor. Orange replied coldly that he was acting under orders and could not enter into any discussion until negotiations with the Pope were authorized. Buondelmonti warned him that the city was better prepared and garrisoned than he thought, to which the Prince retaliated with a picture of the destruction which would take place in its territory. Nevertheless, for old acquaintance's sake, the envoy was allowed to stay on in the camp, where he made careful observations as to the enemy's forces, sending home prudent but encouraging reports. At the same time, he attempted to fulfil the other part of his mission by doing his best to mollify the Prince. He procured for him and the other commanders a regular supply of provisions from Florence, of which they stood in great need owing to the wretched state of their commissariat ; and the comparison between their own penury and the affluence of the enemy they were going to attack was intentionally accentuated. Similarly he obtained for Orange and the Marquis del Vasto the gift of a pair of Turkish horses each—" the best that can be found." But in spite of all this they showed no sign of mitigating their attitude, and on the fall of Cortona he accompanied the army on its onward march without having been able to send home any more satisfactory report.[64]

His experience showed that it was necessary after all to modify the city's attitude in one cardinal matter. One of the fixed points in the policy of the Republic ever since the revolution had been to enter into no sort of negotiation with the Pope.

It was this that had led to the bitter dissensions in the time of Capponi and to his fall ; and nothing had availed to rid the city of its deeply rooted prejudice. Recent attempts of the English envoys to bring about a direct understanding had failed utterly, detestation of Clement being accentuated in this case by suspicions of Henry's sincerity and aims.[65] The invariable reply of the Emperor and his agents to all representations, direct or indirect, had, however, emphasized the fact that to consent to treat with the Pope was the only method by which the advance of the armies might conceivably be checked : and the advance of the armies was growing more menacing each day. From the end of August, therefore, a less intransigeant spirit began to show itself.[66] On 11 September the matter was regularly discussed, and it was suggested as a compromise that some Florentine citizen already in Rome should be appointed to sound the ground. Four days later, a further step was taken by determining to save appearances by sending a representative (" mandatario ") instead of an ambassador ; and the Bishop of Tarbes, French envoy at Rome, was to be asked to use his good offices. Francesco Nasi was chosen for this delicate mission, but with his equivocal position he was obviously able to do nothing. On the same day, however, Rosso Buondelmonti reported on the uncompromising reply of Orange ; and the lingering hopes which centred upon him were destroyed. The news brought an immediate change in the Florentine attitude. Even the Captains of the Guelph Party, who the day before had been unanimously opposed to the idea, were now unanimously in favour of sending ambassadors to the Pope. The proposal was carried with only eight dissentient votes : and four representatives were immediately appointed, though their departure was delayed. The receipt of further despatches confirmed the impression that it was of no use to treat with Orange, but held out the possibility that something at least might be secured by approaching Clement. In addition, the Bishop of Tarbes gave good hope of favourable terms should they open negotiations. Accordingly, on 19 September it was determined that Pierfrancesco Portinari, late ambassador in England and at Siena, who had been already selected for this mission, should depart at once, leaving his colleagues to follow him.[67] Upon the same day he received his instructions, drawn up by Donato Giannotti himself ; and he set out immediately, travelling, in order to save time, without the usual pomp. He had the instructions which might have been imagined—to protest the city's fidelity and respect to the Holy See and to exculpate its conduct ; but he was given no authority to make any sort of concession.[68] His colleagues followed at intervals — first Jacopo Guicciardini, and then

Andreuolo Niccolini with Francesco Vettori—the last an especially conciliatory choice.[69] Their voyage was adventurous. The roads were bad and unsafe. Their departure from Siena was opposed by the Spaniards, and their baggage rifled. In spite of a safe conduct, Portinari was actually arrested, while Niccolini and Vettori were held up until permission was sent from Rome for them to pass.[70] Portinari nevertheless arrived first, on 22 September. The Pope, grateful at this first sign of a change of attitude, received him benignantly, and insisted on his benevolence towards the city.[71] Yet neither side was prepared to make any concession, and the conversations brought matters no nearer an agreement. Peace, however, began to be confidentially expected in Rome as at the camp ; and Nicholas Schomberg, Archbishop of Capua, was sent to Orange in order to conduct negotiations from nearer at hand.[72] Thither, too, went some of the most prominent among the exiles from Florence to act as intermediaries. Meanwhile, Lorenzo Strozzi, brother of Filippo, had been sent from Florence to strengthen Buondelmonti's hands and to dally with Orange, while the city was being put in a state of defence. He was instructed to request that the advance of the army should be suspended at least pending the result of the negotiations with the Pope. With him in his mission were associated Leonardo Ginori and Bartolommeo Marucelli, who were personally acquainted with the Prince through commercial transactions in the old days.[73] They found him on 12 September encamped at Montevarchi. Though still maintaining his attitude on the main question and professing his inability to go against his instructions, the Imperial commander consented to do as a concession what he had probably already intended for other reasons, and to wait for a day or two at his present station and at Figline. On all other points, however, his attitude was as uncompromising as ever, and he would only advise the city to yield. While Buondelmonti and Ginori remained behind to continue the conversations with Muxetula, the Commissary-General, and the other influential personages, who continued to be conciliated by gifts of provisions, Strozzi returned to Florence almost immediately to report the negative result of his visit. During the time that he was in the camp, he had noted with the eye of a practised observer all that he saw, and was able now to make a comparatively accurate estimate of the Imperial forces. To the patriotic party, always ready to minimize its perils, it seemed that the numbers he gave were exaggerated, especially as compared with the more sanguine reports of Buondelmonti. It was suspected—and his lineage gave support to the suspicion—that he was trying to frighten the city into an agreement.[74] His pessimism, however, had no influence upon the general mind. The Archbishop of Capua, on his way to join Orange, went out of his road to pass through Florence, confident that its imminent dangers would at last have brought the city to reason ; but he found himself summarily escorted outside the walls.[75] On 26 September, the recommendation to come to terms which Strozzi had reported was discussed by the Pratica in a full meeting. Lorenzo Martelli, one of the commissioners over the defence of the city, gave an account of the state of the preparations, with which he professed himself to be fairly well satisfied. Encouraged by this, the general attitude remained unchanged in spite of some more timorous counsels. Only, rejecting the defiant policy of the War Party, the majority approved the more moderate suggestion of Rafaello Girolami that yet another envoy should be sent to the Imperial camp to see whether any accommodation could be made without sacrifice of principle.[76] The choice of representative, however, showed in what spirit the proposal was intended, for Bernardo da Castiglione had made himself prominent as one of the most extreme opponents of the Medici and advocates of war. Before he had left, Orange, spurred on by the indignant Archbishop of Capua, moved from S. Giovanni to Figline, at the very gates of the city. (27 September).[77] It was the last chance to avert a siege ; and a special consulta was held in the democratic atmosphere of the Great Council to decide on Castiglione's final instructions. The Gonfalonier addressed the people, urging resistance to the last, and then put the question point-blank—" whether they should submit to the discretion of the Pope or defend themselves." All knew what depended upon their decision—the negation of their liberty, the destruction of the Republic, and return to the servile conditions of three years previous. The citizens retired as was customary to debate in their Gonfaloni before submitting their opinions. It was the decisive proof. There was plain speaking : and feelings ran high. One Zanobi Carnesecchi, a practical-minded merchant of the party of Capponi, demonstrated the physical improbability of victory and the immensely greater losses that would accrue as a consequence of defeat. In spite of the inviolability of the Council and the freedom of speech it was supposed to guarantee, he was mocked and even menaced for his mercantile spirit by Leonardo Bartolini. The same person openly threatened other citizens who counselled sending an " open mandate " to their representatives—that is, opening negotiations with the Pope ; and the Gonfalonier allowed this breach of the peace to pass unpunished.[78] At length the citizens came together again to declare the result of the private deliberations. Bartolini for the Gonfalonieri of the Companies set the tone. " All, unitedly and with one voice, are resolved to defend

themselves and to risk their property and their children, and
not to submit themselves at discretion to one who has never
kept faith, and now wishes to deceive all by this means ; and
they would rather submit to sack than yield at discretion." The
other bodies reported in the main to the same effect, though not
all with such unanimous determination. It was determined
that, though the negotiations with Orange and the Emperor
should continue, no compromise of any sort should be made
with Clement.[79] It was with this errand that Bernardo da
Castiglione went out to Figline, where Orange and the
Archbishop of Capua received him with the stereotyped
formula asking for surrender. " Florence in ashes rather than
under the Medici," was Bernardo's grim retort, which represented the final decision of his fellow-citizens.[80] In addition,
however, to his ostensible mission, he had been given, through
the influence of the Gonfalonier, secret instructions to attempt
to come to separate arrangement with the Emperor, who was
to be mollified by the promise of an alliance coupled with a heavy
money payment. But, though this might have been accepted
some months before, the obduracy of Orange on the one side
co-operated with the boundless optimism of the citizens on the
other to defeat the arrangement. Another compromise was
said to have been put forward—that the city should be governed
by a commission of eighty, half to be nominated by the Pope and
half by a Great Council restricted to 500. It was a proposal
which, in spite of the suspicious delicacy of the balance, might
have recommended itself to some of the aristocrats. But their
day was over, and the people were in the ascendant. Even
without the manipulation which could naturally be expected,
Clement's influence under this system would have become so
strong as virtually to restore his hegemony ; and this no patriot
could accept.[81] The Prince made a final attempt to find a way
out of the impasse by suggesting that the city should give hostages and submit to the Emperor, trusting in his sense of justice
to make a fair settlement. Leonardo Ginori was sent back to
Florence to communicate the proposal. It was discussed at
an unusually full Pratica where no fewer than fifty-nine persons
submitted their opinions. Though the desire for a peaceful
settlement was not concealed, nobody seemed inclined to trust
the Prince's offer. It was characterized as " Spanish trickery " ;
and many insisted that to negotiate only encouraged the enemy
and weakened the confidence of the citizens. " When you draw
the sword, there will be a better effect," cried Simone Gondi at
the close of a fiery speech ; and almost all remained in full agreement that nothing should be done to endanger their liberty,
" which, once tasted, is sweeter than any human thing."[82] Later

on in the same day, and again half a week later, the matter was
again discussed but rejected even more decisively ; and the
general opinion was against so much as considering the question
further.[83] Nothing was left but to recall the envoys from the
camp. Buondelmonti and Castiglione returned, with nothing
to show for their exertions. In spite, however, of recommendations to the contrary, Bartolommeo Marucelli was allowed to
remain with Orange in case of future eventualities.[84] All that
was left, after such a gesture of defiance, was to await the enemy
at the gates.

To the general astonishment, they did not immediately arrive.
Though his troops continued their skirmishings and their depredations, for over a fortnight Orange lay inactive between Figline
and Incisa, within an easy day's march of the city : so inexplicably that he was suspected of having been bribed to do so.[85]
There is good reason also to believe that he had been influenced
by a letter from his mother who implored him to withdraw from
so unjust an enterprise, in which she had a presentiment that he
would meet with disaster.[86] But the main explanation of his
delay lay in a different direction. The Imperialists had advanced
with every confidence in an immediate victory, not imagining
that they would meet with resistance ; but their leaders were
conscious that if they did, they were in no condition to cope with
it, owing to the lack of preparations and especially to the discontent of their troops. Orange himself in the midst of his
successful advance had sent a gloomy report to the Emperor
in which he envisaged the total debacle of his forces if he were
not better supplied with money and anticipating that the Italians
and Germans at least would go over to the enemy outright.
" Sire," he wrote, " I beg you, look well at the date of this letter,
and think that we are at the eighteenth of the month (September).
You know what this means."   Only twelve days were left before
matters would come to a head ; and Charles could do no more
than advise the useless expedient of recourse to the Pope.[87] As
each day passed, Orange's financial straits became more acute.
The experience of time and his intercourse with the Florentine
envoys convinced him of the futility of his lingering hope in
a bloodless victory through menaces alone. His appeals for
proper support became more and more desperate. His artillery
had not yet arrived, the thousand pioneers promised at Rome
had not begun to appear, the scanty papal provision for the
month of September was exhausted. On the other hand, the
city was well provided, and, even though he should succeed in
capturing it, sack at the hands of his famished soldiery would
be inevitable. The Pope, informed of all this through the Archbishop of Capua and his confidant, Giambattista Montebona,

would consent to modify his claims only as a pawn in the game, reserving his right to reassert them when his enemies were disarmed. But he failed to persuade Orange, who sent one special messenger after another to the Emperor to lay the matter before him. If it was desired to persevere in the enterprise he must have his pay guaranteed for three or four months ; though with the forces at his disposal, he said, it would take him ten years to capture the city. If he could not be adequately supported, he urged the Emperor to allow the Florentines to come to terms and so secure himself an honourable peace while he might.[88] From every quarter similar reports reached Charles of inadequacy of preparation, lack of discipline, and unlikelihood of success. Even the Marquis del Vasto, virtually second in command, bluntly informed him that the army could hope to conquer only through its reputation and advised him to avail himself of it by making a profitable peace while he could.[89]

Charles was at this time at his wits' end to help his brother against the Turks in Hungary and to find troops for other enterprises. The expedition against Florence was a serious diversion at the best ; and these reports commenced to convince him of its futility. Antonio da Leyva, commander-in-chief of the Imperial forces in Lombardy, had proposed to him that a duchy should be carved for Alessandro de' Medici out of the Milanese befitting the position of the Emperor's son-in-law.[90] Influenced by the pessimistic despatches from camp, Charles allowed himself to be persuaded, and addressed a letter to Clement urging him to come to terms with Florence, and to accept compensation for Alessandro in the direction suggested.[91] Orange's efforts were henceforth seconded by the Emperor himself. The Archbishop of Bari was actually instructed to attempt persuasion at Rome : and competent observers, who saw the various envoys hurried " up and down, from Court to camp and from camp to the Pope," thought that an agreement was imminent.[92] Meanwhile, the army was delayed at Figline.

In spite of the influence that was brought to bear upon him, Clement remained implacable. It was not for him a mere question of profit and loss. His material interests were not in question so much as his pride ; and this could receive no territorial compensation. He was resolved to reduce the city which had inflicted upon him such deep humiliation : and he could not be expected to abandon his hopes precisely when their fulfilment seemed nearest. He saw with a statesman's eye that his family had far greater probability of founding a dynasty at Florence where it was rooted in the soil and numbered many adherents than in a new state, artificially formed and fortuitously acquired, to which it could offer no personal or traditional appeal. And, above all, he realized that once Charles was definitely committed to the enterprise of Florence, he would be compelled for his credit's sake to carry it through to the end, however arduous the path. He therefore replied that he could not commit himself to so great an undertaking as that of Lombardy, productive as it would be of perpetual difficulties to his house : and the continued efforts of Charles to persuade him met with no success.[93] Nevertheless, it was necessary to make some superficial change in his attitude out of respect to his ally. Hitherto, he had refused to receive the embassy from Florence as a whole when, after many vicissitudes, it had at last succeeded in assembling ; and he had informed it with much asperity that he was determined that their city should be captured even though he would have to sell or pledge his tiara.[94] Now he consented to put forward his terms. He demanded apparently the surrender of his niece, the restitution of his palaces, the restoration of the erased arms, and the freedom of his family from taxation ; pardon for his adherents, and the immunity from taxation of the clergy ; and finally, the payment of an indemnity, the reformation of the government, replacement of the Gonfalonier, and the acceptance of a resident to represent his interests. With these reservations, he would respect their liberty.[95] Clement must have known that much less than this would have been insupportable to the Florentines and could have no result excepting to drive them to break off negotiations, as was proposed immediately upon the receipt of his terms.[96] It was, indeed, a mere gesture to justify himself in the eyes of the Emperor, into whose hands for the rest he professed to surrender all his claims, leaving it to him to decide whether the enterprise should be persisted in or no.[97] But at the same time he did not conceal his real opinions and stigmatized Orange's proposals as unworthy of his reputation and of the Medici.[98] He arranged even to supply the army with 100,000 ducats.[99] Clement's friendship was at this time still very precious to the Emperor, who was forced in consequence against his better judgment to adhere to the Treaty of Barcelona. In response to his importunities he sent Orange in a single day three letters urging him to satisfy the Pope and not to endanger his friendship.[100] Orange's views and requirements did not change and he continued to express them with all freedom, while the discussions were not at an end.[101] But the Pope's inflexible will became his law. On the receipt of the Emperor's instructions, the army began to move forward at last from Figline, and on the next day was at S. Donato. On 12 October, the first forces entered the plain, where they were saluted with artillery fire. A steep slope leads up to Apparita, the last obstacle on the road. As the Spaniards breasted the high ground, the whole city came suddenly into view in its rich plain with the Arno winding through it ; and they saw the commercial capital of Europe, famous the whole world over for its beauty and its wealth, lying out before them like some exotic flower. A cry arose from their ranks, " Prepare your brocades, Dame Florence, for we come to buy them at pike's measure ! " Brandishing their arms, they hurried down the slope to the goal of their lust. On the same day, Orange lodged at Ripoli, barely a mile from the walls : and his troops daily closed up in the teeth of continual skirmishing. The siege of Florence was begun.[102]

NOTES TO CHAPTER VII

[1] Ulysse Robert, *Philibert de Chalon, Prince d'Orange, Vice-roi de Naples*, 2 vols., Paris, 1902, published on the tercentenary of Orange's birth. Minor authorities are Sandrier, *Philibert de Chalon, Prince d'Orange*, Poligni, 1889 ; P. Giovio, *Elogia virorum bellica virtute illustrium*, Lib. VI ; cf. Bardi, *Carlo V e l'Assedio di Firenze*. These reports of the Sienese envoys in Falletti, Vol. II, give a most graphic description of Orange's impetuous character, especially letters 26 and 27 (" Quella collera bestiale che suole "), borne out by his own despatches in Bardi and Robert. His gambling losses while under the walls of Florence are curiously illustrated in *Giornali del Principe d' Orange*, ed. Dom. Pierrugues (Firenze, 1897), pp. 29–30. The remarkable instance recounted by Varchi II, 417, is denied by Robert. Article 28 of the Treaty of Cambrai had reinstated him in his principality.

[2] Varchi, II, 44–5.

[3] Bergenroth Transcripts, VII, f. 187. Micer Mai to Charles (N.D.). Cf. also *State Papers, Spanish*, IV, i, 106 (*id.* 11 August).

[4] " En Florencia abren todas las cartas " (Bergenroth Transcripts, VIII, f. 43). Cf. also *ibid.* f. 191, and *State Papers, Spanish*, IV, i, 77, 106, 121.

[5] Pratiche, 3 July.

[6] Foscari, *Relazione*, p. 91.

[7] Bardi, *op. cit.* p. 12.

[8] *Ibid.* p. 39.

[9] Pastor, X, p. 63.

[10] *State Papers, Spanish*, III, ii, 659 (23 March 1528/9).

[11] Bergenroth Transcripts, VII, f. 328 *seqq.* " Relacion de las cartas del Embaxador Miguel Mai." (Not calendared in *State Papers, Spanish*.)

[12] Falletti, I, 105–9 ; Pastor, X, 54 ; Pratiche, 6, 31 May ; 8, 16, 23, 25, 27 June ; 14, 16 July, and 8 August. Cf. also letters of Capello for same period.

[13] *Ibid.* and Dieci, Missive, XLVIII, to Malatesta, 31 August.

[14] Capello, letter 30.

[15] Dieci, Missive, XLVII, 4 July, to R. Girolami (Deciphered) " . . . Il Papa cerca con ogni industria di guadagnarsi Malatesta la qual cosa noi guidichiamo di non piccola importantia, pensando che tal prat ca possa essere facta ad altro fine . . ." and *ibid.* 6 July ; Capello, letter 20 ; and instructions to Bernardo da Verrazano, envoy to Malatesta, of 14 July (Dieci, *ibid.*).

[16] Pastor, X, 63–4 *n.* Cf. Capello, letter 31.

[17] Varchi, II, 42–3. Cf. letter to Trivulzio in Molini, *Documenti di Storia Italiana*, II, pp. 230–1, and Capello, letter 32.

[18] For this and above, see Vermiglioli, *op. cit.* pp. 74–5, and citation from Bottonio, p. 186.

[19] Bardi, p. 50 ; Pastor, 66 ; *State Papers, Spanish*, IV, i, 106 (11 August 1529). The details in the text are the official, and decide between the wide variations in those usually reported. According to rumour, Clement promised Orange for himself Avignon and the Comtat Venaissin in addition. Cf. Robert, 282–4, for these transactions ; and Ammirato, VII, 51.

[20] Varchi, II, 49. Cf. *Letters and Papers, Henry VIII*, IV, 5780.

[21] Capello, letter 41.

[22] Cf. Nerli, p. 191.

[23] On the Feast of the Assumption of the Virgin (15 August). Signoria, CXXXI, f. 148 ; Paolo Paoli, p. clxxxvii.

[24] Signoria, *ibid.*, f. 169 (1 September).

[25] Varchi, II, pp. 27–9 ; Signoria, *ibid.*, ff. 140, 160, 195.

[26] Varchi, II, pp. 29–31 ; Capello, letters 26, 27, 29, 39 ; Pratiche, 20 June *seqq.*

[27] Varchi, II, p. 31.

[28] Pratiche, 10, 22 August ; Capello, letters 28, 39, 49. It was only on 22 September that the mistake was realized and the evacuation proposed (Pratiche, *ad diem*). From the despatches of Sergardi, it would appear that the line of advance was changed to the Valdarno, the only alternative route for artillery, at the very pressing entreaties of the Sienese. Cf. his letters in Falletti, II, Nos. 3 (P.S.), 7 and 18.

[29] See Capello, *passim*, and especially No. 33 *seqq.* ; Sanuto, LI, 138, 206, 274, 280–1, 307–8, etc. ; and Dieci, Missive, XLIV, *passim*.

[30] Cf. Vitale, *L'impresa di Puglia, ubi supra*, p. 128 *seqq.*, 165 *seqq.*

[31] Sanuto, XLVIII, 326–9.

[32] *Ibid.* XLIX, 505.

[33] Capello, *passim* ; Varchi, II, pp. 39–41.

[35] Robert, 292–3 ; *State Papers, Spanish*, IV, i, 119, and Varchi, II, pp. 32–5. Baglione had also solicited the aid of Urbino ; cf. his letter to Duchess of 17 July (Sanuto, LI, 140–1).

[36] Dieci, Missive, XLVII ; 23 June (to Pandolfini at Ferrara) ; Pratiche, 22, 23 June ; 19, 27 July, etc. ; Capello, letters 31, 42, etc.

[37] Instructions of Jacopo Guicciardini of 30 July (Dieci, Missive, XLVII) ; Varchi, II, 211 ; Sanuto, LI, 415. Molini, *Documenti*, II, 296, 298 (Ercole d'Este to Montmorency, 23 July, 8 August).

[38] Robert, p. 293 *seqq.*, and documents there cited. Cf. also earlier despatches of Sergardi, the Sienese envoy, in Falletti, II ; Bardi, pp. 42 (de Praet to Charles, 18 August) and 53 (Orange to Charles, 31 *id.*) ; Varchi, II, 124. The youthfulness of the Imperial commanders was noteworthy—Orange was 26, Vasto a year older, and Gonzaga no more than 22. For the life of the latter, see Alfonso Ulloa, *Vita del Valorosissimo e gran capitano Don Ferrante Gonzaga, Principe di Molfetta*, Venice, 1563 ; Giuliano Gosellini, *Vita dell' illustrissimo et generosissimo sig. Don Ferrando Gonzaga, Principe di Molfetta*, Milan, 1574 ; and *Gesta militari di Don Ferrante Gonzaga*, Turin, 1832. For notices of the commanders and captains under Orange, see Pierrugues, *Giornali del Principe d'Orange*, pp. 41–79.

[39] Robert, 295–7, with *pièces justificatifs* ; Giovio, pp. 143–4. Cf. Report of Dieci to Gualterotti of 4 September in Sanuto, LI, 494 ; *State Papers, Spanish*, IV, i, 133. The whole of this campaign is fully illustrated by the despatches of the Sienese envoys at the Imperial camp,

published by Falletti, II (for this, especially Nos. 2, 3 and 8) ; and by the rhymed *Assedio di Firenze* of Mambrino Roseo da Fabriano—one of Malatesta's captains (Perugia, 1530 ; republished by Pierrugues, Florence, 1894). This is one of Varchi's principal sources. The Sienese captain, Borghese, employed at Spello, was thought to have been responsible for its surrender. The Romans are said to have considered the death of Urbina as retribution for his share in the sack of their city, following on the like fates of Bourbon and Moncada (Giovio, *ubi supra*).

[40] Despatch of Praet and Mai to Charles of 11 August in *State Papers, Spanish*, IV, i, 106. Cf. Robert, p. 293.

[41] Despatch of 5 September in Bergenroth Transcripts, VIII, f. 122 *seqq.*: (Cipher) " . . . *Malatesta el tirano esta en Perosa cerca de concertar con el papa*, y dixonos S.S. que no lo queria hacer sin nuestro parecer e parecionos que conviene al servicio de V.M. y ansi pensamos que se hara lo qual va remitido al Principe de Orange ante quien se ha de tratar y finir el concierto . . ." Cf. Sergardi, letter 5 (Cannaia, 4 September) : " Ivi—(at Bastia)—si aspetterà la risoluzione di Malatesta, il quale cerca di accordarsi " ; but he did not believe that he would succeed. See also letter 6, and Capello, letter 47.

[42] Robert, 297 *seqq.* ; and Sergardi, letters 6, 8. An important list of authorities for the capitulation of Perugia is to be found in Pastor, *ubi supra*, p. 70, *n.* 2. The text of Malatesta's pardon (13 September) is given by Falletti, I, 104–5 (*f.n.*) ; and the text of the Capitulation (10 September) by Robert, II, *n.* 194, and Vermiglioli, App. XIV. Cf. Malatesta's own account in letter to Montmorency of 28 September in Molini, II, 253. An historical document of some value for Malatesta's march from Perugia is Vasari's fresco in the Palazzo Vecchio at Florence, described also in his *Ragionamenti, n.* 7 (*Opere*, VIII, 165 *seqq.*).

[43] The circumstances reported by Varchi, II, 132–5, do nothing to disprove these conclusions, though read by him in a very different way. Cf. Falletti, I, 104–5. From the letters of Sergardi, especially Nos. 3 and 7, it appears that as late as 7 September Orange was contemplating passing Perugia by, in which case the quandary of the Florentines, cut off from their general and a large body of their troops, would have been even greater. This was anticipated by them as early as July. See Capello, letter 30.

[44] " One of the strongest places in the world," according to Orange, excusing his severe casualties to the Emperor (Robert, II, *n.* 202).

[45] Despatch of Orange to Charles (from Castiglione Fiorentino) of 18 September in Robert, II, *n.* 202 (Bardi, 56–7) ; reports of Buondelmonti of 14–17 *apud* Capponi, II, 553 *seqq* ; Varchi, 135, 147–51 ; Robert, 301–3; Capello, letters 50, 51 ; Sergardi, letter 15 ; Roseo, pp. 24–9 with notes ; Giovio, II, 145–6. The Pope was not satisfied with the capitulation, which he considered unnecessarily harsh. Cf. despatch of Praet and Mai of 22 September in *State Papers, Spanish*, IV, i, 163. The surrender of Cortona is described by one of the defending captains, Goro of Montebenichi, in his *Ricordi* printed by Pierrugues in *Francesco Ferrucci e la Guerra di Firenze*, p. 322 *seqq.* Other contemporary accounts of varying importance may be found in the same volume.

[46] Varchi, II, pp. 16–19 ; Patents of Bartolini of 10 August and those of Albizzi of 31 August are to be found in Signoria, Carteggio, Missive, Registri, LVIII.

[47] Dieci, Missive, XLVIII, 29 August (to Orators with the Emperor). 5,000–6,000 is the force there mentioned—either in error or in intentional exaggeration, as this was the total of the Florentine troops in that direction.

[48] Varchi, II, 135–6. Cf. despatch of Rosso Buondelmonti of 14

September (Capponi, II, App. (X), *n.* 3).   Capello, letter 49 *seqq.* ; and
Ammirato, VII, p. 53.

[49] The so-called treason of Albizzi is examined by Falletti, *op. cit.*
I, 79–84, and found to be groundless.   Giannotti devotes a chapter in
the " Della Repubblica Fiorentina " (*Opere,* I, 139–40) to explaining his
conduct, considering him to have been made the scapegoat of the Dieci.
For the other side, implicating Carducci, see Giovio, II, 146 ; Nerli, p.
192 ; and Segni, I, 198–9.

[50] Varchi, II, pp. 136, 185 ; Segni, I, 200, says that he saved himself
from capital punishment by producing the Gonfalonier's secret instructions.   Pratiche, 27 September (he had already spoken in favour of accord
on the previous day. *Ibid.*).

[51] Signoria, CXXXII, pp. 180, 198 (7, 18 March).

[52] Varchi, II, 525, 531 ; III, 89, 95, 124, etc.

[53] Robert, 304–5, and Varchi, II, 151–6.   Cf. letter of Orange to
Sienese of 19 September (Robert, II, *n.* 203), and despatch of Sienese
envoy of same date (Sergardi, letter 15).   The government of the city was
taken over by one of the citizens hitherto in exile, Francesco Aldobrandini,
self-styled Count of Bevignano, and called because of his red hair the
Conte Rosso.

[54] He was reported to have said, in the hearing of the Pope's and the
Florentine envoys, that " he would fail him or no, just as he pleased "
(Sanuto, *Diarii,* LII, 89–90).   Robert considers these suggestions, p. 285.

[55] Robert, 310 *seqq.* and docs. 195, 204, 218 (in Bardi, pp. 56 *seqq.,*
64 *seqq.*).   The lack of foundation in the suspicions against Orange can
be seen from the Sienese reports in Falletti, II, pp. 21, 42, 55, 76, etc.

[56] Capello, letter 52.

[57] Robert, I, 305 and docs.

[58] Varchi, II, 169 ; Giovio, II, 147.

[59] Varchi, II, 192 ; Capello, letter 55.

[60] Varchi, II, 171–2 ; Sperino, *ubi supra,* pp. 357–8.

[61] *Cronica di Fra Giuliano Ughi,* pp. 146–8 ; Varchi, II, 126.   Cf.
Sanuto, LII, *passim,* especially 45–7 ; Capello, letter 54; Nardi, p. 208.

[62] Pratiche, *ad diem.*

[63] Cf. his *Lettere Testimoniales* to Orange of 12 September in Signoria,
Carteggio, Missive, Registri, LVIII, and his instructions reported by
Falletti, I, 370–1.

[64] See the despatches of Rosso Buondelmonti (already cited above)
in Capponi, *Storia di Firenze,* II, App. X.   They had already been
published with some omissions by Rastrelli, *Alessandro de Medici,* I,
Appendix.   Cf. also *Ragguaglio di Baccio Carnesecchi, ubi supra.*   The
Imperialists were under no delusions as to his real objects.   See despatch
of Praet and Mai of 15 September in *State Papers, Spanish,* IV, i, 150.

[65] See my article, "England and the Last Florentine Republic," *ubi
supra,* p. 184.

[66] The first breath of negotiations with the Pope was from Bartolommeo Tedaldi on 28 August: " Che non saria fuorj di proposito che li
or[i] comminciassino ad intendere la mente di N[ro] Sig. et però si conceda
loro el parlare co' e' legati " ; and others came round to this point of
view on 7 September.   Cf. Pratiche, *ad dies.*

[67] Pratiche, 11, 15, 16, 19 September ; Capello, letters 50, 52.   Nerli,
pp. 192–4, reports the efforts made by Carducci first to prevent and then
to impede the embassy.   Cf. Giovio, II, 118–19.

[68] His " Notula " is reported by Falletti, I, 374 *seqq.*   Nerli and
Giovio (*ubi supra*) assert that a regular commission was deliberately
withheld by the influence of Carducci.

[69] See their credentials in Signoria, Carteggio,Missive, Registri, LVIII ; for Portinari and Lorenzo Violo (perhaps the Florentine resident at Rome), 19 September ; for Guicciardini on 20 ; for Niccolini and Vettori on 23.

[70] Varchi, II, 157 ; Sanuto, LII, 71.

[71] Falletti, I, 377, reports reply of Pope. The despatches of the envoys are to be found in Dieci, Responsive, CLI, pp. 1–23, and 53 seqq. Cf. Capello, letter 52.

[72] Sanuto, ibid. 40 ; Rossi, op. cit. I, 141–2, and sources there cited.

[73] Busini, p. 107.

[74] Vita di L. Strozzi, in Uomini illustri di casa Strozzi, pp. xxi–xxii ; joint despatch of envoys of 22–27 September, ubi supra, n. 8–12 ; Sergardi, letter 18 ; and Sanuto, LII, 15.

[75] Capello, letter 53 ; Busini, p. 108 ; Varchi, II, 181 ; Ragguaglio di Baccio Carnesecchi, ubi supra.

[76] Pratiche, ad diem. The report of Martelli is printed by Falletti, I, 106–8.

[77] Capello, letter 54.

[78] Cf. the account of Zanobi Carnesecchi's kinsman, Baccio, ubi supra, Vita di N. Capponi, p. 976 seqq. ; Busini, p. 33 seqq. ; Segni, I, 176–93, and Nerli, pp. 194–5, report similar treatment of Lorenzo Segni.

[79] Pratiche, 28 September. Falletti (I, 381) is inaccurate in stating that only the Gonfalone of the Nicchio (" conch "—so named after its standard) was absolutely unanimous for defence. What could be more determined than the response of the Ferza (" whip "), which was typical of others ? " All unitedly are of one opinion, and all judge without reservation that liberty should be preserved, and for that purpose they should undergo any peril ; and therefore they conclude that they should not surrender to the Pope, hoping that the city can defend itself, confiding in their cause and in God, and therefore they all together offer all their substance and their own lives that there should be no relaxation in the defence of liberty . . ." Actually, there was some more timorous opinion in the Nicchio itself.

[80] Varchi, ibid. 168 ; cf. joint despatch with Buondelmonti and Ginori of 29 September, ubi supra, n. 13. His attitude on this occasion was one of the charges against Castiglione for which he paid with his life after the capitulation. See Bardi, Filippo Strozzi (da nuovi documenti) in A.S.I., ser. V, vol. XIV, 1894.

[81] Varchi, II, 168–9. Outside Tuscany the monetary composition was rumoured as having taken place (Sanuto, LII, 32, 37). Varchi gives the improbable version that this was rejected on the Florentine side. It may have some connection with the matter discussed in the Pratica on 30 September. The restitution of the Medici was apparently treated of, but by a misunderstanding : " the Capuan saying that it was the Prince who first suggested the idea, whereas the Prince himself writes that it came from the Florentines " (State Papers, Spanish, IV, i, 180).

[82] Pratiche, 30 September. The text of the proposals is missing, but their general effect can be gathered from the course of the discussion.

[83] Ibid. 30 September (ii) and 4 October.

[84] Last despatches of envoys at camp (n. 13–14), ubi supra.

[85] Relazione di Angelo Sperino, in F. Ferrucci e la Guerra di Firenze, p. 357. Cf. Varchi, II, 169, who suggests that the gifts of provisions, etc., gave colour to the suspicions. Giambattista Cei had indeed suggested in the Pratica of 7 September, " Che con prestezza si mandi al Principe, et bisognando ugnerlo, si faccia." (Pratiche, ad diem.)

[86] This is reported by Busini (p. 107) in the name of Marucelli, who was told it by the Prince himself. See also Nardi, p. 215.

[87] Robert, p. 309 *seqq.*, and Doc. No. 202.   Cf. also Bardi, *Carlo V e l'Assedio di Firenze, ubi supra,* sec. III, " Impresa di Firenze."

[88] Robert, p. 314 *seqq.*, and Doc. No. 222 (instructions to Montbardon for Charles of 5 October) ; 230 (8 October) ; 234 (Instructions to Vaury of 9 October).   See also Bardi, *ubi supra.*

[89] See his despatch, probably typical of others, in Appendix of Documents, No. 8.   Cf. report of Marquis Fernando de Alacese (?) on discipline of army summarized in Bergenroth Transcripts, VIII, f. 105, and the advice to come to terms, *ibid.* 103.

[90] Varchi, II, 231–2.

[91] *Despacho que el Emperador Carlos V mando escribir a sus Embajadores en Roma, para que procurasen arreglar con Su Santidad los asuntos de Milan y Florencia,* 1 *Octubre* 1529. (Published by G. de Leva, Padova, 1859, *per nozze.*)

[92] Sergardi, letter 30.

[93] Pastor, X, 86.

[94] Despatch of Guarini of 7 October in Rossi, *op. cit.*, I, 148, *f.n.*

[95] See despatch of Guarini of 30 October, *ibid.* App. IV.   Cf. also despatch of Praet and Mai of 19 October in Bergenroth Transcripts, VIII.   " . . . Respondionos que no se gane florencia en casa de concierto no porfiara por tener el govierno ni quiere sino que el Consejo de Florencia estuviese en su libertad como era antes, y que el confalonere si mude, y que hagan alcun hombre de bien, y que lo que se ha de pagar se pague sin respecto a comun contribucion, porque el Papa tiene mucho miedo que no carguen todas las gravezas sobre sus amigos . . .   Tambien nos dixo que el mesmo lo tractaria con los Embajadores de Florencia que son aqui. . . ."

[96] Pratiche, 11 October ("Havendo per le lettere di Roma vista la durezza del Papa. . . .").

[97] Cf. despatch of Archbishop of Bari to Emperor of 16 October in *State Papers, Spanish,* IV, i, 190.

[98] Robert, *ubi supra.*

[99] Praet and Mai, 19 October, *ubi supra* ; cf. Sergardi, letters 32, 39.

[100] Robert, II, *n.* 229–31, of 8 October, *et seqq.* ; cf. also Sergardi, letters 28, 29, 31, for the resolution of Pope and Emperor.

[101] Robert, p. 324 ; Docs. 237, 242, etc.

[102] Sperino, *loc. cit.* p. 257 ; Varchi, II, 193.   Cf. Sergardi, letters 26–30 ; Capello, letter 57.

CHAPTER VIII

FLORENCE BESIEGED

THE city which the Spanish soldiery saw at their feet from Apparita was virtually the same as that which the pilgrim admires to-day. Modern vandalism has not succeeded in marring to any appreciable extent the distant view of the city of flowers. Thickly populated extensions have indeed grown up in recent years ; but though the city was still restricted on the whole by the third line of fortifications commenced in the time of Dante, where the present-day Viali run, even then some important suburbs lay beyond. The crowded line of roofs was broken by more towers than are at present standing ; but the most prominent were those which attract our notice to-day, with the Campanile above all in its ethereal beauty. Then, as now, the whole was surmounted as with a crown by the majestic cupola of the Duomo. A difference might indeed be noticed in the Arno, which ran perennially like a silver ribbon through the plain before its waters had been diverted for irrigation purposes in the upper valley. The city was surrounded by all the amenities which nature could lavish or wealth procure. " I do not think," wrote the patriotically hypercritical Venetian envoy, " that (for a town of the *terra-ferma*) there is in Italy, nay in Europe, a position more beautiful or more delicious than that of Florence ; for it is situated in a plain surrounded with hills . . . all fertile, cultivated, and pleasant, laden with most beautiful and sumptuous palaces constructed at excessive expense with all the delights which may be imagined—gardens, thickets, fountains, fishponds, baths, and views which seem pictures." [1]

The population had been terribly diminished by the plague of two years previous and now amounted in all probability to no more than 57,000, or, with the suburbs, to perhaps 80,000. In addition, the inhabitants of the surrounding countryside, who had taken refuge within the walls upon the approach of the enemy, came to some 15,000, to which must be added about 10,000 mercenary soldiers. Deducting those who had left before the siege commenced, to escape the dangers of war, the total population during the period must be reckoned at something like 110,000. It was this city, almost negligible in size according to modern standards, which now made ready to resist unaided the combined forces of the greatest potentates of Europe, lords of Italy, of Flanders, of Germany, and of Spain, backed up by the growing resources of the New World.

Apart from all numerical considerations, Florence was in no position to make war. Her constitution, based upon a cumbersome mediæval system of checks and balances, was unsuitable for a period when decision, speed, efficiency, and secrecy were of paramount importance. The rulers of the city were amateurs in the art of government, and bi-monthly changes rendered it impossible for them to gain, excepting in exceptional cases, any adequate experience. Moreover, they lacked final authority, having to refer to an external body for all more important decisions. The deliberations in the Consulte and Pratiche were interminable and indeterminate : the Great Council was paralysed for efficient action by its infinite divisions. Through continual reference to these ever-widening bodies, secrecy became impossible and state matters were known to the city almost as soon as they were brought up.[2] Confidence, whether at home or abroad, could not be completely placed in a government which so frequently changed its composition and even its policy. Military operations could not be efficient if they had invariably to be submitted to the arbitrament of unwieldy civilian boards. These defects were realized by such able contemporary critics as Guicciardini and Giannotti, who proposed remedies for them ; while Machiavelli himself had recommended the Roman practice of electing a dictator in time of crisis. Nevertheless, the city continued during the period of the siege to be governed in the same slow-moving manner, and only towards the very end was any sort of inner council set up for the direction of military operations. In contrast to this, the besiegers were guided by a single will, with no authority above it save the wishes of two absolute sovereigns who granted their general a free hand at least in military affairs.[3]

The lack of vision and co-ordination in the government had recently been shown in the preparations to cope with the dangers gathering round the city. In spite of constant alarms, no serious provision had been made and the whole question had been regarded in an almost mercantile spirit. To the end, the policy of a large number of the citizens remained—to trust in the mercies of God and in the advantages of procrastination. While the fate of the city was being decided in the conversations at Rome between Clement and the Prince of Orange, the Captain-General of the Republic was in Lombardy, the Governor-General with the majority of the forces about Perugia, and the director of fortifications at Ferrara. Even at this juncture, opinion was not unanimously in favour of serious preparation ; and one citizen, well read in ancient literature, adduced classical example to discourage active provision and to rely rather upon the possibilities of seducing some portion of the enemy's forces from their obedience.[4]   Outside the city, military preparations were in an even worse state.   There was not a single cannon at Pietrasanta or Mutrone, two fortresses occupying vital strategic positions, where the towers were without artillery emplacements or even ladders.[5]   Pisa was similarly ill-provided, though its position was peculiarly precarious owing to the notorious infidelity of the inhabitants and the Medicophile leanings of those among them who adhered to Florence.   As early as May her commissary, Cecotto Tosinghi, had begged for some provision, but without result : and permission to deport suspected persons was accorded only in July.[6]   The fortress of Livorno was under two constables opposed to one another, while the other strong places of the dominion were similarly ill-provided.[7]

From the consequences of this lack of foresight, the Florentines were saved by the long delays of Orange, which had been so providential as to seem the work of God.   Had the enemy pushed on immediately after the occupation of Cortona and Arezzo, he would have found the city in a state of panic and unpreparedness and would almost certainly have been able to enter almost without opposition.[8]   For, in spite of the continual alarms of war during the past years, the fortifications even of the capital had been criminally neglected.   Before 1527, indeed, something had been done to bring them up to date.   According to the plans of Antonio da Sangallo, a line of bastions had been commenced on the south side of the river stretching from the gate of S. Miniato to Giramonte.   At the same time Federigo da Bozzolo and Count Piero Navarra had introduced certain modifications in the system of defence in accordance with recent theory.   The towers which crowned the walls at intervals were thrown down, at infinite trouble and expense ; but it was generally thought by the suspicious inhabitants that the city was the poorer for it from the military point of view as well as from the æsthetic.   At the same time, the principal gates—eleven in number—were strengthened with earthworks ; and the course of the Mugnone, which fell into the Arno to the west of the city, was again changed so as to encircle a great part of the walls on the northern side with an effective moat.[9]   After the revolution, the fortresses of the dominion had been put in order, but the defences of the capital had been neglected.[10]   At the commencement of 1529, however, the growing perils of the foreign situation led to a resumption of the work.   Florence was fortunate in having at this time a citizen who, in the heroic age of Leonardo da Vinci, was naturally indicated as a military engineer.   Michelangelo Buonarotti, famous already as painter, sculptor, and architect, was elected in January to the Nove della Milizia, the board over the defence of the city restored in 1527. In this office, he was supposed to have the fortifications as his special care. Yet the timid nature of Niccolò Capponi feared the effect which any sort of warlike preparation might have upon the animosity of the Pope; and Michelangelo found his work hampered, if not nullified, by the head of the government himself.[11] The apprehensions of the Florentines were, however, continually increasing. In the following April, accordingly, the Dieci, " considering the strengthening and fortification of the city . . . necessary in order to resist the perils which are seen imminent each day," elected their " excellent architect " Michelangelo to the specially created post of " Governor-General and Procurator of the Fortifications " at a regular salary (hitherto, as a member of the Nove, he had worked gratuitously). In this capacity he did some work at the fortresses of the Dominion, as, for example, Pisa. But his main occupation was at Florence, especially at the completion of the works at San Miniato.[12] In May, the threatening news from Naples and Perugia led to an intensification of the labours. In the next month a special tax was levied, and payments were authorized, to defray the expenses; while compulsory expropriations at the cost of the state were authorized.[13] At the report of the coming of the Emperor, it was again decided to hasten on the work. Yet even now it was not pushed forward as the situation demanded, and it was only with the news of the treaties of Barcelona and Cambrai and the conviction that " these two princes design to sell us by auction " that the matter began to be taken really seriously.[14] Michelangelo, who had been working at a disadvantage owing to the hostility of the former Gonfalonier, commenced hurriedly to throw up the bastions with fascines of tow. With a modesty rare in an artist, however, he was not satisfied with his work or his qualifications. At the end of July, he was therefore sent to examine what were considered the model works at Ferrara, where the Duke, still titularly ally of Florence and the greatest authority on such matters in Italy, accorded him all facilities, conducting him personally round the walls.[15] The Imperial army had meanwhile begun to move, and he was hurried back to Florence after only a cursory inspection to push on the defence works. In this he was aided by other eminent architects. Though Antonio da San Gallo was in the service of the Pope and working for the besiegers, his nephew, Francesco, was employed by Florence as Capo Maestro of the fortifications, and his namesake Giovanfrancesco had been constantly active during the past two years at various places of the dominion.[16]

The work of Michelangelo was, as we have seen, a continuation of that initiated in the last years of Medicean rule. Yet the original plan was modified by him in important respects. The defences as then planned had embraced the hill of Giramonte. This, however, besides its technical disadvantages, demanded too great an expense both in the construction and in the maintenance, and would have required a larger garrison than could be conveniently spared. He therefore restricted the scheme so as to comprise San Miniato alone. Thence the works went down along the line of the steps—

> "Carved in that old and simple age when still
> The registry and label rested safe"—
>
> (*Purgatorio*, XII, 104–5)

to join the old city wall. To the west, a number of other bastions continued the defences towards the river in that direction. All the way round the walls there were similar lunettes and earthworks, inside and out, to strengthen the existing fortifications. Weak points were safeguarded by bastions, platforms, trenches, and other works, and were specifically defended with troops and artillery. Special measures were taken too to defend the houses abutting upon the river. All this was besides the existing walls, which were of great height and still turreted at intervals, with a platform masking every gate. The principal point remained about San Miniato, where modern Florence has commemorated the architect by the Piazzale bearing his name and adorned with a reproduction of his David looking down over the city, glorying in his young strength. At this spot the foot-hills of the surrounding mountains approach near the river and almost overhang the city and the plain ; and it was obviously the key to the whole position from the military point of view. The old church and monastery upon the height were built with a fortress-like strength and solidarity, and lent themselves to adaptation for the works of defence of which they formed the kernel. The outer walls of the bastion were composed of unbaked bricks, the clay of which was mingled for consistency with chopped tow : the thickness was filled in with earth. This passed through the orchard of the monastery, in the middle of which was constructed an artillery emplacement for three guns. On the campanile of the church, rising almost to the height of the neighbouring mountains, were placed a couple of light pieces which commanded the enemy's camp. It was objected that, in designing these defences, Michelangelo multiplied flanking lines and embrasures beyond what was either necessary or safe. But they stood the test : and such was their strength that they defied even the hard usage of the siege. After the war, they received the compliment of being reconstructed on a more permanent plan. During the next century and a half, the art of fortification made great strides ; yet it is said that Vauban, the most distinguished military engineer of his age, visited with admiration and profit the works of the great Florentine architect.[17]

The whole affair had indeed been left till dangerously late. The city was, however, saved by the slowness of Orange's advance, coupled with the extraordinary activity displayed in the last moments. In the critical days after the fall of Arezzo the work was carried on almost frantically under the personal direction and encouragement of the Gonfalonier himself, " without respect for substance and with great courage, in preparedness for any sacrifice." The peasants previously employed, who were accustomed to such labour, were forced to go home to attend to the vintage ; but their place was taken by the ordinary citizens. Implements and provisions were requisitioned to be taken up to the workers. A licence was given to cut down trees as the Nove thought fit, to be used as material. The services of master-builders were commanded under pain of the gallows. Shops and workrooms were closed while those employed went to labour at the bastions. At a later stage, the whole city was ordered up to the works, so that for some days every adult from fourteen years upwards was employed. The work continued not only in the daytime but also at night, by the light of torches. There seemed to be a friendly competition between soldiers and civilians to see who could do the most. " The preparations," wrote an eye-witness, " are a marvel to see " ; and while the men worked, the women prayed.[18] By the time Orange approached the walls, his opportunity had passed and the city could no longer be taken unprepared. Throughout the siege, and in the first months particularly, the work was continued in weak points, and peasants from eighteen years upwards were still conscripted to labour while the citizens were fighting.[19] As a result, the city became wellnigh impregnable. The fortifications were under the control of the Governor-General and three Commissaries-General with other commissaries dependent upon them. Later, commissions of survey were elected, whose function it was to inspect the defences and to report upon requirements.[20]

By the time the siege was formed, however, Michelangelo was no longer in Florence. It is a mysterious and not wholly creditable episode in the history of the great artist. According to his own *contemporary* account, some unknown person came to him as he was superintending the work on 21 September and whispered in his ear a warning that he should escape for his life. Before the day was over, he had left the city. The truth of the whole affair is difficult to make out. Apparently his sensitive mind was hurt at some imagined offence from the Signoria added to the niggardly support which he had in the past received, and perhaps also by a premature suspicion of treachery within the city.   It is quite conceivable that one of the Medicean partisans who knew the importance of his work and the sensibility of his nature tried to play upon his fears so as to rid the city of his aid, and that this was the origin of the menace which decided him to leave.   In any case, he made his way to Venice with the intention of continuing his journey to France, but did not do so owing to the troubled state of affairs beyond the Alps.   On 20 September his name was included in a list of prominent Florentine citizens who were proclaimed outlaws if they did not return to the city within the week.   He allowed the time to pass, but later his conscience began to smite him.   Battista della Palla, an old friend and correspondent, sent him a noble appeal urging him to come back.   His more recent acquaintance, the Florentine ambassador at Ferrara, wrote a letter of intercession on his behalf ; and as a result a pardon was issued on 20 October.   A month later he belied all suspicions of cowardice by returning to Florence under a safe-conduct.   He was fined 1,500 ducats for his offence, and excluded from the Great Council for three years. Yet, in spite of this, he gave proof of his real patriotism and courage by remaining in the city, giving valuable assistance, until the close of the siege.[21]

An integral part ot the scheme of defence was to destroy everything around the city which might serve the enemy for protection or in any other way.   As early as July the heroic resolution had been taken to destroy the villas and suburbs which had been built without the walls.[22]   In the wealth and luxury of Renaissance Florence, these were of extraordinary magnificence, so much so that it had been generally thought that the citizens would never adventure them in the hazards of war.   " The palaces are the hostages of Florence, which the enemy holds in his hand," wrote a contemporary ; and the sentiment was pro-verbial.[23]   The unflinching determination of the Florentines belied this opinion.   Nevertheless, though a commencement was immediately made, matters were not yet carried to the extreme. At the end of September, however, on the approach of the enemy, the Gonfalonier asked whether the work should be continued. " With tears in their eyes," the Ottanta gave a unanimous con-sent.[24]   All edifices within a mile of the walls, small or great, secular or ecclesiastical, were to be razed without pity to the ground at the expense of the state.   The order was executed ruthlessly—almost jubilantly.   Fire was deliberately set to stately palaces, and the flames devoured priceless treasures of luxury and art.   Troops of youths worked with battering-rams

to break down the walls and to destroy villas to the value sometimes of as much as twenty thousand ducats. The proprietors
themselves were sometimes to be seen working among them to
pull down their own houses. But, as usual, the poor suffered the
most, and ten thousand unfortunates, it was reckoned, were left
roofless to suffer the rigours of the approaching winter. At least
four monasteries, erected at great cost, met their fate with the
rest of the buildings. The very gardens and vineyards and
orchards were destroyed, fruit trees and shrubs ruthlessly up-
rooted, and the branches were carried tied up in bundles to be
used in constructing the fortifications, which for the moment
were made lovely by their verdure. Nothing which could be of
any conceivable service was left to the enemy.[25] There was one
glorious exception. It is a story incredibly characteristic of the
time and place. It was some months later, and the siege was
already far advanced, when it was reported in the city that the
Prince of Orange, unable to put up any longer with the dirt and
squalor of his present billets, was contemplating a removal to
the monastery of San Salvi outside the Porta alla Croce—the spot
where Henry VII had his headquarters two centuries before. A
body of pioneers was sent out to forestall him by destroying the
place together with its surroundings. They set to work without
remorse. The church was battered down, to be followed by the
campanile, and a commencement was made upon the monastery
itself. One of the sides of the Refectory was breached, revealing
a Last Supper by Andrea del Sarto, recently painted on the
interior of one of the walls, in all its fresh glory. The very
workmen were disarmed at the sight. Destruction, and even
sacrilege, might be committed on behalf of the city ; but vandalism not even in these straits was permissible. The tale may
not be correct in all of its dramatic particulars, but is certainly
true in its main details. San Salvi and its fresco remain a
monument of Florentine self-sacrifice and of exquisitely Florentine
sensibility.[26]

The example of destruction was, however, infectious. It
was not natural while destroying the homes of friends to spare
those of enemies, even though they were situated at some distance
from the walls and were without military importance. The usual
band of riotous young men, headed by Dante da Castiglione and
prompted, according to rumour, by the Gonfalonier himself, took
matters into its own hands. The magnificent Medici palace at
Careggi was burned : that of Castello was saved only by the
diligence of a servant. The costly villa of Jacopo Salviati at
Montughi was completely destroyed, and it would have been
followed by the most famous of Medicean dwelling-places at
Poggio a Caiano had it not been for the proximity of the enemy.

The Signoria intervened to prevent further destruction.[27]   Yet what was deliberately ruined now was saved a similar fate at a later stage.   There was virtually no place, great or small, which during the course of the war did not endure the horrors of destruction or of sack, frequently more than once.   Not a door or window was left in any building, all woodwork being carried off for fuel by the one side or the other.   Many years later, the marks left by the iron hooks and rings which had been wrenched away could still be seen.[28]

Besides the city itself, the Florentines continued to defend some few essential fortresses, leaving the rest of the dominion to fend for itself.   Livorno was on the coast and ensured communications by sea.   Pisa was the first city of the dominion and an important centre for corn supply.   In addition it commanded communications with France and the outside world through Livorno on the one side and Lucca and Genoa on the other.   Empoli, Pistoia, and Prato were further vital links in the chain of communications.   The first was also an important agricultural centre, and the others too near the capital to be allowed to pass lightly into the hands of the enemy.   Through the delays of Orange there had been time for these places also to be put into a state of preparation by Amadio d' Alberto and other engineers.[29]   Nevertheless, the Florentines could not feel really secure of any one of their possessions.   The Medici had commenced to form a state about Florence: Savonarola had destroyed it, and the last Republic followed in this also in his footsteps.   Her acutest and most enlightened observers could see the necessity for the extension beyond the walls of the duties of citizenship only, and not its privileges.   Where the commune was the unit of government, and the representative system unknown, this was perhaps inevitable: yet Republican Florence, in contrast to the Principality which succeeded it, shows up at its worst in this aspect, which almost justifies, as it in part explains, its fall.   The old maxims of government were still current—to control Pisa by fortresses, Prato by poverty, Pistoia by factions.   It was a military as well as a moral weakness.   It was necessary to maintain a considerable force of as many as 5,000 soldiers scattered about in all the more important centres, instead of leaving the defence to the inhabitants.   The public deliberations and official despatches breathe a continual uneasiness lest there should be another series of uprisings.   As an additional pledge of fidelity, hostages were ordered to be sent to Florence.   From Pisa, the memory of whose great revolt was fresh, no less than fifty-seven persons were exiled for the sake of security.[30]   The Imperialists on their side were able to overrun the dominion without meeting any really serious resistance, in spite of the immense natural strength enjoyed by the majority of the cities of Tuscany. All of the more important places gave in without striking a blow, though it is significant by contrast that in many cases the citadel, garrisoned by reliable troops, was able to hold out long after the city had surrendered.

The direction of the war was controlled by the various magistracies—the Signoria, the Gonfalonieri, the Buonuomini, the Otto ; and especially the Nove della Milizia and the Dieci di Guerra, whose name was changed by a traditional euphemism to Dieci di Libertà e Pace at time of war.[31] In addition, there was a special commission over the defence of the city in all its details, of which the most important members were Rafaello Girolami and Zanobi Bartolini.[32] Acting commander-in-chief of the forces was the Governor-General, Malatesta Baglione, with an immediate following of Perugians. Second in command was Stefano Colonna of Palestrina, an old condottiere of the Pope and later of the King of France, who had accorded his services to the city at the time of the Treaty of Cambrai.[33] The artillery, of which there was no lack (the soldiers themselves being surprised at the quantity), was under Leonardo Signorelli, a kinsman of Baglione.[34] At the opening of the siege there were nominally about 9,200 soldiers employed for the defence of the city, making an effective force of about 8,000.[35] The number was continually increasing till in the next year it came to over 10,000, though, according to convention, many more than this were on the pay-roll.[36] During the course of the siege, however, there was natural wastage through casualties, sickness, and desertion, so that by April the number of effectives was reduced to 7,000, and in July to little more than 6,000.[37] The total of the defenders was augmented by a provision whereby exiles from the city were pardoned if they returned within eight days and " shall serve without any stipend the Florentine Republic in the defence of her liberty."[38] No fewer than six hundred persons availed themselves immediately of this permission, many even leaving the ranks of the enemy—" fine troops and in good order " ;[39] and in the first days after the lapse of the period they were followed, by special licences, by nearly two hundred more.[40] At a later stage all unattached professional soldiers residing in the city were compelled to serve.[41] There was a strong force of cavalry, to equip which the horses of the citizens were commandeered.[42] The soldiers of the Republic were ordered under pain of death to wear as their device a white cross, to distinguish them from the Imperialists, who wore one of red.[43] A commission was appointed with plenary authority to requisition billets.[44] This whole force was under six colonels and about eighty captains, of whom only seventeen were Florentine subjects. The rank

and file was similarly composed, with perhaps a smaller proportion of natives. Practically all, however, apart from some
few Gascons, were Italians, with a fair number of Corsicans, and
thus enjoyed a certain degree of cohesion as well as of patriotic
feeling, in striking contrast to the mixed multitude beneath the
walls. They were, too, the pick of the Italian soldiery, being in
large part veterans of the Bande Nere, " good and valiant
troops," wrote the Dieci, " and much disposed for our defence,
both because they are well paid and because it seems to all that
we are fighting for the honour of Italy." [45] Of these, as many as
3,600—about half of the whole—were stationed at the key position
of S. Miniato—under Stefano Colonna to the east and Mario
Orsini to the west. At each one of the gates, with the exception
of three which were definitely closed, one company of soldiers
was maintained, while 2,000 more in two divisions were held
ready as reinforcements to succour any threatened position. This
was sufficient for the defence according to the opinion of the
captains, who declared that 6,000 men, with perhaps an extra
1,000 for sudden emergencies, were all that was required. [46] As
we have seen, the actual total exceeded this number at the commencement of the siege by 1,000 or more. In contrast, however, to this, the forces of Orange had been swollen by now to
300 men-at-arms, 500 light horse, 2,500 Germans, 2,000 Spanish,
and 6,000 Italians—over 11,000 in all, and they were constantly
increasing so as to amount ultimately to as many as 30,000. In
addition, pioneers and camp followers hoping for a chance of
booty brought up the total to twice that number. [47]

The force of professional soldiers defending the city was,
however, supplemented by the militia established by Niccolò
Capponi and reorganized in details at the commencement of the
siege. [48] Each quarter of the city was divided according to
ancient usage into four " gonfaloni," each distinguished by its
own flag. This was adopted as the framework of the new citizen
force, which was recruited and divided upon the same basis.
Each of the four companies was commanded by a Sergeant-Major
experienced in arms, aided by a civilian commissary elected
every six months and serving gratuitously. [49] The Palace guard
was reorganized so as to set free for more serious duties those enrolled in the militia : while those eligible for it were not allowed
to take service with the mercenaries. [50] Even from outside the
city men of military age were ordered back to serve. [51] Arms
for them, originating perhaps in Germany, had been smuggled
in from Brescia and its neighbourhood despite the vigilance of
the Venetians, in addition to what was imported by more open
methods : and this continued to be the source of supply. [52] But
they suffered from the paucity of their numbers. Only men of

eighteen to thirty-six were originally included, making a total
of some 4,000, of whom 1,700 were armed with arquebuses
—less than had been expected, owing to the ravages of the
pest.[53] Little trust was placed in them at the commencement
as not being a professional body—indeed, even the Italian mercenaries did not enjoy complete confidence, it being considered
that " without lanzknechts or Swiss it is impossible to rout the
enemy." [54] It was only after the militia had given proof of its
mettle that public opinion began to change, and its scope was
extended. In November, the age limit of those called to arms
was extended from thirty-six to fifty, and in March to sixty.[55]
The *non-beneficiati*—the unprivileged citizens—were included by
a special provision at about Christmas time.[56] By this means,
the number was increased from under 5,000 at the commencement of the siege to twice that number at its close.[57] It could,
however, have been raised still higher had there been a more
liberal spirit on the part of the citizens. It was only in the very
last days that ancient prejudices could be overcome and orders
given for the general arming of the whole population of the city.
The resources of the contado and the dominion, treated with a
contemptuous disdain, were never tapped. This was a mistake
of the gravest order from the political point of view as well as
from the military. Apart from the thousands of able-bodied
fighters whom it would have enrolled beneath the Marzocco—
the traditional lion of Florence—it would have formed a valuable cement between the city and its possessions. But the
proudly independent Florentine spirit could not appreciate the
same qualities in others ; and outside the walls patriotism de-
generated into a species of tyranny, or, at the best, intolerance.
Donato Giannotti alone had the acumen to suggest the arming
of the contado, but even he lacked foresight to envisage the
extension with it of political privileges. As a result, in spite of
the small beginnings of a national army under Cosimo I, the
noble ideals of Machiavelli ran to seed, and all military spirit
died out in Tuscany until the period of the Risorgimento.[58] In
spite of these reservations, the militia proved an immense success
and was the salvation of the city in the critical days of autumn.
It was placed under the able command of Stefano Colonna. At
night part went up to assist in guarding the fortifications while
others patrolled the streets : as the soldiers, excepting those on
duty, were not supposed to leave their billets without orders till
dawn.[59] All were assigned stations to repair to in case the alarm
should be given.[60] Every time that they were in action, they
covered themselves with glory. The most gifted as well as the
noblest of Florentine citizens served in their ranks. Report
mentions the name of Andrea del Sarto, at this time only forty-

three years of age.   Benvenuto Cellini tells us how he provided himself with a rich outfit and went about with the highest nobility of Florence, who showed unanimous desire to fight for the defence of their liberties.[61]   An eye-witness relates how the gilded youth, who used to waste their time lolling about the streets or in the shops exchanging criticism and scandal, suddenly experienced a miraculous change and commenced to think only of their own honour and the welfare of the state.   All contemporary reports unite in their praise and speak of the excellent discipline which they shared with the regular soldiers " as though this very numerous militia were a most strict order of Franciscan friars." [62]

The martial preoccupations of the citizens manifested themselves even in fashions and in habits of life.   The long ringlets hanging down to the shoulder which were invariable before the siege were too effeminate for a city of soldiers, and were cropped short as an offering to Mars.   In compensation, men began to affect the beard, a more masculine adornment as well as one which required less time for attention than the shaven chin which was always to be seen before.   Similarly the hood was regarded as an impediment, and was discarded in favour of hats or caps.[63]   The taverns, puritanically closed as places of resort for the past two years as in the first flush of revolution, were reopened for the benefit of the soldiers who were continually coming and going.[64]

A factor which must always be reckoned with in the Italian character is a love of pageantry.   This had been amply provided for when the militia was set up and regulated.   Two annual celebrations were established—for 16 May, the day of the expulsion of the Medici and the restoration of the Republic ;   and 9 February, the anniversary of the election of Jesus as King of Florence, and the establishment of true liberty.   Each year the Ottanta was to select some young man between the ages of twenty-four and twenty-six who should make an oration on the first of these dates in the Great Council—open for the occasion even to non-privileged citizens—in favour of arming the public, recommending discipline as the true preservative of liberty, and eulogizing the liberty recovered on this day.   The ceremony, attended by all the officers of state, was to be preceded by a solemn mass.   Meanwhile all shops were closed ; and the militia, parading at Santa Maria Novella, was to march through the streets to the Duomo.   Here, facing the Baptistery, an altar was to be erected at which two priests administered a solemn oath of allegiance.   While those present reverently knelt, a Bible was passed from rank to rank, and all swore to use their arms for the glory of God, the common good, and the defence of liberty.

A similar ceremony took place on the other occasion, when an oration was delivered in honour of Jesus as King of Florence, and a solemn procession was made, with all the officers of state participating, from the Duomo to the Annunziata, and so back to the Duomo.[65] Another festivity was observed on the day of San Salvatore (9 November), " on which was made by Omnipotent God the beginning of the salvation of this city," being the anniversary of the expulsion of the Medici in 1494.[66]

In order to sustain the burden of defence the one thing needed, in ancient wars as in modern, was money. This was peculiarly so in Italy where mercenary soldiers played so large a part. Guicciardini, at the commencement of the war, had clearly seen that the whole question of success or failure would turn upon this factor, and had warned the Pope to that effect.[67] To this end, therefore, the efforts of the Florentines were largely directed. Before the siege the annual revenues of the city were about 300,000 florins, of which rather more than half was devoted to ordinary expenditure.[68] Yet the continual wars and other troubles from 1526 onwards had prevented any surplus from being laid aside, and we have seen the constant recurrence to special levies and to forced loans. From the summer of 1529 one expedient succeeded another, especially to defray the crushing cost of the fortifications, and commissions were appointed to study ways and means. The sums gathered soon disappeared under the continual strain. It was even proposed to modify the plans so as to save expense. But the proposal was unanimously rejected owing to the danger which it might entail,[69] and it became increasingly necessary to raise money. Ordinary methods failing, a special commission was appointed to explore fresh methods and to raise a compulsory loan at 12 per cent.[70] Still demands for money continued to be of almost daily occurrence.[71] Finally it was decided in the teeth of strong opposition to sell the property and estates of all gilds and fraternities on the understanding that they were to be compensated for at a subsequent date. So as to ensure success, purchase was compelled by private and public bodies whose deposits in sacred edifices were seized and devoted to that purpose. From this and similar measures a sum of 100,000 ducats was hoped for.[72] From the Badia alone—the abbey of Dantesque memories in the very centre of Florence—over 8,000 florins were expected from deposits ; yet this would barely suffice to defray the expenses of a single day.[73] To this was added the sums raised by selling the property of declared outlaws and of recalcitrant citizens who refused to pay what was required of them even at the penalty of imprisonment. All was put up to auction at sales which were held almost daily in several points of the city. The common people were able to acquire the splendid household appointments of the rich. Estates were sold which the purchasers could not visit in the present state of affairs and perhaps had never seen ; while half of the payment was accepted in receipts for the latest forced loan. Other property was disposed of by the medium of a lottery.[74] This included the precious stones from the mitre of Leo X, long conserved as a pious relic in the Duomo, and now confiscated.[75] Yet, in spite of all, expenditure exceeded the revenue : and recourse had to be made to private aid to make good the shortcomings of public finance. One patriotic citizen had gone so far as to place all of his property at the disposal of the government : and he arranged to provide a fixed sum weekly for the prosecution of the war.[76] It was this example which it was hoped to propagate. The Signoria issued an appeal to the " charity and love of good citizens, more efficacious than any ordinary provision," in which each man was invited to intimate the sum he was prepared to advance to " his sweet mother country " upon the security of the goods of the Gilds.[77] The appeal was launched before the Great Council on 28 September, the day of the high-spirited rejection of the Pope's terms. It was unanimously determined to support the expenses of the war and each citizen made a written statement of his personal offering if he had not enough with him. Within a few hours 30,000 ducats were subscribed in sums of from 20 to 250. Money, reported one enthusiast, was taken by the lapful to the Palazzo every day. By such means, the first months of war were tided over.[78] During the whole course of the war, the expenses totalled at least 100,000 florins monthly, or 1,400,000 in all, for the city alone—nearly ten times the ordinary expenditure, and three times the amount of the unusually high expenses of the previous two years of Republican government put together. At a hundred florins to the pound, the total comes to 14,000 pounds in bullion, or something like £600,000 sterling in gold, at a time when that commodity was worth perhaps fourteen times as much as it is now. This was no mean achievement for a city which by modern standards would not be considered of any great importance.[79]

The determination of the enemy to persist in the attack had been sharpened by confidence in an early victory. It was difficult for contemporaries to believe that the Florentines would defend themselves if it came to the pinch. Just now, too, it was the autumn. The corn harvest had just been gathered in, but could not yet be transported to the cities : the vintage of wine and oil had not yet arrived, and much must be irretrievably lost. This was one of the main reasons for Clement's hope in a bloodless victory on the mere report of the advance of the army.

It is said even that he refused Charles's offer of ample reinforcements from the troops he had brought with him from Spain, for fear they might cause needless damage in the contado.[80] The Venetian envoy, Foscari, had considered the Florentines strong in position, but the reverse in themselves. They were weakened, he declared, by internal strife and divisions. They had too much to risk in the case of hostilities. The very atmosphere and climate engendered timidity. The citizens were mere merchants and craftsmen, and the rulers of the city themselves—here speaks the haughty patrician—might be seen at work in their shops.[81] Varchi himself wonders that such men, accustomed from their youth upwards to shoulder bales of wool and to balance baskets of silk on their heads like the lowest manual labourer, and to work like slaves all day and much of the night at the shuttle and the spindle, could show such grandeur of spirit.[82]

But, if merchants, the Florentines were of a notoriously independent character. A people which would not doff the hat to any below the rank of bishop or Gonfalonier [83] was not likely to yield to mere threats. They were, in addition, borne up by a buoyant optimism which encouraged them to dare everything. Just as they had previously refused to credit the voyage and destination of the Emperor, so they continued to discount all the further perils which overhung them. They persisted, in spite of all indications to the contrary, in trusting in the good faith and ultimate assistance of France, if not of the other allies, even after the Treaty of Cambrai. They refused to believe that the ancient enmity of Pope and Emperor could be smoothed over so easily, or that the latter had sufficient determination to persist. They hoped for relief from his distractions north of the Alps—from Germany, torn by the Lutheran heresy, and from Austria, where the very capital was menaced by the Turk. At the same time, they turned for comfort to the experience of history. They had before them the example of a number of recent sieges all of which had ended in failure—from Padua in 1509 to Naples in the previous year. They had faith, too— and foreign observers shared their opinion—in the natural strength of the city and the invulnerability of its fortifications. One of their proudest memories was the resistance—unique in Italy—to the Emperor Henry VII, two centuries before. They had defended themselves with success against Gian Galeazzo of Milan. They had made themselves respected by Charles VIII. An enemy had never stayed for long in the valley of the Arno. If he were small in numbers he would be unable to form the siege; if great, he would have difficulty in obtaining supplies. As a result, the Florentines were prepared to brave matters out to the last. Neglecting defence, they tended to indulge in speculations rather than in preparations ; and the whole motto of the initial period—found time after time in the records of official deliberations—was " *godere il beneficio del tempo* "—to enjoy the advantage of delay. But this optimism, if it weakened their preparations, only served to strengthen their resolution. It is largely due to this that they had the courage to withstand the menaces and dangers to which they were exposed ; and it gave rise to a stupendously high morale. It is this which makes the siege of Florence so memorable. The area in question may have been insignificant, the numbers engaged small, the fighting some-times a mere travesty and the casualties negligible by modern standards. Yet the spirit which was displayed elevates the whole thing above the trivialities of the moment, and makes the petty Republic as worthy of our study and consideration as the mightiest empire in her hour of trial.

Battista della Palla, earliest perhaps of modern art-dealers, may be taken as a typical case. " I assure you," he wrote to Michelangelo in urging him to return, " that I am not only without any fear, but also full of confidence in a glorious victory . . . I contemplate in these our fellow-citizens a noble spirit of disdain for all their losses and the bygone luxuries of villa life ; admirable unity and fervour for the preservation of liberty ; fear of God alone, confidence in Him and in the justice of our cause ; and innumerable other good things, certain to bring the age of gold. . . ." [84] Foreign observers were no less enthusiastic. " The whole city is of good courage, and every day becomes more intrepid and desirous of showing its worth," wrote the Venetian ambassador.[85] " Certainly, this city deserves to be celebrated for all centuries," echoed Vincenzo Fedele, his secretary. " It is a marvel, or rather a miracle, to see. . . ." [86] Even the enemies of the Republic were lost in admiration at the courage displayed by the Florentines, and bear eloquent testimony to their deter-mination and resolution.[87] Once during an assault Varchi saw an old man with his little grandson hastening to the battlements hand in hand to share in victory or in death.[88] The greatest order reigned in the city. Excepting that the sounding of bells at night was prohibited, the reports of the artillery being heard in their stead, nothing abnormal was to be noticed. The shops were opened and affairs transacted, though the assistants, and, at a later stage, the owners themselves, grave men who had sat in the highest magistracies, went about their business in helmet and hauberk, with weapons at their side and sometimes with the arquebus on their shoulder.[89] Every house kept a light burning in the window all night to ensure order in the streets ; and this was perfectly maintained.[90] The public squares were thronged, the markets well frequented, and the streets filled with music and song. On all the principal corners was scrawled up the motto " POOR BUT FREE." Sharp justice was rendered to malefactors, though the civil courts were closed and private disputes postponed till better times.[91] The children went to school as if nothing were happening, and the Great Council reached a thousand members at its meetings as in normal times. There seemed to be more money about than before the war. Victuals continued to enter the city by water as well as by land, and there was shortage of nothing within the city with the exception of wood. Steps were indeed taken to control and even to requisition supplies : but it did not seem to be necessary, owing to that year's unusually heavy yield. The table of the Venetian ambassador remained well furnished, and he had no qualms about extending his usual lavish hospitality. Persons were actually making bets that within twelve days the enemy would be defeated. In the middle of the siege, when the pinch of war had already commenced to be felt, the carnival season was observed in the usual manner. For the traditional game of *calcio* (a species of football with twenty-five on each side) the Piazza Santa Croce was selected, as the point nearest to the enemy ; and so as to attract his attention the more surely, instrumentalists were placed on the roof of the church to provide music. A cannon shot was sent to disturb them, but it failed to do any damage or to break up the game. " I swear to God, Father," declared more than one Spanish noble to Fra Giuliano Ughi, " that we had heard that the Florentines are skilled with the pen in trade ; but certes, they are more skilled with the arquebus and with arms in war." [92]

No small part of this patriotic ardour owed its origin to religious fervour. Over thirty years before Savonarola had foretold, " *Firenze flagellebitur, et post flagella renovabitur.*" Among the Piagnoni, the memory of this prophecy was still alive ; and it seemed that it was being fulfilled before their eyes. Florence was being chastised ; would it not withstand and as surely be renewed ? The spirit of the Friar came back to the city full flood. It was not only the credulous populace who believed in him. The feeling was general, and shared by men like Lorenzo da Credi, perhaps the most charming among the painters of his age, who was spending his declining years in his native city in serene confidence in " Fra Girolamo da Ferrara."[93] Even by those who did not admit his sanctity, the matter was regarded with intense seriousness. An old partisan who had changed his opinions felt impelled to renounce his errors formally and before witnesses in the Duomo, and to burn his writings publicly.[94] While such a spirit was abroad, small satisfaction could be felt with the cloud which still overhung Savonarola's name by reason of his judicial condemnation. Many, especially among the

women, believed that it was by reason of this that the anger
of God was kindled against the city.   One of the most prominent
among the Piagnoni, the cultured Girolamo Benevieni, actually
approached the Pope at an even later date begging the revision
of the sentence ; and he represented a large body of the citizens
who reckoned that matter an important detail of practical
politics.   In the Pratica itself its cancellation was formally
proposed, " as that which is done against Fra Girolamo is done
against God."[95]

The solemn ceremony of 25 June had marked the rising of
this tide of religion : and it continued without ebb.   There was
no lack of representatives to continue the function of prophet.
The populace, and not the populace alone, gave credit to the
ambiguous forecasts of a poor wool-carder, " Pieruccio," almost
a simpleton but of exemplary life.   Even the Palleschi were
influenced in their actions by the more moderate prognostica-
tions of Suor Domenica del Paradiso.[96]   That S. Marco should
regain some part of the influence which it had enjoyed in the
lifetime of its great Prior was inevitable.   Though the power
which it wielded in the state was openly denounced by some
citizens as excessive, the whole city looked to it for guidance.
Its Prior, Bartolommeo da Faenza, who had taken some considerable part in the revolution, continued to encourage the
people from the pulpit ; and one of its friars, Zaccheria da
Treviso, preached inflammatory sermons in the Duomo in imita-
tion of his great master.   But, above all, the mantle of Savonarola seemed to have fallen on Benedetto da Foiano of the rival
convent of Santa Maria Novella.   At the time of the revolution
he had been in exile, but one of the first acts of the new government had been to invite him to return, and he now presided over
his house as Prior.   His venerable age and imposing personality,
combined with his deep learning and great eloquence, attracted
vast congregations to listen to his sermons, and he exercised
enormous influence over the masses as well as in affairs of state.[97]
At one of the critical moments of the siege, he was chosen to
preach in the hall of the Great Council before an audience
crowded to excess.   He played upon the impressionable Florentines as on an instrument, making them laugh or weep as he
desired.   The substance of his sermon has come down to us.
He showed from the Bible how the city was to be liberated from
the perils which overhung it, and should thereafter enjoy sempi-
ternal liberty and happiness.   Finally, with a theatrical gesture,
he presented the Gonfalonier with a banner embroidered on one
side with a Christ triumphant over His enemies, and on the other
with the Cross of the People, with the words " In hoc et cum hoc
vinces."[98]   " Sermons," wrote one of the Palleschi, almost with

a sneer, " were continual, work-day and holy-day, exhorting the people to maintain the popular government and telling them that even if they had to sell their lives for it they should do so, and not live under tyrants ; and with many exclamations and examples they showed that God would preserve them and help them and not abandon them, and that anyhow they would conquer. And all the ill that could be recounted of the Pope and Emperor they recounted on the said open-air pulpit. . . . And thus they maintained them with the said sermons in their said perfidy, rather to die than to change their minds, and that whosoever died for this would die a martyr, and that anyhow they would conquer. . . . And the said preachers were cause that the city did not come to terms with the Pope six months sooner." [99] So much was the influence of these religious leaders recognized even by the Palleschi that steps were taken to prevent them from preaching ; and pressure was put upon the timider Prior of S. Marco to prohibit Fra Zaccheria from continuing his sermons in the Duomo. [100]

These exhortations fell upon fruitful ground. " That recourse should be had to God " is a phrase of daily occurrence in the deliberations of the Pratica, and concrete methods were continually suggested and tried. The atmosphere was that of a revivalist camp. The churches and monasteries were thronged with women and girls who prayed while the men fought. [101] For over a week, wrote Fedele on 2 November, the city had been engaged in fast and confession with a religious procession each day—on the first of the Signoria, and then of the elders, the militia, the women, the children, and so on. [102] A moving proclamation was issued showing how all the inhabitants, without distinction of sex or age, could assist in battle. " . . . Considering how in every human action we should always and principally seek divine aid, and hoping that the arms of the militia, when accompanied by prayer and divine help, will always achieve victory and every good result, we do therefore proclaim and notify all persons not adapted and fitted for arms, such as priests, friars, monks, nuns, children and women of whatever age, that every time our soldiers go to battle with the enemy, this sign shall be made from the Palazzo, viz. the sounding of the Ave Maria by the great bell of the Palazzo with which summons is given for the Great Council : and then, hearing this sign, all the above-mentioned persons not adapted or fitted for arms shall be held and obliged to kneel, both in churches and in convents and in their houses, and to make continual oration while the battle aforementioned shall continue, and to pray the Omnipotent God to give strength and courage to the arms of the Florentine soldiers and militia, and to give them victory against the enemies of the city of Florence, hoping that through the infinity of the mercies of Our Lord Jesus Christ, King of our city, and through the intercessions of His most holy mother, our aforementioned city shall obtain the abovenamed grace." [103]   As was their invariable custom, too, the minds of the Florentines turned at this juncture to the Madonna of Impruneta. This had never been brought to remain in Florence owing to a legend that on a previous occasion it had shown its disapprobation by retiring of its own volition. Now, however, there was the excuse of the proximity of the armies, in the German part of which native violence was accentuated by Lutheran animosities. It was therefore judged safer to have the miraculous picture brought into the city. It was escorted with all solemnity and devotion to the Duomo, where it was lodged, not without a soothing effect upon the population. Similar objects of veneration, such as the Madonna della Quercia, were brought in from other outlying districts. [104]

In spite of the general courageousness, the advance of the armies, and the crowds of fugitives who sought refuge within the walls, caused widespread alarm. The superstitious had noted with apprehension how in those very days one of the lions kept at the back of the Palazzo, where is now the Via de' Leoni, had broken the bars which kept it from the neighbouring cage and there killed a lioness. This occurrence, last recorded at the time of the death of Lorenzo the Magnificent, was supposed to be a most inauspicious omen. [105] The news of the fall of Arezzo increased the alarm into a panic, especially among those who knew how vulnerable the city as yet was to attack. In spite of the gates being guarded, a large number of citizens fled, including many of military age, and others commenced to put their women-folk and property into places of security. The total number of fugitives by the time the siege had commenced was put down at as many as 1,500 ; while it was alleged that in a single morning, dismayed at the bad news and a couple of notable departures, no less than five hundred of the noblest and wealthiest of the citizens had fled. Only the militia, kept constantly paraded, restored calm ; and confidence was re-established when the Madonna of Impruneta was brought into the city. Many indeed who had fled from timidity rather than from bad faith, reassured by the safe completion of the fortifications, returned spontaneously to their posts. Nevertheless, a large number of the more timorous and less devoted stayed away or continued to withdraw, together with many declared Palleschi who had apprehensions from the violent feeling abroad in the city. Francesco Guicciardini was one of the first ; but he was about to return when the menacing reports from Florence drove him first to the Casentino and ultimately to Rome. He was followed by Alessandro de' Pazzi, Roberto Acciaiuoli, Palla Rucellai, and many more.[106] The fugitives were continually pursued with proclamations ordering them to return under pain of exile or outlawry ; and one list included no fewer than twenty-eight of the noblest and most gifted citizens of Florence.   Only a few—among them Michelangelo Buonarotti and Tommaso Soderini—obeyed the summons ; the rest preferred to await the penalty.[107] The majority of the fugitives made their way to Lucca, the neutrality and vicinity of which made it an ideal city of refuge. Here they were joined by Filippo Strozzi, now returned from France, and by Antonfrancesco degli Albizzi.[108] Here, too, they found Baccio Bandinelli, the puny rival of Michelangelo and butt of Benvenuto Cellini, who had retired thither in apprehension ever since the revolution of 1527.[109]   Cellini himself, to his eternal shame, actually deserted the ranks of the militia and went, by invitation of the Pope, to work for him at Rome.[110]

Others showed their hostility more positively.   The Prince of Orange received active assistance from a large number of Florentine subjects (especially from the dominion, where sympathy for the Medici was always strongest), many of whom were captured and suffered condign punishment.   Some entered into communication with him, or carried treasonable correspondence.[111]   Others showed active sympathy by frequenting his camp and supplying him with provisions.[112]   A number assisted him in local warfare and were partly responsible for some of the devastation caused in it.[113]   There were some who joined the besieging forces beneath the walls without reserve, bearing with them arms stolen from the city.[114]   A few went so far as to raise against Florence various places of the dominion.[115]   Even the fidelity of some who filled offices of trust was proved doubtful.[116] Worst of all, Baccio Valori actually entered the Pope's service and acted as his commissary with the besieging army.   A price was put on his head, alive or dead, by his enraged compatriots. In addition—a traditional punishment and of easier execution—a breach three yards wide was driven through his palace from roof to ground, to mark it as the habitation of a traitor.[117]

It was not natural that known partisans of the Medici should be allowed to leave the city unmolested or to remain at large within the walls to intrigue and work on their behalf.   A special commission was therefore appointed to supervise them.   Twenty-five prominent citizens were declared suspect, among them Ottaviano de' Medici.   All those upon whom hands could be laid were confined strictly to the Palazzo della Signoria till the close of the siege ; and it was thus that Filippo Nerli, the historian, was able, through the garrulity or infidelity of his guardians, to obtain such intimate knowledge of the official deliberations.

Some managed to flee in time—for example, Luigi Guicciardini, the pliant Gonfalonier of the Tumulto del Venerdì, who escaped from Pisa wrapped up in a quilt.[118]   The number of those confined became swollen during the course of the siege by other arrests.   Persons who refused to pay their quota of taxation were imprisoned elsewhere, and not all survived it.   The hostages from those subject cities whose fidelity had not stood the test were shut up in the common prisons.   The Spaniards in Florence, of whom there was a considerable number, mostly merchants, also gave rise to suspicion : and one at least was known to have joined his compatriots outright.   They were therefore similarly segregated and placed under surveillance.[119]

It was inevitable that there should be at this period a fresh outburst of suspicion and of violence against the Medici and their adherents.   Much of it must have been justified.   Meetings of more than ten persons, excepting for religious purposes, were prohibited without special licence.[120]   Suspicious characters were publicly insulted, or even assaulted by hot-headed representatives of the Arrabbiati.[121]   The tribunals were constantly engaged on cases of comparatively trivial importance in which they imposed disproportionate punishments.[122]   The Quarantia especially was convoked with alarming frequency and was kept busy trying suspected citizens and launching sentences of outlawry upon fugitives.[123]   One Carlo Cocchi was beheaded for having asserted that Florence belonged to the Medici, and that a Parlamento should be called to re-establish them : " for if we decide otherwise, it means calling in the Medici into Florence and running the danger of sack by reason of sullying the law." [124] In a different category was a Franciscan friar, Vittorio Franceschi, who had framed, according to report, an audacious plot against the city—to corrupt part of the guard, to spike the guns, and to introduce the Spaniards by way of his monastery of S. Francesco.   The plot was discovered in time ; and the friar was saved from being fired from the mouth of a cannon by the populace only by being hanged and quartered by order of the Quarantia. " As he had no consideration for the hurt of the city, so have we none for him " run the grim words of his condemnation.[125]   The Pope complained bitterly of these acts of violence ; yet as no person of great prominence suffered the extreme penalty, he was easily consolable.[126]

The same spirit of nervousness and suspicion manifested itself also in purely political matters.   On 1 November a new Signoria entered into office—the first since the opening of the siege—without the usual pomp, owing to the extraordinary times.[127]   Its first function would normally have been to secure the administration of internal order by conceding the Otto di

Balia its usual plenary authority to try malefactors and to inflict any penalty up to death. This was, however, withheld ; and on the evening of the same day the Otto was dismissed from office and a fresh election was ordered. Moderate opinion had been too strongly represented in its composition ; and Jacopo Gherardi, who happened to be one of its members, had insisted that efficient administration of justice was impossible under such conditions. Similarly, on another occasion, a suspected member of the Dieci was driven from office.[128] It is not to be wondered at that partisans of the Medici alleged that the constitution of the city was being strained to a breaking-point by such irregular conduct of public affairs, or even that the city had fallen under the terrorism of a few extremists.[129]

While this was the spirit shown towards their adherents, the Medici themselves could not fare any better. Of those most closely connected with the ruling line, there were not many left in the power of the city. The little " Duchessina " remained shut up in the convent of the Murate where she had been removed on the outbreak of the pest, enjoying the pittance allowed her by the government. Party spirit, however, penetrated even among the nuns, who were found one day to have sent her a basket of comfits and flowers into the arrangement of which the well-known arms of her family had been traced. An ugly spirit was aroused among the extremists, who commenced to threaten her with exposure on the battlements to the enemy's balls, or with worse violence. For mutual security the government had her moved back to the surer atmosphere of the convent of Sta. Lucia. There is a pathetic description of the child's tears as she heard this decision, which she thought to be the prelude to her death.[130] A detachment of soldiers was sent to secure Maria Salviati, widow of Giovanni delle Bande Nere, with her son Cosimo, future Grand Duke, at her villa at Trebbio in the Mugello. The captain to whom the affair was committed had, however, served under the boy's father and showed no enthusiasm in his task. As a result, they were able to make timely provision on their side to avoid capture, and ultimately succeeded in making their road to Venice.[131] Upon the Pope himself it was impossible to lay hands : but a descendant of the great Ghiberti, who inherited some of his ancestor's artistic ability, used it to design a cartoon on the façade of the headquarters of the *Lione d' Oro* in the Via Larga. Clement was depicted with full pontifical robes and mitre upon the steps of the gallows, with Jacopo Salviati bandaging his eyes, the Archbishop of Capua administering the fatal push, and the Emperor mounting guard with a sword on which were inscribed the words " Amice, ad quid venisti ? "[132] During the siege, when an intensive bombardment was directed against one of the towers, a Florentine gunner scrawled a mitre on a dirty piece of canvas as a banner and stood by its side, indecently exposed, to show the enemy the scorn he had of their marksmanship and of their pontifical patron alike.[133] " Papa chimente "—" Pope who lies "—was the punning title by which he was generally known.[134]

How widespread was the interest aroused by the siege of Florence may be seen from the unusual literary output, particularly in verse, to which it gave rise. One of the most important of the original authorities for the events of the war is the long and not very elegant poem written at intervals of fighting by Mambrino Roseo da Fabriano, otherwise known as a prolific translator, one of the captains serving under Malatesta Baglione, to whom the work was dedicated.[135] Luigi Alamanni, most distinguished of living Florentine poets, while principally occupied in a sphere of greater utility, commemorated the siege and its consequences in his verses.[136] Attributed to him also is a political poem of considerable length upon the events of 1529–30, in which the Pope is bitterly reproached for venting his spleen against his native city and the Emperor is urged to spare Italy and to turn his arms against the common enemy of Christendom.[137] More popular in character was the Lament of Florence, intended to be sung in the streets, in which the enemy is implored to show consideration and the powers of Italy are asked for help.[138] Of a different nature was the composition of Lorenzo Buonafedi, a humble dyer, whose sole passion was for peace and who inveighed against all, within the city or without, who were responsible for her present state.[139] Salvestro Aldobrandini, Chancellor of the Republic,[140] commented on present affairs in cutting verses, in which he warned the Pope that if ever he succeeded in capturing the city, it would be in the condition of a dying person, to administer extreme unction :

> " Ma di tener Fiorenza,
>   Non avrai Papa il vanto
>   O tu l' avrai morente
>   Per darle l' Olio santo."

Far from Florence Pietro Aretino, the scourge of Princes, wrote a sonnet, bitter even for him, upon the course of events:

> " Cristo ci ha in guardia a tre bestiacce dati.
>   A Papa, a Francia, a mastro Imperatorio . . .
> Ser Carlo con gli angeli ci suori guardi
>   Lasciata in preda al Turco ha l' Ungaria
> Per rimetter in casa tre bastardi . . ."

Leandro (Leonardo) Signorelli, who died during the siege in command of the Florentine artillery and fortifications, was generally

deplored as a loss to the Muses as well as to Mars, and must have
been inspired by the events in which he took part.[141]   Even the
Venetian ambassador, Carlo Capello, was infected by the example
and celebrated the heroic defence in Latin epigrams.[142]   On the
other side, Claudio Tolomei composed an appeal of Tuscany to
the Prince of Orange to save her from servitude to Florence.[143]
Ercole Bentivoglio, son of the late tyrant of Bologna, was fighting
in the Imperial camp and described the siege in one of his satires.[144]
Varchi, Nardi and Busini on the one side, Nerli and Guicciardini
on the other, were deeply interested spectators or victims of the
occurrences they described in their writings.   Vasari viewed them
from some little distance, the aged Lorenzo da Credi from within.
Donato Giannotti, Andrea del Sarto, and Michelangelo Buonarotti were active participants.   Centuries later, at the period of
the Risorgimento, the siege of Florence became a principal theme
of the leaders of the national revival, and " with the bell of
Gavinana, Guerazzi and d' Azeglio sounded the alarm against the
successors of Clement VII and Charles V." [145]

While Florence was thus manfully preparing to resist the
masters of Europe, other enemies of older standing, and nearer
home, could not resist the temptation to take advantage of the
situation.   Siena and Florence, the two cities which contested
the hegemony of Tuscany, had long been in rivalry, and each
favoured inevitably the party of opposition in the other.   A
special bone of contention was the border-town of Montepulciano,
originally acquired by Florence, lost to Siena at the time of the
invasion of Charles VIII, but since recovered as a consequence
of her internal disorders.   Friendship had indeed been maintained during the period of the rule of Pandolfo Petrucci, head of
a family which occupied a position similar to that of the Medici.
But in 1525 he had been driven out, and Florence found herself
in automatic opposition to the new popular government.   As a
result, in the following year a combined papal and Florentine
expedition, aided by the neighbouring petty rulers, was carried
out in favour of the Petrucci.   Outside the Porta Camollia it
had met with a complete defeat which ranks second only to
Montaperti in Sienese records ; and the territory was cleared of
the invader save for Grosseto and other places of the Maremma
which continued to be held by Andrea Doria for the Pope.
Ancient enmities had, however, been aroused.   It became a
cardinal point of Sienese policy to recover her lost possessions,
and she became in the following years more Ghibelline even than
before.   She encouraged Bourbon's march to Tuscany in the
hopes of revenging herself against her rival, supplying his army
with artillery and supplies and showing him every sign of honour.
The new Florentine government took over the animosities of the

old.   Though it attempted to enter into friendly relations with
the Sienese as a medium for reaching an understanding with
the Emperor, private enmity was not the least of the causes
which contributed to the failure of the wider negotiations.   Raids
and depredations continued in either direction over the border,
and Florence did not cease to favour the intrigues and incursions
of the Sienese *fuorusciti*.   In consequence diplomatic relations
were broken off, and all Florentines were ordered to leave the
sister-city within four hours.[146]   These unfriendly relations were
maintained until February 1527/28, when the very fact of common
hostility to the Pope and nervousness as to the effect of her
present policy brought about a change in the Florentine attitude.
The maintenance of an ambassador at Siena was decided on, the
encouragement of the *fuorusciti* ceased, a suggestion of Lautrec's
to assist them in an expedition was refused, and overtures were
even made for an alliance.   This seemed probable enough at the
period of the temporary Spanish eclipse, but on the debacle of
the league the Sienese demands stiffened, and the negotiations
kept dragging on without reaching any conclusion.   Nevertheless,
diplomatic relations were maintained, Florence being represented
successively by Francesco Carducci, Pierfrancesco Portinari, and
Bardo Altoviti.   Though it was impossible to prevent brawls and
border-raids from continuing, they were treated with all tact,
and the French proposals to aid Petrucci were consistently
rejected.[147]   From the autumn of 1528, the expedition against
Florence began to be a question of practical politics.   The
Spanish, therefore, to whom the Sienese were devotedly attached,
did all they could to prevent an understanding between the two
cities and worked to bring about a better atmosphere between
Siena and the Pope as a preliminary step towards the *entente*
between the latter and the Emperor.   As the result of an embassy
to Rome, their recovery of Portercole was legitimized, and when
the Florentine expedition was prepared they were inveigled with
half-promises of territorial concessions, especially in the direction
of Montepulciano.   In addition, they stood in a peculiar relation
to the Prince of Orange, who had continued at least since Bourbon's passage to be in close personal touch with the Sienese
government, over which he had acquired great influence.[148]
Hence they not only put no obstacles in the way of the
expedition, which they could have effectively hampered even by
the observance of a strict neutrality, but they gave it powerful
aid.

The Spanish soldiery had at this time won for itself the name
of the finest in Europe ; yet in all that which lay outside mere
military training and efficiency, it left almost everything to be
desired.   The Imperialist arrangements for the Florentine cam-

paign were, as we have seen, wretched. Beyond the troops, virtually nothing was in a state of readiness, and no preparations whatever had been made for a siege. The commissariat and the ordnance had been neglected, so that the most vital necessities of the army were left to chance. For victuals, artillery, and munitions, as well as for sappers, reliance was had upon the papal territories, upon Lucca, but, above all, upon Siena. At the opening of the campaign, Orange had sent a representative to request co-operation. This the government promised willingly, but they did not act as quickly as he desired. He continued to urge them for immediate provision, so that nothing should be lacking on his arrival at Florence; and their delay in sending the artillery was a contributory cause at least of the slowness of his march. Finally, he sent for his Commissary-General from Naples to expedite matters. This was a most remarkable personality. Four years previously, after the Battle of Pavia, Girolamo Morone, Chancellor of the Duke of Milan, had made himself notorious by an audacious scheme to drive the Spaniards out of Italy in the moment of their victory through the medium of their own generals. He had suffered the surprisingly light punishment of imprisonment, and his enemies had done homage to his ability by releasing him to employ his organizing genius on their behalf. It was a strange re-entry into public life to assist in the suppression of the last glimmers of Italian liberty on the part of one who owed his fame to a grandiose attempt to revive it. Early in October, he arrived at Siena and lost no time in coming to an agreement. The city promised to provide 400 sappers with two master-carpenters and two master-smiths; sixteen cannon, with 5,000 pounds of saltpetre; 2,000 to 3,000 pounds of powder daily; 1,000 pairs of oxen; and a large supply of horseshoes, ropes, and similar articles. The bare list shows how dependent the Imperial forces were upon their allies for the most essential military requirements. But their provision was no better for the barest necessities of life. " Here in camp," wrote Orange from Montevarchi, " there is not a mouthful of bread, and the soldiers of all the nations have come to find me and have shouted that if bread does not arrive to-day, they will go to find it wherever it may be." His official despatches were interrupted by crowds of officers who came to clamour for supplies. His anger was excessive, and he was driven to refuge in oaths and blasphemy, " denying God and bursting into continual ' giuradios.' " The Sienese, he swore, were responsible for all, and he would be revenged on them. If he died in the enterprise of Florence, he would endeavour to be resuscitated in order to be the undoing of Siena. He continually rated and implored them to send speedily the succour which lay in their power, despatching as many as four letters in one day to hasten them.

The fault for the delay did not lie, however, in lack of desire on the part of the Sienese. They had been bullied into promising more than they could give, and not all the pleadings of their terrified envoy could make them do more than they did. The continual commissaries whom they appointed and the penalties which they threatened were powerless to remedy inherent defects of organization. Some of the artillery, sent by the wrong road, fell into the hands of the Florentines ; all was seriously delayed. Only a fraction of the powder promised could be provided. Few of the oxen prepared arrived at the camp, and many of the drivers fled with their charges, as well as some which were not theirs. The slender stores which were delivered were in a state of utter confusion. There was a general outcry against the envoy which made him fear for the safety of his city as well as for his own, should the army come and live at free quarters in its territory.

On the arrival of Morone, matters commenced to improve. He threw himself into the work of organization with characteristic energy. He found a master-craftsman to instruct and super-intend the manufacture of gunpowder. He put an end to the raids and guerilla warfare which were disturbing the peace in the rich corn-lands along the Florentine border, promising security to any subject towns which put themselves under the protection of the allies. He organized the government of the conquered territory, prepared defences and secured roads. A meeting of delegates from the various occupied places was held at Poggibonsi to co-ordinate the supply of oxen and of pioneers. Help was similarly exacted from Cortona and Arezzo. The burden was thus more evenly distributed. Provisions began to arrive with greater regularity, though the supply remained far from satisfactory. The quota of Siena, from which the greatest propor-tion was still supposed to come, remained heavy in the extreme. Requisitions on the one hand and excuses on the other continued without intermission ; and one orator after another, unable to support his equivocal position, begged for recall. Nor were her exertions restricted to supplies in kind. Besides all this, she sent her Captain-General, Alfonso Piccolomini, better known by his Neapolitan title of the Duke of Amalfi, to lead her contingent to assist in the active operations of the siege ; and she gave active assistance in clearing the country neighbouring on her borders. At a later stage she had to maintain upon her territories for some time a considerable body of Imperialist troops. In spite of all, she gained nothing out of the war. The integrity of the Floren-tine dominion under its new masters had already been decided. When the coveted Montepulciano was on the point of capitulation, the Sienese claims upon it were ignored : and when its resistance was protracted, they were even refused permission to besiege it. Only in the insignificant town of Foiano they were allowed to maintain their commissary.[149]

The activities of Morone put an end at least to the immobilization of the Imperial forces. A fortnight after the arrival of the vanguard beneath the walls of Florence, the artillery made its appearance—four cannon with one columbrine and three smaller pieces. Part of this had been captured from the Florentines themselves during the ill-fated expedition of 1525 ; the rest comprised some of that which Bourbon had left behind when he made his sudden dash on Rome. This was also the origin of a few more pieces which had been picked up at Foligno during the advance. Some others came from Lucca, together with large numbers of workmen, pioneers and camp-followers, attracted by the prospects of booty. Morone continued his activity in camp, sending information to the Pope, giving advice to Orange, and working to seduce subject cities from their allegiance. His sudden death at Orange's quarters, probably from an apoplectic stroke following on a dispute, was a real disaster to the besieging army.[150]

On the arrival of the artillery, the Imperialists, in the teeth of some opposition, took up their positions for the siege. Their numbers, however, were insufficient to invest the city completely. They remained, therefore, exclusively upon the south side of the river. It was in this direction that their lines of communication lay, and in the absence of bridges beyond the walls this was a most important consideration. Upon that side, too, the hills came closest to the city, almost overhanging it, and the ground was best adapted for operations. Their numbers, moreover, were sufficient to form in that direction a complete blockade, which they would have been unequal to on the north side. Finally, they had before their eyes the experience of Henry VII who had tried, and failed, precisely in that direction. The right bank, therefore, remained comparatively untouched, save for occasional detachments of cavalry who were able to cross the river and inflict some damage. Thus in the more important section of the city, as in the old days, the gates remained open and communications were maintained. The citizens went in and out without interruption ; young men cantered out to hunt ; and lighthearted bands went as in Boccaccio's day up the hill to Fiesole.[151] To the south, however, the city was completely shut in by the Imperialist camp, which lay in the form of a semi-circle commencing and finishing on the Arno and surrounding the walls. The Germans occupied a point of vantage on the high ground towards Arcetri, having the camp market and the headquarters in their midst. The Spaniards in the centre commanded the gate of S. Giorgio, while the Italians were on the left about Rusciano. Their encampments were joined by entrenchments and defences stretching in a half-circle from opposite the gate of S. Niccolò on the one side to that of S. Frediano on the other. The advance guard, under Alessandro Vitelli, had taken up its position on the hill of Giramonte. Here and on the neighbouring heights the greatest activity was shown. If S. Miniato was the key to Florence, Giramonte, which faced and almost overhung it, was, if anything, the key to S. Miniato. It formed, therefore, the centre of the system. Sappers from Cortona and Arezzo were employed to throw up fortifications and entrenchments which converted it into a strong bastion ; roads were made up to it ; and with infinite trouble almost the whole of the heavy artillery was dragged up and mounted there.[152] The Imperial captains took up their residence in the buildings left standing. Orange's own headquarters were established in the Villa Guicciardini in the Pian di Giullari, with Baccio Valori and other representatives of the Pope near by. The palace in question was among those put up in these very days for public auction. By a magnificent gesture, it was bought at the usual market rate, in ostentatious display of the calm confidence which reigned within the walls.[153]

The Florentines had been taking advantage of the delay to complete their preparations for defence. Now, when all was ready, Malatesta Baglione went up to the bastion of San Miniato one day at dawn accompanied by all the musicians of the city with their instruments (27 October ?). Drawn up there in the sight of the enemy, they commenced to play as though to challenge him to come forward. Immediately afterwards, a herald was sent to the Prince of Orange to deliver a formal defiance. On his return, the music was again set to play, and all the cannon, small and great, in the city and the fortifications were discharged into the enemy's camp. The din was terrible, and the whole neighbourhood was darkened with the smoke. For a whole hour this continued, so as to seem a very inferno. Thus, with a mediæval pageantry, the enemy was informed that the city would resist him ; and Florence, that the siege was commenced.[154]

NOTES TO CHAPTER VIII

[1] Foscari, *Relazione*, p. 11. There is a classic description in some detail of Florence and the Florentines at the time of the siege in Varchi, Book X.

[2] Cf. Capello, letter 6 : " . . . Coming home, I went immediately to a friend who is of the Ottanta . . . who told me that they have replied that . . ." Similarly he got to know almost immediately the substance

of the debates of 20 and 21 June, though they had been under a pledge of secrecy (letter 20). The Gonfalonier himself complained (Pratiche, 4 May): "Il segreto delli offici et altro si paleseva." At a later stage, the oath of secrecy became invariable.

[3] Cf. Falletti, I, 38–54 ; with a detailed illustration of the dilatoriness of the government as shown in the endless delays in the delegation of the envoys to the Emperor, pp. 54–68. Giannotti (*Opere*, I, 158–9) inveighs in a very modern spirit against the inefficiency of the greybeards who monopolized the administration, as contrasted with the energy of the younger men who made all the sacrifices. Cf. also *ibid.* 116–17 : " si governavano le cose più con speranza che con ragione." The whole of the *Della Repubblica Fiorentina* is occupied with an examination of the weaknesses of the Florentine constitution, particularly as shown at the time of the last Republic, with suggestions for its betterment.

[4] Pratiche, 10 August.

[5] *Carte Strozziane, Inventario*, I, 338.

[6] Pratiche, 6 May, 23 June, 14 July.

[7] Cf. speech of Albizzi, *ibid.* 18 July. For the above, see Falletti, I, 32–5, who adopts, however, too extreme a view.

[8] See the majority of the contemporary authorities ; e.g. Sanuto, LI, 616–17, and despatches of Buondelmonti, *ubi supra*.

[9] Ammirato, VI, p. 365 ; Varchi, I, 108–9. The bastion was a recent Italian innovation, though first reduced to a theory by Albrecht Dürer in his book of 1527, which led up to Vauban's system. Cf. Wilson, *Life of Michelangelo Buonarotti*, p. 413.

[10] Cf. Gaye, *Carteggio Inedito degli Artisti*, II, 106, 107, 118, 119, 124, 125, etc., for work at Montepulciano, Livorno, Cortona, Pisa, and other places.

[11] Busini, pp. 103, 115–16. Cf. J. A. Symonds, *Life of Michel Angelo*, I, 408 *seqq.*

[12] Symonds, *ibid.* Cf. Falletti, I, 153–6. For the work in the spring and summer of 1529, see the letters of Cartolaio in the *Inventario* (p. 368 and *passim*), and Falletti, I, 29 *seqq.*

[13] Signoria, CXXXI, ff. 115, 131, 146, etc.

[14] Falletti, *ibid.* The phrase is of M. A. Cartolaio in a letter of 18 July.

[15] Gaye, II, 134 *seqq.*

[16] Vasari, IV, 289 ; Gaye, *ubi supra*. Similarly Baldassare Peruzzi, a Sienese artist, was sent by his native city to assist Orange (Vasari, IV, 603). Milanesi disproves by documentary evidence the biographer's statement that he refused to work against Florence.

[17] A detailed account of the defence works is given by Varchi, II, 195–200. Cf. also Symonds and Wilson, *ubi supra*, and other lives of Michelangelo ; Gaye, II, Doc. CXLI *seqq.*, especially CLVIII with its citations ; anonymous writing published by Milanesi in his edition of Vasari, XII, 365 ; Capello, letter 59 ; letter of Donato Giannotti to Tosinghi of 28 October in *Opere*, II, 404–5 ; and other contemporary writings. See also the report of Lorenzo Martelli, one of the commissaries, upon the state of defence, to the Pratica of 26 September, in Falletti, I, 106 ff. The existence of the gun emplacement in the orchard has been generally neglected ; and in compensation that of the one on the Campanile has been denied. Both, however, are amply attested in contemporary accounts. Cf. especially Giovio, II, 170.

[18] Signoria, CXXXI, ff. 146, 179–80, 184–5, 186, 187 (8 August, 13, 20, 21 September) ; Capello, letters 37, 44, 52, and those of his secretary, Vicenzo Fedele, in Sanuto, LI, 615, etc.

[19] Signoria, CXXXII, f. 94 (27 September). A census of peasants, with their tools, was ordered as late as 13 February (*ibid.* f. 150).

[20] Falletti, I, 425–6.

[21] Falletti, I, 143–93 (" La Fuga di Michelangelo Buonarotti "). Cf. the lives of Michelangelo, e.g. Symonds, I, 416–33, and Gaye, II, Docs. CLVII, CLVIII, CLIX. A record is preserved showing how in the middle of the siege the artist was empowered to ascend the cupola of the Duomo with two companions in order to obtain a general survey of the city and its environs (Guasti, *La Cupola di S. Maria di Firenze,* cited in Gotti, I, 197).

[22] Capello, letter 32.

[23] Foscari, *Relazione,* pp. 22–3. Cf. Capello, letter 57, and Ughi, *Cronica,* p. 149.

[24] Pratiche, 29 September ; Capello, letter 54 ; letter of Dieci of same date in Sanuto, LII, 45–7.

[25] Varchi, II, 174–5 ; *Appunti di un fautore dei Medici* (Francesco Baldovinetti), ed. Londi, 1911, pp. 10–11 ; Capello, letter 57 ; Paoli, pp. cxc–cxci ; Nardi, 210. Ughi gives a most melancholy relation of the destruction of the monasteries in particular, *Cronica,* 145, 149. Cf. the poem of Salvestro Aldobrandini, Chancellor of the Republic :

> " Deh ! quanto è gran dolore
> Ruinar di nostri mani
> L' arche de' Padri nostri
> Li templi de Christiani.
> Deh ! quanto è gran dolore.
> Pensar che a tal destino
> Mena la madre patria,
> Un Papa, un cittadino. . . ."

[26] Vasari, ed. Milanesi, V, 47–8 ; Varchi, II, 175. The clue as to the date and precise circumstances, invariably misreported, is provided by Capello, letter 82 (26 April 1530). A striking contrast to this was the destruction by the *besieging* forces of the sepulchre of S. Giovanni Gualberto, fruit of ten years' labour of Bernardo da Rovezzano for the monks of Vallombrosa, of which mutilated fragments may be seen in the Bargello (Vasari, IV, 532–4).

[27] Letter of Fedele of 9 November to his brother in Sanuto, LII, 244 ; Capello, letter 62 ; Varchi, II 175–6 ; Giannotti, *Opere,* I, 123 ; Nerli, 203 ; Segni, II, 212. Giovio (II, 115) most unfairly puts this occurrence out of all proportion by placing it well before the opening of the siege.

[28] Varchi, II, 477–8.

[29] Gaye, II, 148, 150, 152, 160. For the policy of defending these places, cf. Capello, letter 58.

[30] Signoria, CXXXII, f. 94 (31 December). " Comandamento a Comessarij di Pisa che faccino che gli 57 tra pretj e cittadinj sgombrino Pisa . . ." (for Lucca or Bologna). For the troops in the dominion, see Capello, letter 48. The amazing attitude of mind towards the subject cities is graphically illustrated by Baldovinetti, p. 44.

[31] According to Ammirato, they assumed the title in June (*Istorie,* VII, 49).

[32] Varchi, II, 201, 455.

[33] Desjardins, II, 1106–11 ; Varchi, II, 137. He arrived at Florence on 13 September (Capello, letter 49).

[34] Varchi, II, 200 ; Paoli, p. 201.

[35] Report of Martelli in Pratica of 26 September, *ubi supra* ; Capello, letter 59.

[36] *Ibid.* 72 ; cf. Sanuto, LII, 245. From the roll published in *Francesco Ferrucci e la Guerra di Firenze*, pp. 366–8, it appears that at the close of the siege upwards of 14,000 were on the pay-roll.

[37] Capello, letters 82, 90.

[38] Signoria, CXXXI, ff. 188–9 (24 September).

[39] Capello, letter 55.

[40] Signoria, *ibid.* f. 20 *seqq.* (October and November, *passim*).

[41] *Ibid.* f. 214 (1 April), " *Bamnum quod milites qui sunt florentie & non sunt conducti se representur coram Malatesta.*"

[42] *Ibid.* CXXXII, f. 46 (3 December). This was, of course, on payment.

[43] *Ibid.* CXXXI, f. 185 (20 September), " *Bando che e' soldati portino le croce bianche.* . . . *Ciascuno soldato . . . o stipendario . . . non audisca ne presuma da qui innanzi andare senza il segnio della croce biancha sotto pena d' essere svaligiato & amazato . . . volendo che decta* ✠ *biancha . . . sia cucita & appicata in buona forma che non si possi levare . . .*"

[44] *Ibid.* f., 184 (19 September).

[45] Letter to Carducci, *apud* Gaye, II, 158. A detailed list of the Florentine captains, with some biographical details, is to be found in *Francesco Ferrucci e la Guerra di Firenze*, pp. 483–513. Cf. Mambrino Roseo, Canto II and notes.

[46] Report of L. Martelli, *ubi supra.*

[47] Ricci, in *Francesco Ferrucci, etc.*, p. 457, gives figures which are in general agreement with other contemporary accounts. Faleri, the Sienese envoy (letter 48), reckons on 2 January—before the besiegers had reached their maximum—sixty to seventy thousand mouths to feed. To the unfortunate Florentines there seemed to be even more. Cf. the records of S. Maria del Carmine (*R. Archivio di Stato di Firenze, Ricordanze*, XIX, f. 69), " . . . *et intorno alle mura erono accampati più che dugento milia persone del papa e dello imperadore . . .*"

[48] Signoria, CXXXII, ff. 3–4 (2 November) : " *Capitoli per conto della militia.*"

[49] For their " Constitution," see Falletti, I, 427 *f.n.* For the Ordinance of the Militia and its organization, see *A.S.I.*, vol. XV, and the documents cited *supra*, p. 130, *n.* 17. The roll of one *gonfalone* is published in *Francesco Ferrucci, etc.*, pp. 368–70.

[50] Signoria, CXXXII, f. 158 (20 February) ; CXXXI, ff. 223, 236 (22 and 25 September).

[51] Cf. Carteggio Originale, XII, p. 94 ; Signoria to Commissaries of Pisa, 7 December (all Florentines above eighteen to present themselves at the city without delay). Donato Giannotti, father of the Florentine militia, had desired that the system should be extended to the citizens of Florence inhabiting that place, who should raise a separate company on their own. See letter of 13 July 1529 in *Opere*, II, 402–3.

[52] Soriani, *Relazione*, p. 425 ; patent to agent for purchasing arms, of 9 April, in Signoria, Carteggio, Missive, Registri, LVIII.

[53] Soriani, *ibid.*, estimates the numbers at its inception at 3,000–3,200 instead of the 6,000 expected.

[54] Pratiche, 11 November. Cf. Varchi, II, 191, and *supra*, p. 117, with note 12.

[55] Signoria, CXXXII, ff. 5, 7 (4 and 5 November), 163, 166, 198 (22, 24 February, and 18 March). Falletti is not accurate in these details.

[56] Consiglio Grande, Provisioni, 20 December ; Signoria, *ibid.* ff. 76, 86–7 (19, 26 December).

[57] Capello, letters 50, 54, 84.

[58] For the above, cf. Falletti, I, 425–32, 439, 447–49. In details, however, he is not to be trusted.

[59] Varchi, II, 200.

[60] Signoria, CXXXII, f. 227 (12 April) : " Bando del rappresentarsi a luoghi debiti quando si da allarme."

[61] *Memorie*, I, 42.

[62] Fedele, 20 October and 3 December, in Sanuto, LII, 137–8, 346. Cf. Varchi, II, 117–18 ; Baldovinetti, pp. 37–8 ; Roseo, pp. 61–2, 310 ; Varchi, II, 117–18. In spite of this, there was a dispute between the Otto and the Dieci—the civil and military tribunals—on jurisdiction over the soldiers, the case arising out of the homicide spoken of by Varchi, II, 260–1. The Signoria originally decided in favour of the Dieci (CXXXII, ff. 160–2 ; CXXXIII, ff. 22, 37–8) ; but the Otto continued nevertheless to protest (*ibid.* ff. 84–6). Finally, however, cognisance in such cases was given to the Nove della Milizia (*ibid.* f. 89). Other instances of disorderliness among the mercenaries may be found in Varchi, *passim*— e.g. I, 475–6. On the whole, however, discipline remained exemplary. Cf. the unstinted praise of Giannotti, *Opere*, I, 158–9.

[63] *Diario Fiorentino di Agustino Lapi*, p. 96 ; L. Landucci, p. 371. For the dress of the Florentines at this period, see Varchi, II, 113–16. Cf. the graphic phrase of Ridolfo Cei in the Pratica of 27 January 1529/30 (LXXIV), " Saria bene tor via e' Capucci et pigliare l' arme."

[64] Signoria, CXXXI, f. 183 (17 September) :—one month's licence, periodically extended.

[65] For the actual occasions during the siege, see Varchi, II, 255–7, 338–9, and the preliminary proclamations of the Signoria—e.g. CXXXIII, f. 74, *Bando di iuramento della Militia* for 16 May—" il dì piaque allo omnipotente Dio restituire ad qᵃ exˢᵃ Repᵃ la sanctissima libertà." For the regulations for these days, cf. the ordinance of 7 September, *apud* Falletti, I, 432–7. " Orazioni della Milizia " are extant delivered by Luigi Alamanni (*Verse e Prose*, ed. Rafaelli, p. 477 *seqq.*, as well as in a contemporary pamphlet) ; Bartolommeo Cavalcanti (*Prose Fiorentine*, 1731, pt. I, t. vi, p. 49 *seqq.*, with excisions of the parts most contrary to the Medici) ; Pierfilippo Pandolfini and Filippo Parenti (*A.S.I.*, vol. XV). The occasions and circumstances are closely discussed by Hauvette, *Luigi Alamanni*, pp. 69–71 ; and Alamanni's oration is analysed, *ibid.* 409–15. Hauvette considers this discourse to the whole people an innovation for modern Europe.

[66] Signoria, CXXXII, f. 7 (5 November).

[67] See letter of 30 September *apud* Rossi, I, App. (iii). For the question of finance during the siege, see Falletti, I, 399–419.

[68] Varchi, II, 108–9, where he gives the actual departmental budget, and Foscari, *Relazione*, are in virtual agreement upon the amount.

[69] Pratiche, 5 July.

[70] Consiglio Maggiore, Provisioni, 6 August.

[71] See Pratiche, 2–27 September, *passim*.

[72] Consiglio Maggiore, Provisioni, 13 September ; Pratiche, 19 August ; Capello, letters 49, 52, 59 ; Varchi, II, 137 *seqq.*, where he gives an imaginary speech by Lamberto Cambi justifying the levy on ecclesiastical property —probably not altogether fictitious.

[73] See requisition in Falletti, I, 408.

[74] Nerli, p. 202 ; F. Baldovinetti, pp. 49–50. It is perhaps this method of payment which explains why they differ from Capello (letter 65) and other contemporary accounts in saying that property was sold for below its usual rate.

[75] Signoria, CXXXII, f. 60 (10 December) : " *Commessione a dua*

Coll.j per conto della mitria papale (. . . che vadino a canonici di S. Maria del fiore et commandino a decti Mazieri che faccia consegniare nelle manj di decti Collj la mitria che e nelle manj di decti cannonicj che lasciò loro Papa Leone). . . ." The same fate befell a silver cross in S. Giovanni (Nerli, 208). See also Capello, letter 70, and Giovio, p. 188.

[76] Giovanni Rinnucini in Pratiche of 10 August, 30 September.

[77] Signoria, CXXXI, f. 190 (25 September).

[78] Cf. letters in Sanuto, LII, 20, 45–7, 174–6 ; Paoli, p. 189. Even in those days, the type of the war profiteer was not unknown. The case is on record of a citizen who wrote to his wife to pray to God for a continuation of the war, that they might the more handsomely marry their daughter ! (Varchi, II, 414).

[79] Falletti's calculation of the expenses of the siege (I, 449 *f.n.*) is in close agreement with the information of Segni (*Vita*, p. 285), and of Rastrelli (I, 120–9, " Nota delle Imposizioni fatte al tempo del Popolo dall' anno 1527 all' anno 1530 "). For Florentine currency in relation to European commerce, see Francesco Balducci Pegolotti, *Della Decima e delle atre gravezze* (Florence, 1766), written in 1440. Perrens (III, 230–7) gives some account of the wealth of Florence at this period.

[80] Varchi, II, 49–50 ; *Letters and Papers, Henry VIII*, IV, *n.* 5841.

[81] *Relazione*, pp. 20–3.

[82] Varchi, II, 117.

[83] *Ibid.* 116.

[84] Letter to Michelangelo referred to above, *apud* Gotti, I, 195.

[85] Capello, letter 57. Cf. also Nos. 52, 54, 55, 59, etc.

[86] Sanuto, LII, 215–16 and 345–6. The same impression is gathered from despatches from all quarters in this volume.

[87] E.g. Nerli, f. 208, etc. ; Giovio, II, 148–9 ; Baldovinetti, pp. 33–4, etc. It is noteworthy that the bulk of the testimony for the morale of the citizens during the siege comes from non-Florentine sources—e.g. Capello and Fedele.

[88] Varchi, II, 214.

[89] Baldovinetti, p. 39. His statement that the shops were kept only half open is opposed to Fedele's contemporary account (see next note), and refers probably only to the latter part of the siege.

[90] Signoria, CXXXI, 113, 199 ; CXXXII, 41, etc. Sanuto, LII, 345–6. (Fedele, 3 December) ". . . Who would believe . . . that by night one may go more securely than by day, nor has the least shortcoming been heard of . . ."

[91] See Pratica of 29 March 1530, when, after consultation with representative merchants, it was determined not to reopen the ordinary tribunals.

[92] *Cronica*, p. 149. For the above details, see the contemporary accounts in Sanuto, LII, 165, 174–6, 216–17, 220, 327–31, 345–6, 546–51 ; Baldovinetti, 42 ; Varchi, II, 295–6 ; and for instances of the administration of justice, *ibid.* 259–61, and Sanuto, LII, 327–31. For the control of supplies, cf. Signoria, CXXXI, 189, 190, 195–6 (24–30 September).

[93] Vasari, IV, 569.

[94] Varchi, II, 282.

[95] M. Lorenzo Ridolfi for the Quarter of Santo Spirito in Pratica of 20 April 1530 (LXXIV) ; Varchi, II, 414. Benevieni's petition is printed by Milanesi in appendix to his edition of the same author.

[96] Busini, 33, 53 ; Varchi, II, 19, 415 ; Segni, *Storia*, p. 190.

[97] Busini, 77, 178, 232 ; Baldovinetti, 52. Varchi, I, 474 ; II, 258, 414–15, where he stigmatizes Fra Zaccheria as over-credulous, and Benedetto as over-astute. It was he, for example, who had been largely

responsible for the condemnation of Brucioli.   Another name which may
be added to these is that of Fra Alessandro da Brescia, of the Order of
Ognissanti, an oration of whose, commencing " Maria mater gratie advo-
cata florentie," was ordered to be printed on 30 July 1530 (Signoria,
CXXXIII, f. 99).

[98] Varchi. II. 297 ; Sanuto, LII, 584–6 (9 February).   For a different
view of Fra Benedetto, cf. Lorenzo Buonafedi, the dyer (*apud* Rastrelli, I,
193–5) :

> " Io mi ricordo pur di quel marrano
> Che fu dell' Ordine de Predicatori
> Che fu quel fra ribello da Fojano
> Che sempre confortava i suoi Piagnioni
> ' Non dubitate che saranno rotti,
> Se voi verrete alle mie processioni,
> Andate sempre mai co' colli torti,
> Non dubitate che voi vincerete.' . . ."

[99] Baldovinetti, pp. 51–2.

[100] Signoria, CXXXI, f. 190 (25 September): "*Auctoritas coll : in-
veniendj prohibentem predicari* . . . che . . . habbino auctorità circa al
trovare . . . tucti quelli che hanno operato o spaventato o in alchuno
altro modo indecto il R^do Priore di San Marco di Firenze a prohibire al
R^do padre predicatore che al presente predicha in Sancta Maria del Fiore
di Firenze che non predichi et commandare al dicto R^do predicatore che
predichi liberamente." *Ibid.* f. 201 (6 October): Authority to punish
offenders. *Ibid.* f. 238–9: Condemnation of Jacopo Tedaldi to fine
and perpetual exile, " qui impedierit . . . F.rem Zacchariam de Fivizano
ne predicaret. . . ."

[101] Sanuto, LII, 345–6.

[102] *Ibid.* 215–16.

[103] Signoria, CXXXII, ff. 4–5 (2 November 1529).

" E prefati Magnifici et excelsi Signori Signori priori di libertà et
Gonfaloniere di Justitia del popolo fiorentino insieme ragunati ec. ut supra
Considerando quanto in ogni actione humana si debba sempre principal-
mente ricercare il divino aiuterio et sperando che l' arme della loro militia
quando sarà acompagnata colla oratione et col divino aiuto ne succederà
sempre la uictoria et ogni buono effecto Pertanto fanno publicamente
bandire et notificare a qualunque persona non habile et non ydonea all' arme
come sono preti frati monaci monache fanciulli et donne di qualunque
età che ogni volta si venisse da nostri soldati alla battaglia colli Inimici
che si farà per il palazo questo segnio cio è si sonerà l' avemaria colla campana grossa del palazzo colla quale si suol suonare a consiglio maggiore et
alhora sentito questo segnio tutte le sopradette persone non habile et
non ydonee all' armee sieno tenute et obbligati inginocchiarsi sì nelle chiese
come ne' convencti et nelle case loro et fare continua oratione insino a
tancto che durasse la battaglia predecta et pregare lo omnipotente Iddio
che dia forza et virtù all' arme de' soldati et militia fiorentina et victoria
contro li nimici della città di firenze sperando che per l' infinita miseri-
cordia del nostro signore Re della città nostra et per le intercessioni della
sua sanctissima madre la città nostra predecta conseguiterà la sopra decta
gratia.

" Domenico Banditore rapportò addì 4 di decto mese havere ne luoghi
publici della città di firenze havere facto decto bando."

[104] Baldovinetti, p. 53 ; Varchi, II, 188–9. Cf. Landucci, *Diario*,
p. 368. " And on the second of October, there came to Florence the
Virgin Mary, and she was borne to Santa Maria del Fiore into the chapel

of S. Zanobi that she might guard her city from this war prepared against it. And after she was there, fear and alarm fled from all the city."
    ¹⁰⁵ Varchi, II, 136–7. He mentions other omens of the period—the tearing down from the Palazzo by the wind of a banner inscribed "Liberty" and the eclipse of the sun of 28 March 1530 (*ibid.* 312–13).
    ¹⁰⁶ Rossi, *op. cit.* I, 138 *seqq.*, with documents there cited, and letter of Guicciardini and Pazzi of 30 September in App. III ; Capello, letter 52 ; Varchi, II, 157 ; Paoli, CLXXXVIII ; Busini, pp. 78, 102 ; and letter from ambassadors at Rome to Charles V of 23 October in *State Papers, Spanish*, IV, i, 193.
    ¹⁰⁷ Cf. Signoria and Otto for this period *passim*—especially the latter, CCVI, ff. 23, 28, 29. A large number of formal permissions to withdraw from the city were nevertheless granted. (Signoria, CXXXII, September and October, *passim.*)
    ¹⁰⁸ Varchi, II, 182–5. Strozzi was, however, authorized to remain there or at Pisa. Signoria, CXXXII, f. 68 (16 September).
    ¹⁰⁹ Vasari, VI, 152.
    ¹¹⁰ *Memorie*, I, 42.
    ¹¹¹ O.G., CCVI, f. 24 (27 September), condemnation to be hanged of Battista Borco (?) of Borgo S. Lorenzo because "inventus et captus fuit portare licteras ad principem oranges inimicum civitatis florentie et quia hostiliter cum exercitu venit contra dittam civitatem, que littere emanaverunt a petro antonii a burgo ad S. Laurentium. . . ." It is to be regretted that the records of the Otto are not extant for the whole period of the siege.
    ¹¹² *Ibid.* ff. 47–8 (6 November), condemnation *in absentia* of six craftsmen of Monte Spertolo because "a pluribus et pluribus diebus et citra conversati sunt et continue conversantur in castris ispanorum et inimicum civitatis florentie et ad ditta castra multa vittuaria portaverunt, et plures incursiones et assassinamenta contra homines et personas communis florentinis [commiserunt]. . . ."
    ¹¹³ *Ibid.* ff. 49–50 (10 November), Luigi di Bivigliano de' Medici, sentenced for aiding and favouring the enemy in his incursions in the Magello ; Signoria, CXXXII, f. 69 (16 December), condemnation as *rubello* by a Quarantia of Giovanni de' Taddi and Nero de' Pulci, "atteso l' errore commesso et l' arsione facta . . . venuti contro alla Patria." Cf. also instance in previous note.
    ¹¹⁴ *Ibid.* CXXXIII, ff. 101–2 (3 August 1530, but it must have happened long previously), condemnation as *rubello* by a Quarantia of Francesco de' Riccalbani because "ipse furatus est et abstulit quam plura arma et munitiones communis florentini et de palatio dominorum, et quod fuit et est inter exercitum inimicum et hostiliter seguit contra patriam." Cf. Varchi, II, 189, for other cases. A proclamation was even issued ordering such persons to return, as a prelude to more severe action (Signoria, CXXXII, f. 12, 6 November): "*Bando che chi è nel campo de' nimici torni.*" Segni (*Vita*, pp. 966–7) reports the case of Filippo Valori, a captain of the Florentine militia, who went to Rome disguised as a friar to offer help to the Pope.
    ¹¹⁵ *Ibid.* CXXXII, f. 154 (17 February), Quarantia declares *rubelli* Andrea de' Pucci and others who "venerunt contra civitatem florentie et ribellari fecerunt plura castra & villas in comitate pisarum." *Ibid.* f. 157 (19 February), Quarantia on Niccolò de Montaguto "qualiter reperitur in oppido Signie ordine Imperialium cum inimicis istius civitatis et contra civitate et popolare statu . . . visa eius contumacia . . . alla vita trista et scelerata di questo Niccolò de Montaguto sarebbe da dargli bando del fuoco, ma perchè questa pena non confa con quella che dice la querela

giudicho che gli si dia bando delle forche et confiscatione. . . ." *Ibid.*
ff. 186–7 (10 March), Pierfrancesco Ridolfi " quia ribellari fecit multa
castra et oppida in partibus Romandole " condemned as *rubello* " come
inimico capitalissimo della sua città & inimico di questa santissima libertà."
Similarly, *ibid.* f. 320 (8 April), Roberto Acciaiuoli and Lorenzo Ridolfi
" visis litteris Francesci de Ferruccis commissarii Emporii et commissarum
Pisanorum."

[116] O.G., CCVI, ff. 53–4 (18 September), death sentence on Bernardino
de Podio, Vicar of Anghiari, convicted with another person on the 8th
(*ibid.* f. 49) for favouring the enemy and frequenting his camp.

[117] Signoria, CXXXII, ff. 55–6 (8 December). A price for a smaller
amount was similarly put on the head of Antonio Taddei (Nerli, p. 206).

[118] Signoria, CXXXI, f. 207 (12 October). " Auctorità di sostenere
cittadinj a 7 " ; Gentile, *Storiografia, ubi supra* ; Varchi, II, 182–5.

[119] O.G., CCVI, f. 52 (17 November), condemnation to death of
Castro da Siviglia, a Spaniard and " miles," for waging war against the
city. Varchi, *ubi supra* ; Baldovinetti, pp. 49, 50–1.

[120] O.G., CCVI, f. 9 (9 September). On the next folio is a case of
one such permission.

[121] Varchi, II, 164–5.

[122] Cf. O.G., CCVI, ff. 8–9 (9 September), Lorenzo de' Menucci sentenced to strappado for " quedam verba inonesta et non decentia in vere-
cundiam civium florentinorum et consilij maioris " ; ff. 29–30 (30 September), Alessandro Corsini sentenced for writing a treasonable letter ;
ff. 46–7 (4 November), Francesco and Becho (?) de Gelloria, butchers,
fined for possessing two flags with the arms of the Medici, and boasting
it ; f. 73 (30 November), Alamanno de' Medici exiled for contumacy
and on a charge of leaving the territory and aiding the Medici ; Varchi,
II, 183, torture and imprisonment of a citizen who had seen Valori and
Guicciardini write a letter in secret ink ; *ibid.* 186, and Busini, 36, torture and imprisonment of a singer in the Pope's chapel who came from
Rome to the city ; Sanuto, LII, 461, the case of a Venetian who was
charged with bringing letters and false reports from Bologna, and punished
probably by death. For another instance of suspicion, see Falletti, I,
p. 73 *n.* It is refreshing in the midst of these condemnations to find the
light relief, as when Francesco Baldovinetti—presumably the diarist—
was fined a gift to charity since his action " sia stata più tosto viltà et
dappocaggine " (O.G., CCVII, f. 142 (9 February)).

[123] See O.G. and Signoria, *passim.* Thus on 18 October (Signoria,
CXXXI, ff. 216–7) four persons were condemned to outlawry by the
Quarantia in a single day.

[124] *Ibid.* ff. 212–13 (15 October). Cf. Nerli, p. 199.

[125] *Ibid.* f. 222 (22 October) ; Sanuto, LII, 104, 152, 174–6. That he
was entirely guiltless, as Pallesco historians assert, is inconceivable in
view of this contemporary evidence. Pulinari's chronicle, cited in Ughi,
Cronica, p. 153, gives the curious view that, as a Franciscan, he was
immolated in revenge for Savonarola.

[126] Letter to Charles of 23 October in *State Papers, Spanish*, IV, i, 193.

[127] Signoria, CXXXI, f. 251.

[128] Nerli, pp. 200–1 and 206 ; Varchi, II, 202–3 ; Capello, letter 61.

[129] This is the view of Nerli, Baldovinetti and Giovio (especially II, 219),
as well as of the private despatches of the papal side.

[130] Reumont, *La Jeunesse de Catherine de Médicis*, caps. IX and X ;
Varchi, I, 356–7 ; Nerli, p. 227 ; Nardi, 220–1.

[131] Giovio, II, 173–4 ; Varchi, II, 261. Cf. Booth, *Cosimo I, Grand
Duke of Tuscany*, cap. I.

[132] Varchi, II, 259.

[133] *Ibid.* p. 312.

[134] Busini, *Lettere, passim.*

[135] *Assedio et Impresa di Firenze, con tutte le cose successe* . . . *Peroscia MDXXX.* Edited by Pierrugues with biographical note by Canavari, Florence, 1894.

[136] Cf. Sestina in Rafaelli, *Verse e Prose*, I, 340. " Ch' or convien fabbricar lo studio e l'arme Da potersi covrir dal fero artiglio . . ." (of the Imperial eagle).

[137] " *Manuscrit 5853 de la bibliothèque de l'Arsenal*," ascribed by copyist to Alamanni. It is closely analysed by Hauvette, *op. cit.* pp. 426–30, who doubts this attribution.

[138] " *Lamento di Firenze, qual supplice la Santità del Papa ad unirsi con essa lei con invocazione di tutte le potenze Christiane* " followed by a further ballad on " *L'Assedio di Firenze.*" Republished in *Scelta di Curiosità Letterarie,* Disp. XLVII.

[139] " *Capitolo sopra l'Assedio di Firenze di 1529, di Lorenzo di Santi di Stefano da Prato de Buonafedi, Tintore di Drappi, abitante in quel tempo nella Città di Firenze.*" (Published in Appendix by Rastrelli, I, 190–200, and separately, Florence, 1868.)

[140] For Aldobrandini, as well as Donato Giannotti and Jacopo Nardi, cf. Marzi, *La Cancelleria della Repubblica Fiorentina* (Rocca S. Casciano, 1910), and the biography of Passerini (Rome, 1878).

[141] Roseo, *op. cit.* p. 52 (with note 35), and p. 90.

[142] Sanuto, LI, 231.

[143] Printed by Arbib and Milanesi in appendix to their editions of Varchi, Vol. II.

[144] " *Satira a Messer Pierantonio Acciaiuoli* " (see *Francesco Ferruccio,* etc., p. 102). According to a legend which owes its origin apparently to Guerazzi, this was found on his table in his tent in camp during a sortie by Ludovico Martelli, who added, *impromptu*, a stanza which shamed the other poet of the part he was playing and drove him to retire from the siege ; but see *infra,* cap. X, *n.* 126.

[145] Guerazzi's famous novel, *L'Assedio di Firenze*, is the most important of these, embodying a vast amount of historical research. D'Azeglio's *Niccolò de' Lapi* is very similar though less vehement and more readable. Ademollo's *Marietta de' Ricci* is another important novel of the period, which enriched by Passerini's learned notes, has become an authoritative work of reference for Florentine history. Among the modern poets inspired by the Siege of Florence may be mentioned Alessandro Poerio, who lost his life in the defence of Venice in 1848.

[146] For this account and what is to come, see Falletti, vol. I, cap. v, *Siena e Firenze*; and Capello, letter 30. Details and instructions with regard to the depredations and counter-depredations over the border in the autumn of 1527 may be found in the despatches to Carlo Strozzi, Commissary of Volterra, in Carteggio Originale, XII, especially ff. 71–9, for the month of December.

[147] Falletti, *ubi supra*, and pp. 220–3. Cf. instructions of Carducci of 8 July 1528 in Dieci, Missive, XLIV, and of Portinari of 1 April 1529, *ibid.* XLVI, with his credentials of following day in Signoria, Carteggio, Missive, Minutari, XXI. Those of Altoviti, of 12 May 1529, are in *ibid.* Registri, LVIII, where (20 April, 7 May) are complaints addressed to Siena through Portinari over the treatment of Florentine subjects. The expedition was discussed and rejected in the Pratica of 3 May (Pratiche, LXXI).

[148] See his letters in Robert, II, *passim.*

[149] See Falletti, I, cap. v, *Siena e Firenze*, and the preface to Vol. II, pp. x–xix, illustrated by the letters there published of the successive Sienese envoys at camp (Sergardi, Faleri, Vannini, and Bardi, referred to henceforth by the name of the writer and number of the despatch), of Morone and of Jano Calvo Salimbeni. Cf. also Robert, *op. cit.* cap. xv, esp. pp. 306 *seqq.* and 337, and letters of Orange to Balia of Siena in vol. II, esp. Nos. 181 *seqq.* and 247; Bardi, *op. cit.*, sec. III; and Sanuto, LII, 45–7. For the raids over the border into Florentine territory in October 1529, cf. the complaints from Colle and elsewhere in Dieci Responsive, CXLVI, ff. 33–7, and the complaint registered through the ambassador at Siena, f. 59. A schedule of the provisions supplied is printed by Falletti, II, 106–7, *f.n.* The same authority (I, 352) shows that Varchi (and, following him, Robert) is inaccurate in supposing that the Sienese obtained possession of S. Casciano.

[150] Falletti, II, xxiv–xxxvi, with the illustrative letters ; Sanuto, LII, 69 ; Varchi, II, 227.

[151] Varchi, II, 248–9.

[152] For the disposition of the troops and captains, see Varchi, II, 310–11 ; Roseo, pp. 65–9 ; Giovio, II, 169 ; Nardi, p. 209 ; Capello, letters 57, 58 ; and above all the fresco of Vasari in the Palazzo Vecchio, an historical document of the utmost importance, with his *Ragionamenti* upon it, in *Opere*, VIII, 165 *seqq.*

[153] One would feel inclined to doubt the veracity of this commonplace of classical poliorcetics but for the contemporary testimony of Fedele in his letter of 2 November (Sanuto, LII, 215–16).

[154] Report of G. B. Pessi in Sanuto, LII, 174–6 ; Varchi, II, 201–2 ; and *Ragguaglio di Baccio Carnesecchi, ubi supra.*

CHAPTER IX

THE INVESTMENT

ON 29 October 1529, the first artillery shot was discharged against the city. The brunt of the bombardment was directed against S. Miniato, and more especially against its Campanile. This had already proved itself a thorn in the side of the Imperial forces. The old bombardier in charge of the couple of light pieces mounted there had the whole country-side lying out beneath him like a map ; and he was able to descry and to disturb the slightest movement in the camp, down to the changing of the guard. It attracted, therefore, the greatest part of the enemy's fire. On the first day alone, it received no less than fifty balls—a large number for that age : and the tornado continued unabated for three days. It was a slight object to hit, but in the intensity of the bombardment some of the shots found their billet and not many would be necessary to bring it down. Michelangelo had, however, the idea—not uncommon in those days—of reinforcing and protecting it with bales of wool which he obtained from the Arte della Lana. No less than 1,800 were used, either piled up on the ground to protect the foundations or hanging from the summit to receive and deaden the shots. Later on, mattresses filled with wool and tow were used for the same purpose. It became a point of pride with both sides, and thus acquired an importance beyond its military value. Salvestro Aldobrandini condoled with it in a sarcastic sonnet " *Povero campanile sventurato!* " Once, rendered combustible by reason of its protections, it was set on fire. But the damage was soon made good, and the enemy was reported to have despaired of doing it any injury. Ultimately, an immense earthwork, constructed in a single night, put it out of danger, and the attempt to destroy it was finally abandoned.[1] On 4 November, fire was opened on the Palazzo della Signoria, but the shot fell short on the Bargello.[2] In general, indeed, the execution was slight : and though this was the first occasion that Florence had ever experienced a bombardment, little alarm was caused. In time the reports of the various pieces began to be familiarly recognized even by the women. It was not till the spring, when a cannon ball fell in the Piazza S. Giovanni, that any material damage was done in the city.[3] Nevertheless, great execution was occasionally

done. Thus on 16 December—" a day ever to be wept by the
Florentines "—a single chance shot brought down a building at
S. Miniato, killing Mario Orsini and another of the best Florentine captains, together with five private soldiers and three young
citizens, who had gone to inspect the fortifications.[4] Yet, on
the whole, the artillery from Siena was of little use, for, old and
worn, half of the eight pieces burst after two or three shots,
and there were insuperable difficulties in the way of repairing
them.[5]

Besides the artillery battle, almost every day saw skirmishes,
especially about Giramonte and S. Miniato, where the brunt of
the fighting occurred. Thus on the night of 2 November a
strong party of Florentine troops assaulted Orange's pickets all
along the line from S. Niccolò to S. Giorgio, and retired only after
burning about twenty houses and inflicting some casualties. In
another engagement, the enemy lost three captains and about
seventy men, and Alessandro Vitelli was himself wounded. In
spite of the disapproval of Malatesta, the militia insisted on going
out to reconnoitre with the regulars, and skirmishing continued
uninterruptedly and with some bloodshed. Further afield, there
were constant cavalry engagements with some deposit of supplies
as the usual point of dispute. The losses were greater than might
be imagined, for the campaign was carried on mercilessly. Of
those wounded at all seriously by arquebus shots, few could ever
hope to recover. Both sides had agreed to " wage good war "
and to spare the lives of professional soldiers who were captured.
Orange was, however, enraged at the irregular warfare carried
on by the Florentine peasantry, and, in consequence probably of
this, the arrangement was not observed by the Imperialists. The
Florentines followed suit, and as a result no quarter was given
by either side. Any exceptions made were in favour of the
militia, from whom rich ransoms could be expected. Some of
them, resenting being treated otherwise than as professional
soldiers, made a special point of killing their prisoners.[6]

Matters continued thus without any outstanding engagement
until the vigil of St. Martin's Day. It was the universal custom
to celebrate that night (10–11 November), as the end of the
vintage, by copious drinking ; and Orange determined to take
advantage of the occasion to deliver an assault. The dense
darkness and heavy rain favoured his design. An attack was
accordingly prepared along the whole line of the walls on the
south bank. His troops stole silently up to the ramparts with
scaling ladders, hoping to find the Florentines off their guard and
heavy with wine. They were, however, mistaken. The sentinels
were alert and ready to receive them. While the first attack
was being met, the alarm was given in the city. With remark-

able order and precision, the militia paraded, and all the roads and bridges become thronged with persons hurrying to the scene of battle. Contrary to expectations, the artillery came into action and fired into the ranks of the assailants with good effect. The surprise was a manifest failure : and Orange reluctantly ordered the retreat to be sounded. It was a serious reverse, but outside the city its consequences were exaggerated. In far-off Paris it was reported that the army had met with a crushing defeat, that its artillery was lost, and that the commander-in-chief had been forced to flee on foot.[7]

While military operations at Florence remained virtually at a standstill, there was greater activity in the dominion. It had indeed been determined to hold only the few vital fortresses ; yet the Imperialists were not allowed to occupy the other places without opposition. Thus Montepulciano had on 23 October agreed to surrender if no help came within eight days. Florence could promise no assistance : the mission which had been delegated to ask it went immediately to arrange the terms of surrender : and already the conquerors were quarrelling over the spoil. At the last moment, however, a force of a few hundred horse and archers under the Abbot of Farfa came into the city, and its defence was protracted.[8] Poggibonsi was less fortunate, and, summoned to surrender by the Duke of Amalfi, appealed in vain for help ; as also did Castelfiorentino, Montaione, Gambasso, and many other places.[9] The hill country to the north of the city known as the Mugello fell to an old soldier of base birth named Ramazotto, self-styled Count of Tossignano, and an influential local leader in the Apennine regions. He had obtained an irregular commission from the Pope, and had assembled a force of about 3,000 ill-disciplined followers from his native mountains. These wrought the greatest depredation in the whole neighbourhood, carrying off whatever they could find and infesting the highways. Fiorenzuola, Scarperia, and Borgo S. Lorenzo fell an easy prey ; other places were sacked and then abandoned. Excepting for the citadel of Marradi (one of the keys to the passes of the Apennines) and the fortress of Vicchio, the whole region was overrun by these and similar irregular bands. Nevertheless, Ramazzotto himself experienced a severe check at the hands of an extemporized native force— a first military success which served to restore confidence at Florence. Other troops, operating from Prato, inflicted a reverse, insufficiently pursued, upon the enemy at Barberino. On the other hand, an expedition to recover Borgo San Lorenzo, and thus re-establish communications along the Pistoia-Bologna road, was beaten off with some loss and not without suspicions of complicity.[10] The President of the Romagna on behalf of the

Pope adopted methods more befitting an ecclesiastic, and sent an envoy to seduce the Casentino—the hill country of the upper Arno towards Arezzo—from its allegiance. Florence ineffectually asked help from Venice, and sent an emissary to the spot to collect a force. Bibbiena, always inclined to the Medici, consented without much demur to supply the besieging army with provisions. Poppi, the chief town of the district, was more faithful and sent to Florence for succour. Alessandro Vitelli and Sciarra Colonna were despatched by Orange to reduce it. Brisk operations followed ; and at last it surrendered and fell into line with Bibbiena.[11]

The acid test of war brought out a new personality upon the Florentine side. Francesco Ferrucci belonged to an old Florentine family which had given a Gonfalonier to the Republic as early as 1305, and had founded a chapel in the church of the Carmine. Since those days, however, it had become reduced, though it never lost a modest place in public life. Francesco was born on 14 August 1489, in a house in the Via Santo Spirito, and he was thus at the present time just forty years of age. His father, far from wealthy, had been forced to set him at the early age of twelve to learn business in the bank of Rafaello Girolami, with whom he was afterwards to be so closely connected. He had the usual introduction to public life, enjoying his first experience as " Podestà " of some minor Florentine possessions. In 1527, on the occasion of the expedition of Lautrec, he obtained permission to accompany the Florentine envoys to camp as paymaster. This was the turning-point in his career. He became attached to the Bande Nere and served with them through the unfortunate Neapolitan campaign. This first trial of military life was disastrous for him. He was made prisoner during a skirmish ; and he had to sell all of his inheritance in order to pay his ransom and be free to return to Florence. This military experience led to his being sent in the summer of 1529 to Pesaro to act as Florentine agent in the engagement of some lanz-knechts from the Abruzzi who had been led over to the service of the league. On the conclusion of this mission he was sent as assistant to successive Commissary-Generals, acting finally as liaison officer at Perugia with Malatesta Baglione. As yet he had been given no opportunity to show any unusual merit : and in an age which trusted only the professional soldier, one who was by upbringing a mere merchant was neglected. Donato Giannotti, however, had already learned to appreciate the man whose biography he was afterwards to write, and urged his employment on the Dieci. They sent him, therefore, to fill the minor position of commissary at Prato, which the enemy had recently attempted to get possession of by treachery. Here he was subordinated to

Lorenzo Soderini. The two did not get on well together. Soderini
was impatient of divided control, while Ferrucci objected to the
licence which the soldiers were allowed by his colleague to enjoy.
Yielding, therefore, to requests from either side, the Dieci recalled
the new officer after less than a week, replacing him at Prato by a
more easy character. They already had, however, proof of his
ability, and sent him as commissary with full military authority
to Empoli, which had been asking for reinforcements. This
became from this date the most important centre of operations
outside Florence.[12]

Empoli was, as we have seen, one of the vital fortresses,
occupying a crucial position on the line of communication with
Pisa and the outside world. Ferrucci realized its importance
and with characteristic energy set about perfecting its fortifications as well as securing the fidelity of the inhabitants by
sending hostages to Florence. He put himself into constant
communication with Pisa on the one side as well as with the
capital on the other : and with the greatest difficulty he succeeded
in obtaining powder, ammunition, and even some reinforcements.[13] With these he was able to make some headway in a
direction where hitherto the Imperialists had met with little
opposition. Colle d' Elsa, Lari, Peccioli, S. Gimignano, and S.
Miniato al Tedesco had been occupied at the first assault, and
from them incursions had been made upon the whole of this rich
district.[14] They could no longer continue with impunity. A
series of attacks was made on outlying detachments,[15] and a
brilliant raid followed on Castelfiorentino, though there were not
enough troops to hold it.[16] On 6 November there followed a
highly successful operation against an enemy column, which
resulted in the sending of a hundred prisoners under escort to
Florence, as many again having been killed or wounded.[17] This
led up to an attack on S. Miniato al Tedesco, from which easy
capture the enemy had been infesting even the vital road from
Pisa to Florence. Ferrucci himself led a carefully prepared
assault and was the first to scale the ramparts. After a fierce
fight, the Spanish garrison surrendered and the place again
returned to the shelter of the Marzocco (10 November).[18] A
week later he sent to scour the road to Siena ; and in a cavalry
engagement between Lucardo and Tavernelle a further sixty
prisoners were captured.[19] At about the same time Cecotto
Tosinghi, commissary of Pisa, inspired by this example, sent to
cut off an enemy column returning from Lari laden with booty.
It was dispersed, the spoil recovered, and many prisoners captured.[20] On the other hand, Lastra, an important position on
the road to Empoli and Pisa which had been fortified in order
to hamper the provisioning of the camp, was captured by the

Imperialists after a gallant defence, an attempt to relieve it from Prato and Florence having utterly failed ; and the whole garrison was butchered in spite of the terms of surrender (6 December).[21] Similarly, Colonel Pirro Colonna with a flying column relieved Peccioli, which was being besieged by Count Ercole Rangone for the Florentines, just in the nick of time. Rangone, in conjunction with Tosinghi, avenged himself by a successful ambush near S. Romano. Colonna was able to recover sufficiently to overwhelm in his turn another Florentine detachment, and marched to relieve Monopoli. On the way he fell into an ambush set by Ferrucci, who was awaiting an opportunity to avenge the capture of Lastra. His forces were overwhelmed, 200 men were killed or wounded, and seven standards captured, almost without loss to the Florentines ; while Pirro himself had a narrow escape for his life (13 December).[22] In addition to these major actions, Ferrucci continued a constant activity in minor operations and raids, continually urging the central government to support him in some more daring enterprise. His successes were in themselves of no peculiarly great importance. But they showed that a new star had arisen in the Florentine firmament, and went far to strengthen the morale of the citizens. His despatches breathed confidence and determination, and were read out publicly amid the general applause in the Great Council. Some asserted that as a commander he was over-fierce and irascible, or even cruel. Those who were acquainted with him personally, however, realized that, though severe to a degree, he was invariably just. If his discipline was hard, he nevertheless gained the confidence and affection of his soldiers, who knew that he was always first in danger and recognized that his ability as soldier outweighed his mercantile training. Above all, he was able to inspire them with that restless energy and indefatigable activity which were the greatest of his military virtues.[23]

This example, and the experience of some weeks' siege, gave the city confidence to assume the offensive herself. A careful plan was prepared by Stefano Colonna in conjunction with Malatesta. On Saturday, 11 December, towards midnight a force of five or six hundred soldiers stole out silently from the Porta S. Niccolò. With them went one company of the militia —the Gonfalone of the Unicorn under Alamanno de' Pazzi. They were supported by Giovanni da Torino from the Porta S. Giorgio and Ottaviano Signorelli from S. Piero Gattolini—the present-day Porta Romana. All wore over their corselets a white shirt to distinguish them in the darkness—a circumstance from which these night sorties were afterwards called " *incamiciate*." In spite of the provision of a hundred arquebuses, the assailants used no fire-arms, so as not to betray their presence ; and the obscurity of the night, enhanced by the rain, concealed their movements until they were at the enemy's camp. Passing through the depression between Rusciano and Giramonte, they arrived unobserved at Sta. Margherita a Montici, at the camp of Sciarra Colonna, with whom Stefano, his kinsman, had, as was natural, a private quarrel. It was fortunate that he himself was absent through sickness. The surprise was complete. Many were killed in their tents or in an attempt to escape. A number of swine, let loose by accident through the forcing of the doors of the slaughter-house, rushed wildly about with terrified grunts, tripping up the soldiers and adding to the confusion on both sides. For two hours, wrote one who witnessed it all from the tower of the Palazzo Vecchio, an utter inferno was raging without, in striking contrast to the calm which reigned within the city, where we may imagine all to have been on their knees in prayer. Meanwhile the alarm was given and succour commenced to arrive, led by Orange himself. According to a pre-arranged signal, two cannon were fired from S. Miniato and the assailants commenced an orderly retirement without bringing their reserves into action. The result was not very remarkable: yet it was generally believed that more execution could have been done had fuller support been given and had not Malatesta, prematurely as was alleged, given the signal for retreat. The casualty figures were nevertheless fabulous. The besiegers were said to have lost over 200 killed; the besieged, no more than a single person wounded. But the rumours which got abroad enhanced the victory still further. It was reported that the Imperialist camp had been destroyed and the siege broken up. In many places in the dominion, the people rose at the news and expelled or sometimes killed the Imperial and papal commissaries who had been set over them. Other honourable but fruitless sorties followed on the 19th and 20th of the month. As a result, the enemy captains were instructed to entrench themselves in their quarters instead of lying in the open as they hitherto had done.[24]

The longer the army lay outside Florence, the more acute its necessities became. Besides the utter destruction carried out in the immediate neighbourhood of the city, the Florentine captains had been scouring the countryside. Whatever supplies had not been taken into the fortified places owing to the incurable optimism of the inhabitants or the unusual exuberance of the year were ruthlessly wasted, the wine and oil being poured out on the ground, the corn and fodder burnt. Even the mills were destroyed so as to rob the enemy of the opportunity to grind what grain he had. Every now and again one of the detachments sent out on these errands was intercepted and a sharp fight would ensue. In addition, an unusually wet season had put the roads, already insecure through the licentiousness of the troops, in an impassable condition. Much of the provisions sent from outside failed to arrive in the camp. It was not long before the slender stores which had been discovered round the city were exhausted ; and the army, half drowned in a sea of mud, began to suffer systematically from actual want. From every point of view matters were as bad. Pioneers were still lacking : but when at last some arrived the majority lost no time in escaping. Money was short, and Orange was supplied with barely half of what he needed. His troops were too few for their task, and his artillery hopelessly inadequate : but, tired of demanding reinforcements, he was at last reduced to ask for a promise of them merely to encourage those under his command. There were no doctors in camp, and Alessandro Vitelli himself was forced to ask for one from Malatesta, who ungraciously replied that he might seek medical attendance within the walls. Orange was worried, in addition, by the condition of affairs in Naples and by the activities of the Venetians in Apulia. There were daily desertions to the city, and whole bodies of Spanish troops broke out into open mutiny. Matters, he was convinced, stood at the point of " extreme unction " : and on St. Martin's Day, the morrow of his defeat, he set off to Bologna to lay the matter before his master.[25]

The war thus continued unrelieved by any startling event as autumn passed and the rigours of winter commenced. The shortage of wood in the city began to make itself felt in the intense cold : but the enemy, still suffering from the heavy rains, was in the worse plight. The time had meanwhile arrived for the creation of the new Gonfalonier, as on the fall of Capponi it had been determined that his immediate successor should hold office for eight months only. In order to minimize the possibility of intrigues, it had been expressly stipulated that no second term of office should henceforth be allowed. Carducci, however, had ever since his election been endeavouring to get round this provision by courting the favour of every section of the city. In a harangue before the Great Council he had endeavoured to show, after the manner of the demagogue in war-time, that a change of government in the midst of such a crisis would be fatal, and that authority should be left in the hands of the man who was fully conversant with affairs and had shown himself capable and determined to bring them to a suc-cessful conclusion. It seemed indeed as though the spirit which he had shown in the defence would carry him to office again ; and a recommendation of a sub-committee of the Ottanta that an ex-Gonfalonier should be accorded special precedence and a voice in the secret councils of the Republic, but still remain ineligible for re-election, was rejected by the Great Council. Yet the original provision stood, that he could not become a candidate a second time ; and for one reason or another it was not changed. The function was held on 2 December, at a meeting which easily exceeded the minimum of 1,500. Of the old favourites not one survived the first ballot with the exception of Alfonso Strozzi, whose aristocratic connections were out-weighed by his notoriously hot republicanism : all the rest were new personalities who had recently risen to prominence, like Bernardo da Castiglione and Andreuolo Niccolini. At the second ballot Rafaello Girolami was found to have been elected, as had been foreseen by some acuter observers. By a new arrangement, he entered immediately into semi-official state ; and a month later, on 1 January, he commenced his term of office. His place as commissary over the defence was given to his predecessor, who was also, by an unprecedented concession, accorded a per-manent voice in the Pratica.[26]

Rafaello Girolami, last Gonfalonier of the free Republic, had been for some time prominent in the public eye. A member of a noble and wealthy family which had opposed the rise of the Medicean hegemony, he had been left an orphan in his early youth and had thus come under the influence of the former rulers, for whom he had acted as envoy in Spain. Yet this did not prevent him from showing his sympathy with the movement for independence, and he had been removed from his post as commissary of Poggibonsi as a result of his equivocal conduct at the time of the Tumulto del Venerdì. After the revolution, he had served as Commissary-General with the Florentine forces. His position was at this time already so well established that, according to a contemporary, he was in mind when at the time of the last vacancy it was resolved that none should be elected to the supreme office if more than a certain distance from the city. Since then he had enhanced his reputation by the embassy to Genoa ; and he was the only one of the four members who had actually returned to Florence. As one of the commissaries over the defence he had shown untiring vigour and organizing ability, it being due mainly to his exertions that no serious disorder of any kind had occurred in spite of the influx of alien soldiery. He thus counted on support from all sides—from the nobles and Palleschi for his birth and antecedents, from the war-party for his more recent record.[27] He was, however, distinctly less of an extremist than his predecessor, and his election betokened a more moderate tone in the city as a whole. Yet the change had no influence upon the government. The very fact that one who was not of themselves took the place of Carducci had a strong effect upon the extreme republicans. They acquired a cohesion which they had previously lacked, and the *Setta*, as it was called by its enemies, began to have the dominant position of a Jacobin club in the state. Its leaders acquired an immediate ascendancy over the mind of the new Gonfalonier : and the policy of his predecessor was continued in its entirety.[28]

Never, however, was conciliation needed more than now. There had already commenced at Bologna between Pope and Emperor that fateful conference which was to determine the future of Europe and to shape the destinies of Italy for many generations to come. One of the main purposes of Charles' voyage to Italy had been to receive formal coronation as Holy Roman Emperor—he had been called so hitherto only by courtesy. It had been the invariable custom that this ceremony should take place at the hands of the Pope, and at Rome. The threatening internal situation in Germany and the advance of the Turk had, however, rendered it impolitic that Charles should go so far out of his way : and immediately after his arrival in Italy he had sent to Clement asking that the function should take place at Bologna. In spite of the lack of precedent and the opposition of the Curia, he was too dependent upon the other, especially in the matter of the Florentine expedition, to dare to refuse. On 7 October, therefore, he left Rome. The obduracy of Florence rendered it impossible for him to take the direct road through Tuscany : and he went instead by a longer route through the Romagna, finally making his state entry into Bologna on 24 October. Twelve days later, Charles, who had meanwhile been delaying at Piacenza, arrived to meet him amid the greatest pomp.

The meeting of the two potentates would obviously not be confined to the formal business of the coronation. There was a score of matters to be discussed between them. Charles needed Clement's moral support to settle the affairs of Germany, as well as in the thorny question of the projected divorce of his aunt, Catherine, by Henry VIII of England. Clement needed the other's material assistance in his territorial and dynastic disputes in Italy, with Venice, with Ferrara, and especially with Florence. There were, in addition, several outstanding questions to be decided regarding the execution of the Treaty of Barcelona. The two were continually together discussing these matters, and the meeting developed into a conference. It was not until 24 February, anniversary of his birth and of his victory at Pavia, that Charles was crowned. In the intervening weeks the fate of Italy was decided, and the shackles were forged which kept her enslaved until the nineteenth century.[29]

The minor powers of the peninsula were aware that it was their destinies which were being settled in these conversations. Bologna began to be crowded with the delegates of the various states, who hastened to make the best terms they could. Florence thus saw herself abandoned by the last of her nominal allies. From Venice, even after the Treaty of Cambrai, she had hoped for some assistance, as with her fall Charles would have become omnipotent south of the Alps. The Dieci were accordingly continually asking help in every despatch to their orator at Venice and in every conversation with Carlo Capello at home. The Doge and his council replied with benevolent words and specious promises, and stimulated the defence in every way possible, sedulously discouraging any move which might lead to peace.[30] Their envoy at Florence took an active part in word and deed in encouraging the city to resist, sending away none of his family or property, paying visits to the bastions, and entreating the Signoria in "magnificent orations" to resist any temptation to come to terms. His secretary, the obsequious Fedele, waxed enthusiastic over the determination and spirit of the city as long as his employers did not reveal their hand on the other side. Bartolommeo Gualterotti, the Florentine envoy at Venice, questioned if they would ever fulfil their promises. The Doge replied haughtily that Venice had never acted dishonourably yet and would not now commence. Nevertheless, nothing was ever done. There was indeed no community of interest between the two powers—only one of apprehensions. Florence had no concern in the aggrandisement of Venice, nor Venice in the maintenance of the popular government in Florence. Her sole aim was to protract the war, keeping the enemy engaged until she put herself into security. The only concrete help therefore that she offered during the whole course of the siege was to send the sum of seven hundred ducats for the defence of the Florentine Romagna, on her own borders; but this exiguous assistance was contemptuously refused.[31] The Florentines, seeing their suspicions confirmed that "the Venetians naturally promise much and fulfil little," gave up asking for direct help, which might implicate them too far, and requested merely a diversion towards Arezzo on the part of the Venetian forces at Urbino, which would imperil Orange's lines of communication. With tears in their eyes, the Signoria begged this or other assistance, and Capello urged it in eloquent despatches. Yet, though they were still technically at war and could have lost nothing by compliance, the Venetians refused to compromise their position by any unfriendly operation, however much they were pledged to the reverse. Even at Bologna, where their diplomatic support might have been of use, they neglected their promises and acted for their own hand in spite of all the Florentine requests. As late as 7 December, there were still some hopes of stirring them to assist. Little more than a fortnight later, they became party to a virtually general Italian treaty of peace and alliance, in which the hostility of Pope and Emperor was bought off by the cession of Cervia and Ravenna to the one, and the Apulian towns with a money indemnity to the other. Thus the name of Venetian loyalty, proverbial since Boccaccio's days, was justified.[32]

The Duke of Ferrara was now the only member of the league who had not come to terms. He had already abandoned Florence in deed. As we have seen, he had not permitted his son, Ercole, to take up effectively his position as Captain-General of the Republic. Nevertheless, he had encouraged the Florentines to continue their resistance and had been prodigal of promises of help. He had sympathetically viewed the activities of their ambassador, Galeotto Giugni, in his territories. Though he gave passage to the Imperial troops and supplies, he had been instrumental in securing for Florence the services of a force of mercenaries. He had even given hopes that in spite of everything a pretext would after all be found of sending his son to aid the city. Yet even while he was doing this he was striving his utmost to come to terms. As his danger became imminent, he had lost no time in attempting to secure his position. He had gone to meet Charles at Parma before his arrival at Bologna, and had succeeded in enlisting his sympathies. Though it was still some time before the Pope could be persuaded to pardon this arch-enemy and to grant him mild conditions, he could already be considered as completely out of the quarrel. As an earnest of his good faith, he withdrew Count Ercole Rangone, who had represented him at the commencement of the campaign with a small troop of horse, and had done some good work. Florence was thus left absolutely alone. It was the refractory city's last opportunity to come to terms.[33]

Negotiations had, as a matter of fact, never been entirely broken off. In spite of their ungracious reception, the four Florentine ambassadors had left Rome for Bologna in Clement's train. On the road, at Cesena, he relented in his attitude. His recent correspondence with Orange and with Charles had argued anything but well for the future of the enterprise; and they were continuing to urge him to come to terms. It was necessary to make at least a show of reasonableness. A pretext was given by the exiles from Florence, headed by Guicciardini, who were imploring him to have pity on their common native city. Accordingly, he consented to grant an interview (20 October). His tone on this occasion was milder than usual. He insisted on indemnities and compensations for what had been done against him, but declared that he would show the whole world that he, too, was a Florentine and professed that he would be content with only a " reform " in the government. Francesco Nasi, the under-ambassador, was again sent back to Florence to report.[34] It was found that in spite of the change of tone the substance of the reply was as uncompromising as ever, and so hedged about with conditions as to provide no basis for negotiations. Instructions were therefore sent to Bologna that the envoys should break off all relations with the Pope, but should make representations instead to the Emperor in a last attempt to dissuade him from his decision.[35] Diplomatic relations with him had indeed continued almost without interruption ; and his generals, conscious of the weakness of their own position, had done their best to forward them. By their recommendation the Florentines had again attempted their fortune with Charles by sending Lottieri Gherardi to him at Parma, with instructions to clear his mind of any misapprehensions which he might have as to the dynastic rights of the Medici, and to express their willingness for a reasonable peace. Through the influence of the papal agents, however, he had been refused audience, and even put under restraint for a short time.[36] Early in November, again, Orange had put forward—possibly in order to exert pressure upon the Pope—suggestions for a monetary composition such as had been refused a month previous. It was suspected however, and not without reason, that this was not meant seriously but intended merely to create discord in the city ; and this led to a summary rejection. Nevertheless, in consequence of Orange's advances, the recent instructions to the orators at Bologna were modified so that they might treat again with the Pope as well as with the Emperor.[37]

The Florentines had all along been encouraged in their attitude by the assurance that Charles would be forced by the Turkish advance in Austria to relax or to abandon his efforts in their direction. On the eve of the meeting, however, the news arrived that the attack on Vienna had utterly failed. The close of the campaign in Naples rid the Imperialists of another serious distraction. Thus these optimistic calculations were reversed. Not only was Charles free to retain his troops before Florence, but he was in a position to augment them. It was indeed to his interest to maintain a standing army at the expense of another in readiness for all eventualities. He was thus able to consider the question from an angle more akin to that of Clement. He saw in the Florentine attachment to France a standing menace to his supremacy in Italy, and in their obduracy a flouting of his Imperial authority. Moreover, in their rejection of recent advances they had given to his mind decisive proof of the un-reasonableness of their demands. The amity of the Pope was still so vital a consideration as to outweigh any minor objec-tions. Finally, his advisors were urging him on. Accordingly, Charles definitely abandoned his scheme of investing Alessandro with the Duchy of Milan ; and the embassy found the two sovereigns completely in accord in their determination not to be worsted by a city of merchants. At the commencement the Emperor refused to receive them without the consent of the Pope : and when that was finally obtained he replied in the old strain, ordering them to give satisfaction to his ally. Accordingly, the negotiations were broken off and the envoys returned. [38] Only Francesco Vettori, who in the original revolution had represented the most Medicophile element, and had been brought back from retirement at Pistoia to go on this mission, elected to remain with the Pope and became one of his most trusted advisers. [39] When, accordingly, on the morrow of his defeat of St. Martin's Eve, the Prince of Orange followed up his pessi-mistic despatches by going to Bologna for a personal colloquy, he found a changed atmosphere. He needed, as he had con-tinually insisted, about 70,000 ducats monthly for his pay-roll, and an additional force of at least 12,000 men in order to carry on effective siege operations. Whatever he asked was promised. Clement undertook to find the pay, and Charles, who had the whole army of Lombardy set free by his decision to allow Fran-cesco Maria Sforza to retain Milan, ordered it to move against Florence. [40]

Confident now more than ever before in the determination of Charles, Clement seems to have made an attempt to save the expense as well as the horrors of war by encouraging another embassy on the part of the city, which he imagined now cowed and discouraged. At the end of December, the Bishop of Faenza entered Florence and dismounted at the palace of the Torrigiani occupied by Malatesta, whom he asked on behalf of the Pope to act as intermediary for peace. The latter communicated this to the Signoria, inviting them to send fresh envoys to the Pope in confidence of excellent results. This was the first task with which Girolami was confronted on his entry into office. The Pratica, which discussed the matter, was divided [41] ; and it was then brought up before an extraordinary meeting of the Great Council. A most heated discussion ensued, but ultimately the proposal was carried by the overwhelming majority of 1,000 votes to 375. [42] Simultaneously the King of France was attempt-ing to ingratiate himself with both sides by negotiating an agree-ment ; and his representative in Italy, the Bishop of Clairmont, was sent to Florence to offer his services as mediator. [43]   It seemed now as if peace was a certainty, and its conclusion was believed imminent on both sides. Instead of the secret relations with the Prince of Orange, which had never been interrupted, heralds and even private citizens now went to visit him daily, bearing rich gifts, while Marucelli was sent back as regular agent. The Bishop of Faenza meanwhile, though not quite satisfied, having expected a more submissive tone, returned to Bologna with the news. The envoys elected were Luigi Soderini and Andreuolo Niccolini, both determined republicans. With them went a number of young Florentines anxious to witness the Imperial coronation which was to take place on 24 February— among them Benedetto Varchi, the historian. Thither, too, there went from his refuge at Pisa the young Giorgio Vasari, to paint his well-known picture of the two potentates in conference.[44] Immediately, however, on their arrival at Bologna, it was seen that the high hopes with which they had set out had no foundation excepting if they were willing to humiliate themselves. At the very gates of the city, in spite of their quality of ambassadors, they were examined and their luggage ransacked. When they were received in audience, the Pope overwhelmed them with abuse for the spirit of the government and raked up against them all their old misdeeds and the slights which had been inflicted upon him. Of the present constitution he spoke in insulting terms, reaffirming his intention to abolish the Great Council. Finally he expressed his amazement that the city imagined that he had invited her to send him envoys, which was far from his mind. The Emperor was no more conciliatory than his ally, and refused to hear the deputies unless they had more to say than their predecessors. They became the laughing-stock of the whole city, crowded as it was with delegations from all Europe ; and they returned home to report that their mission had not only been a failure, but had been intended as a deliberate and insulting farce.[45] It was the last time that the Florentines consented to negotiate with the Pope ; and when, on 8 February, the Gonfalonier reported another tentative on the part of the French ambassador, it was almost unanimously recommended to make an end of negotiations and to order Malatesta to do the same, " since in peace there can be no more hope."[46]

With the Emperor, however, there was to be one. more attempt before he left Italy. Galeotto Giugni, orator at Ferrara, who had already been in conversation with the Grand Chancellor,[47] had come into contact with the Duke and Duchess of Savoy, connections of Charles, who had gone to Bologna to be present at the coronation. He had naturally recommended the city to their benevolence, and in reply had received an offer to act as mediators with the Emperor. At the same time, the Prince of Orange, through the medium of Marucelli, who had not left his camp, encouraged the city to enter into negotiations. After a couple of discussions, therefore (conducted under a pledge of secrecy so as to have no evil effect on the city), it was determined by the Ottanta by 83 votes to 39 that Giugni should be authorized to accompany the Duke of Ferrara to his approaching colloquy at Mantua to treat for peace. Reservation was made, as always, of the three main considerations—the liberty of the city, the integrity of the dominion, and the republican constitution. On hearing these limitations, however, the Emperor refused to go further ; and the Duke of Ferrara was instructed to inform Giugni that it was useless to seek audience.[48] In addition, it had been intimated that as an indispensable preliminary it was necessary to stop the guerilla warfare on the part of the Florentine peasantry, and to punish those who had indulged in it.[49] Thus, as was to be expected, the negotiations again fell through.

The reiteration at Bologna of the warlike intentions of the Pope and the impossibility of coming to an agreement rendered it advisable to make good one anomaly in the military organization of the Florentines. Malatesta Baglione held the position of Governor-General of their forces ; but the supreme office of Captain-General had been left empty since the defection of Don Ercole, as though in the hope of ultimately securing his services. His father's negotiations with the Emperor showed finally that this was out of question. Malatesta was meanwhile intriguing to secure the supreme command. He had enough savoir-faire to make himself acceptable to every shade of opinion. The death of Mario Orsini had removed one powerful rival ; another, Stefano Colonna, though he had his reputation enhanced by his successful *incamiciata*, was too aloof in manner and regarded himself, somewhat over-pedantically, as in the service of the French king. Hence when Malatesta put himself forward for the office, there was no other candidate in consideration. He was proposed therefore for the office by the Gonfalonier, in spite of the fact that there were four months of his original agreement still to run ; and he was elected " to the great contentment of all the city, it seeming to all that the rank is worthily filled in him." His position was henceforth that of commander-in-chief of the Florentine forces for a period of two years at a salary of 9,000 ducats yearly and with a personal following of 200 men-at-arms. He on his side was bound to assist the city with his property and person " even against the Apostolic See." To Colonna, in partial compensation, was given the supreme command of the militia. On 26 January, the new Captain-General

was solemnly invested in office with great pomp and ceremony.
The militia paraded and escorted him in state from his lodging
in the Palazzo de' Torrigiani beyond the Ponte alle Grazie to the
ringhiera outside the Palazzo della Signoria.   Here the Marzocco
—the traditional lion of Florence—was crowned with garlands
in honour of its new defender ; and the Gonfalonier presented
him with the standard of the Florentine people with appropriate
words.   The ceremony was marred by a heavy storm of rain,
variously interpreted as a good or evil augury.   Nevertheless, it
could not but be noticed that, in spite of his mental and vocal
vigour, Malatesta was so racked and contorted by the disease
from which he was suffering as to be suited for almost no active
function. [50]

The military reorganization in the face of the new turn of
events was paralleled in the civil spheres of government.   The
number and quality of the burghers who had abandoned Florence
before the siege or in its first weeks, refusing to answer all sum-
monses to return, had been noteworthy, and had given rise to a
natural, if ignoble, desire for revenge.   At the same time the
crushing military expenses rendered it necessary to explore new
channels for raising money to which the exiles, fortified by the
shrewd counsels of Guicciardini,[51] made no contribution.   There
was created accordingly a board of five *Sindachi dei Rubelli*, to proceed against these " putrid members calculated to rot the body
politic."   These were invested with complete authority over the
goods and property of the many outlaws, whose number was
continually increasing through the condemnation of fugitives
who refused to return.   They were empowered to sell by auction
all of their goods, or to enforce purchase at reasonable prices,
treating recent deeds of alienation as null and void.   Any resistance to their authority might be opposed by vindictive
punishments culminating in death at sight, not only on the
principals, but even on their remoter accomplices.   This was,
says Varchi, the most outrageous measure of the whole siege,
proving that republics may be as tyrannical as princes or more
so ; but it was in addition a tactical blunder of the gravest sort,
ranging the exiles, many of whom had fled merely from nervousness, definitely on the side of the Pope. [52]   Even from the financial
point of view the measure was not satisfactory.   The high rates,
little less than normal, which had previously obtained did not
continue in the face of diminished confidence and an overloaded
market.   It is from this period without doubt that prices began
to slump and that the populace was able to purchase these objects
for a fraction of their real value.

The tide of suspicion and violence in the city of which this
was a symptom was continually rising, and the abortive trans-

actions with the Pope increased it. It was suspected that the
Bishop of Faenza during his brief mission had actually entered
into a secret intrigue with some of the inhabitants. As a result,
a further sixteen distinguished citizens were put under restraint.[53]
The brother of the Gonfalonier himself, who was a chamberlain
of the Pope, was not allowed to enter into the city for fear of
treachery.[54] The number of cases brought before the Quarantia
increased by leaps and bounds. On 26 January that body was
convoked for four cases ; on the 31st, for no fewer than six,
for three more on 10 February, and for five in the first days of
March.[55] So great did its activity become that serious alarm was
caused, and it was formally proposed to suspend its action. In
spite of the universal opinion that it formed a powerful weapon
for the defence of the state, it was generally agreed that it
should be prorogued for a single month.[56] In future, in spite
of a recrudescence in April and May, its activities became more
moderate.[57]

Popular resentment was directed especially against those
renegades who were now to be found in the Pope's immediate
entourage. Francesco Guicciardini had left Florence just before
the siege through fears for his own safety, and had been one of
the band of exiles who had striven for agreement at Cesena. At
Bologna, he had become prominent about the papal court, where
according to report he visited Clement twice daily, communicating
to him immediately the secret correspondence which he received
from Florence.[58] He was cited before the Otto to explain his
conduct, but excused himself by letter instead of making a personal appearance.[59] For some time further action was suspended,
but in the end neither his conciliatory attitude nor his republican
brother availed to save him. He was tried *in absentia* before
the Quarantia, a proclamation was made inviting evidence
against him, and finally he was declared *rubello*.[60] The sentence
was confirmed as the result of a second process two months later
on the information of Lorenzo Carnesecchi, commissary of the
Romagna ; and on this occasion Francesco Vettori, the ambassador who had elected to remain with the Pope at Bologna,
shared, with Jacopo Tornabuoni, the charge and the condemnation.[61] This led to automatic confiscation of all property,
and reduced the culprits to utter penury. We know how Guicciardini was driven definitely into the Pope's arms and had to
sue him for some office. Thus were recruited the ranks of the
band of exiles about the papal court who " daily excite him
to pursue his enterprise, telling him that otherwise they are
destroyed for having done him service."[62]

On this occasion, no exception was made even in favour of
the highest. The tapestries and hangings of the Medicean Palace,

so far spared, were confiscated for the use of the Palazzo della Signoria.[63] This, however, was the least of the manifestations. One morning there was found in one of those boxes, which in Florence as in almost every Italian city were placed to receive secret accusations, a charge against Clement himself and the four Florentine cardinals at his court—Sanga, Cibo, Ridolfi, and Salviati—as traitors to their country. The penalty demanded was that ordained for traitors—outlawry with confiscation of all property. The Otto, reluctant to proceed in the matter alone, referred it to the Gonfalonier, who asked the Pratica whether the charge should be pressed. The general opinion was against it. " If it is kept alive or proceeded in," said the representative of the quarter of Santo Spirito, " it will be a verification of that which the Pope is accustomed to say, to wit that this is a government of madmen, and that we look out for accusations in order to take away the property of citizens ; especially since against a Pope it is impossible to proceed except with arms, which seems to be the determination of all this people." On a division, only twenty-nine were in favour of letting the case run its normal course, while fifty-six voted to annul it and ninety-two to suspend it.[64] A month later the question was once more discussed and the case was again, and finally, prorogued.[65]

Reason for these rising feelings could be seen in the state of affairs beneath the walls. The Prince of Orange had returned from Bologna on 29 November with sums of money in hand or in prospect which, if nothing like so much as was actually required, were sufficient to serve at least as a sop for his soldiery.[66] In other respects, the Emperor could be more lavish. Preparations were made and help solicited in every quarter of Italy. Artillery was collected from Milan and Ferrara, comprising about twenty-five additional pieces, and the mules of the cardinals were requisitioned for its transport. Powder and munitions were sent to the camp in vast quantities. The melting snows of the Apennines delayed these supplies on the road, and the cannon arrived in bad condition without finding any master-craftsman to put them into repair. To remedy this, however, was merely a matter of time.[67] Above all, at the end of December there commenced to move down through the Mugello the reinforcements for which Orange had so long been clamouring, comprising the army set free by the peace in Lombardy, numbering some 8,000. The Pope was supposed to furnish 4,000 more, though Orange would have preferred to have the money to pay some of his Neapolitan veterans. Others continued to be expected during the coming months, though their advance was irritatingly slow. The total of the besieging army now amounted to over 30,000, of whom nearly one-half were Italians.[68] As a result of this increase in number, the investment of the city could be completed. The newcomers remained on the northern bank, where the Marquis of Vasto took over command. The Germans under Count Felix of Wittenburg encamped to the westward about the monastery of S. Donato in Polverosa and towards Peretola; while the Spaniards occupied Fiesole and the neighbourhood. A further body, taking up its position a little later at a villa of the Sassetti, was able to harass the gates of S. Gallo, Pinti, and Faenza. The two forces were joined by a bridge of boats over the Arno above the city, though two were originally intended.[69] Thus the north bank, hitherto relatively immune from the ravages of war, began to be wasted like the south. Every day there were cavalry raids or encounters up to the very gates. On 25 January a council of war held at Lastra determined to close up still further, and to establish their lines at no more than two arrow-flights from the walls; and new artillery emplacements were constructed nearer the city.[70] The siege now commenced to be a reality. The comparative liberty to come and go as they pleased which the Florentines had hitherto enjoyed was at an end, and the pinch began to be felt within the walls. At the last moment the government began to rush into Florence the supplies left concentrated in important centres of the dominion. It should not have been left so long. As the circle closed round the city, all communications with the outside world became cut off. Single messengers could only get through with the greatest difficulty, even so sometimes falling into the enemy's hands, while for larger parties it became impossible. Thus a convoy bringing in fodder from Prato was assailed by Gonzaga with about equal numbers. After a two hours' fight it was worsted, and the supplies were captured. From this point, therefore, the city commenced to suffer from dearth, which had hitherto been the prerogative of the besiegers. Meat almost immediately began to run short, eggs were not to be had, and the absence of fuel commenced to be felt all the more acutely in the cold days of January.[71]

With the arrival of these reinforcements, the enemy had forces at his disposal to proceed against the remaining portion of the Florentine dominion, more especially that portion to the north of the Arno which had hitherto remained virtually untouched. The greater part was overrun almost without resistance; the government of the captured places being assumed wherever possible by the Pope, who replaced the Spanish military governors by Florentines of his own faction.[72] These operations were actually facilitated by a sudden panic in Florence, where in a moment of alarm there was ordered the evacuation of Prato and Pistoia, two important cities close to the capital, centres of food-supply and situated on vital lines of communication. Pistoia, which an old proverb recommended Florence to hold down by factions as it did Pisa by fortresses, was now as ever torn between two families—the Panciatichi, who favoured the Medici, and the Cancellieri, who supported the popular government. Hostages from either side had been ordered to be sent to Florence, but in spite of this the Panciatichi raised their head under Niccolò Bracciolini. The Florentine commissary, finding all military support withdrawn and his authority undermined by an admixture of threats and inveiglements, thought it safer to retire to Lucca. Bracciolini was left supreme, and by combining an appeal to the apprehensions of the people with a display of bloodthirsty violence against his adversaries, persuaded the city, which could still have held out independent of outside help, to surrender to the Pope. Prato, left similarly defenceless, was occupied by the Marquis of Vasto, and a large part of the provisions in it, which could not be evacuated or destroyed, fell to the enemy. It was not long before the Florentines realized their mistake and sent to reoccupy at least the latter place. Half-way on the road, however, it was discovered that Calenzano had already been captured, and nothing remained but to return.[73] The circumstances were such that treachery was again suspected, and among the highest.[74] Signa, on the road to Empoli, was similarly occupied by collusion.[75] Pietrasanta, which commanded the coastal road to Lucca and Genoa, was lost with all the territory in that direction; and in connection with this Alessandro de' Giacomini was tried and condemned by the Quarantia for treachery.[76] From Prato, the Marquis of Vasto proceeded against the stronghold of Vicchio in the Mugello, which had been for some time a thorn in his side.[77] In the same direction Orange had captured Nipozzano on his way back from Bologna, as well as defeating a body of cavalry sent to destroy the mills of Vicano.[78] To the south, the Abbot of Farfa had some time previously succeeded in throwing himself into Montepulciano just as it was on the point of surrender. From that position he could have harassed the connections of Orange through Arezzo, and indeed gave him considerable ground for nervousness. A strong force was therefore sent against him under Alessandro Vitelli, and an engagement took place near Anghiari (17 December). The Abbot showed suspiciously slight energy in defending himself, and was defeated without any difficulty. As a result Montepulciano was lost, and with it the remaining Florentine territories to the south in the Valdarno and Valdichiana.[79] It was soon followed by the important city of Volterra, one of the few which still held out for Florence. Acquired as early as 1372, it had remained faithful since its great revolt of a hundred years later, put down in blood

17

by Lorenzo the Magnificent, and resisting even the temptation of the weakness of the Second Republic. At the opening of the war it had shown every sympathy, armed its inhabitants, and put itself into a state of readiness. Its attitude had, however, gradually assumed too great an independence, so that a Florentine commissary had to obtain entrance and recognition almost by force.[80] After the fall of Montepulciano and its neighbourhood, Vitelli, accompanied by Taddeo Guiducci as commissary for the Pope, overran the country about Volterra and summoned the city itself to yield. The Florentine garrison, insufficient for the defence, retired into the citadel ; and the inhabitants, taking matters into their own hands, pacifically surrendered (24 February). Roberto Acciaiuoli was sent to govern the place as papal commissary, succeeded a little later by Guiducci. This was an outstanding instance of how little reliance could be placed by the Florentines in their outlying possessions.[81] The territories to the south were now almost wholly in the hands of the Imperialists. The citadel of Arezzo held out for some time in spite of all attempts to capture it, inflicting much damage on the city and surroundings by sorties and bombardments. Ultimately, however (22 May) it was forced to give in, though its garrison was allowed to retire to Borgo S. Sepolcro. Barely a fortnight later, however (3 June), that place too surrendered, though its fortress continued to resist.[82] On the other side of the Apennines, Lorenzo Carnesecchi, commissary at Castrocaro, was holding out in the Florentine Romagna like another Ferrucci. Almost completely isolated from the main seat of war, he was conducting a campaign of brilliant success. Florence supplied him only with casual and irregular assistance ; he had few troops and almost no money to pay them with : yet by dint of great activity he continued to hold his own and more than his own against the papal forces. He put down in blood the rebellion of Marradi ; relieved the fortress of Castiglione ; routed enemy columns sent against him ; and refused to treat for peace. He was even said to have put a price on the head of Clement himself. Operations against him were finally trusted to Cesare Maggi, a well-known Neapolitan soldier of fortune whom the Florentines paid the compliment of trying to lead over to their own service. Assisted by the active sympathy of the inhabitants, particularly of Marradi, he had some initial success. Dovadola and Modigliano were occupied through the treachery or apathy of the defenders, and a considerable force, well equipped with artillery, was assembled against Castrocaro. An attempt at assault was heavily defeated. Again invited to come to terms, Carnesecchi refused so long as the hostile force remained on Florentine territory. He realized, however, that material assistance from Florence was unlikely, while the discontent of the inhabitants rendered his task increasingly difficult. Accordingly, when the enemy had consented to retire, he opened negotiations and signed a truce maintaining the *status quo* until the end of the war (2 April). " It does not seem little to me," he wrote proudly to the Dieci, "that a Commissary, without resources, deprived of all hope from the city and elsewhere, should have conducted a malignant Pontiff to sue for a truce." But he exaggerated. It was certainly a dignified manner of retiring from activity ; but his province was out of operations until the end of the siege. The only places of importance which continued to resist were Pisa, Livorno, and Empoli.[83]

The general debacle in the dominion had little or no effect in the city. In particular, the attitude of the mercenaries, whose temptations were greatest and patriotic sentiment least, continued to demonstrate their complete confidence in victory. On 16 January, before the high altar of the church of S. Niccolò, all the captains, with the newly elected Captain-General at their head, joined in a solemn pledge to defend the Republic—" a thing truly fair and honourable to the city, which has treated, and treats, its soldiers so well that they have spontaneously moved to make such an oath." The Abbot of Farfa, after his suspicious defeat at Anghiari, had set about coming to terms with the Pope, and ordered those captains who were of his following to go over to the enemy's camp. They preferred, however, to join their comrades in the oath of fidelity.[84] Only three of them, all Orsini like himself, seized the opportunity of being sent a few days later on escort duty to Fiesole to desert to the enemy. Orange received them gladly, though at his wits' ends how to supply their pay. Before long, however, his difficulties were solved, as 250 of the 300 followers they had brought with them returned to the service of the city.[85] The deserters had a price laid on their heads ; but they suffered another punishment more typical of the place and age. One morning the city awoke to find them depicted hanging from a gallows, and so naturally that it seemed real, upon the façade of the Mercanzia facing the Palazzo della Signoria—the handiwork of Andrea del Sarto, most illustrious of living Florentine painters. The same artistic execution, and at the same hands, was inflicted outside the Bargello upon certain Florentine citizens who had fled the city, and continually through the siege on other traitors. Only, in order to avoid the moral stigma of the work, it was performed by night and in the name of one of Andrea's pupils. The fugitive captains were also counterfeited by scarecrows hanging by one foot in the position they had abandoned at S. Miniato with their faces towards the enemy's camp.[86] If individual desertions took place,[87] they were amply counterbalanced by those from the besiegers, where conditions remained far from satisfactory. At this very period Anguilotto da Pisa, one of the foremost Italian captains in the Imperial forces, passed over through some personal pique to the Florentines, bringing with him the majority of his company (21 January).[88] Orange seized the first opportunity to take revenge. It was not long before Anguilotto was sent out in the direction of S. Salvi to protect a party of peasants foraging for wood—still the greatest necessity of the city, both for fuel and for the fortifications. The Imperialists fell upon him in overwhelming force, cutting off his retreat. He fought bravely; but his troops were cut to pieces and he himself paid for his treachery with his life. There was almost a worse result, as the captain at the Porta alla Croce came out to succour him, leaving his position defenceless: and he narrowly escaped hanging by Malatesta for his foolhardiness (11 February).[89]

This was typical of the military operations which continued to take place about Florence; for while able to overrun the dominion without meeting with much opposition, Orange was unable to make headway against the city itself. It was to be imagined that with the arrival of reinforcements and supplies he would at last have delivered the grand assault. His astrologer, it was said, encouraged him in the idea, staking his life on the result; the Emperor was begging him to decide the issue immediately; the Pope suggested the plan of action; and every preparation was made in the camp. On its side, the city had doubled the guards and was prepared for all eventualities, expecting that a Friday would be chosen as a day especially auspicious to the Spaniards.[90] For the moment there was still some lack of provision, especially as the artillery was slow in arriving and the supply of sappers was still inadequate.[91] Accordingly, though one night at the end of January the whole army approached the walls, it retired without doing more. In April, preparations were again pushed forward, but for some reason or other the assault never materialized.[92] Instead, there were constant skirmishes around the city, increasing in frequency as time went on. Thus at the commencement of January a newly constructed artillery emplacement opposite S. Miniato was stormed, though it was not held.[93] Detachments met every day. On one day of the Carnival (28 February), there were as many as three engagements, one of them of some importance. The first Sunday in Lent was signalized by a cavalry encounter at Astrico (6 March). Some days later, a party of the enemy was driven back by artillery fire from the Porta S. Gallo (21 March). Even Easter Sunday was not free from fighting; and the next day saw an important engagement in which Orange and Vasto themselves took part against Jacopo Bichi of Siena, one of the foremost Florentine cavalry captains, outside the Porta al Prato (18 April). Ten days later what might have developed into a general engagement near S. Gervasio was interrupted by heavy rains (29 April). On one occasion (28 March), Malatesta ordered a simultaneous sortie all along the line on the south side of the river in the hopes of destroying a newly constructed artillery emplacement near S. Giorgio, where the enemy was engaged in constructing strong defence works ; but the attack, betrayed by one of the soldiers, failed in its purpose. On another, Nippozano was retaken, but it was soon lost again.[94] Meanwhile the artillery duel continued and the bombardment of the city became more intense. The first day of the New Year, according to the Florentine style (25 March), was signalized by a heavy cannonade directed against a gun-emplacement on one of the remaining towers near S. Giorgio, but it was given up owing to the failure to do any considerable damage. From this period dates the first serious execution done inside the city in the Piazza S. Giovanni.[95] One night a stretch of the bastion of S. Miniato fell of itself, but repairs were commenced so promptly that the enemy was unable to take advantage of the occurrence.[96]

The monotony of these events was relieved by one of the most picturesque happenings in Florentine history. The affair contained all the elements of romance. With the besieging forces was a certain Giovanni Bandini, a Florentine, enamoured of the beautiful Marietta de' Ricci, wife of Niccolò Benintendi. Lodovico Martelli had been his unsuccessful rival for her favours, and saw the opportunity of fixing a quarrel upon him. Salvestro Aldobrandini composed for him a cartel—the last probably drawn up in the full mediæval style—in which Bandini, together with all the other Florentines fighting in the enemy's ranks, were accused of being traitors. The challenge was accepted, not over-enthusiastically. Lodovico chose as his second Dante da Castiglione, Captain of the Gonfalone of the Vaio and chief among the young ardent republicans.[97] On 11 March the Florentine champions left the city in solemn state, accompanied by a numerous train and bearing their own provisions so as not to be forced to accept the hospitality of the enemy. Upon the next day the fight took place amid the admiring Imperialist troops in the special lists set up at Baroncelli, the Prince of Orange himself acting as umpire. The youthful Bertino Aldobrandini, who was acting as second to Bandini, early proved his inferiority to Castiglione, but continued fighting until two more wounds put him out of action. Martelli, on the other hand, badly hit, was forced to surrender to the man he had provoked. He was allowed to go back to Florence, but twenty-four days later he expired, his sufferings perhaps acerbated by the lady's indifference. Aldobrandini had died of his wounds on the same evening.[98] Many others of the Florentine youth were inspired by this example, and similar duels became the order of the day. It became necessary to prohibit formally the despatch or receipt of challenges for private combat.[99]

NOTES TO CHAPTER IX

[1] Capello, letters 59, 60, 66, 67 ; Sanuto, LII, 345–6 ; Gaye, II, 158 ; Varchi, II, 204–5 ; Condivi, 48. Falletti, I, 188, cites a payment authorized to four persons on 28 May for fastening mattresses on the Campanile.

[2] Not the building known by that name at present, where visitors still shed tears over a purely supposititious place of execution—this was then the Palazzo del Podestà ; but an annex at the back of the Palazzo della Signoria, with which it communicated.

[3] Sanuto, LII, 327–31 ; Varchi, II, 258, 301 ; Guicciardini, IV, 248.

[4] Sanuto, LII, 461 ; Varchi, II, 226–7 ; Ughi, 151, asserts that Orsini's death anticipated a plot against the city on his part in conjunction with the captains who later deserted.

[5] Robert, p. 326, with docs. ; Faleri, letter 38 seqq.

[6] Sergardi, letter 26 ; Guicciardini, IV, 248 ; Roseo, Canto III, p. 100 seqq. ; Varchi, II, 206–7, 219 ; Sanuto, LII, 174–6 ; Falletti, I, 125 ; Giovio, II, 148–70 ; Capello, letters 59–62, 65, 66.

[7] Capello, letter 62 ; Varchi, II, 213–14 ; Journal d'un Bourgeois de Paris sous le régime de François I, 292–3 (apud Perrens, III, 261). The fact that this engagement is not mentioned by Giovio, Nerli, and especially Roseo, probably indicates that its importance has been exaggerated by the patriotic writers.

[8] Sanuto, LII, 216–17 ; Faleri, letters 34, 35.

[9] Dieci, Responsive, CLI, f. 212 (9 October) seqq., 305, 315, 322, etc.

[10] Ughi, 147–8, 148, 152–3 ; Faleri, letter 40 ; Sanuto, LII, 45–7, 176 ; Paoli, CXCI–CXCII ; Robert, 325 ; Giovio, II, 173–4 ; Francesco Ferrucci, etc., Despatch, I, pp. 143–4. Ughi's assertion that the captain Otto da Montauto was tried for treachery in connection with the failure to liberate the Mugello, is not accurate (though supported by Capello, letter 70), as he was actually condemned for homicide (Signoria, CXXXII, ff. 160–1 ; cf. Varchi, II, 261). Suspicion may, however, have prompted the prosecution. It was this case which led to the conflict for jurisdiction between the Otto and the Dieci referred to in the preceding chapter, note 62.

[11] Sanuto, LII, 45–7 ; Faleri, letter 29 ; Varchi, II, 173–4. Letter of Leonello Pio de Carpo, " Ravennæ provinciæ Romandiolæ præses," dated 27 September, in Sanuto, LII, 47–8.

[12] There is a full bibliography for the life of Ferrucci (till 1886) in the quatrocentenary volume, Francesco Ferruccio e la Guerra di Firenze (ed. Dom. Pierrugues, Florence, 1889), pp. 517–30. For details of his career, see the nearly contemporary biography of Filippo Sassetti, ibid. p. 56 seqq. According to the review by Giorgetti of V. Piskorski's work on Francesco Ferrucci and his age (Kiev, 1891), nothing is lost in this connection by ignorance of Russian. G. de Luca di Melpignano, in Discorso su Francesco Ferrucci (Trani, 1896), prints six documents hitherto un-

known—including his instructions and two letters on his mission to Pesaro, and (No. 4) an agreement for the loan of money from one Francesco Nati, dated at Naples, 7 December 1528—probably in connection with his ransom. Guerrazzi's biography (*Vita di Francesco Ferrucci*, 2 vols., Milan, 1875) embodies besides interminable rhodomontades much sound research, now superseded with the exception of passages from despatches addressed to Ferrucci. The purely military aspect is treated of in an article, weak from the historical point of view, of Eugenio Barbarich, "L' opera di Francesco Ferrucci da Aversa a Gavinana (1489–1530)," in |the *Nuova Antologia*, LVI (January 1921), pp. 134–49. His brief activity at Prato is illustrated by Nos. I–IV (8–13 October) of his despatches, printed by Pierrugues in the excellent compilation cited above ; the body of the remainder (V–CIX) are dated from Empoli. For other points, see Dieci, Missive, XLVIII (31 August) ; Dieci, Responsive, CXLVI, ff. 43, 176, 293.

[13] Despatches, *ubi supra*, No. 5 seqq.

[14] *Ibid.* No. 11, Paoli, CXCIII–CXCIV ; *Francesco Ferrucci*, etc., p. 432 *f.n.*

[15] Despatches, *ubi supra*, Nos. 26, 30, etc.

[16] *Ibid.* 24–5. For an attack on Montespertoli, held by a renegade son of Machiavelli, see *Priorista di Giuliano de' Ricci* in *Francesco Ferruccio*, etc., pp. 458–9.

[17] *Ibid.* despatches 36–7, from which it is clear that the operation was on the 6th, and not on the 7th as Varchi says (II, 210). Cf. also Sanuto, LII, 191.

[18] Despatches 38 and 41 ; Varchi, II, 211–12.

[19] Despatches 44 and 45.

[20] Varchi, II, 210.

[21] Robert, 335–6, and despatch of Orange of next day (Doc. no. 259) ; Giovio, II, 172–3, adds other details. There is no need to suspect, as Varchi (II, 217–18) inevitably does, that the event was due to treachery, though Giannotti (*Opere*, I, 253) alleges utter incompetence both in the defence and in the relief. It is the castle of Lastra which is to be seen in the distance in Vasari's fresco ; cf. *Ragionamenti*, *ubi supra*.

[22] Robert, 340–1 ; Roseo, 190–202 ; Giovio, II, 174–5 ; despatches of Ferrucci, 69, 70, 72.

[23] Cf. Varchi, II, 208–9, and his despatches, *passim*.

[24] Robert, 339–40 ; Roseo, 127–32 ; Varchi, II, 221–4 ; Giovio, II, 171–2 ; Ricci, *ubi supra*, 458 ; Fedele, in his account of the following day (Sanuto, LII, 379), confirms the improbable figures of the casualties given by Varchi. Cf. also *ibid.* 291, 546–9, and Capello, letter 68. This sortie is among those depicted by Vasari in his frescoes ; cf. *Ragionamenti*, *ubi supra*.

[25] Robert, cap. XV and docs. there cited—esp. 237–42, 248, 250, 254 ; letters of Faleri, the Sienese envoy (in Falletti, vol. II), *passim*, esp. Nos. 55, 81, etc. ; Sanuto, LII, 174–6, 216–17, 245. Cf. Varchi, II, 214–15, and Gaye, II, 158. Varchi's tale of Orange's leaving the camp on the morrow of his defeat is confirmed by Capello, letter 63. He thus anticipated by one day the summons addressed to him by Charles on 12 November (Robert, Doc. 257).

[26] Sanuto, LII, 244, 327–31 ; Paoli, CXCIII ; Varchi, II, 219–20, 283 ; Nerli, 205–6, 209.

[27] Nardi, 211 ; Sanuto, L, 206 ; LII, 327–31. For his character and policy, cf. Giannotti, *Opere*, I, 123–4.

[28] See Nerli, 212–15, and Giovio, II, 175–7, for this view.

[29] For the above and much of what follows on the Conference of Bologna, see Pastor, *History of the Popes*, vol. X, cap. 3.

[30] See despatches of Dieci to Gualterotti in Sanuto, LI and LII, and those of Capello, *passim*, esp. letter 71.

[31] Sanuto, LI, 476, 616–17, and LII, 104.

[32] Varchi, II, 238 *seqq.*; Sanuto, LI, 494 and LII, 44, 45–7, 249; Capello, *passim*, esp. letters 53, 55, 59, 62, 63, 66, 80; original despatches in Dieci, Carteggio, Missive, vol. XLVII; and Pratiche, 6 December. Cf. Falletti, I, cap. iv (*Firenze e i Collegati di Cognac*), and Robert, 344–7.

[33] Despatches of Giugni of 19, 24, 29 November in Dieci, Responsive, ff. 93, 95–6, 102 ; cf. also f. 48 ; Varchi, II, 211.

[34] Rossi, I, 148–59 ; Varchi, II, 146, 157 ; Nerli, 203–4 ; Capello, letter 63. If indeed the Pope was willing to concede the Great Council, it must have been under the nominated form previously outlined. Otherwise the unceremonious rejection of his terms cannot be understood.

[35] See instructions of 25 October in Falletti, I, 383–5.

[36] Capello, letters 55, 57, 58 ; Varchi, II, 181, and Falletti, *ubi supra*. Seeing that he left Florence on 7 October and returned on the 20th, he could not have been imprisoned for any length of time.

[37] Pratiche, 4 November.

[38] Falletti, I, 386–7 ; Varchi, II, 157 ; Pratiche, 11 November. Cf. Bardi, *ubi supra*, sec. III, *Incoronazione di Carlo V a Bologna*, esp. pp. 33–4 (to Margaret of Austria, 22 January). J. Guicciardini and Niccolini had returned to the city on 19 November ; Portinari only on 9 December (Capello, letters 65, 68).

[39] As a consequence, he was tried before the Quarantia and declared *rubello*. See Signoria, CXXXIII, f. 20 (21 May) (Notification by Otto) : f. 25 (25 *ibid.*) (Quarantia drawn) : f. 31 (1 June) (declared state case) : ff. 45–6 (9 June) (Condemnation) : ". . . visis letteris L. di Carnesecchis Com. Romandiole . . . et visis letteris dicti F^i de Vectoribus scriptis prefatis ex^{is} Dominis datis Bononie sub die XXV mensis Novembris 1529 prox. preter . . ." and his medical certificate of being unable to be present personally through ill-health, for which reason his kinsman, Bernardo Vettori, was allowed to plead on his behalf. He was encouraged in his position by his kinsman, Filippo Strozzi ; see letter of 29 November in Bardi, *Filippo Strozzi da nuovi documenti*, in *A.S.I.*, ser. V, v. 14, 1894. The monograph of Passi, *François Vettori, sa vie et ses œuvres* (2 vols., Paris, 1914) adds no fresh information as to his career.

[40] See instructions of 12 November in Bardi, *Carlo V, etc.*, pp. 73–5.

[41] Pratiche, LXXIV, 1 January 1529/30.

[42] See the unusually full report in Varchi, II, 268–79, agreeing with Pratiche, LXXIV, 3 January. Cf. Nerli, 210–14, and Giovio, II, 281–3, who assert that it was after this that the *Setta* influenced Girolami, almost by force, to change his tactics. But their partisan account, which neglects the all-important fact of the invitation from the Pope, is *ipso facto* suspect. Giovio's story of the oration of Francesco de' Migliori in favour of the treaty was apparently the consequence of a practical joke of Segni's ! (Lupo Gentile, *op. cit.* 56–7). There is no confirmation to be found of the report that the Signoria determined to neglect the decisions of the Consiglio Maggiore, which had decided in favour of treaty only, not of peace ; and, far from the popular assembly being suspended thereafter, a meeting was held on 24 February. They were for the rest always rare. See also Capello, letters 71, 72. The envoys were authorized to treat also with the Emperor on 7 January; Pratiche, *ad diem*.

[43] Pratiche, 27 January ; Capello, letter 75 ; Dieci, Missive, XLVIII, to orators with Pope (28 January), and to Carducci (9 February). Fran-

cesco Carducci and Alfonso Strozzi were apparently deputed to carry on the conversations. Cf. Signoria, CXXXII, f. 134 (4 February): " Absolutio di apuntar . . . facta a Franc° Carducci & Alfonso Strozzi . . . messi in cameram ad speculum . . . quia . . . iverant ad loquendum ad nuncios seu ambasciadores gallicos . . ."

⁴⁴ Faleri, letters 48–50 ; Varchi, *ubi supra* ; Vasari, VII, 650 seqq. ; Capello, letter 73.

⁴⁵ Pratiche, 7 and 21 January ; Dieci, Missive, XLVIII, to Carducci, 23 January and 19 February ; Varchi, who is in this case an eye-witness, II, 274–9 ; and Falletti, I, 388–9 and 113–16 ; Faleri, letter 57.

⁴⁶ Pratiche, 8 February ; Capello, letter 77. For another reported invitation from the Pope, cf. Nerli, 221–2.

⁴⁷ Dieci, Responsive, CLI, ff. 39–44 (27 October).

⁴⁸ Pratiche, 15 March ; Dieci, Missive, XLVIII, to Giugni, 16 *ibid.* ; Dieci, Responsive, CLI (ff. 351–2), from Giugni, 31 March, and (f. 353) 1 April; *ibid.* (f. 352), Duke of Ferrara to Giugni, 31 March. Falletti, I, pp. 389–92, is, as not infrequently, most inaccurate on this point, asserting that the Duke of Ferrara initiated the negotiations, and giving wrongly the figures of the division.

⁴⁹ Dieci, Responsive, CLI, f. 178. Despatch of Giovanni Rhenieri of 28 March.

⁵⁰ Pratiche, 4 January ; Sanuto, LII, 565 ; Varchi, II, 282–9. He, however, mistakes the day of the ceremony, which he places on 12 January—the date of the formal agreement (text in Falletti, I, 112 *n.*, and Vermiglioli, *op. cit.* App. XIX). For the speech of Alexo Lappacino for this occasion, see *ibid.* App. XXI.

⁵¹ See letter of Guicciardini of 30 September, *ubi supra.*

⁵² Provisioni, CCIX, 16 December ; Varchi, II, 227–8 ; Baldovinetti, p. 50. Another innovation introduced under Girolami, aimed against the inveterate unpunctuality of the Florentines, was to order a bell to be sounded as the signal for the meeting of the executive councils. Cf. Giannotti, *Opere*, I, 235–6.

⁵³ Signoria, CXXXII, f. 167 (25 March) ; Nerli, p. 219. Varchi's figure (II, 298) of 15 is incorrect.

⁵⁴ Varchi, II, 298–9 ; Nerli, 222.

⁵⁵ Signoria, *ibid.*, 5, 6, 8, 15 December, etc., and *ad dies.*

⁵⁶ Pratiche, 15 February.

⁵⁷ Signoria, CXXXII–III, *passim*, for this period. There were four extractions on 3 April, five on 8, three on 21 May (CXXXII, f. 216 *seqq.*, 221 *seqq.* ; CXXXII, f. 20). There was a further suspension, possibly in view of the threatening situation, on 3 August (*ibid.* f. 102).

⁵⁸ Dieci, Responsive, CLI, f. 139 (from G. Giugni, 22 December).

⁵⁹ O.G., CCVI, 3 and 14 December ; Rossi, *op. cit.*, I, 153–63.

⁶⁰ Signoria, CXXXII, ff. 174 (2 March 1529/30), 182 (8 *ibid.* . . . " Audito Jacopo fratre carnale . . ."), 197–8 (17 *ibid.*). Sentence : ". . . Signore in X^ro nostro re & salvatore può egli essere che tutti habbiamo giurato in conspecto di tua Maestà da fare iustitia per il quale juramento dovremmo tutti tendere ad uno medesimo fine, & tanta varietà di pareri non dovrebbe essere. Vorrei sapere chi non gli pare che M. Franc° Guicciardini habbi errato quello che e' vorebbe che gl' havesse facto a errare et che più danni possa havere ricevuto la nostra città salvo che la destructione di essa Aspectate a punirlo che e' convenga col fuoco. Ma spero in X^ro che prima sarete puniti voi e lui, e per tanto dico . . ." In this process, as in the summons of December, Giovanni Benintendi is associated. This condemnation is overlooked by Rossi. It is obviously the cause of Guicciardini's second apology from Lucca of 2 March.

[61] Signoria, CXXXIII, ff. 20, 25, 31, 45–6 (21 May–9 June 1530). Cf. *supra*, p. 238. This is similarly neglected by Rossi.

[62] Letter of Tarbes in *A.S.I.*, App., I, 476.

[63] Signoria, CXXXIII, f. 30 (30 May). They were restored on 29 October (*ibid.*, f. 112).

[64] Pratiche, 1 March. The records of the Otto for the majority of the period of the siege are unfortunately missing—carried off to Rome, according to report, by order of the vindictive Pope (Varchi, *Introduction*). In consequence, the exact terms of the accusation cannot be ascertained, and we are reduced to following the account of Varchi, II, 291–3.

[65] Pratiche, 4 April. This second discussion is not mentioned by Varchi. Robert (p. 351), with his usual inaccuracy in dealing with internal events, asserts that the condemnation as outlaws actually took place.

[66] Robert, p. 334, and Doc. No. 261 ; Sanuto, LII, 248 ; Capello, letter 66.

[67] Giovio, II, 133, 178 ; Faleri, letters 43, 48, etc. ; *Letters and Papers, Henry VIII*, IV, 6106 ; Sanuto, LII, 165, 230, 343 ; Varchi, II, 282, etc.

[68] Robert, p. 353 *seqq.* (with documents). He has utterly neglected the testimony of the Sienese envoy, Faleri, letter 40 *seqq., passim*. In letter 59 (commencement of February) he estimates Orange's army at 14,000 Italians, 6,000 Spanish, and 8,000 Germans, with 800 men-at-arms and 2,000 light horse.

[69] Robert, p. 347 *seqq.*, and Bardi, *op. cit.* sec. III ; Ughi, pp. 150–1 ; Faleri, letters 40, 50, 54, 57, etc.

[70] Faleri, letters 50, 57, 58, 61, 63 ; Varchi, II, 248, 257 ; Baldovinetti, p. 40.

[71] Sanuto, LII, 391, 532 ; Varchi, *ubi supra* ; Robert, p. 341 and Docs. 368–70.

[72] Faleri, letter 57.

[73] Varchi, II, 249–54 ; Ughi, 151–3 ; Faleri, letters 48–9 (2 and 5 January) ; Sanuto, LII, 546–51 ; Paoli, CXCIV.

[74] *Ragguaglio di Baccio Carnesecchi, ubi supra.* " Massime Francesco Carducci die Prato a' nemici e di poi che fu fuori di Gonfaloniere io credo ma nollo dico certo che desse o facesse dare Empoli." Cf. report of legate of Savoy at Bologna printed by Claretta in *Atti dell' Acc. delle Scienze di Torino*, XXVIII, pp. 634–55. " Ora poi si è detto che Pistoia e Prato si sono vendute," and Ughi, *ubi supra*.

[75] Signoria, CXXXII, f. 157. Cf. *supra*, pp. 221–2, *n.* 115.

[76] Varchi, II, 254 ; Signoria, CXXXIII, ff. 95–6 (27 July). Details as to the piecemeal loss of the dominion to the west may be traced in the despatches of Ferrucci from February onwards.

[77] Faleri, letters 50, 53, 54.

[78] Robert, pp. 333–4 and Doc. 259.

[79] Robert, p. 337 and Doc. 268 ; Faleri, letter 43 ; Sanuto, LII, 216–17 ; Varchi, II, 244.

[80] Varchi, II, 367–72. Cf. Robert, p. 396 *seqq.*

[81] *Seconda Calamità Volterrana* del Cav. Giov. Parelli, ed. M. Tabarrini (Firenze, 1889), pp. 15–23 ; Varchi, II, 373–6. The articles of surrender are *ibid.* 376–8, and the papal brief confirming them (26 March) *ibid.* 380. Acciaiuoli was naturally condemned as *rubello* by the Quarantia (Signoria, CXXXIII, ff. 48–9, 13 June). For the exemplary punishment of Guiducci, see *infra*, *n.* 86.

[82] Varchi, II, 246–7, 257, 263–5. Cf. Robert, p. 338.

[83] Terms in full in Sanuto, LIII, 178–80. See Carnesecchi's own re-

port of operations of 2 April, *ibid.* c. 178–80, repeated owing to loss of first despatch in another of 14 April (Albèri, 265–72, and Francesco Ferrucci, etc., 465–9). Cf. also Busini, pp. 113, 116–17; Varchi, II, 359–61; Contile, *La Historia dei fatti di Cesare Maggi*, lib. II; and letter of Fr. Borghini in Dieci, Responsive, CLI, f. 199: ". . . Parendomi che questi passi con pocho nostro honore." Carnesecchi's original patents of 8 May 1529 are in Signori, Carteggio, Missive, Registri, LVIII. Among those condemned for working against the city in the Romagna were Pierfrancesco de' Ridolfi (Signoria, CXXXII, ff. 186–7) and Lorenzo Giacomini (*ibid.* CXXXIII, ff. 95–6), the latter for surrendering Dovadola, of which he was castellan. See *supra*, pp. 221–2, *n.* 115.

[84] Dieci, Missive, XLVIII, 23 January 1529/30 (to B. Carducci); Varchi, II, 291. Cf. Faleri, letter 60; Capello, letter 74.

[85] Robert, Doc. 299; Dieci, Missive, XLVIII, to orators with Pope, 2 February, and to Giugni, 7 February; Sanuto, LII, 584. Ughi, 151–2, suggests that these captains were involved in the intended treason of Mario Orsini and fled for fear of discovery.

[86] Varchi, *ibid.*; Vasari, V, 53–4 and *n.* 2, where Milanesi cites the original authorization for payments to the artist for this purpose. Cf. sentence of Quarantia on Pierfrancesco de' Ridolfi (Signoria, CXXXII, ff. 186–7). ". . . Et di più che sia dipinto al palazzo del podestà impicchato per uno pie allato a Taddeo Guiducci . . ." The original sketches for some of these drawings are still to be found in the Uffizi.

[87] Faleri, letter 48.

[88] Dieci, Missive, XLVIII, 23 January (to Carducci); Robert, pp. 355–6, and Doc. 291; Capello, letters 74, 76, 77.

[89] Robert, *ibid.*; Varchi, II, 293–5; Giovio, 178–9; Capello, letter 78; Vannini (successor to Faleri), letter 63; Roseo, 204–10.

[90] Robert, Docs. 282, 285, 290; Faleri, letter 57, and Vannini, letter 63; letter of Dieci to Carducci of 23 January, *ubi supra*; Varchi, II, 299–300.

[91] Robert, Docs. 290, 294–5.

[92] Bardi (successor to Vannini, and last of the Sienese envoys at camp), letter 92.

[93] Capello, letter 82.

[94] Varchi, II, 300–1, 319, 321–2, etc.; Robert, 363 *seqq.*; Faleri, letter 55; Vannini, letter 85; Bardi, letters 91, 129; Sanuto, LII, 514–16. It is probably the sortie of 28 March which is depicted by Vasari in one of his smaller frescoes.

[95] Varchi, II, 312; Dieci, Missive, XLVIII, 26 March (to Carducci); Nardi, p. 222; Capello, letter 81.

[96] Faleri, letter 57.

[97] Cf. the doggerel description by Stefano de' Buonafedi, *ubi supra.*

> " Eravi in quel tempo un gran Piagnone,
> Contra le Palle fu molto arrogante,
> Che Dante si chiamo da Castiglione,
> Che sempre si vedeva in ogni parte,
> Su per le Piazze tra gli altri soldati,
> Pareva che di nuovo e' fussi Marte . . ."

[98] Cf. the detailed description in Varchi, II, 302–5. The official documents—challenge, safe-conduct, and report of Orange—have been published by Milanesi in *A.S.I.*, N.S., IV, pp. 1–25 (the last also by Robert, Doc. 303). Cf. also Capello, letter 80; Ughi, p. 420; Roseo, 212, 214, 226–8, 230–1. The duel has become classic, and is the mainspring of Ademollo's famous novel, *Marietta de' Ricci.*

[99] Signoria, CXXXII, f. 192 (14 March). " *Bando del non combattere.* Che nessuno ardisca o presuma in alcuno modo per lo advenire mandare ad alcuna persona qualunque lettera scripta cartello o inbasciatore per combattere insieme nè similmente ricevere . . ." For another case of a Florentine who went out to break a lance with the enemy, cf. Varchi, II, 310–12, 313–20.

CHAPTER X

THE BLOCKADE

ALL these futile engagements around the walls of Florence, though sometimes wasteful of human life, brought matters no nearer a conclusion. The gallantry and determination of the Florentine resistance against increasing odds, to which contemporaries paid generous homage, was rendering the siege one of the most memorable in history. Yet while this cannot be minimized, it should not be forgotten that Orange had a peculiarly difficult task. The army which had stormed Rome could conceivably have stormed Florence, and the contingency was continually recognized within the city as well as without. Yet there was another side to the question. Public opinion, if not his own conscience, would condemn Clement if he exposed the treasures of his native place to the lust of an unbridled soldiery. Apart from this, material considerations came into play. It was not to his interest or to the Emperor's that his rule should be established in a ruined state, or that the goose which laid the golden eggs which in the end might recuperate the expenses of war should be killed. Before he left Rome, Orange had suggested that the requisite funds could be obtained by storming the city. " God forbid," exclaimed the Pope, " that it should be said that we have been the cause of two sacks, of Rome and of Florence."[1] Recent history showed that once the soldiers had to fight their way into a city, anything was possible. The examples of Capua in 1501, of Prato and Brescia in 1512, and above all of Rome in 1527, were fresh in human memory. Orange therefore had no opportunity to repeat his solitary attempt of St. Martin's Eve. The more his forces increased and the greater the assurance of victory became, more and more reluctance was shown to bring matters to a violent conclusion. Antonio da San Gallo, the eminent architect, was serving as engineer with the besieging forces, as his namesakes were with the besieged : and he had designed a mine to blow up part of the wall and thus lay the city open to attack. We have it on good authority that the Pope intervened and had the works put under Italian officers upon whose desire to prevent the horrors of sack he could rely.[2] On one occasion a deserter gave information of an uncompleted and unguarded bastion by way of which easy entrance into the city might be obtained. Preparations were made for a grand assault and the whole army was paraded and led up to the walls in the dead of night. It was withdrawn, however, without any attack being delivered. It was afterwards said that Baccio Valori had sent to inform Malatesta of the plan, so that the position had been found defended and alert.[3]   When, on the arrival of his last reinforcement of veterans from Naples, Orange at last proposed to deliver a more regular assault, he was prevented.   It was by indirect means, and not by direct, that it was now hoped that the city would be captured.   The siege was developing into a blockade.

There were other reasons for preferring this method.   Even when his forces had reached their maximum, Orange's numbers were not sufficient to ensure victory against fortifications now brought to perfection and defended with the confidence engendered by months of success.   The promises made at Bologna had failed to materialize.   Sappers were needed for the construction of siege-works : but of 3,000 required, the Pope and Siena between them could provide only 400.[4]   The arrival of the artillery was tardy, and even so it came in bad repair.   Munitions were short, so that there were not more than forty-five rounds for each cannon.[5]   Above all, there was the eternal question of money, which, notwithstanding all appeals, was only forthcoming in reluctant driblets.   In spite of reckoning months of forty or forty-five days, the soldiers' pay was continually in arrears. On one occasion, the relief refused to proceed to its posts before receiving satisfaction.   The Germans menaced departure to their own homes.   A large part of the army was scattered through the countryside to live at free quarters on the inhabitants. There was utter lack of discipline.   " If the enemy were *gens de bien*," wrote Orange, " they could fight us three to one." [6] Under such conditions, he could see no hope of success : and leaving Gonzaga in command, he made a further visit to Bologna to urge the proper prosecution of the enterprise[7] (28 February– 5 March).   The result of his outspokenness was to give rise to fresh suspicions of apathy.   The Pope even contemplated accepting his resignation and committing the enterprise to the Marquis of Vasto, with whom Orange was on the worst of terms, which a formal reconciliation did not greatly improve.[8]   The determination of the Emperor himself was called into question.   Indeed, but for his general's protest he would have handed the whole direction of the enterprise over to his ecclesiastical ally, who was prepared to proceed in it alone.[9]   The storm, however, blew over ; and the Pope provided 60,000 ducats, which was to be regarded henceforth as his monthly contribution.   With this inadequate sum, Orange returned to camp ; but he was unable to satisfy his troops with it for long. They continued to seethe with discontent. Tumults, mutinies, and desertions continued to be the order of the day ; and the occasional subsidies brought by the distracted Baccio Valori were wholly insufficient to quell the storm. A deputation of three captains—one from each nationality—was sent to Rome, whither the Curia had now returned, but failed to procure from the Pope, even in promises, any increase of the sum which he had agreed to pay. " Bone Deus ! quanta celeritate omnibus modis quaeritur pecunia ! " he was heard to cry on one occasion. He was with difficulty dissuaded from degrading his office by selling cardinals' hats to the highest bidder in order to raise funds. Indeed, there was no alternative in sight. He would have been glad, he exclaimed agonizedly to the Bishop of Tarbes, if Florence had never existed.[10] The only conceivable solution of the difficulty lay in a reduction of forces ; and a reduction of forces led necessarily to a change of tactics.[11]

Hitherto operations of the first magnitude had been impeded by the indiscipline of the soldiery, who, even if they could have been brought to make an assault, could certainly not have been kept in hand in case of success. Nevertheless, Orange had thus far continued to display considerable activity and had not given up hopes of victory by force of arms. Henceforth, all idea of this was to be abandoned. A regular blockade was to be instituted, which should ultimately reduce the city by force of hunger. Energy was to be devoted to entrenchments and other works which would prevent food from entering. Thus it would be possible to reduce the Imperial forces to the limits dictated by the Pope's treasury. The troops on the south side of the river were accordingly brought down to 11,000 infantry, of whom 3,000 were lanzknechts, 2,000 Spaniards, and the remaining 6,000 Italians, from whose ranks the principal reduction was made. For this force, it was reckoned that the 60,000 ducats monthly would be sufficient. In addition, it was determined to retain the light horse, for whom a further 10,000 ducats were to be asked. Upon the other side of the river, Charles was to maintain the lesser forces in his pay.[12] Fabrizio Maramaldo, a Neapolitan of ancient family, who had acquired considerable reputation in the recent campaigns and whose arrival at the camp—almost against the will of the Pope—had been for some time expected or dreaded by both sides, was diverted into Sienese territory, where he remained from 15 March to 30 April. Here his 3,000 troops, at whose passage Rome had trembled, lived at free quarters and extracted a rich blackmail, thus relieving the pressure upon Orange's commissariat and at the same time bringing powerful pressure to bear to stimulate a greater enthusiasm in the unfortunate Sienese. That these veterans were not brought to Florence was the clearest sign that the idea of assault had been abandoned.[13]

This drastic reorganization was not so easy as it seemed. Orange had the greatest difficulty in securing the peaceful disbandment or departure of the Italian troops, whose captains strongly objected. Some Albanian horse were sent back to Naples to be dispersed, for fear that if it were done on the spot they would pass over to the service of Florence. Of these, Orange retained only 150 as a personal following. But the most difficult task was presented by the Spaniards, whose patriotism had been imposed upon by keeping them the worst paid. These could not very well be disbanded in a foreign country. The majority were accordingly to be sent to aid Charles in his campaign against the Turk in Hungary, for which he had asked for a couple of thousand : and to these it was proposed to join a thousand picked Italians. Others were to be kept, if possible, at the Pope's expense, to hold places in the dominion, upon which they could live, or to operate against those fortresses which still held out. None of them would move, however, without their arrears of pay. One mutiny followed upon another and Orange's new quarters in the Certosa were more than once threatened by a disorderly mob of soldiers crying " Gelt ! Gelt ! " The majority allowed themselves to be cajoled into submission by sparse advances accompanied by ample promises.[14] Some, however, were not satisfied so easily. A body of some hundreds, ordered to leave the city on active service, rose in mutiny and seized on Barberino, whence they proceeded to Castellina. The Florentines lost no time in sounding them as to their readiness to enter their own service. Two captains were sent into the city to enter into negotiations. The Pratica was diffident of engaging troops who had already shown their infidelity or of admitting them into any fortified town, and approved of the project only for its moral effect. Yet just as the bargain might have been concluded, it was discovered that the two agents were deceiving both the Florentines and their own comrades in hope of receiving and embezzling an advance of pay. They were accordingly hanged ; and the mutineers before long came to an arrangement with their former commanders.[15] Others of the ringleaders were executed by Orange.[16] Yet even so the discontent was not wholly allayed and isolated revolts continued. Henceforth, however, supplied with greater regularity by the Pope and with his expenses sensibly diminished, Orange's more serious troubles were at an end: and he was able to rely upon his troops to carry out the new plan of blockade.

The constant skirmishes which had characterized the earlier

months of the siege grew fewer and fewer with the advance of the spring. No attempt was now made to seek the arbitrament of arms. Instead, the Imperialists drew their defence works closer so as to prevent any victuals from entering the city.[17] Powder and cash were accepted from Siena instead of sappers.[18] The Emperor himself sent supplies of munitions procured from Mantua and Ferrara.[19] Any persons caught coming out of the city for provisions were indiscriminately hanged, whether soldiers or civilians; and peasants carrying in food suffered the same fate.[20] Meanwhile, in obedience to Orange's instructions, all encounters ceased. His soldiers resolutely refused to leave their entrenchments, whatever provocation was offered, saying openly to the Florentine troops who challenged them that they would leave it to famine to secure the victory.[21] Convoys of cattle and provisions were however constantly prepared in the centres which still held out and were sent to the city with varying fortune. Thus on Good Friday one from Empoli was intercepted, and twenty of the peasants conducting it were hanged.[22] Public opinion drove Malatesta to take the offensive. Seizing advantage of the disorder in the Imperial camp owing to the mutiny of the Spaniards, he ordered on 5 May a sortie —the greatest which had as yet taken place—along the whole line on the Oltr' Arno. The principal objective was the convent of S. Donato a Scopeta, occupied by the Spanish troops. About this place a furious fight raged, which extended from Bellosguardo on the right to the Boboli on the left. The artillery of the city came into action and added to the execution—particularly the piece known as the " arquebus of Malatesta." Reinforcements from the Porta S. Frediano attacked the enemy in the rear, but they were succoured in their turn by detachments some of which crossed over even from the north bank. After a furious fight the monastery was captured, together with the hill on which it stood ; but the battle still raged. It was only after four hours' engagement, when the dusk made continuation impossible, that the Florentines drew off in good order. Among their casualties were Ottaviano Signorelli, Malatesta's lieutenant, and Ludovico, son of Niccolò Machiavelli. The balance of the advantage lay, however, with them, and they were able to safeguard an important convoy of cattle and supplies into the city.[23]

The solitary loophole of Florence to the outer world was now Empoli. Here Ferrucci had continued in unceasing activity though without any spectacular achievements, constantly engaged in perfecting his fortifications, raiding and harassing the enemy. defeating detachments sent against him, or collecting supplies to send to the capital.[24] He had, however, the mortification

18

of witnessing his capture of S. Miniato al Tedesco taken by the Imperialists as they overran that part of the territory.[25] Worse still, he saw the important city of Volterra occupied, as he had foreseen, almost without striking a blow in its defence. Only the citadel under Bartolommeo Tedaldi continued to hold out, continually bombarding and harassing the townspeople. The possession of this place, confirming the hold of the Imperialists upon the south-western part of the Florentine territory, was a perpetual menace to the few remaining possessions, including the gateway through Pisa to the outer world. From the beginning, Ferrucci had been chafing for permission to attempt its recovery, in which case he guaranteed that it would be freed from all further danger.[26] While Vitelli was still at large in the neighbourhood, the Dieci was unwilling that any risk should be taken by leaving Empoli. In the middle of April, however, he crossed the Arno, going towards Pistoia, where the inhabitants had recently been giving proofs of their inveterate restiveness. At the same time the Volterrans were making preparations against the citadel, which was now in serious danger. Fearing to lose this last bastion of defence, the Dieci at last complied with Ferrucci's renewed requests and authorized the enterprise.[27] Some reinforcements were ordered from Pisa. Others were sent from Florence and had to fight their way along the road ; but Gonzaga, sent to intercept them, experienced a serious and unexpected reverse.[28] Ferrucci thus had at his disposal a force of a couple of thousand foot. Leaving Empoli on 26 April, before dawn, he arrived late on the same day at Volterra, where, entering into the citadel, he joined hands with the garrison. Hence he fought his way into the town and through the streets. On the next day, the defenders surrendered at discretion. The booty was rich, including—what was most needed—ample supplies of artillery and munitions just received from Andrea Doria for the bombardment of the fortress. The garrison was allowed to retire to S. Gimignano.[29]

Orange had for some time been contemplating the capture of Empoli, which held the really vital position on the solitary line of communications left to Florence and was her sole remaining source of supply. The blockade of the capital could not be really complete until this place was occupied. The very brilliant enterprise of Ferrucci—the most notable exploit thus far of the whole war—had rendered its possession all the more important, in addition to weakening it by the withdrawal of the best part of its defenders. On the arrival of some of their arrears of pay, without which they refused to move, about two thousand Spanish troops under the Marquis del Vasto and Don Diego Sarmiento were sent towards that place. Mutinies such as were now continual broke out on the road or among the troops ordered to march. Ultimately, however, they arrived beneath Empoli, where they were joined by Alessandro Vitelli. Fabrizio Maramaldo, who had by now moved out of the Sienese territory, was ordered to hang about Pisa and Volterra so that neither place could safely afford to send succour. A preliminary attempt upon the town was repulsed. Artillery was therefore brought into position, a destructive cannonade commenced, and preparations were made for a general assault. Without awaiting it, however, Andrea Giugni, brother to the ambassador at Ferrara and an unworthy successor to Ferrucci, weakly surrendered (29 May). The disorderly troops broke the terms of the agreement by commencing a sack, which Vasto was able to check only with difficulty.[30] The loss was a serious blow to the Florentines and more than counterbalanced Ferrucci's victory at Volterra. The place contained many of their womenfolk and children, who had been sent there for safety and suffered from the licence of the captors. In addition they found great deposits of provisions ready to be sent to Florence and more plunder than they could carry away. Strategically the loss was even more serious. It completed the circle of iron around the city, and cut off the sole path through which provisions or succour might reach it. "It seems that one of our eyes has been closed, through which we saw the opening of the way of our salvation," wrote Alamanni.[31] At camp the victory was celebrated by a banquet, for which the civic band was ordered from Siena; and the Imperialists commenced to look forward to the future with renewed confidence.[32] Within the city, the news was received with consternation. No ordinary reason would serve to explain the ignominious surrender. Giugni was accused of treason, together with Piero Orlandini, the principal of his captains. They did not have the courage to face the trial, and were condemned *in absentia* to outlawry. Interim justice was executed in the usual fashion upon their likenesses, as well as on their relatives.[33]

Pisa, the first city of the dominion, both in size and importance, continued to hold out under Jacopo Corsi, to whom special authority and powers had been given as commissary. Memories of its liberty were still comparatively fresh; and under the Savonarolan regime it had revolted and kept the Florentine forces at bay for a protracted period. Even now, but for the strong garrison maintained in it and the hostages kept at Florence, there could be no doubt that the disaffected population would have shown active sympathy with the Imperialists. While either Empoli or Volterra still held out to threaten their lines of communication, a set siege would have been perilous in

the extreme.   A less honourable method of capture had accordingly been tried four months earlier without success.[34]   Now it
was repeated.   Taking advantage of the commercial connections
and frequent journeys of his son, an attempt was made to
tamper with the allegiance of no less a person than the commissary himself, through the medium of Palla Rucellai, who had
assumed the government of Pietrasanta for the Pope.   Whether
treason was seriously intended by him or no, Corsi did not inform
the government of the fact, and gave Rucellai, though *rubello*,
secret licence to remove his property from the city.   The intelligence was betrayed, and caused alarm in Florence.   Corsi and
his son, with some accomplices, were seized and put to the torture ;
and after trial by the Quarantia both were executed.   Meanwhile
a fresh commissary was sent to Pisa, every precaution was taken,
and the city was put out of danger of betrayal or surprise.[35]

It was not only in the military sense that Florence was being
isolated.   The enmity of the Pope and Emperor entailed that of
virtually all the powers with which she had intimate relations.
Her nearest neighbours, Lucca and Siena, were actively assisting
the enemy, as they had done from the very beginning, with every
means which lay in their power—with men and money, munitions and labour.[36]   Further afield, the Pope, who was paramount at Ancona, brought pressure to bear upon that nominal
republic to make reprisals upon the resident Florentine merchants,
who, in spite of the vigorous protests of their native city, were
imprisoned and had their goods confiscated.[37]   With Genoa
every effort had been made to keep on good terms, and in spite
of the pressing local requirements Doria had been allowed to
purchase grain in Tuscany.   There had, however, been some
friction.   French corsairs had been harboured at Livorno after
depredations in Liguria, and great exertions were then required
to prevent retaliation against the Florentines at Genoa.   In
November, however, some of Doria's galleys had been fired upon
by the forts at the same port, and one of them sunk.   He was
not satisfied by the explanation that they had been mistaken for
vessels of the privateering Prince of Monaco, and reprisals were
this time carried out, not only at Genoa, but also at Lucca.
Hence the Pope had not found it difficult to persuade the Genoese
to break off commercial relations with Florence and to refuse
passage to her envoys ; and Doria supplied the Imperialist camp
with artillery and munitions, as well as ordering a couple of
frigates to Porto Venere to complete the blockade by sea.   Luigi
Alamanni had meanwhile remained at Genoa in continuous
activity on behalf of his city.   Though his exertions evoked
protest, he had for some time evaded the consequences owing to
his friendship with the Doge.   Ultimately, however, on return-

ing from a voyage of intrigue to France, he found readmission refused, and it was to his privileged position that he owed even his liberty.[38] The Duke of Ferrara, while continuing to be prodigal of promises, had been forced to withdraw his envoy from Florence on making peace, and had provided the Pope with money, artillery, and pioneers. Galeotto Giugni, the indefatigable Florentine envoy at his court, had done his utmost to impede or delay these supplies, and continued a ceaseless activity in every other conceivable direction; but in the end he, too, was expelled.[39] Virtually every state in Italy, with the exception of Venice, ultimately threw its weight on the side of the besiegers; and the ring round the city became complete.

From the moment of the fall of Empoli, Florence was isolated from the outside world. It was not only that the convoys of supplies which had hitherto intermittently run the blockade ceased to come in. Even the most ordinary communications were interrupted. The only channel still in any way open was that which lay through Pisa. It was by this route that despatches in the diametrically opposite direction—to Venice or to Ferrara—had to be sent. Even so they were constantly interrupted, and though despatched in duplicate or triplicate, failed to reach their destination. Letter-bearers who were captured were hanged as a matter of course. It took on one occasion sixteen days to get a crucial despatch through to Ferrucci at Volterra. One important piece of information from Venice arrived only after a delay of two months. Thus not only were the actions of the Florentines paralysed, but also immediate knowledge of their policy was secured by the Imperialists, who were frequently able to forestall them.[40] But this was only a minor consequence of the blockade. It was in mid-winter, after the commencement of the arrival of the second army which completed the siege, that dearth commenced to make itself felt in Florence. Strict control had been set up by degrees. Citizens were first ordered to declare the quantity of grain in their possession.[41] This was followed by a statement of the wine and vinegar.[42] The machinery for dealing with the situation proved itself, however, inadequate. Prices rose to an extravagant level in January, and the Uffiziali dell' Abundanzia, whose duty it was to supervise the supply of food, were openly charged with treason—the usual explanation of failure in time of war. It was recommended to elect a fresh board and to tide over the period of stress until better provision could be made by the manufacture of an inferior quality of bread.[43] Ultimately it was ordered that every citizen should sell to the proper officials any quantity of grain over three bushels to be found in his house, to be devoted in the first place to the feeding of the troops.[44] This crisis, however, had been largely due to mismanagement, and wine and bread remained relatively plentiful for some time to come. In addition, the roofs throughout Florence were converted into kitchen gardens for the growth of pumpkins and other vegetables.[45] The first commodity in which real scarcity was felt was meat, which began to run short early in the spring.[46] During Lent, scarcely any fish came into the city; and on Holy Saturday, Malatesta set the example of slaughtering an ass instead of the traditional lamb and sending cuts from it as gifts to his friends.[47] As a final precaution the enemy burnt all the grass within a radius of two miles from the walls.[48] As long as Empoli held out, however, convoys of supplies and live-stock were continually coming in to the city in spite of his vigilance. On its fall, dearth began to make itself increasingly felt and reached alarming proportions. Prices rose to unheard-of heights, and were fixed to prevent overcharging; but the result was that any supplies available changed hands privately at far above the fixed rate without coming into the market. Special commissions were appointed to ration individual commodities such as provisions and salt meat. In the middle of June sixteen commissioners were elected with general control over the food supply, having authority to search and requisition indiscriminately in private houses.[49] The soldiers were given the preference in whatever was found, being enabled to purchase at less than the fixed rate. Wine and oil had by now commenced to run out. At the beginning of May there was only rye bread; but ultimately the ordinary population was restricted to bran, purer flour while it lasted being reserved for the fighting-men, who needed better nourishment to sustain their stamina.[50] To meet subsequent requirements, application had to be made for corn to France [51] and even to Turkey.[52] For wine, recourse was made as far afield as Elba, Corsica, and Provence.[53] A premium was offered to those who brought grain or cattle to Pisa or Livorno, with a view to ultimate transportation to the capital.[54] Horse and ass flesh had by now become almost luxuries. Cats and rats were eaten, and were sold at high prices when any could be found. Ultimately, the population became virtually restricted to bran bread and water alone.[55] As a result of the bad nourishment, disease commenced to play havoc within the walls. Sixty to seventy persons died daily in February; twice as many in March; and nearly 6,000 in the brief period between 10 March and 15 April—an average of 190 a day.[56] Ultimately plague commenced and increased the execution.[57]

One way in which the stress could have been relieved was by sending away from the city what were termed the " useless mouths "—that part of the population which could not help in the defence, and increased the drain on supplies. The proposal to convey the poor and indigent to Pisa had been discussed in the Pratica as early as December.[58] Preparations were actually made, and a census was taken of those who had come to the city since the opening of the siege, with the number of mouths in each family.[59] Nothing, however, ensued ; and the time when such an operation would have been comparatively easy was allowed to pass. The closing of the blockade now rendered the matter of extreme peril ; but the military commanders continued nevertheless to favour the idea and to urge its execution, which Stefano Colonna promised to safeguard.[60] The matter was therefore again discussed under a pledge of the strictest secrecy. Opinions were varied, a large body hesitating to display such want of charity or to expose their womankind, in spite of Colonna's assurance, even at this extreme juncture.[61] A commencement was, however, made with one section which could find none to champion it. On 29 June a proclamation was made to all the prostitutes to present themselves upon the following Saturday under pain of the gallows, in order to be escorted out of the city. With a touch of irony, the church of Saint Catherine—the Spouse of Christ—was specified as the place of assembly, being the nearest to the Porta S. Gallo.[62] A special commission was appointed to supervise the deportation of these and other " useless persons." [63] The day specified found the unfortunate women assembled together with all the peasantry who had sought refuge within the walls from the violence of the enemy, women and children predominating. The total number was estimated at as many as 6,000 souls. The unhappy creatures, trembling at the dangers before them and grieving at the loss of home, were driven together from all quarters of the city and presented a doleful sight as they stood in tears awaiting the order to march. The heart even of the callous government officials was touched ; and the poor wretches were informed that those who would might stay. Only some thirty or forty of the women of ill-fame were sent away, and those, as we are informed, the oldest and ugliest. As a result, an even stricter rationing had to be introduced.[64]

After food, the most important requirement of the city was munitions, which had been peculiarly plentiful at the opening of the siege and of which no stint was made. The most difficult to obtain was gunpowder, of which there was no manufactory at Florence. Moreover, saltpetre, the chief ingredient, came principally from the other side of Italy—from Cervia in the Papal Romagna and Comacchio north of it. Since October, Galeotto Giugni had busied himself in procuring it through Ferrara, and was continually despatching large supplies by way

of Pisa and Empoli, in payment for which heavy sums were forwarded to him.[65]   This, however, became impossible after the
commencement of the summer, when nothing remained but to
ask the King of France to forward 50,000 or 60,000 pounds from
Lyons.[66]   Every effort was made to eke out the stocks of raw
material to be found in the city, search being made, not only in
the butchers' shops, but even in the cemeteries.   Three work-
shops were set up for the manufacture ; but at the commencement results were poor, as the secret of the art was not known.
Matters, however, improved with practice, so that a production
of 1,500 pounds weekly was reached.   A further difficulty lay
in the provision of wood, whether for fuel or for carbon.   This
had been scarce from the very commencement, and there was
now no opportunity of foraging for it as before outside the
gates.   It was necessary therefore to pull down and utilize the
wooden protractions of the eaves of houses and the roofs of
shops throughout Florence.   Latterly the woodwork was
seized from the monasteries, the Opera del Duomo being an
especial sufferer.   Over this, too, a special commissary was
appointed.[67]

The essential requirement continued to be money.   " The
side which can endure longest will be that which will obtain
victory," wrote the Dieci.[68]   While the Prince of Orange was
extracting advances with the greatest of difficulty from his
niggardly employers, Florence was straining every nerve to
defray the expenditure for the 20,000 soldiers by now on her
pay-rolls (though their effective number was far less), with munitions and supplies in addition.   From mid-winter one expedient
succeeded another.   The *sindachi dei rubelli* of 16 December
supplemented by what they exacted the *angaria* of 30,000
ducats of 3 November.   A week later a universal *accatto* of
100,000 ducats was ordered, though it brought in so little that
it was revoked after three weeks.[69]   Then followed the greatest
of all—a levy of one-third of all ecclesiastical property, which
might be seized and sold by compulsion.[70]   A special commission
invested with extraordinary powers was appointed to exact it,
housed in the Palazzo de' Pazzi, who had fled the city[71]; and
an appeal was made to the ecclesiastical heads of the diocese to
consent in the name of the Holy See to satisfy this extreme need
of the Republic.   As might have been imagined, they refused ;
but the city after a solemn protest proceeded without their
licence.[72]   In the middle of January the Great Council ordered a
compulsory distribution of salt to the value of 30,000 ducats.[73]
This was followed two days later by a further *angaria* of one
to 1,000 ducats, according to means, which was expected to yield
the immense sum of 200,000 ducats.   It was a crushingly heavy

levy, and payment was tardy; but after a spirited oration from the Gonfalonier it was determined to avoid the fiasco of the previous occasion and to exact it relentlessly. Contributions were levied outside the city as well, Francesco Ferrucci being authorized to use all severity in order to raise them.[74] Though the majority of the representatives in the Pratica continued to profess their readiness to co-operate with their substance, the heavy arrears on the part of many who were unwilling or unable to pay continued to be an outstanding problem of increasing gravity,[75] and the recalcitrant were punished remorselessly by imprisonment and the sale of their property.[76] Compulsory lotteries were instituted for high prizes, consisting of the confiscated property of *rubelli* ; and citizens were compelled to purchase a number of tickets at a ducat apiece.[77] New commissions were repeatedly appointed to inquire into ways and means of raising fresh sums.[78] Money had by now, however, become so scarce that no suggestions could be made excepting to tighten up the exaction of existing taxes, to search out concealed property, or to repeat the old methods—another forced sale of salt, or further *accatti* calculated to bring in 150,000 ducats.[79] It was necessary to have recourse to a further voluntary subscription as at the commencement of the siege. As a result of the appeal, citizens were seen selling their belongings to the highest bidder at the street corners so as not to fail the city in her need.[80] Every step became more and more desperate. In May, to meet the expenses of a special effort under contemplation, the goods of the hospitals and monasteries were seized and sold as those of the gilds had been before, compensation being made from the property of *rubelli*, of which it was more difficult to dispose. From this, 300,000 ducats were expected.[81] In June an order was made for every citizen, even the craftsmen whose living depended on it, to carry to the mint as an advance to the state all gold and silver plate, whether household utensils or personal adornments, the possession of which was to remain forbidden for three years. The order was obeyed, we are informed, with the alacrity and eagerness with which people usually go to draw their dues, to the amazement of the soldiers and foreigners in the city.[82] But at the opening of July it was again necessary to inflict a fresh *accatto* and a property tax of one-tenth, to exact which a new commission with plenipotentiary powers was set up.[83] Finally, after eleven divisions, it was determined to confiscate all church plate and treasure for the service of the state.[84] The occasion was commemorated by a special coinage worthy of the people which had set the standard for purity of money in Europe, and still regarded its currency with pride. A gold ducat and silver half-ducat were struck, the former bearing the cross of the people instead of the figure of John the Baptist, and both with the characteristic inscription "*Jesus Rex Noster et Deus Noster.*"[85] Further impositions and appeals to generosity continued down to the bitter end[86]; and the soldiers never lacked their pay. The few dependencies looked after themselves as far as possible. Thus, in spite of the danger of increasing the ever-present discontent in that city, the commissaries of Pisa were authorized to proceed to similar expedients for the payment of the 800 men under their command. With great exertion, *accatti* were levied, ecclesiastical property confiscated, and the property of *rubelli* sold.[87] It is indeed surprising that a comparatively small city such as Florence was should have been able to raise time after time such incredible sums. But what was paid out had to be spent of necessity in the city itself and at rising prices. The same currency passed time after time from the merchants to the treasury, from the treasury to the soldiers, and so back again to the merchants. Yet this could not have been continued indefinitely. As provisions and merchandise grew scarce and danger became more imminent, it was natural for the soldiers as for the citizens to hoard rather than to spend. This delicate intermural economy must at last have been disturbed; and the growing difficulty in raising funds in the last months gave a clear indication of what must inevitably happen in the end.[88]

In spite of the growing distress, the morale of the city remained unchanged. The despatches of Ferrucci illustrate the spirit of determination which continued to prevail, just as the letters of Capello show what admiration was entertained even by a foreigner.[89] " We are determined to risk all we have before coming under the yoke of tyranny," wrote the Dieci in a characteristic communication to their ambassador in France. " No burden is too heavy in order to maintain this liberty, the sweetness whereof is the more appreciated, the greater the war waged against it. . . . There is none but spontaneously helps to make good the defences of the city with his own hands. . . . We fear nothing. . . . Such love and sympathy has grown up between the soldiers and our young men that they seem all brothers ; and there can be discerned even in the foreigners such readiness for our defence that it seems as though they fight for their own interest no less than for ours ; which comes from their being excellently paid, and lovingly treated by all . . . so that our infantry is reduced to such perfection in number as well as in quality that if it went on campaign it would make the whole of Italy tremble. . . . In order that nothing should be lacking for the soldiers, we are willing to deprive our own mouths."[90] In the dark moment after the fall of Empoli,

Luigi Alamanni reaffirmed his intention to help the city. "I promise you on my side, that if I was warm before I am now most warm . . . to do all that lies in my power." [91] One day an eagle—the symbol of the Empire—was shot down in the city. It was taken as a good omen, and the delighted mob fought for its feathers and tore it to pieces. The head was saved and presented to the Signoria, who had it placed with an expressive gesture upon the lectern before the assembled Pratica.[92] The religious spirit too remained unaltered in all its incongruities. "To have recourse to God" remained the keynote of public policy as it did of the public councils. Excepting for the short-age of fish, Lent had been observed with all solemnity.[93] On 20 April, the Gonfalonier formally asked in the Ottanta whether "the city finding itself in such travail . . . there should be assembled some clerics to consider whether anything should be done to placate the anger of God." The debate which followed was characteristic. The spokesman of the Gonfalonieri of the Companies replied that he could never have had greater joy than on that evening, it seeming that God had inspired all ; and, on behalf of his colleagues, he professed their readiness to walk in procession in their shirts if need be. The other spokesmen were in agreement ; the quarter of S. Giovanni being of the opinion that the Archangel appointed over Princes had counselled the Gonfalonier on that occasion.[94] Five days afterwards, the clerics made their reply. They recommended, as spiritual remedies, mutual pardon of offences, a public kiss of peace, processions and penitence. On the more material side, they suggested better administration of justice, especially upon soldiers, and the sus-pension of the ecclesiastical taxation as levied since the previous December. Finally—most unpalatable of all—they advised "humiliation before the Pope." Another session of the Pratica was devoted to the discussion of these proposals. Upon the matters of spiritual discipline, all were in agreement, though with a spirit of sturdy independence it was held that while ready to pardon they did not wish to hold as other than enemies those who worked against the Republic. The other suggestions met with no such general approval. It was pointed out that the church endowments had been given by their fathers to use in pious causes, precisely as was the present ; while after three humilia-tions before the Pope, they had no desire to make the experiment again. Francesco Carducci added that the religious exercises should be arranged in such a way as not to give any impression of faltering, and finally showed his disapprobation of the political recommendations by declaring that priests should not meddle in public affairs, in which their counsel could not be other than harmful.[95] A few days later one of the proposals was carried into effect by a solemn procession of all the magistracies clad in black, accompanied by the religious orders of the city. For greater decorum, men and women in the Duomo were kept separated.[96] On 15 May, Bartolommeo Cavalcanti aroused the people assembled in the Sala de' Cinquecento to enthusiasm by the statutory oration in praise of liberty and of the militia which he had been appointed to deliver ; and on the next day there followed with every circumstance of religious solemnity the formal oath of allegiance in the Piazza S. Giovanni.[97] But the greatest of all the manifestations was made on the feast-day of St. John, patron saint of the city (24 June). Instead of the careless rustic festivities still usual upon that day, a special religious function was ordered. All the various magistrates took the communion together and walked in procession, barefoot and dressed in sombre clothing, with lighted tapers in their hands. Before them was borne the whole of the hagiological panoply of the city—the crucifix of S. Piero del Murone, the miraculous pictures of the Virgin from Impruneta and elsewhere, the head of S. Zanobi, and other relics. On this occasion, with an excess of decorum, women were not allowed to take part in the procession or even to show themselves in the Duomo or Baptistery.[98]

Nevertheless, as the months passed, desire for peace grew with the stress of war. The tone of more than one of the contemporary records commences imperceptibly to change.[99] It was at this period that the pro-Medicean feeling which had penetrated even into the nunnery of the Murate led to the transference of Catherine de' Medici to Sta. Lucia. Fresh executions marked the rising tide of suspicion. Thus Ficino Ficini, nephew of the great humanist Marsiglio Ficini, was put to the torture, and beheaded for treason after trial by the Quarantia.[100] One Carafulla, a popular buffoon, was committed to prison for deploring the cheapness and bounty enjoyed under the Medici.[101] Some passive sympathies with the enemy turned by degrees into active, and through their means an efficient espionage service was built up. The lack of secrecy in the public councils was now found to be fatal ; and the most important deliberations were soon known not only beyond the walls of the Palazzo, but also beyond those of the city. What with this and with the intercepted despatches, the enemy came to have an immediate knowledge of all that took place or was proposed among the besieged.[102] A canon of the Duomo was discovered sending information to the enemy ; others signalled to him with flags or lights.[103] Some characters hitherto considered irreproachable were discovered among the spies. Lorenzo Soderini, who had been Ferrucci's colleague at Prato, was found to be in correspondence with

Baccio Valori, whom he regularly informed of everything that went on in the city. He was hastily tried by the emergency tribunal which had condemned Jacopo Alamanni, and was hanged from a window of the Bargello before an infuriated crowd which clamoured for his body. So strained, however, had the people's nerves by now become that it fell victim in the middle of the execution to an inexplicable and deadly panic which spread itself through the city. It was noted with approbation that the soldiers on the bastions continued in spite of this to maintain perfect discipline.[104] Special precautions were now taken against the leakage of information. The oath of secrecy became almost invariable at the sessions of the Pratica. Towards the end of May, the two captains, Baglione and Colonna, suggested that for matters concerning the conduct of operations a smaller council of very few members should be introduced which should ensure expedition and secrecy. The proposal was almost unanimously approved and was repeatedly confirmed.[105]

While the inhabitants of Florence were making these extreme efforts, they were not forgotten by their compatriots outside the city. It was an age when the whole of Europe was filled with Florentine colonies settled in all of its greater commercial centres; and these were following the course of events in Tuscany with anxious eyes, " waiting each day that God send us good news of the afflicted city." [106] Without waiting to be asked they raised among themselves by self-taxation considerable sums of money which they forwarded to Florence. Lyons, which had risen to the position of a financial centre of the first importance, largely through the Florentine bankers invited there by the French king, led the way. They were ably seconded by the merchants of Flanders. Even in far-off England, where the colony was numerically small, over a thousand crowns were collected.[107] Only the Florentines at Venice shared the apathy of the city in which they lived, and all efforts to rouse them to emulation were in vain.[108]

Such aid was however only a small part of what might be expected from abroad. The minds of the Florentines were turning in this juncture once again to France. It was thought that it was only for the sake of recovering his sons that Francis had abandoned his allies and had signed the disgraceful treaty; and he had continued to show the city some signs of good-will. Though forced out of deference to the Pope and Emperor to withdraw his ambassador from the beleaguered city, he had left an unofficial representative who kept alive their hopes by promises of help.[109] Clairmont too, after his mission in January, had left vowing to use his influence in their favour.[110] Till the princes were released, however, it was impossible to expect direct assistance, and distance made the difficulties virtually insuperable.   Aware of this, Florence had been requesting since January some pecuniary aid.[111] Baldassare Carducci, still ambassador in France, was the nominal agent for these transactions ; but he was eclipsed by Luigi Alamanni, whose position at Genoa was ideal for an intermediary.   He had already been designated for a secret mission to France to obtain help when this was anticipated by the maturing of an audacious plan between him and the merchants at Lyons.   Francis was their debtor to the extent of 60,000 ducats or more, which they had not much hope of recovering, at all events not without a long delay.   They were willing, therefore, if he could be induced to repay, to devote at least half the sum to the defence of the Republic.   He, on the other hand, professed himself grateful at the opportunity of assisting his former allies in a perfectly legitimate way without breaking his obligations to Charles or prejudicing the chances of the recovery of his sons.   He was willing to waive even his technical advantage that the majority of the sums in question had been advanced to his Treasurer, Semblançay, since condemned for malversation, whose connections were now regarded as his accomplices rather than as creditors of the Crown.   The expectations of the Florentines were heightened by this complaisance, and detailed instructions were sent as to the method by which the money should be despatched, addressed to private merchants, by the sea-route to Livorno and thus to Pisa.   Hardly was the arrangement concluded, however, than Francis commenced after his usual fashion to evolve more grandiose schemes, and to make specious promises of coming to Italy in person with an army at his back.   The papal agents, moreover, got wind of the enterprise and taxed him with it.   His usual preoccupations about his sons came uppermost, and he begged the Florentines not to press him until they were recovered.   Of the subsidies which came from France, therefore, he was responsible for a very minor portion.   Similar advances were made to England, which the Divorce question was driving into opposition to the Pope ; but matters moved slowly and were hampered by political considerations.   As a result, the fifteen to twenty thousand ducats which Alamanni was actually able to forward was made up principally of the voluntary levies which had been collected.[112]

While thus preparing to outwear the enemy, the Florentines were not neglecting more active expedients.   Even though they were unequal in military strength, they could hope to improve matters by diversions in other quarters.   Through the orators at Venice and Ferrara, negotiations were entered into with the late lords of Rimini, recently dispossessed by the Pope. The head of the house was Roberto, natural son of the famous Sigismondo Malatesta, that notorious condottiere who built in memory of his illicit love perhaps the most magnificent church of Renascence Italy. Roberto's son, named after his grandfather Sigismondo, an adventurer and soldier of fortune, was the active representative of his claims together with his brother Malatesta, who later disappeared in the Anglo-Scotch wars. The brothers had already sent to solicit aid just before the commencement of the war.[113] Not discouraged by the refusal which they then experienced, they applied again in the spring through the orator at Venice, undertaking for the modest sum of 400 ducats to create a diversion in the direction of their native city. Owing to the closeness of the blockade, the despatch of Gualterotti took two months to arrive ; and by that time recent events had made it impossible for the scheme as outlined to be put into execution.[114] Almost simultaneously, however, an envoy sent direct arrived at the city with more concrete and more promising proposals, strongly recommended by Galeotto Giugni, who promised that if he were accorded sufficient confidence and supplied with 2,000 or 2,500 ducats he would set the whole of the Papal Romagna into a blaze.[115] The Dieci were better pleased with the scheme as now presented, " because we know that if such a conflagration is kindled in that province, great diversion will necessarily be caused from our affairs." Yet they did not apparently consider it sufficiently certain to justify such additional expenditure in their present financial straits, and contented themselves with promises of a generous support in the event of something happening which they were eagerly expecting—presumably the arrival of the subsidies from France.[116] Sigismondo continued to press for a decision, reducing his request to 1,500 ducats and promising to raise Cervia as well as Ravenna against the Pope ; and he professed that once the enterprise was launched it could be made self-supporting, being financed by the salt of the one place and the trade of the other. Giugni on his side continued to urge on the enterprise, offering like a true Florentine his own house at Florence as a contribution to the expense.[117] His fellow-citizens, however, could not venture to assume immediately even this reduced burden, and they contented themselves with inviting the Malatestas' co-operation in their own affairs.[118] Meanwhile the Pope, getting wind of the intrigues, succeeded after much pressure in having the arch-conspirator expelled from Venice, on the pretext of having forced his way into the house of a lady with whom he was in love.[119]

This was only one of a number of plans which were being

suggested or tried. Other lords who had once possessed lands in the states of the Church were following the example of the Malatesta.[120] The Abbot of Farfa, in spite of his defection, intimated his desire to re-enter the Florentine service, and became once more a thorn in the side of the Pope.[121] Much hope was pinned on a diversion which the Turk had apparently been encouraged to make.[122] The ambassador in France was in communication with the exiles from Naples, who were expected to raise a rebellion on behalf of the French king when the time should be ripe; and it is significant that from " il Reame " only, Florentine citizens had not been recalled.[123] It was seriously suggested that Francis might care to put the Duke of Ferrara at the head of a Swiss force for their relief.[124] There is an indication even of negotiations with the Lutheran faction in Germany, then in the throes of the Diet of Augsburg, from which quarter the Florentines certainly expected some diversion.[125] The indefatigable Giugni entered into secret negotiations with Giovanni, son of Hermes Bentivoglio and grandson of the namesake of his chased from Bologna by Julius II, to make a sudden raid in the hopes of recovering his ancestral city and creating a further distraction for the Pope ; and the Florentines hopefully promised their support.[126] Nearer home, there were schemes to reverse the disastrous outcome of the campaign of the earlier months of the year. Had it been possible to get money from the Venetian merchants for Lorenzo Carnesecchi—and only 2,000 ducats was the sum required—he would have reopened operations in the Romagna and the contiguous territories in spite of the truce.[127] In this he might expectt he co-operation of the Fabroni family, which was predominant at Marradi and offered to return that important city to obedience in spite of its having rebelled and publicly burned the Marzocco. Similar negotiations were entered into with some of the Malaspina, who offered the services of 500 foot to recover one of their castles.[128] Most reliance was placed in the Bardi, lords of Vernio and influential in the Mugello, who were promised not only pardon but also rich reward if they fulfilled their promise of returning to their allegiance and recovering Prato.[129] There were, moreover, grandiose schemes of bringing about a general mutiny in the Imperialist ranks. A captain of lanzknechts at the court of France, and with the secret encouragement of the King, proposed to induce the German mercenaries serving against the city to rebel or even to change sides ; while a number of Italian officers promised to do as much for their own compatriots.[130] A similar plan was set about by Giugni from Ferrara, at the suggestion of the French ambassador.[131] Other negotiations were conducted with some German adventurer.[132] But the main scheme was

betrayed by a Flemish refugee at the French court ; and when
the captains set out to put it into execution, Orange was already
forewarned and had taken all precautions.[133] In addition, one
at least who had travelled about Italy conferring with the
Florentine agents and had penetrated into the city itself as a
welcome guest turned out to be a mere impostor, who immediately
betrayed all the information he could obtain to the Prince of
Orange.[134] From other directions, too, the Imperialists received
serious distractions. At Siena the people rose in arms more
than once and committed acts of violence, not scrupling to show
their antagonism to the Imperial resident himself.[135] Pistoia,
soon tired of its new masters, had come to blows with the Spanish,
setting aside for the moment its internal feuds.[136] Arezzo,
which had expected as the price of its rebellion to regain its
liberty, and was profoundly disappointed at the general determination to leave the Florentine dominion untouched, sent a
delegation to the Emperor to beg him to reconsider his decision.
On his refusal, the inhabitants commenced to make military
preparations, and talked of offering the Florentines effective
assistance in return for the lightening of their yoke. Among
the besieged, there were already hopes of reoccupying that city
and interrupting Orange's communications and supplies along
the Valdichiana.[137] It is hardly to be imagined that all this
happened spontaneously and without encouragement from
Florence.

Above all, hope was pinned in a diversion from the direction
of Pisa. By now it had been realized what a crass error had
been committed in the evacuations of the various fortresses,
which had given the enemy undisputed command of the dominion,
allowing him to concentrate almost without distraction on the
blockade. With four thousand fresh troops, wrote the Dieci,
they could turn again the revolted cities and force the Imperialists
to raise the siege.[138] The execution of the scheme was encouraged,
if not suggested, by the French king and strongly supported
by Luigi Alamanni ; and it came to be the chief preoccupation
of the government.[139] The idea was to raise a strong independent
force at Pisa which should occupy Pistoia, thus cutting off
Orange's communications with the north. Thence it should
advance, joining hands with other detached bodies, to the
relief of Florence. The essential requirements were money and
troops. To find the latter was the easier problem. Though it
would be dangerous as well as difficult to weaken the strength
of the garrison, paymasters like the Florentines never had trouble
in finding fresh mercenaries. In the Lunigiana, captains were
pressing to serve.[140] Galeotto Giugni had ample opportunity to
engage others in the north-east of the peninsula in spite of the

19

opposition of the papal agents:[141] Giovanpaolo Orsini, son of
that Renzo da Ceri who had led the last effort of the league in
the Abruzzi, was peculiarly indicated for the command. He had
followed with distinction the family profession of condottiere,
and was then lying idle at Venice, having already signified
his willingness to enter the Florentine service.[142] It was,
however, considered proper to ask the formal approval of the
King of France, his patron, who was showing a benevolent
interest in the scheme. To him it seemed that the person suggested was too notoriously a French adherent, and he recommended instead a disaffected Genoese, Antonio Doria, whose
cause was espoused by Luigi Alamanni.[143] In the interval
Giovanpaolo had made his way with some Apulian veterans to
Pisa, whence he wrote asking for instructions, meanwhile making
arrangements to raise fresh followers in the Venetia.[144] With
the commander assured, the only thing required, in order to
levy a force of almost unlimited size, was money. Yet the city
had by now commenced to feel the pinch, and found difficulty
in raising even what was vitally needed for the defence.
Moreover, the blockade was so close that the mere question of
conveying bullion out of the city presented a serious difficulty.
It was for this, therefore, that the financial assistance expected
from France was destined.   " If it soon arrives at Pisa," wrote
the Dieci to their ambassador at Paris, " be sure that not long
after you will hear of our liberation." [145] The interception
of the correspondence with France revealed the scheme to the
papal agents ; and their vigorous protests combined with his
own lack of determination to prevent Francis from fulfilling his
promises.[146] Without money, the expedition was paralysed.
In addition, Empoli was by now captured, which complicated
the military situation ; and the decentralization of the Imperial
forces made it necessary for the remaining garrisons in the
dominion to stand on the defensive. The enterprise had therefore to be postponed.

The busy brain of Galeotto Giugni, orator at Ferrara, had
not been content with the conduct of intrigues or the provision
of saltpetre. Before his expulsion, he sent home in grim earnest-
ness a suggestion which serves to illustrate the antithesis which
the Italian character, even in a friend of Michelangelo, might
always contain. " Seeing the obstinacy of your enemies," he
wrote, " and thinking that the length of the siege may cause
many ill-effects, I do not desire to omit to say that which occurs
to me, which is, that I would undertake to send to the Camp
two or three persons with plague-stricken merchandise : by
which means it would be an easy matter to set the fire in that
Camp, since they have suffered somewhat especially in this

winter and since there are there in the Camp, from what I hear, many dead animals, all things which nourish such infirmity : and this would give me the mind to set to work at an expense of a hundred ducats or less : and if it were not that I do not know what intercourse there is between your men and those of the Camp, through which such contagion might transfer itself to the City, I would have put it into effect without your commission. But for this reason I have refrained and await your decision. . . ." [147] What reply he received to his inquiry cannot be ascertained ; yet the government which could deliberately order the poisoning of the wells about Pisa [148] can have had no fixed objection to the proposal on any grounds other than that of expediency. During the next month, the plague suddenly and mysteriously made its appearance in the Imperialist camp.[149] It continued to rage for some time, especially among the Germans ; and as many as forty or fifty were carried off every day. In the Certosa, whither the Prince of Orange had transferred his headquarters from the Villa Guicciardini, three out of the six remaining friars fell victims in a single night. The Prince himself became dangerously ill and was thought to be in peril of his life. The Sienese envoy left the camp in alarm.[150] At the same time there were considerable hopes in Florence that as a result the siege might be raised [151] : and all intercourse with outside, even for bringing in the provisions which were so vitally needed, was forbidden under pain of death. Whatever hopes were built upon this were doomed however to disappointment ; for after raging for six weeks, the plague abated nearly as suddenly as it had arisen, killed perhaps by the extreme but dry heat. It obtained moreover a footing inside the walls, where it added to the casualties among the inhabitants, already weakened by privation.[152]

Similar efforts to those of the Florentines had meanwhile to be made by the besiegers in order to keep their army together : and though supplies were now more regular, they were still far from satisfactory. The 60,000 ducats monthly which the Pope had promised in November continued to be frequently in arrears, and the payment for the month of October was never caught up. The Council of Regency in Naples refused to send the contribution of 50,000 which Charles had promised without a special order. According to report, the troops were not certain of satisfaction even when money had finally arrived at camp, for Orange was said to have gambled away one subsidy painfully scraped together by the Pope.[153] Requirements continued to be in excess of supply. The stipulated income was consumed by the payment of the infantry alone, leaving nothing for incidental expenses. It was through lack of money that Orange had been prevented from marching against Volterra and Pisa after the fall of Empoli, and thus bringing the campaign in the dominion to an end.[154]   No provision at all had been made for the men-at-arms and light horse which had been retained. To the troops quartered in the dominion no thought was given, though the body under Fabrizio Maramaldo alone should have received 10,000 ducats a month—an income which it enjoyed by special grace for two months only.[155]   As a result, they had to support themselves.   The whole region was filled with unpaid Spanish troops living at free quarters upon the countryside, and known as " Bisogni," or " needy."   One body had seized upon Pistoia, and was now lying in its dependencies, paying only a very nominal authority to Alessandro Vitelli, who was now with his regular Italian troops in the city itself.[156] Mutinies continued, though not with the frequency or universality of the previous months.   At the commencement of July a body of Spanish foot lodged at Castina near Pisa refused to go to Hungary and rose in arms.   Orange sent to arrange matters, and succeeded in appeasing the majority.   Nevertheless, a couple of hundred of them were led to Pisa by their officers under the pretext of setting an ambush.   Giovanpaolo da Ceri forced them to give in ; but, enraged with their leaders, who had promised to lead over the whole body, he had them executed.[157]   Even in the camp outside Florence the fidelity of the troops was not above suspicion, and consternation was once caused at the discovery of a plot on the part of one of the Spanish captains to give the Florentines entrance to the lines when he had guard.[158]   Yet these were now the exceptions, and the army remained on the whole reasonably well disciplined and confident.   The Pope had meanwhile been growing more and more impatient at the protracted expenditure.   His finances, always in a delicate condition, were threatened with bankruptcy by an expedition which had already cost him by 3 July 700,000 ducats instead of the 80,000 on which he had originally reckoned.[159]   With progress of the campaign, however, his hopes had risen.   His attitude with regard to Orange changed and he readmitted him to favour.   He became enthusiastic at the course of operations, expressing unmeasured gladness at the fall of Empoli and confidence that Volterra would soon change hands again.[160]   Henceforth it was not the outcome of the war or the method by which the city would fall which exercised the minds of the Imperialists.   The result was regarded as a foregone conclusion, and they were already contemplating how to avoid sack.   It was feared that once the unpaid soldiery should enter Florence they would not only turn to pillage, but also remain there and refuse to move.   Any possibility of her defraying some part of the cost of the expedition would be at an end, the Emperor would lose the service of an effective force, and there would be the blot of the destruction of a great city on the consciences of all concerned. Muxetula, the Imperial commissary, exerted himself therefore to secure the agreement of Orange and of his master and to make all arrangements to avert the disaster. Florence was, however, by no means so near the end of her resistance as they imagined.[161]

For some time past, the blockade had continued without outstanding event: and Orange's desire to avoid an action seemed to be shared by the city's own soldiers. Stefano Colonna, stung by the murmurings of the citizens, took advantage of the absence of the Marquis of Vasto from camp to plan a new attack. This time it was not to be directed, as upon former occasions, against the main body of the enemy upon the south bank, but against the German encampment to the north. Victory here would have led to a reopening of the road to Prato and so to the outer world. On the morning of 21 June, two hours before dawn, he sallied out with about 2,000 men, part of them militia, from the Porta al Prato, while the captain Pasquino Corsi led a smaller number from the Porta di Faenza. The two bodies advanced stealthily towards the hill of S. Donato in Polverosa, where the lanzknechts had their headquarters. In spite of a premature alarm, the entrenchments were passed through without any difficulty, and the enemy was assailed before being properly aroused. There was a scene of the most utter confusion. The nunnery which formed the centre of the German position was entered through the orchard and became the scene of indiscriminate carnage without distinction of sex, many being killed in their beds. After this initial success, desire for plunder got the upper hand, and the soldiers set about sacking the camp. This gave time to Count Lodovico di Lodrone, who had succeeded Felix of Wittenberg in the command of the lanzknechts, to put together a considerable force and defend himself. A stiff fight ensued which continued till dawn. The alarm being given on the other side of the Arno, succour commenced to arrive. Malatesta, who had taken up his position by the river bank outside the Porta al Prato precisely for such an eventuality, feared that he might be cut off from the city. He turned back, therefore, together with the reinforcements which had been held in readiness. Colonna, wounded in two places, was forced to give the order for retirement. The action had been a most brilliant one, as the enemy admitted; but both sides claimed the advantage in point of casualties and insisted that it was only the tardiness of succour which had prevented them from gaining a complete victory. The balance of the advantage and the moral effect were, however, on the side of the Florentines, who returned laden with spoil.[162]

Ferrucci had meanwhile continued at Volterra, which he ruled with a rod of iron. The people was disarmed, corn and supplies were carried off to the citadel, and fugitives ordered to return. The city was forced to admit its rebellion, as a result of which the old agreement with Florence was declared void and it was compelled to subscribe to new and sterner articles of allegiance. A levy of 6,000 ducats was made for the payment of Ferrucci's troops, which was exacted ruthlessly through the medium of imprisonment and menaces, some recalcitrant friars even being put into custody. The inhabitants were deprived of their weapons, and even forbidden to go about in cloaks which might conceal them. As a result Ferruccio held the city thoroughly cowed and subdued, with his own troops confident and well supplied to meet the test to which they were to be put.[163] Fabrizio Maramaldo had immediately made his appearance in the environs, distracting attention from affairs at Empoli by wasting the countryside from Villa Magna. Finally, supplied with reinforcements and artillery by Orange, he advanced with between four and five thousand men to besiege the place. This was to have been the preliminary to an attack on Pisa, with which Florence would have lost the last particles of her dominion. A herald was sent into the city summoning it to surrender. Ferrucci proudly refused, saying that he would pay his respects in person. A fierce but indeterminate skirmish followed beneath the walls, after which Maramaldo again summoned the city. This time Ferrucci, fulfilling a previous threat, hanged the unfortunate envoy.[164] Maramaldo now commenced a bombardment. Ferrucci did not remain inactive, retaliating with his artillery and sending to destroy a mine which the enemy had commenced. His troops meanwhile exacerbated Maramaldo by mimicking his name from the ramparts with caterwaulings, to which a live cat was pressed into service to contribute.[165] The enemy was impeded by shortage of money and supplies until 12 June, when the Marquis del Vasto and Diego Sarmiento arrived from Empoli with the Spanish troops set free by the capture of that place. Two days after they commenced an intensive bombardment at a point where it was not expected, and where in consequence the fortifications had not been strengthened. As a result a breach was immediately made, but a dispute for precedence between the enemy commanders gave time for it to be partly filled with bales of wool and boxes hastily placed in position. When the attack was launched a terrific fight ensued. Ferrucci, wounded in two places, remained seated in a chair animating the defence. At length the enemy was forced to draw off. The news caused some consternation in Imperialist circles, and the Pope himself urged Vasto to persevere. Sending for more artillery, on 21 June at dawn he recommenced the bombardment in other directions and again made two breaches. These were similarly hurriedly fortified and defended, Ferrucci rising from his sick-bed and defending as before. The assault continued at both points simultaneously for two hours, the Florentines defending themselves desperately with boiling oil and stones as well as with more regular weapons. Finally, however, the Spanish acknowledged themselves beaten and gave up the assault. On 29 June, their camp was abandoned. It was the most humiliating reverse experienced by the Imperial arms during the whole course of the war.[166] Volterra was thus saved the experience of changing hands three times in four months ; but it gained little by it. In order to satisfy his troops, to whom he had promised double pay in order to save the city from sack, Ferrucci confiscated and coined all the gold and silver which could be found throughout the city in public establishments or private, lay or religious, besides selling by auction all the fine cloths on which he could lay his hands.[167] To the citizens there was not much difference between this spoliation and the pillage from which they had been saved ; and the experiences of this year were remembered in their history by the side of the disastrous sack of 1472, as the Second Calamity of Volterra. But such severity was necessary in order for Ferrucci to maintain the fidelity and discipline of his troops, now becoming in his hands an almost perfect military organism.

NOTES TO CHAPTER X

[1] Sanuto, LI, 299.

[2] See Cosimo Bartoli, the well-known *littérateur*, who affirms that he acted as intermediary in these transactions (*Discorsi*, p. 213) ; cf. study by Mancini in *A.S.I.*, ser. V, 1918.

[3] It seems natural to connect the information of Bardi (letter 92) with the circumstantial account of Nardi, p. 215, whose testimony is to be the more readily accepted owing to his intense anti-Medicean feeling.

[4] See letters of Sienese envoys *passim*, esp. Vannini, letters 67 and 72 ; Robert, p. 368, and Docs. 265, 294–5, 304, etc.

[5] *Ibid.* pp. 363–4 and Docs. 298, 302.

[6] *Ibid.* p. 351 *seqq.*, and Doc. 268 *seqq.*

[7] *Ibid.* p. 304.

[8] Sanga to Vasto, 4 January 1529/30, in *Lettere de' Principi*, II, 194.

[9] Robert, 371–2, and Docs. 315–17 ; *Letters and Papers, Henry VIII*, IV, 6109, 6244.

[10] Letter of Bishop of Tarbes to Francis I of April 1530 in *A.S.I.*, App. I, 473–8.

[11] Robert, 365 *seqq.* and documents ; Bardi, letters 93–116 *passim* ; Sanuto, LII, 593, and LIII, 11–12, 30, 32, 73, 103.

[12] See instructions to Orange of 27 April in Robert, Doc. 330 ; and

the very important despatch of Muxetula of 2 May from Bergenroth Transcripts, IX, 1 *seqq.*, in Appendix of Documents, No. 9. Cf. abstract in *State Papers, Spanish*, IV, i, 296, and Bardi, letter 120.

[13] Cf. De Blasiis, *Fabrizio Maramaldo e i sui antenati* in *Archivio Storico per le Provincie Napolitane*, I–III (1876–8) ; iii, 346 *seqq* ; A. Luzio, *Fabrizio Maramaldo* (Ancona, 1883) ; Falletti, II, xxxix–li, with documents.

[14] Robert, p. 376 *seqq.* and Doc. 337 *seqq.* ; Bardi, letters 117, 119, 120, 124, 129, 134, 141, and despatch of Muxetula of 2 May, *ibid.*

[15] Pratiche, 7, 8, 9 May ; Capello, letter 84 ; Bardi, letters 122–9.

[16] Robert, Doc. 343 ; Bardi, letter 130.

[17] Cf. Capello, letter 84.

[18] Vannini, letter 78.

[19] Robert, p. 371 and Doc. 312.

[20] Cf. Bardi, letter 106, 116, etc.

[21] Capello, letters 82.

[22] Cf. Capello, letter 82 ; Ferrucci, Despatches 102, 105, 108 ; Varchi, II, 108 ; Bardi, letter 106.

[23] Robert, 378–81 ; Varchi, II, 327–33 ; Bardi, letter 124 ; Roseo, 245–51 ; Giovio, II, 184–7. Ricci, *l.c.* p. 450, states that Ludovico Machiavelli fell in the action of 2 November. A few days after, Jacopo Bichi, who had hitherto been one of the most prominent among the Florentine captains, died as a result of losing his leg by a cannon-shot (Roseo, 281). Another casualty was Amico da Venafro, one of the best-known captains, who was killed on the Ponte Vecchio after the sortie in a fit of anger by Stefano Colonna for not having carried out his instructions (Segni, I, 245).

[24] Despatches 70 *seqq.*

[25] *Ibid.* 74, 89.

[26] *Ibid.* 89, 94.

[27] *Ibid.* 96.

[28] *Ibid.* 109 ; Sassetti, *Vita di Ferruccio*, 87–8 ; Roseo, 240–1 ; Paoli, CV–CVI ; Giovio, II, 191. Bardi, letter 117 (25 April), shows what a serious reverse this was for the Imperialists, who were forced to revise their opinion as to the extremity to which the Florentines were reduced. Gonzaga, who had his horse killed under him, was discredited in consequence.

[29] *Seconda Calamità Volterrana*, pp. 24–8 ; Varchi, II, 388–94 ; Giovio, II, 191–2 ; Ferrucci, despatches 110–11 ; Cambi, 54–6 ; Sassetti, p. 88 *seqq.* ; Robert, 400–2. Cf. jubilant reports to various envoys abroad of 30 April in Dieci, Missive, XLVIII. The Articles of Surrender are to be found in Dieci, Responsive, CLI, ff. 466–8.

[30] See excerpts from *Storietta di Empoli* (published by G. Lami in *Deliciæ Eruditorum*, Odeporico, Pt. I), in *Francesco Ferrucci*, etc., 373–9, and contemporary account in letters of Bardi—129 *seqq.*, 136, 138. Cf. also Roseo, 234, 241, 273–5 ; Robert, p. 380 ; Varchi, II, 342 *seqq.* ; Giovio, II, 194–6 ; and Dieci, Missive, XLVIII, to Gualterotti, 6 June. The siege is depicted in one of Vasari's frescoes.

[31] Letter of 5 June *apud* Hauvette, App. II, *n.* 58.

[32] Bardi, letter 130.

[33] Signoria, CXXXIII, ff. 83–4 (12 July 1530). "*Sententia Quarantie : absolutiones Nicc : de Orlandinis & Condemnationis Andree de Giugnis & Pieri de Orlandinis,*" of whom the former " commisit magnum scelus cum dederit inimicis castrum emporij ut est publica vox et fama et quod fuit causa quod dictum castrum sit incursum in preda inimicorum et a sacco et quod tot pauperes fame peribunt et mulieres honorem ammictent et in effectu diminuit vires reipublicæ et accrevit illas inimicis . . . item quod

Pierus et Nicc.⁴ de Orlandinis idem commiserint. . . ." Declared *rubelli*
"et che sieno dipinti al podestà come traditorj con e' loro nomj. . . ."
Cf. Capello, letter 84. Falletti, I, 85–93, rejects the evidence for treachery
after a close examination ; and the Spanish sources know nothing of it.
Giugni was, however, certainly guilty of a criminal weakness. Capponi,
II, 451, points out that though Piero Orlandini was much esteemed by
Ferrucci (cf. his earlier despatches), his name was mentioned twenty years
earlier in a list of citizens "to be attempted and gained over to the
Medici" (Archivi Toscani, I, 329).

³⁴ Cf. Pratiche, 27 January, when further deportation of malcontents
was recommended as remedy. The negligence of the commissaries at
this time had caused some alarm. One of their shortcomings was apparently to consult the citizens of their place : " Et perchè questi Comⁱ
fanno consigli de Cittadinj, che facessino Comⁱ uno, o più, che non habbia
rispetto."

³⁵ Pratiche, 14 and 25 April ; Signoria, CXXXIII, f. 36 (2 June) ;
Varchi, II, 347–9 ; Nerli, 228–30 ; Cambi, IV, 62. The sentence as
transmitted to Pisa is in Carteggio Originale, XII, ff. 381–2.

³⁶ Even the territorial neutrality of Lucca was violated by the Spanish,
who arrested within its borders Pieradvardo Giachinotti on his way to
take up the functions of commissary at Pisa. Cf. Signoria, Carteggio,
Missive, Registri, XXXVIII, 6 December 1529. " Lucensibus : . . .
Habbiamo con assai maraviglia e non poco dispiacere inteso come a Lastra
ovvero a Lunata, terra di V. Srⁱᵉ è suto facto prigione da alcuni Spagnuoli
Pieraduardo Giachinotti nostro carissimo cittadino . . " In the end,
however, he was able to assume office.

³⁷ Signoria, Carteggio, Missive, Minutari, XXI, f. 185a (8 January
1529/30), Dieci, Responsive, CLI, p. 334 (from Bartolommeo Giovanni,
Consul at Ancona, 20 April), and letter of protest of 4 May in Appendix
of Documents, No. 10, remarkable for its sentiment against the Pope and
its prophetical warning to the Republic.

³⁸ Hauvette, p. 82 *seqq.*, with original authorities there cited ; Brea,
Sulla Congiura del Conte G. Luigi Fieschi (Genoa, 1863), pp. 148, 182 ; Capello, letter 66 ; letter of Doria in Albèri, p. 18, *n.* 2 ; Varchi, II, p. 347.

³⁹ Capello, letter 81 ; Dieci, Missive, XLVIII, to Galeotto Giugni (and
others), 27 March, 20, 27 April ; Bardi, letter 129. Cf. *infra* for some
of his activities.

⁴⁰ See despatches of Capello, etc., of this period *passim*, and especially
one of Giugni of 13 April in Dieci, Responsive, CLI, f. 363 ; and *infra*,
pp. 275, 298. A number of most important despatches are preserved only
in the intercepted copies from the Spanish archives. Cf. also Hauvette,
App. III, *n.* 20.

⁴¹ Signoria, CXXXII, f. 50 (5 December).

⁴² *Ibid.*, f. 153 (16 February).

⁴³ Pratiche, 3 February.

⁴⁴ Falletti, I, 442. Cf. MS., Ricordanze di S. Maria del Carmine, XX,
f. 163: " . . . Ricordo come a dì 15 d'aprile 1530 forzata una (*sc. vendita*)
si venda alli uffitialij del' abondanza stai quaranta di grano per fare el
pane a soldati. . . ."

⁴⁵ Sanuto, LII, 584–6 ; Baldovinetti, p. 47.

⁴⁶ Paoli, CXCVIII ; Capello, letter 76 *seqq.*

⁴⁷ Varchi, II, 317.

⁴⁸ Capello, letter 85.

⁴⁹ Signoria, CXXXIII, f. 42 (6 June). For evidence of activity, see
elsewhere in this volume.

⁵⁰ Capello, letter 88.

[51] Dieci, Missive, XLVIII, 25 July (to B. Carducci).

[52] See Appendix II, *The Turkish Succour.*

[53] See letter of Alamanni of 5 June in Hauvette, App. II, *n.* 58.

[54] Provisioni (Consiglio Maggiore), CCIX, f. 17 *seqq.* (10 June).

[55] For conditions and prices during the siege, see, besides authorities cited above, Baldovinetti, pp. 45–6 ; letter of Gerolamo Benivieni in *Francesco Ferrucci,* etc., pp. 462–3 ; *Diario di Luca Landucci,* pp. 368–70. *Tre ricordi estratti da un libro del Monastero di Ripoli* (I. di Badia) in *Miscellanea Fiorentina,* II, 166 *seqq.* ; Varchi, II, 466–7 ; Cambi, IV, p. 65 ; Sanuto, LIII, 248 ; Stefano de' Buonafedi, *ubi supra* ; and all other contemporary accounts. On 15 April, before prices were fixed, but before the dearth was at its height, bread fetched ten times its normal price ! (Capello, letter 82). According to a legend of dubious authenticity, the popular drink " Zabaione," a sort of egg punch, was invented as a war-time expedient by Malatesta Baglione, to whom it owes the latter portion of its name.

[56] Capello, letters 78, 80, 82 ; Sanuto, LIII, 247–8. Among the victims was Capello's favourite horse, commemorated in a Latin epitaph still to be seen on the parapet of the Lungarno.

[57] Varchi, II, 358.

[58] Pratiche, 7 December.

[59] Signoria, CXXXII, f. 161 (11 December).

[60] Cf. letter of Malatesta Baglione in Falletti, I, 108.

[61] Pratiche, 2 June.

[62] Signoria, CXXXIII, ff. 66–7 (28 June). *" Bamnum meretricum . . .* così descripte allo offitio dell' honestà come non descripte et quelle che volgarmente si chiamono cantoniere . . . per stare et andare in quei luoghi che dalli Sp.[ll] & dignissimi commessari deputati sopra le bocche disutili sarà loro ordinato . . . sotto pena . . . delle forche."

[63] *Ibid.* f. 73 (1 July). "Auctoritas concessa deputatis ad emictendum foras inutiles personas."

[64] Capello, letter 88 ; Varchi, II, 405–6.

[65] See Dieci, Responsive, CLI, from G. Giugni, ff. 38–41, 93, 135–6, etc. (27 October, 19 November, 6 December), and from Tosinghi (at Pisa), 235–6 (12 April) ; Dieci, Missive, XLVIII, to Giugni (1, 27 March, 19 April, 9 May) ; Ferrucci, *Despatches, passim*—e.g. 98 (2,500 lb. just despatched).

[66] Dieci, Missive, XLVIII, to B. Carducci, 25 July.

[67] Paoli (whose dyeing works were requisitioned for use as a powder factory), p. 194 ; Baldovinetti, p. 46 ; Capello, letter 84 ; Varchi, II, 410.

[68] Quoted by Gaye, II, 158.

[69] Provisioni, CCVIII, 20 December 1529.

[70] Signoria, CXXXII, f. 102, 5 January. Cf. Capello, letter 70, and Provisioni, CCIX, 6 April 1530. Nerli, p. 215, asserts that this measure was forced by the " Setta " upon the new Gonfalonier, who thought that the resources of the city were at an end.

[71] Signoria, *ibid.*

[72] *Ibid.* f. 112 (17 January) : *" Protestatio ep⁰ fesulano* (. . . suffragano & vice princ: Domini D[ni]: N. de Ridolfis car.[lla] et ep.[l] florentie) *et D. Leonardo de Guasconibus* (. . . vic⁰ dictj . . .) . . . Considerantes . . . bellum . . . supplicaverunt ut vellent hunc consensum prestere ut tertia pars bonorum . . . vendatur . . . cum eorum licentia . . . Protestantes eis quod civitas & res publica florentina esset parata hoc idem requirere a sede apostolica & cum omni humil..tione qua decet (*nisi ?*) quia presens bellum sit pro summum pontificem contra civitatem istam . . ." Cf. Nerli, pp. 215–16 ; Provisioni, *ubi supra,* f. 5 (6 April).

[73] Capello, letter 73. Cf. Ricordanze di S. Maria del Carmine, XX, f. 163. ". . . Ricordo come l'anno 1529 el commune di firenze nel tempo della guerra et assedio posa el sale a tutto . . ."

[74] Dieci, Missive, XLVIII, to orators with Pope, 23 January; Pratiche, 19 January, and, for tardiness in collecting, 13, 17, 18 February; Capello, letter 78; and instructions to Ferrucci of 7 February quoted by Falletti, I, 409. Exaction of taxes from the refugees at Pisa was recommended on 27 January (Pratiche, ad diem).

[75] Pratiche, 18 February, 1 March, 25 April, 3 May, etc.

[76] Baldovinetti, 49–50; Capello, letter 84.

[77] Provisioni, CCIX (13 April); Signoria, CXXXII, ff. 229–33–4–40 (13–26 April); Baldovinetti, p. 48 (who is slightly inaccurate in his amounts); Nerli, 223–4; Paoli, CXCVII–VIII.

[78] Pratiche, 1 March, 17 May, 1 July.

[79] Ibid. 3 May; Provisioni, ubi supra; Capello, letters 82, 84.

[80] Pratiche, ibid., Capello, letter 84. For collection of arrears, cf. Signoria, CXXXIII, f. 37 (2 June).

[81] Provisioni, ibid. f. 10 (20 May); Pratiche, 17, 20 May.

[82] Provisioni, ibid. f. 15 (9 June) (the preamble, a notable document, is published by Albèri, pp. 203–4 n.); Signoria, CXXXIII, ff. 45 and 58–9 (9, 24 June). Capello (letter 85) says that 120,000 ducats were raised by this, instead of the 20,000 estimated. Special provision was made to deal with the quantity of bullion gathered in. Cf. Signoria, CXXXIII, f. 53 (18 June): "Commandamento a S^{ri} di Zeccha circa il battere argenti. . . . Atteso come per la provisione facta . . . viene di continuo in decta zeccha buona somma d'oro & argento . . . et non volendo per questo in modo alcuno guastare la lega dell' argento fiorentino . . . che mandino a taglio de grossi, o bacili o quinti più libra che al presente non fanno."

[83] Provisioni, ibid. f. 18 (7 July). Cf. Capello, letter 88.

[84] Ibid.; Signoria, ibid. f. 79 (8 July); Varchi, 359. Cf. indignant account in Ricordanze di S. Maria del Carmine, XIX, f. 69: ". . . Stata la città assediata mesi 14 (sic) quale venne in tanta penuria che si mangiava e' cavalli gli asini & simili animali. . . . Ma quella seta pessima da piagnoni . . . e' quali . . . si dettono allj benj della chiesa e di quelli vendreono la terzia parte autoritate propria; e quello non servendo spoglioronlla di tutti gliarienti calicj croce mercililj et altre cose dedicate al divino culto. Dover al nostro Monasterio tolsino diciotto calicj colleloro patere tutte dariente. Dua terxibilj dariento colle sua nacinelle li quali tutti pesorono colmalanno che dio die loro colla loro piagnoreria libere otto et O° I. Ancor hebbono dua bacinj dariento pesorono liber uno & once diciotto un paio danpolle dariento per la messa cantando pesorono una conun paio di poppe da donna di tutte queste cose privorono el convento que' bani e' quali quelli venderono la sanctità del nostro signiore papa clemente li face. . . ." See also ibid. vol. XX, f. 170: "Ricordo come lanno 1530 dalmese di luglio nel tempo della guerra e che la nostra città era assediata per potere pagare asoldatj si vinsa pel consiglio magiore e faciesi una leghe che tutti li arienti e ori diche sorte si fussino si dovessino consegniare e dare a . . . loro ministri infra tutto 15 di detto mese. . . . E a dì 13 di detto mesa e anno consegnia li infrascritti arienti cioè. . . ." Cf. also Tre Ricordi estratti da un libro del Monastero di Ripoli, ubi supra, p. 166 ff. Among the confiscated property were the silver lamps made for the Annunziata by Tommaso Ghirlandaio (Vasari, II, 201).

[85] Signoria, ibid. ff. 55–6, 60, 75 (20, 25 June, 3 July). See Ignazio Orsini, Storia delle Monete della Repubblica Fiorentina (Florence, 1760), pp. liii–iv, with engraving, p. 310. Cf. also note of Pierrugues in Roseo, pp. 298–9.

⁸⁶ Cf. Pratiche, 23 July.

⁸⁷ Signoria, CXXXII, f. 57 (16 December): "Auctorità a Franc°
Zati & Jacopo Corsi di potere accactare danarj in quel di Pisa." Cf.
Dieci, Responsive, CLI, ff. 235–6 (12 April), and f. 281 (19 April):
". . . Come s'è decto per più nostre andiamo al continuo pensando et
examinando et exequendo tutti i modi da poterci valere di denarj per
potere mantenere questa gentj, inche duriamo faticha incredibile . . .
Speriamo V.S. non ci habbino amancare del possibile . . . et . . . facessino d'havere denari in Lucca copertamente . . . Domattina cominciamo
amettere mano in queste cose ecclesiastiche, che dio cene dia gratia . . .
dato che ancora domani scopriamo uno accatto universale di Ducati duo
mila novecento per pagare ottocento fanti per guardia qui della città. . . ."
Cf. also their letters of 21 and 25 July in *Francesco Ferrucci*, etc., 280,
282 ; and Capello, letter 81. The confiscation of a third part of religious
property at Pisa was authorized by the Consiglio Maggiore on 31 March
(Provisioni, *ad diem*).

⁸⁸ For the taxation during the siege, see the special section in Falletti,
I, 409–19. The most graphic contemporary account is that of Paoli,
CXCVII–VIII. According to Carducci's confession (for what it is worth,
having been extracted under torture) some of these monetary provisions,
especially that for confiscating the Church silver, were pushed through
somewhat irregularly, neglecting the requisite proportion of the majority,
owing to the exigencies of the situation. Cf. Bardi, *Filippo Strozzi da
nuovi documenti, ubi supra*. But according to the provision of 16 May 1527
(see App. of Docs. *n.* 2) only a bare majority was required, in the Ottanta
at least; for monetary provisions, instead of the normal two-thirds.

⁸⁹ Cf., for example, Ferrucci, despatch 82 ; and Capello, letters 77, 78,
81, 82.

⁹⁰ Dieci, Missive, XLVIII, to Carducci, 12 March. Cf. also letter to
commissaries of Pisa of 27 January in Falletti, I, 445 *n.*

⁹¹ Quoted *ibid.* p. 447.

⁹² Cambi, IV, 64–5.

⁹³ Signoria, CXXXII, f. 178 (3 March) ; Capello, letter 80 ; Paoli,
CXCVIII ; and especially Cambi, IV, 52–3.

⁹⁴ Pratiche, 20 April.

⁹⁵ *Ibid.* 25 *idem.* Cf. Falletti, I, 411–15, and Varchi, II, 334–8.

⁹⁶ Varchi, II, 433.

⁹⁷ See Cambi's solemn account and Savonarolan observations, *Istorie*,
IV, 60–1. Cf. Capello, letter 84.

⁹⁸ Varchi, II, 355–6 ; decided on in Pratica of 21 June. Carducci's
attitude was again typical. More material expedients, he urged, should
not be forgotten: ". . . che senza intermissione queste forze si esperi-
mentino, perchè non dubitano che quello che non potranno le forze lo
farà iddio. . . . Qui si consuma e danari, viveri, e soldati. Ogni dì importa un anno ; et benchè si habbino a ordinare tali processioni si operi
pure che non si perdi un momento di tempo. . . ."

⁹⁹ Paolo Paoli and the anonymous diarist *apud* Lupo Gentile, *ubi supra*.

¹⁰⁰ Signoria, CXXXIII, ff. 51–2 (17 June) ; Giovio, II, 177. Varchi,
II, 187, hopelessly antedates the occurrence.

¹⁰¹ Giovio, II, 177.

¹⁰² "Del continuo sono ragugliati d' ogni vostra deliberatione," writes
Giugni to the Dieci (18 June), warning them against espionage (Dieci,
Responsive, CLI, f. 505). The sortie towards Empoli was one of the
operations betrayed to the enemy; see Bardi, letter 117.

¹⁰³ Varchi, II, 408. It must not be thought that Florence was wholly
lacking in espionage service ; cf. payments to six spies in O.G., CCIII,

f. 148. It was probably for secret service that 1,000 ducats were granted to Francesco Carducci at the end of October to disburse without giving any account. (Nerli, p. 200: his insinuations that it was for his own personal use may be neglected.)

[104] Signoria, CXXXIII, f. 75 (3 July) ; Varchi, II, 406–8 ; Nerli, p. 233 ; Capello, letter 88 ; Cambi, 64–5. Soderini had been acquitted by the Quarantia only on 24 May (Signoria, *ibid*. f. 21)—presumably for his suspicious conduct in retiring to Lucca after the loss of Prato (Nardi, p. 222).

[105] Pratiche, 25, 30 May, 2 June.

[106] Letter of Pierfrancesco de' Bardi (24 October) from London, in Sanuto, LII, 245.

[107] Hauvette, p. 88 *seqq*., and documents. Cf. my article, " England and the Last Florentine Republic," *ubi supra*.

[108] Cf. despatches to Bartolommeo Gualterotti, orator at Venice, in Dieci, Missive, XLVIII, especially 6, 21, and above all 30 June: " Che voi siate affaticato invano con li mercanti nostri ci dispiace assai, non tanto per il bisogno che havevamo del loro aiuto, quanto per vedere in loro sì poco amore verso la patria. . . ." Cf. Varchi, II, 361–3. It is to be noted that the patriotism of the Florentines at Venice was already seriously suspect. See *supra*, p. 135.

[109] Varchi, II, 279–80. Cf. also Capello, letter 81.

[110] Dieci, Missive, XLVIII, to B. Carducci (9 February 1529/30).

[111] *Ibid.* 23 January, 16 April.

[112] Hauvette, pp. 84–90, with documents ; and " England and the Last Florentine Republic," *ubi supra*. Hauvette's account is supplemented by the despatches to Carducci of 30 March, 27 and 29 April, in Dieci, Missive, XLVIII, and by his despatch of 27 April in Dieci, Responsive, CLI, f. 367 ; and also by the intercepted despatch in *State Papers, Spanish*, IV, i, 237, which should be dated 25 April 1530 instead of 25 December 1529. Cf. my article, p. 187. He has overlooked in addition the very important despatch of the commissaries of Pisa of 12 April in Dieci, Responsive, CLI, ff. 235–6—a deciphered copy: " . . . È comparso qui sino hieri Archangelo Migliorati da Prato Canc.[ro] di Luigi Alamanni : lettere non ci ha portato ma di boccha ricercha in che grado si trovino e' casi di questa città. . . . Referisce non esser comparso altri denari che 4[m] ma dice esser in speranza di XIJ[m]. Ricercha ancora che fanterie si potrebbono fare in questo luogo quando accadessi, et pare che habbi in disegno che qui si dovessi fare sforzo per levare cotesta machia da coteste mura : et noi di boccha medesimamente rispondemmo che dua mila in tre mila fanti si farebbono di buona gente et anco in brevità di tempo. . . . Lo confortammo con questo intendimento in noi medesimi che quando comparissi qui questo mobile non lo tocchare in parte alcuna sanza l'ordine di V.S. perche non sappiamo a che sia destinata questa massa . . . et lui sene ritornerà questo dì o domani alla volta di genova sulla fregata sua come è venuto. . . ." On 26 April (*ibid*. ff. 324–6) they express their surprise at not having heard from him again. It was hoped to obtain a considerable loan from a Florentine resident in France as early as the spring of the previous year. Cf. Dieci, Missive, to Carducci, 31 May 1529: " . . . È ci è fatto intendere come in corte è uno nostro cittadino il quale servirebbe la città d. $\frac{M}{XXX}$ per andare creditore a librij del commune con utilità di 5 per 100. . . ." The idea of financial assistance from Lyons with private and public utility combined goes back to the autumn (*ibid*., to the same, 1 September 1529). There was some disappointment at the meagreness of the sum collected in spite of the great hopes raised ; and the high-minded Alamanni was accused of having lost it at gaming—his solitary vice (Varchi, II, 323). A further 3,000

ducats arrived in July (see *Francesco Ferrucci*, etc., p. 282), which sum would resolve Hauvette's difficulty about the discrepancies of the various records as to the amount received.   The plan was known in the Imperialist camp by 23 April, though the seriousness of Francis' intentions was doubted.   Cf. Bardi, letter 116.

[113] Pratiche, LXII, 20 July 1529.

[114] Dieci, Responsive, CLI, f. 369, from Gualterotti, 5 April ; and Missive, XLVIII, to the same, 6 June.

[115] Dieci, Responsive, *ibid.* f. 486, 3–5 June.

[116] Dieci, Missive, *ibid.* to Giugni, 7 and 21 June, and to Gualterotti, 12 June.   Cf. Falletti, I, 448.

[117] Dieci, Responsive, *ibid.* ff. 504–5, 506–7, 508, etc. (from G. Giugni, 19 and 27 June, 5 July, etc.).   " Et non havendo altra commodità, per una parte V.S. vendino la casa mia di Firenze " (f. 507).

[118] Dieci, Missive, *ibid.*, to the same, 16 July.

[119] Dieci, Responsive, *ibid.* ff. 507–8, from the same, 6 July ; *State Papers, Spanish*, IV, i. 361, 363.   That the plot was known to the enemy is shown by a reference in *Letters and Papers, Henry VIII*, IV, 6476 *ad fin.*

[120] *State Papers, Spanish*, IV, i, 361.

[121] *Ibid.* 306 ; Varchi, II, 245–6.   *Letters and Papers, Henry VIII*, IV, 6489, 6499.

[122] The question is discussed in Appendix II, "The Turkish Succour," at the close of this volume.

[123] See despatch of Mai of 30 July (Appendix of Documents, No. 15) : " Tambien escrive que ayunbavan el Embaxador de Ferrara con el de Florencia que ambos son letrados con los foraxidos del reyno que alli estan." Cf. Robert, Doc. 344, and Signoria, CXXXII, f. 56 (9 December 1529) : " Bando che cittadini che sono fuora del dominio de Firenze per tutta ytalia *excepto a Napoli* tornino in Firenze."

[124] Dieci, Missive, XLVIII, to Giugni, 24 March.

[125] " La Magna è tutta sublevata," wrote the Dieci hopefully to the commissaries of Pisa on 28 February (Carteggio Originale, XII, f. 172). In Signoria, Carteggio, Missive, Registri, LVIII, there are credentials to the Duke of Saxony for Tommaso Lorenzo de' Lapi, a Florentine merchant.   They are dated 15 December 1529—just the period of the proposed advances to England and the Sultan ; and it is the only ostensibly *mercantile* recommendation noticed in this register.   The Lapi were one of the strongest Republican families ; and John, Elector of Saxony, the most influential leader of the Reformers.   All this is significant if not convincing.

[126] Dieci, Responsive, CLI, from Giugni, ff. 504–7 (7 June, 5 July) ; Missive, XLVIII, to same, 19 July ; Capello, letter 79 (4 March).   If Ercole Bentivoglio, the poet, indeed abandoned the besieging army during the war, this is more likely to have been the reason than a sudden remorse.   It might also explain the Pope's hurried departure from Bologna, put down to his fear of Orange's emulating the exploits of Bourbon (Pastor, **X**, 101).

[127] Dieci, Missive, XLVIII, to Gualterotti, 6, 21, 30 June.

[128] Varchi, II, 340–1, 411, 413.

[129] Dieci, *ibid.* to Giugni, 4 June :   " I S.ᵈ di Vernio se faranno quello che dimostrate havere in animo, non solamente troveranno appresso di noi perdono, ma saranno in modo premiati che faranno exemplo a ciascuno che volesse beneficiare la nostra repubblica. . . ." Cf. Varchi, *ubi supra.*

[130] Dieci, Responsive, CLI, ff. 475–6 ; from Carducci, 5 May ; Robert, 384–5, and Doc. 344.

[181] Dieci, Responsive, *ibid.* ff. 487, 499–500 (5, 8 June) ; and Missive, XLVIII, 7, 21 June (to and from Giugni).

[182] Dieci, Responsive, f. 241, 12 April, from Pieraduardo Giachinotti (deciphered copy).

[183] Robert, 384–5 and 392–3, with Docs. 352, 384.

[184] Mai to Charles, 20 June, in *State Papers, Spanish,* IV, i, 356.

[185] Bardi, letters 138, 139, 141 (31 May, 2–3 June). Cf. despatches in *State Papers, Spanish,* IV, i, 342, 385, 386, 559, and Mai's letter of 5 August in Appendix of Documents, *n.* 16.

[186] Capello, letters 80, 81 ; Dieci, Missive, 16 April, to Carducci; Sanuto, LIII, 135.

[187] Despatch of Nino, Ambassador at Venice, of 28 July, in *State Papers, Spanish,* IV, i, 387. Cf. speech of Castiglione in Pratica of 8 May, urging occupation of Arezzo, and Varchi, II, 364.

[188] Dieci, Missive, XLVIII, to Carducci, 24 March.

[189] Responsive, CLI, f. 176, from Carducci, 30 March ; and 235–6, from commissaries of Pisa, 12 April (see *supra, n.* 112). Pratiche, 3, 8, 17 May.

[140] Responsive, *ibid.* ff. 235–6, from commissaries of Pisa, 12 April.

[141] *Ibid.* f. 505, from Giugni, 18 June. Cf. despatch of Mai of 7 June in Bergenroth Transcripts, IX, 125 *seqq.* : " . . . Demas desto tuvo nuevas el papa que en ferrara se hazia gente y en toda la rromaña, y que tambien se hazia en Padua y en tierra de Venecianos por Rrenzo de Chierri, y que en ferrara sacavan municion a beneficio de florentines y que el duque se escusava con dezir que lo compravan por su dinero, y que el Pr^te de la rromaña avia desarmado y derramado algunos infantes que se avian fecho en lugo. . . ." Similarly in despatch of Muxetula of 15 June, *ibid.*

[142] " Even without payment " (Varchi, II, 323–4). For the life of Giovanpaolo, see note in *Francesco Ferrucci,* etc., p. 495.

[143] Dieci, Responsive, CLI, ff. 367, 475–6, from B. Carducci, 27 April, 5 May.

[144] Letter of 7 May in Dieci, Responsive, CLI, f. 406. It would seem that Bardi, the Sienese envoy, was misled when he believed that he had actually come to Florence (letter 129 of 14 May). According to a despatch to Gualterotti (Dieci, Missive, XLVIII, 6 June), Giovanpaolo gathered 3,000 troops in Pisa. The number seems exaggerated—perhaps to impress the Venetians.

[145] Dieci, Missive, XLVIII, 29 April. Cf. Responsive, CLI, ff. 235–6, from commissaries of Pisa, 12 April : " Habbiamo contento assai della buona speranza hanno vostre signorie della liberatione della città, et Dio ne conceda l'effecto per sua gratia."

[146] *Ibid.* from Carducci, 27 April. The plan was soon known to the Imperialists. Cf. Robert, Doc. 344, and Bardi, letters 127, 129; and *State Papers, Spanish,* IV, i, 311 and 335 : " Respecting Renzo's son, they say that he has already enlisted such a force to march to the relief of the Florentines as might even be sufficiently powerful to destroy the Turk." It was recognized, however, that this represented merely a pious hope.

[147] Dieci, Responsive, CLI, ff. 355–6, 6 April (deciphered copy) : " . . . Appresso veggendo la obstinatione dell' animo delli nemici vostri et pensando che la lunghezza dello assedio possa causar molti mali effetti, non voglio mancare di dire quello che mi occorre, et questo è, che io mi vanterei di mandar in Campo due o tre con merce appestate per il qual mezo saria facil cosa mettere il fuoco in cotesto campo, havendo loro maxime in questa vernata patito alquanto et essendo lì in campo per quanto intendo molte bestie morte, cose tutte nutritive di tale infermità : et questa mi daria l'animo di fare con una spesa di cento scudi o manco :

et se non fosse ch'io non so che Commercio sia tra li vostri et li di Campo, mediante il quale tale contagione potria trasferirsi in la Città, io lo haurei messo ad effetto sanza com^{ne} vostra.   Ma per tal causa mi sono restato, et aspetterò la deliberatione di quella . . ."

[148] Carteggio Originale, XII, f. 435 : " Che quanto prima possibile si guastino et attosichino tutti li pozzi e aque buone allo intorno di Pisa." This isolated passage, without date or superscription, belongs by position to the early summer of 1530.   It is presumably the decipherment of a portion of another despatch.

[149] Bardi, letter 132 (22 May) : " . . . Ancor che la cominciasse molti giorni sono."   Cf. Varchi, II, 358 : " Non s'intese in che modo vi entrò."

[150] Bardi, letters 135, 142 ; Robert, p. 394 and Doc. 360 ; letter of Mai of 30 July in Appendix of Documents, No. 15 : " El Principe ha estado malo, y pusonos en sospecha de su persona."   In the Giornali del Principe d'Orange, p. 30 (18 July), there is noted a payment of " six crowns to Robinet, his apothecary, for drugs, syrups, and other medicines."   See also for the plague in the camp, Letters and Papers, Henry VIII, IV, iii, 6511, and State Papers, Henry VIII, VII, n. 276 (Harvy to King, Osburgh, 11 July): " . . . The said Cardynall shewed me also that th' Emperour had worde how as well the town as camp at Florence is infected with the plaghe, and that th' Emperour is in doubt of the Prince of Orange his chief capten, and the residue of his people ther. . . ."

[151] See speech of Bernardo da Castiglione in Pratiche, 2 June : " Sper-ando che per questa via, e della peste . . . potessi venire qualche salute." Cf. State Papers, Henry VIII, I, 200 (Heneage to Wolsey, 18 August 1530): " . . . The Florentynes dothe styll contenew and defende the power of the Pope, and it is supposed that they shall vynce, by meane that ther ys a gret pestylence fallen amongyst them, being in the felde, of the Pope's partye . . .": and ibid. VII, 279 (Wellysburn to the King, Angou-lême, 23 July): " . . . Ther is very great dethe in the campe : ther do dye dayly 2 or 3 hundred a day, wiche is haulf a rescous for the Floren-tines. . . ."

[152] Varchi, II, 350, 412 ; Capello, letter 88 (14 July).

[153] Varchi, II, 418.   The charge is examined and denied by Robert, 408-9.

[154] See letter of Sanga in Lettere di Principi, II, 199.

[155] See report of Muxetula of 21 August in Appendix of Documents, No. 17.   For Maramaldo's troubles, see De Blasiis, III, 358-9, and Doc. XI (letter of Sanga of 2 June).

[156] Varchi, II, 443.

[157] Robert, 407-9, amplified by letter of Gonzaga to Marquis of Mantua of 7 July in Sanuto, LIII, 366-7.

[158] Ibid. 331 (29 June).

[159] Pastor, X, 101.   The expenses which passed through the hands of Baccio Valori alone totalled upwards of 550,000 ducats.   His accounts during the siege have been published by Passerini in Giornale Storico degli Archivi Toscani, I, 1657 (p. 106 seqq.).

[160] Robert, 393-4, and Docs. 357-8.

[161] See despatch of Muxetula of 7 June in Appendix of Documents, No. 11 ; and Robert, Docs. 358-9.

[162] Robert, 389-91, with authorities there cited and Doc. 355 especially : Varchi, II, 349-55, and Giovio, II, 201-3.   Cf. Dieci, Missive, XLVIII, to Giugni, 21 June ; Capello, letter 85 ; Sanuto, LIII, 305 ; State Papers, Spanish, IV, i, 6499.   The dispositions of the troops for the sortie, dated 20 June, are printed in Francesco Ferrucci, etc., 366-70.

[163] Seconda Calamità Volterrana, 27-8 ; Sassetti, p. 100 seqq. ; Giovio,

II, 192–3 ; *Francesco Ferrucci*, etc., despatches 101–4. De Blasiis, III, 354, *n.* 1, examines and confirms the accusation that on the capture of Volterra, Ferrucci starved to death and then hanged fourteen Spaniards.

164 Ferrucci's partisans assert that he was bearing treasonable correspondence. Cf. De Blasiis, III, 356, *n.* 1.

165 " Maramaldo " in Neapolitan is Maramau = Miaou. This was a common sign of contempt. See *Francesco Ferrucci*, etc., 338–42.

166 For the defence of Volterra, see *Seconda Calamità Volterrana*, pp. 28–36 ; Ferrucci, despatches 106–7 ; Robert, 402–5, with authorities there cited ; De Blasiis, III, 354–64 ; Giovio, II, 197–200. It is depicted in one of Vasari's frescoes.

167 Ferrucci, despatches 116–21 ; Varchi, II, 404 *seqq.*; *Seconda Calamità Volterrana*, pp. 36–7.

CHAPTER XI

THE FALL OF FLORENCE

THE brilliant enterprises of Ferrucci provided a solitary gleam of hope upon the Florentine horizons. Elsewhere, there was none. The only friendly gesture forthcoming in Italy was that of Venice, which offered herself as mediator with the inevitable result, but made no other answer to the city's pitiful appeals and Capello's eloquent pleadings to provide even a loan.[1] Some reliance, however, was still pinned in the northerly powers, England and France. The former was the more distant and the less interested, but it had drifted still further into opposition to the Pope and Emperor over the vexed question of the Royal Divorce. The Florentine request for help had accordingly been taken up and encouraged by the party of Anne Boleyn, headed by her father, the Earl of Wiltshire. As a result, envoys had been delegated to the English court and negotiations for a heavy monetary subvention in conjunction with France had been initiated. But the proposals were automatically contested by the pro-Imperial party under the Duke of Norfolk, and were countered by the Pope by a fresh move in the matter of the divorce. As a result, nothing happened for a considerable time. Finally, the powerful advocacy of Wiltshire triumphed and brought about a monetary accommodation with the Florentine merchants in London which should have been to the advantage both of the King and of the city. At the same time, Henry, as part of the bargain and in order to exert pressure on the Pope, seems to have set about preparing an independent mercenary force in Italy to relieve Florence, and was reported to have been ready to assume the burden of defence. But by this time it was too late for his intentions, whatever they were, to be carried into effect. The experiences of the last Florentine Republic with England remained a record of expectations fruitlessly raised and of promises inadequately fulfilled.[2]

The hopes centred in England were, however, in every sense secondary to those based upon France. If the heart of any Florentine were opened, ran the saying, a lily of gold would be found in it in testimony of their one political devotion. And so, in spite of repeated disappointments, the hope lived on that when times were more auspicious Francis I would show in deeds

that he did not forget the fidelity of his old allies.   He continued
to be propitiated during the siege, as before it, by gifts of those
objects of art of which he was such an ardent collector, through
the medium of Battista della Palla.[3]   On his side he did everything to foster confidence, professing to believe that all the worth
and honour of Italy was centred in Florence, and promising that
on the restoration of his sons he would convert his words into
deeds.[4]   The Florentine ambassador was advised to pray to
God for the speedy consummation of that happy event, " for from
that restitution will arise your redemption."   Not only the King
in person but also his ministers, and even the Queen Mother, all
encouraged him to wait patiently and to have confidence.[5]   As
to Francis' ultimate intentions, they were long in materializing.
In spite of the insistence of the Florentines that it was money
and not men of which they stood in need, he persisted in
toying with the idea of sending Antonio Doria to help them,
which would merely add to their burden.   In his more expan-
sive moments he continued to adumbrate grandiose schemes
of coming to Italy in person with an army at his back when the
opportunity arose.[6]   He would have been glad indeed to secure
the gratitude of the Pope by acting as intermediary in a negotiated
peace, as the result of which Clement might perhaps be detached
again from the Emperor.   The Bishop of Tarbes, his envoy at
Rome, exerted himself to bring about a more conciliatory attitude
on the part of the Pope on his return from Bologna.[7]   These
efforts continued without intermission, and Francis was in hopes
that Clement would be so mollified as to render peace possible.[8]
On the receipt of the news of the fall of Empoli, he began to advise
the city openly to come to terms.[9]   As time went on, it appeared
that the delay in liberating the French princes was due to fears
of the help which he might then give Florence, and his desires for
peace became more and more pronounced.   He urged the city to
make the experiment and see whether the Pope's professions
were genuine, as, in spite of Carducci's scepticism, he insisted
they were ; and he requested the ambassador not to approach
him directly for fear of rousing suspicion.[10]   Nevertheless, his
promises of ultimate help were confirmed, and it was still hoped
that once his sons were released he would commence to put his
undertakings into execution.

Finally, on 14 June, the intelligence arrived in Florence that
this long-desired event had taken place.   At last the French
princes had crossed the frontier into their native land, and their
father was unfettered to do as he pleased.   The news was greeted
with incredible manifestations of joy.   The bells rang out all
day long from the towers and steeples, and a solemn mass of
thanksgiving was attended by all the officers of state, though the

extreme needs of the city prevented the display of fireworks and illuminations usual upon such occasions.[11] A special messenger had informed Carducci of the event at Angoulême in the middle of the night, and early the next morning he waited on the King. Francis encouraged him to be of good cheer, but again brought up the idea of coming to an agreement with Clement. Should the Emperor overcome his difficulties in Germany and with the Turk, he would be omnipotent in Europe. Only an alliance between France and England outside Italy, and Florence and the Pope within it, could oppose him ; and if the Florentines would consent to make peace, this might be possible. Count Pierfrancesco de Pontremoli, Grand Ecuyer to the King (a mission on whose part had for some time been contemplated), was delegated accordingly to go to Italy as special envoy to see whether this might be brought about without sacrificing the liberty of the city.[12] Thus, though Francis was free now to do what he would, nothing ensued. His promises of subvention had narrowed down to the 20,000 ducats to be given in conjunction with half that amount from England.[13] Of this sum, however, even if it were actually paid, only half according to the arrangement would have gone to Florence, the other half being destined for the merchants at Lyons ; while the advance actually received while the city was *in extremis* was of the hopelessly inadequate sum of 3,000 ducats.[14] This, with his offers of mediation and his continual talk of leading an army in person to Italy, was the final total of the much-talked-of and long-expected French aid. The Dieci lost their patience. " We are glad," they wrote, " that his Majesty has such good intentions towards the city, and thinks continually of her liberation ; but these do not seem to us the means to save her." [15] Carducci was instructed to congratulate Francis on the recovery of his sons, and to thank him for his benevolent intention in sending Pontremoli to Italy. But they were sure that in their present extremity the Pope would not hear of compromise. They had finished all their money and treasure, down to the silver and gold ornaments, and could do no more. If Francis really wished to help them, he should send his promised subvention by way of Pisa, and make provision of corn and saltpetre for their future requirements from his kingdom.[16] Luigi Alamanni, refused readmission to Genoa, returned to France and helped Carducci to plead at court.[17] He found the old man sick and in desperate straits. Francis had finally answered his appeals by declaring coldly that he did not wish to reveal his intentions so early, and could therefore do nothing. Carducci followed the court about through Aquitaine, where it had remained after the recovery of the princes, hoping to effect a reversal of this decision, or at least to obtain those secret subsidies of which so much had been promised. It was in vain that he overwhelmed Francis' ministers with reproaches, or with threats that Florence would destroy herself or surrender to the Emperor, thus making him omnipotent in Italy, rather than come again under the heel of the Pope. If they were stung by his declaration, it was by the menace rather than by the shame ; and they could only continue to urge that the medium of Pontremoli should be utilized as an avenue for peace.[18] Carducci had been consistently befooled ever since his arrival in France, and through his credulity Florence had been misled. His patriotic spirit could not bear up under the strain. He took to his bed and died precisely in those dark days when the fate of the city was being sealed.[19]

The Florentines were thus cast entirely upon their own resources. Nor in any case could they have afforded to wait indefinitely in hope of some problematic assistance. The condition of the city was desperate. Money was exhausted or nearly so, and, their strict rationing notwithstanding, provisions could not last out for many more weeks. Any delay might be fatal. Relief must therefore be sought immediately, and in their own arms. The victorious Ferrucci is said to have put forward an audacious plan of action. He desired to muster what forces he could and to make a sudden dash on Rome, publishing abroad his intention to submit that city to another sack. He was sure that by this he could swell his forces almost indefinitely, attracting mercenaries of all nations and even the disaffected Imperial troops. Clement would be forced either to come to an agreement with him or else to summon the Prince of Orange to his defence. In either case, Florence would be saved.[20] But the plan was too venturesome to meet with approval. Instead, Ferrucci was instructed to set about operations of a more orthodox character. It was a return to the scheme of a few months previous, which had been abandoned owing to shortage of funds and to the capture of Empoli. On this occasion it was to be attempted without augmentation of forces or of expense by employing the army of Ferrucci in conjunction with the force already prepared. He was to leave a sufficient garrison to guard Volterra, and make his way to Pisa. Here he was to join hands with Giovanpaolo da Ceri, who was placed under his command. Thus, after leaving 800 behind him as garrison, he would have 4,000 men at his disposal—a small force, but not wholly inadequate—to march with him in the direction of Florence. He was to occupy either Prato or Pistoia, which might be used as a base of operations ; or failing this he was to march directly on the city by way of Fiesole and attempt to relieve it. Meanwhile, every effort would be made to co-operate with him from inside the walls.[21]

Such was the confidence and trust now placed in Ferrucci that he was invested with powers such as no citizen of Florence had ever enjoyed—to come to an arrangement with the enemy as he thought fit, to treat for the surrender of cities, to promise any sums of money which he should desire.[22] In this enterprise, the last hope of the Republic was staked, and the Piagnoni commenced to regard their hero as a new Gideon, who should save, as surely as his prototype, the People of the Lord out of the hand of the oppressor.[23] Owing to the closeness of the blockade and the dangers of the road, the instructions took over a fortnight to reach Volterra, and it was only on 10 July that Ferrucci knew what was expected of him.[24] On the 14th, the two commissaries who were to relieve him arrived, and on the next evening he set out with about 1,500 foot and some few horse. The following day he came to Livorno, and on the 18th, by a further night march, he arrived at Pisa, where he was received with much pomp. But here, as luck had it, he fell ill, his constant activity having delayed the healing of the wound in the knee received at Volterra, which now brought on a violent fever. The expedition was immobilized during his sickness.[25] Meanwhile in the city all preparations were made to deliver a sortie on the camp when Ferrucci should have succeeded in diverting the attention of the enemy. Public opinion had hitherto been opposed to arming the lower classes even in this grave crisis. Some nevertheless continued to urge it.[26] Accordingly, a preliminary census had been held, and it was found that there were 7,000 peasants in the city fit to bear arms, and 5,700 artisans.[27] Nothing, however, was done until the commencement of July, when it was ordered that the latter class only, from the ages of sixteen to sixty, should be enrolled.[28] A few days after, the Ottanta formally approved the proposal, though the old diffidence transpired in a recommendation that only picked younger men should be selected to serve, intermingled with the regular soldiery.[29] Finally therefore prejudices were overcome, and artisans between the ages of eighteen and forty, with all householders up to sixty, were embodied in the militia. Thus virtually the whole of the male population, excepting only the peasants, was at last armed.[30] When at last the news reached Florence (20 July) that the relieving forces had joined hands at Pisa, a feverish activity commenced. Arms were sedulously distributed and the artillery put into preparation. The Imperialists, closely watching the city, observed unusual animation ; while at night the number of lights moving about the streets and on the fortifications betrayed an extraordinary activity. Warned by four separate spies of an impending attack, the besieging forces stood to arms all night in expectation, though without anything occurring; for the time had not yet arrived.[31] On the next morning the Pratica was called together and it was approved with unanimity that when the sortie took place the Gonfalonier should put himself at the head of the army and go out to fight with them, setting an heroic example to the city and to the soldiers alike.[32] On the following day, a Sunday, the whole militia, old and new, paraded together for the first time to the number of 8,000 in the Piazza della Signoria, before the eyes of the magistrates, who watched from the Loggia of Orcagna. On the following Tuesday they relieved the regular troops on the fortifications, while these paraded in their turn, 6,270 in all.[33] It was just at this period that a downright refusal was given to the Venetian offer of mediation.[34] The whole city was determined, and ready to meet its fate fighting. It was a forlorn hope, but desperation, backed up by religious enthusiasm and patriotic fire, could work wonders. Fra Benedetto da Foiano and Fra Zaccheria da Treviso had not ceased to promise victory from the church pulpits. Was it not, according to the disciples of Savonarola, precisely at the darkest hour, when no hope seemed remaining in human resources, that the heavens should open and bands of angels descend upon the battlements in full panoply of war to deliver the city? [35] If they were to fall, they could fall at least like men, " having determined that those who remain in custody of the gates and fortifications, should by adverse chance the forces of the city be routed, shall with their own hands immediately slay the women and children, and set fire to the houses, and then go out to meet the same fortune as the others, so that with the destruction of the city there shall not remain anything but the memory of the greatness of soul of its people, and that they shall be an immortal example for those who are born, and desire to live, in freedom." [36]

But if serious fighting were to take place, principal reliance must be placed on the regular soldiery. These still numbered, as we have seen, over 6,000 and had been maintained throughout the siege at ruinous expense and without any cause for discontent, although they had not been engaged in any major encounter. This was due in part at least to Malatesta Baglione, who had never shown himself over-anxious for a general engagement.[37] From the military standpoint this was at least comprehensible ; but there was another angle from which the matter could be viewed. Malatesta occupied a double position, as an independent ruler as well as a soldier of fortune. From the very commencement of his engagement it had been feared that his interests as one would outweigh his duties as the other. Not only did he send, as was natural, an envoy to accompany the Florentine embassy to the Emperor at Piacenza, but also he continued negotiations with the Pope with short interruptions until the fall of Perugia, thus giving rise to some misgivings on the part of his employers.[38] Even after that event he continued to offer his services to the Emperor when his present engagement should be at an end.[39] On his arrival in Florence after his precipitate retirement, he had been greeted with murmurings in consequence of the curiously easy terms which he had received from the enemy and of his complicity with Albizzi in the abandonment of Arezzo. These suspicions were, however, never shared by the government, who trusted their captain and continually followed his advice.[40] The arrangements for fortification and defence had been carried out in consultation with him ; he had been foremost in demanding provision for reinforcements and supplies and the expulsion of the " useless mouths " ; he manfully repulsed the attack of St. Martin's Eve, and performed all that could be expected of a faithful commander. He was known indeed to have been in communication with the Pope as early as October,[41] but there was still so much to settle in connection with his private affairs that it occasioned apparently no distrust. Even when Galeotto Giugni gave, on the strength of this, clear warning of impending treachery, no action was taken ; for though it was fully realized that his double position rendered him liable to corruption, his fidelity was as yet unquestioned.[42] It was no doubt as a consequence of this intercourse that the Pope, acting through the Bishop of Faenza, used him as a medium to invite the futile embassy of January. But the heavy majority in favour of negotiations showed that in this he was interpreting the will of the people. On the discussion of the humiliating failure of the mission, though it was considered that he might be able to throw light on the matter, there was no breath of suspicion against him personally.[43] It was moreover at this very period that he was promoted without any misgiving to the rank of Captain-General, even the most ardent patriots speaking in unmeasured terms of his services.[44] It is true that he continued to be in constant communication with Bologna,[45] but he made no secret of the matter, informing the Dieci of it without reserve.[46] However, the city had become stiffened in its attitude towards the Pope, and when on 8 February it was determined to refuse his application for fresh envoys, Malatesta was recommended to cut off all connection with the enemy and fix his mind on glory.[47]

For some time to come, nothing more was heard of negotiations. All fighting was under the ultimate direction of Baglione, and there is no ground for believing the *a posteriori* theories of his treachery during this period. If he was not perhaps as enterprising and resolute as patriotic citizens might have desired, that was the common shortcoming of all mercenaries, who had no wish to run that by which they gained their living into unnecessary peril. He showed therefore a prudence which was excessive in a situation which could be retrieved only by daring; and in the light of later events it was easy to read actual treachery in his over-cautious action during the " incamiciate " of 11 December and 5 May, in which greater enterprise and more wholehearted support might, it was thought, have brought about complete victory.[48] It was of obvious advantage to the city to avoid the endless delays and lack of secrecy of the old method by creating the " restricted council " over military affairs, and that he and Colonna proposed it in the middle of May cannot be taken as proof of treason. Public opinion, indeed, already accused him of something more than mere apathy. On the receipt of the news of the fall of Empoli, the Gonfalonier complained before the Pratica of the charges which were being openly voiced against the captains.[49] Yet it was unanimous in urging that these slanders should be stopped. Not a single member, though they were better informed than any private person, had a word to say in confirmation; and ardent patriots like Francesco Carducci were most decided in their deprecation. At this very same meeting the restricted council in which the captains had the preponderating voice was confirmed. Almost immediately afterwards, in order to make good the recent defeat, a sortie towards Empoli was proposed. The captains, however, " expressly protested that to fight will be our final ruin," but declared themselves willing to go out to battle if it should be definitely ordered. Outnumbered as their forces were by the besiegers, it was a natural attitude to adopt. Even the most ardent members of the Pratica—men like Francesco Carducci and Bernardo da Castiglione—deferred to this expert opinion and advised waiting for outside co-operation. Only a minority of the representatives of the super-patriotic quarter of Santa Croce still urged immediate assault. The offer of the captains was therefore not accepted, and the restricted war-council was again confirmed.[50] It was three weeks after this date that the great " incamiciata " of 21 June was carried out. However much caution Malatesta may have shown, he could almost certainly have prevented it altogether, as he would decidedly have done had he been already in agreement with the enemy; and it was directed with an irreproachable gallantry by Stefano Colonna, who was his steadfast accomplice in whatever afterwards occurred.[51] Not only did responsible persons inside the city have as yet no belief in Malatesta's ill-faith. What is more important, in the long and virtually complete series of despatches of the Imperialist agents at this period, there is no reference to the possibility of seducing Malatesta from his allegiance. Even Orange himself, with whom all ultimate negotiations were carried on, shows no knowledge whatever of any such scheme.

Malatesta was, however, as has been pointed out, in an exceptional position. Apart from his engagement as a mercenary captain, he was, or had been till recently, an independent ruler ; and he had private interests to look after as well as those of his employers. It was true indeed that for the convenience of the moment the Pope had consented in the previous autumn to forgo all vengeance, to abandon the cause of his kinsmen, and to allow him full enjoyment of his property in Perugia. But it was hardly to be doubted that, at the first convenient opportunity, he would go back on his agreement without the slightest scruple ; and in that case, Malatesta would find himself destitute. His rivals, Braccio and Sforza, were fighting in the ranks of the Imperial army, obviously awaiting this juncture. His whole future was bound up with that of Florence ; but what if Florence should be forced to give in ? The attitude of Clement towards the captain who had directed the defence of the rebellious city might well be imagined. It was far from certain that Florence could hold out by her own exertions. The problem in the situation was the position of France, whose king was for the rest Malatesta's patron and, nominally, part employer. If Francis should intervene, Florence was reasonably safe and Malatesta would even have some chance of regaining Perugia. If he remained apathetic, Florence could hardly hope for victory and Malatesta's personal position would be hopeless. It was necessary therefore to sound the intentions of the French court. Accordingly, early in April, Malatesta sent an agent thither to treat of " certain private affairs." The Dieci were informed of this, and recommended him to their ambassador in France, instructing him, however, to endeavour to be present at any interview.[52] Carducci did as he was told, but was unable to find out that Malatesta's man had any errand excepting to ask whether his master's " condotta " was to continue and what were the intentions of Francis, " because, having already for eight months sustained this siege without impediment, he would not wish in the end to lose his pains, his honour, and perhaps his life ; and therefore he desires to know His Majesty's views and whether he wishes to give assistance." [53] The envoy must have found out what was already painfully apparent : that Francis was most unlikely to carry any of his specious promises into effect.

It was without doubt this knowledge which led Malatesta to disobey the instructions which had been given him and enter again into some sort of negotiation with the Pope. " The practices commenced between His Holiness and Malatesta are getting on better than ever," wrote the well-informed Sienese envoy in camp on 23 May. " A man of Malatesta, come secretly from Rome, is negotiating with his most illustrious lordship (the Prince of Orange). When he is in agreement with the Pope, Florence must surrender, for he has the *bâton* in his hand." After the fall of Empoli the negotiations became even more promising, and the man of Malatesta returned to camp.[54] But Bardi seems to have been too sanguine. Negotiations were indeed going on : but no secret was made of them in Florence, where the only opportunity of sending despatches outside the walls was through the medium of Malatesta's emissary. The only result of the conversations was that a familiar of the Pope's came from Rome and lodged with Malatesta in order to invite the delegation of fresh envoys to treat for peace. The reply was the invariable one— that Florence did not desire to speak of the subject any more, and that if Clement felt so inclined he might send his envoys to her.[55] Nor was there known in Rome, where it was believed that Malatesta was speaking with the authorization of his employers, anything excepting of regular negotiations for peace.[56] It may be presumed, therefore, that these conversations were probably on the old subject of the settlement of Perugia, and that incidentally, in order to ingratiate himself with the Pope, Malatesta had offered his services once again as intermediary. As yet, as we have seen, none of the Imperial agents, however important, had any inkling of agreement : nor was any suspicion felt among well-informed circles in Florence. It is incomprehensible why, if Malatesta was actively conspiring since the commencement of the siege as the older historians allege, or from this point only as a modern inquirer holds, it should have been necessary to sustain the war at ruinous expenditure till the following August.

In the meantime, Malatesta had still been considered a sufficiently formidable opponent to be got out of the way—had he been a traitor it would have been more advisable to maintain him where he was. The Pope was continually expressing his discontent at the attitude of Francis towards the Florentines, and the Bishop of Tarbes, who was angling for a Cardinal's hat, sent a special messenger from Rome to convey Clement's displeasure at the encouragement and support they were receiving from him. Disclaimers were impossible when the three principal captains in the city's employment—Malatesta, Colonna, and Giovanpaolo da Ceri—were technically his men, and showed greater respect to their distant patron than to their actual paymasters ; and he was requested to order them to leave the service of sworn enemies of His Holiness. Francis, fearing for his children, as yet unreleased, did not dare to refuse ; yet he was not so lacking in sympathy as to comply without reserve. He sent back the messenger to Rome with a man of his own to inform

Tarbes of his compliance and to convey to the commanders in question his order to leave the Florentine service. At the same time, he ordered Malatesta's envoy to return immediately to Florence and to instruct his master and the others to continue in their allegiance in all assurance of his approval and support, without paying attention to any contradictory order which they might receive. Carducci, informed of this, wrote confidently home to inform the government how matters stood, and warning them not to be discouraged by any conflicting instructions which might arrive through official channels.[57] He was foolish enough to entrust his despatch to Malatesta's man, to whom Francis had warily given only a verbal message. Returning post-haste to Florence, he was arrested at Asti. Carducci's letters were seized and deciphered, for the code was no longer secret ; and neither messenger nor message ever got through to Florence.[58] The result of the matter was, that Malatesta can have received only those instructions through the medium of Tarbes which had been intended merely as a sop for the Pope ; Francis' true intentions never reached him. It was not long since that, taxed with being responsible for encouraging the hopes of the Florentines, he replied that the encouragement came from a much higher source —from France.[59] Now that encouragement was cut off. He found himself precisely in the position which he had feared. Excepting in the remote contingency of a Florentine victory— not merely of a successful defence—his position and prospects at Perugia and his whole future would be at the mercy of the Pope. He would not even have any prospect of receiving the support of France, for fidelity to Florence meant disobedience to his more powerful patron. Nor was this mere pretence : for we have seen how insistent he had been on the approval of Francis from the very commencement of his engagement.

This intelligence confirmed the growing conviction in Malatesta's mind that victory for the Florentines was impossible. They had tried for nearly a year to outwear the besiegers, but without success. Their expectations of outside assistance had been disappointed. Their food was rapidly running out. Their last hope lay in a general assault. It was very well for ardent patriots, borne up by a religious conviction, to regard the prospect with confidence. Malatesta, however, was a professional soldier, in whose calculations enthusiasm, patriotism, and religion did not enter. With little more than 6,000 soldiers, weakened by months of privation, he was expected to assault in their positions a vastly superior number of the finest troops in Europe.[60] He would be aided, it was true, by the militia ; but a large part of the militia were raw levies, and they were regarded under any circumstance with diffidence by the professional. It was only the eye of patriotic enthusiasm that could see in this forlorn hope any prospect of victory. In the far more probable event of defeat, not only would the army be annihilated, but also the city after its long defence would be submitted to the inevitable sack. That he would find himself defenceless, disowned by his patron of France, and exposed to the vindictiveness of the Pope, was another consideration. Malatesta conceived that, in safeguarding his own interests, he would be at the same time considering the best interests of his employers.[61]

It was precisely at this period that chance or craft threw into his hands an excellent opportunity of entering into negotiations with the enemy on terms of especial favour. A young Navarese groom serving with the Imperial forces had recently been captured. While he was being examined by representatives of the Dieci, the prisoner suggested that by reason of his intimacy with the Pope's cellarer, he might be able to secure his death by poison. " I would get you given a thousand ducats if you did," cried Jacopo Gherardi, Capponi's old antagonist. " A thousand ! " echoed his colleague, Andrea Tedaldi, " ten thousand, rather ! " [62] Arrangements were made : but as was invariable in Florence, the secret got out and came to the ears of Malatesta, who under the circumstances discovered a squeamishness not previously to be noticed in his nature. On 21 June, after the great " incamiciata," he sent secretly to the camp to inform his old comrade in arms, Pirro Colonna, of the plot. He was serving Florence, he said, as a soldier and not as an executioner, and could not tolerate such practices. In consequence special watch was kept, and the Navarese was arrested coming out of the city bearing a couple of flasks presumed to contain poison distilled in pure water, with antidotes for those who were to administer it. On being put to torture, he confessed that they were given to him to take to Rome, and mentioned an innkeeper of that city and certain Papal attendants who were in the plot. Pirro Colonna was sent post-haste to give warning ; and the Pope in great alarm had the persons implicated arrested and put to torture. In that direction, however, it appears that the alarm was exaggerated.[63] Contemporary as well as subsequent apologists set the matter down as a mere fabrication intended to bring the Florentines into discredit. But the evidence to the contrary is too general, too consistent, and too strong. Nor is there anything inherently improbable in the tale.[64] We have seen that the Florentines did not hold the idea of poison in peculiar abhorrence, nor the person of the Pope in any great reverence. Moreover, the combination against them was built up exclusively upon a single individual. The death of Clement would automatically have broken it up, have deprived the war of its whole *raison d'être*, and have secured their deliverance. The Pope professed an extreme gratitude towards Malatesta for the information, by which his life had been saved. It was recognized that his action was not wholly disinterested, especially as he had desired that the Pope should know from whom it had come. From this moment—and not before—it was trusted in official circles on the Imperialist side that it might be possible to force Florence to come to an agreement through the medium of her Captain-General.[65]

These hopes were not belied. Towards the middle of July, Malatesta commenced to take matters into his own hands. Taking advantage of his revived intimacy with Pirro Colonna, he sent to camp (10 July) one of his own Perugian captains, Vincenzo Piccioni, whose unlovely appearance had secured him the sobriquet of Cencio Guercio (i.e. " squint-eyed ") to request an interview with the Prince of Orange. To him he proposed sending an envoy into the city to speak to the people and invite them to make peace, warning them that this was their last chance and threatening the horrors of sack in case of refusal. The person suggested was Fernando Gonzaga, who as an Italian and brother of the Marquis of Mantua was likely to meet with a sympathetic reception. Orange, who thus far certainly had no secret agreement with Malatesta, signified that he was willing to do what was requested of him and to send in an envoy to treat for peace, on the understanding that the Medici should be readmitted with full rights; and Pirro was himself sent to inform Baglione of the decision, which was conveyed by him to the Signoria. It so happened that this coincided with the receipt of the news of the release of the two French princes, which encouraged resistance. But in any event the Prince's condition would have been inacceptable. After two days, therefore, Pirro was sent back to the camp, and the official negotiations were broken off.[66]

This suggestion of Malatesta's was, however, accompanied by a more sinister proposal. He had seen how the sufferings of Florence could be exploited to his own advantage ; and he realized the prospects of regaining at the price of his honour the position from which he had been ousted eleven months previously. He gave it to be understood that on certain conditions he would use his influence to the utmost to make Florence come to terms. So at least is to be understood from the fact that from this moment the Imperialists were absolutely confident in their victory if only they would consent to pay him his price. " The other part of the negotiation concerns Malatesta," wrote the Spanish ambassador to his master, " and I think that the Pope will be forced to return him to Perugia because of this . . ."[67] This is absolutely the first official indication of any treasonable practice : and it shows definitely that no arrangement was as yet concluded. Every reluctance was indeed displayed on the other side to so great a concession, which would again settle an old adherent of the King of France in a key position of central Italy ; and Charles ordered that if possible this should be avoided.[68] There were, however, certain considerations which made it important to utilize Baglione's services if it were possible. The hopes which had been aroused by the negotiations through Pirro were now known to have been premature, and a spontaneous surrender seemed to be as unlikely as ever. Through Malatesta's intervention, the duration of the war with its enormous expenses, and the lengthy peace negotiations which might follow, would be cut short. The perils of sack, which Clement had been dreading as his moral and financial ruin, would be averted. Finally, there seemed a possibility that if matters were much longer protracted the Count of Pontremoli, with his special influence at Florence, might be able to bring about a negotiated peace on behalf of the King of France.[69] By this, Clement would obtain less favourable terms, while Charles would run the risk of losing his most valuable ally. If, on the other hand, Pontremoli failed to negotiate peace, it was not impossible that Francis, now somewhat recuperated after his exertions, would at length intervene in a military sense. Nor was the possibility of diversion from other quarters—England, or Turkey, or even nearer home—to be overlooked. It was of importance, therefore, to reduce the city to terms with the minimum of delay. Ultimately, opposition was modified, and we may imagine that it was signified to Malatesta that his proposals would be entertained.

Accordingly, on 23 July, the day after the confirmation in spite of his opposition of the arrangements for a general sortie, he took the decisive step, sending out of the city his kinsman, Bino Signorelli, on the pretext of going to Perugia. On his way through the camp he " let slip words which led to an agreement," as a result of which it was arranged that the two opposing generals should have a personal interview at some place outside the walls.[70] He sent back to inform Malatesta of the arrangement, but the latter did not make any reply for some time ; and when finally he did, it was confused and indecisive. Meanwhile, Signorelli went on to Rome to confer with the Pope, Orange having sent on before him to prepare the way.[71] Malatesta's nephew, Galeazzo Baglione, was also employed in the negotiations.[72] It was without doubt at Rome during the last days of July that the treachery of Malatesta Baglione was finally arranged.

It was from this point that his conduct gets beyond suspicion. From now, probably, he ceased to attend at the Palazzo to consult with the government and to join in their deliberations.[73] Assured in his own mind of the hopelessness of the war, he commenced to think of his own interests alone. He, too, was aware of Pontremoli's mission to treat for peace ; and he was determined that if this was to come about the credit and the advantage of if should be his rather than another's. Fearing that he might be forestalled, he did his best to effect his object with all speed ; and he altogether disregarded the means. A casuistic mind could even justify his action. He was employed, not by the government of the city for the time being, but by the city itself : and it was his duty to safeguard the city's best interests. In this idea he was encouraged by certain of the Palleschi, and even others, who assured him that the war party represented only a minority of the inhabitants, and encouraged him to refuse to carry out its orders for assault. The growing strength of this moderate opinion was shown by the number of persons who had thanked Capello for his recent attempt at mediation and urged him to continue in spite of the refusal of the Signoria.[74] So convinced did Malatesta become that he was interpreting the views of a majority of the people that he ultimately consented to accept the verdict of the Great Council upon the subject. It was true that he had much to gain by his action. But he carried with him, not only the subordinate captains over whom he had a greater influence, but also Stefano Colonna, whose fidelity and ardour had hitherto been above suspicion, as all the more important actions of the siege had testified.[75] The professional soldier, who saw himself outnumbered by the enemy, abandoned by the allies, and disowned by his patron, had a different standpoint from the citizen, borne up by patriotic ardour and by religious conviction.

Accordingly Malatesta was able to count on the general collaboration of his fellow-captains in his scheme. On 30 July, he sent his old messenger, Cencio Guercio, to propose once again the old plan of sending Fernando da Gonzaga into the city to influence the people and to force them by dint of menaces to come to terms. He would not promise, as Orange had requested him, to compel them to readmit the Medici to their full rights ; but he gave an undertaking that if they would not do what was demanded he would abandon them to their fate, leaving the city together with the regular troops to the number of 5,000 men.[76] On this understanding, Orange was willing to do as was suggested, and sent a herald into Florence asking for a safe conduct for Gonzaga and other gentlemen.[77] The Florentine government realized the intention behind the request ; but they thought it better not to refuse before seeing how matters stood. Accordingly, with the subsequent approval of the Pratica, they sent

back a counter-request asking for a safe-conduct for one of their
own gentlemen on a preliminary mission. The choice of Bernardo
da Castiglione to execute it was significant that this indicated no
weakening in their attitude.[78] As on a former occasion, he found
the Prince obdurate in insisting upon the readmission of the
Medici to all their former rights. That, declared Castiglione,
was the only thing which the Florentines would not concede even
to the Emperor ; and he returned abruptly to the city, leaving
it to be understood that the safe-conduct to Gonzaga would not
be granted.[79] With him he brought back a letter in which
Orange deplored this decision and absolved himself of the ruinous consequences which might ensue.[80] The Pratica, thoroughly
approving of all that had been done, recommended not only that
all negotiations should cease, but also that the communication
should remain unanswered.[81] Malatesta was now finally committed to the treason which he had promised. He awaited only
the opportunity.

Preparations on the part of the city had meanwhile never
slackened. The day before Orange had made his application the
Great Council had been called together and was harangued by
the Gonfalonier, who communicated the decision to resist to the
last and exhorted all to prepare manfully for battle.[82] Upon
the same day that Castiglione had been sent into the camp, a
Sunday, a great communion service was held, especially for the
magistrates and the militia, accompanied by a last religious
procession in which all went barefoot. This was to be the solemn
preparation for the last combat, and afterwards all persons
of military age were to go about with full arms and accoutre-
ment ready for the emergency which was expected to arise at
any moment.[83] The following day, the first of August, was not
observed with any of the usual festivities. Instead, the four
commissaries of the militia addressed their companies, encouraging them to do their duty like men.[84] Meanwhile it had been
intended to hold a colloquy with the captains to decide upon the
day and plan of battle ; and two members of the Dieci were
sent to communicate the resolution to fight and presumably to
invite their attendance.[85] Baglione, who had given up going
to the Palazzo excepting under escort for fear lest the outspoken
suspicions against him should result in an attempt on his life,[86]
replied by letter, in conjunction with Stefano Colonna, who was
still acting most probably in perfectly good faith. The two
captains merely reaffirmed their previous position. They had
always, they said, discouraged the idea of an attack as it would
mean the ruin of the city. The enemy were better trained, they
were more numerous, and they held the better position—to be
silent on that point meant disgrace. Since the city was deter-

mined to neglect their advice, they had reconnoitred and could recommend two plans as being less fatal than others. But even in the improbable event of success in the initial attack, they would be faced with extreme odds and the city meanwhile would be left defenceless. Her ruin would be certain : but nevertheless, if the government insisted, they were willing to brave all and comply with its orders.[87]

If Florence was ever to fight, the time had come. News had arrived that the relieving force had at last left Pisa. For nearly a fortnight, Ferrucci had lain ill. Even from his sick-bed, however, he had continued to direct military preparations. He had squeezed out of the city, not without violence, enough to satisfy the immediate demands of his troops, and had suppressed with vigour a mutiny of the Corsican mercenaries. He had assured himself of the fidelity of the place even when depleted of troops by having some suspects sent away, and selecting others who were to go with him as hostages. The fortifications were put in order, the artillery removed to the two citadels, and provisions collected in magazines. For his own campaign, biscuits, powder, ladders, and other munitions of war were collected, including a number of light field pieces and a large quantity of flame-throwers (" *trombe di fuoco* ") for use against the cavalry ; while pioneers were brought together to accompany his march.[88] Finally, on the last day of July, he found himself sufficiently well to set out. He had with him about 3,000 foot, the majority armed with the arquebus, and 300 light horse, the total falling short by 1,000 of what had been hoped. He left the city, as was his invariable custom, by a night march, making his way according to instructions in a northerly direction, as the direct route along the line of the Arno had been cut off by the capture of Empoli. He passed peacefully, though with some reluctance, beneath the walls of Lucca, thence turning due west in the direction of Pistoia. At Pescia, however, thanks to recent activities of Maramaldo, he was refused entrance. Not wishing to waste time here, he turned again northwards, and lodged that night at the village of Medicina. On the next day, delayed beyond his expectations and hampered by lack of victuals, he arrived at Calamecca. His objective was Montale, midway between Pistoia and Prato in a slightly northerly direction.[89] Here might have been expected the help promised by the friendly Cancellieri and by the Counts of Vernio, and Florence could have been approached on the side where the Imperialist forces were weakest.

As a result of intercepted letters, the Prince of Orange had learned the details of the plan for the relief of the city as soon probably as they were known to Ferrucci himself. Counterarrangements were immediately made. Fabrizio Maramaldo,

who had retired to S. Gimignano after his repulse, was ordered
to follow on the heels of the enemy on leaving Volterra with
all the forces he could muster, and to attack him before his
arrival at Pisa and junction with Giovanpaolo da Ceri.   In spite
of some fierce skirmishes on the road to Livorno, he failed to
interrupt Ferrucci's march.   He fell back accordingly on his
second instructions—to concentrate at Vico Pisano about ten
miles from Pisa, where he was to effect a junction with Alessandro
Vitelli and the disaffected Spanish troops then lying at Alto-
pascio.   With their combined forces they were to interrupt or at
least to impede the advance on Florence.   Meanwhile they would
be co-operated with from camp.   The men-at-arms were sent
immediately to Prato, where they would be on Ferruccio's line
of march ready to oppose him.[90]   On 1 August, just after
Castiglione with a gesture of defiance had left the camp, the news
arrived that Ferrucci had left Pisa and was marching in the
direction of Pistoia.   Orange, who remembered the two serious
defeats experienced by his principal lieutenants, determined to
take command himself on this occasion.   Leaving Gonzaga in
charge at camp, he set out on the evening of the same day with
3,000 infantry.   A thousand of these, however, he sent back
almost immediately, considering that his combined forces with
those he was to pick up on the way were more than enough to
oppose the scanty following of Ferrucci.[91]

The news of Ferrucci's march and of Orange's departure was
soon known in Florence.   It was under the influence of this
intelligence that the Pratica met to consider its reply to the
captains.   Now if ever was the occasion when the sortie could
be made with any hopes of victory.   Only 4,000 men, according to report, were left in the camp.[92]   Nothing but the
attitude of the soldiers stood in the way.   Antonfrancesco
Davanzati for the Gonfalonieri blamed the situation upon those
citizens who had informed the captains that the assault was not
desired excepting by a few, and urged the government to seek
them out and to inflict exemplary punishment upon them.   If
Baglione wished to resign he should be allowed to ; but no relaxation should be made from carrying into execution the effort
which had been prepared.   Every other spokesman agreed that
in spite of all the captains should be begged to fulfil their promise
while Orange was absent from the camp.   The debate was wound
up by Messer Bono Boni for the Quarter of S. Giovanni.   " They
beg that the captains be informed that the will of the people is
that the enemy be assaulted, begging you that besides confiding
in God you confide in yourselves, in whom victory is hoped ;
which will be moreover to your honour and to the good of the
city."   These are the last recorded words in the Consulte of the

Republic.[93] Two of the Dieci were sent to Malatesta to communicate this decision.   Meanwhile his hands had been strengthened by a general meeting of all the captains from which he
had obtained a confirmation of his opinion that from the military
point of view a general sortie would be fatal.[94]   Colonna and
he communicated their views in a second letter.   Without taking
account of the absence of Orange, they recommended that the
city should come to an agreement, for which purpose they proposed that envoys should be sent to the camp to ascertain what
terms would be offered : should these prove unreasonable, they
were willing and ready to fight.   So sure were they that they
were consulting not only the best interests of the city, but also
the convictions of a majority of the citizens, that they suggested
an alternative.   If the Great Council were assembled and proved
still definitely opposed to peace and in favour of assault, they
would consent to lay down their lives amid the ruins of the
state at its command.[95]   They objected, perhaps on the pretext
that it would weaken the city, to the proposal that 2,000
men should be sent to Montale to co-operate with Ferrucci.[96]
Every circumstance seemed to confirm what was afterwards
said, that Orange had received a definite assurance to the
effect that no attack would be made on the camp during his
absence.[97]

Upon this same day, Thursday, 3 August, the fatal battle
had been fought in the hill country of Pistoia.   Ferrucci had as
his guides in this wild and unknown ground representatives of
the friendly Cancellieri faction, who promised to raise succour
for him in the neighbourhood.   Striking camp early in the
morning on that day, he marched with the enemy hanging on
his rear from Calamecca to Brunetta, whence he should have
taken the straight path towards Montale into the Mugello.   His
guides, however, who had private interests in the neighbourhood,
led him out of his way due north to the fortified village of S.
Marcello, which adhered to their enemies the Panciatichi.   The
place was stormed and fired without much difficulty.   After a
short halt for rest and refreshment in a field known thereafter
as the Campo di Ferro, he turned again due east and commenced
to march in the right direction towards the friendly walled township of Gavinana.   This diversion of Ferrucci's had given the
opportunity to Maramaldo, who had hitherto been following
him, to make a detour and place himself on his road, approaching
the same place from another side.   To Ferruccio's right remained
Alessandro Vitelli with his " bisogni " and Italian followers ;
while Bracciolini, head of the Panciatichi, was hanging at his
heels with a thousand of his own faction.   The Prince of Orange
had come from Florence through Poggio a Caiano by forced

marches, and the previous day had surveyed the countryside from the dome of the cathedral of Pistoia. By dint of a further night march he had by now arrived in the neighbourhood with his forces from camp and other detachments collected on the way. With him also was the whole body of the light horse, including the 150 Albanians retained after the disbandment of the rest. Thus he had altogether some 8,000 foot and 1,500 horse without counting Bracciolini's irregulars. On the other hand, the reinforcements from the Cancellieri had completely failed to substantiate, their representatives fleeing rather than meet Ferrucci's anger : so that he had only his 3,300 followers to oppose three times their number. While he was refreshing his troops at S. Marcello, Orange was doing the same at Lagone on the road from Pistoia. In excellent humour in spite of an access of gout, he took a sudden heavy shower as a good augury from God, who was watering their wine so that they should not go drunken into the presence of the enemy. A fugitive priest from S. Marcello informed him of the movements of the Florentines, and he sent his cavalry ahead to occupy Gavinana before they should do so. Ferrucci's troops were marching on, still tired after their exertion and soaked through by the rain, when they heard the bells of the township before them tolling the alarm. The way was still open to him to avoid battle and to take the hill-paths into the Mugello with the sacrifice of his baggage and artillery. He preferred, however, to fight. Leaving Giovanpaolo da Ceri, in command of the rearguard, to tackle Vitelli and Bracciolini, already commencing to attack, he pressed on ahead with the rest of his troops. The three forces were therefore converging on the same point. Just as Ferrucci was obtaining admission on the one side, Maramaldo forced his way in on the other. The streets of the village became the scene of a stern conflict, centred about the market-place. Ferrucci dismounted from his horse and fought on foot, encouraging his followers by word and example, while they were assisted by the inhabitants with stones and blocks from the house-tops. Meanwhile his cavalry, followed by a number of infantry with arquebuses, made their way outside the walls of the village, and were opposing the attempt of Orange's cavalry to force their way up the hillside from the south. Here, too, a fierce fight ensued among the chestnut groves. Owing to the suddenness of the engagement, Ferrucci did not have the opportunity to bring into action more than a few of his flame-throwers, which had been damped by the rain ; but those employed did good execution. The Prince of Orange arrived with the main body of his followers in time to see his forces repulsed from a first attack. He rallied them, and gallantly led another assault. As he was charging up the slope, he was struck by two arquebus-balls, one in the breast and the other at the back of the neck. His followers, seeing him fall to the ground and his steed gallop-ing about riderless, were affected by a sudden panic, and striking spurs to their horses fled in confusion towards Pistoia. His belt was immediately taken to Ferrucci in token of victory. The report soon spread to the camp and into Florence that the battle had ended with the rout of the Imperialists. In another direc-tion, however, the fight had gone less fortunately. In spite of the entrenchments hastily thrown up, Alessandro Vitelli had routed the rearguard by a furious charge upon its flank. It was all that Da Ceri could do, taking advantage of the diversion of the enemy to sack the baggage, to clear his way to join Ferrucci in Gavinana. He found the battle here had nearly ended with the forcing out of Maramaldo's troops step by step beyond the gate. In the two most important directions, the Floren-tine forces seemed to have gained the victory : and Ferrucci at last had the leisure to lean on his pike and look about him.

There was a large body of the Imperialist forces, however, which had not yet been into action. A couple of thousand lanzknechts with other troops had remained in reserve at Forra Armata, a little distance from the actual scene of the battle. Unaffected by the panic caused by the fall of the general, they had received and rallied a large number of the fugitives, with whom they advanced again to the attack. Ferrucci's cavalry had scattered in pursuit in complete confidence of victory ; and the fresh troops were able to enter the village almost without opposi-tion. At the same time Alessandro Vitelli with his victorious followers had made his way round the walls and reinforced Maramaldo, who was thus able to advance to the attack again. Meanwhile his troops had been encouraged by the reading for the second time of the Papal proclamation putting a price upon Ferrucci's head, alive or dead. Under the scorching sun the battle was resumed in the village streets more fiercely than before, until the way to the market-place was almost blocked by the heaps of bodies. The Florentines were over-come by sheer weight of numbers. Ferrucci, proudly rejecting any suggestion to surrender, still continued to fight at the head of the small body that remained ; and with one last superhuman effort he again forced the enemy out of the village. But here they gathered against him in overwhelming number, and he was unable even to get back again into the shelter of the walls. Surrounded by the enemy, and with all his followers either wounded, fled, or killed, he fought his way with Giovan-paolo da Ceri into the nearest house. By now it was the two commanders only who continued to resist. Covered with wounds, Ferrucci finally surrendered. He was taken before Maramaldo, now left in command. The Neapolitan still smarted from his humiliating defeat at Volterra, to which was added the recollection of his herald hanged at that place. He commenced by overwhelming his prisoner with abuse, and finally struck at him with his dagger. "You slay a dead man," moaned Ferrucci as he fell. At a sign from their leader, the soldiers standing by ran in and despatched him. His body was buried outside the church of Gavinana, the peaks of the Apennines serving as a fitting monument for the last hero of the Florentine Republic. That of Orange, stripped on the field, was taken to the Certosa, where a day or two before his departure he had received the patents creating him Duke of Gravina and Prince of Melfi, and whence he had been treating in these last days for his marriage. Hence it was conducted in solemn state into his own country, where it was buried in the Franciscan church at Lons-le-Saunier. In the funeral procession the captured ensigns from Florence were dragged along point-downwards prior to being suspended above the tomb. He was succeeded in his principality by his sister's son, René, who died fourteen years later after first devising his inheritance to his paternal cousin, William, no blood relation at all to Philibert. Thus, by a curious coincidence, the title of the man who was employed to crush the last vestiges of republican liberty in Southern Europe in the interests of Spain passed to the silent hero who set up that same standard against her in the North.[98]

The 4th of August was a day of great excitement in Florence. The refusal of the captains to attack the camp while Orange was absent had become known on the previous evening, and public opinion had been roused. It was openly demanded that the two commanders should be dismissed if not punished. Malatesta sent away the Florentines serving under him and surrounded himself with the Perugian and Corsican mercenaries, in whom he could trust implicitly. Donato Giannotti, sent to intercede with Colonna, found him in complete agreement with the Captain-General. The whole night through both sides stood to arms with every circumstance of distrust and suspicion. On the next morning, the report was spread that Orange was killed and his army routed. This news caused Malatesta to modify his attitude. The interchange of letters stopped; and he allowed both soldiers and militia to go out on either side of the river to reconnoitre. The enemy, however, did not make a move, and it was afterwards reported that the order had been given to retire in case of attack to the strongly fortified positions in the Pian di Giullari, abandoning all the rest. Later in the day, however, the truth of the terrible news was known. No hope was now left but in Savonarola's angels.[99] Even a protraction of the resistance was impossible, seeing that in spite of the extreme rationing there remained in the city food for no more than eight days.[100] Nevertheless there was no weakening of resolve on the part of the government. Public obsequies and the honour of a statue were decreed for the fallen general : and there was no talk of compromise.[101] It was time for the captains to fulfil their promise to Orange, and to lead their troops out of the obstinate city. To do so outright would have entailed some difficulty on either side. They revived, therefore, the old suggestion of some time previous. They pointed out to the Government the necessity to take precautions owing to the lack of provisions, reminding them how they had served for three months without meat, almost without wine, and with very little oil. They were willing of course to set the example of privation by rationing the soldiers too with bread of inferior quality ; but first the " useless mouths " must be got rid of. They proffered their services, in spite of the danger of the task, to escort them out of the city. It does not seem probable that, at the point to which Malatesta's understanding with the enemy had certainly arrived, he meant this offer seriously ; and it can only be imagined that this sortie was intended to justify his leaving the city in the eyes of the inhabitants as well, perhaps, as in those of many of his own followers.[102] So, too, the communication must have been regarded by the government, for nothing ensued. Instead, its determination was reaffirmed by cashiering three out of the four commissaries over the defence of the city, who seemed to be showing lack of enthusiasm. Among them was Zanobi Bartolini, who had served since the commencement of the siege, and had then been so zealous as to talk of financing the whole burden of the war for a fortnight. Latterly, however, he had been suspected of taking advantage of the continual intercourse with Malatesta which his office entailed, and of being at the head of those who were encouraging him to treat with the enemy. The vacant places were filled by three of the most uncompromising republicans, including Francesco Carducci (5 August). The seventy-two captains in the service of the city were encouraged to renew their oath of fealty by a promise that their stipend would be continued wherever they might be employed for the duration of their lives. At the same time it appears that the two commanders were authorized to satisfy themselves if they pleased as to the implacability of the enemy by sending to sound his intentions.[103]

Accordingly on the next day (6 August), Malatesta sent to camp asking for safe-conducts for two envoys.[104] Upon the following morning, they presented themselves : and Stefano Colonna for the first time formally associated himself by sending a man of his own to accompany Cencio Guercio. It was the first occasion that Gonzaga, who had succeeded to the command of the army, had been in communication with Malatesta ; but he showed himself disposed to continue the practices of his predecessor, as indeed special instructions on the road from Rome with Galeazzo Baglione urged him to do.[105] The emissaries played into his hands. They first inquired whether the Pope would respect the liberty of the city and preserve it from sack. To this Gonzaga replied that neither Clement nor Charles had changed his mind in that the liberty of the city should be respected, but that the Medici must re-enter into all their previous authority. It was suggested, however, that it would be advisable for its future status to be submitted formally to the arbitrament of the Emperor, so as not to make the downfall immediately apparent.[106] On this understanding, the envoys returned to Malatesta, who sent Cencio to report the matter to the Signoria, urging acceptance of the terms. This he did with the utmost arrogance. They were the conditions which had been refused time and time again, and they confirmed to the full the suspicions of the government. Instead of agreeing, they sent back to the captains informing them that it had finally been determined to make an assault, which they were ordered to deliver at once, since every preparation which could be desired had been made.[107] Malatesta and Colonna replied in a last letter which would seem almost noble in tone. They protested that they had faithfully fought and suffered for the city during eleven months, and now, seeing that everything was hopeless, had elicited from the enemy an agreement to preserve its liberty. Their employers rejected this offer and insisted upon courting disaster by going out to fight without even submitting the question to the Great Council as they had desired. Under the circumstances, it was impossible for them to associate themselves in the ruin of the city by connivance in this insane desire. They awaited therefore instructions.[108] They were not long in coming. On the receipt of this letter the Pratica was called together, and it was determined to accept the offer of the two commanders, in the hope that the others who had so recently renewed their fealty would prove faithful. A dignified but too respectful document was drawn up gratefully proclaiming Malatesta's services and accepting his resignation.[109] It was given to two of the commissaries, the greybearded Andreuolo Niccolini and the newly appointed Francesco Zati, to consign to him with due solemnity. Malatesta meanwhile had continued to receive encouragement from different quarters in the course he was taking : and in the Oltr' Arno, that hotbed of Mediceanism, a couple of hundred youths of the militia itself had actually taken up arms in his favour. To lose the command, however, would completely ruin his prospects, as his diplomatic value depended upon his retaining the obedience of the troops. It was necessary to carry out his pledge of withdrawing with all the forces. The two commissaries proceeded to his quarters in the palace of the Bini over the Ponte Vecchio, whither he had removed from the Palazzo de' Torrigiani. Here they found him half-reclining on a couch, racked by his infirmity. Hardly had Niccolini begun to read the discharge than the condottiere sprang up and commenced to strike at him furiously with his dagger. In spite of his weakness and the intervention of the bystanders, the blows took effect, and the envoy fell, mortally wounded, to the ground. His colleague, terrified at this sudden outburst, dropped to his knees begging for mercy. Malatesta treated him with contempt. " I did not want you, but that wretch Carducci," he said grimly.[110]

Open war was now declared. Malatesta prepared to carry out his pledge. He despatched some of his trusted Perugians to occupy and break down the gate of S. Piero Gattolino (better known as the Porta Romana), near which his new quarters were situated, and to turn the artillery there upon the city. Communications with the besieging army were thus secured : and he sent to inform the papal commissary to hold his troops in readiness. " I will save Florence in spite of the traitors," he was overheard to say. The idea had become an obsession with him, and it is probable that he sincerely meant it. All of the troops turned out to be with him, excepting only the handful of Gascons. The body of his partisans on the left bank of the river continually swelled. On the other side, the militia was called out, and that part of it which obeyed seized the bridges, brought up artillery, and prepared to avenge Niccolini. The Gonfalonier was with difficulty dissuaded from putting himself on horseback at their head, and leading them to attack. The whole city was in a state of utter panic, some clamouring for battle and others for peace, many seeking refuge in flight and more in prayer. A single spark would have sufficed to commence the blaze. For two hours the patriotic citizens remained in battle array, with their numbers constantly dwindling through the desertion of those who slunk off to their homes or went to signify their solidarity with the party which seemed to be in the ascendant. But it was realized that once fighting was commenced, the fate of the city was sealed. The Imperial troops were drawn up in readiness, and even if headway could be made against Malatesta he would have been succoured through the broken-down gate and sack would have been inevitable. On the other hand, should he be allowed to withdraw uninterrupted, no safeguard would remain against the Imperialists, whose conduct once they entered could be thought of only with the most extreme apprehension. The government had been manœuvred into an impossible position, and all its gallant intentions were rendered nugatory. Zanobi Bartolini was employed as intermediary. Malatesta, who had drawn up his forces for the march, ready to hand over to the enemy, was persuaded to remain on being confirmed in the command and having his declared supporter Bartolini reinstated as sole commissary with him. The city for the moment was safe, but the price of its safety had been incalculable. The meaning of the step was obvious. Florence had submitted not only to Baglione's authority, but also to his terms for peace. All scattered to their homes, including the militia. That night, though Dante da Castiglione's company remained to guard the Palazzo, the streets were patrolled by Malatesta's mercenaries as though by a foreign invader.[111]

Upon the next day the new position was confirmed. In spite of all efforts to make them disband, a body of four hundred young men of the best families assembled in the Piazza S. Spirito almost under Malatesta's guns to protest openly their devotion to the Medici. Among these were seen persons who had been so prominent and enthusiastic under the Republic as the two sons of Niccolò Capponi, together with Pierfilippo Pandolfini, his eager opponent ; Bartolommeo Cavalcanti, the patriot orator, and Girolamo Benevieni, most ardent among the disciples of Savonarola. Decorated with Imperialist devices, they commenced to assume control in the city. Luckily, a conflict between them and the other side was prevented, though the following day nearly witnessed one.[112] The Signoria tried to calm the population by instructing all persons to lay down their arms and open their shops, and commanding the soldiers to keep to their units. The Palleschi were satisfied by an order for all political prisoners to be set free.[113] The prisons were broken into by force, and the Pisan and Aretine suspects were released.[114] Four " orators " were elected to go to the camp to treat for peace—Lorenzo Strozzi, Pierfrancesco Portinari, Bardo Altoviti, and Jacopo Morelli : while Bartolommeo Cavalcanti was appointed ambassador to the Pope.[115]

Upon the next day at sunrise—it was the feast of S. Lorenzo, patron of the Medici family—the four emissaries went out to treat. In spite of all that had taken place they still held out upon two points—not only the integrity of the dominion but also, even at this stage, the liberty of the city. But this was a mere formula to satisfy Florentine susceptibilities. After a full day's conference, the envoys returned bearing with them a draft of the treaty ; and the next morning they were followed by Baccio

Valori, the renegade who had been acting as papal commissary. He was immediately recognized and greeted with cries of " Palle ! Palle ! " ; so short a time had it taken for the complexion of the city to change ! With him came also Galeazzo Baglione, together with others to act on behalf of the Pope. During the day, negotiations with the Signoria continued : and by night an agreement had been reached and approved by the Ottanta. On the next morning it was carried back to the camp for signature.[116]

The first clause was intended to reconcile the honour of the Emperor, the claims of the Pope, and the susceptibilities of the Florentines : that the form of government was to be settled by Charles within the coming four months, saving always the liberty of the city. Other articles provided for the release or reinstatement of Clement's adherents, for a monetary payment of 80,000 ducats in order to satisfy the army, and for the surrender of the remaining fortresses and fifty hostages as a guarantee of good faith. On the other hand, freedom of movement was to be restored to the Florentines, the dominion was to be evacuated, and the army drawn off. Malatesta and Colonna were to remain in the meantime to look after the city in the interest of the Emperor. Finally there was to be a free pardon for all offences, guaranteed personally by Gonzaga for the Emperor and by Valori for the Pope.[117]

On Friday, 12 August 1530, the capitulation was signed at Valori's quarters in the camp. The Last Florentine Republic was at an end. The siege had lasted for about ten months : and it was three and a quarter years since the Medici had been expelled. The total losses of the besieging army by war and sickness have been reckoned at 14,000, while those of the besieged were about 8,000, without reckoning the immense sufferings of the non-combatants. The total number of deaths in the city during the period of the siege must have come up to as many as 36,000, or a third of the actual number of inhabitants. When the war was over and the majority of the refugees returned to their homes, the population did not exceed 54,000 ; and the registers of baptisms show that what with plague and what with war it had been halved in no more than three years.[118] This struck a fatal blow at Florentine trade, already faced with increased competition and interrupted by the siege ; and it spelled the fall of Florentine greatness in commerce. But her more lasting greatness depended on what was even more irrevocably gone— that proud spirit of independence which manifested itself in art and in literature as in politics. Yet it had made a fitting end. It is idle to inquire why the Republic fell. Florence had her faults of policy as of organization, and they were of the gravest. But her fall did not depend on these. Overwhelmed by numbers from without and sapped by betrayal from within, the wonder is that she bore up for half the time. It is this that gives the record of the Last Florentine Republic and of the heroic siege its absorbing and epic interest.

NOTES TO CHAPTER XI

[1] Capello, letter 89 and *passim* (e.g. 85) ; Dieci, Missive, XLVIII, 20 July, to B. Gualterotti.

[2] See my study, " England and the Last Florentine Republic," *ubi supra.*

[3] Della Palla was authorized to requisition the decorations by Jacopo da Pantormo in the house of Pierfrancesco Borgherini, who had retired to Lucca. His wife, however, a daughter of Roberto Acciaiuoli, overwhelmed the enthusiastic collector with abuse (Vasari, VI, 262). Cf. Dieci, Missive, XLII, ff. 165-8 (to Bishop of Santes, 9 November 1527) : " . . . Thommaso vostro ne ha referito el desiderio d'alcune sculture & picture per satisfarne al X^{mo}. Diche s'userà bona diligentia. . . ."

[4] Dieci, Responsive, CLI ; letters from Baldassare Carducci *passim*, esp. ff. 475-6 (5 May 1530) : " Dicendo che tutto la virtù e gloria di Italia si è ristretta nella città vostra . . ." Cf. Capello, letter 81.

[5] Intercepted letter of Carducci quoted by Mai in despatch of 30 July (Appendix of Documents, No. 15).

[6] Hauvette, 89-90.

[7] See despatch of Tarbes (quoted above, p. 283) of April 1530 in *A.S.I.* App. I, Doc. 38 (p. 473 *seqq.*).

[8] Dieci, Responsive, CLI, ff. 477-9, 11 May, from Baldassare Carducci ; and his despatch of 2 June in Appendix of Documents, No. 12 (inadequate abstract in *State Papers, Spanish*, IV, i, 336).

[9] *Ibid.* ff. 494, 491-2 (15, 27 June).

[10] *Ibid.* ff. 493-4, 491-2, 489-90 (11, 17, 30 June).

[11] Cambi, IV, 64 ; Varchi, II, 410 ; Capello, letter 88.

[12] Letter of Carducci quoted by Mai, *ubi supra.* For mission of Pontremoli, see despatch of 30 June in Dieci, Responsive, CLI, ff. 489-90.

[13] Intercepted letter of Carducci of 2 June, *ubi supra* : " . . . Si è . . . ordinato che ciascuna delle dette Maestà concorrà al beneficio et sussidio di quella, questo per una rata e quel per la metà di quella, di modo che essendosi con l'aiuto di dio . . . ottenuta una assegnatione di venti mila scudi. . . ." Cf. "England and the Last Florentine Republic," pp.189-90, and Dieci, Responsive, CLI, ff. 493-4 ; from same, 11 June. " L' assegnatione di $\frac{M}{XX}$ D. fatta in questi mercanti come per altra mia dissi per l'affectione di detti farà quel tanto di frutto che sarà possibile . . ."

[14] Letter of commissaries of Pisa of 25 July in *Francesco Ferrucci*, etc., p. 292. The enemy were, however, on the look-out for twice the amount (letter of Mai of 30 July in Appendix of Documents, No. 15).

[15] Hauvette, pp. 90-1. Cf. Giannotti's bitter reproaches, *Opere*, I, 225-6, 300.

[16] Dieci, Missive, XLVIII, 25 July, to Baldassare Carducci.

[17] Hauvette, p. 91. Molini, II, 324, prints Carducci's letter to Montmorency recommending Alamanni.

[18] See intercepted despatch of 21 July in Appendix of Documents, No. 14 (inadequate abstract in *State Papers, Spanish*, IV, i, 383).

[19] Varchi, II, 280 (6 August).

[20] Nardi, 223–4. Pitti, in the *Apologia de' Cappucci*, ascribes to Ferrucci an even more venturesome plan—to transfer the seat of the Florentine Republic to Pisa, in anticipation of the Sienese procedure of twenty-five years later.

[21] See No. I (16 July) of a series of letters from Federigo da Gonzaga to his brother, the Marquis of Mantua, published in Albèri, 307–20 ; Sanuto, LIII ; *Francesco Ferrucci*, etc., 342–7 ; and Capponi, II, App. XI, pp. 562–8 (fullest text). Part of them were already printed by Varchi. Cf. also Capello, letter 88.

[22] Busini, letter 16.

[23] Varchi, II, 454.

[24] *Francesco Ferrucci*, etc., despatch 120. The letter of 4 July hastening him on arrived a few hours before the instructions of 24 June !

[25] *Ibid*, despatches 121–2.

[26] See speech of Giambattista Cei in Pratiche, 15 March. Cf. for this Falletti, I, 429–30.

[27] Capello, letters 78, 80.

[28] Signoria, CXXXIII, f. 74 (1 July): " *Bamnum quod omnes bene-faciati & artifices non benefaciati si rapresentant.*" (Text of proclamation in Falletti, I, 430.) *Ibid.* f. 75 (4 July): " *Bamnum descriptionis non descriptorum.*"

[29] Pratiche, 6 July.

[30] Signoria, CXXXIII, f. 80 (9 July): "*Bamnum che da 18 a 40 si rappresentino alle chiese di lor Q^{ri}*" ; f. 82 (12 July), " *Bamnum circa il dar l' arme inscriptis et le persone di casa da 18 a 60.*"

[31] Gonzaga, letter II, *ubi supra* (23 July) ; Capello, letter 89.

[32] Pratiche, 23 July. The Dieci, through Bernardo da Castiglione, recommended the recital of the litany every day till the end of the month, and a sortie as general as that of the inhabitants of Nancy against Charles the Bold. The representatives of the Quarter of Santa Croce added a recommendation that an attempt should be made to buy off the enemy captains at the crucial moment ; and in spite of their grey hairs offered to assume the guard of the palace in order to set younger men free to fight. According to Varchi, II, 421–4, Malatesta, Colonna, and the other captains were present at this Pratica and after a patriotic harangue by the Gonfalonier swore with tears in their eyes to fight for the liberty of the city. But the story, unconfirmed by any other account, has an apocryphal tinge about it ; and Varchi's whole account is not only biased but also confused.

[33] Signoria, CXXXIII, f. 90 (19 July) ; Capello, letter 90, clears up the confusion in numbers of Varchi, who admits himself in doubt. His figures of 2,600 for the militia are impossibly small.

[34] Capello, letter 89.

[35] Varchi, II, 414. Cf. Giannotti, *Opere*, I, 233, and Cambi, IV, pp. 65–6 : " perch' era stato profetato du frate Jeronimo, che navamo a venire a termine, che non ci potremmo più aiutare, e che Dio non ci lasceria perire . . ." ; and the more sceptical Paoli (pp. cxcix–cc), " E ancora stavamo un poco in sull' ostinato per i pazzi cervegli che allora regnavano in questa terra, che assai aspettavano che Iddio ci liberassi per via di miracoli . . ."

[36] Capello, letter 88.

[37] The story of the treason of Malatesta Baglione, a justification of defeat, has been accepted by virtually all Florentine historians from the contemporaries downwards. Perugian writers naturally take up another view, though on almost the same data, especially Vermiglioli, whose partisan biography aroused a storm in the violent passions of the Risorgi-

mento. Cf. also Luigi Bonazzi, *Storia di Perugia* (Perugia, 1875-9), II, 120-9. The question was first submitted to a proper study, but on an insufficient documentation, by Falletti, *op. cit.*, in his second chapter (I, pp. 94-139). The letters of Busini, especially numbers 16 and 19, give a detailed and lurid account of the treachery ; but it has been preferred here to study the matter as far as possible from the impartial testimony of contemporary records. Owing to the impossibility of relying upon the sporadic and frequently inaccurate abstracts of Gayangos in the *State Papers, Spanish*, recourse has been had consistently to the original manuscript of the Bergenroth Transcriptions—a magnificent though unappreciated monument of industry and scholarship.

[38] " Dubitando questi Signori non poco di esso," wrote Capello on 22 June 1529 (letter 20).

[39] *State Papers, Spanish*, IV, i, 190.

[40] See Donato Giannotti, *Della Repubblica Fiorentina*, Bk. IV, cap. v, " Che dalla Milizia . . . si può più sperare che dalla mercenaria " in *Opere*, I, 252 *seqq.*, where Malatesta's services are naturally minimized.

[41] Capello, letter 60.

[42] Dieci, Responsive, CLI, f. 139 ; from Galeotto Giugni, orator at Ferrara, 22 December 1529. " Questa mattina, Mag.[d] Signori Miej, per huomo in diligenza ho scritto quanto mi accada, et perchè di poi sono suto a Corte mi è parso conveniente per quello ho ritratto non mancare di replicare il medisimo per più sicurtà. Per quella dissi che qui era suto Gianmatteo vescovo di Verona, quale si è partito non molto contento, & se ne va al vescovado, et sapendo questa mala contentezza sua, missi sotto uno Amico mio per vedere se posseno ritrarne cosa alcuna & discorrer' de' casi vostri, che fece accenno che quantunche fussino quasi che desperati di poterci forzare, haveano non di meno speranza nella lunghezza del tempo, soggiungendo che havendo voi in firenze tanti varie sorte di gente, era impossibile che qualcuno non descendesse alle veglie del Papa, non mancando a S. Sta il modo da beneficiarlo, & così tacitamente accennò quello che di già ho scritto, & lui ancora penso che sia quello che ha detto allo amico mio, che il Sr Malatesta sia in pratica con li Imperali & per tal causa ha mandati de' suoi fuori, et ancora ha avuti delli loro, come per la detta dissi. Perchè il Predicto Amico mio mi dice haverla da Persona degna di fede, et grande, la quale non vorria che il papa conseguisse quello che desidera. Onde havendo detto prima quello che disse allo amico che io gli messi sotto & poi questo a questo altro, possono V.S. giudicare che qualcosa ne sia, & ne habbi lume. . . ."

[43] Pratiche, 21 January (cf. Falletti, I, 116-17).

[44] *Ibid.* 4 January (Falletti, I, 111-12). Varchi indeed (II, 207) suggests that Malatesta had initiated these negotiations in order to put pressure on the Florentines, and thus secure his election to the office.

[45] Cf. Capello, letter 76 (2 February).

[46] Dieci, Missive, XLVIII, 7 February, to B. Carducci.

[47] Pratiche, 8 February (Falletti, I, 117-18). It is from this stage that Falletti dates Malatesta's *treasonable* practices with the Pope.

[48] As Falletti, I, 120 points out, there were enough informers in the city to betray the plans of the Florentines (e.g. Lorenzo Soderini) without accusing Malatesta of having done so, as Varchi and others do. For his conduct at this time, see Falletti, I, 120-8. His opposition to fighting is illustrated by Capello, letter 82, and Giovio, II, 184-5.

[49] Pratiche, 30 May : " . . . dolutosi prima che chi si va sclamando contro e' Capitani e Magistrati." Carducci put it more plainly : " che ciascuno . . . sempre lo bocia di traditori." Portinari some weeks earlier had made a similar complaint : " Ricordano che si ponga freno alle

cicalarie, perche loro intendono esser lacerato, non solo e' magistrati, ma il capitano, che si obvii. . . ." *Ibid.* 3 May.

⁵⁰ Pratiche, 2 June (analysed, though from a different point of view, in Falletti, I, 129–30). Busini, letter 19, gives us one of Malatesta's pretexts for not fighting—lack of various supplies, which were immediately made up by the Signoria—and tells how he consistently tried to minimize his numbers.

⁵¹ The virtual unanimity of the historians—Nerli and Giovio alone excepted—as to Malatesta's treacherous action on this occasion is, after all, *ex post facto* evidence. Giovio (II, 201) says that he was strongly opposed to the sortie on strategic grounds. The Imperialist despatches do not indeed suggest that the prospects of the Florentines were so roseate as they themselves believed.

⁵² Dieci, Missive, XLVIII, to Carducci, 16 April.

⁵³ Dieci, Responsive, CLI, from same, 11, 22 May.

⁵⁴ Bardi, letters 134, 138. Falletti, I, 127, decides on the authority of these reports that the agreement with the Pope was concluded between 31 May and 2 June, as a consequence of the unauthorized communications which had continued since February. This is insufficient basis, however, to build up a theory which is in conflict with the evidence of all the official despatches. These were indeed unknown or inaccessible to him : but he has neglected, too, the important testimony of Capello, cited below, which proves that these conversations were known to the Florentines.

⁵⁵ Capello, letter 84 (31 May, with postscript of 5 June).

⁵⁶ Sanuto, LIII, 268 (Letter of Suriani of 8 June): " . . . Item che Malatesta Bagion havea scritto . . . che fin hora non si poteva parlar di accordo in pena di la testa, et che adesso Fiorentini assentino che'l si possi parlar. Et il papa dice 'Mi duol che Fiorentini vogliano la sua ruina.' "

⁵⁷ See letter of Carducci of 2 June in Appendix of Documents, No. 12. *There is no copy of this in the Florentine archives.*

⁵⁸ Bergenroth Transcripts, IX, 167: Mai to Emperor, 20 June. (Inadequately reported by Gayangos in *State Papers, Spanish*, IV, i, 356, where needless confusion is caused by the erroneous translation, " a secretary of Malatesta *who was going to France.*") " Entre los otros ha tomado ultimamente (en Aste Scalenga que es alli governador) un ombre de Malatesta, que bolvia del Reyno de Francia, y hale tomado dos cartas de dos e de quatro deste Junio, y son del embaxador que esta en Francia de Florentines direttas a la Señoria, las quales Scalenga imbio al principe por no tener decifrador. Las ha imbiado aqui, donde se han decifrado : y por ellas vera V.M.ᵗ lo que escrive aquel embaxador que los reyes de francia y de Inglaterra quieren defender a florentia . . . y porque este hombre esta preso en poder de Scalenga, che despacha en esta misma hora para el principe dandole aviso desto, para que lo embie a Scalenga para que mejor pueda interrogar al dicho hombre con tormentos si fuere menester. . . ." Torturing Malatesta's envoys does not seem to indicate that an agreement with him had already been reached ! For the anger at the French court at the interception of the envoy and the discovery through Carducci's thoughtlessness of the secret, see his despatch of 21 July (Appendix of Documents, No. 14). Cf. also *State Papers, Spanish*, IV, i, 357.

⁵⁹ Letter of Mai of 15 June in *State Papers, Spanish*, IV, i, 352. This detail similarly indicates that no agreement had been as yet reached.

⁶⁰ The besiegers now numbered between ten and fifteen thousand. Busini, letter 19 (p. 203), attempting to minimize the odds, indicates the former number, while exaggerating the forces of the city by a half.

[61] It is hardly necessary to point out that this is intended as an explanation, not a justification, of Malatesta's conduct.

[62] Confession of Gherardi in Bardi, *Filippo Strozzi da nuovi documenti, ubi supra*, pp. 14–15. Though this was extracted under torture, it is so consistent and so well in accord with other better-established facts that it may be accepted in its main details.

[63] Despatch of Muxetula to Emperor of 25 June in Appendix of Documents, No. 13 (cf. *State Papers, Spanish*, IV, i, 361, pp. 607–9), and of Mai of 27 June (*ibid. n.* 363), from Bergenroth Transcripts, IX, f. 190: "Diciendo Malatesta que el serve a Florencia de Capitan y hombre de guerra y no de verdugo." Cf. Robert, 391–2, and Doc. 356 ; Pastor, X, 101 ; Sanuto, LIII, 299–300, 304–5, 367 ; Lanz, I, 359, 390 ; de Leva, II, 631 ; Guicciardini, *Opere*, IX, letter 52, etc. Varchi, II, 358–9, naturally minimizes the whole affair, and later writers put it down to an utter fabrication on the part of the arch-villain.

[64] Just at this time it was reported that a man had been captured in camp who had been sent to assassinate the Prince of Orange (Guicciardini, *ibid.*) ; and a similar poison plot against Baccio Valori was said to have been unearthed (Bardi, *ubi supra, f.n.*). Finally, an attempt of the Florentines to poison the wells was believed to have been forestalled (Sanuto, LIII, 462–7).

[65] See despatch of Muxetula of 25 June (Appendix of Documents, No. 13). Gratitude explains the Pope's sudden reconciliation with Pirro (Varchi, II, 416).

[66] Gonzaga, letter I (16 July), *ubi supra* ; Capello, letter 88 ; despatch of Mai of 18 July in *State Papers, Spanish*, IV, i, 381 ; Varchi, II, 415–17 ; reply of Davanzati in Pratica of 23 July congratulating the Signoria on rejecting Orange's offer. There is no need to regard this (as Falletti, I, 393, does) as referring to a fresh set of negotiations, more especially as no Pratica had been held since the 6th of the month.

[67] See the most important despatch of Mai of 18 July, *ubi supra*. The Venetian ambassador at Rome had some confused idea of what was going on. " Et che'l Sig. M. Baion havia scritto al papa che Fiorentini dariano le forteze di Pisa et Volterra in man soe, et si meteriano ne l'imperator, et il papa vol obstarsi, ne vol levar lo exercito " (letter of Suriani of 13, 14 July in Sanuto, LIII, 360.)

[68] " En lo de Malatesta, que se deve trabajar de reduzirlo sin lo de perosa " (instructions of Charles of 2 August in Bergenroth Transcripts, X, 4). Orange's despatches are unfortunately preserved only as far as 7 July (Robert, Doc. 360). Till that date, however, there is not the slightest indication in them of any agreement with Malatesta. The events of 22 July, when, warned by four separate spies of an impending attack, the army stood to arms all night (*supra*, pp. 298–9), are additional proof that no agreement had been reached till that date. If it had been, such credence was not likely to have been placed in a false report, nor would the medium of spies have been necessary.

[69] Cf. letter of Guicciardini of 22 July in *Opere*, IX, 152–3.

[70] Gonzaga, letter III (25 July), *ubi supra*.

[71] *Ibid.* letter IV (27 July ; Sanuto, LIII, 407, *not* in Albèri, etc.). This proves that Varchi (II, 418), followed by Robert (pp. 412–13), is incorrect in saying that the interview actually took place ; nor therefore could the details of the betrayal have been concluded on that occasion.

[72] " Galeaço Ballion su sobrino, con el qual he siempre tractado io las cosas de Malatesta " (despatch of Mai of 5 August in Appendix of Documents, No. 16 ; cf. *State Papers, Spanish*, IV, i, 398). For the negotiations

of Signorelli, cf. letter of Guicciardini of 30 July in *Opere*, IX, 154–5.
[73] Nerli, 235.

[74] Capello, letter 89. Cf. what must have been the typical case of Paoli Paoli (p. cci) : " E io Pagolo scrittore di detto libro riputo miracolo grande quando Malatesta Baglione qui capitano disse : Io ho fatto l' accordo tra voi e papa, e non avete se non a soscriverlo . . . e questo m' è paruto il miracolo che s' aspettava . . ."

[75] Cf. Dieci, Missive, XLVIII, 23 January 1529/30, to Baldassare Carducci : " Noi non potremo con parole explicare quanto noi ci teniamo satisfacti de S.^re Stephano."

[76] Gonzaga, letter V of 4 August, *ubi supra*. The dates in this letter are obviously confused, and on the strength of this, Ranke (*Zur Kritik Neuerer Geschichteschreiber*, p. 84 *seqq.*) doubts the authenticity of the whole series, reckoning them a forgery intended to implicate Malatesta. Their presence, however, in Sanuto's Diaries makes it virtually certain that they are genuine. The confusion can be largely explained by the supposition that the letter was added to a couple of days after it was commenced ; and the excitement at camp at that time was certainly not conducive to clear thinking. The number 5,000 is somewhat small. Possibly Malatesta was unable to count as yet upon the obedience of the remaining 1,200. As we shall see, some of the troops remained faithful to the end. The papal brief of 2 August, published by Fontana, *Renata de Francia*, I, 460–1, shows that on the receipt of this news Clement was confident that the whole enterprise had now come to a successful conclusion, though it does not peculiarly implicate Baglione, as Fontana alleges and Pastor (X, 101) repeats. Orange was destined never to receive it.

[77] See his letter of request of 30 July in Robert, Doc. 362, and Albèri, p. 305.

[78] Pratiche, 31 July. Luigi de' Pazzi explains for the Dieci. " . . . Fu giudicato che se ci fusse cosa alcuna fussi ben ridurla, et giudicoron la venuta di detto Don ferrando esser per nocere assai ; et però fu giudicato che fussi bene scriver nel modo detto . . ." (cf. Falletti, I, 394). Their request for a safe-conduct is in Dieci, Missive, XLVIII, 30 July ; the credentials of Castiglione, *ibid.* 31 July.

[79] Varchi, II, 419.

[80] Published by Robert, Doc. 363, and Albèri, p. 306.

[81] Pratiche, 1 August (Falletti, I, 395).

[82] Varchi, II, 425.

[83] Signoria, CXXXIII, ff. 97–8 (29 July): " . . . Vedendo la città nostra essere ridotta in termine che egli è guidicato utile e necessario tentare con la forza di liberarsi dalla crudele obsidione et fuggire il durissimo gioogo della tirannide et sapendo che ogni potestà e fortezza e dallo omnipotente e [im?]mortale iddio re nostro. . . ." Cf. Capello, letter 90 ; Cambi, 65–6.

[84] Varchi, II, 426.

[85] Pratiche, 31 July. Luigi de' Pazzi, for the Dieci, declares " Domatina si haranno e' Capitani per ordinare el dove et quando del combatere " (Varchi, *ibid.*).

[86] Busini, letter 19.

[87] Letter of 2 August in Sanuto, LIII, 491–3, and Varchi, II, 427–9. Cf. Roseo, pp. 310–11.

[88] Letters of commissaries of Pisa of 18–25 July in *Francesco Ferrucci*, etc., pp. 277–82 ; Sassetti, *ibid.* 127–31 ; Varchi, II, p. 440 *seqq.* For the " trombe di fuoco," cf. descriptions brought together by Pierrugues in notes to Rosco, *op. cit.* p. 331.

[8][9] See his last despatch (No. 125) of 1–2 August (p. 283), and Sassetti, *ibid.* 131–2.

[90] Gonzaga, letter I, *ubi supra* (16 August). Cf. De Blasiis, III, 365–6. Alfredo Chiti, in *Il Maramaldo nel territorio pistoiese (Bolletino Storico Pistoiese*, anno IV, fasc. 2), describes Maramaldo's activities at this period. He demands provisions and intelligence of Ferrucci's movements from the acting government of Pistoia ; and on 2 August redoubles his pressure and orders it to send a number of spies to secure reliable information. The Florentine general has been criticized for not falling on Maramaldo while he was alone ; but this would have been a dangerous diversion from his primary task, which was to relieve Florence.

[91] Gonzaga, letter V, *ubi supra* (4 August). It was all the Spanish troops, and not part of them, as Varchi says (II, 443), that he sent back. Robert, p. 420, makes an egregious blunder in saying that he sent back *for* a thousand men !

[92] This number, given by Capello, letter 90, is probably too small.

[93] Pratiche, 2 August.

[94] For an account of this meeting, from his point of view, cf. Busini, pp. 172–3. A contemporary writer, however, Ruberti (MS. *Diario*, quoted by Gentile, *Sulle fonti*, etc.) confirms the report that the captains agreed with Malatesta that it was useless to fight four times their number. Cf. also Claretta, *ubi supra*.

[95] Letter of 3 August in Sanuto, LIII, 493–6, and Varchi, II, 430–3. The last Consiglio Maggiore for deliberative purposes had been on 18 February (Pratiche, *ad diem*).

[96] Capello, letter 90.

[97] The promise, according to Busini (p. 173), was found in writing upon Orange's body. But from Gonzaga's letter of 4 August, *ubi supra*, it is plain that an assault on the camp was still expected in spite of this ; and Orange's nervousness as to the situation was shown by his sending back 1,000 of the troops he had taken with him.

[98] For the battle see, above all, Edoardo Alvisi, *La Battaglia di Gavinana* (Bologna, 1881), and *La Battaglia di Gavinana descritta dal Capitano Domenico Cini di San Marcello e dagli storici del secolo XVI* (Florence, 1889)—a Ferrucci quatrocentenary publication, which embodies the majority of the primary authorities. Cf. also Roseo, pp. 285–309, with Pierrugues' valuable notes ; Robert, 420–9 ; a number of contemporary records in Sanuto, LIII, and in *Francesco Ferrucci*, etc., which also contains maps illustrating the battle and Ferrucci's march, with a photograph of the house where he made his last stand ; the biographies of Maramaldo by Luzio, Sforza, and De Blasiis ; despatch of Mai of 5 August announcing the news to Charles in Appendix of Documents, No. 16 ; Rodoni, *L' animo e la fama di Francesco Ferrucci* ; the rhymed *La Rotta del Ferruccio*, by Donato Callofilo, Bologna, 1531 ; and Vasari's fresco and *Ragionamenti, ubi supra*. Alvisi's attempt to rehabilitate Maramaldo from the charges brought against him have been met by Luzio, *op. cit.*, and Villari, in *Arte, Storia, e Filosofia* (Florence, 1884), p. 379 *seqq*. Confirmatory evidence of especial value may be found in the MS. Ricordanze di S. Maria del Carmine, XIX, f. 69, which, in spite of its intensely Medicophile tone, says, in a way which leaves no doubt : " . . . Capitano generale del campo era el principe darange . . . contro al figlio di njcholo ferrucci *allora nostro operaio* detto per nome francesco el quale fu amazato *a sangue freddo* da Alexandro Maramau Napoletano. . . ." Giovanpaolo da Ceri, on the other hand, was held to ransom together with the other captains, excepting one bought and massacred for a private vendetta by one of the inevitable Colonna. The casualties in the battle, which lasted

for three hours, are reckoned by Varchi (II, 451) at about 2,000 dead between the two sides, without counting the large numbers who died of their wounds. Mai, in his letter of 5 August (*ubi supra*), asserts that barely 200 of the Florentines escaped. The cavalry, however, made its way to Pisa almost intact (Cambi, IV, 67). According to a report, in Bardi, *loc. cit.*, the Florentine wounded were massacred by the local peasantry. See also report of Mai to Charles in App. of Docs., *n.* 16.

The death of Orange—ascribed by current scandal (Varchi, II, 453-4) to the intrigues of the suspicious Pope—added a last name to the tale of those responsible for the sack of Rome who met an unhappy end, as was the case with Bourbon, Moncada, and Urbina. For his obsequies, etc., cf. *Giornali*, pp. 31-7, and Robert, 437 *seqq.* The tale of priests and candles who accompanied the body from Gavinana to the Certosa discredits Varchi's account (II, 454) of the unhonoured transport over the back of a mule.

[99] Capello, letter 90 ; Varchi, II, 436-7.

[100] Cambi, IV, 68.

[101] *Priorista di Giuliano de' Ricci* in *Francesco Ferrucci*, etc., p. 460: " 1530. A Francesco Ferrucci furono decretati dalla Città honori di esequie et statue per la memoria di lui quali non furono effettuati et eseguiti ma aboliti et scancellati."

[102] Letter of 5 August (Sanuto, LIII, 496-7 ; not in Varchi). I question, however, whether this does not actually belong to a date some months earlier, with which it would seem in greater harmony. See above, pp. 266-7.

[103] Capello, letter 90 ; Varchi, II, 455.

[104] Letter of Gonzaga of 6 August (Sanuto, LIII, 433).

[105] Letter of Mai .of 5 August in Appendix of Documents, No. 16.

[106] Letter of Gonzaga of 7 August (Sanuto, LIII, 433-4).

[107] Varchi, II, 456-7 ; Roseo, 310-11.

[108] Letter of 8 August in Sanuto, LIII, 497-9, and Varchi, II, 457-60.

[109] Text in Sanuto, LIII, 499-500. According to Giannotti (*Opere*, I, 271) Girolami manœuvred to get a more placatory decision from the Pratica by an individual expression of opinion, but was thwarted by Carducci.

[110] Capello, letter 90; accounts of Girolamo Benevieni and Michele Ruberti in *Francesco Ferrucci*, etc., 460-1 ; Varchi, II, 461-2 ; Nerli, 240 ; Roseo, 312, etc.

[111] *Lettera di Girolamo Benevieni*—the primary authority for these events, of which the chronology is hopelessly confused by later writers— *ubi supra*, 161-2 ; Capello, letter 90 ; Busini, letter 17, pp. 179-82 ; Varchi, II, 464-7 ; Nerli, 240-1 ; Roseo, 313 ; letter of Gonzaga of 10 August in Sanuto, LIII, 461-2.

[112] Varchi, II, 467-71. For the attitude of Benevieni, who thought it the work of God that the city had escaped sack, see letter, *ubi supra*.

[113] Signoria, CXXXIII, ff. 104-5. The unfortunate Benedetto Buondelmonti, first among the victims of the revolution, was forgotten, with Giuliano de' Medici, until 20 August (*ibid.* f. 107).

[114] Capello, letter 90.

[115] Signoria, *ubi supra* ; with their instructions in Dieci, Missive, XLVIII, 9 August, and credentials in Signori, Carteggio, Missive, Registri, LVIII, *ibid.*

[116] *Vita di Lorenzo Strozzi*, in *Uomini illustri di casa Strozzi*, xxiv-xxvi ; Varchi, II, 470-1. A letter of an eye-witness in Sanuto, LIII, 460-1, shows that Valori and the papal agents followed on the day after the return of the envoys instead of accompanying them (Varchi, *ubi supra*) or preceding them (Nerli, 218).

[117] Text in Varchi, II, 471–5 ; Falletti, I, 458–61 ; Sanuto, LIII, 501–3.

[118] Pardi, *Storia Demografica di Firenze, ubi supra*. For the terrible condition of the dominion after the siege, cf. letter of Bongianni Guicciardini, brother of the historian, published by Isidoro del Lungo in *L' amico del contadino*, 1887, and in *Francesco Ferrucci*, etc., 401–2. A popular account of the siege by Del Lungo is to be found in *La Vita Italiana nel Cinquecento* (Milan, 1897), pp. 65–112.

EPILOGUE

BARTOLOMMEO CAVALCANTI, the newly elected orator, arrived in Rome on 13 August: and the Curia, which had learned the news of Gavinana eight days before from a special messenger despatched by Maramaldo, knew that at last Florence had given in after a year of conflict. Though publicly reviled by Guicciardini, the envoy was graciously received by Clement, who signified his forgiveness and his willingness to recommend the city to the Emperor.[1] Nevertheless, the terms of the capitulation could not be considered as wholly satisfactory. It was to the representatives of the Emperor, not of the Pope, that the surrender had been made; it was his ally, and not himself, who was to settle the form of the new government, and even so with vexatious, if formal, restrictions. Both parties were discontented with the comparatively small sum of money which the city had bound itself to pay. On the point of the conclusion of the treaty an envoy had arrived post-haste at the camp, to insist that no arrangement should be made without a promise of at least 200,000 ducats—the sum which had been spoken of all along; and he flew into an immoderate passion on hearing that he was too late.[2] The Imperial envoys indeed hoped that even now that shortcoming might be made good.[3]

All this, however, could be remedied later on. Though grateful to Ferdinando da Gonzaga, whose tact had secured Florence without violence,[4] Clement still had the greatest apprehension lest the city should after all be stormed by the insubordinate and unpaid soldiery, who had at last unsealed the fount of gold and were stimulated to revenge by the death of their leader. Public opinion in Rome thought that sack was certain, and even in distant Augsburg the thought gave preoccupation to the Emperor.[5] For Clement, everything was at stake—his honour, his prosperity, the future of his family. He commenced therefore to show genuine if not altruistic anxiety for Florence, and to exert himself to the best of his ability on her behalf. If her present condition was the result of his vindictiveness, her recovery from it was due to his solicitude.

The most pressing business was to get rid of the tumultuous army lying outside the walls and still interrupting the city's food supply as well as threatening its safety. It was necessary

330

first of all to provide a fully accredited leader. The Council of Regency at Naples had sent back the Marquis of Vasto to take command in compliance with the desires of Clement, who hoped that with the great credit which he enjoyed he would be able to keep the soldiers under control.[6] In the meanwhile, however, the news arrived that Charles had appointed the Marquis of Mantua to the post. In the interval before his arrival his brother Ferdinando da Gonzaga, already nominated by Orange for the post of Captain-General, was to continue in command. The nature of his task was shown by the fact that the lanzknechts refused to give him the oath of obedience until they should have received their arrears of pay.[7] This was not the worst. On 29 August old rivalries and jealousies, long smouldering in the Imperial camp, and no longer restrained by external dangers, broke out in an alarming fashion. The Italian troops fell upon the Spanish and seemed likely to exterminate them ; the Germans, who had hithero been neutral, feared for themselves and entered into action to redress the balance. The results were as sanguinary as those of a pitched battle. Both sides retired into entrenched positions ; and the Italians, moved either by sympathy or by apprehension, commenced to let food pass into the city. From the roof of their lodging, Valori and Baglione had watched the action which a single week earlier would have ruined all their hopes.[8] Muxetula meanwhile returned from Naples to superintend matters. But it was obviously impossible to get the soldiers under control without satisfying their rightful claims ; and one of the main objects of Cavalcanti's mission had been to solicit Clement's aid in raising the army. There was a dispute as to how much the Pope actually owed, but it was certainly not less than 180,000 ducats ; for the expedition had cost him at the very least ten times as much as he had calculated. In addition, there were the outstanding claims of the men-at-arms and light horse ; and Maramaldo's forces which had secured the victory deserved their 50,000 of arrears. In all, the Imperial representatives claimed that the total debt amounted to 280,000 ducats.[9] Muxetula finally came to an agreement to attempt to draw off the army on a payment of only 200,000. Of this, 70,000 could be despatched immediately, including 10,000 from Naples on behalf of the Emperor. A further 50,000 might be counted on in the near future. It remained for the city to raise the sum which it had promised in the capitulation, as well as that which was necessary to satisfy the outstanding claims of its own mercenaries. On the day following the surrender the Great Council—meeting, as it resulted, for the last time—had passed a provision for a forced loan of 20,000 ducats each from five citizens, to be repaid within six months by a hundred others, and these by three hundred more whose claim should remain a first charge upon the treasury. This exaction fell largely—perhaps primarily—upon those who had been living outside the city during the siege (such as Jacopo Salviati), and were in consequence better able to support the burden.[10] An additional *acatto* of 25,000 ducats was levied at the end of August, and another of 70,000 on the next day. There was a further direct levy of from one to twelve ducats at discretion on every householder, this being later doubled. Heavy sums were exacted as ransom for some of the hostages given at the time of the surrender. The accounts of the late government were audited and arrears exacted. A loan was even solicited from Lucca. The greatest efforts were made to collect these sums as a doubly patriotic duty by which the city would be finally relieved from the perils which still hung over it. In spite of all efforts the total fell short by a considerable amount of what was required.[11] Nevertheless, thanks to the exertions of Muxetula, the Spanish and German mercenaries under Gonzaga were induced to leave after the payment of a little more than half of the sums owing to them ; and, on 8 September, they moved off down the Valdarno in the direction of Cortona, accompanied by Florentine commissaries to do them honour and to procure them supplies. A week later the Italians, only half-satisfied, and paid in part in cloths, began to move away. Even so, large sums were still needed before all could be induced to leave the dominion. Part of the troops of Fabrizio Maramaldo had to be bought off from sacking S. Gimignano by a heavy payment, and on the night of 10–11 September the forces under Gonzaga at Figline broke out into open mutiny. They were only partially satisfied by new arrangements by which the dominion was overburdened in order to provide them with provisions. For over a fortnight they remained working off their discontent at free quarters about Arezzo, with the incidental result that the place was forced in spite of its disinclination to return to full allegiance. At length, though they still had some outstanding claims and remained perilously near, they retired to Sienese territory and freed Florence from her immediate preoccupations.[12] With the departure of the army, it was possible to get regular supplies of provisions into the city and to make good the dearth which had continued even after the capitulation. By arrangement with the generals, precarious communications were secured up certain roads, relieving though not removing the scarcity ; while the Pope himself turned in all directions to secure supplies. For some months to come a bounty, constantly decreasing in amount, was paid to merchants who imported grain into the city.[13] Finally, on 18 October, the Tabernacle of S. Maria of Impruneta was taken back, with less than the usual circumstance, to its proper place. It was a sign that the period of emergency had come to an end.[14]

Meanwhile, Florence was being cleared of her own mercenaries. Muxetula, who could not entirely trust the faith of the commander who had shown that he did not keep it, had insisted that Malatesta Baglione should not be confided in too far.[15] Accordingly he was made somewhat reluctantly to evacuate the city with his troops on 12 September, while the Italians were still lying outside for security. At the last moment the disappointed Corsicans and Perugians clamoured for pillage, but were quieted without much difficulty by their commander. In their place, an interim garrison was provided by Count Lodovico di Lodrone at the head of a body of lanzknechts of unusual insolence; and at the end of October they were in their turn replaced by Alessandro Vitelli with six or seven hundred Italians.[16] Stefano Colonna on leaving the city retired to France and continued the unsettled career of condottiere, fighting now under one master, now under another. Ultimately he returned to Florence as an instrument of the tyranny of its Medicean lord; and he died at Pisa in 1547 without apparently having profited from his want of loyalty.[17] The same could not be said of Malatesta. Immediately upon the receipt of the news of the surrender, Clement had sent him a brief thanking him for what he had done [18]; and on the completion of his work he received the stipulated price, now confirmed in a fresh agreement negotiated by Galeazzo. He was allowed to return to Perugia and its dependencies in the same state which he had previously enjoyed. His goods and property were restored. The cause of his kinsmen and rivals was definitely abandoned, on the pretext that they had not observed the terms of the capitulation of the previous year. Finally he with all his partisans was pardoned for any offences committed against the Holy See.[19] He was rumoured in addition to have gained 50,000 ducats by the transaction—"all the which things have been conceded unto him by His Holiness because he hath given him Florence and hath saved her from pillage contrary to the expectation of man."[20] Florentine commissaries were appointed to accompany him through the dominion; he received rich gifts from the Signoria, including six pieces of artillery and a brace of lion-cubs; and he was treated with every mark of honour. He returned home almost in royal state and entered Perugia "in great triumph and gladness." Little more than a year later, before he had reached the age of forty, he died amidst supernatural portents; and popular fantasy expressed its detestation by elaborating the horror of his end.[21] It has perhaps been shown in the foregoing pages that his treachery was not so inexplicable or so deliberately planned as has hitherto been imagined. It is difficult, however, to qualify far the verdict of the Doge of Venice : " He has sold that people and that city and the blood of those poor citizens ounce by ounce, and has assumed the cap of the greatest traitor in the world."

The Pope, to do him justice, had shown the greatest solicitude for the city after the surrender ; and there can hardly be any doubt that but for his efforts Florence would have suffered in 1530 the terrible experiences known by Rome three years earlier. Nevertheless, he could not forget his private interests or his personal feelings. Part of the difficulty that had been experienced in raising money had been due to the fear of a change of government, which everybody knew to be inevitable in spite of the terms of the capitulation. Malatesta, however, whose co-operation was essential, was a novice in the art of diplomacy and overestimated the validity of that document. He showed in consequence some hesitation to comply. A conversation with Gonzaga outside the walls convinced him of his mistake and of the ultimate sanction of the Emperor for anything which might be arranged.[22] On 20 August a proclamation was made calling a Parlamento—that obsolete relic of the older democracy which had become an instrument of the Medicean hegemony and had been abolished with each restoration of the Republic.[23] The old mockery ensued. Malatesta occupied with his Corsicans all the roads leading into the Piazza. The great bell of the Palace tolled for twenty minutes only instead of the usual hour, and a few hundred Medicean supporters were suffered to assemble, any republican who had the hardihood to show his face being assaulted and thrown out. The Signoria, cowed by the menace of force, went down to the Ringhiera. Hence the assembled handful, under the pretext of being two-thirds of the total population, were asked whether they were willing to create a Balìa of twelve persons with full and complete authority over the government of the city. With cries of " Yes " and cheers for the Medici the revolution was completed. The twelve included Baccio Valori, Ottaviano de' Medici, Zanobi Bartolini, and—as a mere formality—the Gonfalonier.[24] On the same day they held their first meeting, as a result of which the Signoria was put under guard and the Otto and Dieci were dissolved. On 1 September, the new Signoria, nominated as in the old days, entered into office.[25]

Baccio Valori, who had represented the Pope as commissary with the besieging forces during the long months of war, now enjoyed the fruits of victory. He virtually assumed the government, and installed himself in the Medicean Palace, where he had the hangings confiscated in the previous May restored.[26] He was assisted by Roberto Acciaiuoli, Francesco Vettori, and Francesco Guicciardini, for all of whom the wheel had turned full circle. Their first duty was to rectify some of the measures of the past three years, as well as to prevent the possibility of a reaction. Condemnations of Palleschi as *rubelli* were quashed and their goods restored without compensation to the unfortunate purchasers. Certain offices, such as the Nove della Milizia, were suppressed ; and all citizens were disarmed.[27] But quite apart from precautionary measures, now that the city was being rapidly nursed back to normal life there were old animosities to avenge, in flat contradiction of one of the most important clauses of the capitulation. Filippo Strozzi, once again an ardent Medicean, was given Girolami's place on the Balìa, where he egged on the spirit of vengeance and acted as Clement's mouthpiece. The mild remonstrances of the Imperialists, which came too late to protect all, merely postponed for a short time the punishment of some. Clement had desired that the hostages who had been given in guarantee of the execution of the treaty should be sent to Rome instead of to the camp [28] ; but ultimately he preferred to rid himself of blame by leaving the execution of his desires to the civil government. Of these, chosen from among the hottest supporters of the Republic, only the most innocuous had been allowed to ransom themselves. The more important, to the number of forty-eight, including men like Francesco Carducci and Jacopo Gherardi, were imprisoned in the Palazzo in the apartment left empty by the release of the Palleschi. One of the first actions of the Balìa was to secure the possibility of laying hands on others by prohibiting any person to leave the city. Some few succeeded in fleeing and were able to save themselves from anything worse than outlawry—among them Dante da Castiglione, who made his way to Venice disguised as a friar. Many more were banished or imprisoned. Six, after examination by torture, were executed upon trivial grounds as a result of their devotion to the Republic. Their names were added to the list of martyrs for the liberty of Florence : Jacopo Gherardi, Bernardo da Castiglione, Luigi Soderini, Giambattista Cei, and Pieradoardo Giacchinotti, headed in death as in life by the heroic ex-Gonfalonier Francesco Carducci.[29] Rafaello Girolami, after being lulled into security by inclusion in the Balìa, was also arrested, thrown into the Bargello, and put to torture. The intervention of Gonzaga saved his life for the moment. He was, however, imprisoned at Volterra and Pisa until, a short time after, he was found dead, not without suspicion of poison. A similar fate befell Battista della Palla, the old plotter and friend of Michelangelo.[30] Fra Benedetto da Foiano, the inspirer of liberty, was arrested by Malatesta and handed over to the Pope. Benvenuto Cellini, eight years later, was committed to the same noisome dungeon in the Castle of S. Angelo where the priest whose blood none might shed had been made to die of hunger. Zaccheria da Treviso, his collaborator, fled to Venice disguised as a peasant, but was poisoned not long after.[31] Salvestro Aldo-brandini was saved by the gratitude of the young Catherina de' Medici, who remembered his gentleness, and was only im-prisoned and fined. Years after, his son rose to the Papacy as Clement VIII.[32] Michelangelo Buonarotti hid himself in the bell-tower of S. Niccolò, but his genius ultimately secured him immunity.[33] About a hundred and fifty persons in all suffered death, imprisonment or banishment, without counting those who anticipated condemnation by flight.[34] Every quarter of Italy harboured exiles from Florence whose only hope lay in appeal-ing to the Emperor to see that the treaty signed and guaranteed in his name should be observed.[35]

Authority meanwhile continued to be exercised by Baccio Valori in the name of the Pope, with an arbitrariness intolerable even to his partisans, until he was ultimately succeeded by Nicholas Schomberg, Archbishop of Capua, who showed a greater tact and moderation. By this time the Balia had swollen to the unwieldy proportions of 147 members.[36] This was essentially however an interim government, pending the final settlement which had been left by the terms of the capitulation to the Emperor. On 17 February the Balia with an effusion of compli-ments elected Alessandro de' Medici, then with his intended father-in-law at Brussels, as one of their number, habilitating him to all offices in spite of his youth, and recognizing him as representative of his family in the city.[37] He showed no hurry to assume control, and arrived after a leisurely journey only on 5 June. Upon the next day, before the magistrates assembled in the Sala de' Ducento, Muxetula, who had accom-panied him, published the Imperial bull antedated from Augsburg on 28 October previous. The Emperor pardoned the city for its rebellion, restored to it all of its privileges and liberties, but at the same time declared that all magistrates should be elected as before 1527, and recognized Alessandro as head of the state.[38] No previous ruler ever had his anomalous power confirmed by Imperial patent; and with his Neapolitan title of Duke and the status of the Emperor's son-in-law, Alessandro's position was more absolute than that of any of his predecessors had been. At the commencement of the next year the great bell of the Palazzo, which had summoned the people together so often to the councils of the Republic or for the defence of liberty, was found to be broken.[39] It seemed to realize that its functions were at an end. Four months later, on 4 April 1532, a Parlamento was held—the last in the history of Florence ; and the invariable mockery ensued. The Balia elected in consequence carried out a complete revision of the constitution. A new council was set up, composed of two hundred citizens elected for life, forty-eight of whom were to constitute the senate. The place of the Signoria was assumed by a commission of three senators changing every three months. They were to be presided over by Alessandro himself, who was to exercise in perpetuity the functions of Gonfalonier and to rule the state under the hereditary title of " Duke of the Florentine Republic." It was thus that the terms of the capitulation were observed. It was thus that the freedom of Florence was suppressed.[40]

Michelangelo Buonarotti, assured of forgiveness if he would re-enter the service of the Pope, was in these years engaged on the tombs of the Medici in S. Lorenzo. The bitterness of his spirit entered into his work. It is not perhaps right that we should read too much into the productions of any artist, but successive generations have agreed in assigning more than the outward significance to these masterpieces. They seem to symbolize the state of Florence. Above sit the two young warriors, the one immersed in thought, pondering over the mistakes of the past and meditating plans for the future : the other roused to action and with his hand tightening over his weapon. Below them lie the famous allegorical figures—Night and Day, Twilight and Dawn. Gigantic male shapes of immense power are shown sinking into a troubled rest or fettered in the chains of slumber, faced by female forms awakening to realize their agony. Whatever the artist's intentions, these may well be taken as symbolical of Florence, her darkness and anguish, waiting for the call of youth and valour to rouse herself to greet a new day—a day which never dawned.

NOTES TO EPILOGUE

[1] Sanuto, LIII, 500–1. That Cavalcanti does not mention Guicciardini's insults in his despatches (Rossi, I, 170 *n*.) is precisely what one would expect, and the traditional story may be allowed to stand.

[2] *Vita di Lorenzo Strozzi*, pp. xxv–vi, where it is stated that the envoy, Giovanni della Stufa, arrived just before the signature of the treaty ; Varchi, II, 475, who says that he arrived just after. Two hundred thousand ducats is the sum stipulated by Charles in his instructions of 2 August (Robert, II, Doc. 365).

[3] Despatch of Muxetula of 21 August in Appendix of Documents, No. 17 (cf. abstract in *State Papers, Spanish*, IV, i, 413).

[4] Sanuto, *ubi supra*.

[5] *Ibid*. 467, 520. Cf. report of Savoian envoy, published by Claretta, *ubi supra*.

338 THE LAST FLORENTINE REPUBLIC

[6] Despatch of Mai of 5 August in Appendix of Documents, No. 16.
[7] Despatch of Muxetula of 21 August ; Sanuto, LIII, 520–1 ; Robert, II, Doc. 369.
[8] Sperino in *Francesco Ferrucci*, etc., 359–60 ; Roseo, 317–18 ; Varchi, II, 500–2 ; De Leva, II, 641.
[9] Despatch of Muxetula of 21 August, *ubi supra*.
[10] Provisioni, CCIX, 26 *seqq.* (13 August 1530).
[11] Rossi, I, 181–7 ; Falletti, I, 471–3. Cf. the contemporary account of Cambi, IV, 74.
[12] Rossi, I, 194–205 ; *Avisi dal Campo presso a Firenze* in *A.S.I.*, App. I, 481 *seqq.*
[13] Rossi, I, 176, 178, 207 ; Falletti, I, 472–3. For the scarcity in Florence after the siege, cf. Cambi, IV, 73–6.
[14] Signoria, CXXXIII, 138–9 (15 October) ; Cambi, IV, 78. For the economic re-establishment of the state, cf. Rossi, I, 244 *seqq.*
[15] Despatch of 21 August, *ubi supra*. Clement's own reported dictum has become proverbial. He liked, he said, treachery, but not traitors (Varchi, II, 505).
[16] Rossi, I, 190, 205–6 ; Varchi, II, 506–7.
[17] See biographical note in *Francesco Ferrucci*, etc., 510–11.
[18] Text in *Cod. Ital. Dipl.*, I, 1159 ; Varchi, II, 489–90 ; Vermiglioli, App. XXXII.
[19] Text in Varchi, II, 482–4 ; Sanuto, LIII, 515–16 ; Vermiglioli, App. XXXIII.
[20] Sanuto, LIII, 514 ; Frollière, *La Guerra del Sale*, in *A.S.I.*, App. XVI (ii), 442–3.
[21] Sanési, *La Partenza di Malatesta Baglione da Firenze*, in *A.S.I.*, ser. V, vol. ix, p. 67 *seqq.*, shows that he received no superfluous gifts, as has been stated, but was given merely what he asked in order to be rid of the burden of his following. Cf. also Heywood, *History of Perugia*, pp. 315–16 ; Falletti, I, 137–9 ; Baldovinetti (one of the commissaries who accompanied him), 71–2 ; Ughi, p. 168.
[22] See letter of Ferraran envoy cited by Rossi, I, 181.
[23] Signoria, CXXXIII, 110, 20 August: " *Bamnum pro Parlamentum* . . . qualiter quilibet qui voluit possit venire in plateam dominorum prefatorum subito statim et ad sonum campane palatij dictorum dominorum ad videndum et audiendum ea quæ deliberabuntur et disponentur per dictos Mag.cos et ex.sos d.nos . . ." *Ibid.*, " *Bamnum quod fiat Parlamentum* . . . non obstantibus quibuscumque prohibitionibus dispositis per quascunque leges et provisiones usque nunc fatas et ordinatas . . ."
[24] Cambi, IV, 71–3. The text of the decree nominating the Balia is printed by Falletti, I, 462–8.
[25] Signoria, CXXXIII, 112 ; Varchi, II, 480–1 ; Nerli, 242–3. The first Gonfalonier under the new dispensation, appointed as in the old days for two months only, was Giovanni Corsini, a refugee at Rome, who experienced considerable difficulty in returning and was much delayed owing to the state of the roads, still infested by the disorderly troops. (Rossi, I, 179–80.)
[26] Signoria, CXXXIII, 112 (27 August).
[27] Rossi, I, 207–14.
[28] Sanuto, LIII, 514. Instead of fifty, sixty-four had been actually selected. For their names, see Varchi, II, 495–7.
[29] Rossi, I, 208, 221–32 ; Falletti, I, 473–6 ; De Leva, III, 93–4 ; Bardi, *Filippo Strozzi da nuovi documenti*, p. 10. He prints (pp. 12–13) Carducci's confession, which, though extracted by torture, convicts him of nothing worse than pushing monetary provisions irregularly through the

Councils during the siege owing to the pressure of necessity. The charges amounted to no more than having fostered the resistance of the city, excepting in the case of Gherardi, accused of having attempted the assassination of the Pope. Giachinotti, according to Cambi, IV, 80–1, was punished for having been responsible for the execution of Corsi and his son at Pisa ; Cei and Luigi Soderini in revenge for the latter's kinsman Tommaso. These half-dozen comprised the principal leaders of the popular resistance, excepting only Andreuolo Niccolini, killed by Malatesta, and Niccolò (di Braccio) Guicciardini, who escaped perhaps because of his relationship to the loyal Francesco.

[30] Rossi, I, 230–2 ; Falletti, I, 477. For condemnation of Girolami, see letter of Balia of 17 November to Alessandro de' Medici in Desjardins, III, 5–7.

[31] Busini (letter XVIII), 187–9.

[32] Varchi, II, 559.

[33] Symonds, *op. cit.* I, 437–8.

[34] Lists of those condemned may be found in Varchi, II, 570 *seqq.* ; Cambi, IV, 87–8, 91–4 ; Baldovinetti, 73–82.

[35] Cf. the " Narration " of Galeotto Giugni published by Gelli in appendix to his edition of Nardi, and the " Discourse " in Falletti, I, 478–81. A minor vexation to the historian at least was the removal to Rome of a number of important volumes in the Florentine archives containing material derogatory to the dignity of the Pope (Varchi, I, 48). No trace of these is preserved in the Vatican.

[36] Rossi, I, 215–21, 254, 266. Their names are given by Cambi, IV, 81–6.

[37] Text in Falletti, I, 405–7.

[38] Text in Lunig, I, 1163 *seqq.* ; Varchi, II, 569.

[39] De Leva, *Assedio di Firenze*, 23.

[40] See Caggese, *Firenze*, III, cap. I, " *L'Organizzazione del Principato*," and the authorities there cited.

APPENDIX I

GUICCIARDINI AND THE TUMULTO DEL VENERDÌ

The part played by Guicciardini in arranging the final settlement of the Tumulto del Venerdì is said on his own authority to have been decisive. It is a minute point; but it is one which exercised Villari and Ranke, through whom the reputation of a great historian has been made to turn in part upon his account of his own share in this matter. It is fully discussed by the former in a note to his life of Machiavelli (Bk. II, cap. xv) where he vindicates his compatriot against the German historian—apparently with success. Nevertheless, an additional point can be added here which deals with the position of Federigo da Bozzolo. If this is elucidated, the truth of the various narratives can easily be tested.

The majority of those who have told of the events of the day have given us to understand that Bozzolo went to the Palace at the lull in the fighting in order to induce the rebels to enter into negotiations. Guicciardini, on the other hand, says that Bozzolo had entered early in the tumult, hoping to allay it, but received only hard words for his pains and had some difficulty in obtaining permission to leave after several hours. This he did full of rage and designing to urge on the attack, but Guicciardini was able to calm him and to induce him to negotiate the surrender. The account that Bozzolo was in the Palace during the whole time is borne out by other authorities—e.g. Casale (*State Papers, Henry VIII*, 3078) who reported from Venice that he with other captains was *detained* there; or Foscari, who tells us in his "Relation" how Bozzolo, with two grooms, spurred to the Palazzo immediately he received news of the revolt, and before the assault was commenced: and again, in his letter to his son of the same day (Sanuto, XLIV, c. 580–2), how he was detained there and was sent out to treat for peace.[1] Most important of all, in his letter, Nardi, one of the leaders of the tumult who was in the Palazzo all the time, leaves it to Heaven to decide how Bozzolo could have possibly entered, and knows only that he called up the stairs offering accord. Without doubt, then, Guicciardini's tale (followed in the text) is true; this last testimony is too strong to controvert. But this leaves the major difficulty. It is generally attested that Bozzolo brought back overtures for peace with him, but Guicciardini depicts him as returning breathing fire against the rebels. The accounts are not very difficult to reconcile. It is true that Nardi saw him leave the Palace as a peace-emissary; but that is the only rôle in which he could have left it. Guicciardini met him on the other side of the Piazza in a mood far from pacific. There is no reason to doubt his word; once the other had succeeded in escaping from the dangerous environment of the Palace, he may well have changed his tone. By the account in the text, the best of the historical accounts are reconciled with the veracity of Guicciardini.

Another point may perhaps be mentioned. As a further detail in the controversy, it has been disputed whether Francesco Vettori or Francesco Guicciardini drew up the actual terms of surrender. The authorities are about evenly divided ; and the question has been much debated. In the dispute, however, it has been overlooked that Vettori was at the time among the rebels in the Palace ; naturally, he does not stress the point in his own account. What more likely than that both were engaged from their respective sides, in the manner suggested in the text ? Thus, without impugning any of the authorities, may be explained the gratitude which the government felt to Guicciardini.[2]

There is one other detail of inconsiderable importance. Nardi, writing to Varchi, tells him that he has no reason to repent for his conduct on that day. Did not his timely guidance in beating off the attack save the Palazzo from sack ? Foscari assures us that the happy salvation was due to his own exertions, together with those of the other Venetian representatives.[3] Guicciardini is no less sure that he was himself principally responsible for that desirable consummation. It is no wonder that under *all* these auspices the Palazzo was saved.

NOTES TO APPENDIX I

[1] So also Agnello, *ibia. ;*82–5.

[2] Rossi, *op. cit.* I, 15–16, quoting letter of Otto di Pratica of 29 April. For references, see Villari's note, *ubi supra*, and the authorities mentioned in the text.

[3] His compatriots, however, remained unappreciative. Cf. Sanuto, XLVII, 63, where we are told that his relation (since become almost a classic) took four hours to read, " to the great tedium of the Council."

APPENDIX II

THE TURKISH SUCCOUR

One of the most romantic traditions about the epic Siege of Florence relates how in a dark moment of its fortunes the city turned for succour to the Turk. This tale has been repeated by one historian after another on the solitary basis of the casual report of the Venetian envoy, Carlo Capello; and even Falletti in his painstaking researches into the official records was able to find no corroboration, much less amplification, of it.[1] It is worth while therefore to go into the matter in some detail.

In spite of the distance from his native city, the ubiquitous Florentine had formed at Constantinople a considerable trading colony. The Last Republic thought it worth while to maintain cordial relations with the Sublime Porte, and on giving Alessandro Sacchetti in April 1528 his credentials to the Sultan as Consul over their merchants in that place, he was particularly instructed to recommend the city to his continued friendship.[2] During the course of the year, communications with Turkey became increasingly important. The autumn of 1528 saw extreme dearth in Florence,[3] and the city was forced to go as far afield as the Levant to satisfy her requirements for corn.[4] The Uffiziali dell' Abundanzia, in whose hands the provisioning of the city lay, despatched Piero degli Albizzi as special emissary to Ragusa to act for them in this important matter;[5] and he was ultimately sent on to Constantinople with special credentials to the Sultan, who was begged in pressing terms to assist the city in this great necessity.[6] Similarly an application was made to Ragusa for a loan of ships to transport the grain arriving there overland, as the city was in imminent danger of famine;[7] and the Duke of Urbino was asked for permission to unload the ships in his port of Pesaro.[8] Ill luck however dogged the transactions. A contract had been entered into with a certain Tommaso di Aiolfo to furnish the city with corn from Constantinople to the value of 8,680 ducats—a considerable sum for those days. But there were serious delays in the receipt of the grain in Florence, and the merchant was accused also of irregularities in his accounts. Alessandro Sacchetti was accordingly commissioned to look into the matter from the other end and speak about it to the erring factor.[9] At Ragusa, too, there died one Federigo da Mensa, who had entered into an agreement with Albizzi to provide transports for the grain; and the Signoria insistently pressed the government of that city to appoint guardians for his infant sons so that the contract could be carried out.[10] For by this time the siege of Florence had commenced, and the requirements of the city had become even more pressing.

In this extremity the minds of the citizens were turning towards the Turk for a different reason. It had been hoped that his advance upon Vienna would have diverted the attention of the Emperor to another and more pressing seat of war and would have forced him to raise the siege. However, the debacle of the autumn of 1529 cut off possibilities from this direction. Nevertheless, there was a continued hope that the mysterious power seated upon the Bosphorus would make some other move which would divert the attention of the enemy to his own affairs.[11] Accordingly, the government were continually making inquiries as to his activities from their various agents, and receiving from them regular reports.[12] Out of this, the idea naturally arose to send some encouragement to the Turk, especially since they were already in regular diplomatic intercourse with him. " Nor are they without hope," wrote Carlo Capello, the Venetian envoy in Florence, " . . . if they see themselves abandoned by the Christians, to have recourse to the favour and aid of the Grand Seigneur." [13] The question was first brought up, according to report, by Jacopo Gherardi, an old enthusiast who paid afterwards with his life for his excessive republicanism.[14] It was formally proposed in a *consulta* held on 7 December 1530, at which the advisability of sending for help to other foreign powers, particularly England and Venice, was primarily discussed. Niccolò Castellani was the first to suggest that " the Turk should be entreated for some favour " ; and after a couple of further speeches Francesco Galuzzi gave his opinion that " being abandoned by all, they should send to the Turk for money " ; with which opinion Simone Gondi agreed. Giovanni Gondi wound up the discussion by advising that " they should have recourse everywhere for help, excusing themselves first to the Pope and Emperor at Rome in the matter of the Turk "—for it seemed to be necessary to justify this action even to their enemies.[15]

There is no certain indication as to whether these proposals were acted upon. With the following spring, however, expectations rose to great heights. " I do not wish to omit," wrote Capello, to Venice, on 24 March, " that these signori are always asking me about the affairs of the Turk, showing that they have great hope in him ; and yesterday they received through Ancona letters of the 14th from Ragusa that this power was preparing a great force, both by sea and by land, and had already sent to Valona 100 galleys and 100 palandre, which news has given the greatest contentment to this whole city, so that it can be taken as almost certain that these signori have informed the Turk of their need ; and of this I have also received report from a good source." [16] Within a few days they certainly did what Capello suspected. On 8 April the Signoria sent a letter to Alessandro Sacchetti, their consul at Constantinople, recommending to him a mission with which he was entrusted by the Uffiziali dell' Abundanzia in which they urged him to proceed with the utmost caution and secrecy, " for otherwise all your industry and diligence will be in vain." [17] The precise nature of his errand cannot be ascertained, nor could the letter of the Uffiziali referred to be traced in the Florentine Archives. But it must have been concerned with something more than the mere purchase of grain. The covering letter from the

Signoria itself, their warm encouragement, their insistence upon its urgency and above all on its secrecy, all point to the conclusion that he was instructed to make at least a subsidiary attempt to send home more substantial succour—probably in money, for which recourse was had at the same time to England. It is to be imagined, too, that he was to remind the Sultan of the straits of Florence and of the preoccupations of Charles and to encourage him to make the effort which he was always supposed to be meditating. In the meantime the expectations of the Florentines continued to rise, and they began to have more hope in diversions from the Turk—apparently towards the South of Italy—than even in the succour of their ancient allies of France.[18] Finally, in May, when perhaps an answer to their request might have been awaited, their expectations rose to a certainty ; and men were offering to bet large sums that within a fortnight the enemy would be compelled to raise the siege.[19] At the end of the month, the return of some Imperialist cavalry from Apulia damped their expectations.[20] Nevertheless, Bernardo da Castiglione, that stout republican, did not give up hope [21] ; and the government continued to inquire anxiously for news from their envoys at Venice and Ferrara.[22] Nothing however materialised ; and the appeal to the Turk for succour had no effect beyond adding another romantic touch to the dramatic history of the Siege of Florence.

NOTES TO APPENDIX II

[1] Falletti, I, 447.

[2] Signoria, Carteggio, Missive, Minutari, XXI, 30 April 1528 : " . . . in ultimo racchomandi alla Maestà Sua Gloriosissima et se et tutta la natione, pregandola si degni per lo advenire comme sempre ha fatto per il passato difendirla adiutarla et confermarla in tutte le sue occurentie, aspettandone eterna gloria appresso li huomini et da tutta questa città et natione nostra obligho immortale." *Ibid.* are Sacchetti's credentials to the retiring consul, Giovanni Lotto ; to the resident Florentines ; and to the government of Ancona, through which place he would have to pass.

[3] Cambi, IV, 35–6.

[4] Cf. Dieci, Missive, XLVIII, 27 February 1528–9, to Bartolommeo Gualterotti, orator at Venice, instructing him to obtain free passage for Luigi Gherardi, who "fa venire certi navj di grani di levante per ancona & altri parti nel Golfo."

[5] Credentials in Dieci, Carteggio, Missive, Minutari, 1º Canc., XXI, 15 September.

[6] *Ibid.* 5 December.

"*Magno Turco*. Serenissime Imperator ; desiderando noi per li bisogni della nostra città far provisione di qualche quantità di frumento del quale certamente habbiamo non mediocre penuria, et sperando trovare nella Maestà Vostra Glorissima la medisima disposizione verso di noi quale sempre per li epochi passati habbiamo in quella per molti benefizii cognosciuta : Mandiamo per lo effecto detto Piero di Bomeo delli Albizzi nostro clarissimo et nobilissimo cittadino alla Maestà Vostra Gloriossisima il quale di boccha li narrerà, qual sia la causa dela sua venuta e quanto noi desideriamo in questa nostra urgente necessità essere da quella come sui devotissimi amici riconosciuti. Pregiamla quanto ad noi è possibile che non solo aggiusti indubitata fede ad quanto in nome nostro gli riferirà el prefato nostro mandato ma che ancora si degni alli altri suoi innumerabili benefizij conferiti alla città et nazione nostra volere aggiungere questo et subvenirla in questa sua necessità ; di che ne harà per ogni tempo obligho immortale."

Ibid., a general commission to Albizzi, "di fare provedimento di grani in tutti quelli luoghi de lui giudichirà esser necessario et opportuno."

⁷ *Ibid.* 6 November.

⁸ *Ibid.* 22 September.

⁹ Signoria, Carteggio, Missive, Registri, LVIII, 28 August 1529. Cf. Signoria, CXXXI, ff. 97–8. "*Preceptum offitialibus abbundantiæ* (. . . Attesa la difficultà del acceptare & pagare nuove lettere di cambio di Thomaso d'aiolpho in Pera . . . et udicto anchora quello che per Piero delli Albizzi (*suo*) mandato per decti offitiali a Ragusa . . .)."

¹⁰ Signoria, Carteggio, Missive, Registri, 5 November 1529, and 8 April 1530.

¹¹ Cf. Carteggio Originale, XII, 381–2 (28 February 1529–30). Dieci to commissaries of Pisa : ". . . La Magna è tutta sublevata, lo Imperadore è necessitato partirsi in brevi da bologna respecto alle gagliarde provisioni che fa il turcho per mare e per terra. . . ."

¹² Dieci, Missive, XLVIII, to Bartolommeo Gualterotti, orator at Venice, 9 November, 24 March ; to Galeotto Giugni, orator at Ferrara, 27 April.

¹³ Capello, letter 66 (26 November 1529).

¹⁴ Giovio, II, 226—the only confirmation, however slight, of Capello's report among contemporary historians.

¹⁵ Pratiche, 6 December. The actual subjects brought up for discussion by Gonfalonier are—exceptionally—omitted in the text ; and it is therefore impossible to tell whether the proposal was an official one or no. It is strange that Falletti, who (I, 264) refers to this very debate, did not notice this part of the discussion. When the proposal to approach Henry VIII of England for assistance, discussed at this same meeting, was finally acted upon, it was on the grounds of the spirit displayed in his invitation to the princes of Europe to act together against "impiissimum Turcorum principem" (*ibid.* I, 265). The necessity for justifying their conduct can therefore be understood, more particularly as the Emperor issued from Bologna one of the usual formal calls to a campaign against the infidel.

¹⁶ Letter 80. (The date is misprinted as 24 *May*, but this is rectified by the order of the letters and internal evidence.)

¹⁷ Signori, Carteggio, Missive, Minutari, XXI, 8 April : "Spettabilis Vir : La presente è solo respecto alla alligata de nostri officiali della Abundantia, per la quale ti commettono alcune cose pertinente al loro Magistrato o più presto al publico : in le quali vogliamo, et così ti commettiamo, che tu proceda con ogni possibile diligentia et sopra tucto cautamente et secretissimamente ; perchè altrimenti saria indarno ogni tua industria et diligentia. Cognosciamo non ti manchare nè prudentia nè affectione alla Città ; et però non useremo teco molte parole. Fiaci cosa grata intendere che detti officiali restino dell' opera da te usata satisfacti. Vale ecc."

¹⁸ Capello, letter 82, 20 April.

¹⁹ *Ibid.* letter 83, 7 May.

²⁰ *Ibid.* letter 84, 31 May.

[11] Pratiche, 2 June: ". . . Sperando che per questa via (*sc.* il bene-fitio del tempo) et della peste, et delle cose del turco, potessi venire qualche salute."

[12] Dieci, Missive, XLVIII, 4, 6 June.   Cf. also Sanuto, LII, 245.

APPENDIX OF DOCUMENTS

No. 1

R. Arch. di Stato di Firenze.
Archivio Mediceo avanti il Principato, filz. CXXVI, f. 80.

Illmo S^r mio,

Hieri per l' Cavallarino scrissi quanto occoreva, et non è dipoi partito per insino al presente ; che scrivo in fretta. E poi ch' io hebbi scritto, nacque 'l tumulto in Firenze, che essendo andati li tre Cardinali incontro al Duca D'urbino verso Castello dove haveva dessinato, et incontrata sua ex.^{tia} nel camino si levò romore per la città con dire che e' Medici erano fuggiti e se incomminciò a gridare popolo popolo libertà libertà corsino alla porta della giustitia et sacchegiorno la monitione del' arme di ppoi in piazza et presono l' Palazzo et feriti doi de' Signori et minacciando el Gonfaloniere d'amazarlo fecino far l' partito che la Città fosse in libertà et Medici ribelli. Inteso questo il R^{mo} Corthona che anchora era di fuori sollicito con l' altri Car^{li} et il Duca, Marchese di Saluzzo et Sor Federico el cavalcar, et mando innanzi el Conte Piernofrio a prender la porta, et così fece ; poi detto Conte ragunate le compagnie andò alla volta della Piazza che tutta era piena di popolo armato la qual alla arrivata di esso conte sentendo scaricar l'archibusi sgombrò la Piazza, et al Palazzo incomminciò a dare la battaglia. In questo mezo gionsino li Car.^{li} el Duca et Signori et con artegliaria incomminciorno a batter el Palazzo : el Signor Federigo qual ha fatto come un Cesare s' accostò al Palazzo et fece chiamare quelli drento dicendo volo chi favellare : et entrato incominciò a exhortarli a dovere che poner l' arme et redursi a penitentia di quello havevano fatto, che lui prometteva di salvarli et farli perdonar ; altramente che tutti sarebbero tagliati a pezzi. Così fu tratatto l' accordo : fu loro perdonato et uscirono del Palazzo quale è recuperato : che non si fece fuocho. E capi del tumulto non stato Piero Giuliano Salviati et Averardo et Nicolò Capponi con alcuni altri. Tandem fu cessato el romor ; et palle palle per tutto non ostante el pericolo grande che habbiamo passato. Questa intendo era una Congiura de più che mille gioveni ; et hora possiamo creder che Lorenzo Salviati sia nel campo de' nemici, et questa sia stata farina sua e che sotto detta congiura l'inimici siano venuti a questa volta quali si ritrovano a Montevarchi et a San Giovanni. El popolo roppe le Stinche : le prigioni del Bargello ; et sacchegiano l' Bargello et fecino scappar tutti i prigioni e tra l'altri Gio. Bapt^a Pitti, el Giachinotto, el l' altri presi parechi giorni sono per el trattato facevano, et così vanno le cose Illmo Signor mio : Hora bisogna attender allo nimico di fuori, poi s' attenderà a quello drento. El M.^{co} Hypp.^{to} è stato questa mattina in Palazzo, et fatto un partito ottenuto che si mandi un bando che ognuno deponi l' arme excetto quelli delle Compagnie o chi havrano licentia dalli otto della practica, et che tutto domani tutte l'arme tolte alla monitione sotto pena di X tratti di corda, et così s'è mandato et pubblicato. V.S. Illma intende hora in quanto pericolo noi siamo stati hieri si che non vi provedeva, basta la presentia del Duca di questi Signori et vi si sono ritrovati : et la prudentia con la sapientia del R.^{mo} Corthona che invero è stato grande et ha salvati tutti et ha hora dimonstrato quanto sa fare et quanto l' voglia. El Conte Piernofrio ha fatto da un Palladino : Agnellaero da Perosia il simile ; morto el suo banderaio, et amazato tre o quattro de suoi : et feriti parrechij, ferito Pieredese da Pistoia malamente ; ferito un Camar.º del R.ᵐᵒ Cibo in una cossa da un Arcobaxo, et dubito che morria. Monsʳ R.ᵐᵒ Cibo li cadde el cavallo adosso, et si fece un puoco di male ad una gamba ; ma è puocha cosa. Qua sono tutti questi Signori et il Duca ritornerà hoggi in Firenze. Perchè aquietata la baruffa uscì fuori : et anchor vi è venuto el Conte Guido et ordineranno el exercito et la gente : et credo che drento ne metterano tanto che basterà per conto del popolo quando volesse romeggiare di nuovo : et nel Palazzo son posti molti fanti et persona che meglio lo guarderà che non fece hjeri el Signor Bernardino Montaguto che se lassò galdar.

Per quanto intendo, manderano V. S. Illᵐᵃ a Pisa o altrove : piacesse a Dio ch'io gli fosse appresso che non sarei in tante ebulatione : et in buona gratia di quella tutto mi raccomando.

Da Firenze alli XXVII d'Aprile 1527

De V.S. Ill.ᵐᵃ Sʳ fidel.ᵐᵒ

FABRITIO PEREGRINO.

No. 2

R. Arch. di Stato di Firenze.
    Balie, vol. XLI, f. 348 seqq.

Die 16 maij 1527 per baliam ultima deliberatione pro nuovo stato.

Desiderando i Magnifici et excelsi Signori per pace et quiete del praesenti governo et pro satisfactione universale della nostra città venire alla deputatione del nuovo mag.ᶜᵒ golfaloniere di justitia et de mag.ᵈˡ Signori acciò che passati tutti li anmi si proceda nella città praedetta in tutte le cose con più dignitate et reputatione et satisfactione che sia possibile et pro non obstante che pro

Die 16 Maij 1527 *Auctoritas data nove mutationis status fiorentiae.*

Volendo el Magnifico gonfaloniere di giustitia et li altri speciali cittadini della praesente ballia pigliare qualche optimo et salutifero ordine pel buono et utile governo della nostra città, acciò che ne' praesenti tanti periculosi tempori per le guerre che vegliano per la Italia, quella si possa in pace et sanza periculo riposare, et hauto sopra diciò parere et consiglio di molti savij et buoni cittadini providono et ordinono

Che per virtù della praesenti provisione s'intenda esse et sia data auctorità a praesenti magnifici Signori et loro venerabili colegii et consiglio di 70 et della praesenti balia di fare quanto più presto si potrà una deputatione di 30 cittadini per qualunque quartiere ; dando la rata alla minore ; in questo modo, cio

Nominisi per qualunque de Magnifici Signori 4 per 1º del suo quartiere et numero (?) et per il Magnifico Gonfaloniere sei, et per li altri dua per 1º d'età d'anii 29 forniti e quali così nominati si debbino sqittinare infra dei Signori Collegii 70 et balia in numero sufficiente ragunati et di quelli chi haranno più fave nere che li altri et chi non havessino obtenuto el partito posino 2/3 sene pigli 30 per quartiere dando la rata alla minore come è dicto e' quali s' intendino esse et sieno electi per dicto consiglio.

A quali così electi insieme con dicti praesenti Magnifici Signori et Gonfalonieri et collegio pro tempori existenti 70 et balia s'intenda esse et sia data per massima auctorità et podestà di ellegere et deputare gli uficii che accorevano haversi affare insino a dì 20 di giugno proxime futuro e' quali si facevano per electione nel consiglio del cento o altrimenti, nel quale tempo comincerà l'uficio del consiglio grande del quale di sotto si dirà.

Et più habbino auctorità di deputare commisarij, ambasciadorij, et far provisioni di danari el altre cose come ha al presente el consiglio di 70 o del cento secondo gli ordini, vincendosi e partiti in dicto numero per 2/3 de praesenti et basti si ragunino e 2/3 di dicto numero et duri l'ufficio loro mesi 4 proxime futuri dal dì della loro deputatione et li altri ufici che s'avranno haversi a fare alla giornata si traghino delle borse che al presente veghiono insino al dicto tempo che 'l consiglio grande sarà deputato..

Item che quanto più presto fare si potrà pel dicto collegio delle tratte et ordini di fare et così si faccia 1° consiglio che si chiami consiglio maggiore. Nelle borse del quale distinte a quartiere et membri s'imborsino tutti quelli che harano le qualità che s'inchiedevano pel consiglio maggiore el quale veghiassi inanzi el mese di settembre del' ano 1512. El numero sufficiente del quale basti che sia 800 almeno delli habili a dicto consiglio ragunandosi al suono della campana grossa, col rintochare come per dicto consiglio maggiore era ordinato et sotto la medesima pena, et habbi tutta quella auctorità circa al fare li uffici et provisione et altre cose che per dicto consiglio maggiore subservava colle limitationij non dimeno deliberationi et ordini che per li XX huomini da deputarsi come di sotto si dirà sarà in una volta o più ordinato et deliberato.

E' quali XX cittadini si debbino ellegiere et deputare nel modo scritto cioè.

Sieno tenuti et debbino e' Magnifici Signori et loro collegi consiglio di 70 et balia et li dicti 30 per quartiere ellegere et deputare XX cittadini cinque per quartiere dando la rata

(Here intervene two pages of provision of 20 May)

Dando la rata alla minore Potendosi nominare dua per 1° per Magnifici Signori et gonfaloniere di justitia et per li altri uno per 1°.

E' quali così nominati si mandino a partito in dicti magistrati insieme ragunati et di quelli che haranno più fave nere et li altri due che non havessino obtenuto el partito per 2/3 sene tolga cinque per Quartiere 1° per consorteria delle più fave nere dando lo rata alla minore et i quali s'intendino esse et sieno electi colla auctorità soprascripta et duri dicta loro auctorità tutto el mese di luglio proxime futuro.

Item che per dopo dicto tempo di mesi et in luogo del sopradicto consiglio de 30 per Quartiere disopra ordinato si deputi pel consiglio maggiore un altro consiglio di 80 cittadini 20 per Quartiere dando la rata alla minore per 1° nūo (?) per vuolta nel modo e forma che si elegienono quelli delli 80 che veghiorono inanzi adicto anno 1512 e con auctorità di ellegiere ambasciadorj et commisarij et fare provisioni di danari et altre cose per dicto consiglio ordinate, vincendosi fralloro e' partiti per 2/3 de ragunati dovendosi ragunare almeno e' 2/3 di dicto consiglio. Ma con la approvatione da farsi quanto alle provisioni de denarj per dicto consiglio grande per la metà delle fave nere et una più.

Item che vinta che sarà la presente provisione s'intenda esse et sia sparita et finita l'auctorità della presente balia excepto che quanto al dare perfectione alle cose disopra ordinate.

Item che durante l'uficio de presenti otto di practica el quale finora a dì X del presente mese di giugno proxime futuro s'intenda rifata e star ferma l'auctorità loro di stantiare insieme co' Magnifici Signori tutti e' denarj et le spese che alloro tempo si saranno fatte secondo el consueto.

Item per conservatione della vera pace et unione de cittadini s'intenda esse et sia data auctorità a dicti 20 cittadinij 70 balia arroti come di sopra et sino atanto che sia fatto dicto consiglio grande di potere ribandire liberare et absolvere qualunque cittadino siendo condemnato per conto di stato alloro dichiaratione.

Et per fare cosa grata alle persone infrascripte si provede che gl' infrascripti della Ill.ᵐᵃ casa et famiglia di medici cioè

El Magnifico Ipolito del duca Giuliano et el duca Alexandro del duca Lorenzo et la duchesa Caterina del duca Lorenzo et loro discendenti sieno tenuti et reputati come amorevoli et buoni cittadini dela città di Fiorenza et nel modo et forma che qualunque altro cittadino è hauto et reputato.

Et non si possa contra di loro ministrj adherenti et seguaci et loro beni procedere per cagione di qualunque cosa seguita dal' anno 1512 in qua per conto di stato o per qualunque altra cagione respiciente al publico, così ancora s' intenda qualunque altro didicta casa de' medici così passati come viventi, nè ancora in dicti modi si possa andar contra alla madre fratelli et nipoti del Ex.ᵐᵒ Cardinale di Cortona o loro benj.

Ancora che a dicti medici sia concessa exemptione che non possa esse importa loro gravezza alcuna di qualunque nome si sia excepto che le decime ordinarie come corrono et correvanno per li altri cittadinj et questo per anj cinque.

Ancora che la habilità della età concessa al dicto Magnifico Ipolito per deliberationj passate s' intenda esse ferma et rata nel suo esse come è al presente.

Ancora che a dicti medici sia lecito ad ogni loro voluntà andare et stare nella città di Fiorenza et fuori di quella et ritornare come alloro parrà et piacerà liberamente.

Ancora per virtù della presente s' intendino esse et sino absoluti et liberati dalle carcere et da ogni pena et preiudicio Bardo di P.º Altoviti Giovannj di Simone rinnucini et Giuliano di f. dom.º da ripa, et di tutti e' denarj el dicto f. giuliano havessi pagati al commune sia fatto creditare in saliarii di dogana dove sono creditori l' altri che hanno prestato danarj in sul cam.º di dicta dogana proxime fut.º non obstantibus, ec.

No. 3

R. Arch. di Stato di Firenze.

Balie, vol. XLIV, f. 343 *seqq.* ; 20 May 1527.

Nominatio Status et officios deput°.

Volendo e' Mag.ᵈⁱ et excelsi Signori et loro ven.ⁱⁱ col.ⁱⁱ et altri sp.ⁱⁱ cittadini del presente consiglio nuovamente deputato in sufficiente numero ragunati dare ordine et principio al nuovo governo della nostra republica et deputatione delli ufici et magistrati di quella et maxime per rimediario a molti sconvenienti et scandoli che si vegono et cominciati et potrebbono seguire nella nostra città per tanto col parere et consiglio di molti altri prudenti cittadini providono et ordinano

Che per virtù della presente provisione la deputatione et auctorità et ordine del consiglio maggiore el quale sotto la provisione obtenuta per la balia sotto dì 16 del presente mese di maggio doveva cominciar a dì 20 di giugno proximo futuro cominci et cominciar debba a dì 21 del presente mese.

Et possasi et debbasi ragunar dicto consiglio dicto dì 21 al suono della campana grossa et rintochi di quella et il numero sufficiente sia 800 almeno delli habili al dicto consiglio Ragunandosi nella sala maggiore dove si soleva in passato.

La quala si rassettj et ridurà per li operai del palagio nel modo che stava prima.

Et dicto dì inanzi che si cominci a fare alchuna altra cosa si canti una messa dello spirito sancto al nome di dio et della sancta trinita et a buono et felice principio de tal consiglio et conservatione di quello.

Et pei Magnifici Signori si possa et debba distribuere per l'amor di dio et per elemosina sacha 100 di grano del cor (?) a munistrej et altri luoghi a persone bisognose a chi loro parrà conveniente et necessario.

Pel qual consiglio si possino et debbino eleggiere deputati et fare tutti quelli ufici et magistrati provisionj electionj et deliberationj i quali et le quali et nel modo et forma che et come si poteva fare et s' observava l' anno 1512 inanzi al mese di settembre di dicto anno.

Et per questa proxima volta possino in dicto consiglio ragunarsi et quelli che fussino descripti ne' libri dello specchio per qualunque cagione et ancora tutti quelli che fussino di minor età d' anj 30 purchè sieno d' anj 24 forniti et da questa proxima volta sola questo alla età delli habili al dicto consiglio subinforma quello et questo s' observava in dicto anno 1512.

Dichiarando primo che in dicto consiglio non possino venire alchunj di quelli che hanno acquistato el beneficio de' tre maggiorj da dì 16 di settembre 1512 in qua Salvo quelli che l' havessino aquistato da dicto tempo in qua et havessinlo hauto el consorteria loro e' quali s'intendissino habili come si aquistato l'havessino hauto inanzi a dicto anno 1512.

Dichiarando ancora che per tempo d'una mese proxime futuro si possa dare et havere qualunque uficio et magistrato et a quelli che fussino a spechio con questo che chi sarà electo al alchuno uficio et fusse descripto ne' libri dello specchio sia tenuto et debba levarsi da spechio infra XX. dì della sua electione et portarne fede alcuno rettore delli tratti ; altrimenti perda dicto uficio et in tal caso si dia l' uficio a quello che dopo luj harà hauto più fave nere in tal partito per l' ufici che si dano per le più fave et nelli altri che s' imborsino quelli che hanno obtenuto el partito si traga lo scambio e' secondarij et non vi essendo si rifaccia secondo gli ordinj.

Ancora si dispone che per ogni tempo advenir el magistrato de X. di balia si deputano in dicto consiglio maggiore per modo di nominatione nel modo et forma et come s' observava inanzi a l' anno 1512 excepto che quanto alla inborsatione et tratta di quelli che havessino vinto el partito in luogo della quale si dia l' uficio a quelli moranti in partito dicto e' quali haranno vinto el partito per la metà delle faue nere et una più et haranno più faue nere che gli altri et dove fussino convenienti si rimandino a partito in dicto con questo tanto che l' uno avanzi l' altro et intendansi electi con tutta quella auctorità più ampla auctorità presente et balia la quale hanno hauta qualunque ufici di X dal 1494 insino al 1512. Dichiarando primo che dicti X non possino fare comissarij nè ambasciadori se non per tempo di XV dì per volta.

Et il medesimo solevi nella deputatione dell' uficio delli otto di guardia e balia per questa volta i quali s' infacciano per resto del tempo di quelli che entrorono dì prima del presente mese.

Et da questa volta in la predicto uficio delli 8 s' observi in tutto per tutto quello et questo s' observava nel consiglio maggiore inanzi al mese di settembre in dicto anno 1512.

Et chi harà nominato uno di quelli et rimarrano electi ad alchuno di dicti dua magistrati habbia el premio consueto et il medesimo s' observi per l' uficio di 3 maggiori per li altri ufici come s' observava in dicto anno 1512 inanzi al mese di settembre.

Ancora si debba per dicto consiglio maggiore quanto più presto fare si potrà deputar el consiglio delli 80 per tempo di sei mesi per volta facendosi per uia di nominatione et dandosi l' uficio a quelli delle più fave nere et togliendosi in luogo di vacanti e' seguenti delle più faue come di sopra dell' ufficio di X di balia è ordinato.

Provisione pecuniarum. Et con auctorità di fare qualunque deputatione di dinari la quale si debba obtenere almeno 2/3 di dicto consiglio maggior per la metà delle faue nere et una più.

Et con auctorità di ellegire ambasciadori et comisari et ogni altra cosa fare la quale et come faceva in dicto anno 1512 inanzi a dicto mese di settembre.

Ancora si debba per dicto consiglio maggiore come prima fare si potra deputare l' uficio de 20 huomini per dicta prouisione ordinati cioè 4 per Q^{re} per la maggiore et 1° per Q^{re} per la minore d' età d' anj 40 almeno.

Nominandosi 20 per la maggiore et 5 per la minore per qualunque quartiere per li electionarij e' quali si traghino d' una borsa che sarà primo ordinata et quelli che sarano nominati si mandino a partito in dicto consiglio, et li 4 per Q^{re} per la maggiore et 1° per Q^{re} per la minore che haranno più faue nere che gli altri s' intendino essere et sieno electi a dicto uficio hauendo vinto el partito almeno per la metà de' ragunati et uno più.

L'auctorità de dicti XX huomini sia di limitare regolare et corregere et aggiungere tutto quello che per loro de dua parti di loro in una volta o più circa al dicto consiglio maggiore et observantia di quello sarà giudicato esse di bisogno.

Possino ancora dicti XX dichiarare per quanto tempo s' abbia affare et deputare el Magnifico gonfaloniere di giustitia purchè non dichiarino per manco tempo d' uno anno ne per più di tre annj et con quello salario auctorità et conditionj che giudicheranno esse et sanza observare in tale electione divieto alchuno commiciandosi tale deputatione al gonfaloniere che hara d' entrar a dì primo di giugno proximo futuro.

Et tutto quello che sarà per detti 20 circa le cose predette dichiarito in una volta o più vaglia et tenga et observare si debbasi et poi che sarà approvato per dicto consiglio delli 80 o le due terze parti diquello in sufficiente numero ragunato et duri l' auctorità di dicti XX per tutto el mese di settembre proxime futuro.

Debbasi ancora fare in dicto consiglio maggiore quanto presto far si potrà la electione et deputatione di tutti quelli ufici che si chiamano postiorj dientro et fuori della città così de' cittadini come de' notai secondo gli ordini.

Et fatta che sarà dicto consiglio delli 80 come di sopra el presenti consigli de 10 balia et arroti s' intenda esse finito et ogni loro auctorità.

No. 4

(i)

R. Arch. di Stato di Firenze.
Otto di Guardia e Balia, vol. CC, ff. 192–3.
Die XXV Novembris 1527.

Prefati spectabiles otto virj simul adunati ut supra loco eorum solite audientie et residentie pro eorum offitio exercendo et exequendo visa quadam querela sive notificatione coram eorum offitio exibita et facta sub die quarta presentis mensis novembris contra ed adversus Reverendissimum presbiterum cardinalem de cortonio et Hypolitum Julianj de Medicis et Alexandrum laurenzij de medicis et in libro querelarum dictj eorum offitii descripte et annotate ad 113 et omnibus et singulis in ea contentis cuius tenus habeatur hoc pro rescripta et inexta et visis citationibus factis de dictis super supra nominatis et eorum relationibus et confentione et responsione coram dictis dominis otto facta per chiarissimum de medicis et quia dicti domini otto pluries et pluries a magnificis dominis dominis prioribus libertatis et vexilliferi justitie et spectabilibus decem viris libertatis et pacis civitatis florentie insimul adunatis vocati fuerunt ad consulendum et practicandum super querela predicta et contentis in ea et attentis persuasionibus eisdem dominis otto factis per dictos excelsos dominos et per dictos spectabiles decem viros de absoluendo querelam predictam et dictos inqueritos et acusatos et maxime pro bono et pace et concordia et unione civitatis predicte et civium eiusdem et attento maxime quod moderna tempora non requunt neque postulant excitare sibi inimicitias dictorum acusatorum et querelatorum et attentis pluribus querelibus similibus per eorum intercessores absolutis et liberatis et attento gradu prorogatiue et privilegij dicti Reverendissimi cardinalis silvij de Cortonio et attento privilegio et indulto facto dictis Hypolito et Alexandro et aliis de eorum familia et eorum ministris adherentibus et seguacibus et eorum bonis per spectabiles homines balie civitatis florentie sub die 16 mensis maij proxime preteritj 1527 absoluent et liberant predictos acusatos de omnibus contentis in dicta querela et attenta conformatione dicti indulti et privilegij postea et facto sub die 6 Junij inter Antonium Francescum de albizis et zenobium de bartolinis comissarios generales reipublice florentine ex parte una et pacionem de pistorio castellanum tunc fortillite civitatis pisarum ex parte altra in recuperatione dicte fortilite et per spectabilos decem viros predictos confermata et rogata manu ex: laurenzii de violis et visis in predictis et ex predicta que videnda et desideranda fuerunt desiderantes maxime parere et obedire persuasionibus et recordationibus et optimis monitionibus eisdem dominis otto virjs factis per dictos excelsos dominos et vexilliferem justitie civitatis predicte una insimul cum dictis spectabilibus decem viris insimul adunatis et congregatis vigore eorum auctoritatis presentis balie servatis servandis et obtempto partito secundum ordinamenta et per otto fabos nigros deliberaverunt sententiaverunt liberaverunt et absolverunt dictos et infrascriptos

Reverendissimum Cardinalem de ⎱ et quemlibet eorum a dicta querela
    Cortonio   ⎰ et contentis in ea et pro absolutis
Hipolitum Juliani de Medicis   ⎰ et liberatis habent
Alexandrum Laurenzij de Medicis ⎰

Voluerunt et mandaverunt omni meliori modo via justa et ferma quibus magis et melius potuerunt et possunt   Mandantes ecc.

(ii)

Signori, Carteggio, Missive, Minutari.
    1° Canc. vol. XXI (27 November 1527).

Car[u] ⎱ Quale sia sempre suta la observantia nostra verso la sede apos-
Car[u] ⎰
tolica et il sacro collegio de R.[ml] Carl.[1] pensiamo essere talmente noto ad ciascheduno che rationabilmente non si debba o possa dubitare.   Per la quale cosa sieno contente la S. C. R.[mo] levarsi totalmente dallo animo se alcuna sinistra opinione havessino conceputa per havere el magistrato nostro delli Octo facto citare Monsig.[r] R.[mo] di Cortona, perchè nelle repubbliche che sono regolate dalle legge non è lecito a Magistrati se non con grave loro preiudicio procedere altrimente che da quella sia disposto ; non possono usare le medesime licentie che sono consueti usare a Principi i quali secondo che a loro pare molte volte procedono nelle loro actioni.   E per tanto tucto quello che si è facto per il detto Magistrato è seguito solo perchè così astrecti dalli ordini nostri ; et per potere ordinariamente liberare el prefato R.[mo] di Cortona dalla querela messa davanti ad loro contro a sua R.[sa] alla quale liberalmente et favorevolmente hanno posto silentio ; non tanto per fare anchora cosa grata

ale S. V. R^{me} quanto per giudicare così esser conveniente et ragionevole. Quelle adunque si degneranno per lo advenire persuadersi che salva la libertà delle ordinationi e legge nostre, per noi sempre si haranno quelli debiti et convenienti respecti, che merita l' antiqua nostra devotione per observatione verso la sede Ap'lica et sacro Collegio di V. R.^{me} S.

No 5

Bib. Nat. di Firenze.
   Carte Strozziane, filz. H.C., f. 191 *seqq.*
   (*Letters and reports, much in cipher, part of which undeciphered.*)

23° X^{bre} (1527) . . . . Admesso all' audientia alla S.^{ria} de Firenze, esposi le commisioni mie et salutargli et offerir di far in ogni loco ogni opera per lor S.^{rie} per raccordarsi sua S^{tà} quella città essergli patria et havergli molti oblighi. Mi dolsi de portamenti del commissario loro in campo, in voler retenir li ostaggi et altre cose ree et del trattamento che facevano le loro genti, nel stato della chiesa quali però su S^{tà} sapeva nascer dal capo proprio del commissario et non de commission loro per molti rispetti, et max^e. per esser tanto obligata quella città allo infinito amor che S.S.^{tà} gli ha sempre portato che fu tale che per coprirla Lei se nudo tanto che poterano lor S.^{rie}, dire di S.S.^{tà}, Langores nostros ipse tulit, et eius livore sanati sumus etc. et qui mi dilatai quanto seppi, aggiungendoli il detto amor essergli perseverato et nelle calamità di S.S.^{tà} et perseuerar di p^{nte}. Mostrandogli quanto habbia vogliuto pater Lei et il suo stato, et prerogato adosso a se lungamente il male, per non lo lassar passar a loro, et come pur sentiendo il lor bisogno gli haveva dato commissario per aiutargli ad haver $\frac{M}{20}$ Ducati dal clero. Ma ben si doler che un tanto beneficio, et concessogli con tanta carità non fosse stato accettato come doveva, ma interpretato sinistramente et che da loro medesimi se havessino vogliuto pigliar indebitamente quello che lei con bon modo li havea dato. Facendogli la conclusione, come ho scritto di supra (che era intendato et di concerte con el dicto gonfaloniere). Così finita la mia riposta, che regratiavano S.S.^{tà} et della salutatione et dalla commissione datami da procurar il ben loro, et che così mi pregevano facessi come speravano per esser stato la sede ap.^{ca} et quella republica sempre in vera amicitia, come io havevo ancora ditto, et spetialmente con S.S.^{tà} qual instamente pensava a credere che del commissario suo haveva fatto cosa alcuna nasceva dal capo suo et non dj commision loro, et per la cosa delli ostaggi sene poteva chiarire che ben può saper, che non potevano havergli data commission in ciò. Benchè dicessero haver lettere dallui, che non gli volso mai retenir et che la risposta che' l fecero al proveditor veneto fu, che non li lassaria, perche non bisognasse perchè mai non erano stati presi (?) et lo escusorno assai, et dal mal trattamento che facevano li suoi soldati non era per dispetto loro d'esso, ne per indole tale(?) ne sua ne di loro, ma più presto per la mala qualità dei tempi che anno messo tal costume in Italia, che non par che sieno soldati ma ladroni; ne per pagarli si possono far desistar da tal ribaldarie. Dal mandare S.S.^{tà} il commissario, non fu accettato per esser venuto con commission di assai manco somma di quello era il bisogno loro, et cosi tardi, che gia havevono fatta quella provisione, non per far cosa che dispiacesse a S.S.^{tà} ne contra la dignità Ecclesiatistica . . . (CIPHER) . . . ma a finirla che fosse per non che potterli(?) . . . (CIPHER)
   . . perchè la toglievano in prestito et con molto cautioni honesti, i quali per saperlo V.S. non scrivo, ma che speravano che come S.S.^{tà} la intendesse et lo urgente bisogno loro, quali erano pur perseverati in ditte spese ancora a servitio alla liberatione di S.S.^{tà}, non solo non se ne doglierà ;

ma perseueraria in concedergli gratuitamente delle cose allei possibile per aiutare quella città. Così con molte bone parole mi licentiorno. Et il gonfaloniere a parte mi seguito e ringratiato d' haver parlato così e disse che non mancava di far prova di far mandar oratori et che ne sperava bene et che si servirrà di questa occasione di questa mia ambassata a disponerli a ciò et mi discorsi molti particulari et delle cause perchè facevano pagar la heredità alla casa ch'erano per debito di Mad.ᵃ Alfonsina et non per alcuna altra impositione, et mi parlo molte cose in simile materia pregandomi che non ne volessi scriver a S.S.ᵗᵃ acciò le lettere non andassero male, et perchè mai li notificaria ogni suo disegno per el dicto Vincenzo Durati ; solo mi muto del parlar fatto avanti, et dubitandosi o penitosi d' havermi parlato così chiaro che' l stato era ancora drizato et incaminato et non si poteva alterare senza la ruina della città ma che perseverando S.S.ᵗᵃ in la bona voluntà tutto se assenaria bene insieme et sempiterni(?) questo fu quanto feci in Firenze.

f. 206 : Hoggi che sono li XXV. (*page in cipher*).

f. 207 : . . . . di parlar privatamente al Gonfaloniere andai tanto a bona hora in palazzo che lo trovai a pena veglito et così havendolo salutato da parte de H.ʳᵉ S. et del mia commissione lo retrovai tanto largo meco che io me ne maraviglai, discorrendomi tutte le cose passate et el suo desiderio et disegno di assetar le cose di Firenze quali però esser di corso lungo et di quasi una hora et per havermi lui detto che Vincenzo Durante Maestro di Casa di Carlᵉ. Ridolfi mandare a dire a bocca a S.S.ᵗᵃ tutto il suo parer lo tacerò et solo li diro la conclusion suo esser stato non già con parole così chiare come scriverò di sotto ma tanti che se possono interpretar nel medisimo senso che non volendo el popolo dominar ma tener le cose in mani de' optimati sperava si potrà far che come fusse commeso questo su questa hora s' ha da S.Bⁿᵉ erano molti homini da buono ch' erano uniti in questo volere quali facilmente tiravano co' lo aiuto di S.S.ᵗᵃ questa cosa a buon fine : però mi pregava poi che no li diceva che S.B.ⁿᵉ non havea altra voluntà, volessi parlando alla Signoria inducerla et mi prego che dicessi a lui prima quello volevo dire all Signoria glielo dissi et gli piacque in tutto, se non che in l' ultima parte dove diceva che volessero talmente portarsi con S.S.ᵗᵃ come con Papa, che come Papa non s'havesse a resentir. Parlando dall' accatto posto alle chiese, mi prego che volessi mitigare piu dolcemente questa parola de' resentarsi, acciò che non fusse chi interpretasse questa comination esser per metterli in bisogna di mandarli a suplicar, et con questo mezzo attacar(?) tratassi de' ritonar al governo, et con questa suspicion se levasse da lui l' occasione de mandar oration a S.S.ᵗᵃ il che si sforzava et sperava di ottener. Io li dissi che volessi prestarli tanto credito che vedendolo alla bona voluntà sua vedeva per non li lavastar(?) mitigarei la commissione mia et direi in cambio di quello, risentindo non li dar occasione di dolersi il che li piacque così.

No. 6

R. Arch. di Stato di Firenze.
Signori, Carteggio, Missive, Minutarii, 1° Canc. XXI, f. 16 *seqq.*

(i)

Frⁱ Thomᵉ Caiano Ord. Predicatorum
Die 4. Aprilis 1528.

Vener : Alla paternità vostra non parrà grave offerire con ogni debita reverentia alla S.ᵗᵃ di N.S. le inserte nostre lettere responsive ad uno breve di sua B.ⁿᵉ el contenuto della quale sarebbe lungho et ancora superfluo al presente replicare : sperando maximᵉ costì in corte haverlo facilmente ad intendere. Et sia contento ad benefizio della commune patria fare tutte quelle opere et non manchare di quelli offitij che da uno buono et prudente cittadino si aspettano et che sono ad uno religioso conveniente. Ne li paia fatica per sue lettere della presentatione darne quanto presto li sia possibile aviso, offerendoci parati sempre in qualunque occurentia di V.P.^{ta}. Que bene valeat.

Dno: Gabrielli Calderonis Faventino
Dno: Alex° Tertio Berghamensi }Singule Singularis Die 7 E.

Mag.^{er} etc. Quod nostrum sit de tua eruditione etc. (Extende ut supra) D^{no} Fabio Lechino Arcis contrar : Eadem die

Mag^{er} etc. Integritas tua etc. (Extende ut supra).

(ii)

F^{ri} Thom^e Caiano Die Eadem (*sc.* 6 *Maij* 1528).

R^{de} etc. Ricevemo alli giorni passati le di V. Pat: insieme con uno breve di N.S. al quale havendo secondo ricerchava el debito nostro fatto risposta conveniente alla devotione nostra verso S.Sta habiamo voluto indirigerla alla Pat. V. ad causa sia presentata per le medesime mani che le altre nostre lettere. Preghiamle che con quella destrezza che altra volta ha fatto, diche noi restiamo assai satisfatti poi l' harà presentato, gli raccomandi la città nostra sua patria, dandoci absolito aviso di tale presentatione et d'ogni altro particulare giudicassi degno della notitia nostra. Bene Valeat.

(iii)

R. Arch. di Stato di Firenze.

Signori, Carteggio, Missive, Minutarii, 1° Canc. vol. XXI, f. 162a.

Clementi VII Summo Pontefici Die 5 Eiusdem (*sc.* Mens. Maij 1528).

Sanctiss^e : etc. Non indigebat summe veritatis testimonio, quod nulli esse dubium in re debet. Cui enim non palam est fuisse semper optimo Pastori, qualis B.^{do}.V. est, prime sue salutem rebus ceteris omnibus potiorem paterna proseque charitate adversus cives suos ? qui certe preces apud eam suas nunquam futuras irritas nullo sibi labore persuadet. Aliter enim de cive, de Pastori, & de comuni omnium Parente, de ipso tandem christi Dei nostri Vicario credere piaculum omnino est. Absit, ut aliud unquam merito in animum inducere cogamur. Oramus quoque S.^{tae} nequid sine causa de civibus filüsque suis aliquanto suspicet vehementer cam oramus atque etiam obsecramus. Nos quidem ut optime sempre de Apostolica Sede deque V.B^{ne} mereamur, dabimus enixe operam. Agimus eidem pretereaque gratias et quidem ingintes, quod animarum saluti consulendo, suas in nos et cives nostros censuras aliquantes persuspenderit. Quo sane munere spem nobis oblatam arbitramur, futuram nobis S^{mo}.V. nommodo placabile, sed exorabile etiam et (ut ita dixerimis) obsequentem. Quid vero aliud indulgentissimum parentem oremus, nisi, ut siquid sorte preter eius voluntate admissum est, id totum necessitati tribuere, et quas ad certum tempus suspendit censuras, sua benignitate penitus abrogare velit ? Illud etiam suppliciter precamur, ut nostrarum necessitatum memor opem filiis suis ferre non neget : sed publice civitatis inopie sua indulgentia obviam ire dignet. Neque enim deerit S^{ri} V. qua nobis opituletur facultas : voluntas quoque parenti tam pio de futura, nephas est credere. Hec sicut confidimus, ab ea impetrabimus, re ipsa quod suis ad nos litteris innuere visa est B^{do} V. testabit : et civitate istius sacre sedis observantissima, suoque nomini deditissima, maximo quodam beneficio demerebit.

(iv)

Sumo pontefici Die 28 *Junii.*

Sanctissime etc. Docet nos Christus Jesus rex et salvator noster peten-
dum esse ut accipiamus, pulsandum ut aperiatur nobis. Cuius
R^ta ne nos in necessitatibus nostris preceptorum obliri videatur, colu-
imus nostris his letteris opem clementissime V.B^nis implorare. Non
facile dixerimus B^me P^r quod attenuate sint civitatis nostre vires
quod imminuti ciunsciunque generis redditus quod denique crebris
exactionibus quod tributis defessi omnes. Nequeunt illi ulterius
tam grave tantorum sumptuum pondus, alieno presertim arbitrio
susceptum, suis tantum humeris sustinere. Succumbant cito
oneri, aut nil tandem sibi ad communes vite usus reliqui faciant
necesse est. Laborat iampridem civitas nostra atque ager fere vis
miserabili pestilentia. Laborat, caritate annorum. Premitur
gravissimo ne diutino bello. His in rebus quid nos dispendij
facere cogamur facilius et existimare atque ferre. Poscunt cives
nostri et forse non iniuria poscunt ut ubi de comuni omnium salute
atque incolumnitate agit, omnis pariter opem ferant. Hoc quidem,
bellum non sponte a nobis aut esse temere initium nemo qui
nesciat ab eo tuto discendere non possumus, si re publica salva
cupimus, si agrum nostrum, si civitatem, sacraque omnia et pro-
phana nolumus prede esse militibus. Non nostra tantum res agit,
B^me P^r non sit ne tantum observamus, belli huius sumptas. Sed
in partem illius nobiscum veniant quorum bona una cum nostris
eque tuemur nec sint immunes onerum omnino qui beneficiorum
fieri participes diffiteri non possunt. Audiati B.V. civium suorum
preces ; quod egenti prime quod potest sua benignitate subveniat.
Oramus nos quidem quod quanta debemus humilitate precamur
exorari se patiatur ut Florentinus clerus aliquam subeat nostrorum
sumptuum partem difficillimo hoc tempore quod imminentibus
tot undique non modo secularibus sed ipsi etiam clero periculis.
Agnoscet civitas nostra hoc potissimam beneficio vero paternam
erga se pietatem. Quod quam alteris in letteris restata e B^do V.
erga filios indulgentia. Et si quod alias de Apostilca sede deque
S^re V. benemerita fuit dubit posthac quoque operam ut ufficio.
quod denotium erga eam sue S^atis esse actum omnes cognoscant.

(v)

165B.

Iachinotto de Serraglis. Die . . . . .
    (per uno nostro cavallere apposta la presenti quod insieme).
    Spettabilis etc. Mandiamti una alla Santita di Nostro Signore per
lo effecto che costi ti fia manifesto, per servici della opera tua nella pre-
sentantione di essa. Faraci cosa grata a darla in propria mano, non
manchendo di quelli reverentii che fussino convenienti. E in tutto
quello che tu potrai operare al benefitio della citta, ti ricordiamo quale sia
l' ufitio d' uno buono cittadino verso la patria sua benche pensiamo per le
tue bona qualita non saria di bisogno. Daraci subito risposto di quanto
fussi occorso, cosi della presentatione come d' ogni altro particulare che
ad questa materia in qualunque modo appartenessi.

No. 7

British Museum, Add. MS. 28579.
    Bergenroth Transcripts of Spanish State Papers, VIII, f. 6 *seqq.*

Emperor to Grand Chancellor Gatinara (2 September 1529).

Monsr le Chancellier.

Les ambassadeurs de Florence ont yci envoye lung de leurs consors. Est Celuy qui premiers vint vers moy a Savona Nomme Lalamant. Lesquelx mont montere ung povoir a eulx envoye par la comunaulte dudit Florence/quest seulement pour traicter avec moy/et encoyres commil semble assez cruz touteffois ils ont dit que quant a ce qui me concerne ils se faisoient fort davoir tel mandement quil me plairoit. Et quant a ce que touche a n^{re} sainct pere ilz navoient autre mandement e leurs sembloit que aussi ne fut besoign pour ce quilz ne pensent avoir riens affaire avec ledit S^t pere. Et jacoit ce que jaye persiste par tous bons moyens dassentir deulx sils avoient autre pouvoir e voudroient entendre a traicter les affaires dudit Sainct pere nen ay peu tirer plus synon quils nont charge ne pouvoir de traicter en lendroit dudit sainct pere. Quoy voyant et ayant le tout communique au Nunce e longuemont divise avec lui sur cestuy affaire avoit semble le mieulx de vous remectre de faire la responce a tous lesdits ambassadeurs ensemble, pour austant mesment que ledit nunce tient celluy venu divers moy plus contre aux choses de n^{re} sainct pere e aussi ledit Lalamond. Et que ladite responce fust en effet quils scavent bien comme je leur ay dit et declare par plusieures fois que je ne vouloye ne pouvoye traicter avec eulx sans leditt sainct pere. Mais que ayant pouvoir pour joinctment traicter des choses concernans le sainct pere e myennes je y entendroye voluntiers et mintremictroye dappoincter ce quest en difference entre nre sainct pere et eulx. Et que sur ces propoz ils avoient despeche comme ils disoient pour avoir ledit pouvoer, et scavoir la finale intention et determination de la comunaulte dudit florence sur le tout. Et puis que le dit pouvoir ne comprent de traicter et appoincter ce que concerne notredit St pere et quilz dient ne avoir nulle charge, je ne voys moyen de pouvoir traicter. Et quil nest besoign quilz se restent en ces termes ainsi sen pourront aller ou fere quilz verront le meilleur. Et neantmoins que pour riens dellaiser en tout ce que par raison et honestite leur puis ouffrir. Et que toutes et quanteffois quils appourteront pouvoir souffisant et vouldront venyr a moyen raisonable pour traicter joinctement avec nre dit Sainct pere et moy, feray tousiours office de bon prince, et cognoistront par effect lentiere affection que jay dappaiser et pacifier lytalie et dabondant afin de non perdre temps que silz veullent ils se peullent adresser a mon cousin le prince doranges pour comme dessus joinctement traicter de ce que touche ledit sainct pere et moy. Et que mondit cousin a tout pouvoir de moy. Et si a des agents de nredit sainct pere avec luy. Du maniere quil ne restera que a ceux dudit florence de cy on la traicter sels veullent estre raisonnables.

Depuis ce que dessus ainsi advise, e que javoye remys ledit responce a vous, lesdits ambassadeurs et Lalamand mont dit quilz que doubtoient que seriez party de gennes avant leur retour illec. Quoy voyant et afin quilz ne pensassent que ce fust une deffaicte/pour les entretenir leur ay fait dire ladite responce. Et si les autres ambassadeurs dudit florence sont encoires ou liue on recevrez ceste ou ce trouvent devers vous la leur pourrez faire en ceste substance. Je me pars de ce lieu/pour aller a tortona, e sil survient quelque affaire ou autre chose nouvelle, vous en advertiray.

Jay reçu lecters de Anthoine de leyva qui m'escript que il a receu lettres du conte felix contenant que le XXVIIJ daoust les pietons allemans e les hommes d'armes de flandres e de bourgoigne commencoient a marcher tous ensemble. Et parce jespere quilz arryveront/tost vers moy, et en bonne opportunite, et les actendes de jour a autre.   A tant Monsr le Chancellier n^{re} S^{eur} vous tienne en sa sainct garde.

Escript a Gavy le 1j^e daoust MDXXIX.

CHARLES

A Monsr le Grand Chancellier   *A Perrens*
Comte de Gattinare.

No. 8

British Museum, Add. MS. 28,579.

Bergenroth Transcripts of Spanish State Papers, VIII, ff. 249–50.

Muy manifico Señor,

Por una carta mya que el otro dya escreby al Comendador juan batysta castaldo,/haura entendido vuestra merced alguna parte de las cosas deste exercito y de aquellas que seryan necesaryas para el fyn desta empresa/y sy con el tiepo no crecyesen nuestras necesydades remityerame con esta a la otra, mas parecyendome que soy obligando hazer entender a su magestad las cossas que toccan a su servycyo he quesydo con esta escrevillas a vuestra merced, porque las acuerde a Su magestad, a la qual no me atrevo a escrevyr, pues dudo que asy como no me se responde no se deven tanpoco leer mys cartas, y por esto me parece tomar este trabajo con vostra mad, pues se que su mag^d las entendera, y yo cumplire con lo que debo a su real servicio/este exercito es mas para conquistar con la reputacion de las cosas pasadas que con la fuerças presentes y por esto se deve pensar obrar sus fuerças los menos que se pudiere, y too hazello con la reputacion y esta preservar quanto fuere possible pues con ella se pueden hazer mas servicios/que con ningun otro qualquier medio/digo esto que nosotros estamos aquy sobre esta ciudad, y mas nos sostenemos con el nombre que con las obras/porque nos falta todo lo que puede faltar a un exercito/ començando del numero de la gente, que en verdad pocos son menos los enemigos que estan dentro/el dinero no sera cosa nueva mas como aqui no puede aver el remedio que en otras partes se ha havido/es imposibile que la gente sufra la hambre/y tanto mas, que agora ay muchos ytalianos los quales no suelen tener aquel sufrimiento que espanoles, y faltandole su paga pensaran de yr a tomalla con los enemigos los quales cada dia se la ofrecen/los alemanes aunque no agan lo mismo, no dexaran de amotinarse, porque la mayor parte dellos estan riccos y desean de yrse en sus casas/y a la fin deste mes/que sera despues de manana cumple su paga y el tiempo del juramento que han hecho de servir y no ay un carlin para dalles de modo que tampoco se les puede tomar nuevo juramento/ asi como es costumbre hazer con ellos/los espanoles en el misono termino se les devran dos pagas sin las reçagades/y con esto passan tanto trabajo, que es una pyedad en vello y si por servicio de su magestad dexaran de motinarse, y de demandar sus pagas, por pode hazer el misino servicio es menester que piensen de comer por bivyr/y lo mismo digo de la jente darmas y cavallos lygeros que estan en el mismo trabajo/pues no siendo pagados crea vra. mrd. que son forçados de salyr al camino a tomar por fuerça la vitualla que vienne al exercito/y esto siguendo a tres dias no hauremos un pan/y vernemos todos a morinos de hambre, ende mas que el tiempo entra tan fuerte que dara mucha ocasyon a las cosas susodichas/ e quesido dezir todas estas razones por dar entender a vostra mrd. la ympossibilidad de sostener este exercito/y el poco frutto que deste modo aca puede hazer/porlo que me paresce que Su Magd : deve resolutamente procurar con Su S^d el acordio/siendo tan justo, y en tiempo tan conveniente, pues su magestad se halla con peso de defender la Christiandad, y de socorrer a su ermano, Cosas tan importantes por las quales se deven posponer todos los interesses particulares destos principes Christ-

ianos/y Su S^d devrya ser el primero que prepusiese este santa elecyon/si
lo desta empresa se pudiesse tener alguna esperançia de acaballa por la
fuerça que aqui se le puede hazer, podrian, ansy Su Mag^d/po lo que ha
prometido como Su S^d por lo que le va en ello/procurar con obstinacion el
fyn della/mas syendo esto ymposyble porque no consentyran al acordio,
con el qual su Mag^d sacara dinero y Su S^D mostrara de ser aquel pontefice
justo que le conviene ser/pesame que a la fin se verna a este punto/mas
sera tan tarde que ni Su Mag^d havra la parte del dynero que pyensa, ny Su
Sant^d mostrara la sana voluntad que devrya tener, digo esto, porque florentines conoceran que se hara por pura necessidad/con la qual muy mal vernan
a consentyr a nada que les paresca fuera de razon/y con el tiempo ellos haran
sus hechos/porque esperan que este exercito poco podra sostenerse/y enter-
tenerse en este cerco, y sy Su Mag^d querra resolverse en embiar mas gente
y dinero conocen el gasto que le yria en ello/y el tiempo que pasarya en
medio/y la yncomodidad/que se le syguiria en esta coyuntura estas razones
no las dygo a V^{ra} Mrd. porque crea que no las pyensa mas hagolo por
satysfazer a mi mismo de lo que soy obligado/. El Señor Principe trabaja mas de lo possible/y es parte para que muchos esperen el trabajo con
mucho sufrimiento/y con esta no me ocurre dezir otra cosa a vra Mrd.
syno suplicarle que se acuerde de quan suyo soy, y de lo que en my tyene.
Pues con esta memorya terna recuerdo par enderecar mys cosas como en
el espero/y nuestro Senor de a Vra Mrd. lo que dessea/del campo sobre
florencya a XXVIIJ de Otubre a servicyo de vra mrd- el marques del
gasto-*Rubrica*.

Sobre Al muy magnifico Señor el Señor Cobos. Comendador mayor de
Leon. Secretario y del Consijo de la Ces^a y Cattolica M^t.

No. 9

British Museum, Add. MS. 28,580.
   Bergenroth Transcripts of Spanish State Papers, IX, f. 1 *seqq.*
   Copia de carta original de Muxetula al Emperador fecha 2. Mayo 1530.
Carpeta : A Su M^{at} de Muxetula dos de Mayo.
Testo : Sacra Cesarea y muy Catholica Majestad.
   Humilmente besando las imperiales manos y pies de V.M^{tad} asta oy
he sperado el despacho de V.M^{tad} que apponto embiarme despues de mi
partida, y llegho por cierto bien a tiempo y pareciendome en este medio
que venian las carthas de V. Mtad, no dexiar de practicar lo que V.Mtad
me havia mandado able muy largho al principe del todo. Y quanto a
lo del exercito, il principe havyendo visto lo que el papa acia entender
sobre no querer pagar mas de los lx^{il} escudo y lo que V.Mtad sobre esto
dicia, aunque se hallava en mucho trabajo, porque esta jente que era
aqui era mucha, y da otra parte le parecia que por lo mucho recaubdo que
se habian dado los de dentro, en fortificarse y bien repararse, y la poca
manera de gastadores de los quales cada dia se avian aqui menor forma,
que era lo mas siguro y cierto esforçar esta tierra por via de tenella byen
acercada y con quitalle la maner de entrar en ella la vittuala y cosas
de comer, ende mas que segun lo que que de los de dentro se sentia, en ella
es gran estrechura de hambre y solo pan le queda : y porque la sola esperança dellos era en algun muttin de esta jente a la qual fallando el dinero
speravan que se disolviesse, y con esto se les abriesse puerta de algun
rimedio y siendo bien acordado al principe, quanto cumplia al servitio de
V. Mtad que se diesse buen fin a esta empressa, y quanto esto parecerya
byen por lo honrra del mismo principe, y por lo que complya tambyen a
este exercito, pareciole juntamente con obedecer a V.Mtad restringir el

numero de la jente que estava aqui demasiada, por la pagha dela qual era
menestir mas de los lx[ll] escudos al mes, y con esto tambien strengir mas
el cerquo de la tierra, partiendo la jente en lugares muy buenos y mas a
cerqua de Florentia por quitalle en todo el entrar que alguna veç se acia
de algun soccorro de comer, y esto tambien tanto mas le la parecido byen,
porque el dia adelante que aquy lleghe, salieron da una parte de la Ciudad
seycientos enfantes y cyen cavallos y se juntaron con otros que estavan en
empoli, y se furon en Vulterra lexio de aquy quarenta millas y por via
de la fortaleça que tenian florentinos cobraron la tierra, de la qual podrian
aun se no se diesse remedio de mas strengir el cerquo de la tierra, llevar
alguna vittualla y carne por soccorro de la Ciudad, y visto todo esto y
otras raçones que le han movido se ha resolvido tener de toda esta gente
de aqua de rio once mil enfantes, es a saber, tres mil alemanes, dos mil
españoles, que venieron de Napoles, y seys mil ytalianos, quitando da
cada coronel de Italianos el numero que fuesse demas de lo dichos seys
mil, por los quales once mil infantes ya son bastantes lor lx[ll] escudos que
paga el Papa. Es verdad que por los caballos legeros que son muy neces-
sarios por munchos respectos, y por otros extraordinarios serian menestier
almeno por otro mes x[ll] otros escudos, los quales yo me forçare procurar
con el papa, que de su grado y buena voluntad los dea, demas. Y estos
once mill enfantes con los otros que paga V.Mt da la otra parte del rio,
los partira de manera, muy acerca de la Ciudad, que podran tenella mas
estrecha, y le quiteran la esperança de subsidio de cosas de comer, tambyen
ha determinado, con parte desta gente, cercar a Empoli, que esta en medio
del camin de Pisa y da Vulterra, porque se le quicte la esperança de haver
soccorro de aquellos lugares, y a este efecto y tambyen por quitar este
peso a los de Sena que lo no querian mas sufrir y aun porque no se junten
tantos despedidos, en una veç y aghan algun gran desorden, ha pensado
de embiar el coronel de fabricio marramaldo contra Pisa y Volterra y
entertenello alla en alguna manera por algunos dias, entretanto se despedi-
ran estos ottros enfantes ansi los demasiados de estos coroneles ordinarios
come muchos aventureros, que estan por las tierras y las destruen todas,
a cuya causa faltavan las vittuallas y lo exercito no se puede aprovechar
dellas, en muchas cosas y tambyen se despedia la jente, que tenia
Cesare de Napoles que era llegada en estas partes y despidiendo esta
gente a parte, a parte, y no toda junta se espera que no havra inconveniente ende mas que se ha mandado a los coroneles que quedan que en
ninghuna manera consientan que los despedidos entren en sus coroneles
que otramente ellos mismos, correran peligro de ser despedidos, y se le
ha hecho entender que con esto seran byen pagados de los que le quedara,
y assy el principe had empeçado a poner esto en efecho que ya ha llamado
los coroneles ordinarios, y con muchas y buenas raçones le ha eccho entender
el numero que quyere que tiengan y que dispidan los otros, y provean que
los dispedidos se vayan sin hazer disorden, y aunque se ha hovido en esto
artho trabajo con todo se ha eccho y effectuado esto : y se dispidiran los
aventureros y despues de esto se dara a un remedio a los enfantes de
Fabricio que es la mas jente, y se V.M. la oviesse menester en Ungria,
podriase embiar ahy, porque fabricio tiene voluntad de servir a V.Mtad
en todas las partes, y quando no hoviesse de yr entonces se vera con algun
medio dispedir parte dellos, y la otra parte se intertenera sui costa del Papa
ny de V.Mt da estos mismos lughares del paes, que quederan en nuestro
poder, y servyran tambyen a tener estrechos los inimighos que estan en
Pisa y en Vulterra, que no saleran a su placer, ny tanpoco se aprovechan
de los lughares abiertos los quales haviendo a entertener jente mejor sera
que intertengan la de V.M. que no la enimigha.
    Tambyen el principe ha con buena manera embiado muchos cavallos

legeros albaneses en el reyno, y al entrar dello seran despedidos, y se yran a sus casas, segun la orden de V.Mtad porque si se dispedian aqua muchos dellos serian ydos a servir a Florentia, que come son griecos lo acostumbran acer, y los florentines no tenian menestier dellos y todos no se podian mas entertener aqua, y ha hecho quedar da cientos y cinquenta cavallos de los mejores dellos y a los que ha hecho partir por el Reyno por dispedillos les ha dado el principe mil ducados de los que ha dado Sena, ne le parecia que fuessen buenos por Ungria. Los mil enfantes espanoles dispedidos se juntaron, y yban amuttinados aminaçando, y habia tanbyen aparejo y trampa que con ellos se querian juntar muchos otros questavan da qua del rio sperando con crecer el numero esforçar al principe de tenellos aqua : yo come llegue dixie tan claro quanto V.Mtad se havia sentido de este muttin y que determinava no sufrillo dexiandose obedecer (en demas en tal tiempo) a los ordenes de V.Mtd y aciendo byen entender a muchos principales de este exercito quan mala cosa era esta, y que gran verguença de la nation y de los buenos que se suffrisse tal inobediencia havyendo estos tentado no querer servir la persona a V.M^t lo que syn dinero lo havyan de ofrecer y diciendole en esto muchas rasones y que pensasen que V.M.^{tad} no havia con estos terminos a floxiar, syendo su proprio castigar los ruynos y porfiosos y perdonar a los humiles. No son y dos mas deste exercito a juntarse con estos enfantes, mas antes muchos dellos se son apartados del numero y muttin y vanse derramados esperando algun medio y son quedados obra de quinientos hombres, los quales estan en un lugar que tomaran y ahy byven y todavia se trata concertallos y obrar o que sieguan su camino obedicindo lo que fue mandado o se buelvan en espanna, o se dissolvan todos, porque no hagan danno al paes ny a las vittualas del exercito ; esto se trabaja con toda diligentia.

Despues dado principio, a todas estas cossas llegharon las cartas de V.Mtad de XXVIJ de Abril, con el despacho que yo esperava y con el calor dellas se dio muy buena mano a todo lo que yo havia hablado al principe en nombre de V.M^{ad} y quanto tocca a lo del exercito, esta byen concertado todo, y ansi spero se egequitera, porque ya tiene determinado tenello siempre muy obediente, y que no se desmande, y esta el principe muy conforme con lo que V. Md le ha mandado, ansi de no turbar la mente del Papa en pedille mas dineros, come en todas las otras cosas, solamente desearia los x^d escudos de mas por los cavallos legeros y otros extraordinarios los quales, o por una via o por otra espero que se havian.

Esto de los enfantes despedidos se trabaja concertar que aun estan muy duros en andar en ungria, y se le ha ofrecido por el pagador de V.Mtad la pagha en bolona, y otra en trento, que assi dice que tiene orden de V.Md y por que dician que no tenean un real aqui para moversi tanbien se le ha ofrecido un ducado en quenta de la pagha y que vayan : estan duros, y al principe tambyen le parece recio proceer contra ellos con açelle dano a sus personas : hoviendo servido siempre a V.Mtad con todo esto se trabaja de concertallos endemas siendo venidas hoy la postreras carthas de V.Mtad de XXVIII de Abril en las quales V.Mtad escrive haver ya mandado que los enfantes que eran partidos dal campo per su orden vayan a Ungria, y que queria otros dos mill o al meno mill espanoles, y por esto se trabaja que vayan en todo caso, estos con otros que hay aqui demasiados, y piensa el principe que los inbiara con otros mil Italianos buenos. . . .

. . . Muy bien ha parecido al principe lo que V.Mt manda que hagha entender a la gente sobre las mercedes que ellos esperavan aghora de V.Mt y come estavan algo mal contentes estos capitanes con la cartha che lliegho de V.Mt que se le podia leyr y con las palabras que accudi conforme a la orden de V.M^t y a su cartha, quedaron muy contentos y con muy buena esperança, y no faltaran byen servir come han bien servydo y assi lo dizen todos en verdad que son por azer.

Los recaudos de los xx^{ll} escudos por la gente venieron a muy buen tiempo, y ansi se son enbiados dos hombres con ellos, lo uno a Jenua lo otro al Duca de Milan por cobrallos, porque ya la gente ablaba de muttin, yo por orden del principe y del marques able a los coroneles y capitanes y espereran este dinero porque bien conocen la buena provision de V.Md.

Hase embiado luegho el poder al Cardinal Coloña por haver los xxxx^{ll} escudos. . . .

. . . Hable de forma con el marques del gasto, y tambyen con el principe come da mi sobre estos malos contentamientos del marques, que ya el marques servira de buena voluntad y espero havellos entreghados en amistad y haunque entrellos passe algun recelo por los malos medios que han ovido entrellos, yo espero havellos bien concertados, y pienso que no terna V.Mt desto mas trabajo. . . . . .

Fabricio Maramaldo con su coronel en llegando yo nel campo se levanto da lo de Siena, y por orden del principe se va sobre Pisa, y piensa acer algun byen/al meno quitara el remedio de comer que podia venir a Florentia da aquella parte y aun aprovechera mucho que los de Vulterra no hagen rebolver otras tierras que le estan a cerqua, que si non era esta gente se havian empeçadas a alcar, y estos commissarios del papa que ya sienten gran comodidad de esto, les place mucho que se enbie esta gente nel pisano, y por muchos respechos ha byen parecido todo esto al principe y se que plaçera al papa endemas, que si se podiesse ganar Pisa, seria ganar Florentia, y V.Mt se accuerda que lo desseava mucho Su S^d.

Sena paga unos cinco mil escudos, porque el coronel de fabricio se sea partido de sus tierras, pero vienen en esta Thesoreria del exercito, para las necessidades del y no en benefitio del dicho coronel. . . . Mañana con la gratia de dios me partire por Roma, y ahy exequutare la orden de V.M^t y asimismo hare despues lo que me mando de mi yda en el Reyno, y de la bolvida pora servir V.Mt in presentia. Chedo humilmente besando las imperiales manos y pies de V.Mt la prosperosa vida dela qual con acrecimiento de quanto justo desea. N. Señor dios conservi y felicite come ella y sus buenos y fieles vaxallos y servidores desean. Dal felicissimo exercito de V.M^t sobre Florentia, a ij de Maio MDXXX—de V.Ces. e Cath. M^{ta}—humil siervo chi soi Imperiali piedi e mani basa Jo. Ant° Musectula.

Sobre : Sacre Ces^a multumque Cath^{ea} M^{ti}.

No. 10

R. Arch. di Stato di Firenze.
Registro di Lettere Esterne agli Ambasciadori dal 1529 al 1554
Signori, Carteggio, Missive, Registri, 1° Canc. LVIII, 4 May.

Anchonitanis. Mag^{cd} Dnj: etc. Quantumque non ci sia nuovo nè ci habbia posto maraviglia alcuna che chi ha cercato e di continua non resta sanza causa alcuna et fuori d' ogni justitia di spogliare questa nostra città della libertà sua habbia operato che in cotesta città siano facte rapresaglie delle robe de nostri merchanti, ci ha ben facto maravigliare assai che dalle M. S^{rie} V. sia stato non solamente consentito contro alla publica fede datane, ma quello che molto più ci ha facto maravigliare et ce ne ha facto dolere è, che per V.M. S.^{rie} sia stata facta tale exequtione il che non ci saremo mai persuasi, pensando che per V.M.S. si fussi dovuto ogni extrema resistentia di non essere adoperato per instrumento di fare contro alla fede loro una cosa tanto vituperosa quanto e questa ; dal quale modo di procedere si puo trarre una certissima coniectura, che non sia più possibile confidare nella parola et nelli ampli capitoli di quelle per alcuno che si sia solito negociare in cotesta città. . . . Siamo certissimi che V.S. (non) sopporteranno di lasciarsi tanto vilmente tyranneggiare contro ad ogni Justitia per nuocere a chi in publico et in privato vi ha sempre giovato. Il quando segua ne haremo piacere grandissimo per lo utile nostro et per honore di V.S. le quale habbiamo sempre amato da fratellj; così come non succedendo (il che non ci puo però esser capace) saremo forzati insentircene et farne quella demostratione che merita la ingiuria, della quale per non esser morti (come si stima chi ha procurato farsi tal cosa per V.S.) haremo speranza poterci valere. . . . Risentinsi adunque V.S. et non voglino in uno medesimo tempo nuocere ai Merchanti nostri, alla città loro . . . non dovendo una Magᶜᵃ Città tale sendo libera et capitolata, lasciarsi però comminciare ad somettere con la sedia appostolica.

No. 11.

British Museum, Add. MS. 28,580.
(Bergenroth Transcripts of Spanish State Papers, IX) f. 123 *seqq.*
Carpeta : A Su Mᵗ : de Muxetula VIJ de Junio 1530.
Testo : S.C. y C.Mᵗ.

Humilmente besando las imperiales manos y pies de V.Mᵈ las cosas de Florentia a mi parecer son en buenos terminos, y segun algunos avisos que hay de la Ciudad, si lo de Vulterra se gana como yo espero y vyvamente se va sobre Pisa con la misma gente que es aghora en Volterra y con la que ha servido a Empoli, y se vehe que nuestra gente tiene forma de estar en el cerquo quanto tiempo sera menestir ; florentinos han de ceder por fuerza a mi parecer creciendo como ya cada dia le crece la ambre y necessidad y faltando la speranza de remedio : y porque podria ser que las cosas lleasen a estos terminos por muchas razones creho que el verdavero servicio de V.M.ᵗ seria que la Ciudad cediesse a lo que V.Mᵗ mandasse della y que no entrasse lo exercito dentro y la sacheasse y destruysse mas que se conservasse. He avertito desto el principe, che seria muy byen que se piensen desde aghora los medios come se lleghe a este fin, el qual dexiando aparte el deseo, que desto y con razon tiene el Papa, mas porque sino me ingano, esto cumple tambyen al servicio de V.Mᵗ, pienso que se ha de procurar porque si una vez lo exercito entra en Florencia, y la saquea cierto esta que sera imposible sacallo mas dalla, sin mucho dinero porque nunca ha quesido contentarse que saqueandose la tierra no puedan pedir el dinero que se les deve por el passado, y veyendo su determination, al principe no parecio tentallo mas. Por esto digo que si ellos una vez entran y saquean, demas de destruyr una tierra tan principal y que siendo a la orden de V.Mᵗ podra aprovechar a las cosas que puedan suceder, claro esta que se llevara la gente despues sin dalle mucho dinero, el qual la Ciudad deshecha no puede pagar, y el papa esta tan pobre que pienso que sera imposible que la paghe, y detto manera se fuesse menester sacar la gente, V.Mᵗ puede pensar, a quien esto daria trabajo. Por esto a mi parecer pues las cosas se acercan al fin de la victoria, se han de trajar los medios con los quales se lleghe ad aquel fin que sea mas servicio de dios, que es no destruyr tantos probres hombres mujeieres monasterios y otros tantos que no tienen culpa, y sea tambyen mas servitio y honora de V.Mᵗ la qual pienso que sera mas servida desta manera, que de lo otra, y tambyen porque es conforme al deseo del Papa, por ser su patria y a un papa, al qual pareceria muy mal hazer destruyr una tal ciudad, podiendose salvar y ganar ; que quando no se pudiesse hazer lo uno sin lo otro, la causa excuseria l'effetto, y porque pienso que si se trabajan los medios en esto, podrasse venir a esto buen fin, demas de havello todo advertido al principe, me ha parecido tambien escrivillo a V.Mᵗ porque seria arto bien que V.Mᵗ por cartas lo advertiesse tambien al principe, que podiendose ganar la Ciudad y reducir que no stea mas en su porfia, que lo trabaje y ponga todos los medios porque no se destruya. Digbo esto que podria ser que la Ciudad, segund algunas palabras que se entienden, perdiendose Volterra y sabiendo que no se ha de deviar este cerco venira a tractar su concordia y darse. Y porque quando la voluntad de V.Mᵗ no sea tambyen conocida dal Principe, podria ser que no se mirasse tanto a este fin que digho y assy los soldados gozarian de la victoria no a servicio de V.Mᵗ mas por mas trabajo : yo como me allo en esto por my descargho y por el servitio de V.Mᵗ me ha parecido azerselo entender todo, y assy pensando que esto sea conforme a su voluntad lo ho procurado y trabajado, y ansi lo trabajare, quedo rogando a Nuestro Señor dios por el acrecymiento de la felice vida y Reinos de V.Mt como por ella y por sus buenos y fides vaxallos y servidores se dessea. De Roma a VIJ de Junio MDXXX.

Despues escripta esta, todavia se entiende que florentines stan porfiosos y esparan quanto puedan y che tienen trigo por ogosto : y che la mayor esperanza de eglos es el rey de Francia, rompiendo las paces despues de aver los yscyos. De V.C. y C.Mᵗ—humil servo que sus Imperiales manos besa—Jo/ Ant° Musectula.

Sobre : Sacre Cesarᵉ y Catᶜᵉ Majestati.

No. 12

British Museum, Add. MS. 28,580.
(Bergenroth Transcripts of Spanish State Papers, IX) f. 108 *seqq.*

Copia de un documento en italiano en cuya carpeta dice : Las Cartas que se tomaran en aste que de Francia se escrevian a Florencia que se embiaron de Roma.

Dentro.

Di Baldassara Carduccio alli Sʳˡ X : di Francia, de 2 giugno.

Magᶜˡ Do: Dni: observanᵐⁱ : Fu l' ultima mia delli XI del passato, la quale secondo che ho aviso da panciatichi fu per loro indricciata all via di Genova, e da Genova facilmente per via di Luigi Alamani sarà condotta a Pisa a salvamento pero non repplichero altro. Arrivarono dipoi le di X detto congli mandati allo effecto in esse contenuto e per non havere pottuto Barnardo Altovetti secondo dice commodamente andare ne et mandare al luogo destinato per quelle, benche io penso habbia più tosto voluto satisfare a Gio: Francesco de Bardi et Giovanni Girardi i quali erono di parer che non fusse bene mandarvi homo aposta, ma che il mandato fusse fatto in loro per non fare dimonstratione, essendo come dicono, cosi la voluntà di quel Re. Mi ha detto Bernardo sigficato che io debbia mandare a quelli tal potere, certificandomi doversi più prontamente expedire questo negocio per loro mano che per altri. Io ancor che non mi dessero specificatamente tal commisione accio che quel bene et comodo che potesse sequire per loro opera non si perda, exeguiro mandandole instruttionj mandatemi. Per quanto detto Bernardo mi significa addio piaccia quanto si desidera habbia effecto et non di manco come per altra dissi non è manco speranza che qui si faccia più commoda e più pronta expeditione che la perche si è stabilito tra questa Maesta et il Signore Conte oratore del Re d'Inghilterra di non lasciare in modo alcuno perire cotesto Dominio tanto loro affettionato et ordinato che ciascuna delle dette Maesta concorra al beneficio et sussidio di quella, questo per una rata et quel per la meta di quella, di modo che essendosi con l'aiuto d'Iddio e con quella sollecitudine mi è stata possibile insieme con Giuliano Bonaccorsi ottenuta una

assegnatione di venti milla scudi, credo absolutamente, che questo S^r
Conte con beneplacito del su re concorrera a Dieci milla intendendo tal
compositione dover durare insino alla totale liberatione di cotesto assedio.
Non dimeno, in qualunque modo detto Re serva, sara approposito per
me qui non si manchera di sollecitare et instare per questo effetto, giudi-
cando maxime per parere di questa Maestà et dell' amiraglio che più apposito
sia instare per questo concorso qui qual sara più efficace et certo et senza
alcuno interesse che per altra via se i mercanti di Lione hanno tal assegnatione benche picciola darano modo di potere su detto fare qualche somma,
dover esser molto pronta et expedita : et quello che verra per una di queste
altre vie sara di non mediocre augmento a pottere sostentare l'impresa
cominciata di fuore, ne per questo manchero di stimulare et importunare
questa Maesta del resto de tale assegnatione per la somma delle dette
cedole, et spero di fare qualche profitto come pure doppo tanta longhezza
si è ottenuto questa.   Dissi altravolta con voluntà di questa Maesta i vari
modi servava il Papa con quella di mostrare di desiderare che essa inter-
ponesse fra V.S. (etiam) di trovare qualche comoda compositione salvando
sempre la liberta della citta et il vivere publico come altra volta opero che
si mandasse Chiramonte il quale hoggi e passato di questa vita, et non
dimeno non opero la venuta sua frutto alcuno salvo che al presente farebbe
il simile : il che allegando hoggi mi fu risposto allhora essere un tempo
per essere l'imperatore in Bologna, et hoggi esserne un altro di che piena-
mente adverti V.S^{rie} di nuovo.   Pare che si proponghi quei medesmi
termini, offerendosi pronto allevare l'assedio et che V. Signorie si desar-
massero et simile cose nelle quali facendo io poco fondamento non instaro
altramente.   Ultimamente, per uno huomo expedito da Tarbes move detto
Papa altro modo di procedere, querellandosi gravemente di questa Maesta,
dicendo che essa è causa de tenire la città gagliarda, havendo dato loro
capitani et homini oppositi al bisogno suo, et in altre soccorendola etiam
di danari, in modo che non repputava havere manco la guerra da Sua
Maesta che da Vostre Signorie, et volendo che si conosca essere il contrario
la conforta e priega che voglia mandare al Signor Malatesta et Signor
Stefano et Signor Gio: Paolo, tutti homini di quella, che si partino di
stipendi di quelle, il che affermano, non dubitare che farrano quando Sua
Maesta lo faccia di bono animo : onde che volendo quella dimonstrare non
lo volere impugnare de alcuna sua impresa, ma essergli obsequente come
sempre è stato et molto contento perquanto si aspetti a lui non essendo
in verita detti Signori suoi homini comandarli che per conto suo non
servino V.S^{rie} contro al Papa, benche gli paia essere certo che non l'ubidir-
anno, pure ne fare prova, et mandera con detto homo di Tarbez uno a
posta a tale effecto costi.   Quale habbia ad essere questo homo non so
ancora perche affermano non haverlo ancora deliberato et non dimanco
per non mancare di quello ha havuto sempre et e per havere in intentione
non solamente di non nuocere in cosa alcuna a V.S^{rie} ma di giovare in
tutto quello che li sia possibile, ha expedito l'homo di Malatesta, sinon con
fatti, almen con bone parole et bonissime promesse di non mancargli in cosa
alcuna di quello che gli ha promesse, et circa la condotta et circa l'ordine
grande non fusse per altro obligo che per lo havere visto quanto egregia-
mente se è portato verso cotesto Dominio che certamente non gli potria
havere fatto cosa più grata confortandolo a seguitare virilmente non
obstante alcuna sua comminatione o mandati fatti o da farsi par S. Maesta
a petitione del Papa ; et il simile volle che detto homo di Malatesta faccia
intendere al S^{re} Stefano et S^{re} Gio: Paolo.   Anchor, che riccercasse S.
Maesta di due versi, saltem per modo di credenza non ha voluto fare,
dubitando non accadi a lui come al Cavalero Dasperetto.   Anche l'ha
advertito che si torni con tutte la cautelle possibile perchè pensa che il

Papa li habbia attendere le reti ad ogni passo. Sarebbe detto homo già in camino sinon che aspetta di essere spedito di alcuni danari che S. Maesta gli ha ordinati per suo viaggio. Ho voluto prevenire con questa acciò che quando detto homo riccevese impedimento alcuno, o soprastesse in alcun luogo V. Signorie habbiano questa pocca notitia avanti l'arrivo del homo del Re et di Tarbez.

De la restitution de figliuoli non ho altro che significare a V.S. salvo che del continuo questa Maesta e in moto per accostarsi a luegho dove si debbe fare, et essendo rescate tutte le dificulta, si spera che in brievi giorni saranno in Francia che è quanto al presente mi occorre far noto a quelle. A la bona grazia dele quali mi raccomando que bene valeant. Di Myrambco il giorno ij di Giugno MDXXX.   E.D.V.

BALTHASSAR CARDUCCIUS.

No. 13

British Museum, Add. MS. 28,580.
(Bergenroth Transcripts of Spanish State Papers, IX) f. 187 *seqq.*

Carpeta.
A Su M^t. de Muxetola XXV de Junio 1530.
Testo.
Sac : Ces^a y Cath. M^{ta}.

Humilmente besado las Imperiales manos y pyes de V.M^{ta} digho, que ya V^{ra} M^d por la posta que pochos dias sonse le enbyo de aqui havra intendido lo que se ha descubierto de las platicas del Rey de Francia et Rey de Inglaterra, y como por el ombre de Malatesta Baglione que prendio Escalenga se ha visto como no solamente dan esperancas y favor a Florentines mas aun dinero porque no se pierden esto mismo se ha confirmado despues con otras cartas que son venidas de Francia del nuncio del Papa, el qual escrive que el embaxador de V.M^t que ay rreside lo ha tanbien descubierto y lo ha dicho a el que lo avertiese al Papa. Crea tanbien que lo avra escripto a V.M^t.

Tambien aqui se ha descubierto otra cosa que por diversos rrespectos importo mucho ; y es que Malatesta Baglion muy secretamente averttio de dentro Florencia al Coronnel Pirro que es un de los coroneles de V.M^t y su amigo que Florentines tenian platica de envenenar el Papa, y que embiarian un ombre con los instrumentos y aparejos desto, y le dio las señales porque lo tomassen y le dixo que avertiesse al Papa porque ahunque el servia a Florentines como capitan de que hera y hazia lo que convenia a onbre de guerra, pero que estos medios como deshonrrados y malos no le plazian ende mas siendo el vasallo y servidor de Su S^t en todas las otras cosas, y ansi se exeutto por el dicho coronel Pirro che saliendo aquel hombre y rreconocidos las señales le tomo y le hallo las rredomitas llenas de veneno con algunas tabllillas de cierta mistura que se avian de tomar./primero de los que havian de hazer la salva al Papa, porque a ellos el veneno non danasse. Y traydo este ombre en poder del yllustre Principe saco del todo esto cierto y nombra algunos servidores del Papa muy intrinsicos que cabian en ello. Y luego el principe me ha avisado aqui a Su St y le ha enbiado el dicho coronel Pirro con los dichos instrumentos y aparejos que el Papa es quedado tan obligado al principe quanto decirse puede y tambien arto satisfecho de la obra de Malatesta y piensa tambien que Malatesta haviesse quesido en esto obligar al Papa por poderse fiar del en algund concierto que se oviesse de trattar de las cosas de Florencia ; y como en aquel tiempo Malatesta no havia podido saber lo que llevava este onbre de Francia se haviesse determinado a concordia Florencia y con este medio oviesse quesido ganar la voluntad del Papa la qual por cierto discubriendose mas la verdad deste mal que se procurava la tiene por ganada.

Su Sd con grandissima diligencia mira en llegar a cabo la verdad desto veneno y quien cabra en ello y va todo muy secretto endemas porque no se sepa como se ha empeçado a descobrir y se dara aviso a V.M^t de todo, ha escripto all Ill^{me} principe palabras muy eficaces y grandes por las quales muestra agradecer en grand manera este servicio a Malatesta porque tambien asi ha parecido al dicho Principe que se haga podra ser que esto descubrir de un tan grand mal fuesse tanbien principio de gran bien. . . .

De Roma a XXV de Junio MDXXX de V.Ces. y Cath. M^{ta} humil siervo. che sus imperiales manos besa Muscetula.

Sobre : Sacre Ces^{e} et Cath^{ee} M^{ti}

No. 14

British Museum, Add. MS. 28,580.
(Bergenroth Transcripts of Spanish State Papers, IX) f. 286 *seqq.*

Carpeta : Copia de carta del orator florentin que sta en corte de Francia. Es la misma que embio Don Hernando de Gonzaga.

Testo : Deciferato di lettere di Messer Balthassare Carducci oratore Fiorentino in Francia a Signori Dieci di Firenze, di XXJ luglio 1530.

Magnifici Domini Domini mei observantissimi, ecc.

Come per l' ultima mia di XV con dispiacere per homo a posta dissi a V.S. la resolutione di questo Re esser stata di non si volere scoprire, et d'essermi necessario seguitare il camino con questa Maestà per intendere et procurare quelli secreti subsidii qual intendeno prestare a cotesta povera Città, onde transferendosi da Bordeo a Borgo per la Dordona il seguitai, et a levare del Gran Maestro ricercar lo come di sopra, dolendomi gravemente della sinistra sorte di quella et del poco ricognoscimento si trovava in loro rispetto a meriti et fede suoi tanti verso la Maestà Sua non dimittendo di replicarli il termine nel quale quella si trovava et ancor che patientemente mi ascoltasse, come quelli che pure cognoscono il mancamento loro, non dimanco stava ancora sul honesta del non dovere questa Maestà cosi subito precipitare in venire contra a si fresca conventione del Papa et del Imperatore : dolendosi molto delle mie, trovate al homo di Malatesta et deciferate dove si vedevano le promesse di questa Maestà. Al che risposi non haver mancato de scrivere in cifra, et di haverlo advertito del camino che fu condutto in Asti contra l'intentione nostra, et pero possano V.S. vedere quanto sarebbe necessario mutare la cifra come più volte ho scritto ; et non se n'è fatto nulla. Alla parte dell'honestà risposi essere molto maggiore dishonesta mancare delle promessi tante volte fattaci, et tanto debite, anzi che tutto il mondo li harebbe per tal causa in pessimo concepto nè mai più sarebbe prestato fede a loro colligationi et confederationi, mostrandoli il fine de V/S. non havere mai riguardato ad alcuno suo commodo, o adquisto da farsi per alcuna impresa con questa Maestà dove si sono spese immoderatamente le facultà della Città, ma solo a la protettione et defensione dello stato et libertà loro della quale questa sola volta, benche per causa loro erano caduti in tanto bisogno. Et volendosi persuadere doversi pro loro con l' Imperatore et col Papa fare ogni sforzo che si dovesse cessare da questa si iniusta obsidione mostrando essersi col Papa et col nuntio suo qui molto exasperatosi, detestando questa sua impresa, havennuti i principi Christiani deposto le arme et fatto pensiero di viver Christianamente sola teneva l' Italia tutta in perturbatione et quel che è molto più vituperabili, la p.nia sua jl che sperava, mediante tali opera et la diligentia dello scudiero Pier

Francisco, dovessi succedere qualche buona compositione. Dissili esser ridotte le cose a termine di non dovere nè potere sperare compositione alcuna buona, et se havessero desiderata la quiete et sicurtà di V.S. per via di compositione la devevano procurar col Imperatore nella Combraia, ma che sempre il fin loro era stato et ancora è in proprio interesse, et non in quello delli amici, et confederati loro, come si vidde allhora, et se vede hoggi molto più dove è, cessato l'interesse de Figliuoli, non dovea restare maggior interesse che la conversatione delli amici ; da quelli pericoli et incommodi ne quali li haverano messi, certificandolo che tanta era la iusta indignatione di cotesta universalità, che prima che comporre col Papa, et ridursi ad un evidente termine d' una sevissima et barbaria servitu consentira di mangiarsi li figli et incendir tutta la città et offerirsi voluntariamente alla morte et fuoco quando temessero quella non mancava loro animo di insignorire l'imperadore de più nobili di quel Dominio, come è Pisa, Livorno, Volterra, accio non se n'habbia ad insignorire il Papa, appetendo più presto d'esser absolutamente servi et subditi di Barbari che d'un Giuliano de' Medici, il che ne dubitono esser grato et accetto per li effetti che evidentemente se ne possono conoscere infra quali era di guada-gnarsi il più bel dominio d'Italia, et il più al proposito della desiderata monarchia sua, o al manco ne succederebbe effetto contrario a quello che si procura per loro Signoria del tener il Papa, et non si dechiarare amico loro come disegnono et sperono, tenendo l'Imperadore nutrito di speranza di renderli le cose predette.   Tanto che composse le cose de Allemagna, ritornandosi in Italia, possa parlare et operare più sicuratamente con lui di questa cosa tutto per turbarlo, talche me disse Ambassadore, il luogo dove di presente ci troviamo, non è da poter fermare cosa alcuna sopra è casi vostri : voi vi transferirete in Angulem, dove subito sara questa Maestà et senza necessita si dara ordine di provedervi di qualche somma di danari per la dipesa vostra et non mi exprimero la quantità.   Dissi Signore il mal nostro a bisogno di buona provisone, perche horamai è tanto durato che la città è propinqua alla morte in modo ch' una piccola quantità la manterrebbe sul tisico et alla fine ne la conducerebbe, et penso che sara forsi più a proposito di quella apertamente disperarla della speranza nostra, che farla consumare in questo modo, potendo forsi con l'aiuto di Dio salvarsi dalle mani del Papa et della sua crudeltà col modo detto.   Et partendosi da esso con la resolutione del trovarmi in Angulem distante XIIIJ leghe, mi richiamo in drieto et me disse (credo pensando alle parole dettoli).   Ambassadore, non vi andate cosi disperato, im-peroche io credo resolutamente che sarete aiutati ; il che mi conferme nella opinione detta di sopra che la parole dette lo pongessero nel vivo, dispiacendoli tanta grandezza dell' Imperatore et molto più che se codesto dominio (che è Dio guardi) pervenisse nelle mani del Papa sperandovi manco offensione, massime procurandosi le amicitia sua, come è detto potissime, per l'interesse del Re d'Inghilterra, col quale costoro conoscono haveri tanta obbligatione, quanto sia possibile, di maniera che, io tengo per certo, che questa sia la causa della si repente variazione, havendo come credo, vedutosi il Papa a mal termine, se recuperati e figliuoli, dato nuova speranza di questo maledetto divortio, per tener fermi questi dua Re a non si scuoprire contro di lui.   Havendosi, come per altre dissi, trovato quel conte di Vilser nel suo ritorno di Roma tutto perturbato, et scandalizzato contro il Papa, et offertosi de operare a benefizio della città con quel Re, con tutto l' ingegno suo, e di già haverne scritto e mosso questa Maestà, al medesimo offerendo far sempre concorrere il suo Re per la metà di quello che contribuisse questo et inoltri quelle Maestà havea dato larghissima intenzione a quelli di Londra di servire la città, mostrando bravamente dolersi che si ingiusta impresa del Papa.   E non di meno in un subito da ogni parte ogni cosa raffreddò usando di dire, come di sopra di non si voler scuoprire, come per più mie significai. Et cosi com' io temeno che questa Maestà differitigli et prorogatali la restituzione dei figliuoli ogno volta che li fossero stati offerti, sarebbe deposta ogni indignatione, et remessegli nel buon di cosi Inghilterra, ogni volta che li sarà dato speranza del divortio etiam che fusse commesso a cielo contra del Papa tornerebbe in amicitia con lui come si vede ora in fatto. Et però V.S. sapientissime giudicheranno quello sia expediente, benchè sia tardi per la salute loro ; perchè temo, come ho detto che questi sperati subsidii non sieno piccoli et tardi secondo il costume di qua. Non però si manterrà per me di seguitare, come di sopra ed tutto darne notizia a V.S. Non voglio mancare di fare intendere a quelle come qua si è sparsa voci mediante alcuni lettere di Roma, dello haver la Città procurato veleno al Papa, cosa che pare contro a quella opinioni la qual universalmente si ha del universi hogge costi tanto rettamente. Sonmi ingengato, come credo esser il vero, mostrare questa essere un calumnia procurata per li inimici di V.S. affermando questo non esser stato mai in consuetudine della città nostra il che facilmente si dimonstrava nella nipote del Papa, ma che vuol aggrave l'opinione, et fama buona di V.S. trovava simili calunnie ; et quando la bontà di Dio giudicherà, dovere esser il tempo di detto Papa senza alcuna procuratione humana opera quanto sara necessaria, ch' è quanto al presente ne ocurre significar a V.S. alla buona grazia delle quali mi raccomando, quae bene valeant. Di Angulem.

No. 15

British Museum, Add. MS. 28,580.
Bergenroth Transcripts of Spanish State Papers, IX, f. 321 *seqq.*

Carpeta : A Su M^t del Embaxador de Roma XXX y ultimo de Jullio 1530.
Testo : Muy alto y muy Poderoso Señor. . . . . . .

En este dia llegaron dos cartas interceptas del Embaxador Florentin que esta en Francia en que dizia que antes de la restitution de los hijos el se quexava con el Christianissimo porque les abandonava, siendole tan devotos : y que Su Alteza le respondio que debia tener mas compasion del que no quexa, viendo quanto le iva en la recuperation de los hijos y que por esto no le devia venir a hablar a el por no causar nuevas sospechas pues el mesmo effecto haria hablando con el Almirante, pero que cobrados los hijos no les havia de faltar y que en esto mesmo estava el Rey de Anglaterra, al qual havia rogado que les soccoriese con diez mill ducados agora, y que el acudiria a la portion concordada entrellos que es como parecio por otra letra del mesmo tambien intercepta la mitad mas segund lo escrivi los dias passados a V. M^d y dize que el Angles quiso saber si havian de ser prestados o dados ; y porque el Christianissimo dixo que dados parecio que al Angles se le hizo de mal, y que por remediar esto luego el mesmo embaxador Florentin fue al de Anglaterra y le dixo que no los querian sino prestados, y que el tenia poder para obligar a sus principales a ello, y que le dio el poder el qual fue imbiado en Anglaterra ; y respondieron de alla al Embaxador que no era bastante ; de manera que dize el que escrive que teme no sea cautela.

A este mesmo respecto escrive que le dixo Robertet Rogad vos a Dios que se restituian los hijos del Rey, que de alli depende vuestro bien, porque aquella restitution ha de ser vuestra redemption. Y por esto escrive que el mesmo Robertet en la mesma noche, que a la corte de Francia llego la nueva de la entrega de los hijos se lo embio a hazer saber a la media noche, y por la manana siguiente el fue a hablar al Almirante sobre sus cosas y que le dixo, que no le aquexase tanto, y le dixo que estuiviesse de buena gana que pues eran cobrados los hijos, sus cosas irian bien.   Y que despues hablo al Christianissimo, el qual le dixo lo mesmo ; el qual tambien le dixo que se devian acordar con el Papa y unir todos, y que el Papa tambien se contentasse dello, y que pensasen que si Vra Majestad componia las cosas de Alemaña y las del Turcho que seria absoluto Señor de todo, y que si ellos se unian al Papa y Florentines con el Rey de Anglaterra y con el, que no ternian miedo a Vra Majestad. Esto dizia la carta por estas palabras mesmas que por ser substanciales, trabaje que no se me obvidasen.

Tambien avisava como en Francia se tratava casamiento del Vayvoda con la hermana del que ellos llaman Rey de Navarra.

Escrevia tambien en la mesma letra que venia el Conde Pontremolo para este effecto y para dar aviso a los Florentines de la dicha resti-tution. . . .

Tambien entiendo por las mesmas cartas quel orador de florentines fue a hablar a Madama que estava fuera de la corte en una casa y que no allandola, hablo a un su muy grand privado que dizen que se llama Larocche Beaucourt, el qual le dixo que tuviesen buena esperança porque pues tenia sus hijos antes que pasase un mes veria que el Christianissimo haria buenos effectos en beneficio de Florencia y mas dixo que al Rey de Francia cumplia de hazerlo asy, y que en caso que no estoviese alli aquella ciudad devia de procurar el Christianissimo de hazer otra, sola para este effecto.

Tambien escrive que se ayuntavan el Embaxador de Ferrara con el de Florentia que ambos son letrados con los foraxidos del reyno que alli estan. . . .

Tambien ha pocos dias que vino nueva como esperaban en Pisa seis mill ducados imbados de Francia, y luego escrevi a Genova para que tomassen el vergantin que los havia de traer a Pisa y lo mismo tornare a escrevir esta noche, para que se provea lo mismo si aportaren por alli unos salitres que por cartas nuevamente ynterceptas de Florentines se sabe que ymbiavan a demandar a Francia juntamente con mas dineros.

El Principe ha estado malo, y pusonos en sospecha de peligro de su persona, agora ya esta bueno y es ido a caça y entiende en aquel cerco y empresa con mucha diligentia.   De dentro de Florentia ha salido un hombre que dizin que viene a tractar de paz, ahunque por otras partes se entiende que los mesmos Florentines quieren diz que salir y pelear, pero no creo que lo haran.   Ntro Señor muy alto y muy poderoso principe Soberano Rey y Señor nos guarde y ensalce a V.Mt por tan largos tiempos y con tanta felicidad y gloria como sus buenos servidores vassallos y criados desseamos.   De Roma XXX de Jullio de MDXXX.

No. 16

British Museum, Add. MS. 28,581.
Bergenroth Transcripts of Spanish State Papers, X, f. 21 *seqq*.

Carpeta : A Su Mt de Micer Mai V de Agosto 1530.
Testo : Sacra Caes : Cath. : M^{ad}.

En este puncto he recibido una carta de Don Fernando de Gonzaga, hecha ayer IIIJ deste, en la qual me dize como antes de ayer a los II, el Principe de Oranges se encontro con la gente que salia de Pisa, que eran IIJ mill hombres y CCC. cavallos segund dize el que trahe la carta, y desbara-toles con tanto estrago de los enemigos que no escaparon vivos apenas CC. hombres y tras estos ivan los villanos, como en Italia se acostumbra tan encarnizados que se piensa que no escapara ninguno.   El Principe como era valeroso cavallero compro esta jornada a V.M^d con la vida.   Cierto el ha muerto a mal tiempo y V.M^d pierde en el un buen capitan de guerra : plega a Dios de levarle a Parayso.   En lo demas el ha acabado sus dias valerosamente y en servicio de su principe y creo que los enemigos o deservidores de V.M^d sentiran pena del daño que han recibido los Florentines y de la reputacion que ha crescido al felicissimo exercito de V.M^d y tambien de la muerte del Principe, pues saben que no le faltan a V.M^d capitanes y personas bien qualificados para este y otro qualquier cargo, y esto he començado a sentir aqui en este poco espacio que ha que es venida la nueva.   Supplico a V.M que mire mucho en esta provision como suele en todas las cosas ; porque a la verdad este es un cargo que no lo ay igual del en Christianos.

Porque el Consejo que V.M^t tiene en Napoles ha de ordenar las cossas que se offrecen no he querido hazer ninguna provision sino que a la mesma hora he despachado una posta haziendoles saber como al Papa y al Cardenal de Osma con quien lo he comunicado parece, y a mi tambien que deve venir volando el Marques del Vasto porque con el credito que tiene entre los soldados servira mucho haviendose de hazer lo mas que desta empresa queda con ellos, que es, excusar el saco de Florentia, es persona que fenicida la empresa podra ir a Hungria o hazer lo que V.M^d mandare, porque no pretendera posession ni tendra fin a mayores cosas.

Tambien parece que venga Micer Jo: Antonio Musetula y con todo pienso que seria bien que imbiasse de alla V.M^d alguna persona bien qualificada para dar calor al negocio, y a lo que ha de hazer el exercito porque tanto quanto mejor se proveera agora para este entretanto, terna mas espacio V.M^t para proveer lo demas que si lo de Florentia y lo del exercito toma assiento parece que las cosas de Italia daran harto espacio para lo demas algunos dias.

Porque assentado lo de Florencia, conviene al servicio de V.M^t asentar lo de Sena con la mesma autoridad y calor del exercito como ayer lo escrivi a V.M^t viviendo el Principe bastava el por los poderes que tenia para assentarlo todo agora pienso que sera necessario que V.M. lo cometa particularmente porque aquello tiene necessidad de remedio y si agora no se assienta no solamente no se assentara despues pero quedara aquel humor movido y con el tiempo podria accarear algun mal.

Porque una grand parte de las speranças de lo de Florentia era la fe que Malatesta tenia al Principe, porque esta no manque yo procuro de inbiar alla a Galeaço Ballon su sobrino con el qual he sempre tractado io las cosas de Malatesta, para que le assegure que todo lo que se tractara con los ministros de V.M^t se le observara.   He scrito a Napoles que den la mesma comission o instruction al Marques, o al que viniere, y pienso que sera servicio de V.M^d que mande proveer lo mesmo.

Entratanto yo escrivo a Hernando de Gonzaga con hombre proprio exhortandole a proseguir y sostener aquella empresa porque ansi los soldados nuestros como los enemigos le tengan en autoridad y por persona legitima ; y he escrito a Napoles que hagan de alla los mesmo por que pienso que conviene darle autoridad entretanto que alli estuviere solo ; y si V.M^d no da orden mas presto pienso que sera su servicio escrivir esto mesmo.

No escrivo a V.M^d particularmente como fue lo de la batalla desta jornada porque no se mas desto, y Don Fernando de Gonzaga no lo escrive sino que con otra carta me dara aviso della.   Quando le tuviere le dare a V.Md. Solo he sabido que es muerto el Capitan Ferrucho que los traya que es el que defendio y se salio despues de Vulterra y entro en Pisa, y agora venia a socorrer a Florentia, y tambien diz que fue preso Jo: Paulo hijo de Renzo de Chieri.

Rodrigo Nino me ha escrito con carta que he recibido agora que el Rey de Anglaterra ha imbiado dineros a Venecia a su embaxador hasta VIIJ o X mill ducados, porque es una letra de cambio de iiij⁰ y D. y otra de credito de todo lo que el embaxador pidiere para soccorer, segun dizian, a Florentia ; y si esto es verdad, no seran solos que no vengan con ellos los xx⁰) de la contribution de que con otras cartas mias he dado aviso a V.Mᵗ Pero como quier que sea dios lo ha hecho mejor que no sean llegados a tiempo que a la verdad si esta gente engrossara mas havia mas que hazer.

Tambien podria ser que estos dineros que han llegado de Venecia sean para sobornar al mundo en la causa de Anglaterra. La cosa se abrira presto, yo estoi siempre lo mas vigilante que puedo para entender y dar aviso a V.Mᵈ desto y de todo lo demas que se offreciere. N.S. muy alto y muy poderoso Señor nos guarde y felicite a V.Mᵈ como sus buenos servidores vassalos y criados desseamos. De Roma V de Agosto MDXXX. —S.D.V.S.C.C.R.M. Humilde y devoto vasallo y criado que sus imperiales pies y manos beso. Mai. *Sobre* A la Sacra Caes y Cath Maiestad.

No. 17

British Museum, Add. MS. 28,581.
Bergenroth Transcripts of Spanish State Papers, X, f. 42 *seqq.*

Carpeta : A Su Md de Muxetula XX, de Agosto 1530. Respondidas de Augosta XXIIJ de Setiembre.

Testo : Sacra Cesᵃ y Cathᶜᵃ Mᵗᵃᵈ.

Humilmente besando les Imperiales manos y pies de V.Md ; por las otras carthas mias he escrevido, come por mucha instantia de la Sta del Papa, y carthas del embaxador May me parti por Roma, adonde siendo llegado han quesido da mi dos cosas ; la una que diesse mi parecer a los capitulos que se eran tractados y ahun firmados en Florentia, de los quales pienso que Vre Mᵈ haya havido traslado, y quando no, con estas lo enbyo a Vra Md, y tambien, que diesse mi parecer de come se havia y podia despedir l'exercito sin encorrer en algun inconveniente, y che se havia de azer por serse bien seguro de la Ciudad por el servitio de V.Mᵈ y su Sᵗᵃᵈ, y tambyen Su Sd y el dicho embaxador mucho me apretaron que quessiesse yr asta Florentia assi por las cosas de la dicha Ciudad y reformar el Regimiento, come por lo del exercito encareciendomelo mucho. Jo en lo primero dixie mi parecer, y primieramente que me pesava que se haviesse capitulado tan pocha suma de ochenta mil escudos que saliessen de Florentia, y que se provesse lo que fuesse menestier por l'exercito, por Su Sᵈ y por Vra Mᵈ, porque lo que l'exercito devia haver era artha suma y que segun la cuenta que enbyava el scrivan de ration del Campo, toda la gente devia haver, por el solo mes de Julio, docientos y ochenta mill escudos, y carghar lo demas a Vra Md y a Su Sᵈ no se come se hazia, porque V. Md no havia de pagar mas de su rata que era cinquenta mill escudos, sin lo que corria de este mes que aghora corre, y que si Su Sᵈ queria pagar lo demas que era byen, otramente no sabia como esto podia byen salir. Despues desto no me parecia byen cautelado lo de la seguridad de la Ciudad por la sola promission de Malatesta y Stefano Colonna, haviendon ellos a tener su gente dentro la Ciudad y querer que nuestro exercito se dissolva por las cosas que podrian entrevenir, las quales los prudentes piensan y las maldades que havemos visto nos fuerzan a remediallos ; y pareciame que la razon querria que pues Malatesta y el Colonna dizen y quieren tener la Ciudad por V.Mᵈ que demas de los Rienes dela Ciudad diessen ellos rienes por lo que tocca a ellos ; echando tanbyen la mayor parte de la gente de gherra que ahy tienen o que hechandola toda, recebiessen por guarda de la Ciudad unos mill o dos mill hombres de los de V.M^d, o espanoles o Alemanes o Italianos o de qualquiera nation su parte para que con ellos se defendiesse la Ciudad de los que quisiessen contra la orden de V.M^d dañarle ; y este medio era mexior que no lo que esta capitulado y que estando la Ciudad ya por perdida y no haviendo otra manera de mas sostenerse por falta de victualla, y por ser perdida la esperansa del soccorro, era muy certo que havia da venir en mejores partidos y mas provechosos assi por la siguridad, come por la mas summa del dinero, y que si la una e la otra condition adelante que Su S^d ratificasse se podiesse mejorar era muy bien ; y asy a Su S^d ya todos parecio quel marques del Vasto aghora que iba en el campo mirasse de azer mas assegurar lo de la Ciudad, o que con azer echar la gente de gherra della y entrar de la nuestra tantos quantos serian menestier por su defension, o per haver las fortalezas de Pisa o de Liurno entre las manos, o por rienes, o por otra mejor manera con alguna buena manera no mostrando desazer lo echo, mirasse de concertarla mejor, y quanto a io de la pecunia dize el papa que mudandose el Regimiento de la Ciudad y aziendose a su voluntad haria de maniera que lo promectido por Su S^d a la gente se paghasse. Es verdad que en esto devido tenemos harta differencia con el Papa, porque Su S^d dizia que dal mes de Noviembre ha promectido sexenta mill escudos cada mes, que por todo el mes de Augusto son seycientos mill escudos, y que pagado lo que havia ya pagado no quedaria por todo Agosto a pagar si no cyen y veynte mill escudos. Yo averti Su S^d que aunque haviesse pagado todo lo que dize, devia mas una otra mesada que fu del mes de Octobre, que V.M^t byen se accuerdera que siempre quedava vazia, y aunque el Papa no pretendia devella pagar con todo esto despues quando yo concerte esta differentia que fue en el Campo se contento que accordandoso Florentia haviesse de pagharse por Florentia, e por Su S^d y Su S^d me lo ha actorgado aghora, de manera que havrasse de pagar tambien la dicha mesada que seran otros sexanta mill escudos, que desta manera havian de cierto salir de Florenta o del Papa cyentos y ochenta mill escudos.

Mas con todo esto faltaria artho por pagar todo l' exercito, y esta falta viene quel Papa no queria pagar sino los sexenta mill escudos al mes, y la gendarme y cavallos lejeros quedan a ser pagados de muchos meses, y la suma que era necessaria para ello era demas de los lx^{il} escudos al mes ; y come sabe V.Md el Papa nunca ha quesido passar esta summa, sino por dos meses que pagho veinte mill escudos de mas que serviron por los Italianos que vinyeron posteramente dal Reyno, si que queda esta differentia porque yo querria que se pagasse esto dal Papa o da Florentia, y el Papa dize que no esta a su cargho, y por esto me pesa que en la capitulation se hayan contendados los nuestros de los ochenta mill escudos de Florentia por questo de la gendarme, y cavallos lijeros y otros extraordinarios que se deven al Campo, que son mas de lx^{il} escudos el mes con mas razon se podrian pedir a Florentia que gana no ser saqueada y destruyda, que no dal Papa que no es oblighado ni V.M^d lo ha querido obligar a mas que a los lx^{il} escudos el mes.

Con todo esto espero que el papa hara pagar sino todo esto que deve a la gendarme y cavallos lejeros al meno la mayor parte ; esto estoy agora trabajando porque no sigua disorden por esto y se puede esto venir en provecho de V.M^d non havra de pagar por este tiempo la giente de cavallo de suyo.

Demas desto pide pagha la gente de Fabricio Maramaldo ende mas que ha servido mucho, y fue causa de la victoria, y tambyen somos aghora en plattica con Su Sd que pienso que de las cinco paghas que dize la gente que ha servido pagara Su Sd las tres che son mas de XXX^{il} escudos.

Circa el dispedir de la gente se ha mucho ablado y parece a Su Sd que

asigurado lo de Florentia en buena forma tal que quede en poder de V.Mt
se empeze a despedir la jente no toda justa mas que se empeze da los alemanes que estan a cargho de Su S^d a los quales provehera luegho de todo
lo que se le deve, y tambyen se empezen a dispedir quatro o cinco mill
Italianos, y despues los otros Italianos, y despues se paghen los espanoles,
y tambyen se despidan los tudeschos, que estan a cargho de V.M^t y se
paguen los espanoles que estan tambyen a cargho de V.M^d, y porque
V.Md no me mando quando yo me fue de Mantua que se despediessen los
espanoles, y no se sabe adonde han de estar se esta con mucho trabajo,
adonde estos espanoles podrian estar, o yr, porque sy se pagan han de
salir de tierra de Florentines ; y por esto V.M. sera servida mandar que se
ha de hazer de todo esto y de los espanoles adonde han de estar ; y se que
V^{ra} M^d sabe come queda el Reyno destruydo con los que ahy estan, y por
esto V.M. mande lo que en esto se ha de hazer.

De my yda en el Campo, yo dixie que no tenia desto orden de V.M. y
que poco en esto podia azer, haviendose de azer por los capitanos y por
los otros que tenian el cargho da V.Md ende mas que yo havia da venir
a la corte por servir V.M. come me mando, y que se me se mandasse por
V.M. que de passada yo haziesse ahy alguna cosa procuraria egequuntar
lo que se me mandaria ; otramente no podia ni convenya yo azer en esto
algho, endemas no trayendo el dinero que fuesse necessario por concertar
la gente ; y asi parecio al Papa y al embaxador que partiesse hoy el Marques
con aquel dinero que era presente que heran lx^{ll} escudos del Papa y diez
mill dal Reyno ; y empezasse ad tractar y egequuntar las cosas sudichas,
y que si despues era menestier que yo fuesse alla con l'otro dinero, que
quedasse que se haria por mi lo que me fuera mandado, aunque Sobrano
Señor yo no pienso yr sin que V.M^t me lo mande o mirasse que esto fuesse
servitio de V.M. y que podiesse provechar en algo.

Esta manana partio el marques con el dicho orden y estando escriviendo
esta el marques se e bolvido da veynte millas de aqui porque dize que ha
allado un hombre que le truxio letras del campo que V.M. ha proveydo de
Capitan General el Illustre duque de Mantua, y en su absencia por governador del exercito a Don Fernando su hermano, y porque dize que el yva
por servir ahy V.Mt y ha proveydo en aquel exercito y cargho de otra
persona, no se ha de azer sino lo que V^{ra} M^d ha mandado, y ansi se ha
excusado con el Papa, el qual visto la dicha provision, no le ha parecido
estrengerlo que vaya, ende mas andar debaxo de Don Ferrando y assy
todo lo que se avia concertado que el aziesse en el exercito see scrivera por
su S^d al dicho duque, y en su absentia al dicho Don Ferrando.

El Marques ahunque de principio le parecia azersele afruenta por lo
del Don Ferrando, que de lo del Duque dizia, que era muy bien echo, y
que no tenia causa de quexiarse, todavia quedo contento porque se le
acordo que esto no se havia proveydo ni pensado proveher en su prejuyzio ;
mas que esto V.Md lo havia assi echo, y mandado no sabiendose que el
estuviesse aun sano ny para yr tan ayna al Campo nel qual por la muerte
del Principe y por las cosas que entonces quedavan assi abyertas y l'exercito sin ninguna caveza convenia proveherse lueghto del quien ahy residia,
ende mas siendo Don Ferrando hermano de qien Su M^d hazia in general
en Italia, y dadas estas razones quedo el Marques muy satisfecho y con
aquel sabor que debe un buen servido de V.Md ende mas que se le dixio
que haviendole proveydo del cargho de Ungria V.Md no havia da creher
que haviesse deseado este govierno del exercito que en absentia del duque
se deve al hermano.

Aghora tambyen quel Señor Duque se allara en el exercito, no se a
que sea menestier que yo vaya alla sino venirme drecho a V.Mt come
pienso azer se no me lo mandasse tanto el Papa, y requeresse l'ambaxador

y me pareciesse ser servitio de V.M^d que esto come razon pudiesse en mi mas quel desseo y comodidad.

No dexiare dizir a V.M^t quanto a lo del dinero que es menestier por lo que esta a cargho de V.M^d veho muy mal recando en el reyno, come el Cardenal tambyen ha escricto a V.M^d sino sale de las compositiones las quales como muchas vezes he escrito por mucho que haya mostrado las carthas de V.Md a los Commisarios sobra esto, no han quexido azellas sin particular orden de V.Md dirigida a ellos y come esto no es venido no se a echo nada, y sino fuesse estado que V.M. me lo ha mandado tantas veces por sus carthas, y emportava mucho que no faltasse el dinero en el campo, non havria tanto sollecitado esta materia ; porque no pensassen que fuesse esto porque me plaziessen que se haviessen ecchas las compositiones, yo no he curado desto, pues que se my intencion, que es el verdadero servitio de V.M. y egequuntar sus mandados ; y quien tiene lempias las entranas y tractasse de servir su amo no deve dexiar procurar su servitio porque no lo tengan en suspecho ; porque en este caso procediendo con estos respectos adande va el servitio de V.Mt non haria servitio a V.M^t mas a my mismo porque me quitaria de trabajo y falsas suspictiones. Yo se que V.M. y todo el mundo conoce mi intention y tambyen mis servitios poco curare de otras falsas calunias Vra Mt por esta via o por otras mande de manera esto que se puedan enbyar los dineros dal Reyno se queda servido que se embyen que mas de sollicitarlo procurarlo y emportunallo no tiengo poderes. Accabo besando las Imperiales manos y pies de V.Mt y rogando a Ntro Señor Dios por el acrecimiento de la vida reynos y Señorios de V.Md come por ella mas complidamente se desea. De Roma a XXJ de Agosto MDXXX. De V.Mt Ces y Cath. humill^o siervo che las Imperiales manos y pieis besa

Jo: Ant^o Musectula

Sobre : Sacre Cese et Cath^e M^{tt}

INDEX

(References are given to the notes only where they contain substantial amplification of the details in the text.)

379